THE MEANINGS OF MODERN ART

THE MEANINGS OF MODERN ART

JOHN RUSSELL

THE MUSEUM OF MODERN ART, NEW YORK

HARPER & ROW, PUBLISHERS

Designed by Nora Sheehan, assisted by Wendy Byrne

ISBN: 0-06-013701-0 81 82 83 10 9 8 7 6 5 4 3 2 1
ISBN: 0-06-430110-9 pbk 81 82 83 10 9 8 7 6 5 4 3 2 1

LIBRARY OF CONGRESS CATALOG CARD NUMBER: 80-8217

To the memory of THOMAS B. HESS 1920-1978

CONTENTS

Preface **9**
The Secret Revolution **13**
The Emancipation of Color **42**
History as Nightmare **69**
Reality Reassembled **97**
The Cosmopolitan Eye **126**
An Alternative Art **157**
The Dominion of the Dream **192**
A World Remodeled **222**
A Lost Leadership **258**
America Redefined **291**
The Great Divide 1950–70 **329**
How Good Is Modern Art? **362**
Suggested Readings **406**
Index **417**

PREFACE

This book is built upon two beliefs. One is that in art, as in the sciences, ours is one of the big centuries. The other is that the history of art, if properly set out, is the history of everything. As the case for these beliefs is argued on every page of this book, either directly or by implication, I shall not defend them here. But I owe it to the reader to explain that this book itself has an unusual history.

Rather more than ten years ago I was asked by The Museum of Modern Art and the Book-of-the-Month Club if I would write for them a general survey of modern art. It was to cover the period from 1875 to the present day. It was to be acceptable to the Museum, in terms of art history, and it was to be acceptable to the Club, in terms of general interest and readability. Beyond that, I was on my own.

The book that resulted was published in 1974–75 in twelve monthly parts. It was distributed by the Book-of-the-Month Club and could be had by mail subscription only. In preparing the present edition, which appears under the joint imprint of The Museum of Modern Art and Harper & Row, I have made a radical change in the presentation of the text. While the earlier edition had captions which in many cases were so lengthy and so elaborate as almost to constitute a parallel text, I have now eliminated them. I have, however, felt free to integrate them, wherever it seemed desirable, in the text proper. That text is therefore substantially longer—and, I hope, richer—than it was in the original edition. I have also revised and updated the text here and there, though this is not a text for which I would claim a fugitive up-to-dateness.

As work on the original edition proceeded, the true nature of the book seemed to me to declare itself more and more clearly. It was intended to meet the severe standards of the College Art Association, which subsequently was kind enough to present me with its Frank Jewett Mather Award for art criticism, but it was not a mainline art history. Nor was it a directory, a dictionary or an encyclopedia. Whole countries, whole schools, whole categories of artists (some of them individually dear to me) appeared in it either momentarily or not at all. In art, as in most other things, I hold by what André Gide once said: "The world will be saved by one or two people."

Insofar as *The Meanings of Modern Art* is modeled upon any other book or books, they date from quite some time ago and have nothing to do with art history. They are examples, that is to say, of the democratic Enlightenment that came into being in Victorian times and was a force for good at least until the outbreak of World War I. It had to do with the notions of self-help and of adult education, but it also had to do with a moral obligation that was felt by many good writers, even if they did not always put it into words.

It was a point of honor with these writers to make the best of themselves available to the largest possible public at the lowest possible cost. John Ruskin, the greatest of all English writers on art, was wholeheartedly of that persuasion. The ideal of universal education was at hand: how could good writers address themselves to the privileged only?

In the first years of our century, book after book was animated by this noble ambition. Three that I cherish especially are *Our Knowledge of the External World* by Bertrand Russell, *Landmarks in French Literature* by Lytton Strachey and *An Outline of Russian Literature* by Maurice Baring. These could have been no more than primers, but in point of fact they have quite another character: and it was that character, or something like it, that I hoped to annex for *The Meanings of Modern Art.*

It was fundamental to that character that every book should be an act of commitment. We never doubt that Ruskin would have put his hand in the fire for J. M. W. Turner. Freshness and lightness of touch are fundamental also: Bertrand Russell made us aware not of the hard work that had gone into his book, but merely of the barely audible hiss of glee with which the final formulations were set down on paper.

These books had, finally, an element of covert

autobiography. Their authors did not write as deskmen or as high-grade copyists. They wrote as men made and marked by what they were writing about. When Lytton Strachey wrote about the terrible insights of Racine, he did not make us think of Racine as "a classic," but as a friend and confidant whose every word left a brand. When Maurice Baring wrote of the great Russian novelists, it was not as a man who had graduated from a language laboratory. He wrote as someone who had sat long and late over the table in Russian country houses, and argued this way and that with Russians on weeklong railway journeys, and plunged into Russian rivers at the time of year when bathing in those rivers was like bathing, he tells us, in hot tea.

These things were not paraded, but they were present. They did not validate what was said, but they brought with them a sense of involvement that communicated itself as the single most desirable characteristic in books of that kind. I have no illusions as to how far *The Meanings of Modern Art* may fall short in this matter, but I like to think that its subject matter has been as much lived as studied. My opinion of Gustav Klimt was formed in Vienna before World War II. My opinion of Henry Moore was formed in the early 1940s, at a time when he could barely keep himself in stone or wood. My opinion of the great masters of the School of Paris was formed during visits beyond number to that city from 1946 onward, and my opinion of the Russian avant-garde was formed in Moscow and Leningrad during the 1950s. I hope that in dealing with more recent art—and in particular with art that originates in New York City, where I now live—I am as attentive as ever to considerations of time and place and cultural context. Immediacy is not everything in such matters, but where it exists it should be put to work.

None of the things I have mentioned can make a foolish man wise or a bad book good. But when they are properly used they remind us that the act of reading is an act of confidence, and almost of conspiracy, between one human being and another. That conspiracy can get nowhere, and that confidence can be betrayed. But if all goes well the reader may put down the book at the end and say what the author—and this author is no exception—most wants to hear: "I learned a lot from your book, but what is more to the point is that I had a very good time."

Perhaps I might add that the human conditions in which I worked on the original edition were outstandingly happy. It is a grief to me that among the officers of the Book-of-the-Month Club who did so much to make those years agreeable neither Warren Lynch nor that most stringent of editors, Ralph Thompson, is here to see the book in the stores. At The Museum of Modern Art I benefited beyond measure from the professionalism of Frances Keech, Patricia White (now Mrs. Bradford A. Warner, Jr.), Nora Sheehan, Francis Kloeppel and Clive Phillpot.

THE MEANINGS OF MODERN ART

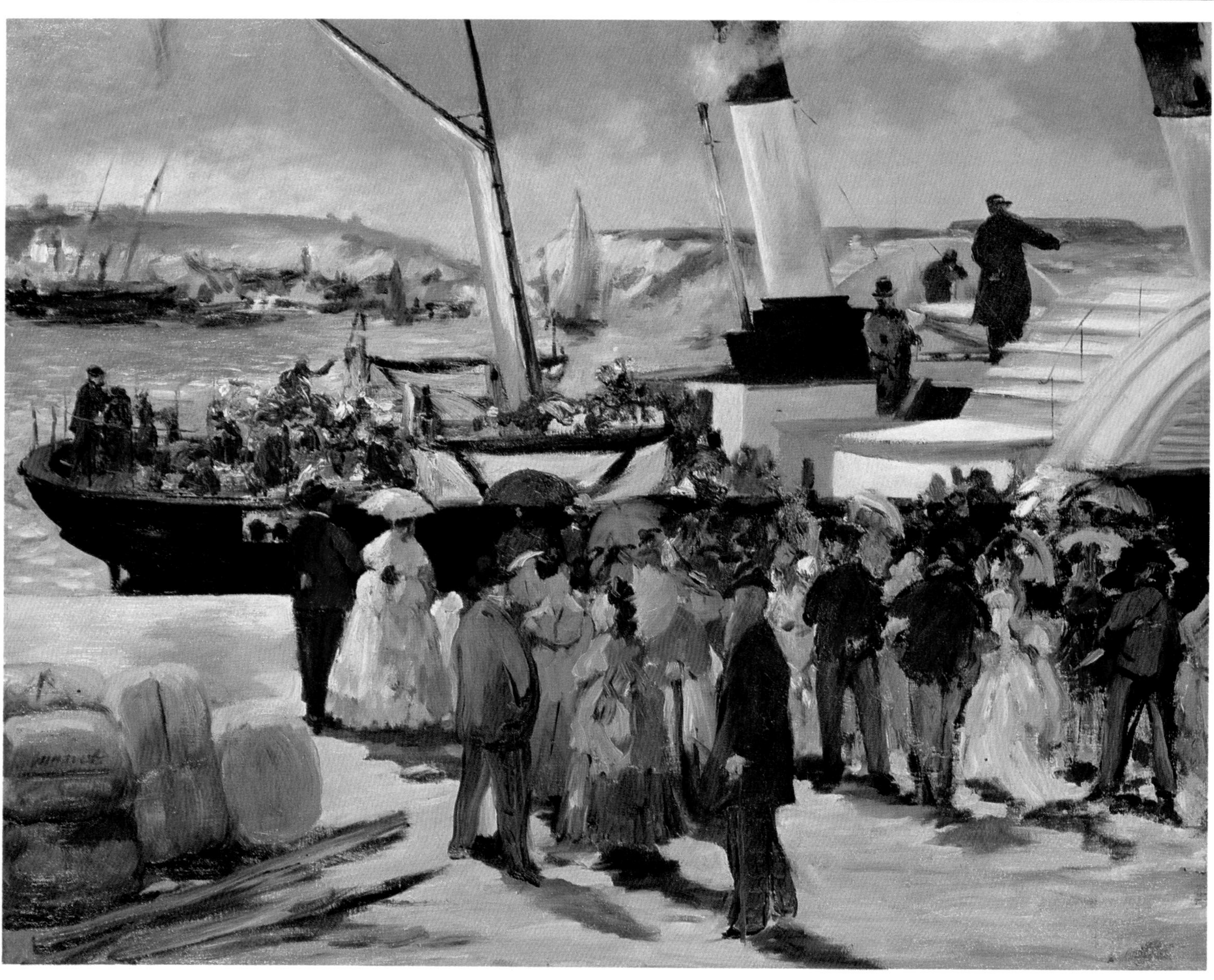

Edouard Manet.
The Folkestone Boat, Boulogne. 1869.
Oil on canvas,
23½ × 28⅞ inches.
Philadelphia
Museum of Art.
Mr. and Mrs. Carroll
S. Tyson Collection

THE SECRET REVOLUTION

When art is made new, we are made new with it. We have a sense of solidarity with our own time, and of psychic energies shared and redoubled, which is just about the most satisfying thing that life has to offer. "If that is possible," we say to ourselves, "then everything is possible"; a new phase in the history of human awareness has been opened up, just as it was opened up when people first read Dante, or first heard Bach's 48 preludes and fugues, or first learned from *Hamlet* and *King Lear* that the complexities and contradictions of human nature could be spelled out on the stage.

This being so, it is a great exasperation to come face to face with new art and not make anything of it. Stared down by something that we don't like, don't understand and can't believe in, we feel personally affronted, as if our identity as reasonably alert and responsive human beings had been called into question. We ought to be having a good time, and we aren't. More than that, an important part of life is being withheld from us; for if any one thing is certain in this world it is that art is there to help us live, and for no other reason.

It was always so. Art is there to tell us where we are, and it is also there to tell us who we are. It gives pleasure, coincidentally, but primarily it is there to tell the truth. For hundreds of years, and on many matters of supreme importance, it had the edge over all other sources. It gave out the truth about this world and the next one. It encapsulated history. It told us what people wiser than ourselves were thinking. It told the stories that everyone wanted to hear, and it fixed, once and forever, the key moments in our evolution. Art answered the great riddles, filled in the gaps in our general knowledge, and laid Eternity on the line. Above all, it gave reassurance; it told us what we wanted to hear—that experience was not formless and illegible, that man could speak to man without the obstructions of language, and that we were at home in the world, and with one another.

That was long the function of art. Art restored

to us the lost wholeness, the sensation of being at one with Nature, and at one with society, which we crave from the moment of birth. Many and desperate are the expedients which we devise for the recapture of that lost wholeness; art restores it completely and forever. So we are quite right to be dismayed when art seems to shift its ground in ways that we find difficult to follow. Still less do we like to think that art might one day peter out. We do not care to echo what was written more than three hundred years ago by Sir Thomas Browne: " 'Tis too late to be ambitious. The great mutations of the world are acted." We should prefer to think—and in my opinion we are quite right to think—that the masterpieces of our own day can perfectly well stand comparison with the great achievements of the past.

But the anxiety remains. And art *has* shifted its ground, and recoded its messages, and questioned its own nature, and reshaped the ordeal by initiation to which we are subjected before we can understand it completely. Indignation at all this masks feelings to which we dare not give their true name. E. H. Gombrich, with his *The Story of Art,* has taught millions of people how to look at old pictures; and he put this point very well when he said that European Expressionism before 1914 sprang from the fear of "that utter loneliness that would reign if art were to fail and each man remained immured in himself." If the two words "modern art" are enough to start an argument almost anywhere, it is because this fear of the eventual and hypothetical failure of art has come to haunt even people who have never been to a museum, let alone bought a picture.

It was in the second half of the 19th century that art was relieved of certain of the duties which it had been carrying out on society's behalf and became free to look into its own nature. The duties in question had been many and varied. Philip IV of Spain never doubted that when his troops won a famous victory his court painter Velázquez was the best man to commemorate it. When Marat was murdered in his bath in 1793, it was by popular demand, almost, that Jacques-Louis David made haste to paint *Marat Assassinated.* When the Houses of Parliament burned down in London in 1834, art gave us our most memorable account of what happened: J. M. W. Turner was on hand to tell how the great scarf of flame unwound itself high in the night sky. Art had no rival on such occasions. It gave us what we could get nowhere else. Nor was the artist simply a passive recorder: when the French frigate *Méduse* was lost in particularly ghastly circumstances in 1816, it was a painter, Théodore Géricault, who brought the matter out of the newspapers and onto a deeper level of concern.

In paintings such as the ones I have named, people were told what they wanted to know, and told it in a way that allied power to concision and eloquence to understanding. These traits in combination inspired a collective confidence in art. A recent example of that confidence is the first line of a poem by W. H. Auden: "About suffering they were never wrong, the Old Masters." Though not wholly true—some Old Masters were platitudinous and histrionic, others had an attitude toward suffering that was distinctly equivocal—this line does indicate one of the ways in which art helps us to live.

That is to say that we have a deeper understanding of old age and are the readier to meet it ourselves if we have studied Joseph Wright of Derby's *The Old Man and Death.* We have a deeper understanding of what it means for one person to give himself to another if we have studied Rembrandt's *The Jewish Bride.* We have a deeper understanding of what it means to love the world and lose it if we have studied the valedictory images of the dying Watteau. Marcel Proust was one of the most observant men who ever lived, but he spoke for all of us when he wrote, "Until I saw Chardin's paintings I never realized how much beauty lay around me in my parents' house, in the half-cleared table, in the corner of a tablecloth left awry, in the knife beside the empty oyster-shell."

Behind this collective confidence in art is our

trust in the archetypal attitude, the stance before life, which is exemplified for us by each of the great masters in turn. It is a common dream that one man's life should be the measure of all things and that it should make sense of the complexity of experience in ways which are valid for everyone. Reading Tolstoy, watching a play by Shakespeare, working our way through the canon of Schubert's songs, looking at a Titian, or at a Dürer, or at Poussin's *Four Seasons*, we find that dream fulfilled. One man can master life. He cannot shield us from misfortune, but he can teach us to bear it better. And while we are under the spell of his art we feel invulnerable, as Brünnehilde was invulnerable when Wotan spread around her the magic circle of fire.

Invulnerability: that is what people ask of art. It would be a bad day if such achievements, and such men, could be talked about only in the past tense. No one likes to think that there lies before us only a long littleness. If rage and dismay enter so often into reactions to new art it is because of what is at stake: our capacity to make sense of life as it now presents itself. The Old Masters are still there, and they may well be present to us more vividly than many people whom we meet in "real life"; but we need the new masters, too, and it is very uncomfortable to feel that they may not be there.

The poet Charles Baudelaire realized this as early as the 1840s. He foresaw that the conditions of life were going to change faster and faster, and that the duty of modern art would be "to express that specific beauty which is intrinsic to our new emotions." Our *new* emotions, he said; for there were going to be new emotions to make new sense of. Baudelaire knew that there would be drastic readjustments for all, both in the public and in the private domain, and that art would have to come to terms with them. And that is what has happened; Tolstoy in his novels said all that there is to say about many aspects of life, but we needed Solzhenitsyn to tell us in *Cancer Ward* and *The First Circle* how much of human dignity can survive when a great adventure is perverted and the vision of a just world brought to nothing. Beethoven in *Fidelio* gave us once and forever an ideal image of human loyalty; but not until Schoenberg's *Erwartung*, more than one hundred years later, did music yield a definitive image of the dissolution of personality under stress.

In art, equally, we had needs which could not be satisfied by the Old Masters, because those needs did not exist when the Old Masters were around. Poussin in his *Massacre of the Innocents* gave us an unforgettable image of a human mouth wide open in a scream; but because he was a great classical artist that scream was incidental to his Olympian overview of the scene as a whole. It fell to Edvard Munch, in 1893, to give us an image of a shriek which (in Munch's own words) "pierced the whole of Nature" and stood for a sudden, vast and quite irresistible sensation of panic and dismay. Europe needed just that picture at just that time, and nothing from the past could have taken its place. In 1945, when the complete facts about the Nazi concentration camps were available for the first time, Europe needed Picasso's *The Charnel House*, which was the more powerful for its sobriety of color, its condensed, pressed-down, claustrophobic imagery and its refusal to itemize what was so readily to hand in print. The best art of the past hundred years came into being on occasions when nothing from the past would fill the bill. What those occasions were, and what art did about them, is the subject of this book.

As to exactly when new art came in and old art went out, several opinions can be upheld. There is a case for those who believe that the change came in the second half of the 1860s. Those five years were pregnant with the future: these were the years when Marx began to publish *Das Kapital*, Nobel invented dynamite and Bismarck drew nearer, step by step, to the domination of Europe. In painting, not-yet-named Impressionism was beginning to dissolve the Old Master tradition of modeling from dark to light in a simulated deep space. The "subject," as previously conceived, was

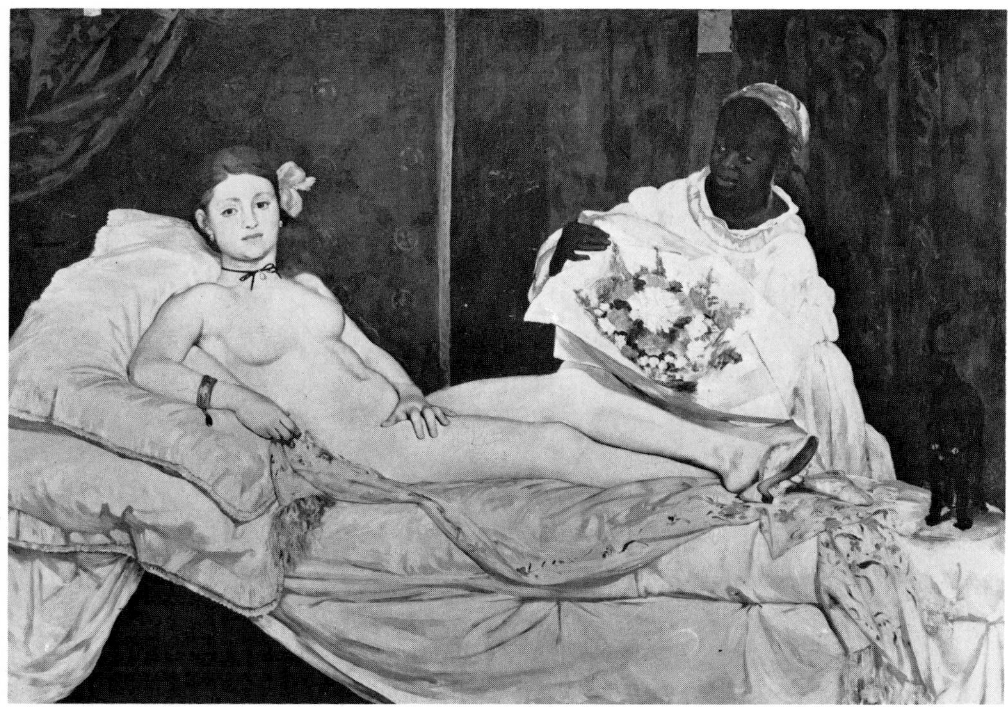

Edouard Manet.
Olympia. 1863.
Oil on canvas,
51⅜ × 74¾ inches.
Musée du Louvre,
Paris

giving way to a new conception of painting, in which the artist's sensations *were* the subject, no other being needed. One of the most challenging pictures of the century was put on view at the Paris Salon in 1865: *Olympia* by Edouard Manet. *Olympia* was challenging in every possible way. It stood for a new kind of candor as between the painter and painting, as between the painter and his subject matter and as between the painter and his public. Manet in 1863 had annoyed people very much by transposing motifs from the Old Masters into modern life and showing, in his *Le Déjeuner sur l'herbe*, how it was possible for a pretty young girl to take off all her clothes while picnicking in the open air with two fully dressed men. That painting had been rejected by the official Salon; but two years later *Olympia* was hung among the 3,559 canvases which had officialdom's sanction.

We do not, of course, see *Olympia* as our great-great-grandfathers would have seen it had they chanced to be in Paris in 1865. The picture has aged, as a physical object. Where once it looked blank and blatant it now looks what it is: an Old Master of our time. More than a hundred years of rougher, more coarsely provocative painting of the female nude has made us aware that Manet was essentially an aristocrat. We also know, as the public of the 1860s mostly did not, that the pose is taken from Titian's *Venus of Urbino,* which Manet had copied nine years earlier. The treatment of the naked figure now seems to us a model of tenderness and delicacy; but at the time it looked two-dimensional and incomplete ("Like the Queen of Spades just out of her bath," said Gustave Courbet). We enjoy the cat, and we find it wonderfully true to the facts of feline behavior, and we know the symbolic role of the cat in the poetry of Manet's friend Baudelaire. In fact, we find the whole picture strongly Baudelairean in its frankness, its overtones of luxury and indulgence, and in the contrast between the white of the flesh, the white of the sheets, the dazzling still life of the bouquet of flowers, and the dark face and hands of the attendant. We relish the uninhibited way in which the naked girl looks straight at us, as much as to say, "Here I am. What are you going to do about it?" The public of the 1860s sensed that the girl was saying it. But they also sensed, even if unconsciously, that the way of painting was saying it, too. *Olympia* was a declaration of war. The public was presented with a new way of seeing and a new way of setting down the thing seen. "Here I am," was the message, "and what are you going to do about it?" The mid-1860s were crucial in that respect. In 1867 both Manet and Courbet exhibited on their own at the World's Fair in Paris, thereby indicating that an alternative must soon be found to the art circuits of officialdom. These were the years in which Claude Monet and Pierre-Auguste Renoir began to paint regularly in the open air; and in which Camille Pissarro put it about that black and bitumen should be outlawed by every painter worthy of the name; and in which the young Zola began to champion the young Paul Cézanne. If we are simply looking for the new, we need look no further.

The case for the late 1860s is the stronger in that Impressionist paintings of the top class have made so great a contribution to human happiness. Looking at them, we think better of life and better of ourselves. Nor are they simply a school of pleasure, and one from which we have all graduated; they are also a school of truth. Impressionist painting

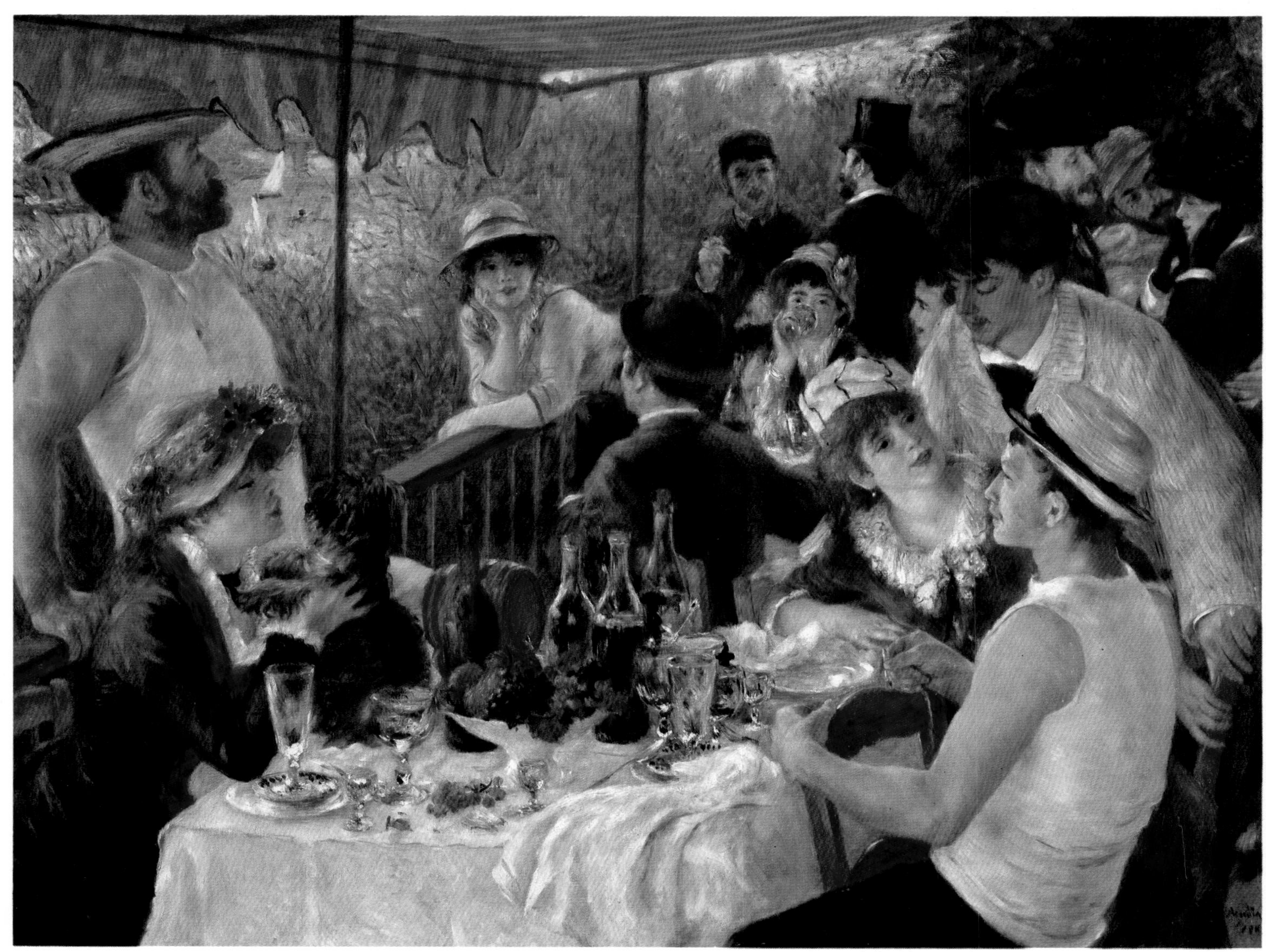

Pierre-Auguste Renoir. *Luncheon of the Boating Party.* 1881. Oil on canvas, 51⅜ × 69¼ inches. The Phillips Collection, Washington

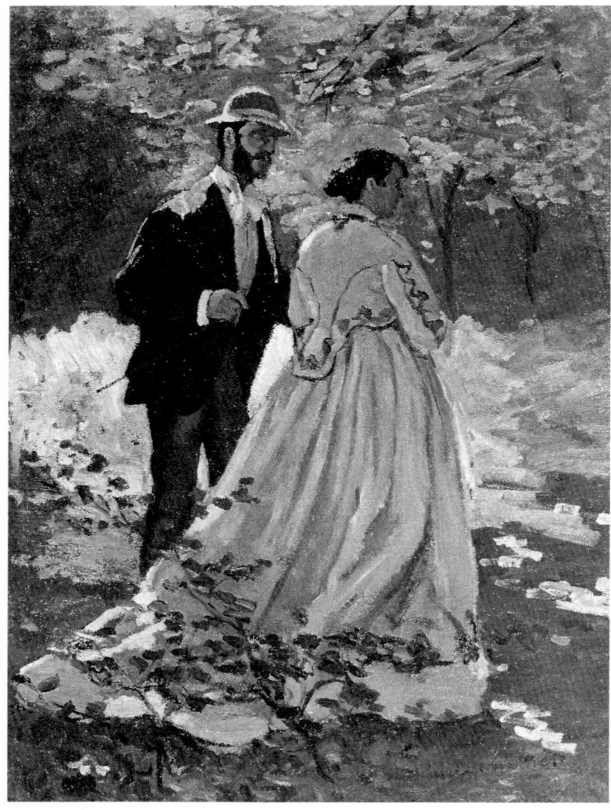

Claude Monet. *Bazille and Camille.* c. 1865. Oil on canvas, 36⅝ × 27⅛ inches. National Gallery of Art, Washington. Ailsa Mellon Bruce Collection

was true to everyday experience in a way that painting had not been true before. This is how light falls, this is how color is broken up, this is how the fugitive moment presents itself. These pictures have a physical beauty, but they have a moral beauty as well: free and independent human beings have said "No" to pictorial tradition and set themselves instead to tell the truth about what happens when they set up their easels in front of Nature. It was the truth about what the eye saw, and it was also the truth about what happened on the canvas. The allover flicker of Impressionism mimed the very act of putting paint on canvas, where the suaver, blander and, in intention, seamless procedures of earlier painting had tended to conceal it. Impressionism said "No" to the mind, with its apparatus of received values, and put its trust in intuition. That does not sound, in today's terms, like too momentous an undertaking. But then we say things every day which would have got us banished or burned alive in earlier times; in art, equally, we take it for granted that we can do just as we like, with impunity. The painters of the 1860s were the prisoners of a very different set of historical conditions. Edmond Duranty, one of the most discerning of French writers on art, had said in 1855 that "It takes immense genius to represent, simply and sincerely, what we see in front of us." That had never been what art was about; for the tens of thousands of people who went every year to the official Salons in Paris, art was one of the learned professions, and it was not the function of the artist to teach people to look around them.

The Impressionists thought just the contrary. They were living in an extraordinary time: a time when the conditions of life were changing more radically than in any previous era. They saw, for instance, that between them the steam train and the steamboat were putting a completely new style of life at the disposal of everyone. At once rakish and imposing, convenient and yet the emblems of an imperious masculinity, they were the great new subjects of the day. When Gustave Flaubert began to write *A Sentimental Education* in 1865, he chose for his opening scene the departure of a steamboat, with all its attendant bustle and activity, as a symbol for the way in which human relationships are continually forming and re-forming. Manet in his *The Folkestone Boat, Boulogne,* 1869, and Monet in his painting of *The Gare Saint-Lazare, Paris,* 1877, found in the steam age an ideal subject matter. The scene on the quayside allowed Manet to employ what looked at the time like an almost improvisational method of composition; the rapid, nervous movement of the brush corresponded exactly to the vibration of the ship's engines, the brisk to-and-fro of passengers and crew and the sense—never absent from the most conventional departure—that a decisive moment in life was at hand. People were about to pass from the known to the unknown, from *terra firma* to the open sea; and painting was in the same situation.

In Impressionist painting, the eye has a new

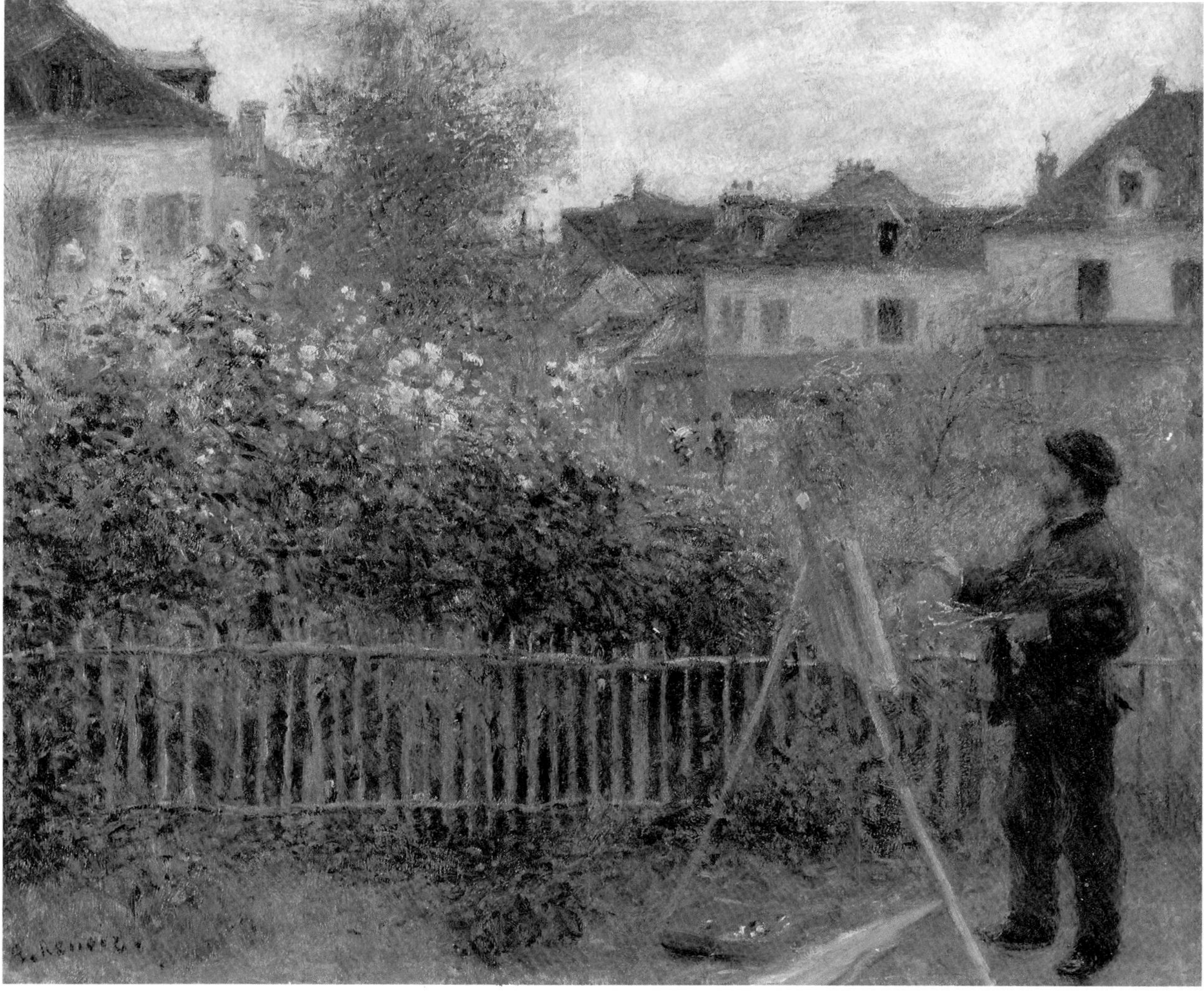

Pierre-Auguste Renoir. *Monet Painting in His Garden at Argenteuil.* 1873. Oil on canvas, 18⅜ × 23½ inches. Wadsworth Atheneum, Hartford, Conn. Bequest of Anne Parrish Titzell

privilege: that of concentrating on aspects of experience which had previously been thought to be too disorderly, too freakish, too seemingly accidental to qualify as material for art. Manet found this material on the quayside, where the spectacle changed from moment to moment. Monet, in the Gare Saint-Lazare series, took the huge iron-and-glass structure of the station, which had only lately been opened; he took the locomotives, which a generation earlier would have seemed like visions from an unimaginable future; and he took the element of steam itself—the mysterious, tinted exhalations which ballooned up and up beneath the unprecedented roof. The Gare Saint-Lazare was a startling enough sight even in the 1930s, when the steam locomotive had not yet been ousted; in the 1870s, and for painters who had known the countrified look of a preindustrial Paris, there can have been nothing to cushion the shock of modernity.

But if Monet was painting the new world, he was also painting the new way. He was using the element of shock in the experience of the Gare Saint-Lazare to cover and justify the element of shock in Impressionism itself. In the painting now in the Fogg Art Museum, for example, he used the swerving movement of the right-hand set of tracks in the foreground to draw the observer into the center of the painting. That center is defined as a space like a diamond laid on its side, with the flattened and inverted V of the roof as its top; the

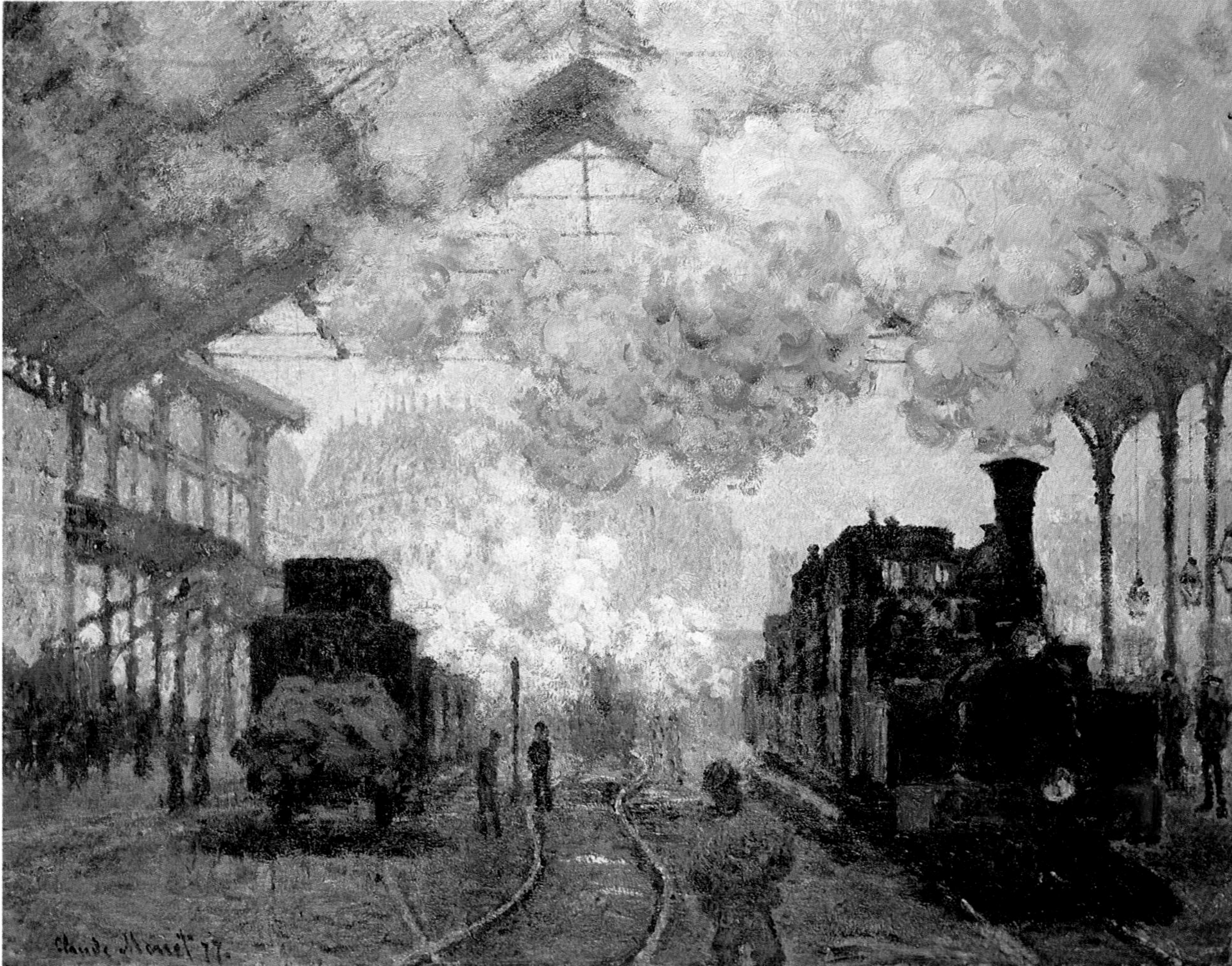

Claude Monet.
The Gare Saint-Lazare, Paris.
1877.
Oil on canvas,
32½ × 39¾ inches.
Fogg Art Museum,
Harvard University,
Cambridge, Mass.
Bequest the
Collection of
Maurice Wertheim

lower half of the diamond is formed by two invisible lines that run through the upper section of the two locomotives in the foreground and meet up in the spectral locomotive that can be glimpsed in the center and at the rear. Within this diamond is the true subject of the painting: the play of light on something never before recorded—the iridescent cloudscape of steam as it forms and re-forms within a confined space. Such a thing had never been seen before, and it will now never be seen again.

No one relished the new subject matter of Impressionism more completely than Edgar Degas, in the series of music-hall and café-concert studies which he made in the second half of the 1870s. In the café-concert he found an ideal combination of the things that most prompted his imagination—faces and bodies in vigorous movement, artificial lighting that turned the most humdrum scene into carnival, strange and aggressive combinations of color. The scene lent itself to abrupt, asymmetrical, snapshotlike images which threw the emphasis everywhere but where it was expected. It was a continual challenge; faced with hardworking professionals, Degas in his turn gave all that he had.

A capital example of this is the *Café Singer Wearing a Glove* of 1878. Degas at this time was using tempera mixed with pastel to produce little paintings, at once astringent and feather-soft, which he could carry through quickly after long and careful preparation. "Pastel colors" in every-

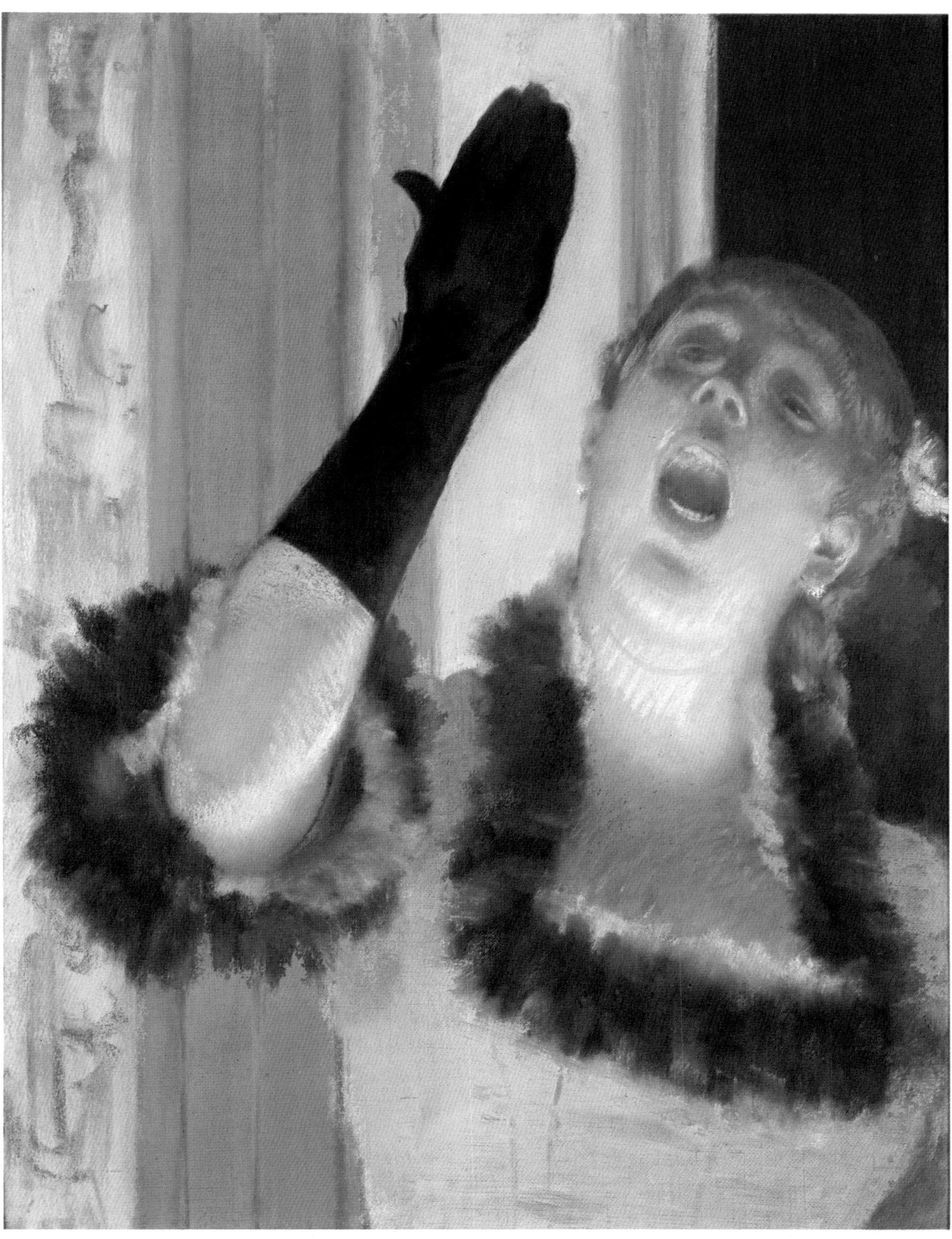

Edgar Degas.
Café Singer Wearing a Glove.
1878.
Pastel and distemper,
20⅞ × 16⅛ inches.
Fogg Art Museum, Harvard University, Cambridge, Mass. Bequest the Collection of Maurice Wertheim

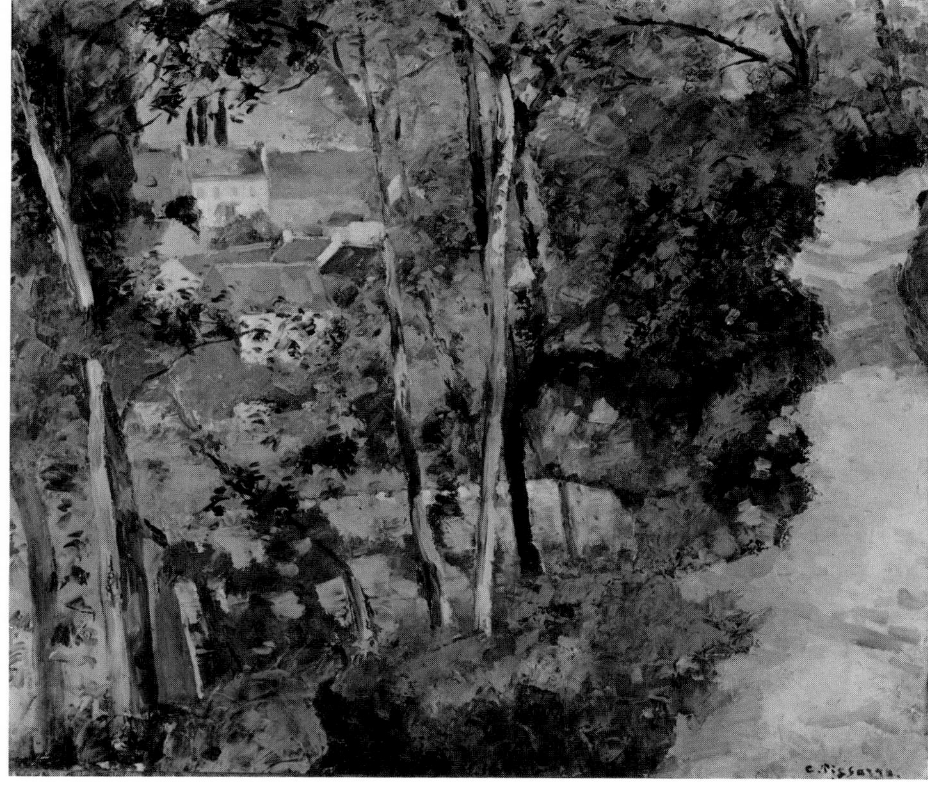

Camille Pissarro.
The Climbing Path.
1875.
Oil on canvas,
24½ × 25¾ inches.
The Brooklyn Museum. Gift of Dirkan G. Kelekian

day speech have connotations of the washed-out and the effete; but there was nothing of that when Degas matched palest lilac against salmon pink, as here, and set up a sharp apple green to sing out against the black of the glove. Where other painters might have portrayed the singer as a dignified figure in the middle distance, Degas gives us a dentist's view of her wide-open mouth, allows her to slip sideways as if at any moment she would move out of the frame altogether, turns her black glove into the most powerful single image in the picture and makes of her outstretched and bent-back thumb an unforgettable image of effort and strain. Degas spared nobody; but he didn't diminish anybody, either.

Man as a seeing animal has few monuments that can compare with the masterpieces of Impressionism. But man is not only a seeing animal. He is also a thinking, an imagining, a cross-referring and a systems-making animal; and none of these latter traits could be accommodated by pure Impressionism.

Impressionism was by definition dependent on the fugitive and the contingent in human experience. The beauty of the sunlight on the climbing path in the painting of that name by Pissarro is something that once seen is never forgotten; we see such things, ever after, as he saw them. But there are other kinds of experience, and other ways of marshaling them; and to the extent that Impressionism cannot deal with them it has, in the end, its limitations.

When Cézanne said of Monet that he was "only an eye—but what an eye!" he did not mean to put Monet down. An uncorrupted eye is a wonderful thing, and many a later painter has set a very high value on Monet's robust energy, on his open and candid procedures and on his readiness to break with the past when instinct told him that it was the right thing to do. Where Manet hedged his bets on modernity with learned allusions to this great master or that, Monet simply went ahead on his own. He did much more editing than was formerly supposed, but fundamentally he was a master of the single idea. And to the extent that a great compound idea is more resonant in the end than a great single idea, I myself would nominate the late 1880s as the moment at which new art came in and old art went out.

What I mean is this: nothing could be more delectable than the masterpieces of Impressionism. But a work of art is not simply an object of delectation; it is also an ideas-bank. A work of art is an emblem of the good life, but it is also an energy system. The ideas and the energy in question are not those of the artist alone, though he may well be uniquely alert to them; there is no warrant for the legend of the major artist as a man who acts on inspirations peculiar to himself and owes nothing to earlier art.

So the place, the time and the current ideas all had their part to play in the 1880s. When the period is one of crisis and the current ideas are outstandingly rich and complex, the role of the place becomes decisive. It is a very great help to make art in a place which has had an uninterrupted tradition of great art for several hundred years *and is still producing it.* There was not much to be said for being a painter in Madrid after the death of Goya, or in Venice after the death of Tiepolo, since in both cities a great tradition then collapsed. But in Paris the tradition held firm and was never firmer than in the second half of the 19th century.

In the 1880s, a world new beyond all prediction was coming up over the horizon. Not for many years did people learn to make the right cross-references among all that was going on. Certainly there was a large audience for the three-word pronouncement "God is dead" when it came out as part of Nietzsche's *Gay Science* (1882–87). But few people can have foreseen that Krafft-Ebing's *Psychopathia sexualis* (1886) would cast so long a shadow into the 20th century, or that that century would look back with awe to the paper with which in 1881, as a young man of only 25, J. J. Thomson set physics on a new path. The Michelson-Morley experiment of 1887 established, among other things, that there is no such thing as the absolute velocity of a material body, as distinct from the relative velocity of any two material bodies. As such, it was not without its parallels in the work of Cézanne, where the identity of any given object is often most subtly varied and adjusted by the fact of its proximity to other given objects. The historian of ideas should point also to Freud's meetings in Paris in the winter of 1885–86 with Charcot, the great specialist for cases of hysteria, which led eventually to a completely new phase in our understanding of human nature. Few knew of all this, just as even at the turn of the century there were reputable histories of French literature which did not mention Rimbaud's *Illuminations,* first published in 1887.

Ibsen and Strindberg in the 1880s were dynamiting pretty well every accepted idea of private and public morality, even if plays like *Ghosts* (1881), *An Enemy of the People* (1882), *Rosmersholm* (1886), *The Father* (1887) and *Miss Julie* (1888) were not widely seen till the 1890s and Strindberg was known to his friends in Paris less as a dramatist than as a keen and perceptive student of painting. The emergence in 1888 of the word "chromosome" signaled an important shift, elsewhere, in human understanding. Given as a name to the minute bodies which had been detected in the dividing cells of which animals and plants are composed, it led directly to one of the most significant generalizations in modern biology—the chromosome-gene theory, which posits that all living things have a common unit of structure. Once again, science and art turned out to have affinities as yet unsuspected. Such things were crucial in their field—as was, for that matter, the publication in 1890 of the first two volumes of J. G. Frazer's *The Golden Bough.* Imminent and radical changes could be descried in almost every department of life, and more especially in our notions of human nature, of space, time and causality, and of the structure of the universe and the structure of ourselves.

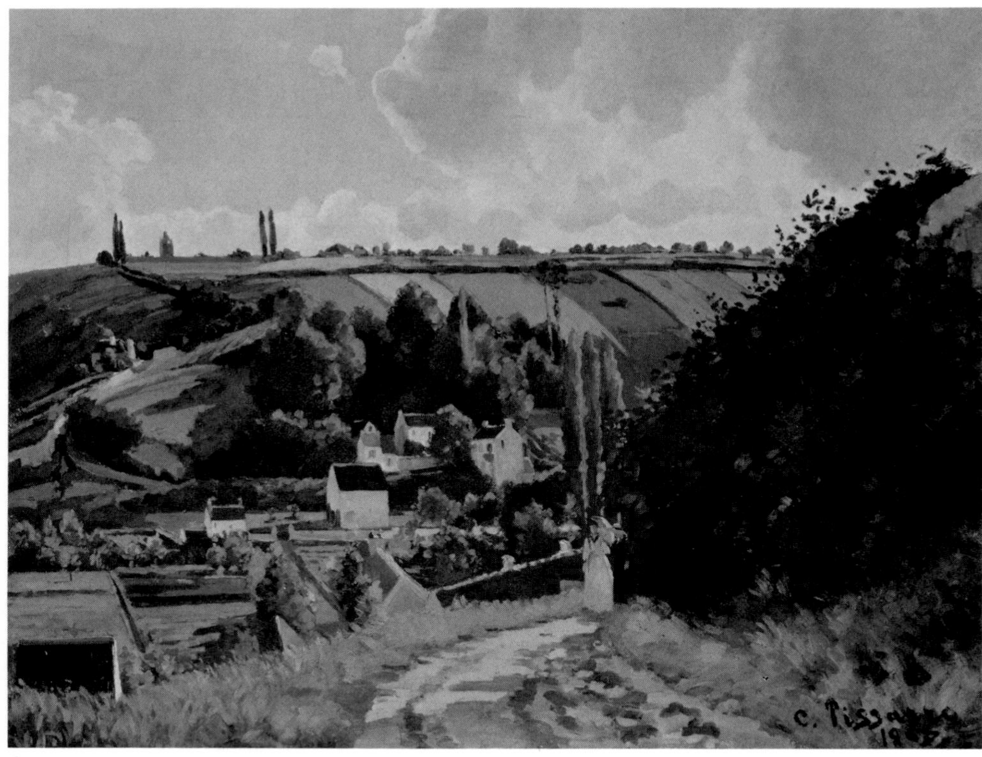

Camille Pissarro.
Jallais Hill, Pontoise. 1867.
Oil on canvas,
34¼ × 45¼ inches.
The Metropolitan Museum of Art, New York.
Bequest of William Church Osborn

There were, furthermore, elements in the general situation which every intelligent person should have been able to decipher. From the time of the Franco-Prussian war in 1870–71 it had been clear that Europe was bent on tearing itself apart. The French financial crisis of 1882 was trifling by the standards of the crash of 1929, but it was unpleasant enough for those—Gauguin among them—who earned their living by the stock market. Kropotkin's *Paroles d'un révolté* (1884) was one of many signs of radical activity in Europe. In Russia the increased persecution of the Jews, in Germany Bismarck's demands for an ever larger army, in Africa the establishment of the Congo state as the personal property of King Leopold II of the Belgians—all these were events of the 1880s that went on reverberating well into our own century. The world was getting into big trouble, quite clearly. All over Europe broad new boulevards were being cut through capital cities; but to what purpose? And what kind of life would be led in those cities? No one knew, but everyone was free to guess. People looked at the mechanized armies, and they heard about the ironclad warships, and they saw the armed police going out about their business, and they knew something—not too much, but something—about the plight of the disinherited masses. They could draw their own conclusions.

Art would not be art—would not, that is to say, be one of the most acutely indicative barometers of human activities—if it did not react, and did not adjust, to a situation of that sort. Very great and quite new ambitions were forced upon art in the 1880s, and the question to be answered was: what language would be adequate for these ambitions? Did it exist already, or must it be created?

It was a good question. Impressionism had proved that great art could be made from the most ordinary experiences, with no references to earlier art, no deft allusions to the Bible or Virgil or Ariosto, no search for "significance" in subject matter. Even so, its prime characteristic was a certain passivity before the free-flowing, unstructured *données* of optical experience: the *donnée,* the thing given, was the only thing that it took account of. This had its heroic side: the glorious impartiality of Pissarro's procedures had not been achieved overnight. Zola got the point of Pissarro when he wrote of his *Jallais Hill, Pontoise* in 1867 that "a beautiful picture by this artist is the work of an honest man. I cannot better define his talent."

"Perhaps we all come out of Pissarro" was how Cézanne summed up the matter. But it was not enough to come out; they had to have somewhere to go afterward, and they also had to have a greater freedom of maneuver than Impressionism could offer. The future of mankind and the future of art both called for that freedom. Only someone who was close to art and to artists could intuit the extent to which art was about to lose, one by one, the near-monopolies which it had enjoyed for centuries. The swing away from Impressionism was above all an instinctive, unstudied defense against art's then-imminent losses: a survival strategy for art, and a removal to positions in which art could keep its place as one of the most meaningful of human activities.

To count up the losses in question, we have only to look at the position today and see how many of art's former prerogatives have vanished. In the lifetime of Titian or Rembrandt it was a rare and an almost magical experience for people to come into contact with images at all, outside of a church. Till well into the 19th century the European street was for the most part a matter of bare walls and long empty prospects with only a house number or the name of a tradesman to animate the scene. Any metropolitan photograph of 1885 or later will show the difference. Our lives today are spent in almost continual contact with images of one sort or another. In all this, art's privileges have been withdrawn, one by one. For fact, people go to the newspaper, the news magazine or the television screen. For fancy, they go to the movies. Since Freud, the unified, unhesitating procedures of formal portraiture look obsequious and incomplete; the camera's offhand stalking seems to us almost always to give more truthful results. After the great war-photographers, battle paintings look stagy and squeamish. Even Eternity has been taken from art; and as for our place in the universe, a camera set down on the moon is more compelling than anything that art can come up with. In these contexts art has for years been a second-class activity.

If those contexts had been the only ones in which art could operate, painting and sculpture would long ago have abdicated, moved to the peripheries of life, accepted the archaic status of handweaving or custom shoemaking, or gone

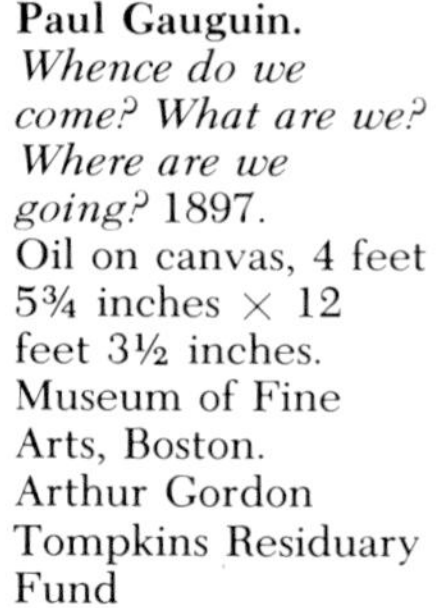

Paul Gauguin. *Whence do we come? What are we? Where are we going?* 1897. Oil on canvas, 4 feet 5¾ inches × 12 feet 3½ inches. Museum of Fine Arts, Boston. Arthur Gordon Tompkins Residuary Fund

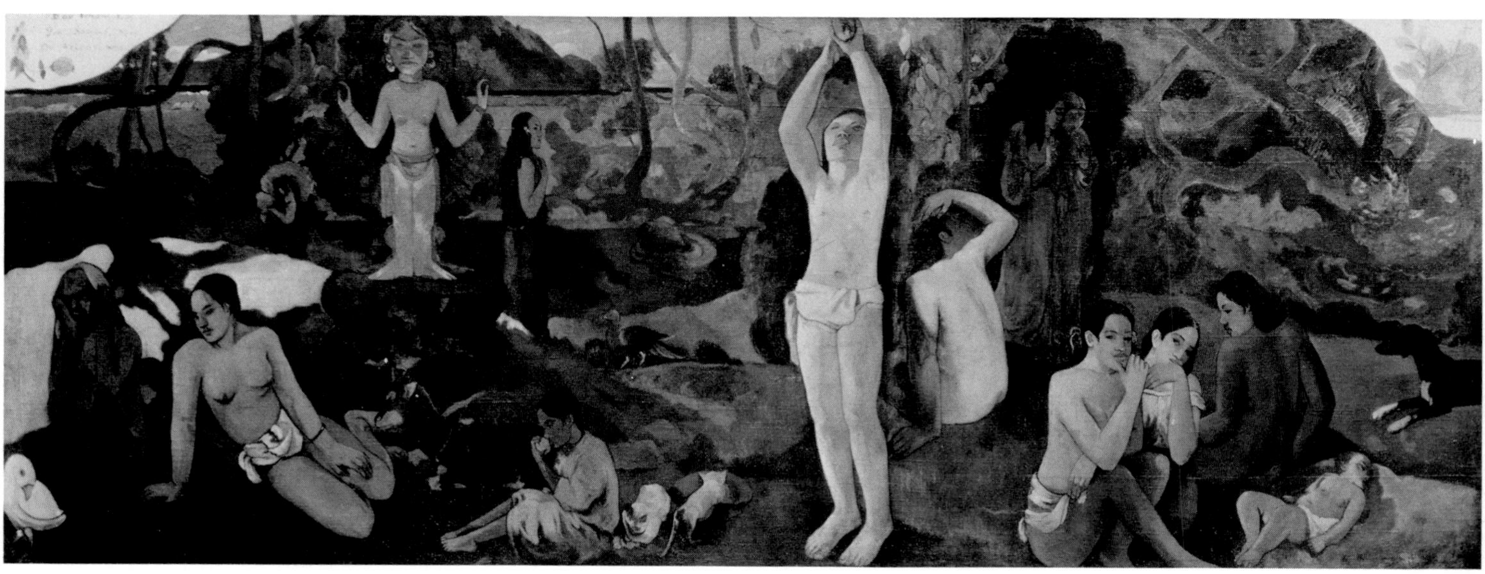

down altogether, the way the alexandrine vanished from the theater when people wanted a more informal way of speaking from the stage. We owe it to Courbet, Manet, Monet, Pissarro and Degas that this was never really in question, and to Cézanne, Georges Seurat, Vincent van Gogh and Paul Gauguin that in the late 1880s a whole set of new options was opened for art.

Not many people cared at the time. For one reason or another the work was not easy to see, and Authority was in no hurry to relieve the condition of physical and moral isolation in which Cézanne, van Gogh and Gauguin were working. Authority was at best indifferent, at worst actively dismissive: Nietzsche could have had Cézanne in mind when he wrote in 1885, "It is not the strength, but the duration, of great sentiments that makes great men."

Officialdom was quite right, from its own point of view. Napoleon III judged his interests correctly when he took his whip to a painting by Courbet. Kaiser Wilhelm II knew best when he fired the director of his National Gallery for buying too many modern pictures. Emperor Franz Josef had second sight when he told his coachman never to drive past a new and wholly unornamented building by Adolf Loos. These sovereigns knew what Plato knew: that the state of art is bound up with the state of society, and that when the laws of art change the laws of the state are likely to change with them. Courbet was a republican, a freethinker, a friend of Proudhon, the anarcho-socialist philosopher who invented the phrase "property is theft." He detested everything that emperors stand for, and he was later to go to jail for his beliefs. The Emperors and the Kaisers were absolutely right when they sensed that there was an imminent shift in the laws of art. That imminent shift stood for a freer, more spontaneous, more independent and less biddable state of mind—just the sort of thing that emperors should be nervous of. Authority thrives on submission, and the message of art in the late 1880s was that each man should decide for himself how to live.

What Then Must We Do? The title of Tolstoy's little book, written in 1886, could stand as motto for the whole decade. Both van Gogh and Gauguin were obsessed with the implications of that title—so much so, in fact, that when Gauguin came to sum up his whole career in the huge painting which is now in the Boston Museum of Fine Arts, he gave it a name which has a slashing, panoramic, Tolstoyan quality: *Whence do we come? What are we? Where are we going?*

Gauguin began work on this huge canvas at a time when he could be in no doubt that, as he wrote to a friend in November, 1897, his days were numbered. "Living and partly living" on mangoes, guavas and an occasional shrimp, with no money to buy bread and a steadily worsening physical condition, he nonetheless put such strength as he had into a three-part panorama which would sum up certain themes which had long preoccupied him. "The landscape," he wrote later, "is blue and Veronese green from one end to the other, and the naked figures stand out against it in bold orange." The general theme of

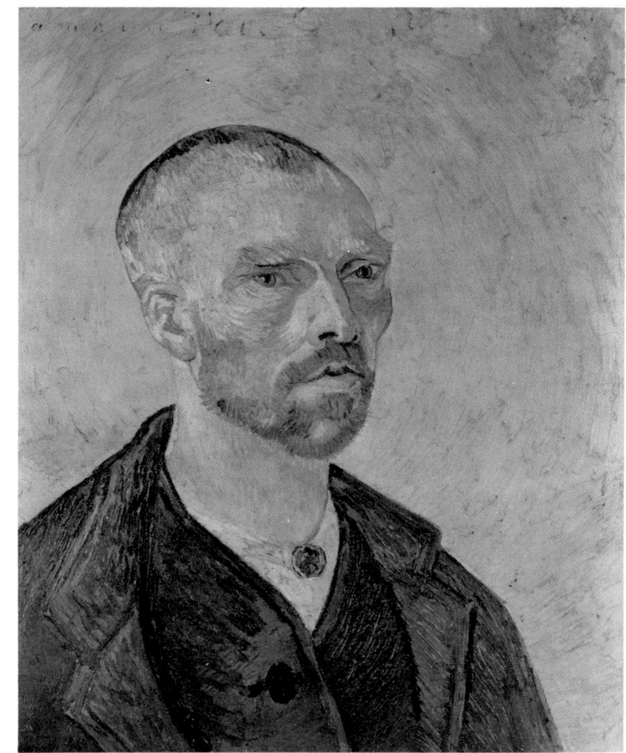

Vincent van Gogh. *Self-Portrait.* 1888. Oil on canvas, 24½ × 20½ inches. Fogg Art Museum, Harvard University, Cambridge, Mass. Bequest the Collection of Maurice Wertheim

the painting is the irresponsibility, the ignorance of destiny, the general lack of focus and understanding, which leads human beings to go on living in an aimless day-to-day way while inscrutable forces, stronger than ourselves, look down on us.

It was, Gauguin said, "a philosophical work, comparable to the Gospels." He admitted that it had "enormous mathematical faults"; but he refused to adjust them, prizing above any mere correctness the fact that the big picture had been done "direct from imagination, straight from the brush, on sackcloth full of knots and wrinkles." In a letter written some years after the picture was completed, Gauguin summarized the subject matter by saying that in the left-hand section an old woman sits, near to death; that in the central section "the man of instinct," still in his prime, meditates on the meaning of human existence; and that in the right-hand section life begins again with a little child lying beside a stream. Not the least touching thing about this huge ramshackle painting is that in time of supreme stress Gauguin, the Parisian know-all, should have reverted to so old-fashioned a scheme.

Tolstoy's *What I Believe In* came out in French in 1882, and one of the people to whom its ideas appealed especially was van Gogh. "Tolstoy suggests," he wrote to his brother Theo, "that whatever may happen in the way of a violent revolution there will also be a private and secret revolution in man. From this there will be born a new religion—or rather something entirely new, for which we do not have a name. It will give comfort, and make life possible, in the way that Christianity once did."

This idea mattered a great deal to van Gogh, who had tried his very best to be an evangelist and had had no success at all. Better than many a more worldly individual, he understood the apocalyptic implications of industrialization. He was convinced that "through revolutions, through war, through the bankruptcy of worm-eaten states, disasters are bound to fall like a terrible lightning on the modern world and on civilization." But what if art could bring about the "private and secret revolution" which Tolstoy had in mind? What if he, van Gogh, could help to avert disaster by touching men's hearts with his paintings as he had once hoped to touch them with his words? Van Gogh died before he could see his pictures put on show; but when we look at the lines of people that stretch round the block when those pictures are on exhibition today, we know that he did indeed get through to them.

More could be got out of art: as to that, the dreamer and the scientist were of one mind with the student of society. Art's potential had been underrated, underused, undersystematized. Art was not a boutonniere to be worn once a year; it was, on the contrary, one of the most fundamental of human activities. So that Seurat was aiming high, but not too high, when he said that he wanted his studies of metropolitan life to be the modern equivalent of the Panathenaic frieze on the Parthenon. The Parisians, like all other peoples, revealed themselves in their pleasures; and it was in their pleasures that Seurat sought them out —*en masse* on a hot summer Sunday afternoon, in *La Grande Jatte*, in ones and twos in *Une Baignade à Asnières*, at the theater in *Le Chahut*, at the circus in the painting of that name and at the street fair in *La Parade*.

Seurat was only 31 when he died. His output of oil paintings was small by comparison with that of van Gogh or Gauguin, and he has none of their universal celebrity. There are those who find his speckly procedures mechanical; even in his lifetime he is reputed to have been called "the little chemist" on account of the deliberate, laboratory-like manner in which he calculated the dosage of this color or that. Nor did the dot prove to be in itself a very rewarding instrument in the hands of others.

There is, even so, a grotesque injustice in this view of Seurat. Of course he was an eager theoretician. Like many another clever man in the 1880s, he believed that applied science could do a great

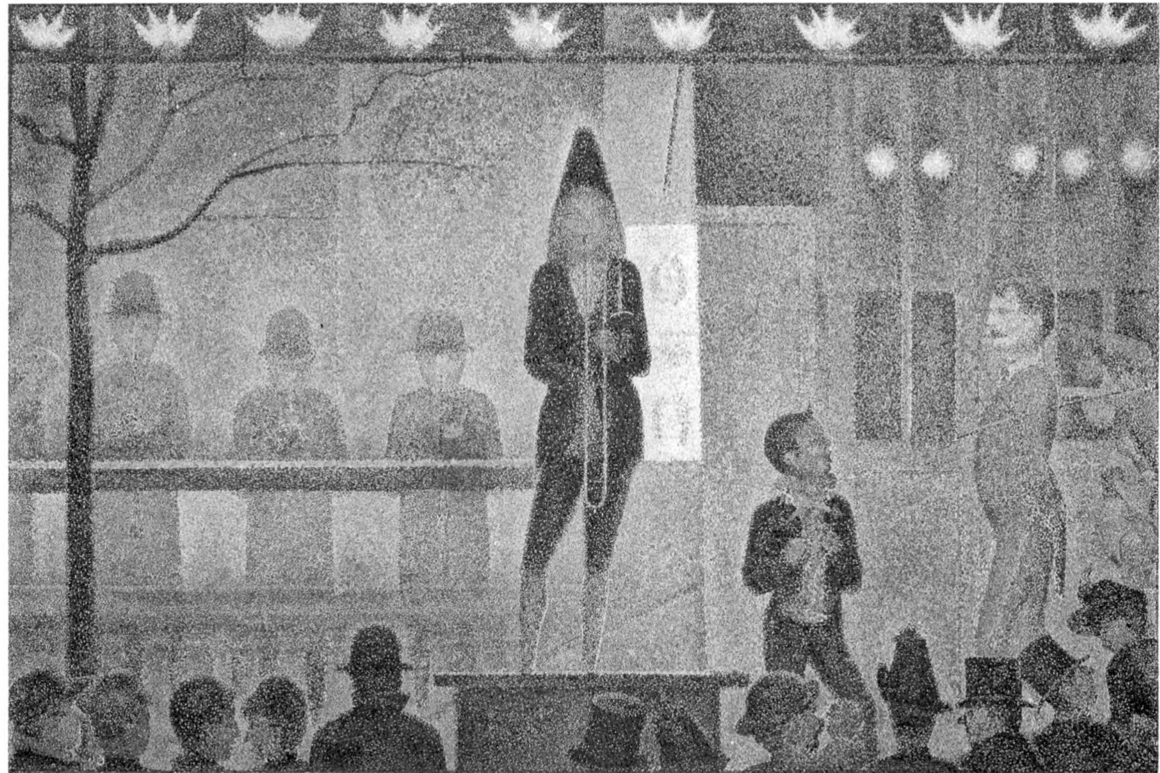

Georges Seurat. *Invitation to the Sideshow (La Parade).* 1887–88. Oil on canvas, 39¼ × 59 inches. The Metropolitan Museum of Art, New York. Bequest of Stephen C. Clark

deal for art. To that end, he studied the composition of color, and the emotional properties of mathematics, and the significance of ascending and descending lines and many another para- or pseudo-scientific formulation. Above all, he believed that, as the French theoretician David Sutter had argued in his *Phenomena of Vision* in 1880, "the laws of color harmony can be learned as one learns the laws of harmony in music." In this Seurat followed a number of earlier French 19th-century theoreticians, but with the difference that where their vision of a grammar of the arts did not really get off the printed page, Seurat was one of the great picture-architects of all time. He was also a penetrating social observer, with a particularly keen eye for the compulsive pranks to which his contemporaries subjected themselves in the name of pleasure. The governing principle behind his metropolitan subjects was this: that places do things to people, and that new kinds of places do new kinds of things to them and that it is the painter's privilege to sort all this out.

La Parade is full of scientific devices. The idea of using the dot as a basic unit agreed with the 19th century's many attempts to estimate the size of the smallest unit of matter into which physical phenomena can be broken down. Baudelaire in 1846 was already analyzing Nature in terms of its molecular structure and likening it, in its color relations, to "a spinning-top which revolves so rapidly that it looks gray, even though it embraces within itself the entire gamut of color"; and Seurat's contemporaries noted that although he applied his colors in small touches of the utmost purity and intensity, the optical mix which resulted often had the grayish look which Baudelaire attributed to Nature in its molecular aspect.

In its architectural construction, *La Parade* is based on mathematical theories put forward in 1885 by a Frenchman called Charles Henry, who was regarded at that time as a universal genius, as ready to pronounce on the best method of training for a bicycle race as on whatever lofty and abstract question was the topic of the day. A pleasure-pain

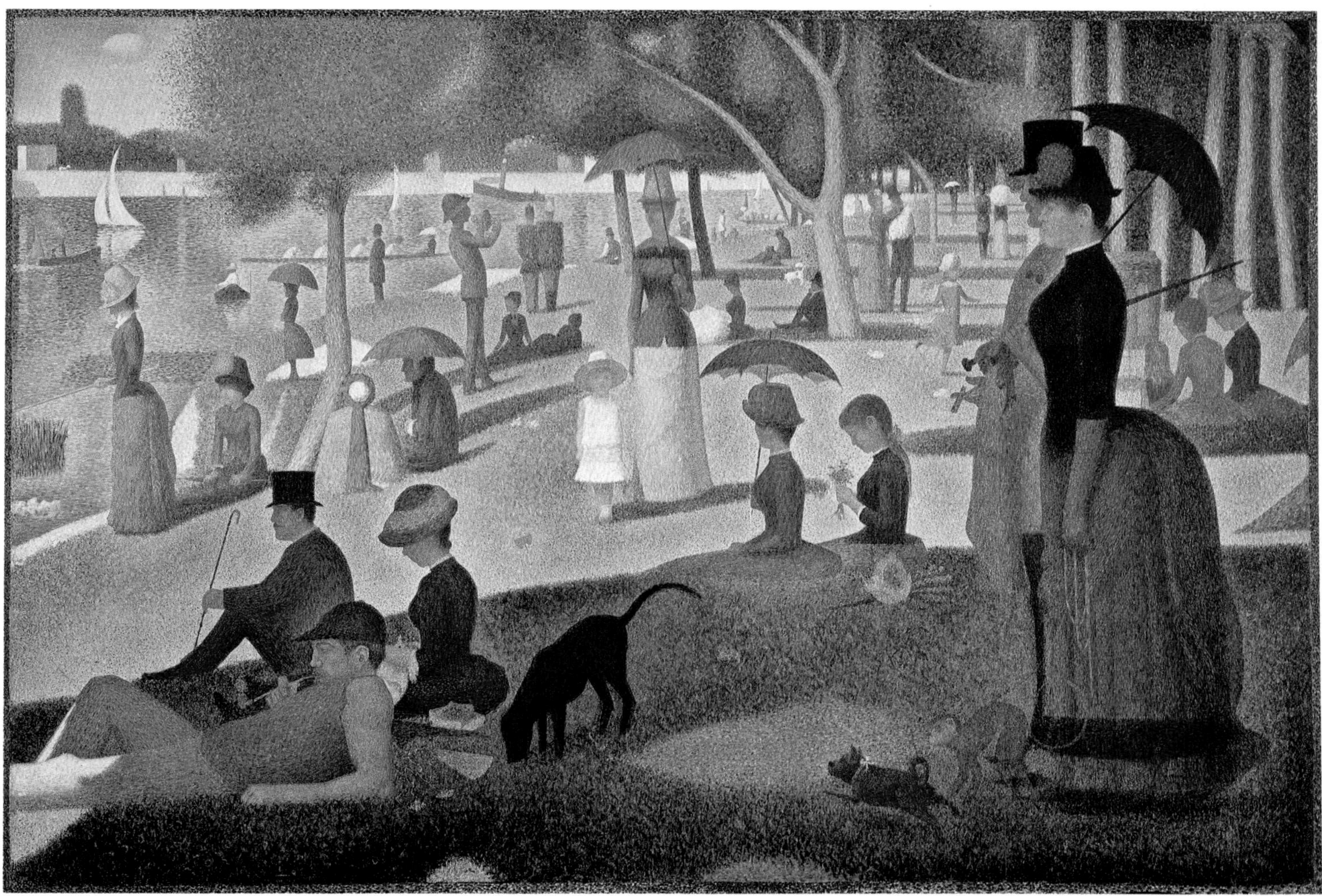

Georges Seurat.
Sunday Afternoon on the Island of La Grande Jatte.
1884–86.
Oil on canvas, 6 feet 9 inches × 10 feet.
The Art Institute of Chicago.
Helen Birch Bartlett Memorial Collection

theory much in favor in the 1880s can be linked to Seurat's use of a meandering line here and there, just as the form of the gas lamps at the top of the painting corresponds to the idiosyncratic, flower-like forms that Seurat prized as an emblem of festivity.

Art history thrives on details such as this. But the real message of the painting relates more to the dehumanization of big-city life than to systematic ingenuities of color and line. Anyone who compares an earlier treatment of the same theme—Gabriel de Saint-Aubin's *La Parade du boulevard* in the National Gallery in London, for instance—will see that where Saint-Aubin speaks for genuine, unforced, unsophisticated enjoyment, Seurat is almost ghoulish in his detailing of the metropolitan scene. His trombone player might be an executioner, and his auxiliary musicians defendants on the stand, while the director of the circus, in his cutaway coat, might be a prison warden ready to strike out at the nearest offender with his cane. Artificial light pollutes the environment, and the scene as a whole reminds us of what had lately been published in Rimbaud's *Illuminations*—the portrait of a big modern city as a place where trees bear no leaf, where people prefer not to know one another, and where the air is fouled by the leavings of industry. (On this last subject, Seurat's drawings of Paris have much to say.) *La Parade* is a masterpiece of ordered statement; but it also calls for a change of heart before the big city gets out of hand.

Seurat looked in many directions: back to Piero della Francesca, out of the studio window to the posters by Chéret which were turning the boulevards into one enormous picture gallery and forward toward kinds of art as yet unimagined. The ramifying tendrils of Art Nouveau derived in part from Seurat's use of arabesque; Marcel Duchamp, in his *Nude Descending a Staircase,* developed an idea of serial representation which was already present in Seurat's *Le Chahut;* Paul Klee by 1912 had mastered Seurat's color doctrine, even though his own work was then still primarily in black and white; Robert Delaunay took the systemic use of pure divided color and worked it up into Orphism; Wassily Kandinsky wrote that Seurat had aimed to show "not a fragment of Nature chosen at random, but Nature complete and entire in all her splendor"; and although Henri Matisse did not go along with the programmatic element in Seurat's work, he saluted "those other, truer values—those human painterly values which today seem ever more profound."

It would be hard to work up much opposition today to the proposition that Cézanne was one of the greatest painters, and by extension of that one of the greatest men, who ever lived. No one has had more influence on later art. Yet a mature painting by Cézanne has neither the immaculate and inexorable organization of a painting by Seurat nor the importunate pull of a painting by van Gogh or Gauguin. The subject matter is likely to be sober and conventional; the manner was for a long time thought to be tentative and overlaid with second thoughts. (Cézanne "couldn't draw," people said.)

This was because Cézanne had dismantled, one by one, the beliefs on which the practice of art had previously been based. That was in itself so momentous an ambition that he did not need, and could not have encompassed, the hectic high color and the patently symbolical subject matter of Gauguin or van Gogh.

There was nothing in Cézanne of the willful iconoclast. He revered the French classic tradition—as it had been exemplified by Poussin, above all. He revered it for its clarity, its complex, masterful organization, its noble and fastidious utterance, its disdain for the private and the accidental. Everything in Poussin happens the way it is meant to happen; never does he permit himself a loose end, a second thought, a momentary whim or caprice. A price was paid for all this, as it was paid in the plays of Poussin's near-contemporary, Racine. In Racine, nobody sneezes; the disorder of everyday life is outlawed by classic tradition. In Poussin, equally, we never come across a passage that is awkward or unfinished or a piece of drawing that has been flubbed.

Cézanne was alive to all this, but he knew that it was his destiny both to let in the things that had been left out of the French classic tradition and to let drop, one by one, its grave certainties. "Is that really how we look at the world? Or is there something in the nature of painting itself which has not yet been explored?" Those were the questions which Cézanne was to ask, and to answer, in the paintings of his last 29 years. He did not ask them in an abstract or schematic way. He *lived them,* in front of the motifs which Nature provided. No painter was ever more attentive to the outward and ostensible subject of his paintings: the portraits, the still lifes, the Provençal landscapes whose beauty Cézanne hoped to reveal for the first time. But fundamentally from the late 1870s onward he was also preoccupied with the notion of painting as a constructive act.

Cézanne took nothing for granted. He knew that style in art is like style in life: there is a moment at which it allows us to do what we have never done before, and there is a later moment at which it simply walls up the unknown and cuts us off from our own potentialities. Cézanne took down that wall; and he worked not as a dynamiter works but minutely and patiently, chip by chip, until in the end everything could come in. Prizing above all things a certain equilibrium of the vital faculties, Cézanne never aimed to let instinct rip.

It must, for instance, have been very painful for him when he gradually came to realize that traditional perspective would have to go. He knew how for more than four hundred years perspective had been the painter's automatic pilot, marshaling on his behalf no matter how large a quantity of visual information. By taking as its first premise a single point of vision, perspective had stabilized visual experience. It had bestowed order on chaos; it allowed elaborate and systematized cross-referencing, and quite soon it had become a touchstone of coherence and evenmindedness. To "lose all sense of perspective" is to this day a synonym for mental collapse. Yet perspective, before Cézanne, was fundamentally one of the sanctified frauds that keep the world turning: a conspiracy to deceive, in other words.

Of course it had brought great rewards. The expressive potential of perspective had been enormous. Cézanne acknowledged that his ambition was "to do Poussin over again from Nature"; and nothing in Western art is more moving than the godlike assurance with which Poussin argues that perspective is the right and natural way, the harmonious and logical way, in which complex statements can be spelled out on canvas. Yet Cézanne had in mind something more truly and more completely expressive of human capacities. Whether or not he knew it, his stance before life was characteristic of his time—and, more especially, of the attitude defined by Henri Bergson in a famous essay of 1889 on the nature of intuition: *Les Données immédiates de la conscience.* "We have to express ourselves in words," Bergson begins, "but most often we think in space." In French the word *conscience* means "conscience" in our sense, and it also means both "consciousness" and "knowledge." To a Frenchman, therefore, consciousness *is* knowledge, and to be conscious is to be learning, continuously. Bergson's ideas about duration and contingency, and about the interrelations and interpenetrations of objects, are often strikingly similar to Cézanne's procedures. We soon realize that whereas Tolstoy in the 1880s was asking "What Then Must We Do?" Cézanne was asking, "What can we know?" and asking it in terms which will always be relevant.

He let in, one by one, the things that had been kept out of painting: the fact, for instance, that in our knowledge of a given object time plays a part. We do not see it once and for all from a given point; nor does the given object have a given identity, once and for all. Monet also was aware of this, in his Cathedrals series of 1894; but the particularity of Cézanne was that he could work the effects of serial vision into a single canvas, thereby showing how everything is relative, in questions of identity, and subject to time, and movement, and change. Renaissance and post-Renaissance practice had given art stability; but stability and equilibrium are not necessarily the same, and when stability is spurious—willed, that is to say, and arbitrary—bluff enters into it. Cézanne called that bluff.

It was the same bluff that lay behind all the other pseudo-immutable systems—Euclidean geometry, for one, and Newtonian physics, for another. All the bluffs got called, between 1880 and 1914, and nowhere more thoroughly than in art.

Cézanne rebuilt the experience of seeing. He rebuilt it on the canvas, touch by touch, and he made each touch do a threefold duty. It had to be true to the object seen. It had to be true to the experience of seeing it. And it had to play its part in a grand overall design. That design was not carried out in the sweeping, unified and clearly eloquent style of the earlier masters. It was *built up,* piecemeal. All this is shown to perfection in his *Still Life with Peppermint Bottle,* which is a majestic amalgam of traits derived from French classical tradition, on the one hand, and forays into completely new territory, on the other. Since the 17th century French still-life painting had been remarkable for the weight, the solidity and the sense of a classical equilibrium with which household objects were rendered. Cézanne was faithful to this: never was fruit more monumental, never glass more artfully transparent, never the neck

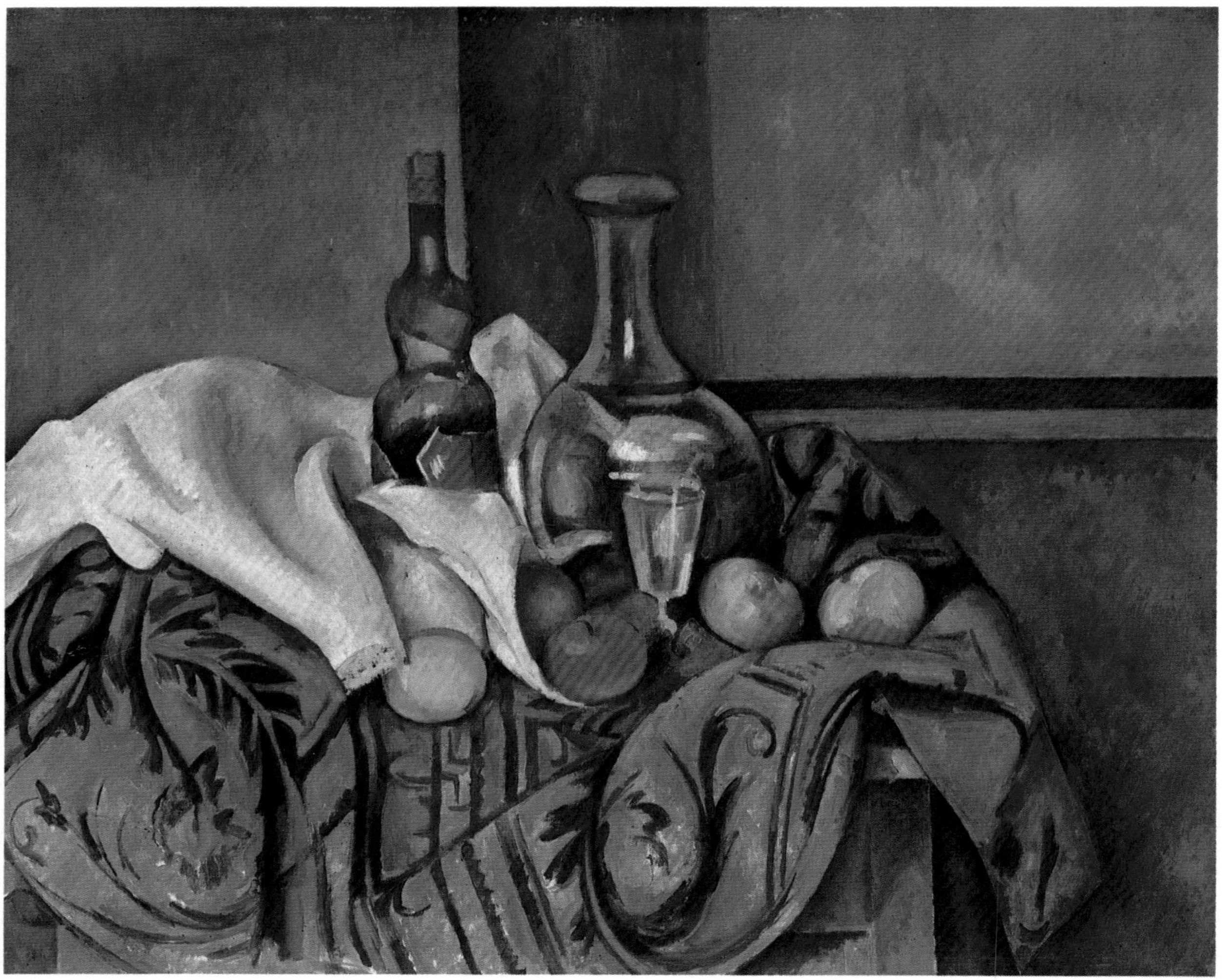

Paul Cézanne.
Still Life with Peppermint Bottle.
1890–92.
Oil on canvas,
26 × 32⅜ inches.
National Gallery of Art, Washington.
Chester Dale Collection

and shoulder of a bottle more thoughtfully aligned to their surroundings.

But there was no authority in classical French painting for the peremptory way in which the top of the table had become invisible and illegible; for the way in which the decanter was made to belly out on the right; for the tumult of the drapes, which rear up from the top of the table like waves on a rough day at sea; or for the way in which the composition as a whole is both a portrait of stability, in which everything is balanced, somewhere and somehow, by every other thing, and at the same time a portrait of perpetual motion. Those drapes did not come from earlier painting but from the recesses of a riotous imagination; and yet, as always, Cézanne was minutely attentive to such details as the particular shiny red of the seal at the top of the bottle. There are portents of later painting in the way, for instance, in which the drapes mysteriously form, in the lower right-hand folds, into the likeness of a musical instrument much favored by the Cubists. There is a quick-moving, widely ranging system of echoes in the patterning of the drapes; Matisse was to pick this up and use it to great effect before 1914. Paintings such as this one stand on a high plateau between the past and the future of European painting. Cézanne was always true to what Bergson called *la conscience immédiate:* the facts of his own awareness. Anyone who doubts this should look at his monumental and yet totally human paintings of card players: everyone in them is, as D. H. Lawrence said of one of his characters, "like a piece of the out-of-doors come indoors." Cézanne never took a formula

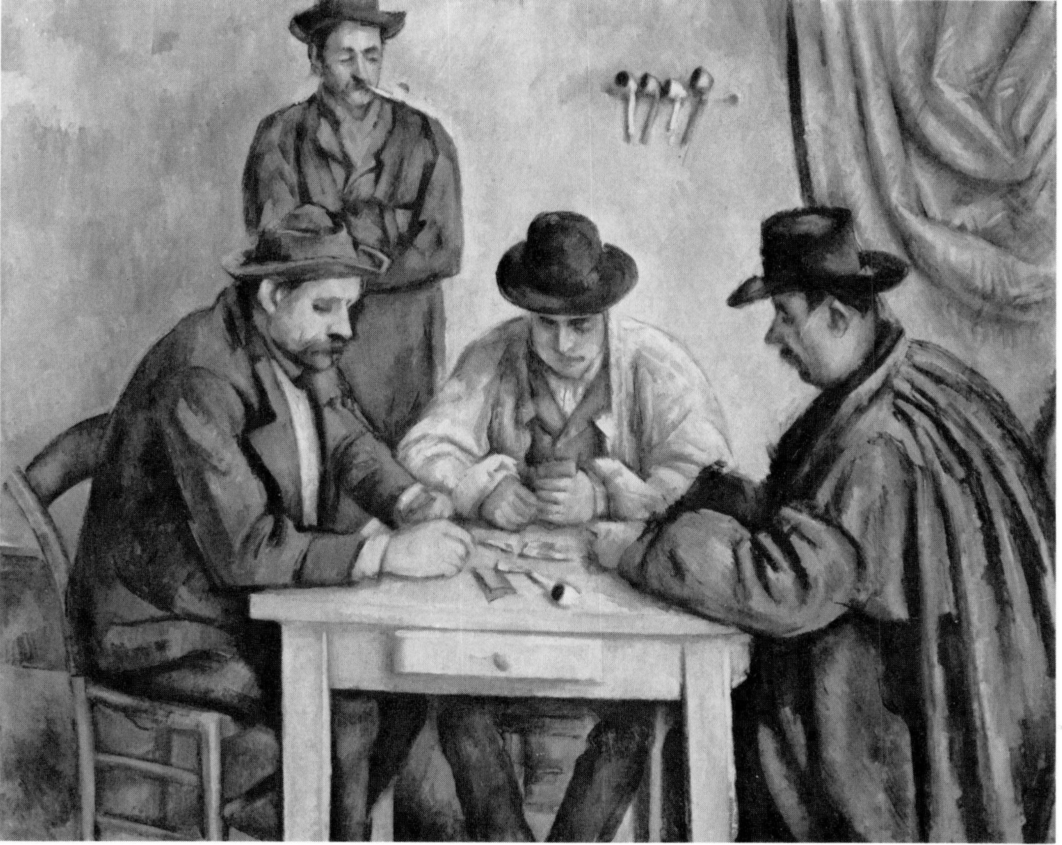

Paul Cézanne.
The Card Players.
1890–92.
Oil on canvas,
25½ × 32 inches.
The Metropolitan
Museum of Art,
New York.
Bequest of Stephen
C. Clark

from stock; every mark on the canvas had to prove itself. But he also personified the organizing intelligence; and as he grew older there developed an ever greater tension between the demands of this organizing intelligence and the evidence which was brought to an eye that grew continually more acute. It was a part of the French tradition that order and stillness and lucidity should be bestowed on scenes which in themselves were in continual flux. When Louis Le Nain painted his *Peasants in a Landscape,* for instance, he devised a grand mathematical structure for his figures; his picture is a triumph of the grand style, and yet it does not abate the individuality of his subjects. Their dignity as human beings is enhanced by it. When Corot painted his *Breton Women at a Well,* he too gave the scene a severe, pyramidal structure in which the element of chance was ruled out. Cézanne, in the big *Grandes Baigneuses* now in Philadelphia, was as concerned as either of his predecessors with the august harmonies of triangular form—in fact he used the triangle three times over: once in the trees and twice among the bathers—but he also let in all the paradoxes, the contradictions and the irrational emphases which abound in our everyday experience. Cézanne included these too, and in doing so he gave an altogether grander dimension both to art itself and to the cognitive act. It is for this reason that Cézanne now seems to have given us, in words used by Henry James in another context, "the strongest dose of life that art can give, and the strongest dose of art that life can give."

That quotation might seem to relate, and in its original context in *The Tragic Muse* did relate, to a key moment in classical drama, when violent emotion is made bearable, but only just, by art. In Cézanne it might seem to apply more to the early imaginative subjects, where rape and murder are taken for granted, than to the work of the later years. But Cézanne from the 1880s onward was on to one of the fundamental truths about our life on

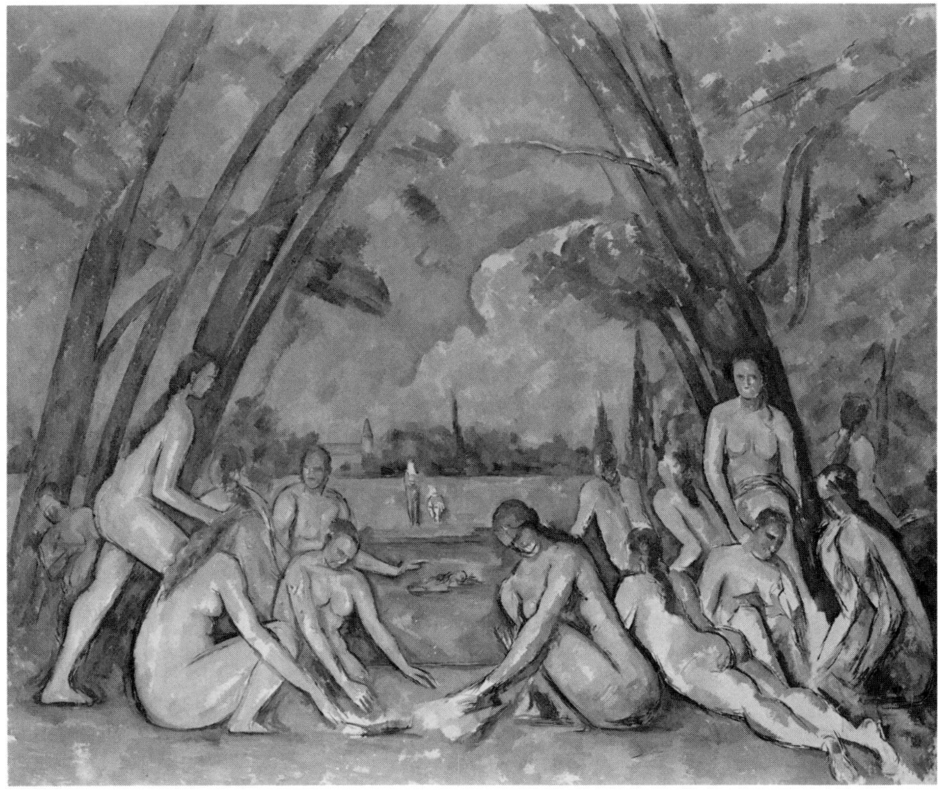

Paul Cézanne.
Grandes Baigneuses.
1898–1905.
Oil on canvas, 6 feet 10 inches × 8 feet 3 inches.
Philadelphia Museum of Art.
W. P. Wilstach Collection

earth: that *an idea is the most exciting thing there is.* Imagined melodramas about one man killing another cannot compete for enduring interest with the restructuring of the act of cognition which was Cézanne's deepest concern during the last years of his life. In one way or another, there is hardly an artist of consequence in the 20th century who was not affected by Cézanne's handling of the fundamental question "What can a man know?"

Gauguin was a very good judge of painting, and when he had the money, between 1876 and 1880, he formed a collection of Impressionist paintings which would have got him into art history even if he himself had never touched a brush. But when he became a painter himself his instinct told him that European art needed reinvigoration and that that reinvigoration would come from sources untapped in the schools. His memories of a sojourn in Peru in childhood had convinced him that in so-called primitive art there were inherent forces that could somehow revitalize the European imagination. Working in Brittany in the 1880s, and trying to build a picture language that would be distinctly his own, he remembered the hieratic and antinaturalistic presence of the Egyptian, Assyrian and Far Eastern sculptures which he had seen in the Louvre. He had Japanese prints pinned up in his room, alongside reproductions of Manet's *Olympia* and paintings by Botticelli and Fra Angelico; he looked hard at the Romanesque carvings which were to be seen in Brittany near Pont-Aven. Painting his *Breton Eve* in 1889, he took her pose from a Peruvian mummy which he had seen in Paris; painting his *Yellow Christ,* in the same year, he took both color and pose from a polychrome wooden sculpture in the chapel at Tremalo, near Pont-Aven. By taking the statue out of the chapel and putting it in the Breton landscape he gave it, however, something specifically Gauguinesque, the sense that mysterious forces, sometimes Christian in origin and sometimes not, are at work in landscape. Where the Impressionists saw landscape as fundamentally wholesome and benign, Gauguin saw it as the henchman of the unknown, and he made us aware of this by treating the landscape, as in the *Yellow Christ,* in terms of flat bands of color that had none of the Impressionists' regard for probability. "The mysterious centers of thought" were what Gauguin wanted to reach; and with that in mind he deliberately broke with the conventions of visual experience, circumscribing the principal elements of the picture with a firm, bold line, heightening and sharpening the color and flattening the planes until we are in no doubt that a new experience in a new kind of country is at hand.

Gauguin's personality in general was strong to the point of aggressiveness. But in one very beautiful painting done in Brittany in 1890, Gauguin subordinated his own edgy, incisive and at times almost hectoring approach to portraiture. *Marie Lagadu* is in fact an act of creative homage to Cézanne. More than anything that could be said or written, it shows with what a tender submission Cézanne was regarded by those of his fellow painters who had got close to him. Gauguin gave his sitter the monumental stillness and solidity for which Cézanne strove in his own portraits. He modeled her with a sculptural fullness and firmness, building the head with rich, fat color areas. Just behind her he placed a still life by Cézanne himself. ("I cling to that picture," he once said, "as I cling to my own life.") Re-creating a part of that still life on his own canvas, he went on to modulate almost imperceptibly from it to the real still life—the fruit and the tablecloth—in front of it. With a noble reticence quite foreign to his own nature, he integrated the real still life and the interpreted still life into a single, unbroken image. There was nothing of Gauguin's arbitrary, heavily outlined handling of color; the color was Cézanne's, just as the majesty of the pose was Cézanne's. Gauguin for once did not think of himself.

Marie Lagadu was an act of creative assimilation. If Gauguin's methods were usually more abrupt, it was because he believed that desperate situations called for desperate remedies. When he went to the South Seas it was not to "escape forever" but to save himself—and perhaps Europe too—from inanition. "A great thought-system is written in gold in Far Eastern art," he wrote in June, 1890. "The West has gone to rot, but a strong man could redouble his strength, like Antaeus, just by setting foot in the Far East. A year or two later he could come back as a new man."

Gauguin did not come back as "a new man," but the idea of the transplantable energies inherent in primitive art was to spread to Picasso, to Matisse, to Derain, to Kirchner and his colleagues in the group called Die Brücke (The Bridge) in Dresden, and to many another young artist before 1914. Gauguin saw the artist as a lord of life who could pick and choose from the past whatever would best release his own inmost nature. In this he pioneered one of the archetypal attitudes of the 20th century.

Gauguin also showed how color could be heightened in the interests of truth to individual human feeling; and in this, once again, his example was of primary importance to later painters. It is crucial to remember that what we call "influences" in art are not always linear. The people who profited most from Gauguin's example were not his immediate followers. Nor were they the people who tried to imitate what he had done. They were artists of quite other persuasions: Edvard Munch, most evidently, Bonnard and Vuillard in the 1890s, Picasso in his Blue Period, Matisse in 1905, Kandinsky in the years 1908–10. "Heighten color, simplify form" was the essence of what Gauguin told his admirers. It was Maurice Denis who said later: "The idea of having to copy Nature had been a ball and chain for our pictorial instincts. Gauguin set us free."

What Gauguin did in the last years of the 1880s was to specify the conditions in which the artist of the future could go to work. "My own work may be only relatively good," he said later, "but I have tried to vindicate the right to dare anything." Like Nietzsche in *Beyond Good and Evil,* he wanted to

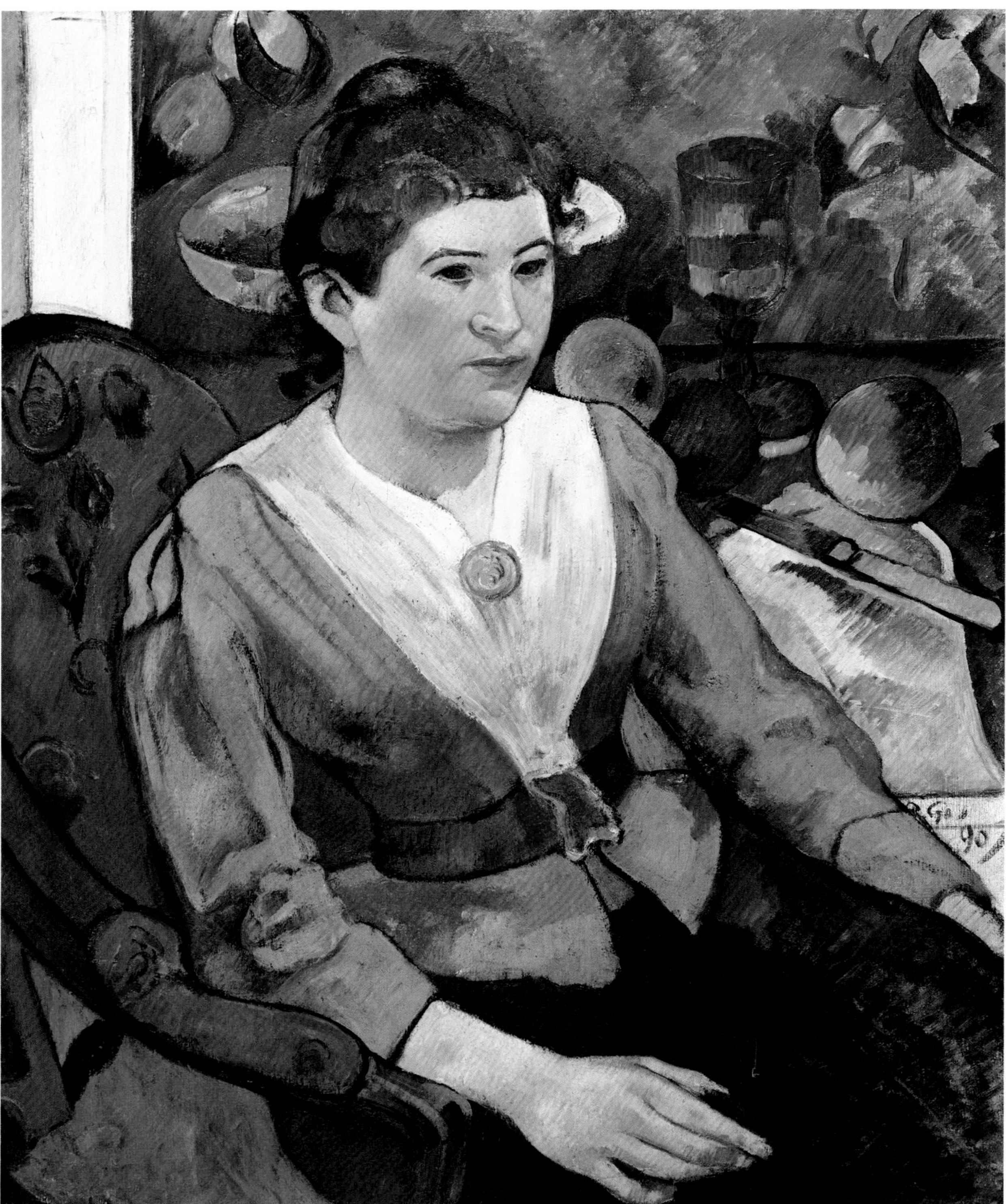

Paul Gauguin.
Marie Lagadu. 1890.
Oil on canvas,
25⅝ × 21½ inches.
The Art Institute of Chicago.
The Joseph Winterbotham Collection

get back to "the terrible original text, *Homo natura.*" "Two natures dwell within me," he wrote to his wife in 1888, "the Indian and the sensitive being. And now the sensitive being has dropped out and left the Indian to stride out ahead on his own." But the "sensitive being" in Gauguin kept coming back, unbidden, even if the Indian agreed with Nietzsche that Christian principles were "mere enfeeblement: witchcraft and sugar." But Gauguin was in touch with Paris till the end; the pictures he painted in the South Seas owed as much to Puvis de Chavannes (1824–98) and the tradition of European pastoral as to anything he picked up in Tahiti. This is true even of paintings which, like *The Moon and the Earth,* seem at first sight entirely non-European in their terms of reference. Gauguin did not like people to press him for a literal "explanation" of his South Seas paintings. He preferred on such occasions to quote the poet Stéphane Mallarmé: "Music needs no libretto." "The essence of a work," he wrote to one of his critics, "lies precisely in what is not expressed. . . . It has no material being."

So we may not be a great deal further forward for the knowledge that *The Moon and the Earth* represents an encounter between Hina, the moon, and Fatou, the earth. Hina stretches to her full height in order to ask Fatou if man cannot be reborn after death. When he says "No," she replies, "As you wish, but the moon will be reborn." The two figures dwarf the surrounding jungle. Gauguin has in fact given Hina the full-bodied power of one of Courbet's forest girls, while rendering the landscape in summary and miniature style, thereby reinforcing the suggestion that these are superhuman beings, personified Fates whose dialogue affects every one of us. But, once again, elements from earlier French painting keep coming in. The giant head of Fatou, for instance, is a descendant of the statues that look down on the mortals' goings-on in more than one major painting by Watteau. Degas bought this picture when it got to Paris in 1893; and as no one could have been less interested in images of the

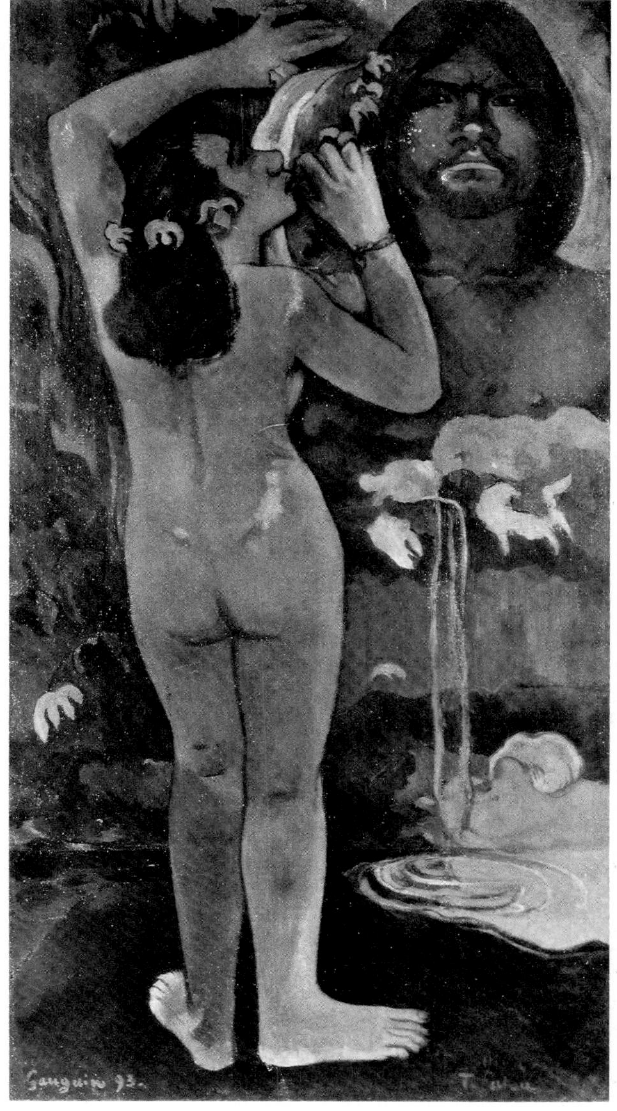

Paul Gauguin.
The Moon and the Earth (Hina Tefatu).
1893.
Oil on burlap,
45 × 24½ inches.
The Museum of Modern Art, New York.
Lillie P. Bliss Collection

supernatural, I suspect that what he responded to was the strength and assurance with which Gauguin had reinvented the notion of pastoral.

The breakthrough that mattered to later art was the one he made in Brittany in 1888—to an abrupt, peremptory, self-willed sort of painting, in which perspective was flattened, forms were outlined with none of the continuous modeling of earlier times and color was used with unprecedented simplicity and force.

That is what Matisse, for one, took from Gauguin: flat tones, radical contouring and the readiness to let unaccented color areas overwhelm the

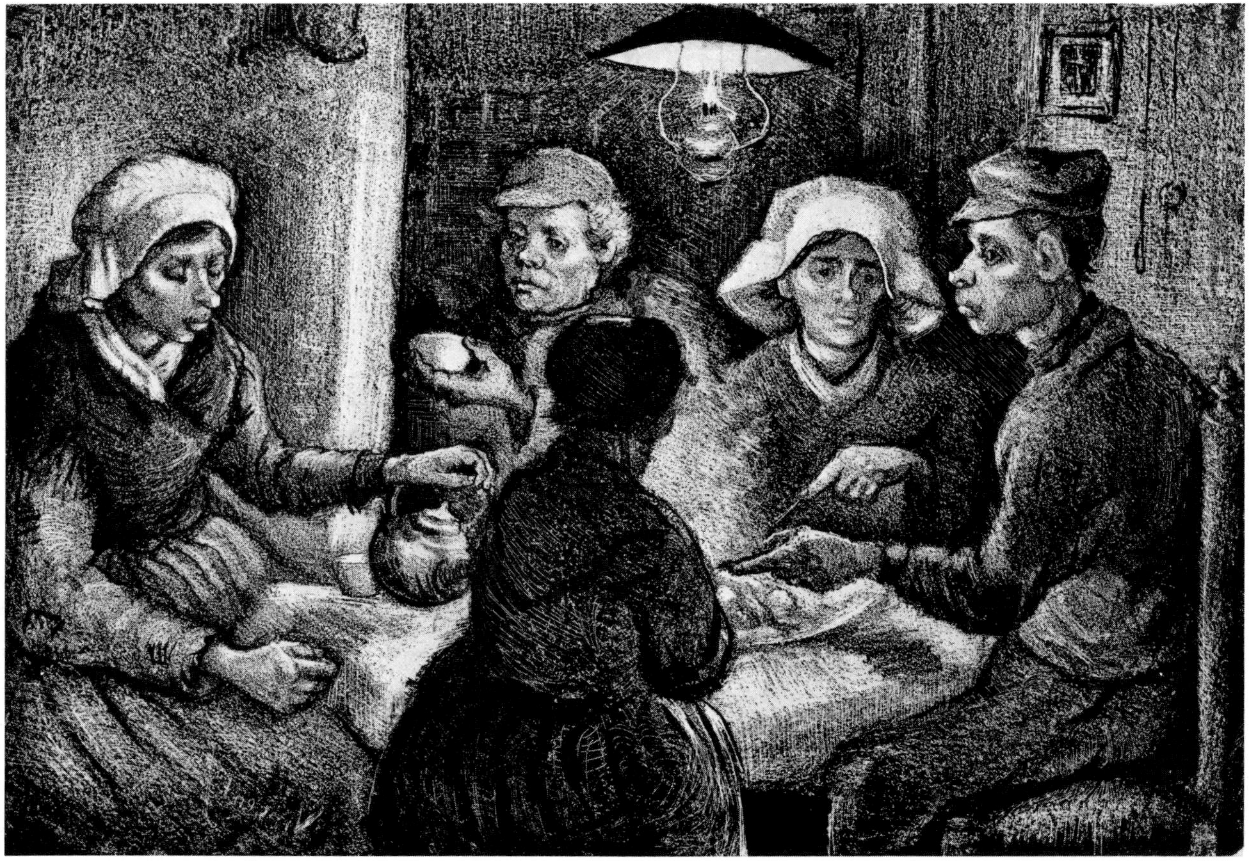

Vincent van Gogh. *The Potato Eaters.* 1885. Lithograph, 12¼ × 15¾ inches. The Museum of Modern Art, New York. Gift of Mr. and Mrs. A. A. Rosen

spectator. Bonnard and Vuillard could not have been less like pre-Columbian Peruvians, but they saw what could be made of Gauguin's arbitrary flat patterning and disregard for conventional perspective. When Gauguin used heightened color to express emotional truth, he got through to Kirchner and his colleagues in Dresden not as an "experimenter" but as a free spirit who used painting to redefine the dignity of man. We know now what Picasso meant when he said, many years later, that from a certain time onward "every man could re-create painting as he understood it from any basis whatever. . . ."

Gauguin in later years did not demur if people thought that van Gogh was fundamentally a simpleton, a Dutch dunce who had been picked up and put on the right road by him, Gauguin. Some of the facts were on his side: Gauguin knew the Impressionists when van Gogh was still toiling over his perspective-frame in The Hague, watching the workmen shambling out into their courtyards at four o'clock in the morning while the first fires were starting to smoke all over the town. In 1885–86, when Gauguin was about to make the decisive jump toward an arbitrary, inner-directed manipulation of color, van Gogh was still pondering how, in Dutch painting, "one of the most beautiful things has been the painting of *black,* which nevertheless has *light* in it." Black, which Pissarro had outlawed 20 years before!

Yet van Gogh in his Dutch years was already, even if only in intuition, the progenitor of much that is best in the art of our century. The year 1885 was, for instance, the year of the *Potato Eaters,* the dusky masterpiece of his years in Holland. But it was also the year in which instinct told him that color could be set free. Before he had ever seen what we call "modern painting"—that was reserved for his arrival in Paris in February, 1886—

he was writing to his brother in terms that even today have kept their explosive power. Holed up in the Dutch village of Nuenen, where his father had been a pastor, he developed on his own the idea-structure which gives him so firm a hold on later art.

"Color expresses something by itself," he wrote. "Let's say that I have to paint an autumn landscape with yellow leaves on the trees. If I see it as a symphony in yellow, does it matter whether the yellow that I use is the same as the yellow of the leaves? *No, it doesn't."* So much for the ancient convention by which every object has its "local color" and must bring it everywhere as evidence of its identity.

The culmination of van Gogh's views about the moral potential of color is *The Night Café,* which he painted in Arles in 1888. For the Impressionists, the café was a place where people went to enjoy themselves; Degas, for one, looked at it from the standpoint of an unshakable social assurance. Van Gogh saw it quite differently: partly because it was in his nature to solidarize with the poor and the lonely, partly because he was never rich enough or assured enough to go to places where the customers did not have to count their every penny. He saw the café as "a place where one can ruin oneself, or run mad, or commit a crime." He sensed "the powers of darkness" in what was probably a straightforward French working-class drink shop; and he tried, when painting it, "to express the terrible passions of humanity by means of red and green." His account of the painting is explicit enough to deserve quotation. The room, he said, was "blood red and dark yellow, with a green billiard table in the middle." Four lemon yellow lamps cast a glow of orange and green. The blood red and the yellow and the sharp green of the billiard cloth contrasted with "the tender, soft, Louis XV green of the counter, with its pink bouquet of cut flowers." The atmosphere was full—or so it seemed to van Gogh—of pale sulphur, "like a devil's furnace"; and the owner's white coat was changed to "lemon yellow, or a pale, luminous green," as he stood on duty in the corner.

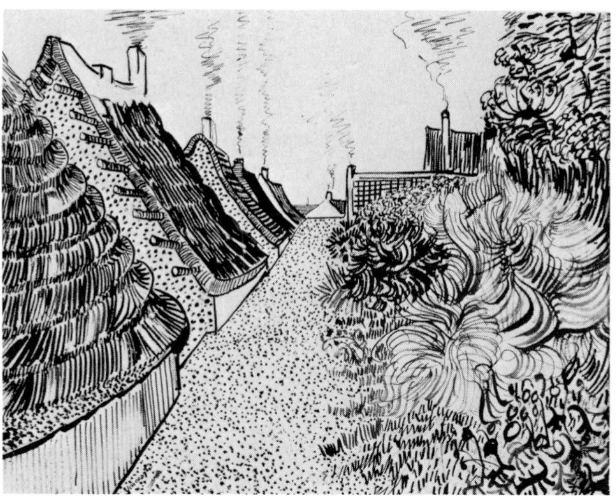

Vincent van Gogh. *Street in Les Saintes-Maries.* 1888. Ink and reed pen, 9⅝ × 12½ inches. The Museum of Modern Art, New York. Abby Aldrich Rockefeller Bequest

Now, it is quite clear from a painting which Gauguin made of this same café that van Gogh misrepresented its basic nature, which was that of a place where people sat not too far apart and stared boldly around them. Van Gogh's inner distresses caused him to present the café as a place where a few cheerless patrons were swept to the perimeter of the scene, the way snow is swept into the gutters of a roadway. All possibility of an amiable human intercourse seems excluded, and we genuinely feel, as he wished us to feel, that "the terrible passions of humanity" have run their course behind the half-drawn curtain at the back of the room. Even the billiard table, that robust old stand-in for a more active and constructive way of life, suddenly looks like a bier. Van Gogh achieves all this in part by manipulations of perspective; but it is above all the color that projects a sense of the most penetrating inner anguish. Truth to feeling had never come out more strongly in painting. By setting truth to individual feeling above truth to objective fact, van Gogh gave the colorist his charter. Those words of his in 1885 are the beginnings of much of Matisse, much of Munch, much of early Derain and Vlaminck, much of Kandinsky, much of Chagall in his early years, much of Klee. To this day, when artists talk about color, they owe something, directly or indirectly, to van Gogh.

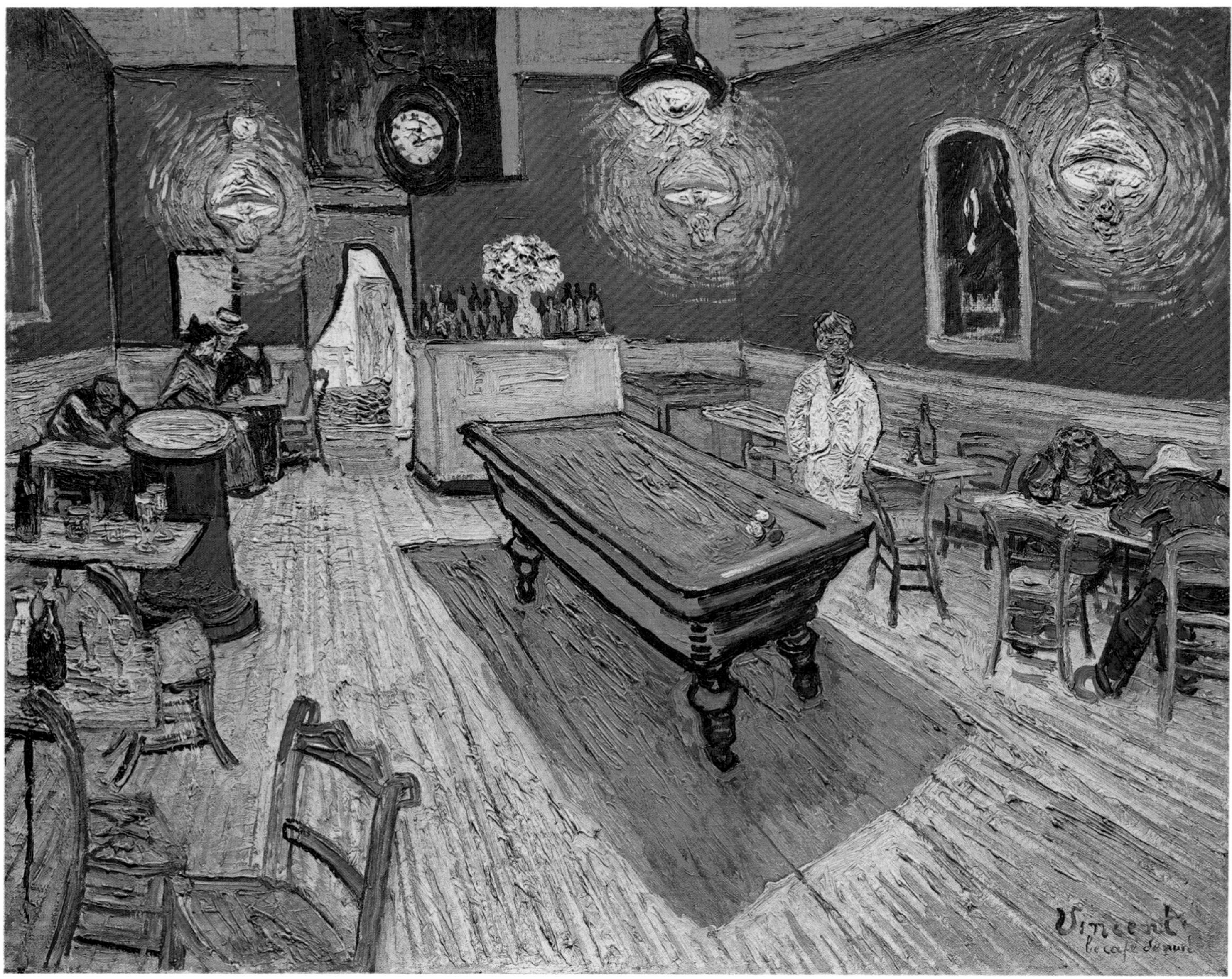

Vincent van Gogh.
The Night Café.
1888.
Oil on canvas,
28½ × 36¼ inches.
Yale University Art Gallery, New Haven, Conn.
Bequest of Stephen Carlton Clark

Van Gogh was also coming to terms at that time with what is for the layman one of the most bothersome aspects of modern art: distortion. Distortion is, or was, a sore subject with young and old alike. We remember, for instance, how in 1913 the art students of Chicago burned Matisse's *Blue Nude* in effigy when it came to the city as part of the Armory Show. And it was an "artist" who complained to van Gogh's brother about the distortions in the *Potato Eaters.* "Tell him," van Gogh wrote, "that I should be in despair if my figures were 'correct,' in academic terms. I don't want them to be 'correct.' Real artists paint things not as they are, in a dry, analytical way, but as *they* feel them. Tell him that I adore Michelangelo's figures, though the legs are too long and the hips and backsides too large. Tell him that what I most want to do is to make of these incorrectnesses, deviations, remodelings or adjustments of reality something that is—yes, 'untrue,' if you like, but more true than literal truth."

This was, once again, written in the year 1885, and in the depths of the Dutch countryside. Again van Gogh hit on just the turn of phrase that could stand as a motto for the century that is now in its last decades. To "paint things not as they are . . . but as *they* feel them" is an ambition so nearly universal in our time that van Gogh would deserve immortality for that phrase alone. Yet he went on finding, to the end of his short life, the right words for the kind of work which would bring to light the buried life of man. Before how many great paintings of this century do we not remember van Gogh saying that "the painter of the future will be a colorist such as there has never been," and that the unit of expression for the new art would be "a form of brushwork that would cut out stippling, and the rest, and offer simply the varied stroke"?

In pictures like *The Starry Night,* painted in Saint-Rémy in June, 1889, van Gogh showed what he meant. The paint in *The Starry Night* is not applied in polite, well-judged, art-school style. It forms itself into ideograms of convulsion: emblems of an apocalyptic vision which includes stars brighter than the sun at midday, a huge horned moon that seems to hold the sun in its embrace, and a spiral nebula that flies through the air like a serpent from the Book of Revelations. Even the moonlit woodlands behind the little town are rendered with a ferocious, nonstop, over-and-over movement of the loaded brush. Just once or twice before, others had got somewhere near to the intensity of *The Starry Night:* Leonardo da Vinci in his drawings of a storm, the German Old Master Altdorfer in his portrayals of a tormented northern sky. But van Gogh was out on his own for the sheer visionary intensity of his new "unit of expression." This is painting that refers not to earlier painting but to areas of our experience to which art had not previously had access.

To Cézanne's "What can a man know?" van Gogh added a question of his own: "How can we best unlock the valves of feeling?" To one or the other of these questions, or to both of them in conjunction, modern art has the answers.

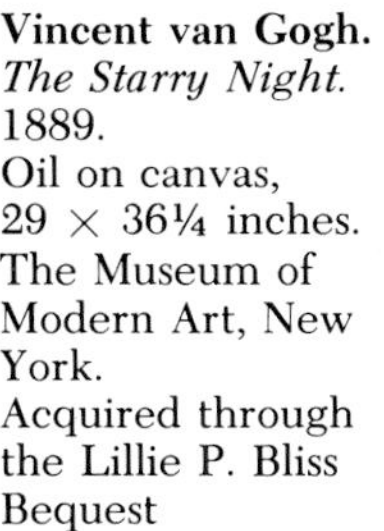

Vincent van Gogh.
The Starry Night.
1889.
Oil on canvas,
29 × 36¼ inches.
The Museum of Modern Art, New York.
Acquired through the Lillie P. Bliss Bequest

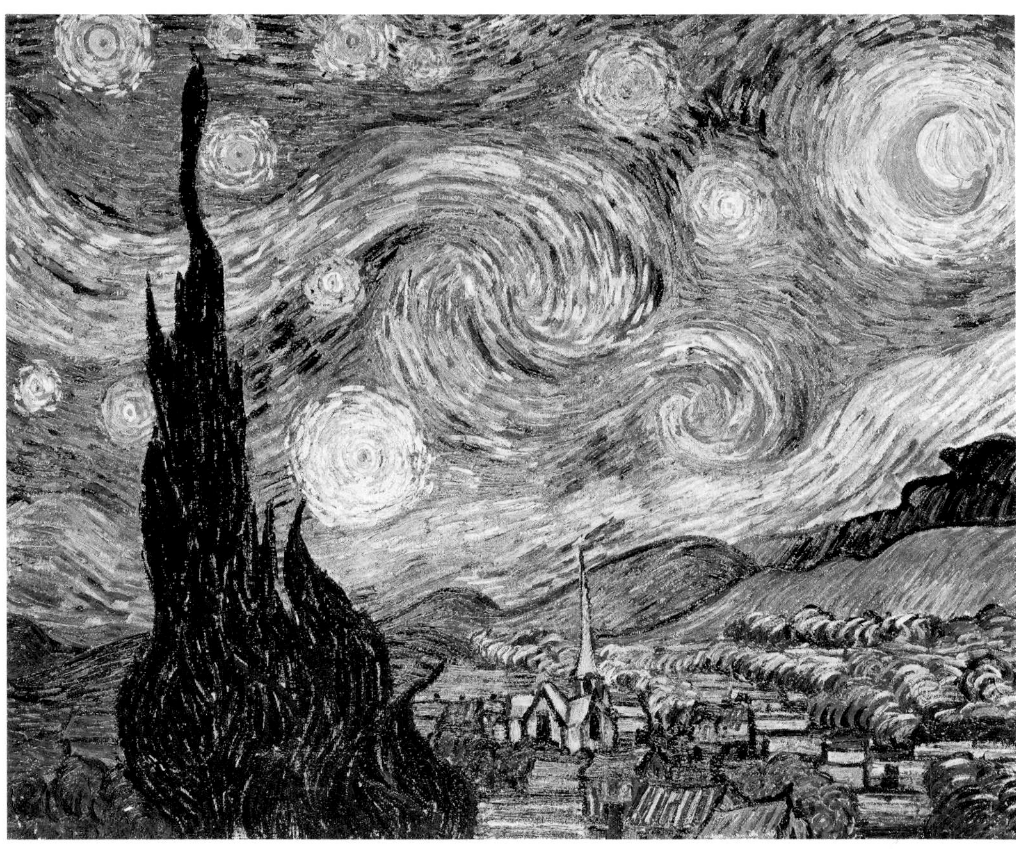

THE EMANCIPATION OF COLOR

Between 1890 and 1905 the emancipation of color was completed.

Like most of history's upheavals, this one looks inevitable when surveyed from a safe distance. Emancipation had been in the air for a long time: you couldn't open a newspaper, sit through a play by George Bernard Shaw or put your nose inside a factory without realizing that radical changes—some peaceful, some not—were on the way. The 1860s had provided the Grand Design: people remembered 1861 for the emancipation of the serfs in Russia, 1863 for the emancipation of the slaves in the United States, 1867 for the emancipation of the Jews—in principle, at any rate—throughout the Austro-Hungarian Empire. The emancipation of women would take longer, but by the late 1880s it had become clear that society was moving toward it. It was unthinkable that in art, that most sensitive area of life, equivalent emancipations should not occur.

And occur they did, though not quite fast enough to save Pissarro and Monet from near-martyrdom by poverty in the late 1860s. Gradually it became clear that the traditional patronage of the state and the church was giving way to a freer and more informal relationship between the painter, his dealer and just one or two informed collectors. The tyranny of the big annual official exhibition loosened around the same time, and a new tradition began: that of the little back room to which the fortunate few were admitted by pioneer dealers like Ambroise Vollard and *le père* Tanguy. Subject matter was set free, now that the favor of a frock-coated official was no longer essential to an artist's advancement. The fine arts were released from obligations to society which could better be carried out by photography; as a result, their natures could be explored without either inhibition or surveillance.

In all this, color was the conspicuous element. Its emancipation was foreshadowed as early as 1885, when van Gogh put it in writing that "color expresses something by itself." That color could send coded messages in a cipher not yet cracked was clear to Gauguin by 1888 and quickly got through to his disciples. That color could make volume and define form was being proved by Cézanne all through the 1880s and 1890s. That patches of color laid flat on the canvas were the prime constituent of painting, and should take rank as such, was argued by Maurice Denis, then just 20 years old, in a now-classic article, "A Definition of Neo-Traditionism," first published in August, 1890. The more men looked into the fundamentals of art, the more consistently did color turn up at the center of their inquiries.

But when color finally came out strongly at the Salon d'Automne of 1905—in the room given over to Henri Matisse, André Derain, Maurice Vlaminck, Albert Marquet, Henri-Charles Manguin and others—people were dumbfounded, all the same. They were dumbfounded all over again in Dresden in 1906, and in Munich in 1911, and at the Armory Show in New York in 1913. As in other departments of life, it is one thing to talk about emancipation and quite another to meet it face to face. There were local and auxiliary motives for their stupefaction: many of those who were appalled by Matisse's paintings at the Salon d'Automne in Paris in 1905 had never seen a Gauguin or a van Gogh and knew nothing of the historic fatality which had brought those particular Matisses into being. But there was also a general and a more rational reason to raise the alarm.

Color is a constant: one of the standards of excellence and normality by which we judge Nature, judge much that is of our own making and judge one another. Color is also a differential: one of the things that help us to find our way about the world. We don't like to feel that either of these two main functions of color is subject to alteration. Color is fundamental to life: to call a man "colorless" is as rude as we can get without descending to particulars. Color has a hot line to instinct, and its messages take priority even over those of language: the hunter doesn't need to speak if he can point to fresh blood in the snow. Our first reaction to change in all this is one of defensive rigidity; if the traffic lights turned blue at the next intersection, a conservative driver would put the gears into neutral and sit by the side of the road.

But we also know, and our predecessors knew already in 1905, that color is one of the affirmative elements in life. Color is energy made visible. Energy in itself is not necessarily good; anyone who has been within range of a hurricane will have seen for himself that energy can be vicious and destructive. But in the context of art, heightened color usually brings heightened energy of a euphoric sort; and I don't think it was an accident that Matisse in 1905 was painting in a world that wanted to get more out of life than people had been getting before. What was the message of Henry James in *The Ambassadors,* first published just two years before? "Live all you can—it's a mistake not to."

Heightened color came into art at just the time when heightened energy of an environmental kind was becoming available to everyone. This is not to say that there was a self-evident relationship between science and art from the 1880s onward. Gauguin in Pont-Aven and van Gogh in Arles were about as innocent of up-to-date scientific knowledge as intelligent human beings can be. But they knew that there was more to color than had yet been got out of it, and that somewhere in color there was energy, waiting to be released. Color had to be made to work for everyone as electricity was working for Edison, as the gasoline engine was working for Gottlieb Daimler, and as Niagara Falls was beginning to work for those who knew how to tame it. These things had to have their equivalent in art; and Gauguin knew before he died that he had opened new color options for painting, just as van Gogh knew that the great artist of this century would be a colorist of a kind never seen before.

Matisse, as much as anyone, was that colorist. By 1909, when he painted the first version of his *Dance,* he was able to make a plain, bald, unhesitating affirmation of color-as-energy. *Dance*

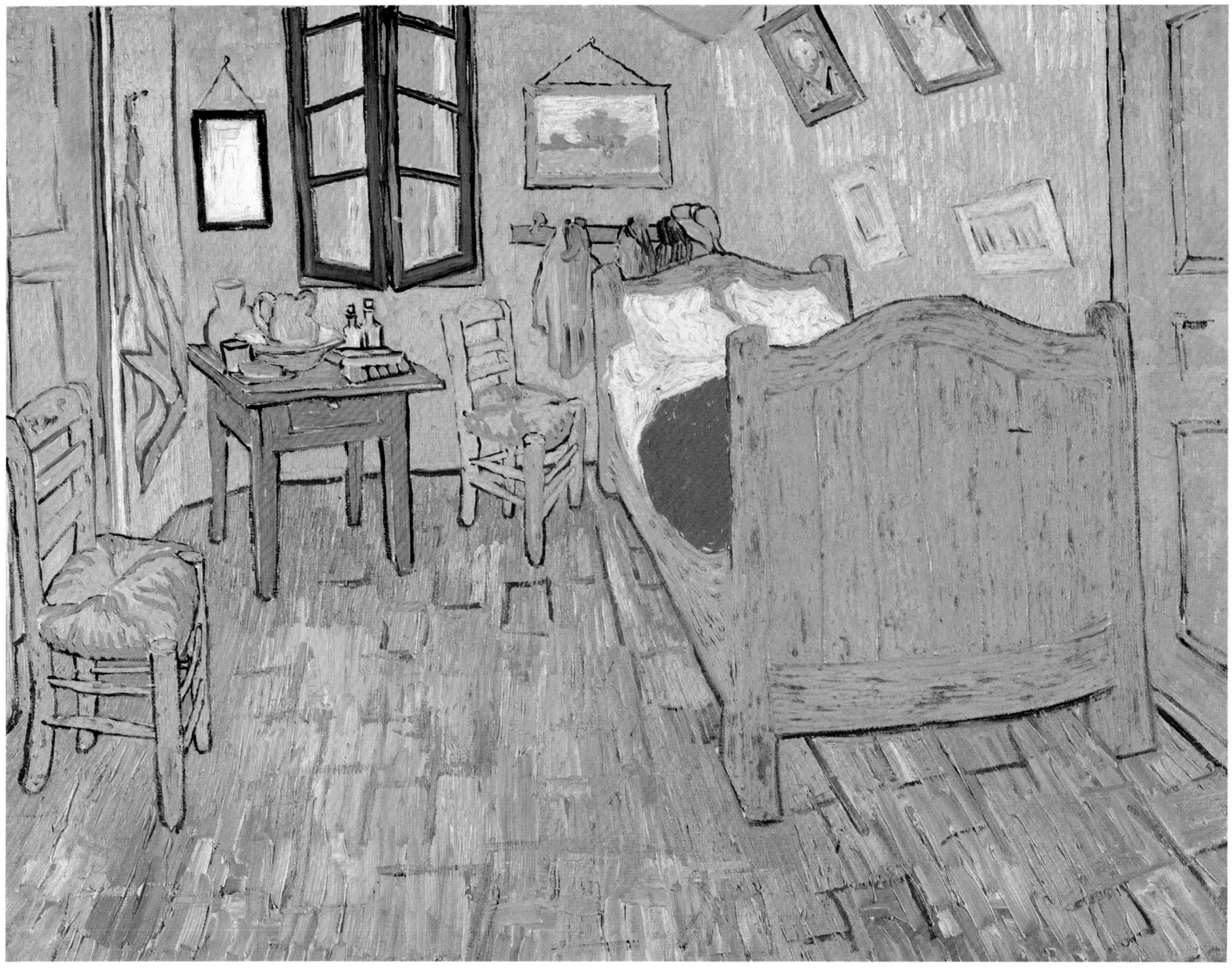

Vincent van Gogh.
Bedroom at Arles.
1888.
Oil on canvas,
28¾ × 36 inches.
The Art Institute of Chicago.
Helen Birch Bartlett Memorial Collection

looked (and still looks) so spontaneous that many people believed that Matisse had simply trusted to instinct and let rip, like a "great artist" in a movie. When Matisse opened a private art school in Paris in 1908, his students thought to please him on the first day of the term by daubing their canvases at random with the hottest colors they could lay their hands on—only to find that Matisse disliked this very much indeed and sent them right back to the formal beginnings of art education.

He also knew that the Old Masters were neither ignorant nor timid when it came to the use of color. Everyone has heard of Titian's way with red, Veronese's way with green and Vermeer's way with a lapislike blue. But the conditions of art in their day were such that color had to stay down in the kitchen as the servant of form and the henchman of design.

There was even a socio-philosophical prejudice against color. Immanuel Kant, in his *Critique of Judgment,* first published in 1790, gave classic expression to the subjection of color. "In painting and sculpture," he said, "the *design* is the essential thing. . . . The colors which give brilliance to the

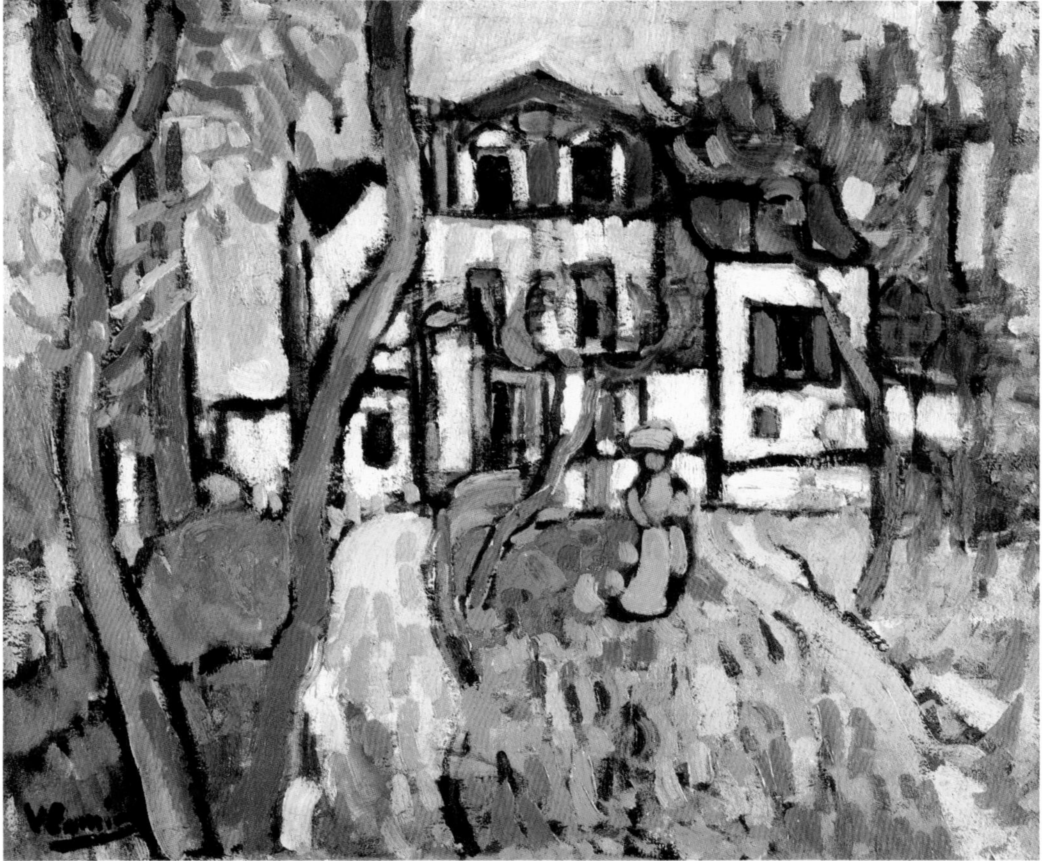

Maurice Vlaminck.
The Blue House.
c. 1905.
Oil on burlap,
21½ × 25½ inches.
The Minneapolis
Institute of Arts.
Bequest of Putnam
Dana McMillan

sketch are part of its charm and they may, in their own way, give an added liveliness to what we are looking at. But they can never, in themselves, make it beautiful." This was, admittedly, a philosophical position rather than the view of a man who had spent much of his life looking at pictures. Kant had hardly ever left his native city of Königsberg and was so indifferent to the pleasures of sight that it was several years before he even noticed that he had gone blind in one eye. Kant was predominantly cerebral in his orientation, and he ran true to psychological type in preferring line to color; the sensitory freedom for which color stood was of no interest to him. But, quite independently of this innate predisposition, he spoke for educated European opinion at a time when color was thought of as a dispensable additive; and Matisse could almost have had Kant in mind when in 1945 he looked back, as a man in his late 70s, on the evolution of color.

"The whole history of color," Matisse said then, "lies in the recapture of its powers of expression. For centuries it was no more than the complementary of drawing. Raphael, Dürer and Mantegna were like all the painters of the Renaissance in that they built their pictures on drawing and added the local color later. The case was quite different with the Italian primitives and with the painters of the Orient. With *them,* color was the principal means of expression. . . . From Delacroix to van Gogh (and, in particular, to Gauguin) by way of the Impressionists, who cleared the ground, and by way of Cézanne, who gave the definitive push when he showed us how to make volumes with pure color, we can trace the rehabilitation of color and the recovery of its power to work upon us directly."

Matisse, when he said that, had been painting and drawing and sculpting for over half a century. There lay before him, in his 80s, a terminal period as fruitful as any in the history of modern art. No one ever knew more about color than he. So what he has to say has great weight with us and, once again, the upheaval which he describes now looks inevitable.

But changes of this sort correspond to profound, hard-won changes in social attitudes. The long subjection of color stood, for instance, for a fear, or at the very least, a distrust of the instinctual life. By the 1890s Nietzsche had spread throughout Europe a contrary point of view: instinct was marked *plus* in his work, whereas for centuries it had been marked *minus.* When Kant wrote his *Critique of Judgment* it was with art as it was with property, and with monogamy, and with authority in all its forms: the instinctual life had to be kept down, lest anarchy should supervene. There was no such thing in the 1790s as a "pure colorist," in our modern sense; but any such person would at that time have been put on the official list of subversives, along with the seducer, the freethinker and the democrat. If such people were not kept under control there would not be in all Europe a great house unsacked, a church without its Tree of Liberty or a husband without horns: that was the idea.

Like most ideas, this one was thoroughly raked over in the 19th century. It wasn't altogether foolish, by the way. There really is such a thing as the demagogy of color: Hitler's use of black and red at the Nuremberg rallies soon proved that. But the 19th century's investigations into color were conducted for the most part in a liberationist spirit: the question to be answered was "Can color set men free, and if so how?" It seemed to Goethe, and to those who came after him, that the understanding of color was an important subdepartment of self-knowledge. Color might provide the grammar that was needed if we were to speak a new language and the keyboard that we needed if we were to draw new music from our life on earth. Ingres spoke for a steely and unalterable rearguard when he reiterated that "drawing is the probity of art"; but John Ruskin carried the century before him when he wrote in 1851 that "the purest and most thoughtful minds are those which love color the most."

The emancipation of color was linked, moreover, to the emancipation of art in general from social duties which had by then become obsolete. If we look at a masterpiece of Kant's day like David's *The Oath of the Horatii,* 1784, we shall see at once that it carries a load of anecdote, of precise documentation and of learned pictorial reference which could not be borne by the color language of 1905, even had that language been available. Interiors painted by Edouard Vuillard in the 1890s now seem to us not only ravishing in themselves but remarkably precise in their references to costume and decoration; and if, at the time they were painted, they seemed sketchy and approximate even to quite sensitive people the reason is that those people were conditioned to expect color of a tight, predictable sort. Every painting is a duet, after all. If the man who is looking at it can't keep time with the man who painted it, then the painting is incomplete; even the most radical moves in modern art were always made to an audience of not less than one.

So color was not set free in any one moment of time, as Florestan is set free in *Fidelio.* It took well over a hundred years to resolve the antithesis between the English connoisseur Sir George Beaumont, who said, "A good picture, like a good fiddle, should be brown," and a painter like Derain, who in 1905 took a plain red, a plain blue and a plain yellow from the tube and put them straight on the canvas in rectangular dabs that subverted the whole notion of "good painting." Color was set free in a disorderly and coincidental way: by Constable when he set out to show things that "exist in Nature but have not been seen before"; by Delacroix when he noted in the 1850s that painters should "banish all earthen colors" and remember that shadows cast on the ground, by no matter what object, are violet; by Turner when he came back from his first visit to Italy and prompted Constable to say that "Turner is stark mad with ability

—the picture seems to be painted with saffron and indigo"; and by Pissarro, the White Knight of Impressionism. "Such things *are*, though you mayn't believe it" was Ruskin's answer to those who could not adapt to the changing role of color in art; but there were many such people, and it took a very long time to convince them.

However, it was one of the good things about the French art scene in the 1890s that officialdom was losing its power. There were still young artists who put in for the Rome Prize, just as there were still older artists who longed for a success at the Salon. To win the Rome Prize augured lifelong success of a sedate and unadventurous kind. With this in mind, art teachers for generations had vaunted the grand formal picture for the grand formal occasion as the apotheosis toward which all studies tended; and in the 1890s Rouault, for one, did his best to comply. But for Matisse, as for Bonnard and Vuillard, the basic social relationship was more intimate. It was, in fact, the audience of not less than one: the dealer who had faith in him and showed his work to just a few people, the patron who saw him privately and not at the Salon, the like-minded friend and contemporary who fed him ideas. Those were the contacts that counted; the state could keep its medals, its commissions for town halls and post offices, its appointments-with-tenure at provincial schools of art.

All this favored the beginnings of modern art as a secret revolution: an experience shared initially by only a few and as often as not quite modest in format and scale. It also favored the emancipation of color, in that color is a private matter, direct in its communications and urgent in its appeal to experiences which cannot always be shared with others. Color spelled out in public, as at the Salon d'Automne of 1905, was color spelled out to a disbelieving crowd. Set free in private, on the other hand, color had the fascination of a secret society: Stendhal's "happy few" were not more happy than the first patrons of Bonnard and Vuillard and Matisse.

It was by the most fortunate of dispensations that the future of French painting lay in the 1890s with very clever men. The groundwork had been done by colossal natures: people like Monet, Cézanne, van Gogh and Gauguin, who had in effect offered themselves as human sacrifices so that art should continue. Theirs were most cheerless courses, in human terms: transposed crucifixions made bearable, insofar as they were bearable at all, by the awareness of an exceptional destiny. They brought to their task something more resistant, more elemental, than intelligence; but it was to intelligence, all the same, that art looked afterward. Without it, art would have foundered, no less surely than it would have foundered had not one or two gigantic natures brought it over the hump of the 1880s.

What was available in the 1890s to a French painter born in 1870 or thereabouts was an idea structure exemplified by Monet, Cézanne, van Gogh and Gauguin and put into words, perhaps better than he knew, by Maurice Denis. Denis wrote in 1890 that before a painting was a portrait, a battle piece or a Mother and Child, it was a flat surface covered with patches of color assembled in a certain order. There were two basic ideas in this remark, and both of them were important to the future of art. The first idea was that two contradictory elements had to be harmonized in picture-making: the fact of the flat surface of the canvas covered with flat patches of paint, and the fact that that flat surface was read by the public as a magic window, a window that opened, as all other windows open, onto a deep space in which everything has its allotted location. Pictorial practice hitherto had discouraged the observer from becoming conscious of the flatness of the canvas; art had been conceived as the power to make the observer—the partner in the duet—forget altogether that he is looking at a flat, vegetable object which is at most a quarter of an inch thick. If that fact was now brought home to the observer it was because color had assumed a new importance. It was also because painters had come to believe that more

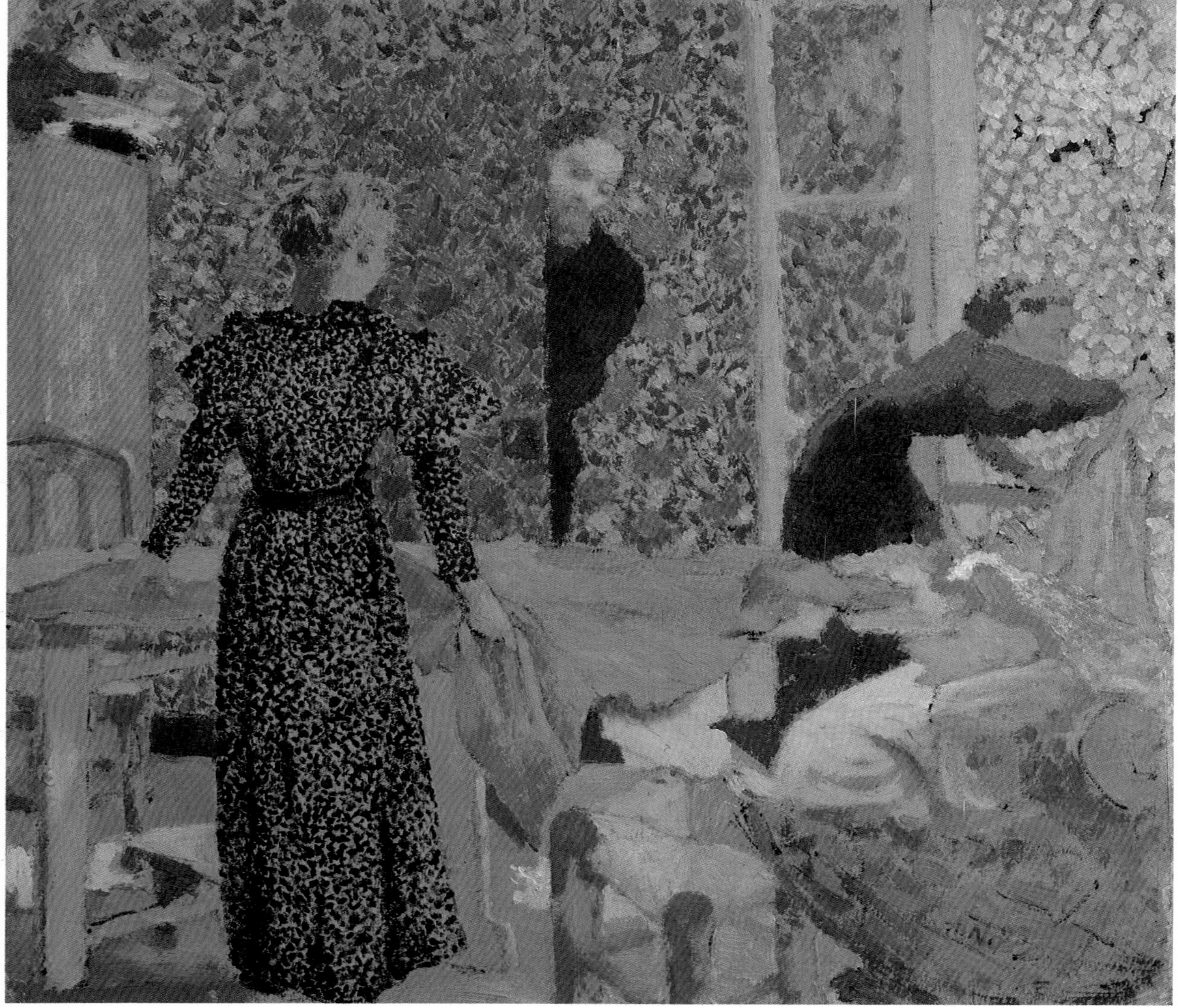

Edouard Vuillard. *The Suitor* (also called *The Workshop;* formerly *Intérieur à l'Etang-la-Ville).* 1893. Oil on millboard panel, 12½ × 14¼ inches. Smith College Museum of Art, Northampton, Mass.

was to be gained by bringing that fact into the open than could be gained by concealing it.

One of the basic blunders that we can make, from our privileged point of vantage, is to suppose that the artists of 1890 knew what we know today. We have our great museums, and we have art books by the truckload, and we have tables of dates to tell us just what was happening at this moment or that; what we don't have and cannot reconstruct is the amalgam of ambition and ignorance, inner necessity and random exterior spark, which prompted certain pictures. We incline to think that a great painting is like an earthquake—something that makes itself felt at once and over a wide area—whereas it could be better likened to a murder or an act of love: a private episode that may be discovered 20 years later or not at all.

We must also remember that in modern times no artist of consequence will accept a general directive. The people who imitated Gauguin were second- or third-rate painters like Charles Laval or Meyer de Haan. The people who *benefited* by Gauguin in a profound evolutionary way were the major artists who didn't paint like him at all. The last thing that Bonnard and Vuillard and Matisse wanted to do was paint portentous allegories about the destiny of mankind, as Gauguin did. Equally, it would not have occurred to them to

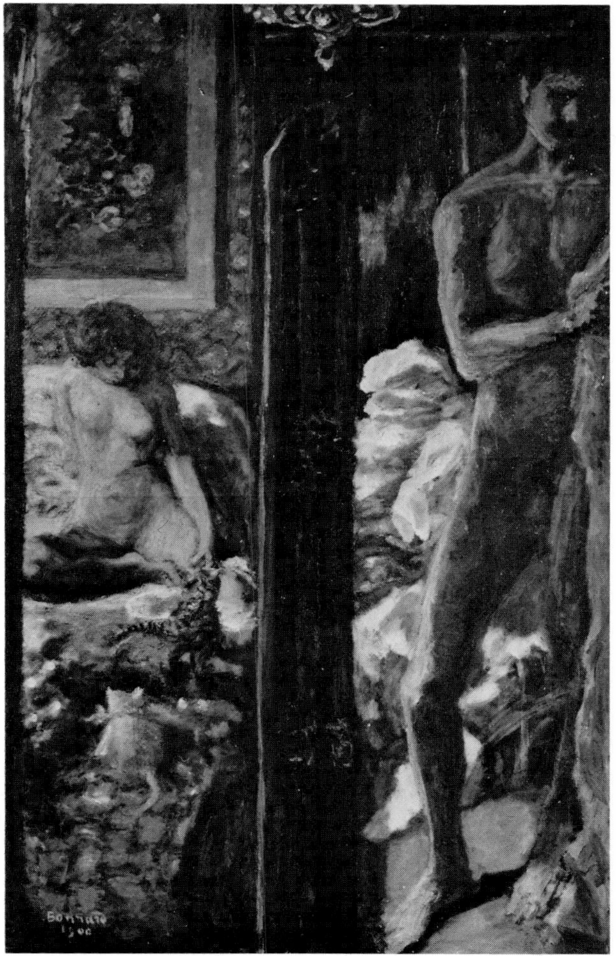

Pierre Bonnard.
Man and Woman.
1900.
Oil on canvas,
46 × 28½ inches.
Musée National
d'Art Moderne,
Paris

take the symbolism of color as van Gogh took it: to see "the terrible passions of humanity" in terms of an acid red and an acid green. Life simply did not appear to them in such terms. Bonnard and Vuillard had been to schools (not art schools, but top-class general schools) at which the education offered was just about as good, and as exacting, as at any school in the Western world. When they came to make art, they made it in the image of that education. In other words, their art came out behind a shield of wit, and mischief, and elegant turn of phrase. It was not short of either feeling or sensibility, but those qualities came mostly in disguise. Bonnard and Vuillard in the 1890s had the kind of intelligent and undeceived high spirits which often follow, whether paradoxically or not, from a rigorous and demanding education. They knew what they could do and what they couldn't. Neither of them was cut out to be a preacher, like van Gogh, or to raid, like Gauguin, the mythology of peoples remote from ourselves. The life around them was their subject: whence the name of "intimist," which was given to Vuillard in particular.

An intimist is a person who studies life at close quarters. Vuillard took the life around him and broke it down in terms of flat patterns and chromatic vibrations; but he had seen a great deal of good acting and heard some of the best talkers of his day, and these two elements in his experience stayed with him when he sat down to paint. To paint was torture for Vuillard, but he never let it show: not for him the deeply worked whirlpools of paint which mimicked the motor energies within van Gogh's nature, or the dramas of alienation behind a Tahitian sky which Gauguin sent back, batch by batch, to his friend Daniel de Monfried in France. Vuillard's dramas were of another kind: moments of social interlocking most affectionately observed and set down in an environment which owed something, beyond a doubt, to the scenery which he had so often painted for his friends in the theater. He did not have to force or readjust his experience to get the flat colored areas desiderated by Denis; he had them around him in the workshop where his mother carried on her dressmaking business—in the patterned screens, in the long flat bolts of patterned cloth, in the patterned papers on the long wall in the background. Matisse was later to become the supreme master of this kind of subject: the domestic interior, that is to say, in which the pull back and forth between what we see (the richly patterned paint surface) and what the artist set out to depict is particularly rich and vivacious. But Vuillard was achieving just that, and with the utmost apparent composure, well before 1900.

Color was not, of course, the only constituent in all this. Both Vuillard and Bonnard could draw very well in a way that was peculiar to themselves: brisk, insightful, epigrammatic. They had evolved —from Japanese prints, above all—an off-center,

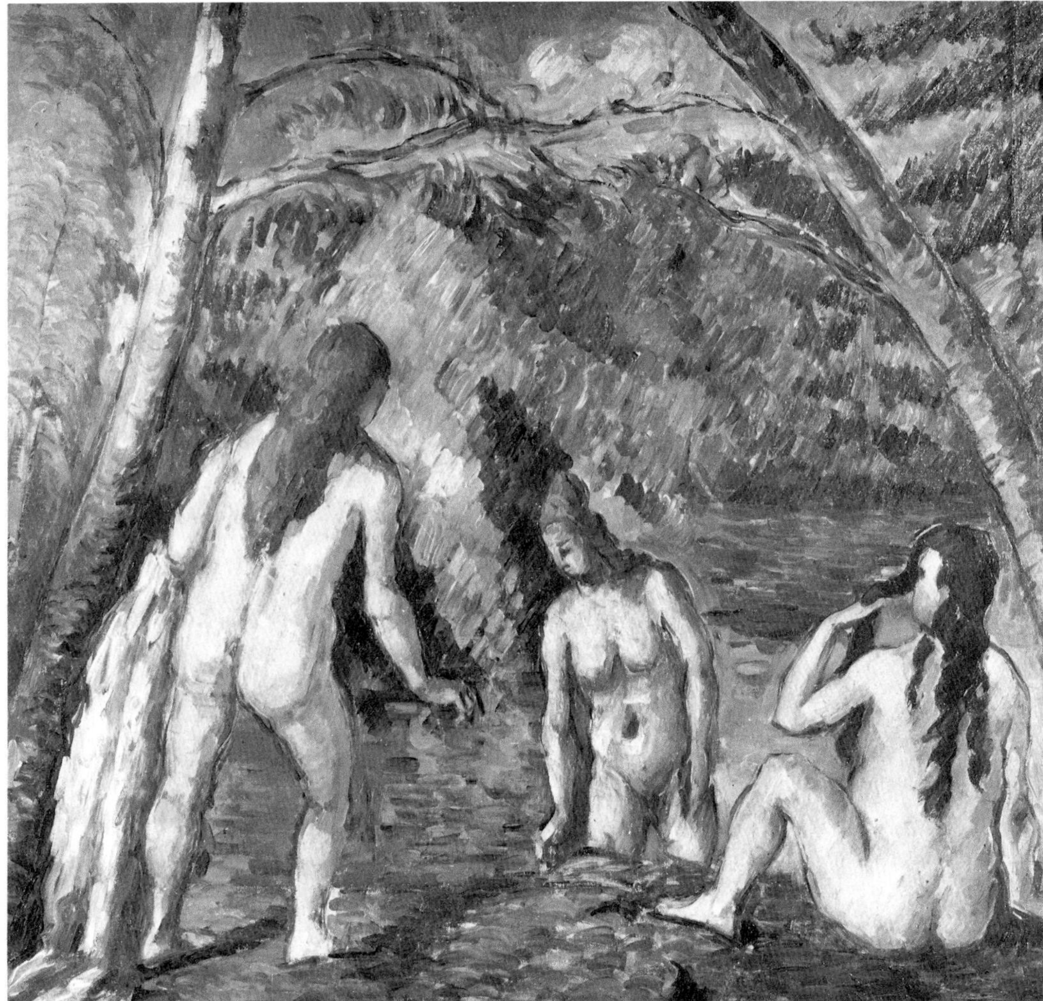

Paul Cézanne.
Three Bathers.
1879–82.
Oil on canvas,
19⅝ × 19⅝ inches.
Petit Palais, Paris

casual-seeming form of composition that allowed them to capture the intimacies of everyday life with a freedom and a penetration which had not been brought to such a pitch before.

There had never, for instance, been a picture quite like Bonnard's *Man and Woman* of 1900. At first glance the two figures could almost be statues niched in a wall, or butterflies framed behind glass. But at the same time they are completely and most artfully rendered in a space that is divided and made vivid to us by the screen that rears up in the middle of the canvas and gives each figure its privacy. The two figures, both naked, bring into painting what is called in French *le naturel:* a lack of inhibition so complete that at first we barely notice it. Of course there had been bedroom scenes in painting before, but they had been of quite other kinds: gamy and equivocal, if the painter was out to titillate, or noble and generalized, if mythology was in question. Bonnard brought in a new fullness of statement and psychological grasp which made it possible for the woman to probe her big toe and the man to dry his hands on a towel without our doubting for a moment that there was an intense, continuing sexual relationship between the two. The new candor of color, and the frank acceptance of the ambiguous nature of the painting as a physical object, made possible other candors and forms of frankness.

Something was owed in all this to the specifically Parisian turn of mind which both Bonnard and

Vuillard had perfected at school: the nimble curiosity, the belief that there was no such thing as an experience which could not be processed in terms of one more witty remark, and the Proustian sensibility which must normally be kept hooded from the world. Matisse had none of all this. He was a year younger than Vuillard and two years younger than Bonnard. During the years between 1891 and 1895, when Bonnard and Vuillard were already painting pictures which are fundamental to the modern movement, Matisse was simply a painstaking beginner. Vuillard in his self-portraits of 1892 was an audacious colorist; Matisse at that time was still copying the Old Masters in the hope of sorting out one gray from another. Bonnard and Vuillard were in touch with the liveliest minds in Paris from their school days onward; Matisse got to know what had been going on in roundabout ways, or by chance. It was not until the middle of the 1890s that a painter friend introduced him to Impressionism. He was interested in Gauguin—to the point, in fact, of buying a small painting by him in 1899—but once again it was by chance that he came to see a large body of Gauguin's work when he was taken to call on Gauguin's confidant, Daniel de Monfried, in the summer of 1905.

Matisse was slow to begin, slow to get through to the great painting of the immediate past, slow to decide as to precisely what he should do about it. He had certain traits still common in northern France: he was tenacious, ruminative, almost insanely hardworking. A trained lawyer, he looked very closely at every side of a question. He had no blazing natural gift to give a deceptive assurance to his earlier work; he had, on the contrary, a set of innate psychic checks and balances which warned him to go slow, and sometimes to stop altogether, when the moment was not ripe.

All this came out in the work. From the moment that he came into contact with the Impressionists, he could see that there was something important for him in the Impressionists' palette, which was, in musical terms, all treble and no bass. He rejected the methods in favor with the followers of Seurat on the ground that "the splitting-up of color meant the splitting-up of form and contour. The result: a jerky surface. Everything is reduced to a mere retinal sensation, and one which destroys all tranquillity of surface and contour." But before coming to this decision he made a characteristically sustained and individual attempt in the summers of 1904 and 1905 to get out of that system all that could be adapted to his own purposes.

He revered Cézanne, and in 1899 he bought a little *Bathers* by Cézanne which he refused to sell even at times of great financial need. Already in 1900 he proved that he could model the human figure with great slabs of pure color that owed everything to Cézanne's example; but then, characteristically again, he drew back and turned to painting of quite another kind. He tested the possible modes of painting, one by one, against his own needs and his own potentialities. He even brought some of those modes to a new degree of fulfillment: his *The Dessert,* 1897, is the apotheosis of the Impressionist interior, and his *Luxe, calme et volupté,* 1904, the apotheosis of the outdoor scene as realized by Seurat's followers. His was, as

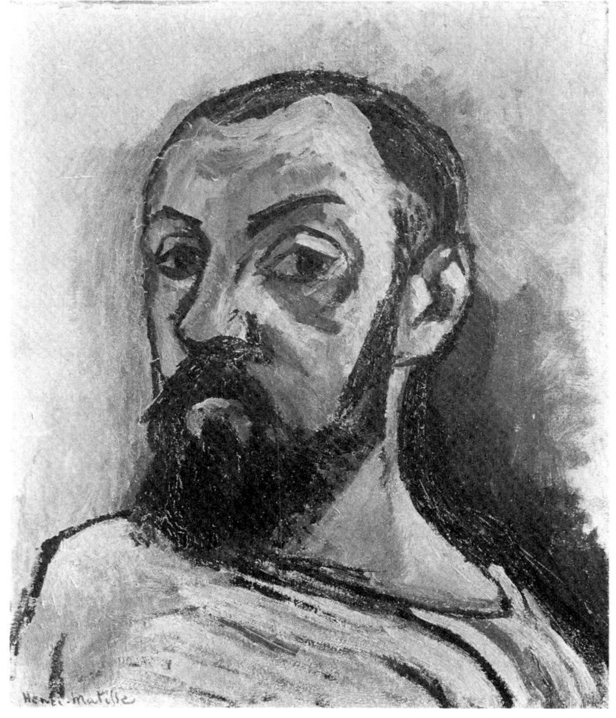

Henri Matisse. *Self-Portrait.* 1906. Oil on canvas, 22 × 18 inches. The Royal Museum of Fine Arts, Copenhagen

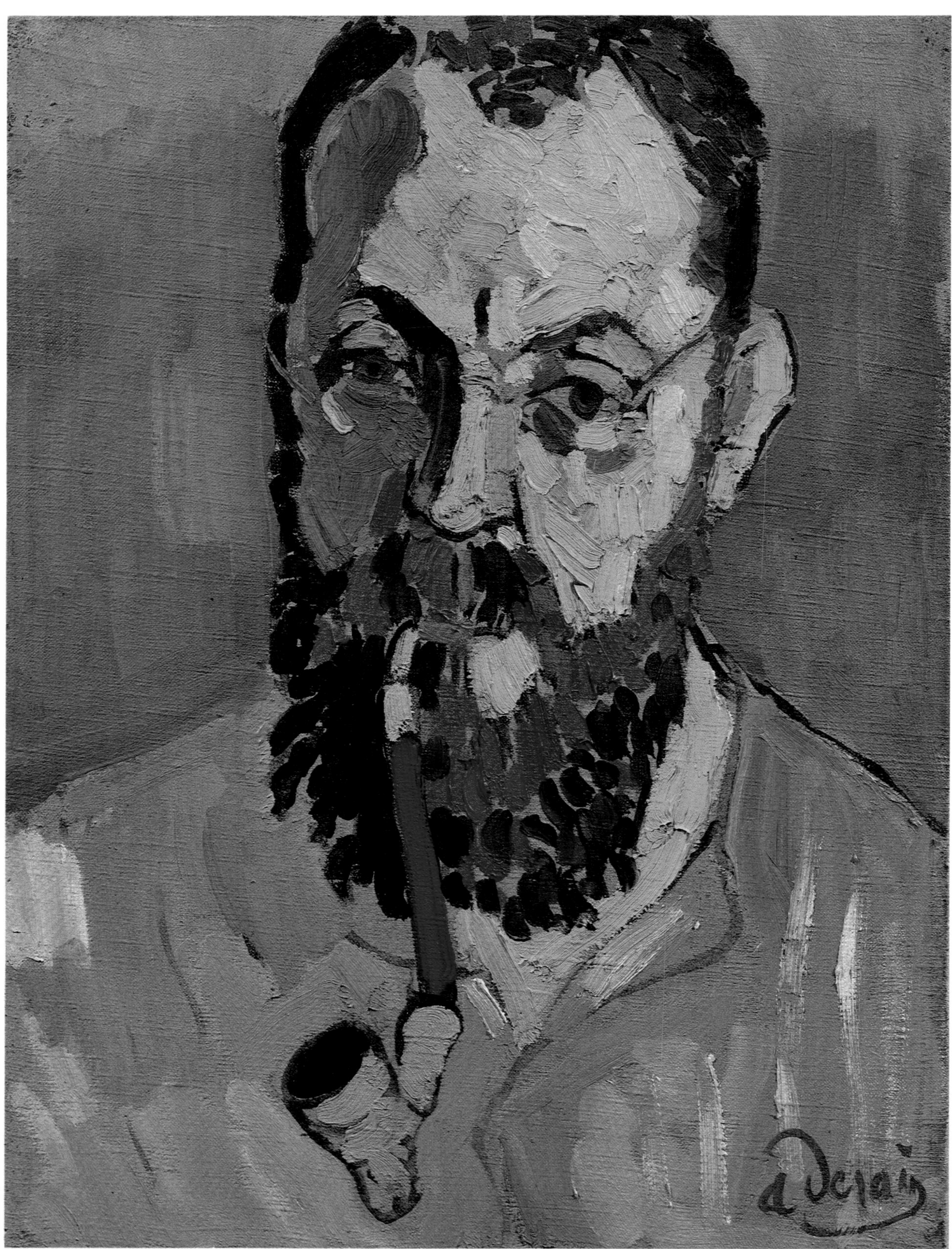

André Derain.
Portrait of Matisse.
1905.
Oil on canvas,
18⅛ × 13¾ inches.
The Tate Gallery,
London

much as Gauguin's or van Gogh's, an exemplary destiny. He spoke, as they did not, for certain permanent traits of the French genius: the inspired conservatism, the power of lucid analysis, the ability to objectify. When instinct said "Drop all that and think only of yourself!" Matisse could always say "No."

Among Matisse's friends and contemporaries before 1901, none were of his own caliber. But in 1901 he happened to see Derain at an exhibition of van Gogh's work in Paris, and through Derain he met Vlaminck. Matisse had never looked young, and in the company of Derain and Vlaminck, who were extraverted giants of a generation later than his own, he must have had an almost exaggeratedly careworn and professorial look. (Derain captured something of this in the portrait of Matisse which he painted in 1905.) The encounter was important to Matisse because he soon found that Derain and Vlaminck had arrived at a position very similar to his own. They wanted to let color come through, in other words, without any of the constraints which the history of art had imposed upon it. Derain wanted this because he was an immensely well-educated young man who had looked at everything in the museums and decided that that was the way art had to go. Vlaminck wanted it because he was a coarse brute with just one brief spark of genius, and he wanted to prove that the art of the museums and the Salons was all washed up and could be ignored without loss. Matisse did not go along with Vlaminck in this, but he did undoubtedly derive very great comfort from the allegiance of his two juniors. (One of them wrote that Matisse "looked ten years younger" at the end of his first visit to them.)

Those first meetings in 1901 led eventually to what is called Fauve painting. ("Fauve" is the French word for a wild and dangerous beast.) It is in some ways a silly name, and it certainly does not suit Matisse; but it does suggest the ferocious energy with which the public as a whole was confronted, head-on, at the Salon d'Automne of 1905.

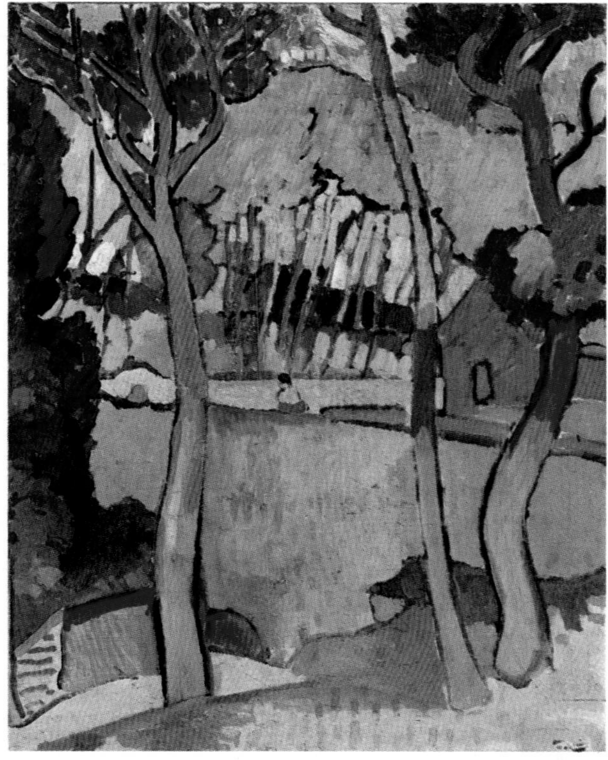

André Derain. *Three Trees, L'Estaque.* c. 1906. Oil on canvas, 39½ × 31½ inches. Art Gallery of Ontario, Toronto. Gift of Sam and Ayala Zacks

(This was, by the way, the last confrontation of its kind that Paris was to see. Later developments in painting were first shown in dealers' galleries, and some were not shown at all: Picasso's *Les Demoiselles d'Avignon,* probably the most famous painting of this century, was not seen in public until 30 years after it was painted, while some of Matisse's greatest works went to Moscow before 1914 and were not seen in a French museum until 1970.)

Chromatic energy found in Fauvism its strongest and least ambiguous expression. An aesthetic of pure exhilaration could ask for no finer monument than Derain's Fauve landscapes. In them, a robust and for the moment undivided nature fulfills itself completely. But as Derain was a deeply intelligent man he may have sensed that only at that moment in his life, and only at that moment in the history of art, was such a fulfillment possible. For just two or three years the compass needle of painting turned toward an art that was all spontaneity, all heightened and simplified sensation. Nuance was banished, and the order of the day was "All systems go!" Derain and Vlaminck at

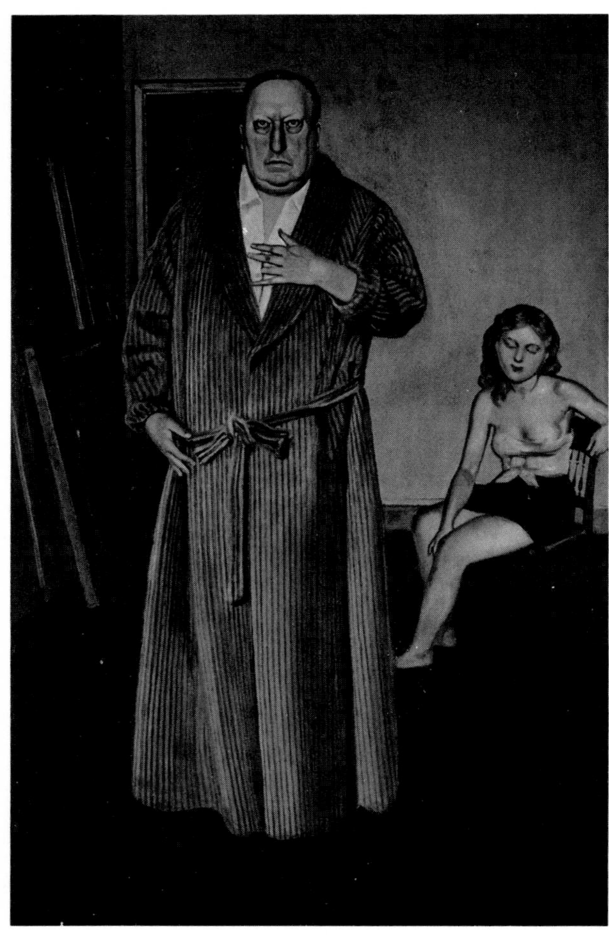

Balthus.
André Derain. 1936.
Oil on wood,
44⅜ × 28½ inches.
The Museum of
Modern Art, New
York.
Acquired through
the Lillie P. Bliss
Bequest

that time disdained the gloss of "fine art": their paintings had to be seen as what they were—and for what they were.

That was never quite Matisse's position, and even Derain and Vlaminck could not maintain it for long. The rest of Derain's long career was a 40-year attempt to recapture the qualities for which Fauvism had no place: long-pondered composition, Old Masterly craftsmanship, learned allusion to the art of the past and the search for a well-carpentered equilibrium. Only rarely, and above all in his stage designs and illustrated books, did the delicious, unballasted chromatic energy of 1905–07 return to Derain's art in later years. Derain, for almost all his life, was a man mismated with his time and mismated with himself: something of his wracked intelligence, his overwhelming but somewhat tumbledown physical presence and his tendency to smother self-doubt with histrionics comes out in Balthus's portrait of him.

Fauvism was like a forest fire: everyone who was anywhere near got singed. This applied as much to Georges Braque, a painter of supreme gifts, as it did to minor masters like Albert Marquet and Raoul Dufy. It also applied to someone like Kees van Dongen, who for just a year or two was hoisted right out of his class by the fact of participating in an important moment of art history. That moment could not be prolonged, however. Fauvism was an art of maximum statement, and although its crashing, undifferentiated oppositions of pure color were thrilling in the hands of Derain and Vlaminck, the thrill was bought at a very high price.

Braque put this clearly when he discussed many years later the period in the fall of 1906 when he followed the example of Derain (and of Cézanne before him) and went down to paint at L'Estaque, near Marseilles. He had responded, just for one season, to the violent change of color and light. "But I couldn't have done it again," he went on. "I'd have had to go to the Congo the next time to get the same effect." Of course this was in part a temperamental reaction; Braque was one of the most fastidious men who ever touched a brush, and he could neither think, feel nor act to the drumbeat of pure Fauvist practice. But he adapted it, all the same, to his own nature. He brought in lavender blue as well as Prussian blue, Veronese green as well as emerald green, pink as well as vermilion, violet as well as orange. With all these, and with ivory laid on a priming of white lead, he nuanced his way across the canvas and yet stayed loyal to the Fauvist ethic: there was nothing on the canvas but the approved lozenges of unbroken color. Yet a Fauve landscape by Braque is never aggressive in the way that a landscape by Vlaminck can be aggressive; the return route to other kinds of expression is always kept open.

Braque at that time—1906—was barely 24 years old; one of the most fruitful careers in 20th-century painting had hardly begun. He was young enough and inexperienced enough not to chafe at what may now seem to us the evident shortcoming of Fauvism—the fact that it pushed color into an untenable and self-defeating position. By 1907 Fauvism for everyone except Matisse was like an army that had got ahead so far and so fast that it had run out of supplies, and run out of gas, and lost contact with headquarters. Color had been set free, but in such a way that it had nowhere to go but backward.

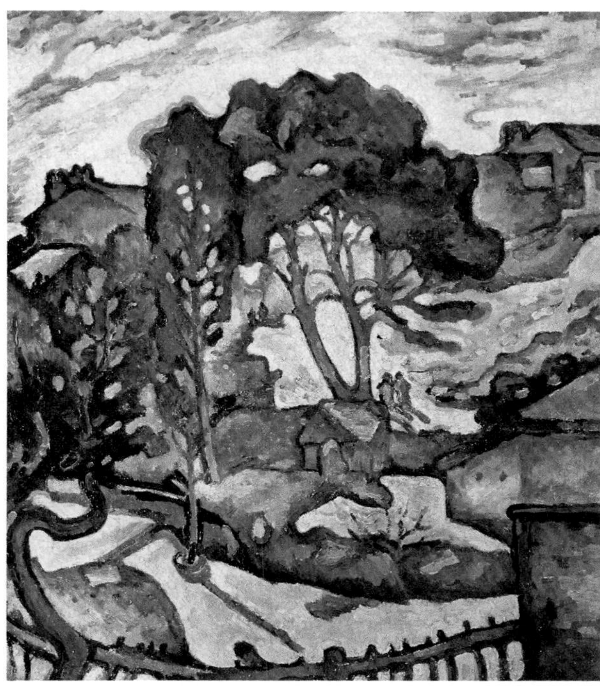

Georges Braque. *Landscape at L'Estaque.* 1907. Oil on canvas, 32⅝ × 28 inches. Private collection, New York

This was clear to Derain, who even in 1907 was reverting to forms of art in which the gamut of color was restricted in the interests of monumentality. Dufy by 1912 was working with royal blues and bottle greens and a system of tightly interlocking, Cézannesque formal units, whereas in 1906 he had concentrated on the chromatic to-and-fro of the billboards along the promenade at Trouville. Fauvism had been a sprinter's style: a 100-meter dash in which quick response and animal vigor were all-important. But great art is the province of the distance runner; and one by one, from 1907 onward, the painters worth talking about remembered this.

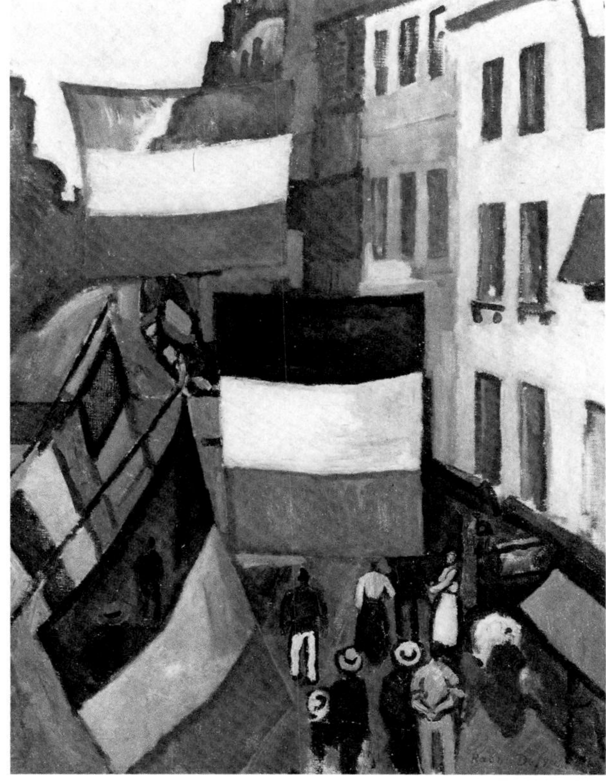

Raoul Dufy. *Beflagged Street, Le Havre.* 1906. Oil on canvas, 31⅞ × 25⅞ inches. Musée National d'Art Moderne, Paris

Matisse was the only one who never needed to backtrack or to disengage himself; he had never imagined that a progressive attitude toward color could be combined with a reactionary attitude toward other departments of art. In formal terms, the Fauve paintings of Derain and Vlaminck were conservative and unambitious by comparison with a great Gauguin. What they had to say in terms of the complexity and contradictoriness of human experience was infantile when set beside what van Gogh had had to say in Arles, in Saint-Rémy and in Auvers. Color was given its head in Fauvist painting, but it was not free in any deeper sense, any more than a steam locomotive is set free if we take it out of its shed and put it in a meadow. Fauvism had made a great contribution to the natural history of exuberance; but by 1907 people were beginning to look around for something less limited.

They found it in the threefold revelation of Cézanne which took place in the fall of 1907. Cézanne had died in Aix-en-Provence in October, 1906. Just a year later, what had been known to only a few was made apparent to everyone—that the new century had everything to learn from Cézanne. There was a retrospective of 48 oil paintings at the Salon d'Automne; there were 79 watercolors at the Bernheim-Jeune gallery; there was the publication in the *Mercure de France* of his letters to a young painter, Emile Bernard. Nothing was ever the same again in living art.

All this was a surprise to most people, but it was not a surprise to Matisse, who for eight years had studied his own small but masterly Cézanne hour by hour. Quite possibly it was because of the uproar around him that he agreed to set out his own ideas, once and for all, in a now-famous article called "A Painter's Notes," which came out in *La Grande Revue* in December, 1908. Like most pronouncements of its kind, this one has been pored over, and turned this way and that, and tilted to suit every imaginable purpose. But there does emerge from it, even so, a coherent picture of what Matisse was trying to do.

Matisse did not see it as the function of the painter to describe what he saw, or to confirm the teaching of conventional vision, or to record immediate sensation in a vivid and garrulous way. On the contrary: he thought of each of his paintings as an object new-born into the world. It was, in his own words, a "condensation" of experience, not an imitation of it. In earlier painting there had usually been gradations of intensity, with areas of maximum interest and focal points toward which everything in the composition tended. Meanings had been signaled in ways universally understood by what Matisse called "passions mirrored upon a human face or revealed by a violent gesture." In a Matisse there was nothing of this. Every part of the painting ranked as equal in meaning with every other part; the expression—and Matisse valued expression above all things—lay not in the thing portrayed but in the organization of the surface of the painting. The quintessentials of the act of painting were that it was considered, steady and deep; each painting was to be a portrait of human nature at one with itself.

The role of color in all this was fundamental. Color was to be full, weighty, individual and perfectly judged. Color was to be allowed to build *on its own;* it was to work on the flat, with an august personal rhythm which came from the painter's inmost nature; and it was to work in depth, building the forms, situating them in space, making them free citizens of an ideal republic of the eye. And that republic must endure: whatever was built must stand up forever.

Matisse in all this was opposing himself to everything in painting that was descriptive and pedestrian, on the one hand, or fugitive and undigested, on the other. Above all, the emancipation of color must be linked to the emancipation of all other constituents of painting; the artist must be as free to reinvent space, and to restructure form, as he was to release color. If he succeeded in all this—if he justified, among other things, the abandonment of literal representation—there might come into existence "a higher order of beauty."

After a hundred years of the "modern movement," we know that that higher order of beauty of which Matisse wrote is likely to present itself in guises unfamiliar to us. This causes us to be, if anything, overenthusiastic: to confound the novel with the new, in other words. Before 1914 this was not the case. The "audience of not less than one" was quite often reduced to an audience of not more than one; and in 1905, when Matisse's Fauve paintings went on show, the reaction of the public was so violent that Matisse had to forbid his wife to go into the gallery in question.

This hostility was directed against Matisse in large part because his new methods were applied not only to landscape and to still life but to the human face. People very much dislike the idea that the accepted look of the human face on canvas can be dismantled and discarded. Something of their own identity is at stake, whereas landscape and still life can be taken apart and restated with much less menace to the individual psyche. Ma-

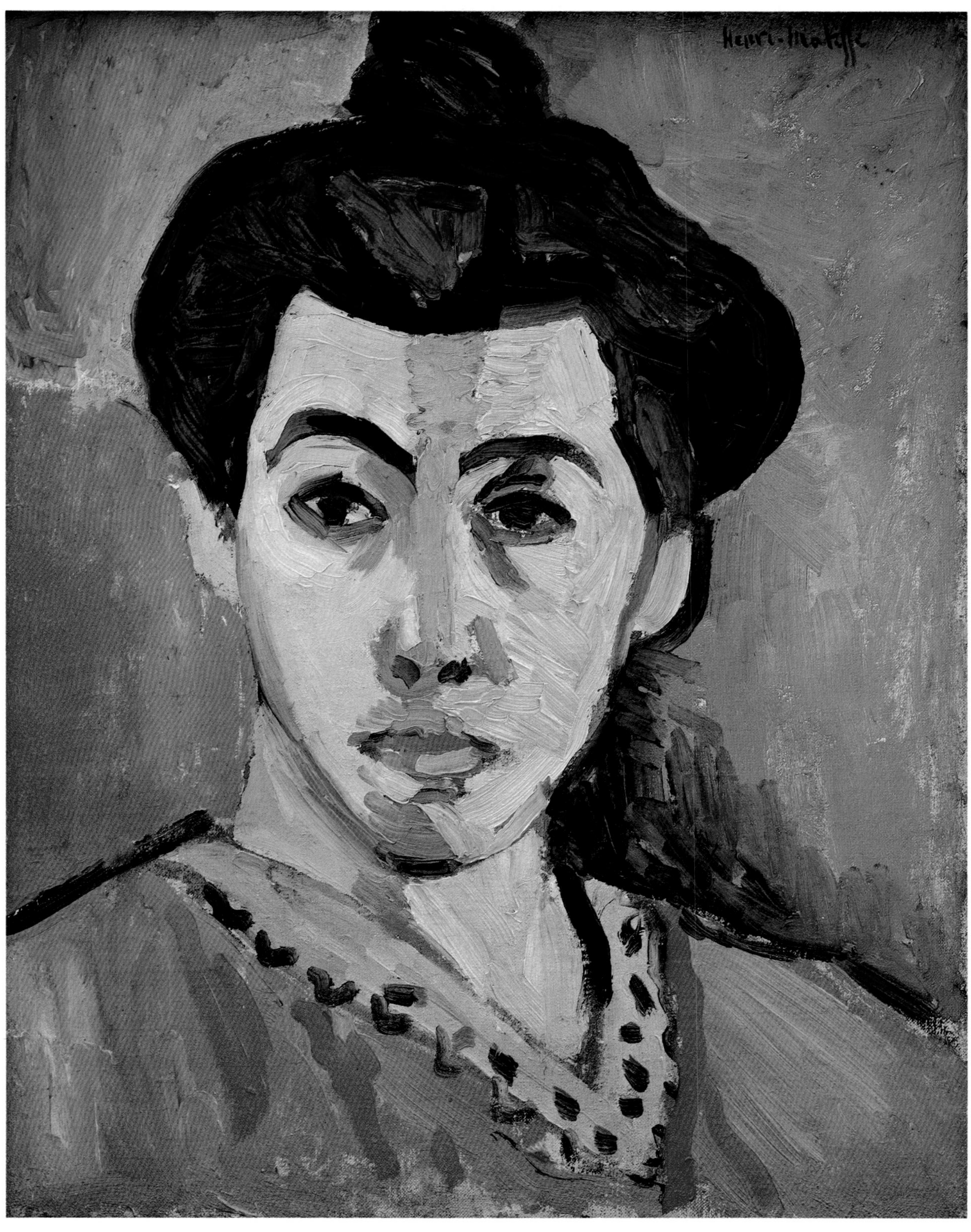

Henri Matisse. *Portrait of Mme Matisse with a Green Stripe.* 1905. Oil on canvas, 16 × 12¾ inches. The Royal Museum of Fine Arts, Copenhagen

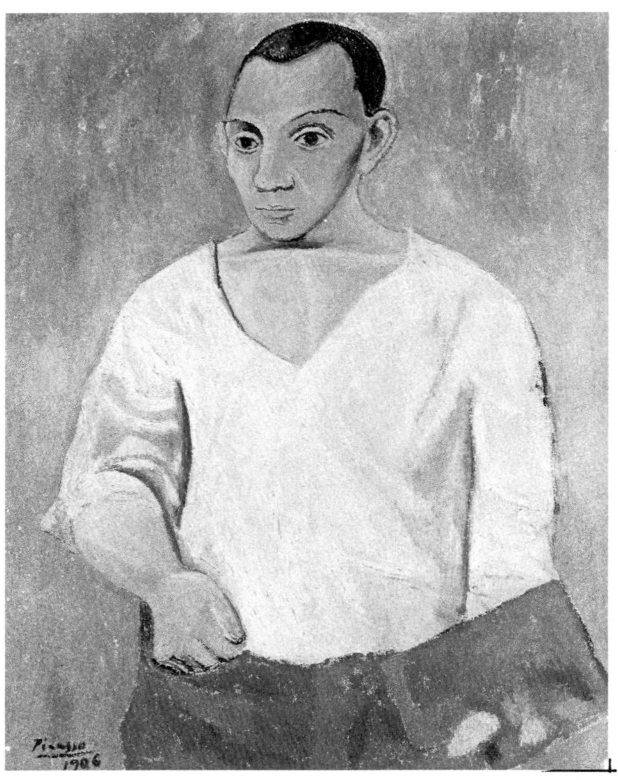

Pablo Picasso. *Self-Portrait.* 1906. Oil on canvas, 36¼ × 28¾ inches. Philadelphia Museum of Art. The A. E. Gallatin Collection

tisse offended by putting a broad green stripe down the middle of his wife's forehead, by putting a bright red boundary mark where forehead gives way to hair, and by dividing the face into sharply delineated color areas; and his offense was compounded by the fact that those color areas related more to the empty spaces adjacent to the face than to any conventional idea of the unity of the human complexion. People simply didn't realize every part of the picture was as expressive as every other part; refusing to see this, they missed the point—which was that the painting was a tender and recognizable likeness of an individual human being.

The chromatic issue was not, to Matisse's way of thinking, something that could be detached from the other considerations which govern the making of a major work of art. Nor did he think that any one color was "beautiful" or expressive on its own. What interested him was the interrelation and the interdependence of a whole group of colors. In his Fauve period he never transcribed his color literally, as his colleagues did when they chose subjects which had vivid color built into them: billboards, or a street decked out with the red, white and blue of the French national flag. His color was based on feeling, not on imitation; Madame Matisse is said to have posed in a black dress for some of the most brightly colored of his portraits of her.

Matisse in a quiet way was one of the most ambitious men who ever lived. His ambitions extended, moreover, to every department of art: there was not one of them that he did not intend in time to hump on his shoulders and haul bodily into a new phase of its development. To this end he would spend years on a single small sculpture, drag himself across Paris night and day from one art school to another, and ruminate on the art of the past—European, Islamic, "primitive"—as if wondering against what to measure himself next. As he was also, in terms of his work, a late developer, it came about that the great pictures which he painted in his late 30s and early 40s were quite remarkably rich, dense and various.

In this he was prompted by the ancient and honorable tradition of the masterpiece: the big-scale work into which the artist puts all he has got. Matisse in the 1890s had lived through the time when painters were haunted by the idea of the wall-sized decoration. The 19th century had been possessed throughout by the idea of the very large picture: Géricault's *The Raft of the "Méduse,"* 1818–19, Delacroix's *Death of Sardanapalus,* c. 1827, Courbet's *Burial at Ornans,* 1849, Monet's fragmentary *Le Déjeuner sur l'herbe.* Cézanne in his *Grandes Baigneuses* carried into the 20th century the notion of the very large painting as a mark of manhood; now someone had to take up the torch that had fallen from Cézanne's hand.

To an extent which we can now never define, Matisse was affected at this time by the fact that since the summer of 1904 Picasso had been living and working in Paris. Picasso himself will figure so often and so largely in this book that I need only say of him here that he too manifested, during the years in question, a most resolute intention to

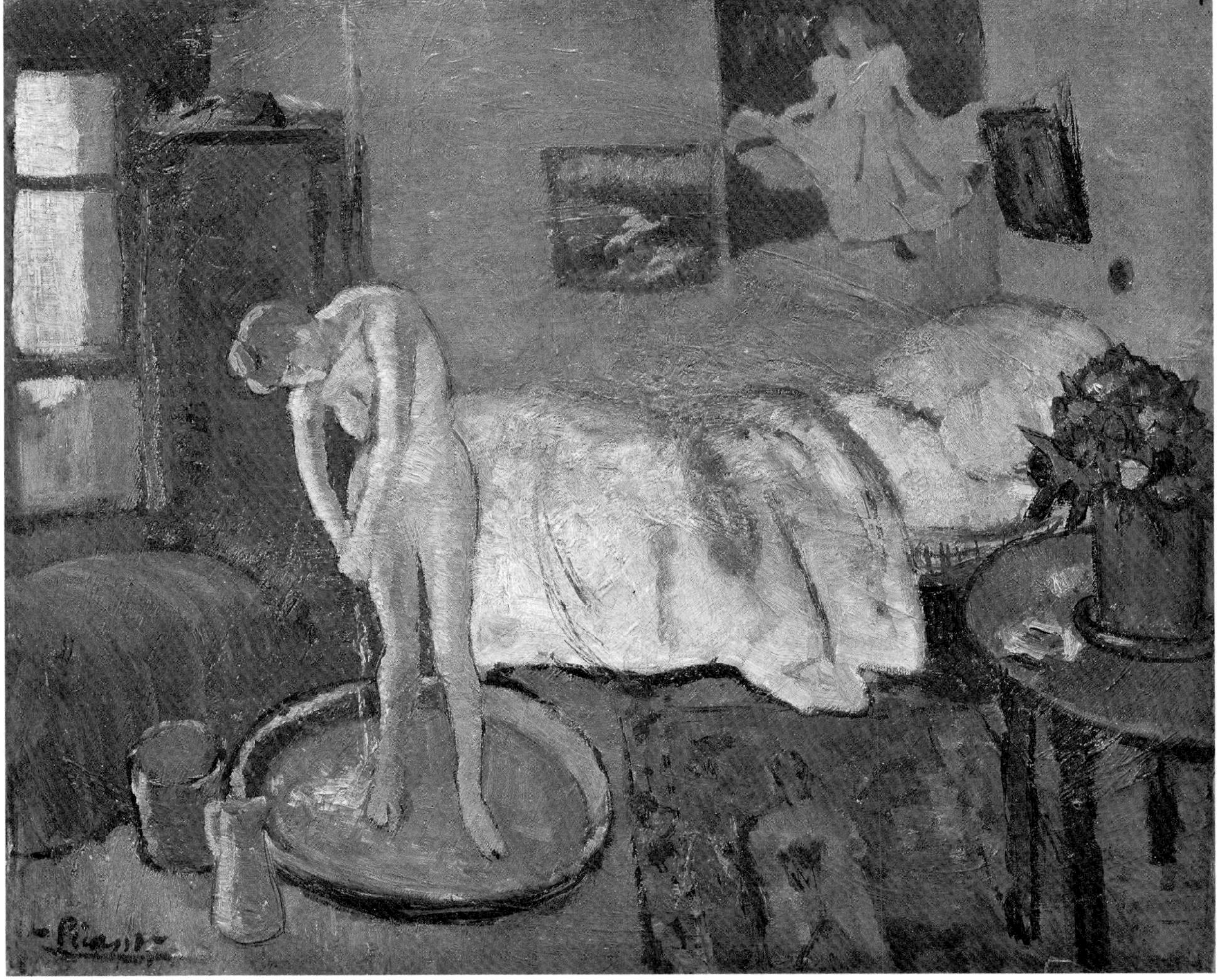

Pablo Picasso.
The Blue Room (La Toilette). 1901.
Oil on canvas,
20 × 24½ inches.
The Phillips Collection, Washington

draw a firm black line beneath the history of painting to date and head out toward the future in which his role would be predominant. This was clear from his general deportment: in the *Self-Portrait* of 1906, for instance, he holds the palette as a Greek warrior might hold his shield. It was also clear from the series of major paintings which he undertook between 1903 and 1907: *La Vie,* 1903, the *Acrobat with a Ball,* 1904–05, *Family of Saltimbanques,* 1905, *Boy Leading a Horse,* 1905–06, and above all, *Les Demoiselles d'Avignon,* 1907. Picasso was out to capture art as a great general captures a walled city: by storm.

There was no question, where Matisse and Picasso were concerned, of crude rivalry or thick-witted emulation. After Matisse died, Picasso said to a friend, "I have to paint for both of us now"; and the remark indicates to what an extent, for over half a century, the two great men were aware of one another—never competing, but never forgetful, either, of the colossal contribution of the other.

They were never friends, in the sense that Picasso and Braque, or Matisse and Derain, were friends at one time. There was no direct influence, of the kind that Seurat had had on Signac, or that Cézanne was to have upon a whole generation. Temperamentally, they were as distinct from one another as it is possible for two men to be. Matisse was measured in his utterance, slow and thorough in his approach to any new idea, unbending in his insistence on the privacy of the home. Picasso was direct and piratical, acquisitive and quick to take fire: no one has ever been faster to process a new idea. He was a predestined autobiographer, a confidant who kept nothing back from his public; and whereas Matisse went into his apartment as Noah went into the Ark, seeing it as a sanctuary indispensable to life, Picasso regarded his friends, male and female, as a kind of traveling repertory company which could go through its paces in the street, or at a café table, and did not need any more formal environment.

Matisse and Picasso were not so much opposites, therefore, as complementaries. When Picasso spoke of Matisse and himself as "the North Pole and the South Pole," he doubtless meant that they were a long way apart; but he also meant that they were landmarks indispensable to the map of modern art. Without them, that map would make no sense.

Picasso was not a "colorist," then or later, but he was a man who used color, as he used every other constituent of art, with a kind of ferocious sufficiency. He did not aim to reinvent the whole notion of color, but he could make color do what he wanted. From the time of his second visit to Paris in 1901 he used color in a direct, allover, instantly recognizable way. Color in his Blue Period paintings operates as a strong rinse that tells the observer just what is demanded of him. (The little painting called *The Blue Room,* 1901, shows how well Picasso took the point of the poster by Toulouse-Lautrec which figures in it: Picasso had already learned to signal with color in the way that Lautrec used blue and yellow to signal the merits of May Milton.)

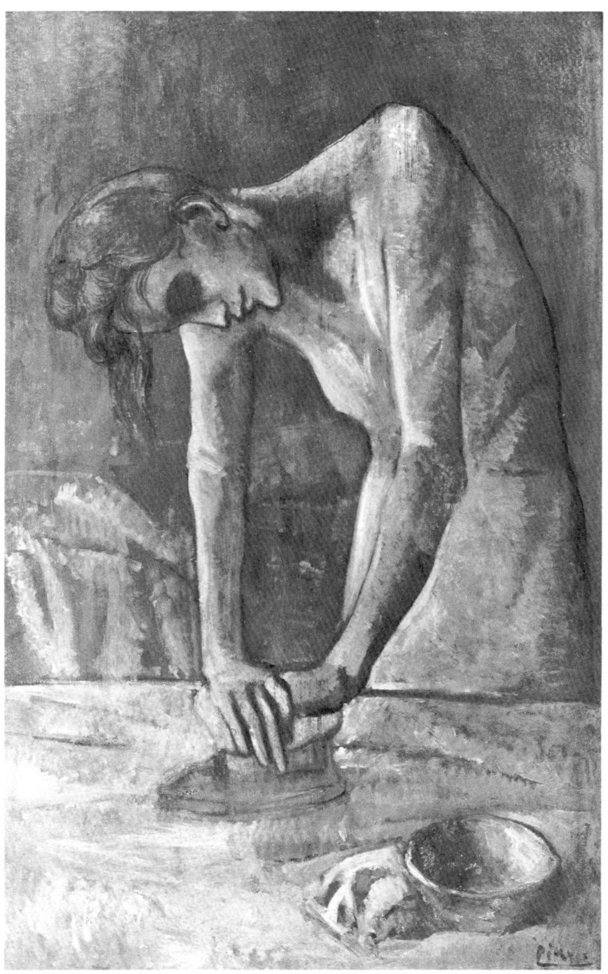

Pablo Picasso.
Woman Ironing.
1904.
Oil on canvas,
45¾ × 28⅝ inches.
The Solomon R. Guggenheim Museum, New York. The Thannhauser Collection

People have always reacted strongly to the paintings of Picasso's Blue Period. Blue in itself has melancholic associations for almost everyone; and the pictures combine poignancy of subject matter and a simplified emotional structure in ways which make them immediately accessible. We don't need Picasso to tell us by his choice of emphatic subject matter that it is a misfortune to have nothing to eat and an even greater misfortune to go blind. It is possible to feel that many of these paintings are discreditably mawkish. Not only is color being used, but we ourselves are being used also. Passivity before misfortune is not in itself an admirable trait, and if we compare Picasso's *Woman Ironing* of 1904 with Degas's two great paintings of a similar subject, there is no doubt that with his robust, caustic and yet deeply human handling, Degas gets much the better of the comparison. Color in a Blue Period Picasso has too often the role of an emotional additive, wished up from nowhere to reinforce a point already well made in black-and-white work of the period.

It is hazardous, at more than 75 years' distance, to attribute motives and reactions to one of the most combustible natures that ever existed. But it is beyond argument that Picasso's almost preternatural intelligence had a great deal more to bite on in Paris, from the summer of 1904 onward, than it ever had in Barcelona. Barcelona, at the turn of the century, was the most stylish and cosmopolitan of Spanish cities; nowhere in Europe was there a wider, richer and more eager intake of ideas from abroad. But there is a difference between living in a place where things are talked about and living in a place where they are done; and Paris in 1904 was the place where things were being done.

What was being done in Paris was powered above all by the belief that the next great thing, in art, must follow logically from the last great thing. Inspiration had its part to play; but the best artist, other things being equal, was the one who made most sense of history. Matisse had always believed this. Picasso had known it ever since he had first been exposed to the crossbred artistic life of Barcelona; and in *La Vie* he had drawn directly on van Gogh in the hope of basing a major pictorial achievement on the art of the immediate past. But at the time when he came to live in Paris, that immediate past was being given a particular grandeur by the appearance of 30 paintings by Cézanne at the Salon d'Automne of 1904, and of smaller but still substantial groups of Cézannes at the Salons of 1905 and 1906.

Such things could not be digested quickly. They corresponded to a profound change in the nature of human understanding. Things looked different, in Cézanne's paintings, because they had become known to be different. Merely to ape the outward appearance of a painting by Cézanne would get nobody anywhere. It was several years before Picasso could deal comprehensively with his reactions to Cézanne; and even Matisse, who lived with a Cézanne on his own walls, had every imaginable difficulty in mastering its lessons. Meanwhile there was something exclusive, something all-devouring, about the preoccupation with what Derain called "color for color's sake." When Matisse and Derain were together at Collioure in the summer of 1905, they were bent on going much further than anyone had been before in the direction of color which was completely dissociated from everyday associations. Here for instance is how Alfred Barr, in his pioneering book on Matisse (1951), described a landscape painted by Matisse at Collioure that summer. The color, he said, "seems completely free of any responsibility for description of natural appearances. The tree trunks, for instance, as one reads the picture from left to right, are blue-green, maroon, bright blue, yellow-green, scarlet and purple, dark green and violet, and at the right, ultramarine. They spring from a ground that is spotted blue, orange, ochre and sea-green, and they carry foliage of vermilion, green and lavender. Only the sea in the distance and the sky retain their natural color."

Color thus used was like a shellburst on the surface of the canvas. Only after a while did the observer learn to read the forms, and read the space; and only if he was very bright indeed would he realize that in this Matisse landscape he was looking at an unpopulated variant of a subject that had been in and out of European art for hundreds of years: the Golden Age.

The idea of the Golden Age is difficult to bring off, under its own name. Too much is asked of it. A world without inhibition, without guilt, without fallings-down or fallings-off! Since Freud, we just don't believe in it. The decline began before Freud, in fact. Even Ingres, even Corot, fell short when they tackled the problem head-on. What we know, but they did not, is that the dream of a Golden Age can shift its ground. Not Ingres's *The Golden Age* but his *Odalisque with a Slave* now fires our imaginations; not Corot's dancing nymphs but his tranced afternoons in the Roman campagna. (Cézanne's Bathers likewise fill the bill.) The dream, in such cases, travels with a new passport; but it is still the same dream.

The high-arching trees which Matisse chose as one of his motifs at Collioure were, coincidentally or not, the kind of background that Cézanne had devised for his *Grandes Baigneuses,* which re-

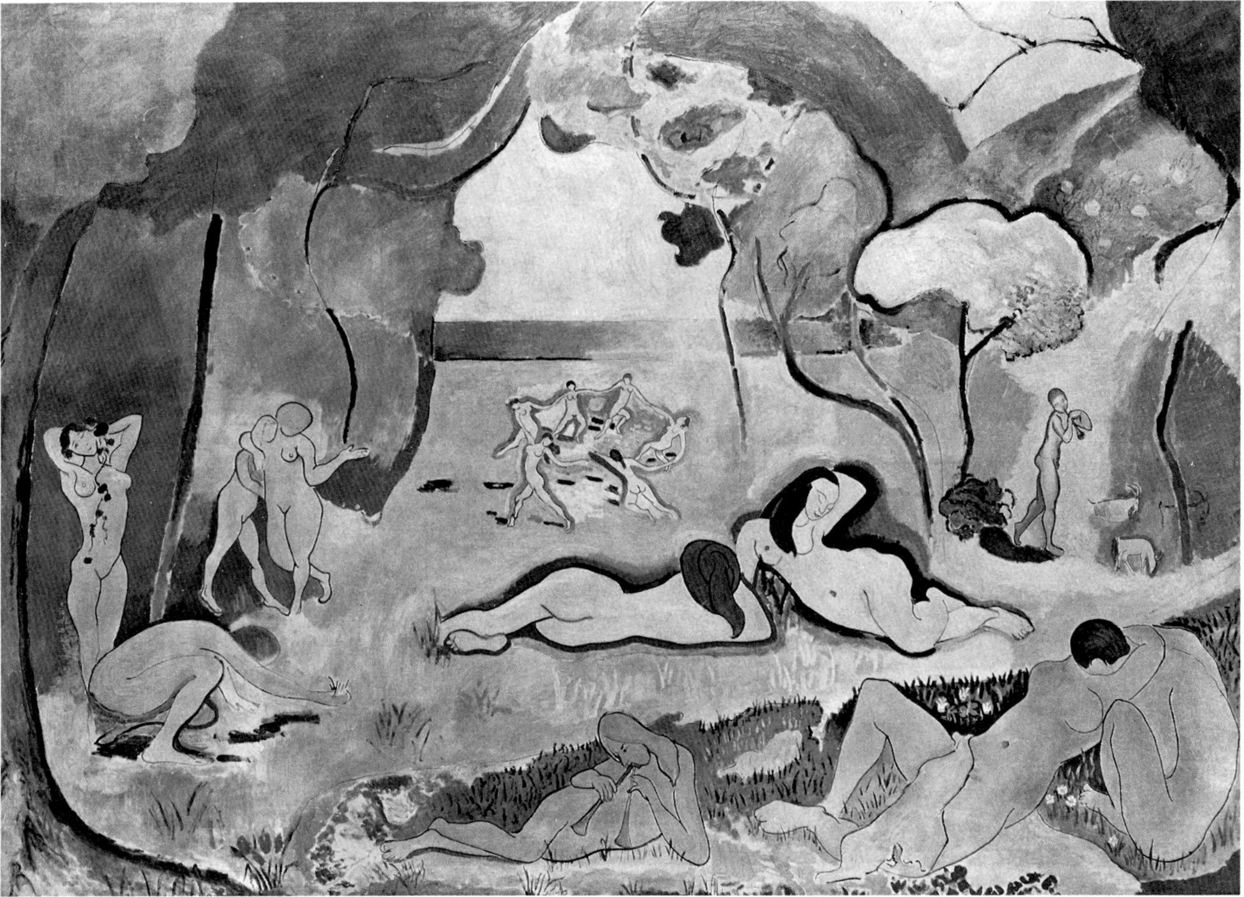

Henri Matisse.
Joy of Life.
1905–06.
Oil on canvas, 69½ inches × 7 feet 11 inches.

mains one of the grandest of all evocations of the Golden Age. To someone as steeped in the history of painting as was Matisse, there must have been a challenge to his inmost being in the idea that somehow the Golden Age could be re-created in terms of the new freedom of color. When he got back to Paris in the fall of 1905 he set about doing just that, with overhanging trees to frame the scene and a distant view of the sea. He was not alone in wanting to re-create in modern terms the secret garden, free of guilt, which is for most people a secular version of Paradise.

People often think of modern art as something that disdains the past and leaves it thankfully behind. That was never Matisse's point of view. His *Joy of Life* is entirely of its date (1905–06) in that never before could color have been used so freely, and in such independence of any descriptive intent. It is also of its date in that the sinuous, Art Nouveau–style drawing of the human body and the freakish distortions of traditional perspective would likewise have been inconceivable earlier. No one in the 19th century would have put up with the woman entwined with ivy on the left, or the loving couple on the right who seemed to have only one head between them. Matisse was handling form as freely as he was handling color: without the least regard, that is to say, for previous conventions. Matisse in his *Joy of Life* took over themes which had haunted the French imagination ever since Watteau had given them supremely poignant expression just about two hundred years before: linked figures on the grass beneath overhanging trees, wind-music in the open air, statues that seem to have turned into flesh and blood. Just how to bring that vision of the Golden Age to life again was a problem that in the 19th century defeated Puvis de Chavannes, for all his compositional skill, and defeated Ingres, whose *The Golden Age* looks congested and unspontaneous when set beside Watteau. The subject preoccupied many of Matisse's contemporaries; André Derain, for one, expressly gave the title of *The Golden Age* to the ambitious, energetic but finally quite incoherent painting which he produced in 1905. It was left to Matisse to restate the subject in terms of the 20th century.

His *Joy of Life* was by no means a break with the past. Those who got over their first astonishment might soon see that the piping boy in the rearground on the right derives from the Titian/Giorgione *Pastoral,* which Matisse had seen hundreds of times in the Louvre. They could go on to acknowledge that the *Joy of Life* is, from beginning to end, a derivative of those major paintings by Watteau in which figures are grouped in landscapes. Finally, they would remember that Matisse admired Ingres for the freedom with which he would reinvent the female anatomy when it suited him to do so. They would think especially of Ingres's *The Golden Age*—stilted as it may be—and they would see that the two paintings are closely allied in their readiness to violate academic anatomy in the interests of a broad, flowing arabesque set against a heavily wooded landscape that was cut open in the center to give depth and admit of a far blue distance.

The *Joy of Life* hung for years in Gertrude Stein's drawing room in Paris, where Picasso was a frequent visitor. He must, consciously or not, have seen the big picture as a challenge to his own capacities; and when he came to paint *Les Demoiselles d'Avignon* he began from a compositional scheme which was strikingly akin to that of the *Joy*

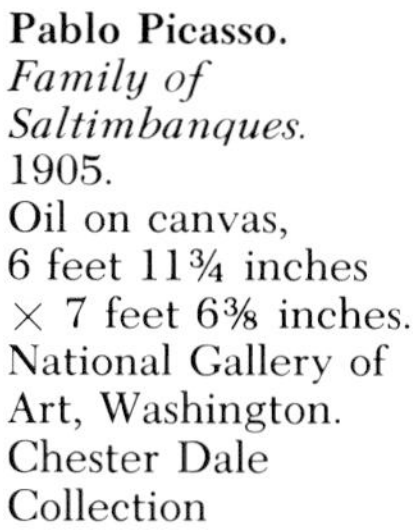

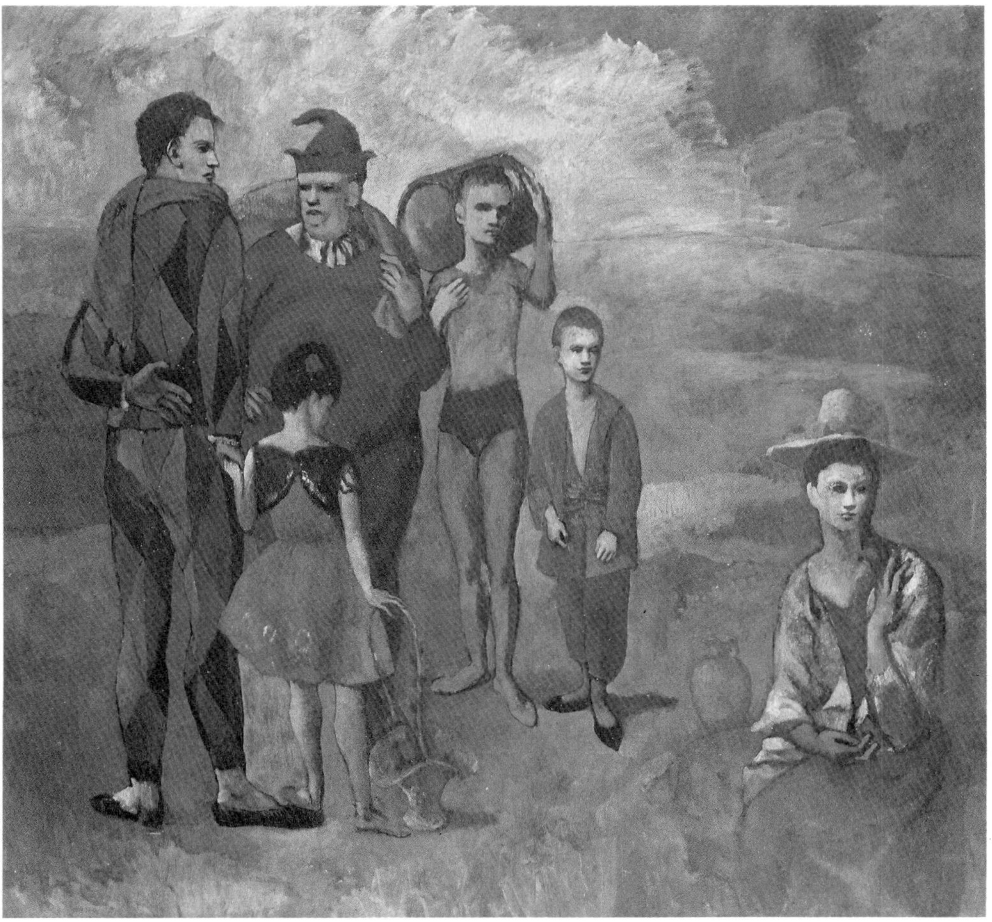

Pablo Picasso. *Family of Saltimbanques.* 1905. Oil on canvas, 6 feet 11¾ inches × 7 feet 6⅜ inches. National Gallery of Art, Washington. Chester Dale Collection

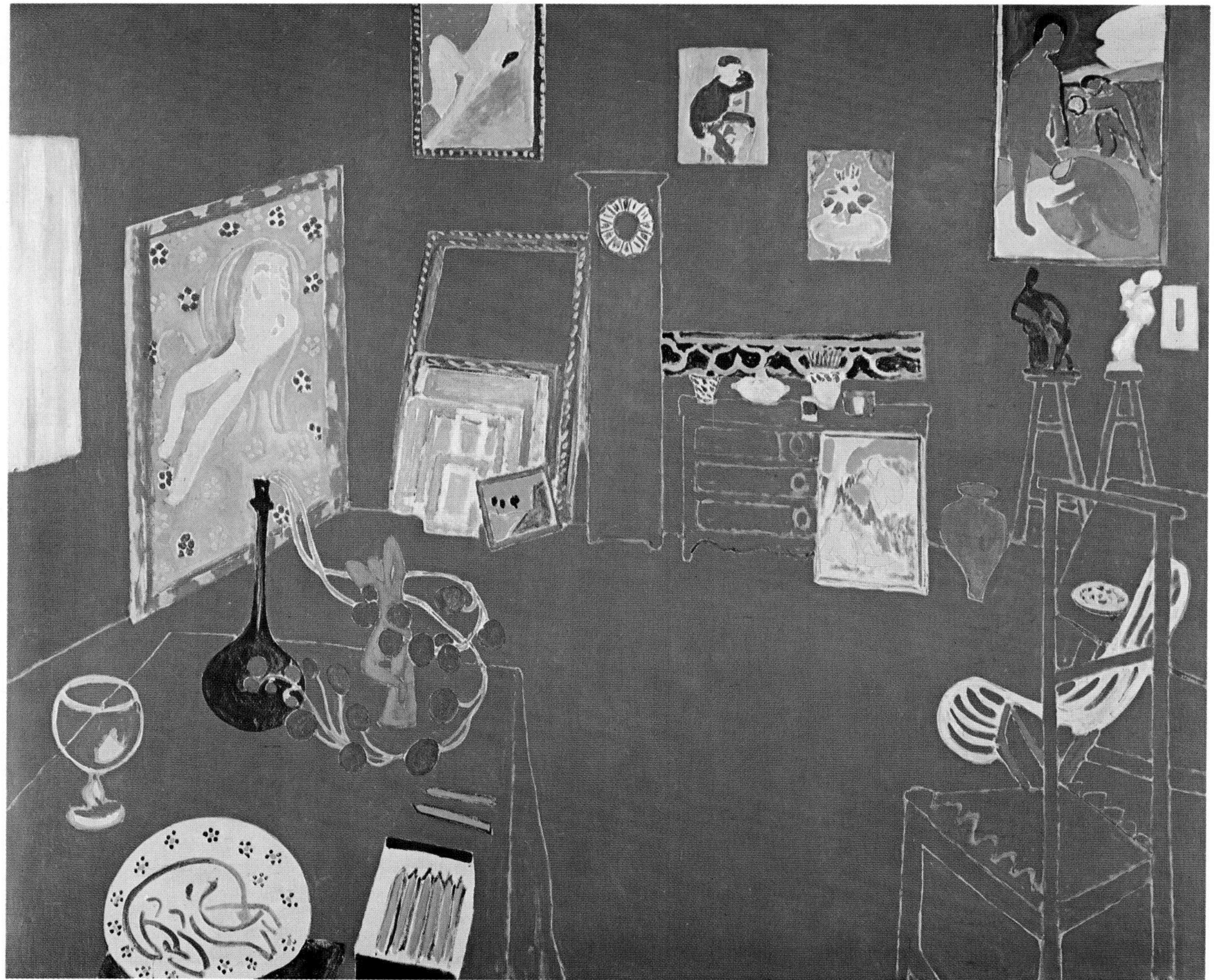

Henri Matisse.
The Red Studio.
1911.
Oil on canvas, 71¼ inches × 7 feet 2¼ inches.
The Museum of Modern Art, New York.
Mrs. Simon Guggenheim Fund

of Life. Les Demoiselles d'Avignon will dominate a later chapter in this book, and I need say here only that, like the *Joy of Life,* it has to do with grouped human figures set in a tripartite formal design that varies in color from warmth on the left to a cooler, sharper climate on the right. Again like the *Joy of Life,* though in a way that is altogether more trenchant, it treats the figures in a variety of styles, with no attempt at internal consistency.

Meanwhile Picasso, in his 25th year, was working on two monumental projects which had in common an instantly identifiable pinkish tonality. Picasso's Rose Period would seem to have begun in March, 1905, with a painting in gouache and watercolor of a young acrobat. Thereafter he produced a substantial corpus of paintings and drawings of circus- and street-perfomers, in costume and out of it. Their general subject was the contrast between the beauty and fragility of the human body and the feats of strength and endurance which it can be trained to carry out. With this came a subsidiary contrast: between the enclosed world of the performers and the world which we ourselves inhabit. The poet Rainer Maria Rilke knew Picasso's *Family of Saltimbanques* very well, and he wrote about it in one of his "Duino Elegies." He saw the little family as having been tormented from childhood onward by the will toward a brief, hard-won perfection: a fugitive beauty which few would notice and fewer still would stay to applaud. The *Family of Saltim-*

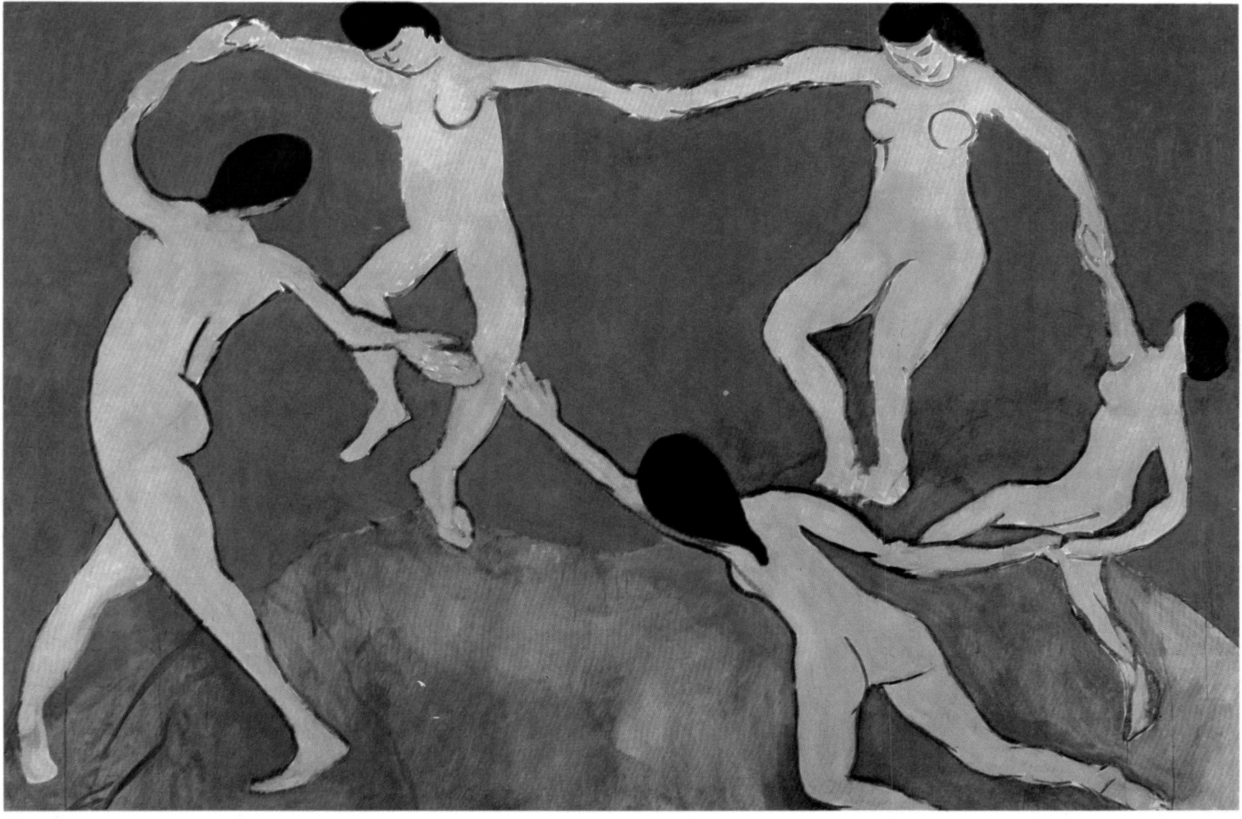

Henri Matisse.
Dance (1st version). 1909.
Oil on canvas, 8 feet 6½ inches × 12 feet 9½ inches.
The Museum of Modern Art, New York.
Gift of Nelson A. Rockefeller in honor of Alfred H. Barr, Jr.

banques was intended in this sense, beyond a doubt; but it is also a metaphor for the painter's position in society.

Picasso in the *Saltimbanques*, and in the never-finished project of 1906 for a large painting of horses and their attendants, was carrying forward a tradition in which Manet, in particular, had excelled: that of the complex figure composition in which people, often costumed beyond the demands of everyday, were grouped in an informal manner. The paintings in question can be read as portraits of disconnection, though there is no reason to think that Manet (or Watteau before him, in his theatrical paintings) so intended them. "Alienation" is, even so, our current name for the look of apartness which Manet gives to the old musician and his companions; and it recurs in Picasso's *Family of Saltimbanques*. Color in the big Picasso defines the emotional climate of the picture—and how subtly! Those faded pinks and subdued terra cottas, those echoing blues are picked up by the colors of earth and sky; the flowers in the child's basket index them all over again; even the pitcher on the ground plays along.

We would suppose that all this was as much a product of Picasso's imagination as the recurrent washes of moon blue in his paintings of a year or two earlier. But it has been pointed out that some of the Rose Period paintings deal—in terms of straightforward local color—with the facts of life among circus performers. It was a matter of literal truth that the interior of the most popular circus in Paris was painted "a tender red, shading slightly into gray," and that acrobats traditionally wore what one writer called "pink tights tinted the color of fresh roses." Indeed, Degas and Seurat had treated that same circus building in tones of rose, pink and red. There is therefore no reason to think of the color in these paintings as a bid to preempt our sympathies. Touching as it is, it remains primarily descriptive.

The delectable paintings of circus performers

which figure so largely in Picasso's Rose Period were linked to life, therefore, by their use of color which was, in effect, a mark of professional identification: circus pink was as specific, in this context, as "navy blue." But the Rose Period also corresponded to a basic change of mood in Picasso's output; and that change of mood persisted in the more directly autobiographical work of the period —the self-portraits, the affectionate variations on the looks of his best friends and the sideways allusions to the role of the artist in society. Matisse was altogether more detached—more cool-hearted, many would say—in his choice of subject matter. And whereas Picasso could manipulate circumstantial detail to most poignant effect, Matisse tended between 1905 and 1910 to eliminate more and more of those elements in his figure paintings which could detract from the central role of color.

When Matisse's Russian patron Shchukin asked him, for instance, for a decorative panel on the theme of music, he began with a sketch which showed people in the standard attitude of enraptured concertgoers; standard flowers grew at their feet, and a standard mastiff completed the scene. But before long he cut out the flowers, cut out the dog, cut out the self-awareness of the listeners. Color had been set free, and now it must be *left* free: that was the message of the two big decorations, *Dance* and *Music,* which Matisse sent to Moscow.

The Museum of Modern Art possesses the first version (1909) of *Dance.* From the study of this, and more particularly from the study of *The Red Studio* of 1911, we can see exactly what "color for color's sake" could mean at that time. It meant—as Matisse told his students—building the picture in terms of color. It meant getting the colors to support one another without anecdotal references or any resorting to "local color." Nature must be made to submit to "the spirit of the picture"; and that spirit was to be expressed in terms of pure color, as intense as the painter could make it. Color must do all the talking.

Matisse decided to build *Dance* with three colors: in his own words "a beautiful blue for the sky, the bluest of blues (the surface was colored to saturation, that is to say, up to a point where the blue, the idea of absolute blue, appeared conclusively) and a like green for the earth, and the vibrant vermilion for the bodies." Matisse had experimented with maximum saturation the year before with a single bathing figure. Now he took a group of dancers from the middle ground of the *Joy of Life* and brought them up front, on the kind of anonymous promontory that Picasso had used for his *Family of Saltimbanques.* The Museum of Modern Art's version has not quite the chromatic intensity of the Moscow version, and some of the drawing is more felt than realized: the detailing of hands and feet, for instance. The New York painting is about an uncomplicated form of high spirits; the Moscow one, about what could almost be a dance to the death, such as was to be portrayed in the music of Stravinsky's *The Rite of Spring.* But the two big paintings should be contrasted rather with the classic bacchanalia of European painting than with one another. Poussin's *Bacchanalian Scene* in the National Gallery in London has, for instance, a comparable round dance, with comparable positioning of hands and feet and a comparable circular pounding swing, round and round, as if naked figures had picked up Energy itself, as one might pick up a ball, and were flinging it from hand to hand. But Poussin upholstered the image with allegorical byplay in ways which Matisse by 1909 felt free to discard; in *Dance* there are no garlanded satyrs, no overhanging foliage, no distant mountains, no bunches of symbolic grapes and no cherubs to lap up the symbolic juices. The picture is presented to us undressed, just as the dancers themselves are undressed; whatever is not indispensable has been dispensed with. Both dance and dancers burst out of the frame; and in the simplifying and concentrating of the image the role of color is primary.

As much as any of the great altarpieces of the past, Matisse's *Dance* is a painting that can be seen

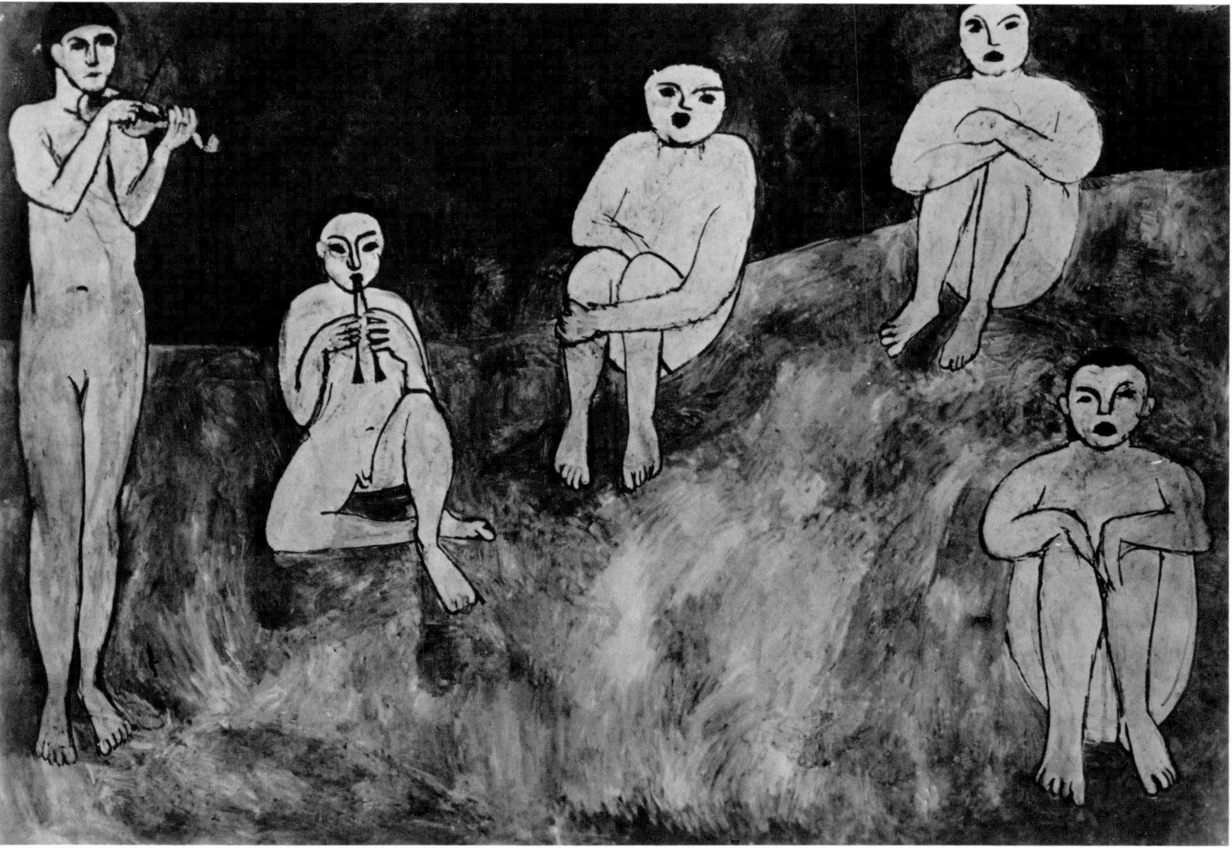

Henri Matisse.
Music. 1910.
Oil on canvas, 8 feet 5⅝ inches × 12 feet 9½ inches.
The Hermitage, Leningrad

from a great distance and still dominate the surroundings. But it differs from those altarpieces in that there is reserved for each of us a place in the very middle of the dance: it is for us, if we feel like it, to fill the gap between the outstretched hands of the two foreground figures.

Even more irresistibly are we drawn into the picture space of *The Red Studio,* 1911: the box of crayons in the foreground seems in some mysterious way to be already under our hand, and we wouldn't be surprised to see our own two familiar feet somewhere on view along the lower rim of the canvas. Color in *The Red Studio* is used to bend space in a way more radical than had been seen before in painting. Matisse takes the classic, rectangular deep space of the studio and treats it as we treat a miscellany of objects presented to us on a jeweler's tray. Certain things he picks up and puts under our noses. To others he says, "Keep your distance!" On the far wall, four identifiable pictures face us frontally, setting up a clear idea of the distance involved. Two identifiable statues by Matisse define, again, the space immediately in front of the far wall; but the double-A shape of the stools on which they stand is not related to the floor beneath them, any more than we can identify, in the top half of the picture, the point at which the left-hand wall meets the far one. Matisse's own paintings, and his own ceramic plate in the foreground, retain their own chromatic identity. But other objects in the room have been bled of that identity and restated in terms of the glorious, uniform red which gives the picture its name. What we see is, in fact, an unbroken field of red on which certain incidents have been laid, or incised. Delectable as they are in themselves, these incidents are the captives of that one resonant, imperious, inescapable field of red. It is a crucial moment in the history of painting: color is on top, and making the most of it.

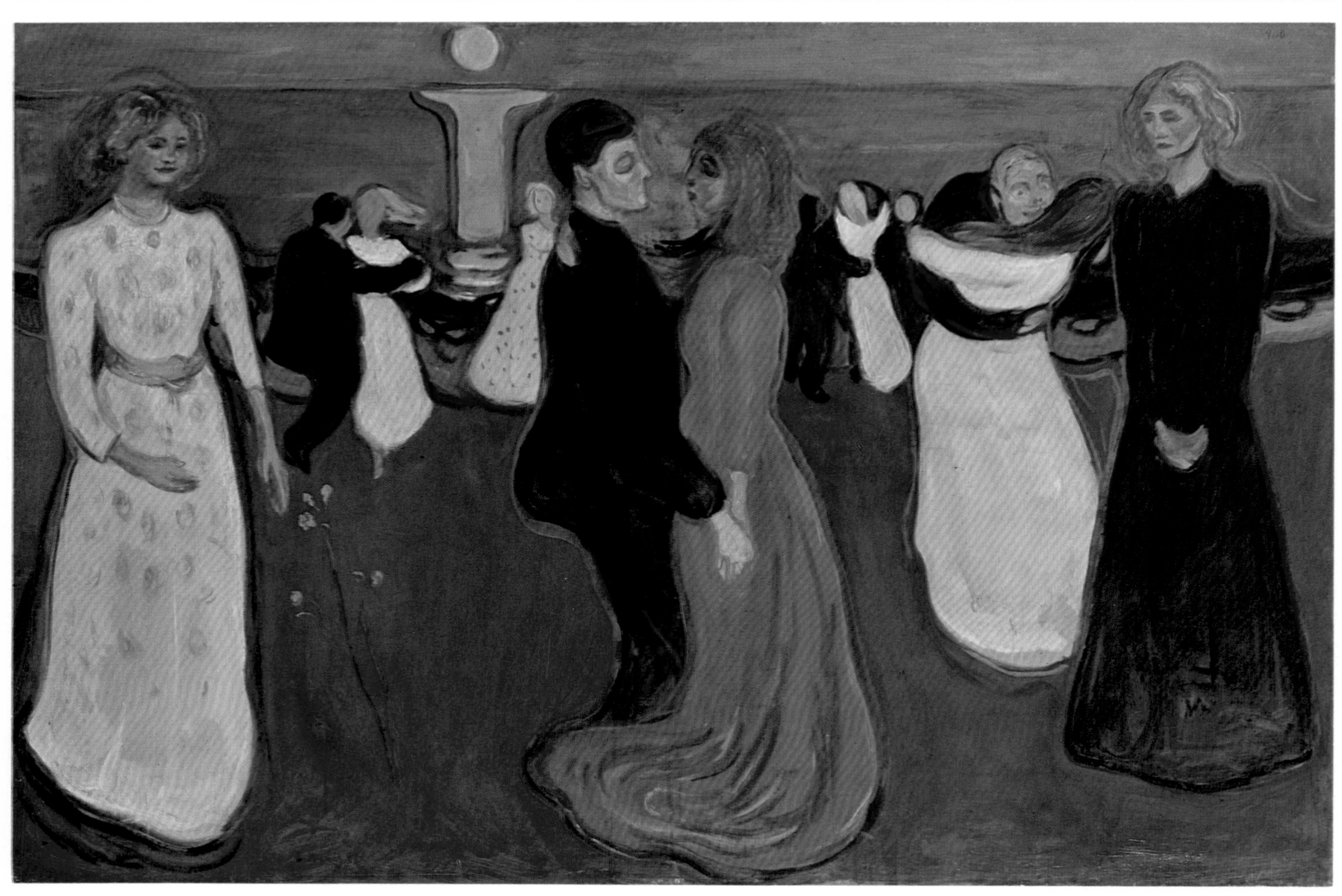

Edvard Munch.
The Dance of Life.
1899–1900.
Oil on canvas,
50 inches × 6 feet
4 inches.
Nasjonalgalleriet,
Oslo

HISTORY AS NIGHTMARE

One of the key remarks of this century occurs in a very long novel which was begun in 1914 by an Irish writer who had yet to make a name. James Joyce was the writer, the novel was *Ulysses,* and the remark was all of 11 words long. "History," said Joyce's Stephen Dedalus, "is a nightmare from which I am trying to awake."

I take "history" to mean, here, a sense of the past as something that determines the present to an intolerable degree. To be born in a certain place, at a certain time, and of a particular parentage, can be a disadvantage from which it is impossible to recover completely. I take "nightmare" to mean, here, the state of mind defined in 1931 by Ernest Jones, the eminent psychoanalyst and biographer of Sigmund Freud. Jones described the classic symptoms of nightmare as "agonizing dread, a sense of oppression or weight at the chest which alarmingly interferes with respiration, and a conviction of hopeless paralysis." A sense of history as nightmare, thus interpreted, is as severe an affliction as can be wished upon us.

Yet we can all think of times at which that sense was mandatory among intelligent and sensitive people. The calendar of the recent past is full of such times, and very often they are linked to particular places: Prague in 1968, Dallas in 1963, Budapest in 1956, Hiroshima in 1945, Leningrad during the seige of 1941–43, Pearl Harbor in 1941, Paris in 1940, Berlin in 1933. To be aware of what was going on in those places at those moments was to experience in our waking life the terrors attributed in 1834 by a Scottish savant, Dr. Robert Macnish, to the nightmare state: "The whole mind is wrought up to a pitch of unutterable despair; a spell is laid upon the faculties which freezes them into inaction; the wretched victim feels as if pent alive in his coffin, or overpowered by resistless and unmitigable pressures."

At such times, and in the face of such thoughts, we realize how high van Gogh was aiming when he said that he wanted his paintings "to retain their calm even in the midst of catastrophe." Art and literature are there at such times to steady us: to remind us that night thoughts, even when warranted, are not the whole of life. But art and literature are also there to remind us of aspects of existence, and of ourselves, with which we have not dared to come to terms.

Someone who knew this was Franz Kafka. Kafka in 1903 was only 20 years old, and he was still some way from writing the novels and the stories—among them *The Trial, The Castle* and *The Metamorphosis*—which were to earn him a unique place in the history of the European imagination. But he already knew what was worth writing (and reading) and what wasn't. He sensed that a state of emergency would shortly be declared within the European psyche, and that a new kind of awareness would be needed to deal with it. The old order might seem to be intact in the Austro-Hungarian Empire of 1903, and the concept of the collective unconscious had not yet been formulated by C. G. Jung. But Kafka also sensed that someone would have to force that new kind of awareness upon us. Meanwhile, it was not the writer's first duty to help the reader to pass the time as agreeably as possible. "A book must be an ice axe," Kafka wrote to a friend, "to break the sea frozen within us." "If the book in our hands does not wake us, as with a fist that hammers on the skull, then it just isn't worth reading." That was the message.

Kafka and his ice axe could remind us of a German painting which, though not modern in date, is both a classic of clear-sightedness and the ancestor of much that is memorable in the art of the last hundred years: *The Frozen Sea,* which was painted by Caspar David Friedrich in 1822. This was a new kind of picture, with a new echo to it, and it is still the best image we have of the way in which human hopes and human ambitions can have the life crushed out of them by forces beyond our control. Friedrich took one of the vicissitudes of early Arctic exploration and turned it into a symbol of "history as nightmare." Such was the force of his emotional commitment, when allied to a steadfast and pellucid form of expression, that his private anxieties took on a universal and timeless validity.

Like all the great symbols, *The Frozen Sea* will bear many interpretations and yield something new to all of them. It is a painting to which every age reacts in a different way. Friedrich never sold it. The sailing ship was for him, throughout his career, a symbol for all that was vulnerable and nerve-ridden in human affairs; but I believe that *The Frozen Sea* had a secret meaning for him, and one so poignant that he could not bear to part with the painting. It had an inner subject: the events of the immediate past in Germany. The disaster to which it refers is political as much as maritime. Friedrich was still the man who had painted, ten years earlier, a picture called *The Grave of One Who Fell for Freedom;* and when he painted *The Frozen Sea* he must have had in mind the Carlsbad Decrees of 1819, by which freedom of the press was abolished over a large part of Germany, political agitation was suppressed, the universities were brought under state control and the free-spirited individual laid under suspicion of "conspiracy." That was "history as nightmare" in the 1820s. In how many countries is it not still with us?

Friedrich was the first major European artist to acknowledge the role in his work of the as-yet-unnamed unconscious. "Close your physical eye" was his advice to other painters. "Look first at your picture with the eye of the spirit, and bring to the light of day what you have seen in darkness." It is as if he knew, ahead of his time, that the documentary, illustrative function would soon be wrested from art. Art had still the power, however, to come up with symbols so telling, so universal in their application, that they take rank among the experiences that orient us in life. One such was Goya's *The Colossus.* As much as anyone who ever lived, Goya carried within him the sense of history as nightmare. The offhand brutality of our own times is something to which Goya, in 19th-century Spain, gave definitive expression. Where he trod, it is pointless for other painters to follow; what has been done completely need not be done again.

Caspar David Friedrich.
The Frozen Sea.
1822.
Oil on canvas,
38½ × 46½ inches.
Hamburger Kunsthalle, Hamburg

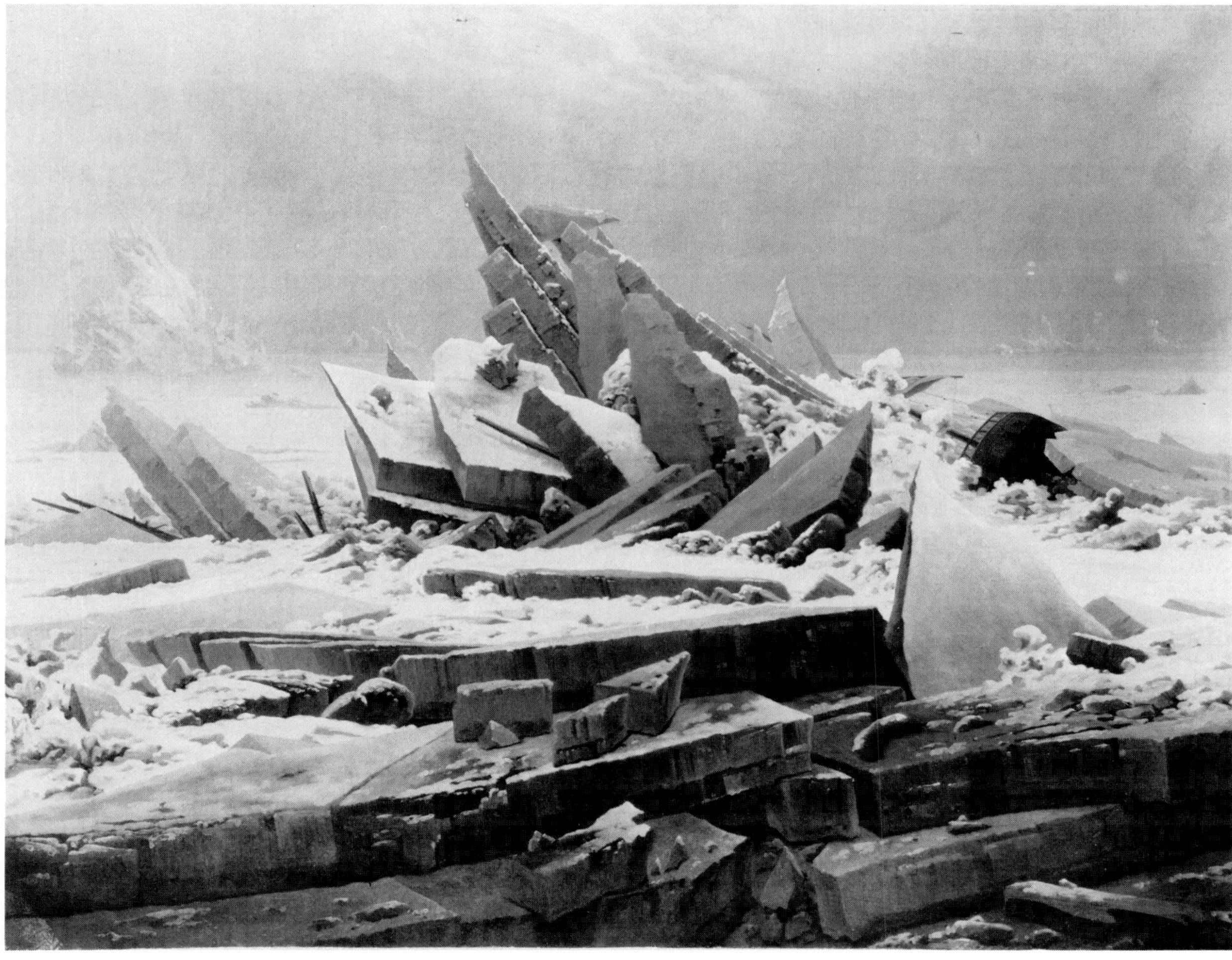

Goya had in an extreme degree the premonitory sense: he knew what kinds of behavior had come to stay. "No one," said Baudelaire of Goya, "has ventured further in the direction of the *possible* absurd." Now that the absurd is everywhere—in behavior so appalling that we have to give it an ironical name before we can bear to think about it all—we realize that to explore the "possible absurd" in such depth was as great a service to mankind as art can perform.

The Colossus gave us a new metaphor for nightmare. Just who the giant was, and just what he was doing, Goya left it to us to decide. He is an archetypal figure of dread; each generation gives him a new set of identity papers. To have some idea of the powers of art we have only to set *The Colossus* beside a comparable image from the 1930s: a still from *King Kong. King Kong* was a good movie, and its image of a giant gorilla standing on top of a skyscraper has entered into the folk-memory of our times. But beside the Goya how flat it is, how banal, how pedestrian! How much less terrifying is King Kong's petulant stance, with its conventional baring of the teeth, than the indifference of Goya's colossus, who does not even deign to look back at the scene of panic and terror beneath him!

Both *The Colossus* and *The Frozen Sea* stand for an important shift in the activities of the human imagination: the shift from allegory to symbol. Allegory in this context is the use of art to tell a story which is already familiar but cannot be told too often. Anyone who went to the Doges' Palace in Venice in the 1580s and was shown the new paintings by Veronese would immediately see that most of the paintings in question were about power, and about the fact that the Venetian Republic had power and intended to keep it. Allegory, in this instance, was doing its job well; Mars and Neptune were on the ceiling, and very fine they looked; but the implication was that Venetian power had the sanction of the gods and woe betide anyone who presumed to challenge it. Allegory had for centuries been one of the prime functions of art. Allegory in public places was confirmatory, by its very nature. If a painting was put up in church, or in the law courts, or in one of the seats of government, it was a safe bet that it would tell people that things were quite all right as they were. The painter was not going to say that religion was a hoax, or that the judges were ignorant and corrupt, or that the ruler was not fit to rule. When Tintoretto worked in the Doges' Palace, and Rubens worked for Marie de Médicis when she was Queen of France, and Tiepolo painted the great ceiling in the Bishop's Palace in Würzburg, they were being asked to uphold the status quo; and they did it, without demur. If they thought that the Doges had got above themselves, or that the Bishops were too free with the excellent local wine, they never said so.

By the 19th century the structure of obeisance, long shaken, fell apart. So did the structure of shared learning on which allegory could draw. The old confidence in society and its rulers, already undermined by the revolutions of the 18th century, was collapsing. ("Casca il mondo"—"The world is coming apart"—said the Papal Secretary of State in 1866, when the Prussians defeated the Austrians at the battle of Königgrätz.) Allegory in its great days depended on shared beliefs, and shared expectations, and allusions universally recognizable. But in the 19th century a new world was coming into being: a world in which many thoughtful people had not read Virgil and Ariosto, and didn't know one saint from another, and were convinced that the only thing in which they could believe completely was their own private emotional experience. Whole sections of humanity felt themselves orphaned. To accommodate all this—to express the poetry of dissent and the politics of disquiet—a new kind of art had to come into being.

Friedrich's had been a preindustrial sensibility: one that functioned in perfect unselfconsciousness before what now seems to us the second Fall of Man. By the 1880s the role of the imagination was in the ascendant, in that symbols alone could stand for thoughts too long repressed in made-to-order painting. Symbol was the free man's revenge upon authority. It was the essence of the symbol, in this context, that it did not tell a familiar story. In fact it didn't tell a story at all. It sowed a seed: of disquiet, wonder, speculation, doubt. It was an invaluable way of saying something very important without pinning oneself down. No tyrant was immune to the symbol; and the 1880s had their full share of tyrants and would-be tyrants. The time was approaching when James Joyce could say that "silence, exile and cunning" were the only conditions in which a major artist could go to work. The silence could be conditional, the exile a matter of inner adjustment, the cunning a strategy to keep out of authority's way. The essential was to keep the work intact. The symbol was the mine with which outdated ideas would be blown sky-high; meanwhile, the vagrant imagination did better to shun company. It is significant that the life style of Symbolist painters like Gustave Moreau and Odilon Redon was private and obsessional, with none of the hearty, outgoing quality which had characterized Monet and Renoir in their youth.

But if the vagrant imagination did not have company in the Paris of the 1880s, it had backers. In poetry and painting alike, it was defended by masters of language: Stéphane Mallarmé, above all, and his fellow poets Jules Laforgue, Tristan Corbière and Jean Moréas. Symbolism is so much a matter of the individual imagination, and so little a matter of theory and doctrine, that groupings of this sort are valid primarily as a matter of historical convenience. Much of what is called Symbolist painting and poetry had nothing to do with "history as nightmare." It was a retreat into a dream world of epicene twitter and recondite allusions not worth disentangling. But many of the best poets agreed with many of the best painters that the dream was the essence of their activity, and that it should take priority at all times. As for fidelity to the experience of everyday—other, lesser persons could take care of that. Painting and poetry were very close; already in 1864, 22 years before Jean Moréas wrote the "Symbolist Manifesto," Mallarmé was using the verb "to paint" when he defined his intentions in poetry.

Mallarmé, in matters of art, was fundamental not only to his own century but to ours as well. Whenever a work of art has a resonance that cannot be explained in literal terms, or in terms of information, Mallarmé is somewhere behind it. At the age of 22, he spoke of inventing a new use of language which would "paint not the thing itself but the effect that it produces." He was neither narrow nor doctrinaire in his tastes. A close friend of Manet, and the subject of one of the most elegant of Manet's portraits, he wrote on Manet in the 1870s with an eloquence and an understanding which have not been surpassed. Artists of many persuasions loved him: when he died in 1898, Rodin, Renoir and Vuillard were among the mourners at his graveside.

He believed that straight description had no place in art. Of course art could teach, tell a specific story, link one fact to another. But the essential lay elsewhere: in the echo, the singular vibration, the symbol which could not be pinned down

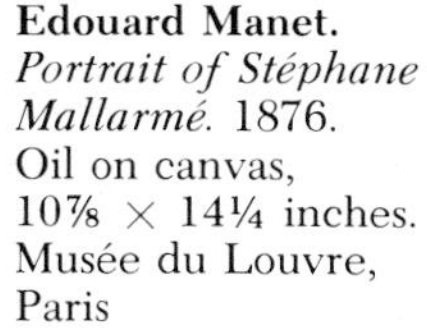

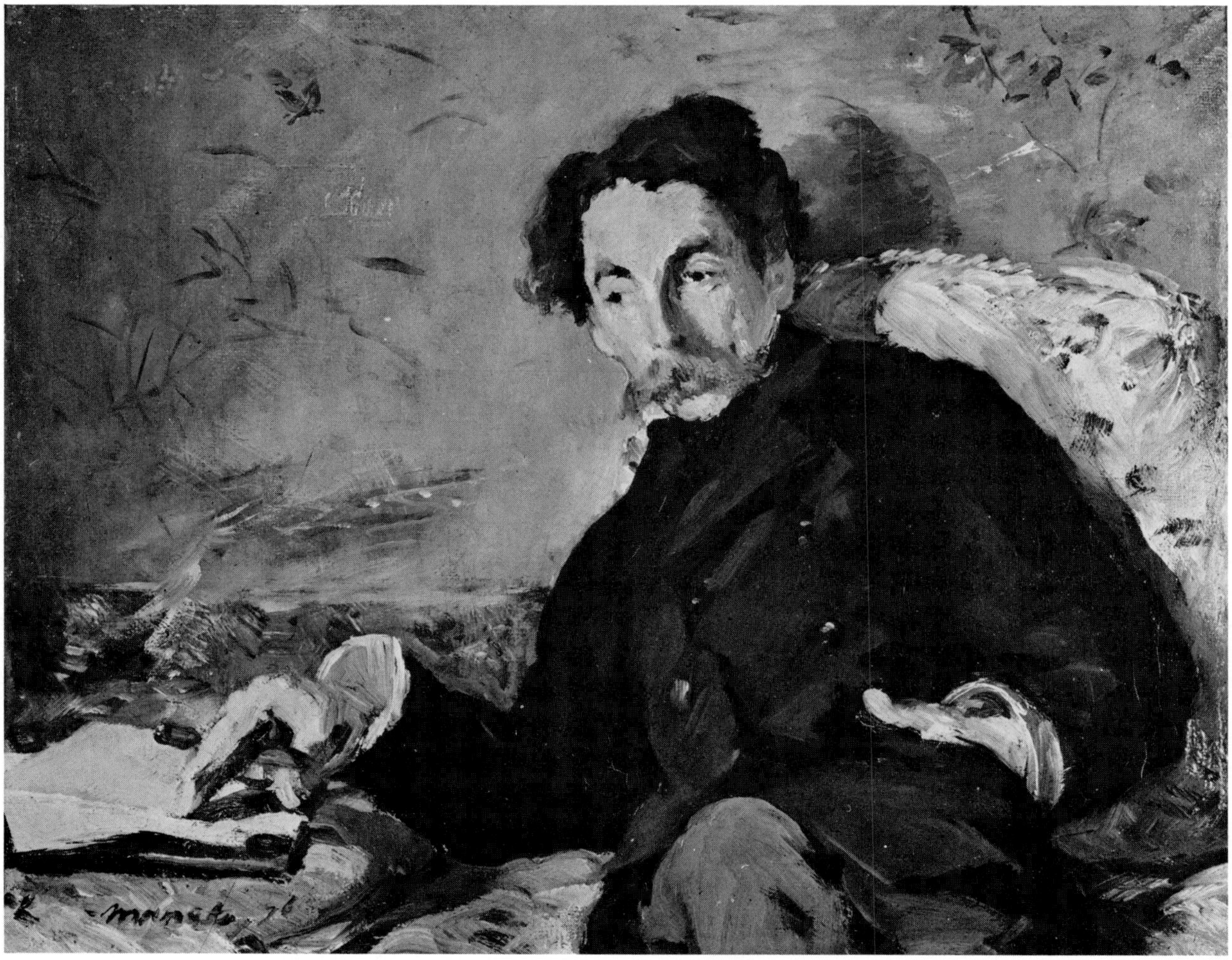

Edouard Manet. *Portrait of Stéphane Mallarmé.* 1876. Oil on canvas, $10\frac{7}{8} \times 14\frac{1}{4}$ inches. Musée du Louvre, Paris

or explained away. "To *name* an object," Mallarmé wrote in 1891, "is to deprive the public of three-quarters of its pleasure. The identity of objects should be revealed gradually. Guesswork should enter into it. To *suggest*—that should be the poet's dream. In suggesting, he makes the best possible use of that mysterious thing, the symbol."

Mallarmé in writing this was out to break the domination of a tightly wrought, tightly metered poetry in which subject matter was precisely defined and images were drawn as if with an etching needle. But the distinction which he drew between naming and suggesting could apply just as much to the difference between painting which relies on what is given to the outward eye and painting which proceeds from an inner vision. Other poets underlined this difference. Tristan Corbière said, for instance, that "the only thing that the painter should paint is what he has never seen and never will see." Gustave Moreau, preeminent among painters of that sort, once said that he did not believe in what he could touch or in what he could see; the only things that he believed in were the things that he could *not* see.

Moreau was neither a bigot nor a doctrinaire, and in his last years he proved to be as inspiring and as liberal a teacher as France has ever produced. He had been close to Degas in his youth, but he never stooped to petty disparagement of painters whose practice differed from his own. Yet his work was anti-Impressionist by implication. In a period when nearly all the great paintings, from Courbet to Monet, had to do with the restatement of observable fact, Gustave Moreau kept open the line to an art of pure fantasy. In his own work he allowed his imagination to drive him to the edge of incoherence, the edge of self-revelation, the edge of delirium. Despising what he called "the sad accountancy of common sense," he offered himself as a living exemplar of its antithesis. For all the idiosyncrasy of his obsessions Moreau was right in there first, as Friedrich in other contexts had been right in there before him, with the obsessions of a later age. Moreau's *Oedipus* is the archetypal fine-boned victim of a dilemma to which Freud gave universal status, just as Moreau's *Salome Dancing before Herod* prefigures Richard Strauss's treatment of the same subject in the opera first performed in 1905. Moreau lived the life of a moneyed hermit—"a hermit," said Degas, "who knows the railroad timetables by heart"—but the frozen seas within him turned out, when melted, to set whole generations afloat.

Moreau was a favorite of the novelist J. K. Huysmans. Huysmans also saw the point of a younger artist, Odilon Redon, whose work he described in 1881 as "nightmare transposed into art"; and Redon did, in fact, pride himself on the idea. He thought that the Impressionists were the captives of their subject matter and that they could look at it from only one limited point of view. His own great wish was to welcome "the messenger of the unconscious, that most lofty and mysterious personage, who comes in her own good time. The vital thing," he went on, "is to submit to the unconscious. . . ."

Looking back at Moreau and Redon, with their admirably cut clothes, their ordered senior-citizens' lives and their circle of eminent friends and acquaintances, we find it paradoxical that they should stand with van Gogh, the outcast, and with Gauguin, the exile, in the Symbolist pantheon. But they were at one with Gauguin and van Gogh in believing that there should be more to art than is encompassed by everyday visual experience. Just what that "something more" might mean to us was put very well by Edvard Munch in 1889, when as a man of 26 he defined the limitations of Impressionism once and for all: "I've had enough of 'interiors,' and 'people reading,' and 'women knitting.' I want to paint real live people who breathe, feel, suffer and live. People who see these pictures will understand that these are sacred matters, and they will take off their hats, as if they were in church."

Munch was not alone, of course, in wishing to create an art of concern. As we have seen, van Gogh was a born preacher. Gauguin tried to take upon himself all the tribulations that western Europe was heir to. All over Europe, artists were aiming to enlarge the preoccupations of their well-to-do public. Some of them were convinced radicals, like Käthe Kollwitz, who in 1897 produced a series of prints in homage to the Silesian weavers who had revolted against their masters in 1844. Some of them were what Ibsen called "pillars of society." Hubert von Herkomer, for instance, was a great personage in late Victorian England, but in 1891 he surprised many of his admirers by sending to the Royal Academy a picture called *On Strike*, which was a gesture of solidarity toward the industrial poor.

These were honorable personal statements, and Käthe Kollwitz was, to the end of her long life (1867–1945), an outstandingly courageous and selfless individual. But she did not change the course of art: that role was reserved for Edvard Munch. Not only did he impose a new kind of sensibility in the 1890s, but he extended the idiom which van Gogh and Gauguin had made available. Munch had always made it his business to know what was going on in art, and when he was in Paris between 1889 and 1893 he looked about him hard and long and at what Rodin, in particular, was doing.

As a sculptor who aspired to work on the grandest scale and to become, in effect, the keeper of the public conscience, Rodin was bound to get into trouble. Sculpture makes people uneasy in a way that painting does not. A painting sits on the wall, and can be ignored. Traditional sculpture occupies the same space as ourselves, mimics our way of standing, and forces us to get out of its way. Sculpture which trespasses upon our inner life is likely to offend against taboos so powerful, so deep-seated in our natures, that we are not even aware of their existence. But Rodin showed with his *Gates of Hell*, 1880–1917, that he was not to be deflected by such considerations. The designation of "Symbolist" is quite inadequate to characterize the full range of Rodin's activity; but he was a true Symbolist insofar as he did not wish his imaginative subjects to have local, finite implications. "The imagination of the spectator," he once wrote, "should be left free to roam at will. That is the role of art, as I see it: the form which it creates should furnish a pretext for the unlimited development of emotion."

That "unlimited development of emotion" was exactly what Munch had in mind when he studied the work of Rodin. In scale and function, Rodin's *Gates of Hell* was the pessimist's counterpart to the great affirmations of faith which had been among the highest achievements of European art for more than fifteen hundred years. Unlike the monumental sculptured doors of Santa Sabina in Rome, San Zeno in Verona and San Lorenzo in

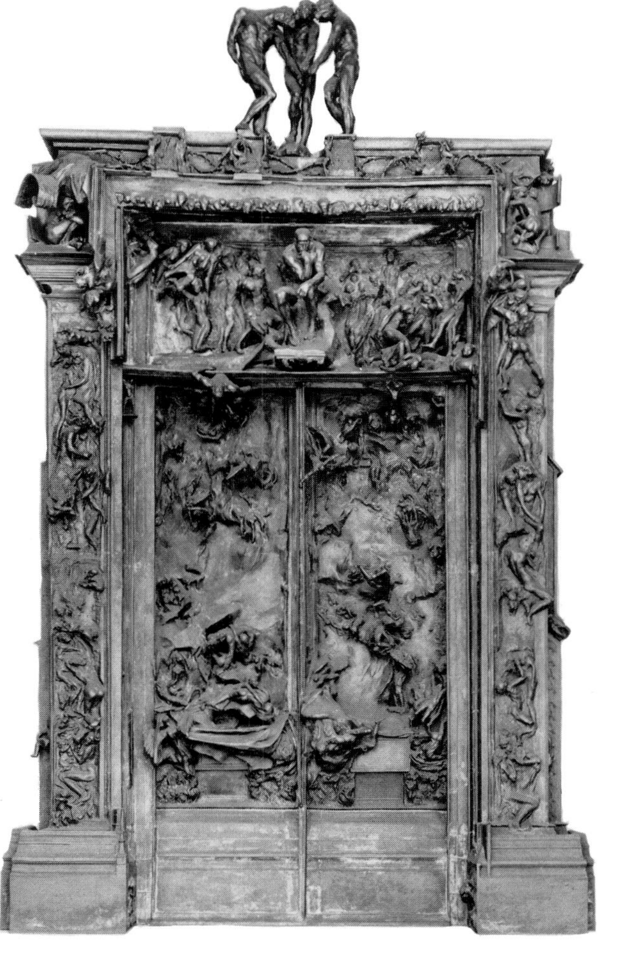

Auguste Rodin. *Gates of Hell.* 1880–1917. Bronze, 20 feet 10¾ inches × 13 feet 2 inches × 33⅜ inches. Philadelphia Museum of Art. Gift of Jules E. Mastbaum

Florence, Rodin's gates were to bring no consolation to those who passed beneath the lintel. His message was, on the contrary, that (as Albert Elsen has said in his book on Rodin) mankind was "adrift in an empire of night; separated from, rather than being the victim of, its deity; born with a fatal duality of desire and an incapability to fulfill it; damned on both sides of the tomb to an internal Hell of passions."

A discouraging point of view, decidedly; but one not easily refuted. Humanity was in a bad way as it trundled toward the year 1914. The conditions of life in industrial society were such as to sunder man from man, condemning each and all to an ever-greater alienation. Rodin did not plan his huge scheme in advance but proceeded according to the imperatives of the unconscious. As he saw it, humanity had no sooner raised itself from the primeval slime than it gave in, unprotesting, to the tyranny of Self; his myriad figures, forever twisting and turning, are emblems of the disconnectedness of modern life.

Munch learned from Rodin how to release the innate expressiveness of the human body. And although Rodin was 23 years his senior, Munch was enough a man of the 19th century to aspire to make a complete panorama—a three-volume novel in paint—of the human condition. He was to get the chance more than once; but meanwhile he displayed certain gifts which we are likely to underestimate now that we no longer question his achievement. He showed that easel painting was still very much alive at a time when the going thing in Paris, with Bonnard, with Vuillard and with their friends, was the big wall decoration. And he showed how to paint Symbolist pictures in which the human body, every bit of it, was as expressive as the body of a great actor on stage.

Munch also had a playwright's sense of economy. Nothing is in his pictures that does not need to be there. And what is there has in the highest degree, even today, the power to disturb and disquiet. Like Friedrich in *The Frozen Sea,* Munch drew on his own circumstances: the fact, for example, that his mother and his sister both died of tuberculosis while he was still a schoolboy. Like Moreau, he allowed his feelings about women to color his work from start to finish. He was not quite so frank as Moreau, who said in an unguarded moment that he found the iniquities of his Salome "not in the subject itself, but in the quintessence of womankind as I see it in life—woman, with her craving for unhealthy emotions and her stupidity, which is so intense that she does not grasp the horror of even the most dreadful situations."

Munch would never have said that, but then he had acted out his beliefs more directly in his work. Nowhere do we find more vividly portrayed the late 19th century's belief in woman-as-sorceress. We come across that belief in the novel, in the drama, in poetry, in the opera house, in the two words *femme fatale.* In this, as in so much else, Baudelaire was a pioneer: his *Les Fleurs du mal* (1857) is stamped on almost every page with the idea of female seduction as something elemental, a force of nature not to be turned aside, much less resisted. That same idea comes out in the character of Kundry in Wagner's *Parsifal* (1882); it permeates the action of Dostoevsky's *The Idiot* (1869) in the character of Nastasia Petrovna; and if it was difficult at that time to be quite so candid in the legitimate theater, there were redoubtable instances of woman-as-willpower in the Scandinavian drama. Who can forget Hedda Gabler in Ibsen's play, burning the manuscript of her former lover's lifework, or the central figure in Strindberg's *The Father,* consigned to a straitjacket by his womenfolk?

Munch's emotional experience was of the kind which can be made bearable only if it is transformed by art. Munch's mother died when he was five. His father turned to the church for consolation and became a prey to religious anxieties which unfitted him for the ordinary traffic of life. (Munch said later that "disease and insanity were the black angels at my cradle.") As a grown man, Munch had great charm, a noble bearing and good looks of a statuesque sort which he retained even

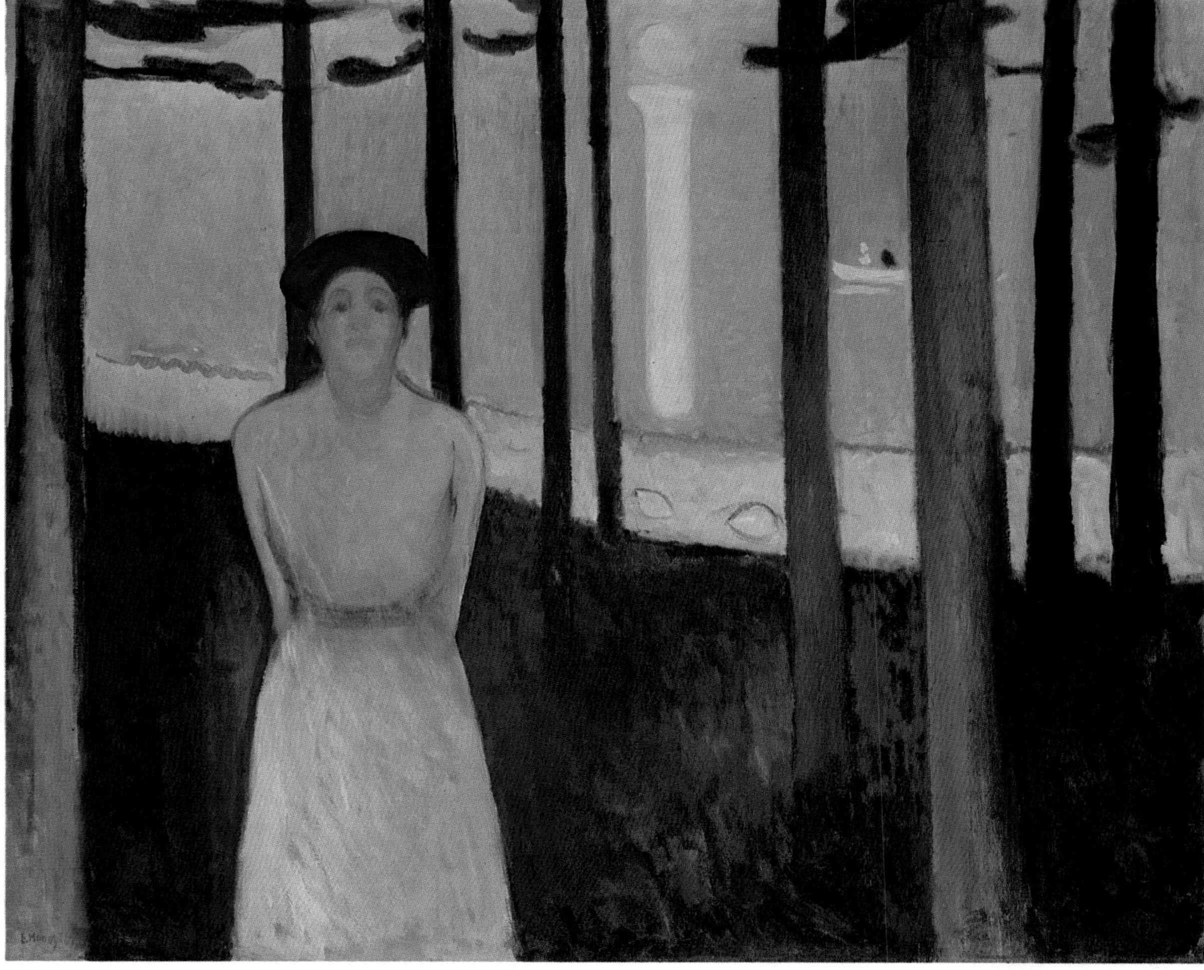

Edvard Munch.
The Voice. 1893.
Oil on canvas,
34½ × 42½ inches.
Museum of Fine
Arts, Boston. Ernest
Wadsworth
Longfellow Fund

into old age. But these endowments did not save him from the most lurid and melodramatic of private entanglements. When he was 40, for instance, he was involved with a girl who had herself laid out, as if on her deathbed, in an attempt to prevent him from leaving her; and when she threatened to shoot herself and Munch tried to restrain her, the gun went off accidentally and he lost one of his fingers in the struggle. Two or three years later he had to leave Norway after a public brawl with another man. As late as the 1930s Munch was still reliving that day in his work—still picturing the look of his bloodied antagonist as he staggered along the narrow lane toward Munch's house, and still picturing the reflex of instinct with which he himself had picked up a gun as if to ward off a second attack.

Munch was able to share these experiences with us in a way that is neither garrulous nor self-pitying. He was also able to give them a universal implication. (A later painter, Oskar Kokoschka, said that Munch had been the first man to enter "the modern Inferno" and come back to tell how it was.) Art was for Munch what the theater was for Strindberg: "a *Biblia pauperum*, or Bible in pictures." He could have said, with Strindberg, that he "found 'the joy of life' in life's cruel and mighty conflicts"—and in the colossal discharges of psychic energy to which they gave rise. In dealing with those "cruel and mighty conflicts," Munch undressed feelings the way bodies are undressed in the act of love.

All this is made clear in such classic Munch subjects as *The Death Chamber, Jealousy* and *The*

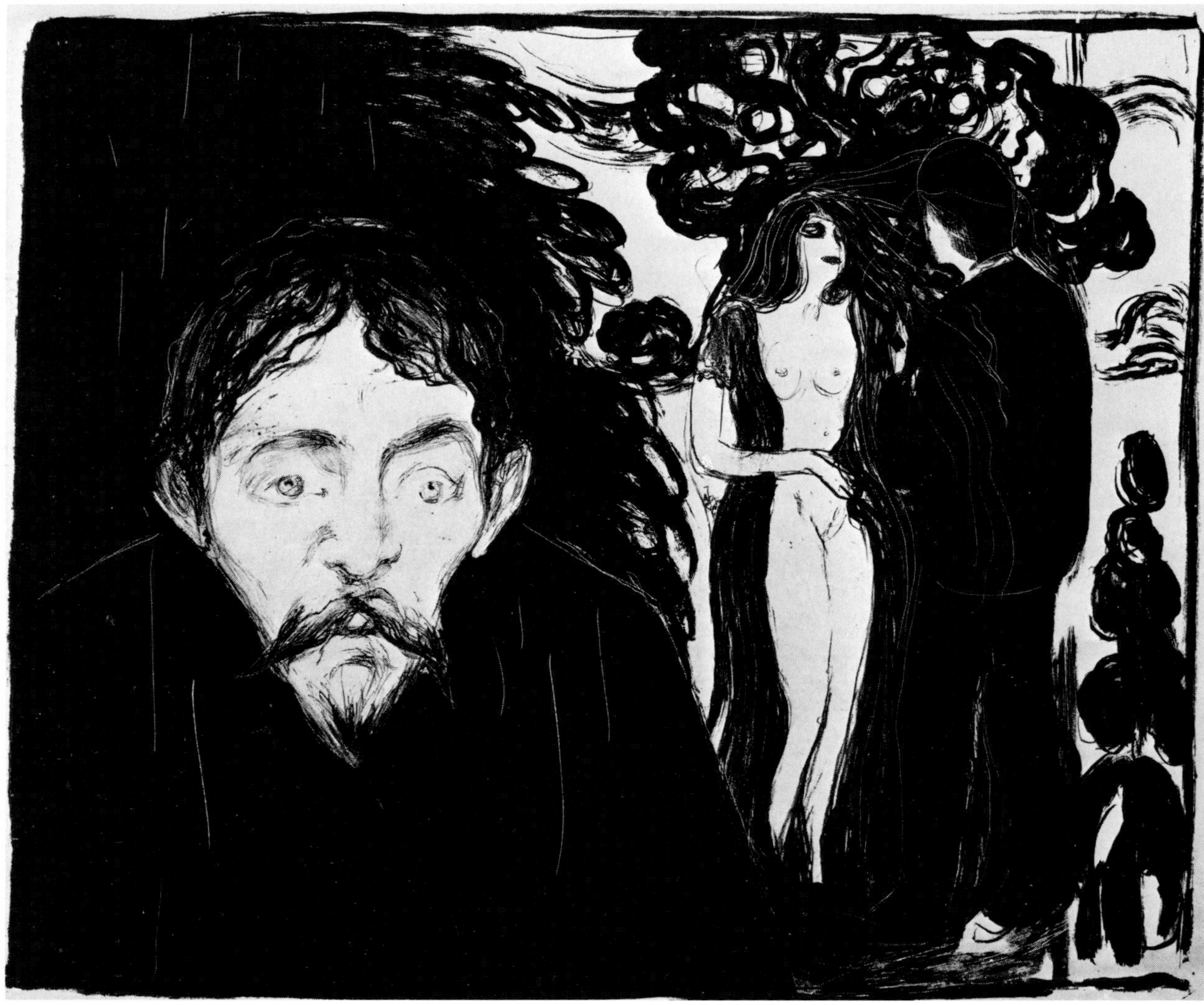

Edvard Munch.
Jealousy. 1896.
Lithograph,
18¾ × 22⅝ inches.
The Museum of Modern Art, New York.
The William B. and Evelyn A. Jaffe Collection

Dance of Life. In a painting like the *Virginia Creeper* of 1898, Munch uses a perfectly ordinary aspect of suburban horticulture to make us feel that the whole of Nature is hemorrhaging in sympathy with the tormented man in the foreground. Munch came from a part of the world in which Nature often seems to side with the extremes of human feeling; and Nature in his paintings is neither indifferent nor hostile. She figures, rather, as the accomplice of mankind and as a commentator who gives a new amplitude (and what Rodin had called "an unlimited development") to emotions which in life are often repressed.

For the greater part of his life Munch was preoccupied with the idea of painting a series of pictures which, when put together, would constitute a complete panorama of human life. He completed a modest version of it for the foyer of a theater in Berlin. Later, in 1922, he tried to compress the idea into a series of 12 paintings for a chocolate factory in Oslo; and sometimes there were single paintings which, like *The Dance of Life,* tried to show the whole gamut of human existence at once. Munch felt so strongly and so deeply for this subject that he was ready to adopt a system of cues which another artist would have rejected as too banal: as in *The Dance of Life,* for instance, where the white dress of the girl on the left stands for an as yet unblemished purity, the black dress and tortured demeanor of the woman on the right stand for mourning and rejection, and the red dress of the woman in the middle stands for a delight in the passing moment. In the background, to left and to right, goatish couples symbolize the baser life. As always, it is the solitary figures who most engage Munch's sympathy.

It is a part of the genius of Munch that he brings us face to face with aspects of life which we would otherwise neglect or ignore. If he shows a crowd streaming toward us along a city street, we sense that the crowd could at any moment be gunned down. If he paints a group of uncorrupted young girls—and no one was ever better at doing this—we see them as hostages on whom life will make heavy demands, sooner rather than later. If he paints a portrait, there is something peculiarly moving about his frank, open, frontal approach: we feel that this is how it should be, but so rarely is, when one human being confronts another. Munch gives us an object lesson in the use of color and in the nature of composition; but, more than that, he teaches us to live with our own experience and not be afraid of it.

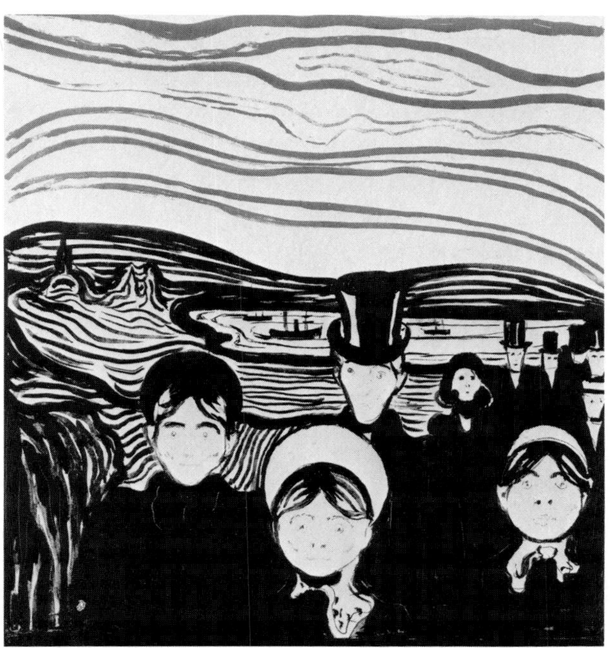

Edvard Munch. *Anxiety.* 1896. Lithograph, 16⅜ × 15⅜ inches. The Museum of Modern Art, New York. Purchase

If someone were to say "Munch" when asked to guess the authorship of the portrait of Erich Heckel and *Street in Dresden,* reproduced here, he would not be so far wrong as to have made a fool of himself. Neither painting could have been painted without Munch's example. The portrait of Erich Heckel has precisely the tall thin format, the open and unambiguous stance before life, and the peremptory outlining of the figure against a light background which we associate with Munch's portraits of men. The *Street in Dresden* has, again, many traits which are characteristic of Munch. It is in that same way that Munch sets his figures to face the observer—as they might face a firing squad, head-on; his, equally, is the way of allowing a blank space to ooze and eddy its way upward from the bottom of the canvas. Munch had no equal when it came to handling metropolitan crowds. Where the Impressionists rendered the Parisian crowd in terms of petals and dabs and commas of pure color, Munch put real people, complete, on the canvas.

In point of fact, these pictures are by Ernst Ludwig Kirchner. Kirchner was 16 years younger than Munch, but he had in common with him the feeling that too much of life was being left out of art. When he was 20 years old, he was appalled by what then passed for "modern German painting." "The content of those pictures, and their execution, were as depressing as the public's total lack of interest," he wrote later. "Inside the gallery there were those pale, lifeless daubs. Outside, there was the flood of life itself, with its color, its sunshine, its sadness. . . . Why didn't those worthy gentlemen paint real life? Because it moves, that's why. They neither see it nor understand it. And then I thought—why shouldn't I try? And so I did."

The intention was not far from Munch's. But the environment, the social situation, the climate of belief—all these were quite different. Munch and the friends of his youth had axed their way through the frozen seas of Scandinavian provincialism, and very few people in Scandinavia had thanked them for it. Munch himself did much of his best work in exile; some of his writer friends

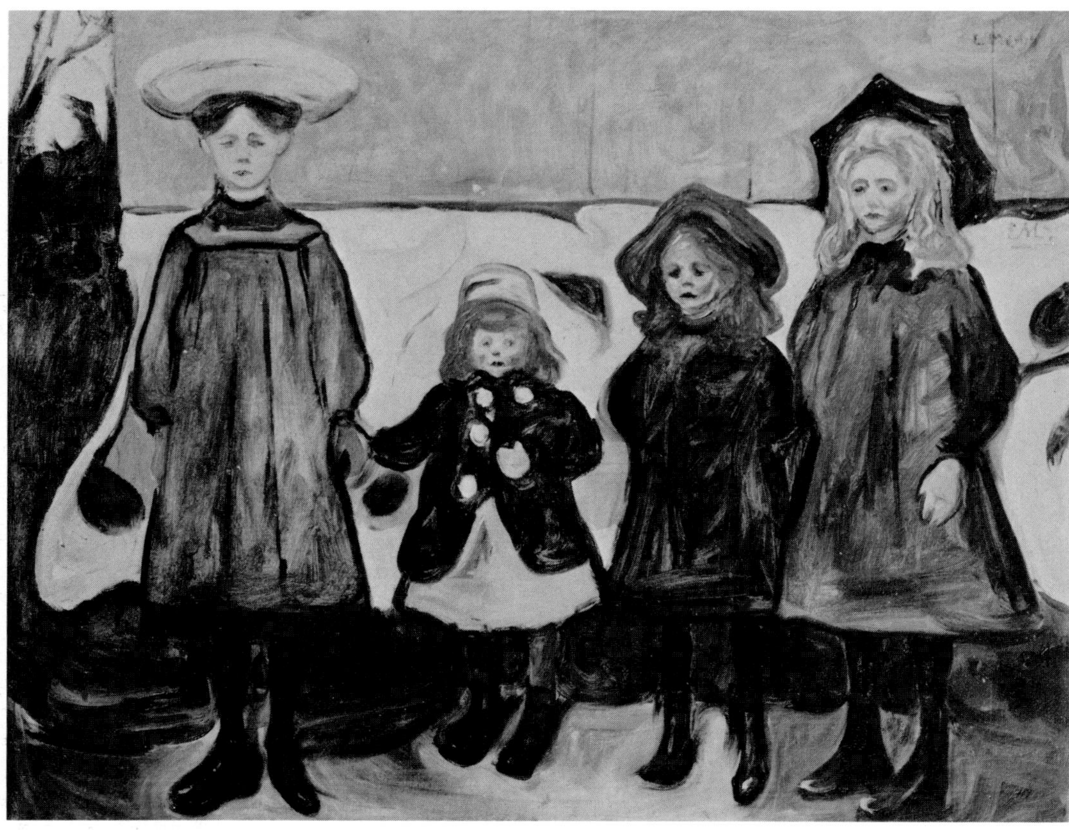

Edvard Munch.
Little Girls in Aasgaardstrand.
1904–05.
Oil on cardboard,
34½ × 44¼ inches.
Munch-museet, Oslo

were sent to jail for novels now forgotten but vital at the time; Ibsen had a very long haul before he became, in old age, a national hero.

Germany between 1900 and 1914 was not at all like that. But it had problems of its own. It had, for instance, an absolute ruler, in the person of Kaiser Wilhelm II, who had fixed ideas about modern art. "Art is not art," he said in a speech in 1901, "if it transgresses the laws and barriers laid down by Me. The word 'liberty' is often misused and can lead to license and presumption. . . . Art should make it possible for the lower echelons of society to raise themselves to the ideals which the German people is now alone in possessing. Art which merely portrays misery is a sin against the German people. . . ." This is the context in which we should view such classics of their kind and date as Menzel's *The Departure of Kaiser Wilhelm from Berlin on July 31, 1870, to Join the Troops at the Front.*

But an insubordinate view of the world did find its way, even so, into German painting, and at just the time (1905–09) when Richard Strauss in *Salome* and *Elektra* was changing the whole notion of what could, and what could not, be done in the opera house. Both works were first heard in Dresden; and it was in Dresden that Kirchner and his friends Erich Heckel and Karl Schmidt-Rottluff invented, between 1905 and 1911, a new kind of German art. Dresden before 1914 was not at all provincial in the sense that Oslo was provincial in Munch's early days. It had a first-rate theater and a first-rate opera house, a waterfront on the Elbe which was one of the most beautiful sights in Europe, and Old Master collections which were worth crossing the world to see. It had dealers' galleries which were particularly active and discerning. Anyone who lived in Dresden between 1896 and 1906 could see the work of Monet, Cézanne, Munch, Seurat, Gauguin and van Gogh not in ones and twos but in bulk; and what they did not see would be filled out by the art magazines which

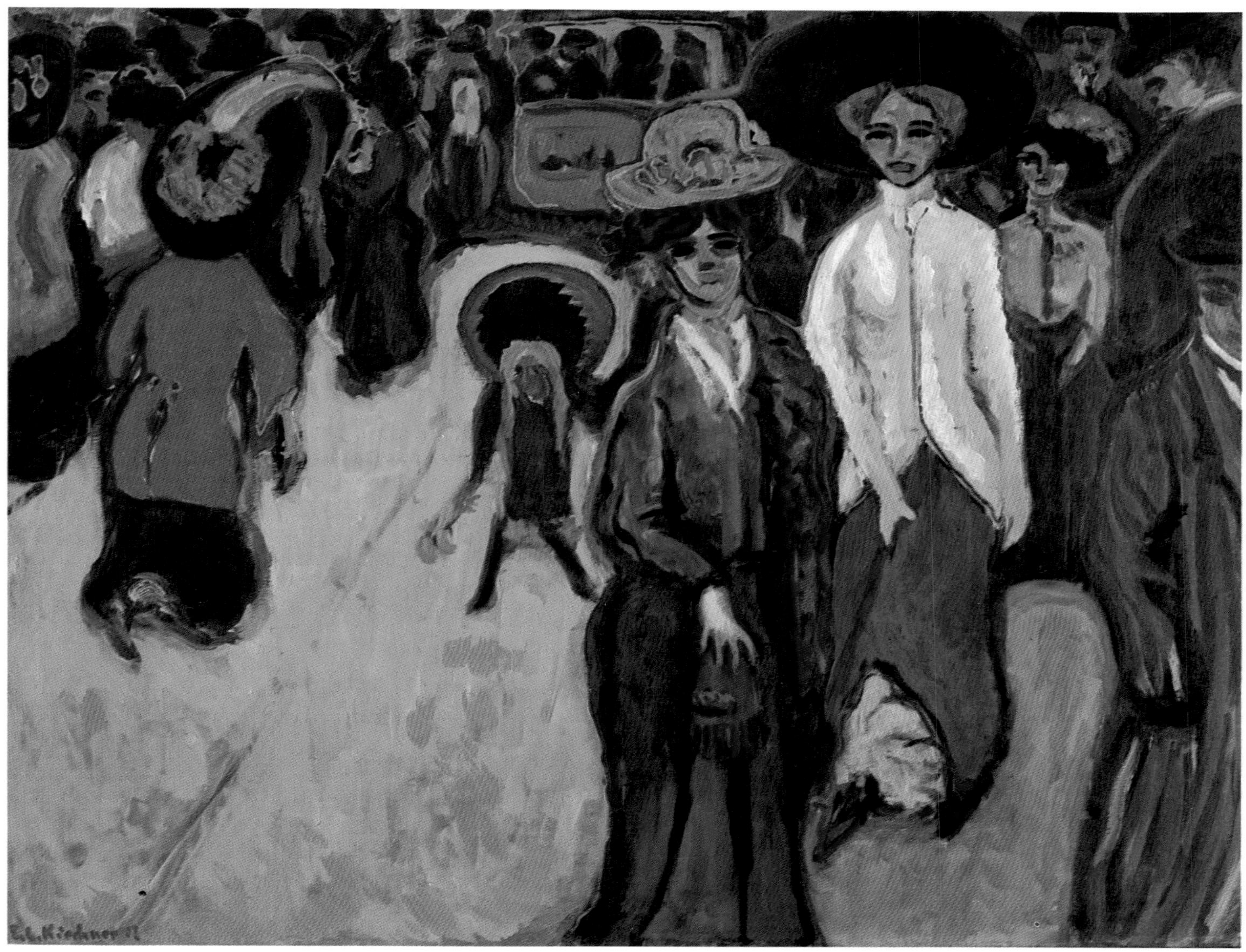

Ernst Ludwig Kirchner.
Street, Dresden.
1908, dated on canvas 1907.
Oil on canvas, 59¼ inches × 6 feet 6⅞ inches.
The Museum of Modern Art, New York. Purchase

in Dresden, as elsewhere, were the accepted currency of the new: *Jugend, Pan, The Studio* and *Insel.*

To exactly what extent Kirchner and his friends were influenced by the European art of the immediate past is not our main concern—perhaps luckily, since they never welcomed inquiries on this subject and were likely to deny that they owed anything at all to Munch or to Matisse, whose work Kirchner saw when he was in Berlin in January, 1909. What we have to examine here is, rather, the extent to which they brought to German art the new kind of awareness which Kafka had posited in 1903. Did they awaken their contemporaries "as with a fist hammering on the skull"? And if so, how?

Their life style offers an initial clue. Instead of a conventional studio in an "artists' quarter," they began by renting an empty butcher's shop in a working-class suburb. Dresden had a very well-equipped school of art, but Kirchner, Bleyl, Heckel and Schmidt-Rottluff were students of architecture, not of art, and they never changed over. When they banded together as a group and called themselves "Die Brücke" (The Bridge), they did not address themselves to an established

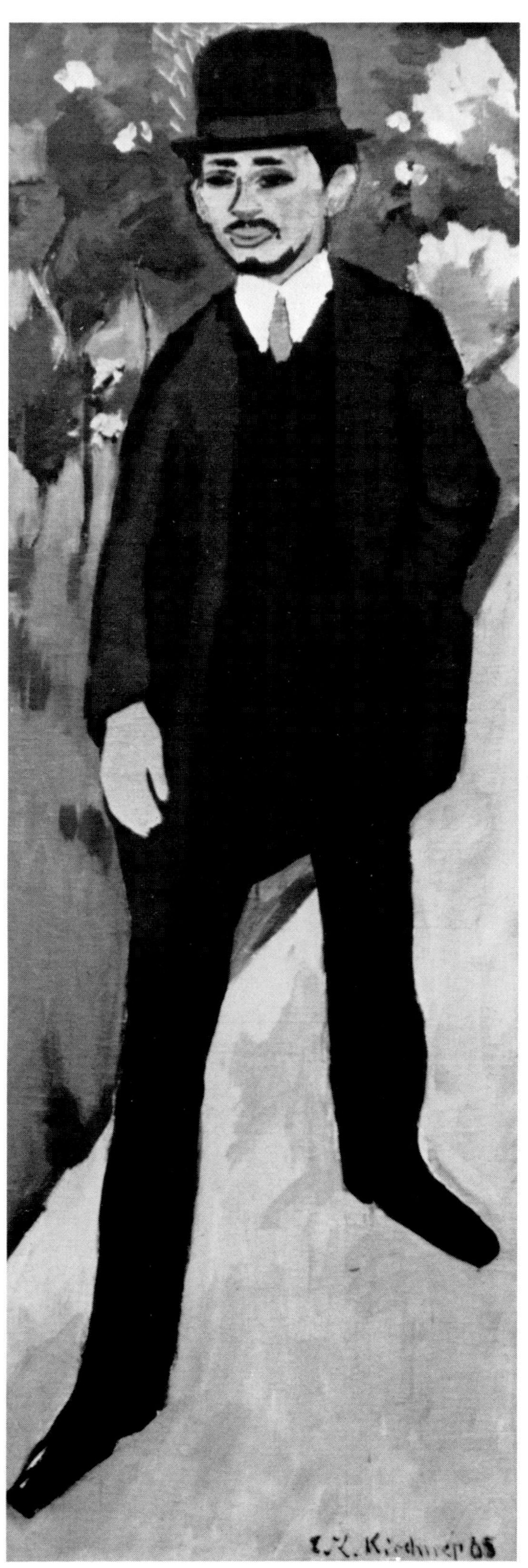

Ernst Ludwig Kirchner. *Portrait of Erich Heckel.* 1908. Oil on canvas, 48¾ × 26¾ inches. Städtisches Karl-Ernst-Osthaus-Museum, Hagen, West Germany

middle class. Their first exhibitions, in the fall and winter of 1906, were held in the showrooms of a lamp factory in the suburban district of Dresden-Löbtau. There were conventions in the Germany of that time as to how an artist's studio should look; but visitors to the former butcher's shop (to which was later added a former shoe shop in the same neighborhood) were met by a way of life which was a deliberate affront to "good society": floors piled high with cigarette butts, naked girls ambling to and fro, subversive conversation at every hour of the day, almost nothing but cake to eat and the risk at every moment of an impromptu reading from Nietzsche or Walt Whitman. A particular favorite was Whitman's "We Two Boys Together Clinging"; and one may doubt if Kaiser Wilhelm would have approved its last three lines:

Misers, menials, priests alarming, air breathing,
water drinking, on the turf or sea-beach
dancing,
Cities wrenching, ease scorning, statutes
mocking, feebleness chasing,
Fulfilling our foray.

Kirchner and his friends took a long time to find what we now call "the Brücke style": so long, in fact, that Kirchner in later life tried to conceal the fact by backdating certain of his pictures. It mattered to him that he should have begun to use flat, strong color contrasts only after the French Fauve painters had been seen in Dresden in 1908; but it doesn't matter so much to us, because we are more interested in the specifically German aspect of the Brücke—the way, in other words, in which they made themselves felt through the great eiderdown of German complacency before 1914.

That complacency was a late manifestation of 19th-century *Gemütlichkeit:* a quality defined by the literary historian J. P. Stern as "a curious and unique configuration of time-honored habits, rich meals, ancient or at least old-fashioned furniture, solid broadcloth and solid moral maxims. . . ." Property and propriety were conjoined in *Gemütlichkeit;* between them, they smothered the free

Hans Baldung (called Grien). 1484/5–1545. *The Temptation of Eve.* Oil on panel, 25¼ × 13 inches. National Gallery of Canada, Ottawa

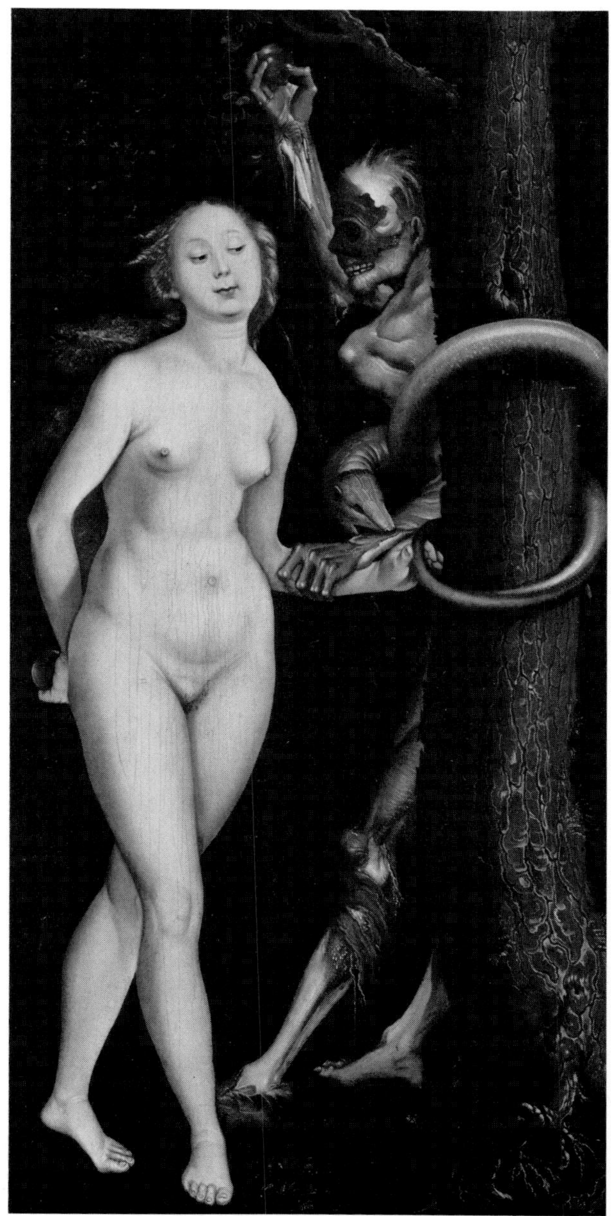

spirit. Just occasionally that spirit revenged itself: in a novel by Wilhelm Carl Raabe, for instance, called *Documents of the Vogelsang District* (1896). Nothing else in contemporary German literature quite equaled the climactic scene in Raabe's novel, where the main character comes back to his native town after making a success of life elsewhere. He has money, he has a house that has been in his family for generations, and within that house he has all the apparatus of *Gemütlichkeit:* a veritable German ark filled with furniture, linen, carpets, heavy curtains, bibelots of every kind. He waits for winter; and when winter comes he steadily and consistently, day after day, burns all his belongings. *"Er heizte mit seinem Hausrat,"* says Raabe, in a five-word sentence that denied the materialistic basis of German life: "He burned his belongings to keep warm."

Kirchner had something of that sort in mind. To achieve it, he springboarded backward in time to the days when German art meant Dürer and Cranach and to the still earlier days when German architecture meant the lean, arrowy forms of German Gothic. He had seen that German Impressionism was fundamentally a compromise rather than a bold break with the art preceding it: greasy in physical terms, it was greasy also in its social attitudes. Kirchner and his friends looked elsewhere for their ideal Germany. Looking at Hans Baldung's *The Temptation of Eve,* or at the bronze figure of Hansel the shawm player, which was made in Nuremberg in the 1380s, we see that ideal made visible. Kirchner saw the Brücke group as *Neudeutsche:* "new Germans." "German creativity is fundamentally different from Latin creativity," he wrote. "The Latin takes his forms from the object as it exists in nature. The German creates his form from fantasy, from an inner vision peculiar to himself. The forms of visible nature serve him as symbols only . . . and he seeks beauty not in appearance but in something beyond."

By "symbol," here, Kirchner did not mean the delicate vibration which Mallarmé had had in mind. He meant something robust, forthright,

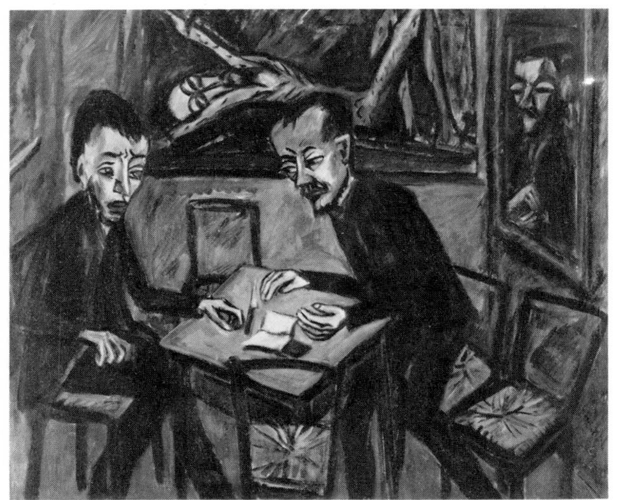

Erich Heckel.
Two Men by a Table
(scene from
Dostoevsky's *The
Idiot*). 1912.
Oil on canvas,
38½ × 48 inches.
Hamburger
Kunsthalle,
Hamburg

provocative. His idea of a symbol was something that said "Live more naturally! It's a mistake not to." Living more naturally meant breaking with the current notion of fine art and relying, for example, on the antithesis of the woodcut, the primeval clash of plain black against plain white, as against the curdled sauces of German Impressionism. It meant using color contrasts that looked both caustic and gaudy when set against the supercivilized procedures of Matisse. The human beings in Brücke paintings often looked as if they had been carved out of wood with a blunt knife; and when the Brücke portrayed big-city life it was rarely without a hint of underlying menace.

All this they did in the name of an undefined but ever-present emergency. History as nightmare presides over just about all the best work of the Brücke group. Sometimes they simply showed an intelligent awareness of what was going on around them: the sexual candor of Wedekind's play *Pandora's Box* (1904) has obvious echoes in their work, as did the first complete publication (from 1907 onward) of Dostoevsky in German translation. But fundamentally the vision of the world which they had to offer was peculiar to themselves, despite its borrowing from the German past, from African and Indian art, and from Munch and Matisse. It is a vision in which the individual is battered about by society and thereafter left to fend for himself.

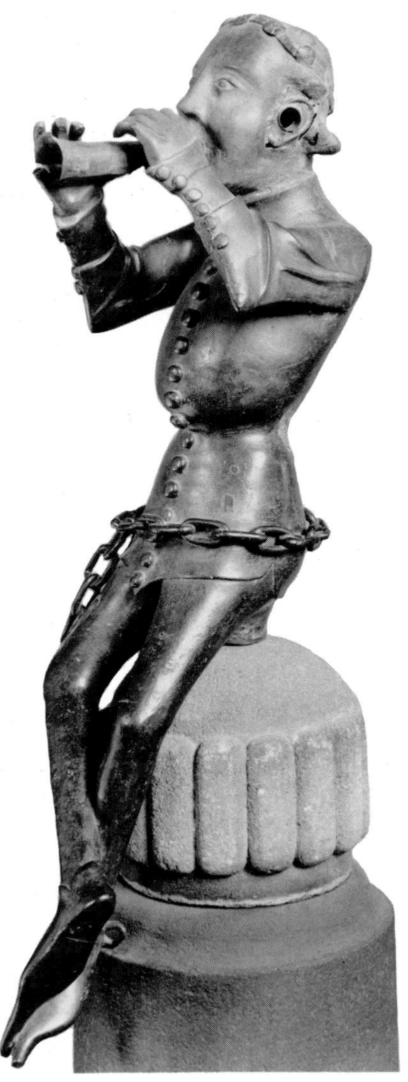

Anonymous.
Shawm Player.
c. 1380.
Bronze, 47 inches
high.
Germanisches
Nationalmuseum,
Nuremberg

Dostoevsky's books were still a novelty in German translation when Heckel painted his *Two Men by a Table,* which relates to the climactic scene in Dostoevsky's *The Idiot,* when Mishkin and Rogozhin talk in secret beneath a reproduction of Holbein's *Dead Christ.* The exact nature of the Expressionist vision could hardly be better summarized than in the taut, nerve-ridden, elongated figures of the two men and the subtly distorted perspective of the room.

Kirchner had been a compulsive draftsman from childhood onward; and when he came to paint his big Dresden street scene, he had no difficulty in finding a graphic equivalent for the quirks of character and deportment which he had been

Ernst Ludwig Kirchner.
Street, Berlin. 1913.
Oil on canvas,
47½ × 35⅞ inches.
The Museum of Modern Art, New York. Purchase

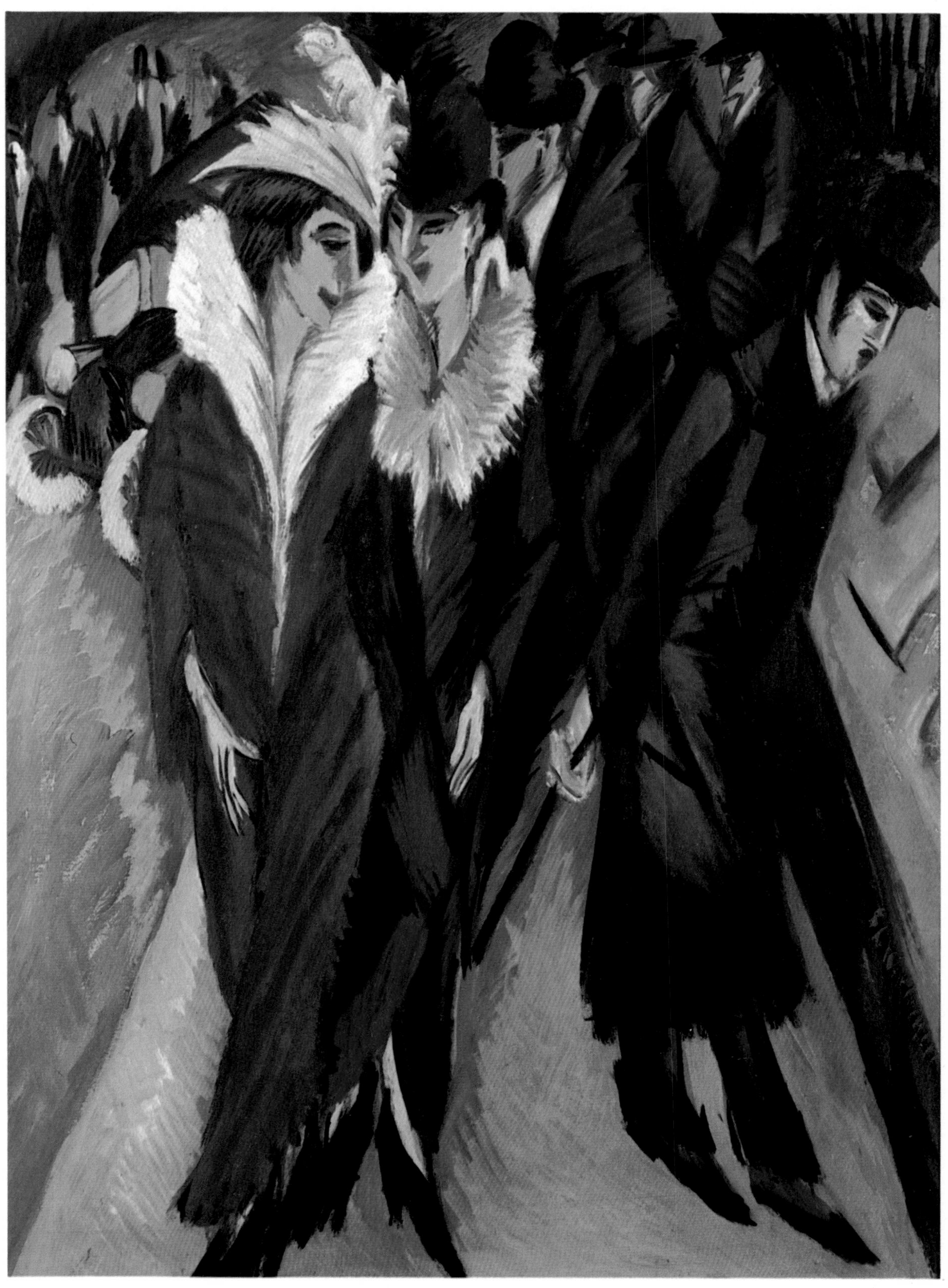

studying for the greater part of his life. He had never drawn "from the model," in the academic sense; what he drew, he had lived. The Dresden *Street* is, on one level, almost dandified in its use of the continually varied hat shapes, back and forth across the upper half of the canvas. Kirchner is no less ingenious in his animation of the shallower space on the right-hand side of the picture; how subtly does he suggest that these are people possessed by the city! Yet the picture is neither decorative nor polemical; the drawing sees to that. Each person is an individual, an identifiable Dresdener hurrying to keep up. If we ask "To keep up with *what?*"—history has an answer.

After six years of collective activity in Dresden, the Brücke moved to Berlin in the fall of 1911. It was a fateful change. Dresden by comparison with Berlin was still slow-moving, almost countrified; Berlin had a rapacious, uncaring, over-energized quality. Whether coincidentally or not, 1912 was the year in which Kirchner "came out" in international terms. He met Franz Marc and was made welcome in the Blaue Reiter, the Munich group formed by Marc and Kandinsky. He met Munch at an international art exhibition in Cologne. He was invited to take part in the Armory Show in New York, Chicago and Boston. Above all, he developed a new way of handling the metropolitan scene.

In the Berlin *Street* of 1913, we find ourselves in the world of pure Expressionism. Bodies are elongated beyond the possibilities of anatomy; color bears no relation to the colors of everyday; distortions take us into the realms of hallucination. This is the Berlin which the Expressionist cinema was to evoke a decade later. (It was an Expressionist painter, Ludwig Meidner, who designed the sets in 1923 for one of the most nightmarish of early German films, *The Street.*)

It should be said that the real Berlin was not at all like this. It had been developed in the second half of the 19th century in terms of broad avenues and generous intersections, with sidewalks wide enough for the most elaborate of sexual maneuvering and really very little that resembled the slot-like streets and converging skylines of Expressionist painting. Kirchner tackled this real Berlin quite straightforwardly in daytime suburban townscapes; but when the night-prowlers went through the routines of appraisal in midtown Berlin, Kirchner presented them as hemmed in by their environment, with barely enough room for one silk-lined marauder to squeeze past another. A long, thin, constantly repeated daggerlike formal motif runs throughout the Berlin *Street;* only the antediluvian taxi is exempt from it. There is, once again, a foretaste of the Expressionist cinema in Kirchner's drastic way with perspective: the sidewalk, for instance, rears up behind the promenaders as if it were about to throw them forward and out of the picture altogether. It is as if the emergency were too great to allow of a third dimension. This is a scene of predation, in which human beings are stalked by other human beings and a hard bargain may soon be struck. Kirchner intensified its effect by using color in a way which was quite new for him. In Dresden he had worked primarily with forthright oppositions of complementary color. In the Berlin *Street* he worked with colors that were adjacent to one another on the color wheel: neighbor was set against neighbor. As Dr. Donald E. Gordon puts it in his book on Kirchner: "The interplay is between the rich dark blues of the central figures and the intense colors of the sidewalk; though ranging from crimson to cerise, they are dominated by an acrid scarlet. The purple robe of the nearest figure (whose hair is red) is the necessary median to these adjacent hues."

The painters of the Brücke epitomized also that particular roughness of expression which has characterized a great deal of radical art in this century. What they had to say was too urgent to be tidied up. If the finished canvas looked like a relief map of the painter's agitation, so much the better: gentility was out. What mattered was truth to the moment and to the unfettered play of instinct. Humanity had arrived at one of the hinge-points of history, and it was the duty of the painter

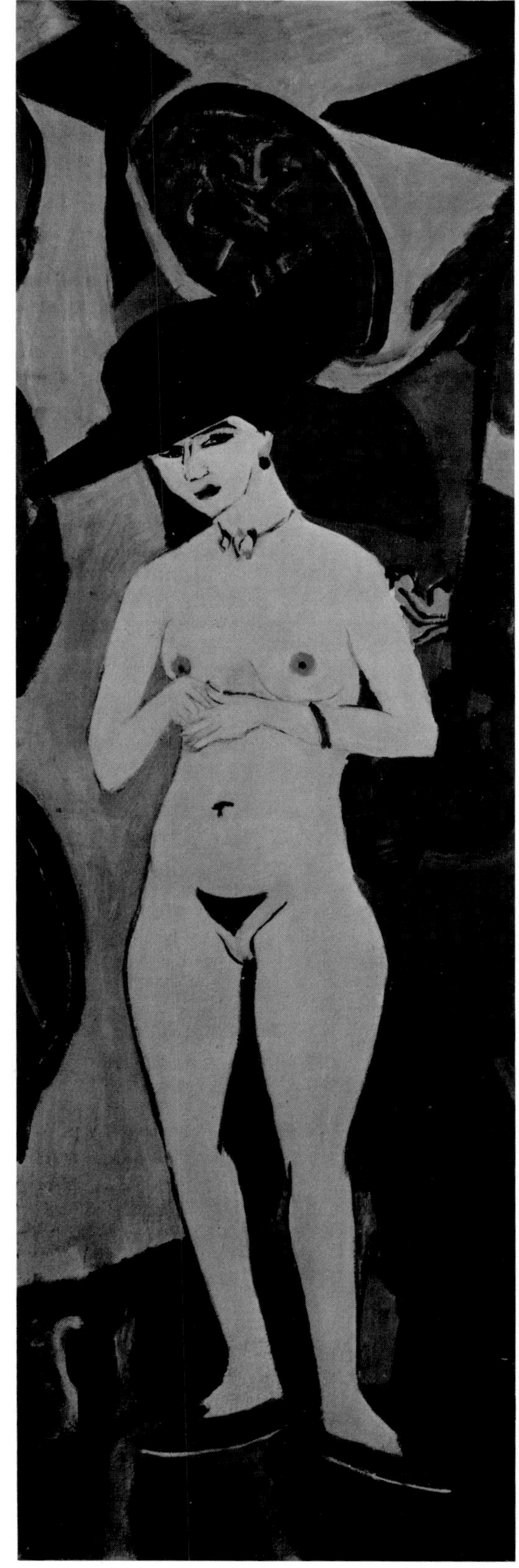

Ernst Ludwig Kirchner.
Standing Nude with Hat. 1910–20.
Woodcut, 6 feet 10 inches × 26 inches.
Städtische Galerie, Frankfurt

to bear witness as best he could. This might seem to rule out—and in the case of Kirchner and his friends it did rule out—those grand panoramic adventures which had always been the supreme ambition of the allegorical painter.

Adventures of that kind were not likely to come the way of radical painters in Germany while Kaiser Wilhelm II was on the throne; but they did come the way of Munch, who spent some of the best years of his life (1909–14) on mural paintings —some of them as much as 38 feet in length—for Oslo University. And a comparable opportunity was given in Vienna to Gustav Klimt when, in October, 1894, he was invited to paint three large panels—*Jurisprudence, Medicine* and *Philosophy* — for the great hall or Aula of the University of Vienna. It must have seemed quite a safe choice; Klimt was known as a reliable young man who could work to order. He was practiced, docile, meticulous, and he turned in his work on time. There was every reason to suppose that his work for the University would go through without incident.

Klimt was in human terms the exact opposite of almost all the artists with whom we have lately dealt. Easy and convivial by nature, he was accepted throughout his life as a man who did honor to his generation: not for him the subterranean political motivation and the eventual exile of Goya. He strode into life as a champion swimmer strides into the sea. Of course such looks can be deceptive, and Klimt in point of fact had his full share of inner anxieties; but these never compared with the alienation of Munch, who in 1908–09 was restored to mental stability only after eight months of intensive care in a clinic, or with the slow decline of Kirchner, who died by his own hand in Switzerland in 1938 after a long period in exile. The crippled emotional life of the mother-bound Moreau was at a far extreme from the royal freedom with which Klimt appeared to move from one attachment to another. Klimt was at one with the world.

Or was he? It did not seem so when the first of

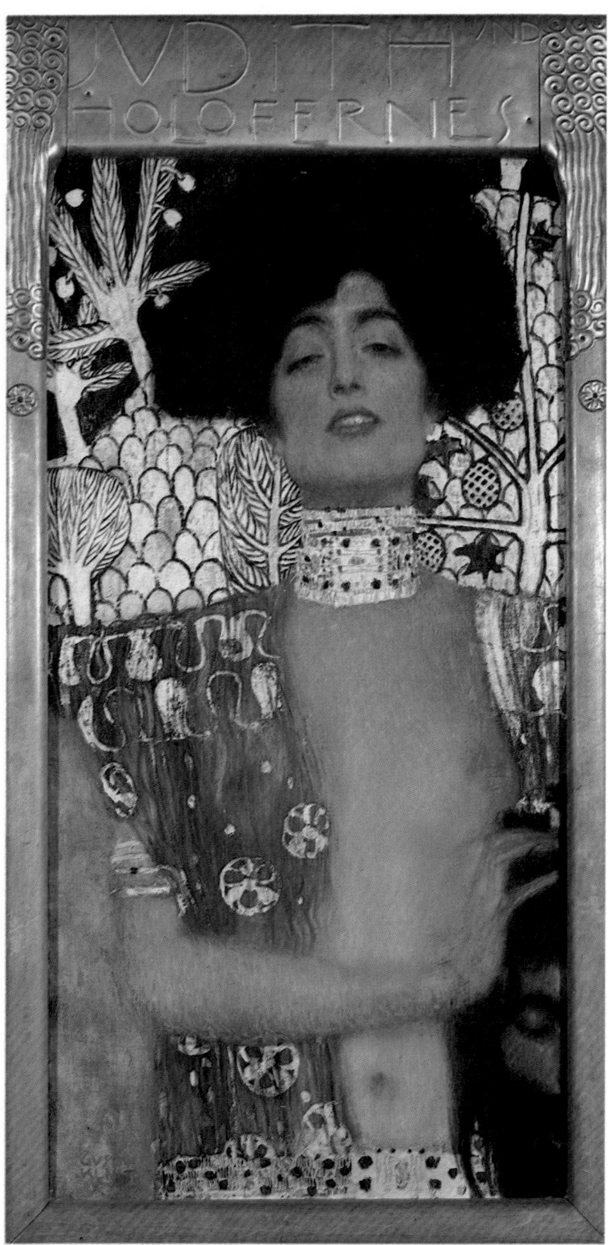

Gustav Klimt.
Judith I. 1901.
Oil on canvas,
33½ × 16½ inches.
Osterreichische
Galerie, Vienna.
© Galerie Welz,
Salzburg

the three panels, *Philosophy,* was put on view in 1900. *Medicine* was shown in 1901; and in 1903 all three were shown together, though *Jurisprudence* was still not finished. There was in every case a most terrible uproar—so much so that in the fall of 1903 the contract was annulled. The three paintings were never installed in the University; and, as they were destroyed in a fire during the last phase of World War II, we can judge them only by the old and imperfect photographs which have survived and by a few working drawings in Viennese public collections. It is clear from these, however, that Klimt did not represent philosophy, jurisprudence and medicine in terms of superior wisdom, or of an intellectual majesty that stood high above the battle, or of a long view that put all our earthly concerns in perspective. The imagery in general was nearer, if anything, to that of Rodin's *Gates of Hell.* What had philosophy to do with families twirling in limbo? Or medicine with an over-decorated temptress who was feeding her pet snake from a glass saucer? Or jurisprudence with the seductive young women, dressed only in their superabundant hair, who fixed the spectator with looks that were anything but judicial? It was all too much for the Ministerial committees, and too much for the outraged faculty members of the University, and too much for the general public.

Klimt had, of course, changed a great deal since the contract came his way. In 1892 he had lost both his father, an engraver by profession, and his younger brother Ernst, who had worked with him on more than one laborious decoration. In ways not yet disentangled, these misfortunes seem to have liberated Klimt; after several years' silence he emerged in 1898 as an artist of a completely different kind and a vastly greater stature. The docile journeyman-decorator became the spokesman of his age—or, more exactly, of that age's unconscious longings and fears. In the Vienna of Gustav Mahler, Arnold Schoenberg and Sigmund Freud, Gustav Klimt was a person of consequence. He was present at table on the occasion when Mahler first set eyes on his future wife, and he was

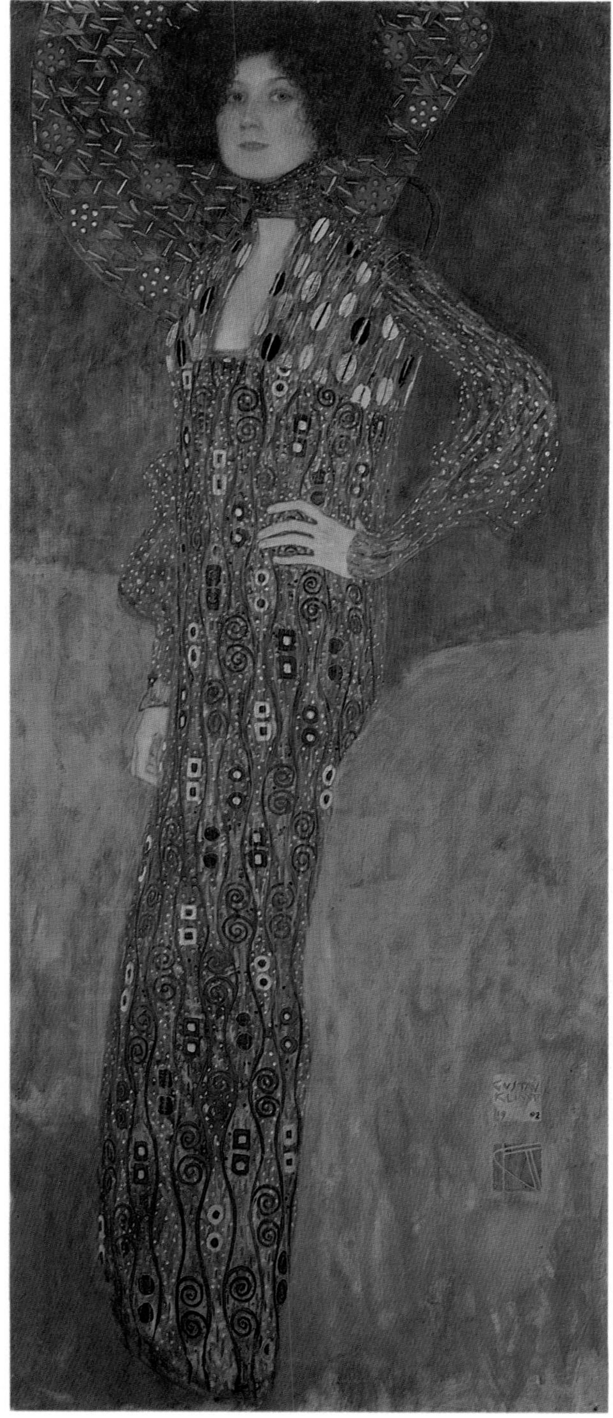

Gustav Klimt. *Portrait of Emilie Flöge.* 1902. Oil on canvas, 6 feet ¼ inch × 33½ inches. Historisches Museum der Stadt Wien

one of the very few people who saw Mahler constantly after his marriage. When the younger Viennese artists formed the Vienna Secession in 1897, Klimt was the natural choice for their first president. The amenable tradesman of the early 1890s had turned by 1900 into a poet who could take a look at the worst and remember its every detail. This is what Klimt did in his three panels for the University: what if medicine and philosophy and jurisprudence had no effect whatever on the conditions of human life? What if medicine could not heal our deepest ills, and jurisprudence had nothing to do with justice, and philosophy could not assuage the inner torments of mankind? Klimt in 1893 had gone along with society in its every detail. By 1900 he had brought that same society face to face with itself. People did not like it, any more than they liked it when Mahler presented them, in work after work, with a fragmented and deeply pessimistic account of one man's passage through life.

The University panels are by no means Klimt's only claim upon us. His position in art history, and in the history of human inclinations, is owed quite as much to his easel paintings as to the three panels which were left to burn by the German SS troops as they withdrew from Austria in 1945. Klimt's mature style was, on one level, a most dexterous amalgam of ingredients from the international style in European decoration at the turn of the century. He took from the decorative paintings of an Englishman, Edward Burne-Jones. He took from the work of a Scottish architect and designer, Charles Rennie Mackintosh, and from the work of Mrs. Mackintosh, the painter Margaret Macdonald. He knew all about the twining and twirling of linear decoration as it was practiced by the artists of Art Nouveau in Germany, in Belgium and in France. He had had on his doorstep in 1898 a survey of the international style at the Vienna Secession. Like most Central Europeans of his generation, he had looked at the work of Aubrey Beardsley; and he knew that there was something of a renaissance in the applied arts, and that that renaissance had made use of gold and silver and enamel and precious stones in a way that looked quite new.

He could have known all this and been no more than a low-powered eclectic: a provincial pirate, quick to sight the spoils but too weak to bring more than a part of them home. But in point of fact Klimt's easel pictures are unlike anyone else's. Not many of them survive, and they are not easy to see. But they have claims upon us which are unique. Nobody, to begin with, has given us so complete a portrait of a certain kind of European womanhood at its apogee.

Vienna has always had more than its quota of beautiful women, but in the period before 1914 they had a particular bloom and a specific poise. They also had a fullness of nature, a psychological complexity, which found the amplest possible outlet in action. Klimt's *Judith* is pure Viennese in physical type. She could be on her way to a costume ball, except for one thing: we have no doubt that the severed head which she holds is a real one, and that she has been to bed for many nights and of set purpose with a Babylonian general, and that hers was the hand that cut off his head.

Klimt does not set himself up as judge, in such cases. He is at the farthest possible remove from Aubrey Beardsley, who chose the subject of Salome because it allowed him to make public his fear and loathing of women. Klimt simply took it for granted that men and women have their way with one another and that from time to time, whether literally or in metaphor, heads roll.

Klimt was without equal, in my view, when it came to portraying women whom he admired and respected. Perhaps his closest friend was his sister-in-law Emilie Flöge, one of a trio of liberated young Viennese women who ran a successful dress shop in Vienna at a time when young ladies of good family were not expected to go into trade. Klimt could never see too much of her, and when he was brought home in January, 1918, after the stroke which was to kill him, his first words were, "Get Emilie here." Not surprisingly, the portrait of her which he painted in 1902 is a masterpiece of delicate insight. It is also remarkable for the amount of flat patterning of a purely ornamental sort which Klimt managed to combine with the naturalistic modeling of the head. Not only did Klimt love densely patterned materials for their own sake, but he was sufficiently a man of his own time to think hard and often about the extent to which the canvas should be presented quite straightforwardly as "a flat surface covered with colors assembled in a certain order." As he grew older, that flat surface played an ever greater role in his paintings; the human body was portrayed, as always, with a most delectable immediacy, but it was set more and more in a jeweled surround that paid no regard whatsoever to plausibility. If that surround could be read in terms of jewelry, or of a wall-hanging, or of a dress elaborated beyond the dreams of even the best designer in Vienna, so much the better. If it couldn't, Klimt didn't care; people must find their way about the picture as best they could. Sometimes the ornamentation was vivid but sparse, and placed with a Whistlerian delicacy. Sometimes it was made an effect of overpowering luxury; the observer might well have been reminded of the barbaric overplus of jewelry which Clytemnestra had on her person in Strauss's *Elektra* when she was cut to pieces by Orestes.

The point is that there were many artists who could transpose onto canvas the formal motifs of Art Nouveau jewelry, or who could raid the world of precious stones for new alliances of color, or who could go to turn-of-the-century architecture and interior design for new ideas about how to compose their pictures. The singularity of Klimt was that he could use these things as symbols, and in an emotional context of his own devising. It is worth remembering that Klimt's paintings were made at a time when pure Expressionism was the coming thing in Central Europe. Pure Expressionism is an art of immediate effect: all sense of distance is abolished, ideally, between the painter

Gustav Klimt
The Park. 1910 or earlier.
Oil on canvas, 43½ × 43½ inches.
The Museum of Modern Art, New York.
The Gertrud A. Mellon Fund

and his public. If people were shocked by Kirchner and his friends—or by Oskar Kokoschka, in Klimt's own city—it was precisely because of this abolition of all barriers. Klimt took down the barriers, too, in one sense: no one was more direct than he about the nature of bodily attraction. But he multiplied the intensity of his insights by setting up, within the same image, a complex and luxurious flat patterning. That patterning had a life of its own; and it enabled Klimt to distance the human entanglements and to give them an air of redoubled fatality. Removed from the melodrama of everyday, they took on an emblematic quality: history as nightmare was taken out of the clinical report and given the antique resonance which it has in high art.

When it was clear that World War I would soon break out, it was natural for Expressionism to give nightmare literal form, as in the Apocalyptic Landscape series of Ludwig Meidner. Meidner spoke of himself later as having been "driven to breaking-point by the approach of world catastrophe"; and his portraits of a great city in dissolution retain even today a certain descriptive force. But they have none of the mystery with which Caspar David Friedrich was able to invest a distant view of the town of Neubrandenburg going up in flames. Literalism does not last, in such a context; only the symbol survives. The apocalypse, when it came, was better interpreted by the ferocious and elliptic methods of George Grosz, for one, in his *Metropolis,* 1917. But it is with Max Beckmann that the concept of history as nightmare found a new fulfillment.

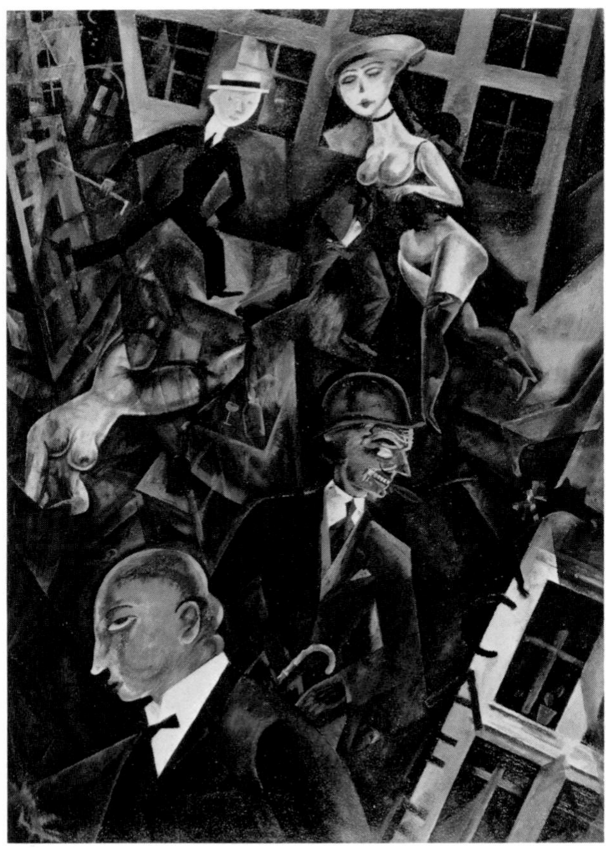

George Grosz. *Metropolis.* 1917. Oil on cardboard, 26¾ × 18¾ inches. The Museum of Modern Art, New York. Purchase, the Stephen C. Clark Fund

Beckmann now looks to us like the predestined successor of the poets of disquiet with whom we have been dealing. In childhood and youth he was distinctly a member of the privileged classes. He was good-looking, self-confident and quite unusually precocious. His parents had a great deal of money and an assured position in society. In 1905, when he was 21, he became known throughout Germany for a large figure painting of *Young Men by the Sea.* He had the backing of two of the best judges of new painting in Europe, Count Harry Kessler and Henry van de Velde; he became a favorite with Paul Cassirer, then the most successful dealer in Berlin; and when Edvard Munch was in Berlin in 1906 it was only natural that Beckmann should be presented to him, as much for his sensational rise to fame as for the Munch-like overtones of *Young Men by the Sea.* (Beckmann, with his robust, outgoing nature, was none too pleased when Munch suggested to him that his real bent was for tragedy.) A self-portrait painted in Florence the following year shows a forthright, well-brushed young man in a high wing collar: a rising young lawyer or doctor, one might think, and in any case a man with nothing to fear.

He was sensitive, even so, to the tormented inner life which is a part of the German heritage. He realized the full stature of Grünewald's Isenheim Altarpiece in Colmar at a time when that great painting found few to admire it, and in general he shared Kirchner's admiration for early German painting. It was from German Gothic, and not from his contemporaries, that he took the pure, thin, tart color, the confined shallow space, the needly, linear drawing and the overlapping zigzag of figures piled on top of one another that were to distinguish his paintings of 1917–20. German Gothic gave him the abrupt narrative style that enabled him to get through to the public of his day with a rare urgency; it also taught him to take the fat off his paintings so that the map of feeling within them was exposed as if in a manual of anatomy.

Beckmann took some years to evolve this mature style; his subject matter, likewise, came along at its own pace and would not be hurried. He was concerned about what went on in the world—to the extent, in fact, of painting imaginary accounts of events which he had not witnessed, like the earthquake in Messina (1908) and the loss of the *Titanic* (1912). But he treated these disasters very much from the outside, and as examples of broad, spectacular and manifestly "effective" subject matter. There is no reason to suppose that he saw them as symbols of anything in particular. But when World War I broke out, Beckmann had from the first a keen and sober understanding of what it meant. His etching *Declaration of War,* 1914, is most revealing in this context. Beckmann set down in a spirit of complete objectivity the facts of what he had seen: that there were people in Germany who greeted the news of the outbreak of war in August, 1914, with bemusement, inertia and dread.

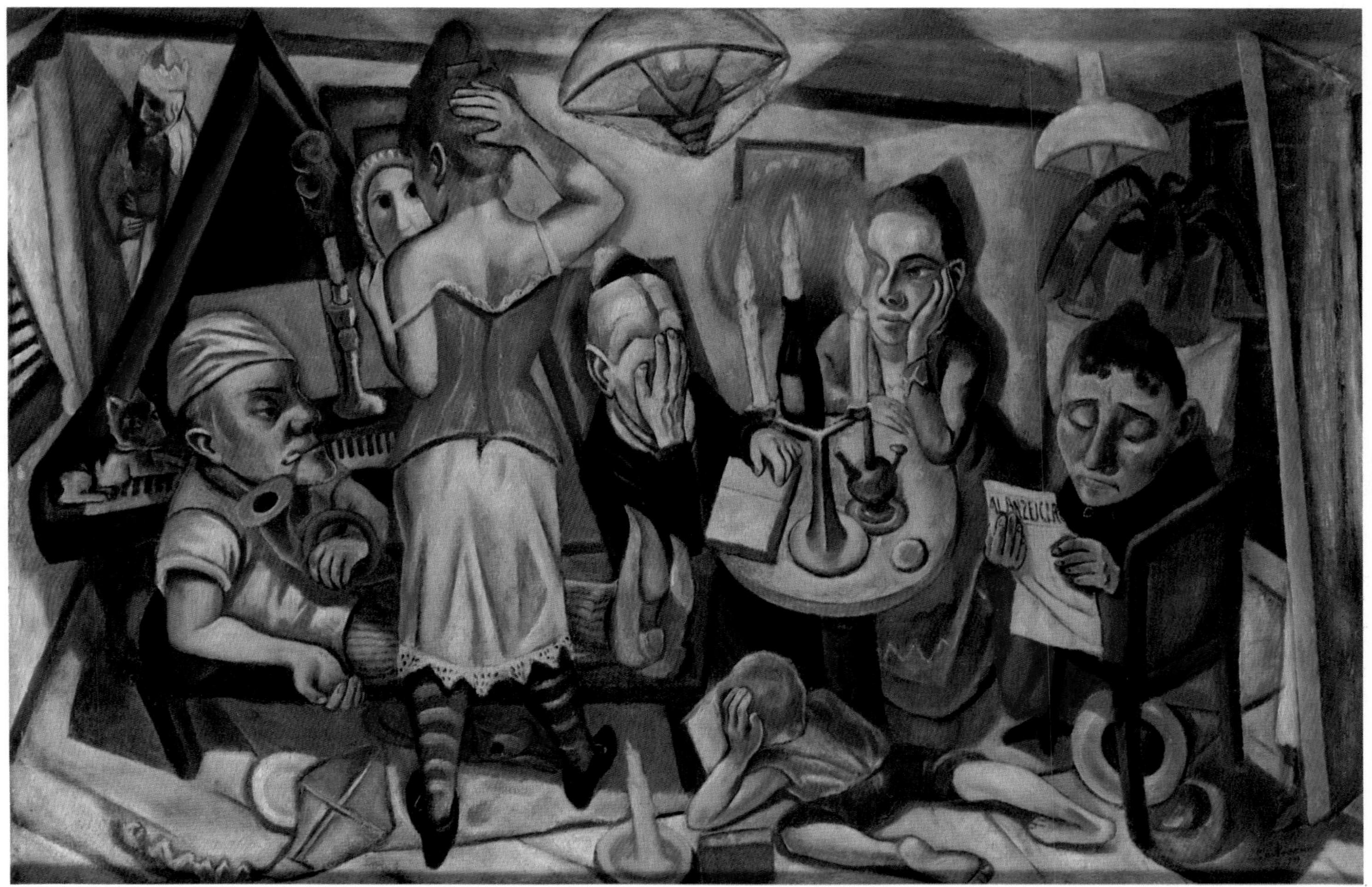

Max Beckmann.
Family Picture.
1920.
Oil on canvas,
25⅝ × 39¾ inches.
The Museum of Modern Art, New York.
Gift of Abby Aldrich Rockefeller

He himself went on to serve in the medical corps on the Russian front and in Flanders. It was at this point that history caught up with him, and the well-built, untroubled young man became a neurasthenic who had to be discharged from the army, after barely a year, as unfit for further service. When he began to paint again it was, as he said in 1917, "to reproach God for his errors." A great part of his new material came from the notes which he had taken during month after month of close contact with men who had been hideously wounded. This experience had given him a phantasmagorical insight into the casual indignities which come the way of the human body; and when the war came to an end in 1918, and it turned out that those indignities did not come to an end with it, Beckmann was able to sum up the situation in a big painting called *The Night.*

The Night is not an objective statement, like *Declaration of War.* It is a symbolic statement: "history as nightmare" is everywhere present in it. It has in it elements from the news of the day: the killing in furtive and underhand ways of people who should have played a lofty part in German life; the swinish conduct of the defeated military; the stealth with which evil deeds were done, and the readiness with which wicked men found accomplices, and the equanimity with which people would stand around and watch. All these things were a part of German life during the months—August, 1918, to March, 1919—that Beckmann toiled away at the picture; and it is, to that extent, a "document of the times." There is, in *The Night,* enough circumstantial detail to flesh out a novel;

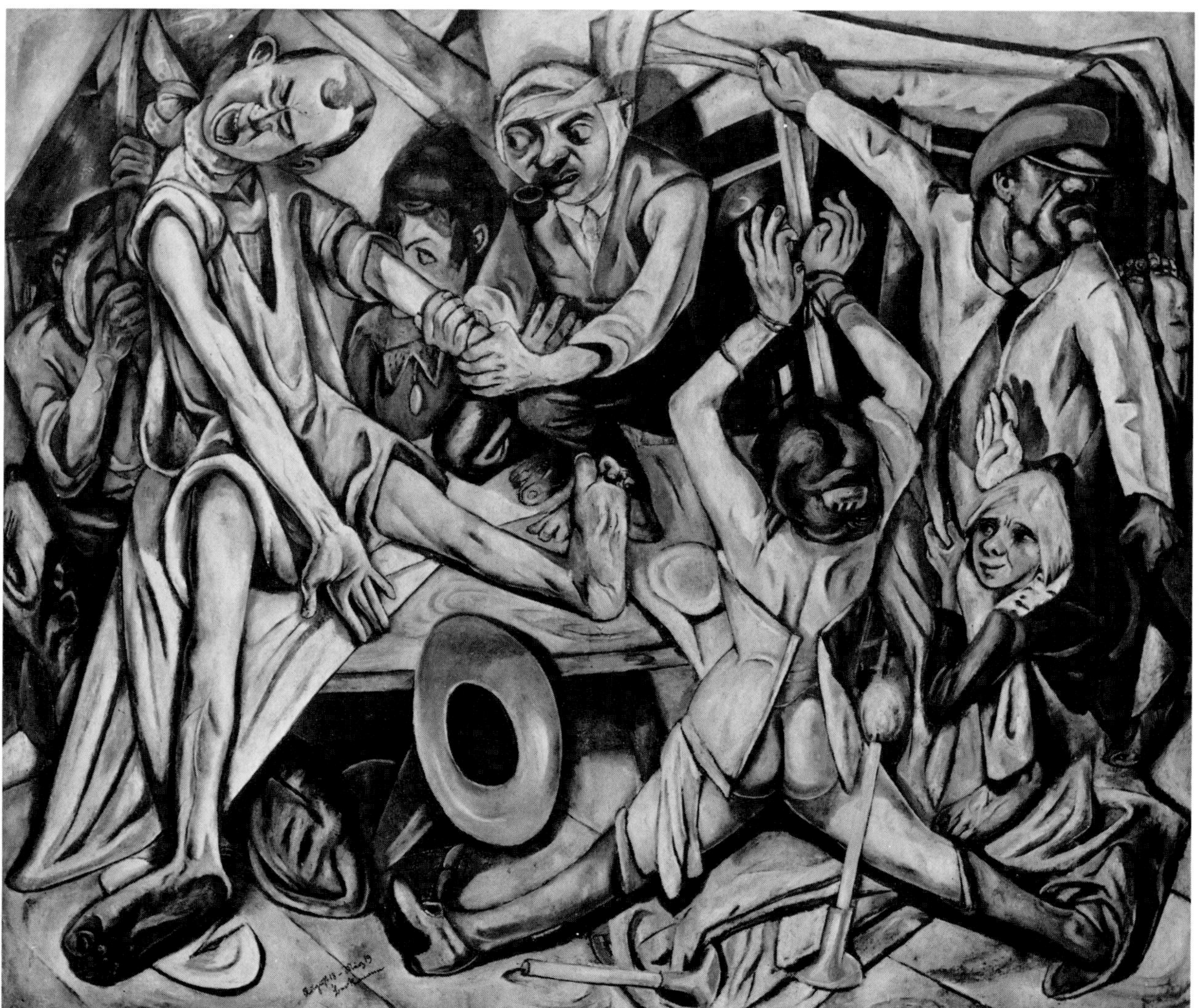

Max Beckmann.
The Night. 1918–19.
Oil on canvas,
53 × 61½ inches.
Kunstsammlung
Nordrhein-
Westfalen,
Düsseldorf

but the peculiar and lasting force of the picture is owed to its pre-echoes of an even more bestial era. This was how it would be when torture was taken for granted as the instrument of state policy, and when millions of people would live in dread of a knock on the door in the night. "You may live to see this" is the message of *The Night.* As in all Symbolist paintings of real quality, the artist spoke truer than he knew.

It is not, however, a self-pitying picture. Beckmann's was not a negative nature. He believed that if the case were put in the right way, and with sufficient force, the course of history might just possibly be changed. But he did not underestimate the role of habit, and of ingrained obedience, in the German nature. In 1920, for instance, he painted his *Family Picture:* a portrait of an enclosed world, a shallow Gothic space updated to the 1920s and inhabited by six human beings, each one of them locked in his own concerns. These are the people who will have to choose, one way or the other. Beckmann himself lies brooding on the piano bench. The auguries do not look promising. His mother-in-law hides her face. His wife thinks only of the possible fading of her good looks. His sister-in-law has drifted into dreamland. The servant is content to sponge up the small print in the local newspaper. Beckmann's young son alone shows something of resolution in the avidity with which he pores over his book. Elsewhere the concept of *Gemütlichkeit* has turned rancid.

Family Picture is not much fun to look at. As for *The Night,* it is one of the most disagreeable images which the art of our century has to show. Yet Beckmann nowhere exaggerates: he makes his effects by enumeration, and by a certain steadiness of mind, and above all by the exact and unsparing draftsmanship which made him so fine a printmaker. One can admire these things and yet feel that these paintings bring bad news. What could be more rash, after all, than to assume that what happened in 1918–19, and what happened thereafter, will never happen again? If we have lived through even part of all that, we can be forgiven for not wanting to think about it. If we are young enough to know it only from hearsay, we are likely to have problems of our own time to preoccupy us. In either case, we may well be glad to let the ice form again over those particular seas. If all this were a matter of record—of keeping a particular body of knowledge in being—we could leave it to the libraries; art could find its material elsewhere. But what if the symbols which art has to offer are vital to our understanding of the world and cannot be found elsewhere? If that is so—and in the case of the works here discussed it is so, beyond a doubt—then what Kafka said about books is no less true about pictures. Here it is again: "What we need are books which come upon us like ill-fortune, and distress us deeply. . . . A book must be an ice axe, to break the sea frozen within us."

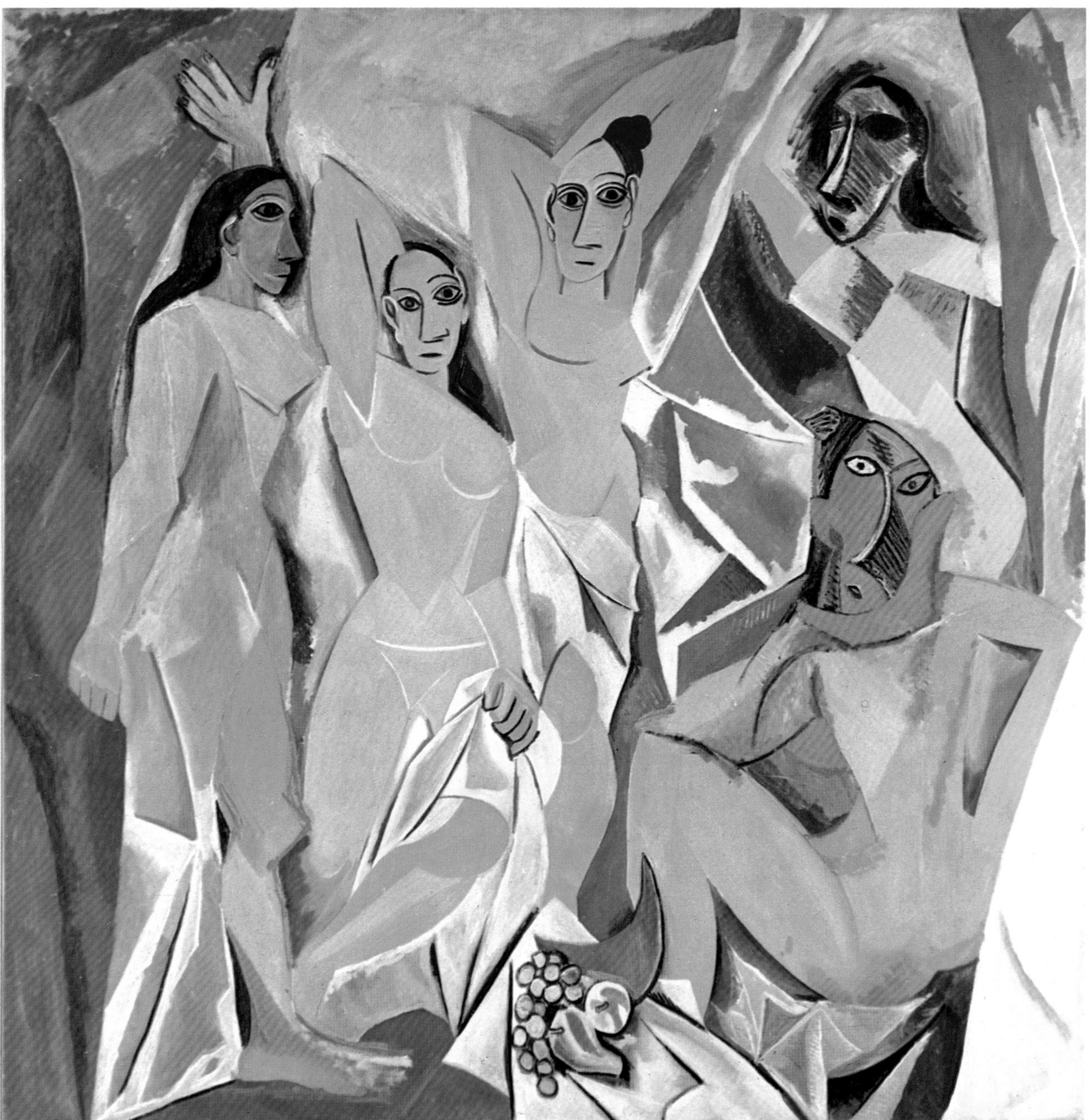

Pablo Picasso.
Les Demoiselles d'Avignon. 1907.
Oil on canvas, 8 feet × 7 feet 8 inches.
The Museum of Modern Art, New York.
Acquired through the Lillie P. Bliss Bequest

REALITY REASSEMBLED

In the art of this century one painting has a place apart: Pablo Picasso's *Les Demoiselles d'Avignon,* 1907.

This in a way is odd; for the *Demoiselles* is not a masterpiece in the old, outright, unarguable sense. By the standards of Raphael or Poussin or Ingres it could even be called a failure. Picasso himself seems never to have regarded it as finished but simply to have turned its face to the wall and got on with other things. It was not seen in public until 30 years after it was painted.

Yet there is no doubt that the *Demoiselles* is the white whale of modern art: the legendary giant with which we have to come to terms sooner or later. It was always, and it is still, a demanding picture. It is an edgy, scary, almost a dislikable picture. It awes, but it does not seduce. And yet seduction is, on one level, what the *Demoiselles* is all about: seduction of a blatant and demystified kind but seduction nonetheless.

The scene is the parlor of a turn-of-the-century whorehouse in Barcelona. The basic subject is one common enough in Old Master painting: beauty on parade. The Old Masters used most often a mythological pretext: the Temptation of St. Anthony, Susannah and the Elders, Diana and Callisto. Above all they used the Judgment of Paris: nothing in the Latin poets was more advantageous for the Old Masters than the moment at which Paris said "Goddesses, undress!" when he was called upon to decide whether Venus, Juno or Minerva was the best-looking. No one has ever had a better visual memory than Picasso, and he would certainly not have forgotten what Rubens, for one, had made of that subject. When he came to paint the *Demoiselles* the three girls on the left were just as Rubens had placed them in the version of *The Judgment of Paris* which is now in London, and the two figures on the right were just as Rubens had placed his Paris and his Mercury: almost too close, all this, for coincidence.

In several of his first sketches for the *Demoiselles* Picasso introduced some clothed male figures: patrons of the house, for whose benefit the

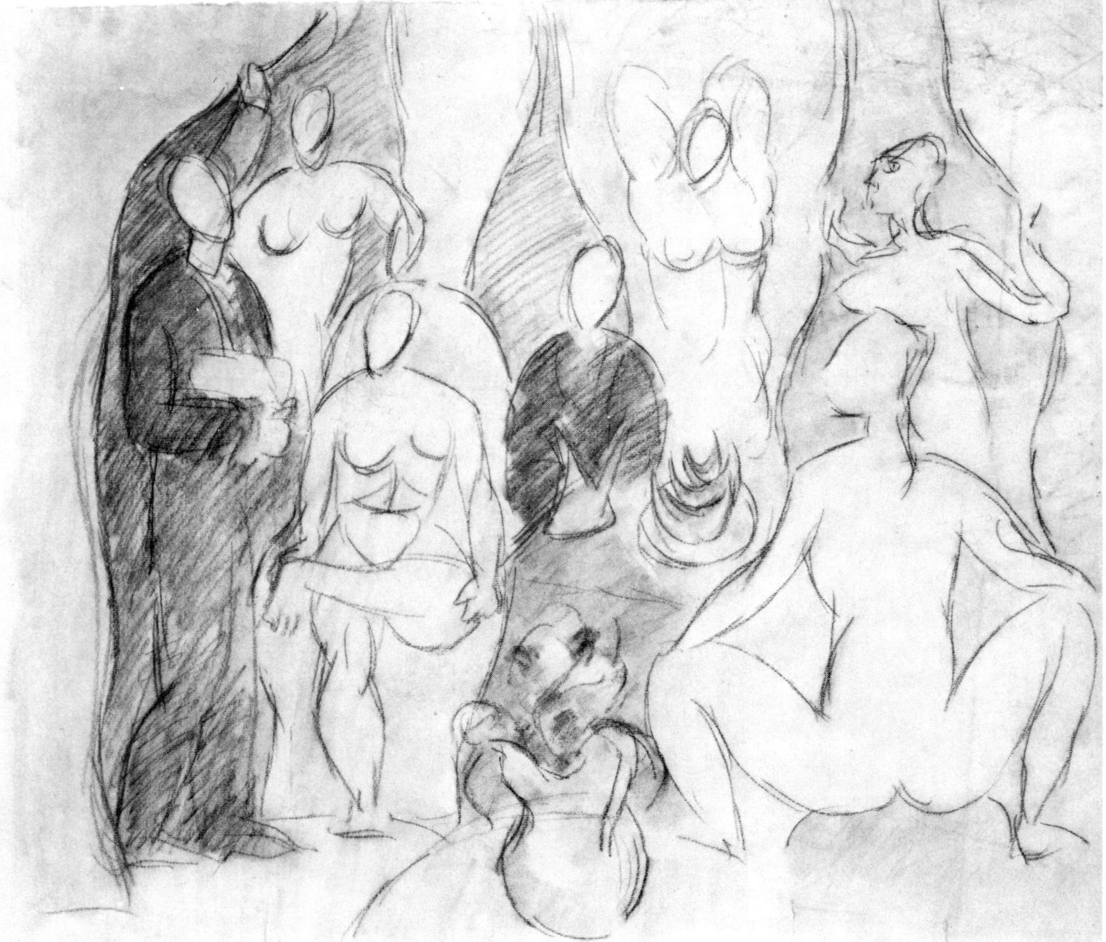

Pablo Picasso. *Study for "Les Demoiselles d'Avignon."* 1907. Pencil and pastel, 18¾ × 25 inches. Kunstmuseum, Basel

parade was being mounted. In the study now in Basel, for instance, the *Demoiselles* still looked as if it might shape up, in the end, like a traditional group photograph in which one or two people happened to have taken their clothes off. The two clothed men, in particular, have an air of unconcern which is quite absent from the painting. In the painting itself the latter-day Paris and the latter-day Mercury are both played by women. The Paris figure glares round at us in a veritable ecstasy of connivance; the Mercury figure parts the curtains, the better to see what is going on. In any enclosed society—ship at sea, barracks, prison camp—the inmates take an intense pleasure in masquerades which distract them from the routines of everyday; and Picasso in the *Demoiselles* shows how the five girls keep boredom at bay. Not only do they reenact their daily task at an exalted level, but they even have on the table before them the legendary apple which Paris will award to the goddess of his choice.

Picasso knew such houses from his years in Barcelona. He was old enough to have verified the prognosis which had been given to him in a palm-reading when he was still a boy: that where women were concerned he would be imperious in his choices and quick to act upon them. Degas and Toulouse-Lautrec had proved that life in a brothel could be endowed with an offhand, lapsed grandeur that had nothing to do with conventional titillation. Yet there remained the fundamental question: how to restate all this in modern terms? How to "make it new" in a way which would be true to him, Pablo Picasso, in the 26th year of his

Peter Paul Rubens. *The Judgment of Paris.* c. 1632–35. Oil on panel, 57⅛ inches × 6 feet 4⅜ inches. The National Gallery, London

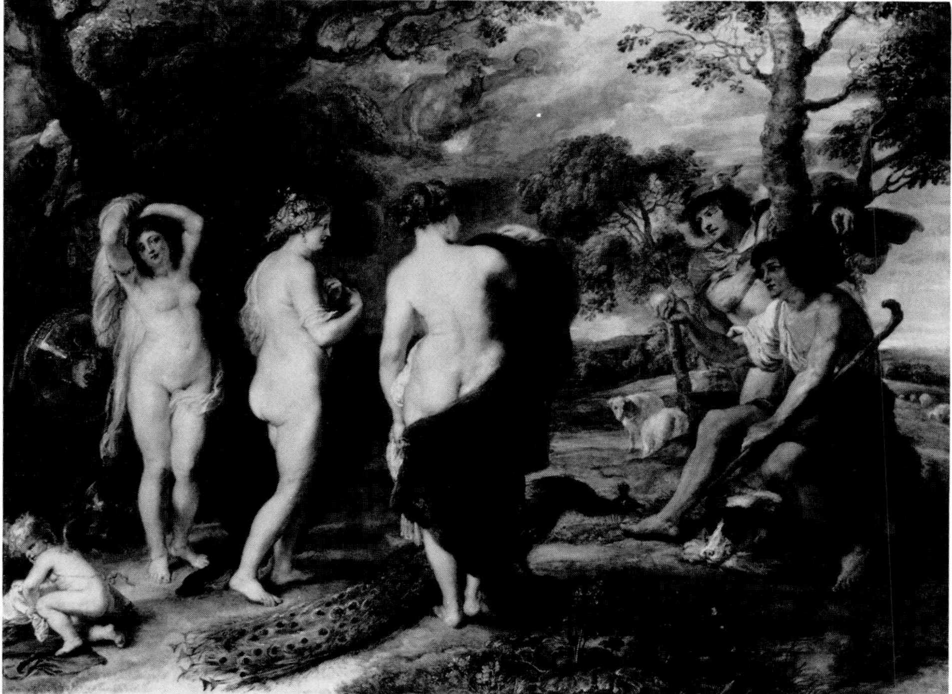

existence, and true to the needs of art in the winter of 1906–07? How to take the future by the throat?

Picasso had in mind the epic scale which Matisse had lately attempted in such pictures as his *Joy of Life.* Cézanne's *Grandes Baigneuses* was the measuring rod for all such enterprises at that time, and as the *Demoiselles* developed it turned out that the composition was anchored by a squatting figure derived from the woman in the lower right-hand corner of the *Three Bathers* by Cézanne which belonged to Matisse. (Whether or not Picasso had seen Cézanne's *Five Bathers,* now in Basel, at the time he was working on the *Demoiselles d'Avignon,* there is an evident congruity between the two paintings: above all, in the juxtaposition of five human figures in a shallow space and the points of resemblance between the figure on the extreme left, with right arm stretched downward in both cases, and the standing figure on the extreme right which, again in both cases, turns our attention inward.) But meanwhile the first drawings for the *Demoiselles* suggested an easygoing linear design with no overtones of emotional stress: a party of pleasure, in fact, set down in calligraphic terms. As entries in a diary, these first drawings would have been ideally lively; but as drafts to be enlarged on the scale of epic they lacked something of monumentality. One of the earliest of the individual sketches that can be related to the *Demoiselles* is for instance a *Head* in watercolor. In its introspective and atmospheric quality, the eyes downcast and the shape of the head adjusted to an elegant and elongated oval, the little picture looks back to the stylish melancholy of Picasso's Blue and Rose Periods. Doubtless it was to exile all feelings of this sort that in a later draft Picasso penciled in, almost unchanged, the majestic, sculptural *Two Nudes* which he had finished painting not long before.

These nudes were very different from the delicate and androgynous adolescents whom he had been painting not long before. From the winter of 1905–06 onward his development accelerated to such a degree that quite often he combined three or four modes of utterance within a single painting. In the head of the *Woman Combing Her Hair* the influence of ancient

Iberian sculpture is as strong as it is in its contemporary, the portrait of Gertrude Stein. The torso has still something of the tender particularity of the bodies of the Blue and Rose Periods; and the ill-defined but richly painted background is a souvenir of another phase in Picasso's evolution—that of the figure groups of 1905–06. In the *Two Nudes* the transition was complete. Anatomies too fragile for the traffic of life were replaced by bodies that seemed about to sink into the ground beneath their own weight. Skins as tender as the paps of a dormouse were replaced by what looked like an outcrop of reddish-brown stone. Buttocks fit for a baby elephant were seen in low relief. Breasts and forearms had a monumental life of their own. Heads were colossal, deep-hewn and suggestive of anything but feminine frailty. The fastidious, all-over play of light that had caressed the human body and given it an ideal harmony had quite vanished. Light and dark were now in the artist's gift, to be granted or taken away at will; and there was something willful and disjunctive about the way in which parts of the body had been put together. The open, shelving backgrounds of the Rose Period gave way in the *Two Nudes* to a narrow ledge and to what looked like a heavy curtain perhaps six inches behind the two giantesses.

These were figures on an epic scale. Cézanne had been mated with Iberian sculpture to produce the first of the elemental women who were to be in and out of Picasso's work for many years to come. But although figures in epic may well be larger than life in physical terms, they should be larger than life in moral terms also; and there should be something of superhuman energy in their articulation. The *Two Nudes* were not right for the *Demoiselles*, and the scene as drawn had neither bite nor bounce; Picasso did not carry it further. Trial and error persuaded him in time to change what had begun as a kind of convivial group photograph into something more angular, more briskly energized. The relaxed curvilinear style of the earlier drawings dropped out of sight; elbows and knees were poised like missiles ready for firing; bodies were shown in vigorous action; draperies, table and still life echoed the tusky, arrowy, sharp-pointed forms which Picasso had stressed throughout the rest of the design. In what now seems to us the final draft, he introduced a more dynamic version of the left-hand figure in the *Two Nudes;* thereafter, he was ready to go.

He had second and third thoughts, even so, while actually painting the picture. In fact it may almost remind us today of the façade of St. Mark's in Venice, so freely and with such abandon did Picasso loot the art of other times and other places for whatever suited his purpose. He manifested in this the stylistic imperialism which is one of the marks of advanced art in this century. As much as T. S. Eliot in the last section of *The Waste Land* or Ezra Pound in the *Cantos*, Picasso in the *Demoiselles* has a pivotal position in time. The picture carries the future within it, but it also carries the past. It has echoes and adaptations of Iberian sculpture, Egyptian art, El Greco, Cézanne and African sculpture, as well as more general affinities with Old Master painting. It also may be said to comment upon the more recent past. It could, for instance, be called the last great Symbolist painting, so heavy is its load of powerful and yet ambiguous subject matter. And it could be called the most haunting of all Expressionist paintings, such is the wrench it gives to all preexisting notions of the expressive potential of the human body. No great painting sits more squarely on the hinge of time.

Throughout the *Demoiselles* Picasso continually shifts his ground as far as visual conventions are concerned. The ever-increasing intensity of the subject matter was paralleled by the mounting complexity of the picture language. What had begun as a Cézannesque parade of beauty ended up as what the art historian Leo Steinberg has called "a tidal wave of female aggression." Correspondingly, what had begun as a figure subject to be rendered in harmonious and unified style ended as a dismantling of a tradition that had ruled since the Renaissance. On both levels the

Pablo Picasso.
Two Nudes. 1906.
Oil on canvas,
59⅝ × 36⅝ inches.
The Museum of Modern Art, New York.
Gift of G. David Thompson in honor of Alfred H. Barr, Jr.

picture was bound to be profoundly disturbing. The women had distinctly got out of hand: there is something in the *Demoiselles*—not much, but something—of the haplessness with which the male faces the female in Munch. But what is borne toward us on that tidal wave is not, in the last resort, a domineering professional sexuality. It is *the future,* made visible. That is why the *Demoiselles* so dismayed the few friends of Picasso who were allowed to see it. It marked the end of something, and his friends could read it only in terms of privation and loss.

In that respect we are in a privileged position. We know that the *Demoiselles* was not only "the end of something." It was also the beginning of Cubism, a movement as fruitful as any in the history of art: between the year 1909 and the outbreak of World War I, Picasso, Braque and Juan Gris produced an almost unbroken succession of supremely beautiful pictures. It also gave us, coincidentally, a whole new range of possibilities for sculpture. The *Demoiselles* did not lead immediately to Cubism, for the ideas within it were too many and too complex for even Picasso himself to exploit all at once. But if Cubism had from 1909 onward a developmental energy which never fails to astonish us, much in that is owed to the proving ground of the *Demoiselles.* Alfred H. Barr in his pioneering study of Picasso (*Picasso: Fifty Years of His Art,* 1946) refers to the *Demoiselles* as "a transitional picture, a laboratory or, better, a battlefield of trial and experiment"; and no one could better this description of a painting which, though in many ways still enigmatic and self-contradictory, will never cease to straddle history like a colossus.

"Les Demoiselles d'Avignon may be called the first Cubist picture," said Mr. Barr, "for the breaking up of natural forms, whether figures, still life or drapery, into a semi-abstract all-over design of tilting, shifting planes compressed into a shallow space is already Cubism." No less fundamental to Cubism is the combination, exemplified above all in the squatting figure on the right, of several

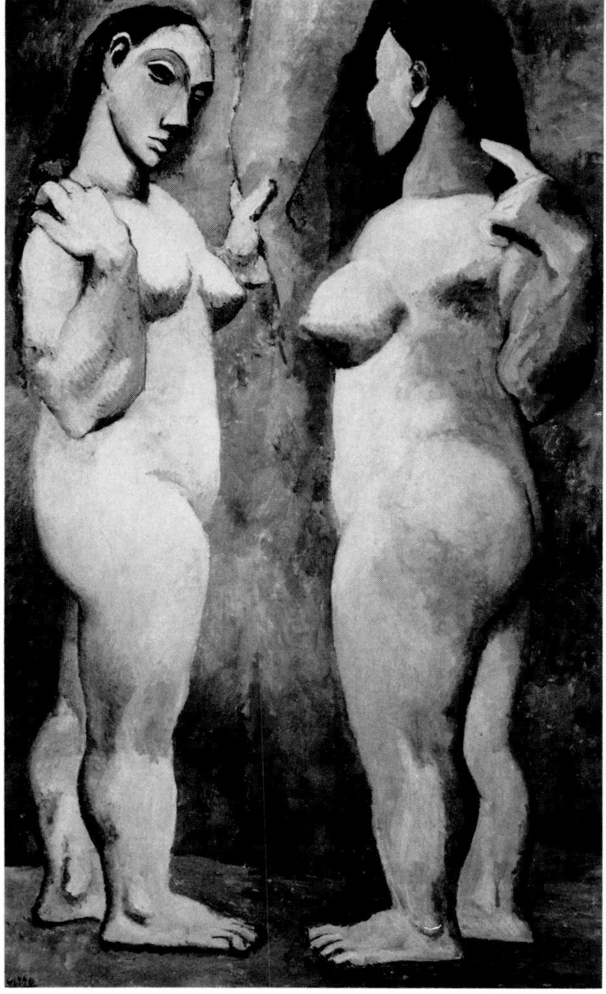

points of view within a single image. There is, on the other hand, little trace in fulfilled Cubist painting of the epic scale, the raunchy subject matter, the hectic emotional tone or the heterogeneous inspiration of the *Demoiselles:* these traits were peculiar to Picasso at a certain moment in his evolution.

A further legacy of the *Demoiselles* was the unquestioned freedom to reorder the evidence of sight. This, once again, was fundamental to Cubism. It is perhaps at this point that we should try to distinguish those characteristics of the initial phase of Cubism which were in the personal gift of Picasso or Braque from those other, more general dispositions which were part of the climate of the age. This is a matter in which the emphasis can easily fall the wrong way. Picasso and Braque were the co-founders of Cubism; and they ridiculed the idea that there was any real correspondence between what they had done and what now seems to us a comparable achievement in other departments of human effort. If pictorial space changed its character at the same time as the physicists were revising our notions of physical space, that was simply coincidence. If our notion of matter as something solid and unchanging was revolutionized just as Picasso and Braque were revolutionizing the presentation of solid objects in art, that was another coincidence. Cubism as developed by them was in their view a purely intuitive art, based on the detached and objective contemplation of subject matter which was for the most part both commonplace in itself and emotionally neutral. They were in tune with the times to the extent of having a boyish admiration for pioneer aviators like Wilbur Wright; but as for Einstein and Max Planck and Ernest Rutherford and Niels Bohr, they had never so much as heard of them.

No one disputes this. But it is also true that we are influenced in our ideas, in our outlook and in our behavior by people we have never heard of. Matisse wrote in 1933 that "our senses have a developmental age which is not that of our immediate environment, but that of the period into which we were born. We are born with the sensibility of that period, that phase of civilization, and it counts for more than anything that learning can give us." Picasso painted the *Demoiselles* at a time when civilization was identified to a considerable extent with the ideology of scientific progress—with the idea, in other words, of a triumphal advance toward a firmer grasp of the conditions of modern life. In one field after another, human frailty was to be eliminated and age-old commonsense convention overthrown. What did Max Planck single out in 1908 as the essential factor in the development of theoretical physics? "A certain emancipation from anthropomorphic elements, and especially from specific sense-impressions." What did the philosopher Edmund Husserl wish to substitute in 1907 for the sumptuous mix of memory and association on which Marcel Proust, for one, had nurtured his gifts? What he called a "phenomenological reduction": an ascetic method of apprehending objects which would arrive quickly and surely at their essence. All this was in the air; and Cubist painting relates to it even if the Cubist painters did not. Cubist painting is central not only to the art of this century but to much of the thought of this century as well. A great Cubist painting ideally illustrates, for instance, the point made not long ago by Jean Piaget, founder of the psychology of intelligence, when he said that it was essential to distinguish between "knowledge as a copy and knowledge as an assimilation of reality." In Cubism, as much as in Piaget, reality is "seen to consist of a series of transformations beneath the appearance of things." "In order to know objects," Piaget goes on, "we have to act on them, break them down, reconstruct them."

Knowledge as a copy has no place in Cubism. But we are dealing here with a most delicate equipoise of internal contradictions. It is true that Picasso and Braque set out from 1909 onward to look at objects simply and straightforwardly, without predetermined notions of what they were like. Everyone agrees that their intentions were what is called "realistic." Courbet was evoked by the poet Guillaume Apollinaire and others as the true father of the Cubists, on the grounds that he too —in his still lifes, above all—had set out to demystify painting. Certainly he aimed at a matter-of-fact, no-nonsense approach; but what emerges from his monumental mounds of apples and pears is, even so, the nobility and generosity of Courbet's own temperament. Objectivity loses out in the end, and we are left not with the matter-of-fact but with a human statement unique for its rich, slow beat and the steadfastness of its underlying beliefs.

In Cubism, equally, we discover in the end that what seemed important at the time—the "rational," "scientific," "objective" element—resulted in large degree from an act of self-deception on the part of sympathizers who wished to apply to Cubism the names then most in favor. If those names went on being applied to Cubism, it was in part because reproductions of Cubist painting emphasize the "rational" or "scientific" aspect of the work. What gets left out of even the best reproduction is the wayward, often hesitant and in any case quite unscientific pressure of the brush as it touches the canvas more or less lightly with a load of paint that is more or less heavy. There are paintings by Picasso and Braque from the years 1910–11 which look in reproduction to be armored against our scrutiny; but when we come face to face with the originals we find that they are sanctuaries of openheartedness in which nothing is kept back from us.

For the founding fathers of Cubism did not aim to create a kind of art for which any preexisting name was appropriate. Their object was to define the terms on which painting could survive in a changed world. Reason and objectivity played their part in this, and so did "science" of a sort. But if Cubism can be said to have saved the dignity and the coherence of painting at a time when those characteristics were in jeopardy, much in that was owed to nonscientific qualities also: imagination, for one, and deep feeling, for another, and truth to self, for a third.

Cubism arose from the notion—and whether it was entirely true is irrelevant—that art was in the doldrums; or, at any rate, that it had far too much unfinished business on its hands. The problems posed by Cézanne were fundamental to the continuance of serious art; nobody had dealt with them in ways which had a general application. It was common ground with many people that single-point perspective had become a hindrance to art; nobody had found a principle of internal organization which could take its place. Cézanne had had no equal in the portrayal of solid forms, but he had achieved this by conceptualization after a very long series of individual acts of perception; the equilibrium involved in this was personal to himself. Cézanne had introduced into his paintings a most delicate spatial ambiguity by what in French is called *passage:* the running together of planes which in the picture space are far apart, so that the old notions of foreground and background are dissolved in a tautly constructed planar structure. This likewise had implications as yet undeveloped.

Other, more general problems remained open. There was the notion of the flatness of the picture surface, so clearly formulated by Maurice Denis in 1890 in a famous article called "A Definition of Neo-Traditionism" and yet so difficult to put into practice; that flat surface so often looked inert and decorative. There was the problem of color; since Gauguin everyone had known that color should be set free, but by the winter of 1906–07, when Picasso began to hatch out the *Demoiselles,* it looked as if color had not so much been liberated as turned loose with nowhere to go. Altogether, painting was in deep trouble. On the one hand, much was expected of it: a new age called for a new art, and people at such times feel personally let down, if not actually disgraced, if art does not

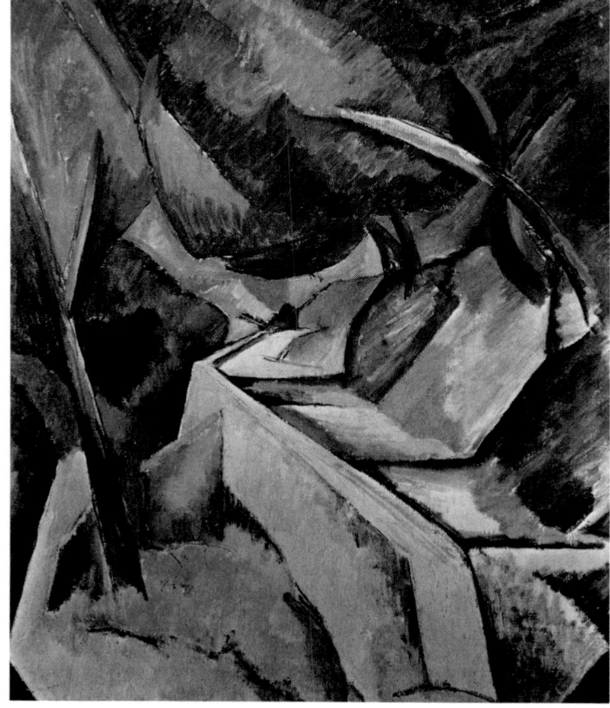

Georges Braque. *Road near L'Estaque.* 1908. Oil on canvas, 23¾ × 19¾ inches. The Museum of Modern Art, New York. Given anonymously (by exchange)

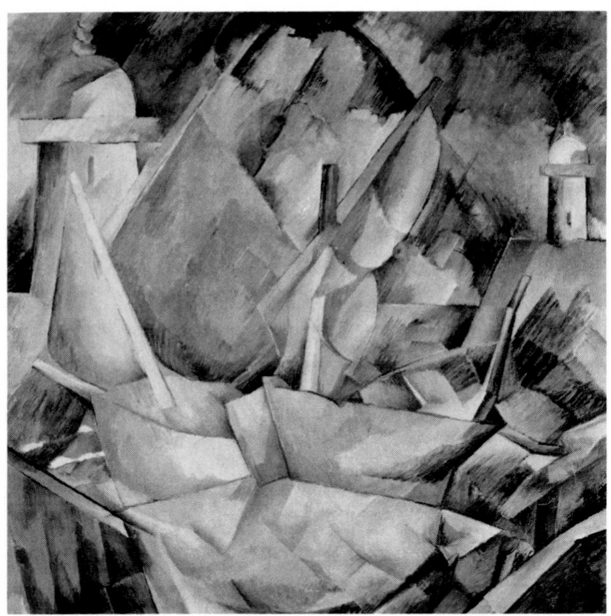

Georges Braque. *Harbor in Normandy.* 1909. Oil on canvas, 32 × 31¾ inches. The Art Institute of Chicago. The Samuel A. Marx Purchase Fund and Major Acquisitions Fund

do what they ask of it. On the other hand, art was manifestly being relieved of many of its traditional functions. A young painter, Fernand Léger, summed this up in 1913 when he wrote that technology had put a lot of art out of business. "How can Salon painting compete," he asked, "with what is available today in every cinema in the world? Each of the arts today is isolating itself and limiting itself to its own field." The function of Cubism, in this context, was to serve as a redoubt —an unassailable fortress for an irreducible art.

Van Gogh had said not long before he died that in future the great steps forward in art would be undertaken collectively, since no one man could be strong enough to bear the burden. He was borne out in this by the history of Cubism, which was from its beginnings a joint operation. Picasso and Braque were its co-founders. It was a partnership of opposites, but it was also a partnership of equals. From time to time their contemporary Fernand Léger worked in ways tangential to theirs; and from 1912 onward a young painter, Juan Gris, continued the movement with an authority and a coherence which were distinctly his own. But fundamentally Cubism was the invention of Picasso and Braque. In its reverberation—in the extent, in other words, to which it made the future possible—their alliance was akin to that of Bertrand Russell and A. N. Whitehead, who at much the same time were producing, in *Principia Mathematica,* a complete deductive system, based on a very few first principles, which laid the foundation of modern logic and led in time to the development of the computer system. Cubism was not "a system," in that sense, but it was an achievement of comparable stature.

Georges Braque had been introduced to Picasso by Apollinaire toward the end of 1907. The friendship was slow to develop, and in background and character the two men could hardly have been more different. Picasso had a fine-art inheritance —his father was for many years a professor in the Barcelona Academy of Fine Arts—and in his first youth he was already the coming man in one of the most sophisticated cities in Europe. Braque, in contrast, was the son and grandson of professional housepainters. The height of ambition in his family had been to become a prosperous master craftsman. By the year 1899 Picasso knew what was going on in art all over Europe, whereas Braque was a sedulous apprentice in the provincial city of Le Havre, learning how to plaster, how to paint and paper a wall, how to simulate the textures of fine wood and rare marble. His was a relatively dull and limited milieu, and even when he finally got to paint full-time in Paris his outward progress was slow. Yet it was Braque, alone among Picasso's friends, who made sense of the *Demoiselles* after a first instinctive revulsion; and it was Braque, in the summer of 1908, who came back from the town of L'Estaque, near Marseilles, with what were later called "the first truly Cubist paintings."

Picasso, meanwhile, had found it difficult to follow the *Demoiselles.* He tackled one after another the formal inventions which had been made to cohabit in that great and terrible painting; but there was an evident and painful sense of stress in many of the pictures which resulted. He was like an engine which is so powerful that no chassis yet developed can house it; and from time to time there were paintings like the *Big Dryad* of 1908 which gave off an almost palpable sense of elemental energies for which no definitive use had been found. It was at this point that Braque with his composed and impregnable nature and his steady, consistent methods of work began to play an ever larger part in Picasso's life. Braque had for some time been awed by the beauty and dignity of Cézanne's achievement; L'Estaque was a favorite workplace of Cézanne's, and had Braque been an everyday "follower of Cézanne" he would have seized, in that summer of 1908, on the first facts about the landscape there, which were the devouring brilliance of the light and the saturated blue of the sky. But in fact he did nothing of the kind. The landscapes which he brought back with him were filled with a hooded light of his own devising. In their compositional scheme the sky played no part. They were severe, tightly constructed paintings in which color was restricted to the most sober of greens and ochres. Contours were broken, contrasts of "near" and "far" were often contradicted, forms opened up into one another, and houses were splayed out in such a way that more was seen of them than could have been seen from any one point of view in life.

It was with respect to these paintings that the critic Louis Vauxcelles wrote that Braque "reduces everything—places, figures, houses—to geometrical schemas, to cubes." The name was never apt, since there are no cubes in Cubist painting, but it stuck. One column-inch in a newspaper dated November 14, 1908, established Braque as the pioneer of the movement; and as he went on his ruminative way he produced *Still Life with Fruit* in late 1908 in which intersecting planes were dramatized by the quite arbitrary fall of the light, and early in 1909 a *Harbor in Normandy,* painted in Paris, which was fundamental to the development of Cubism. The memory of Cézanne still presides over it; the repeated triangles which form up in the sky, the sails of the boat on the left and the detailing of the jetty are related to the lofty, echoing, triangular forms in the *Grandes Baigneuses.* But Braque had evolved on his own a method of unifying the painting by causing the sky, the sea, the boats, the lighthouses and the harbor itself to run on into one another—each coaxing the other, as it were, to take over the burden of structuring the picture. Braque's ambition was to remake space in such a way that each

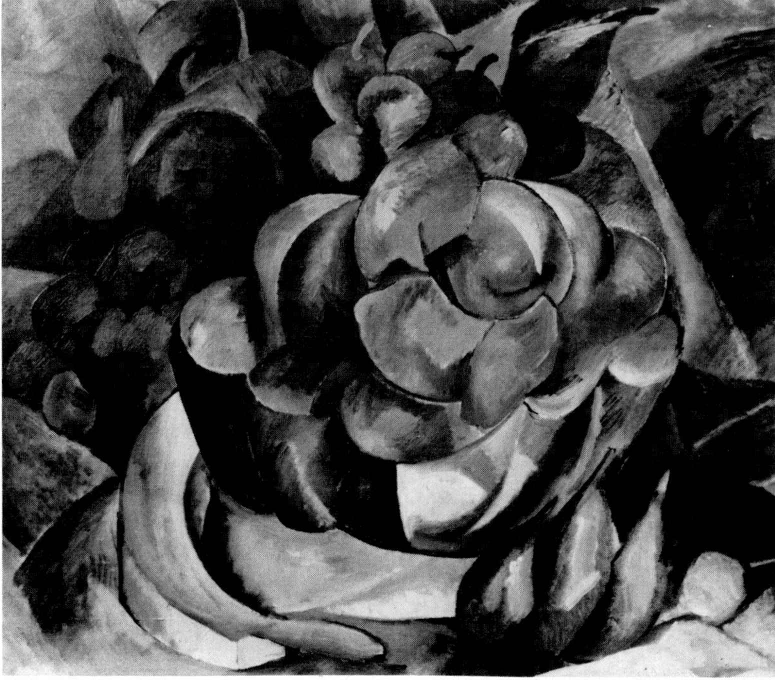

Georges Braque.
Still Life with Fruit.
1908.
Oil on canvas,
21½ × 26 inches.
Moderna Museet,
Stockholm

object would come forward in turn—to be stroked, almost, as antelopes are stroked in a zoo. (The art historian John Golding says of the *Harbor in Normandy* that "the optical sensation produced is comparable to that of running one's hand over an immensely elaborate, subtly carved sculpture in low relief.")

In the preface which Apollinaire wrote for Braque's first one-man show at Kahnweiler's, in November, 1908, he rightly singled out the element of "angelic moderation" in Braque's nature. But to be angelic is not to be characterless; Braque in 1908–09 defined the immediate ambitions of Cubism in a way that testified to the operation of a most powerful and resourceful intelligence. "Angelic" remains the right word, however, for the final effect of Braque's early Cubist work, which is that of a peaceable kingdom of forms, each of which submits with total docility to its presentation in a continually changing space. That kind of thing was quite foreign to Picasso's nature, and when in the summer of 1909 he produced his first group of completely realized Cubist paintings they had quite another character. Alike in landscape and in portraiture, he displayed a power-mindedness and a drive toward total possession which were quite absent in Braque.

Something of the difference between Picasso and Braque comes out in the contrast between Braque's *Still Life with Fruit,* 1908, and Picasso's *Still Life with Liqueur Bottle,* 1909. If the Braque is more broadly and generally conceived, it is more a matter of generous forms generously modeled, and if it has touches of much higher color, that may be in part because it is the earlier picture of the two and because Cubism was not yet so distinctly based on sharp-edged, prismatic planes and near-monochromatic color. But there is something peculiar to Picasso in the use of idiosyncratic objects like the many-faceted bottle of Spanish anisette that is in the lower left-hand half of the painting and the rather less legible ceramic bottle in the form of a cock that is above and to the right of it. Picasso had by this time proceeded much further toward the adoption of an all-purpose, prismatic form, like a folded sheet of writing paper, which paces the image and determines the speed at which information is given to the observer; and it is already quite difficult to read the individual objects in the picture. It is an indication of the dynamic of Picasso's career that the year 1909, which produced such fidgety, prismatic Cubist paintings as the *Still Life with Liqueur Bottle,* should also have prompted the *Still Life with Bread and Fruit Dish on a Table.* Everything here seems larger, grander and more stable than in everyday life. The majesty of the hinged table, the bare, strong outline of the bread, the total lack of fuss or histrionics—all relate back to the ancient traditions of Spanish still-life painting; it is as if, after the agitations of the *Demoiselles,* Picasso had come through to the kind of calm, clear, exact statement which proves all over again that absolute dignity can characterize the fundamentals of everyday. (It is, by the way, in character with the metamorphic energy of Picasso's procedures that this most austere of still lifes should have evolved

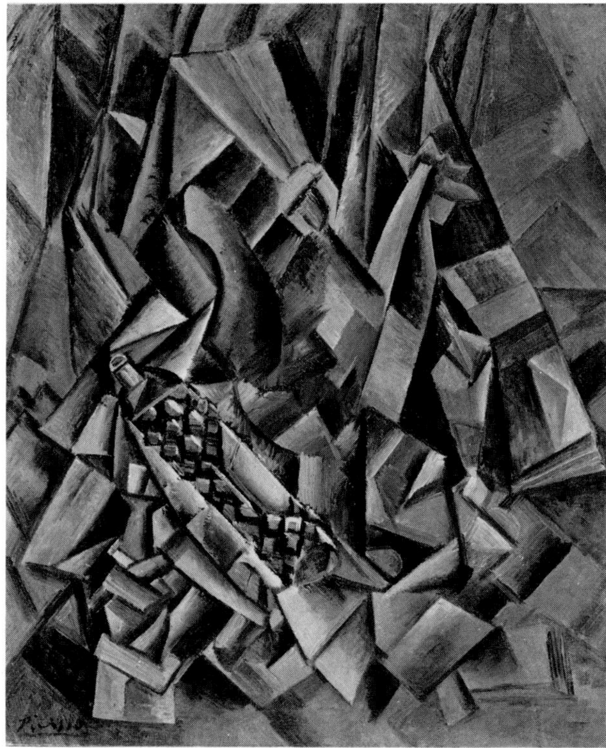

Pablo Picasso. *Still Life with Liqueur Bottle.* 1909. Oil on canvas, 32⅛ × 25¾ inches. The Museum of Modern Art, New York. Mrs. Simon Guggenheim Fund

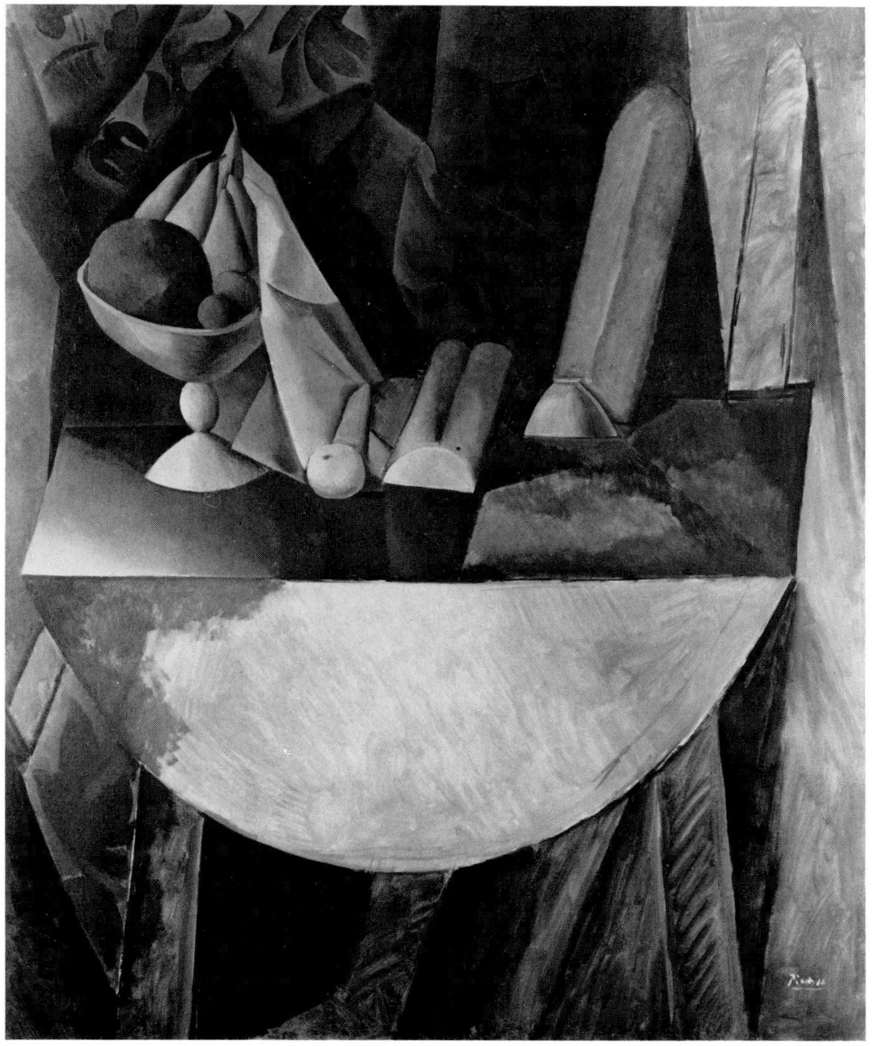

Pablo Picasso.
Still Life with Bread and Fruit Dish on a Table.
1909.
Oil on canvas,
65½ × 53 inches.
Kunstmuseum, Basel

from the initial idea of a group of revelers at a neighborhood café.)

In this same redoubtable year Picasso also addressed himself to the human figure with a renewed energy. The painting *Woman with Pears* and the bronze *Woman's Head* are sister images —reworkings of a shared idea. In the bronze, the twist of the neck and shoulders gives the whole sculpture a specific impetus: a turning motion which is echoed by the general direction of the deeply shadowed angular planes of the head. In the painting, Picasso has modeled the outline of the left shoulder and the left side of the neck, right up to the back of the left ear, in terms of a continuous, girderlike form which tilts over to the left as it reaches the level of the cheekbone. This offsets the many broken, sharp-angled and deftly tilted forms which make up the right side of the head; and both idioms are echoed in turn by the draperies, the fruit on the table, the tablecloth and the table itself. The integration of these many types and varieties of form into a single, harmonious and fully expressive composition is one of the major achievements of Picasso's career before 1914.

Picasso in the summer of 1909 was undoubtedly stimulated by the fact of being in Spain, at Horta de San Juan. Gertrude Stein made one of her more helpful remarks when she said that "in the landscapes which he painted there he emphasized the way of building in Spanish villages, the line of the

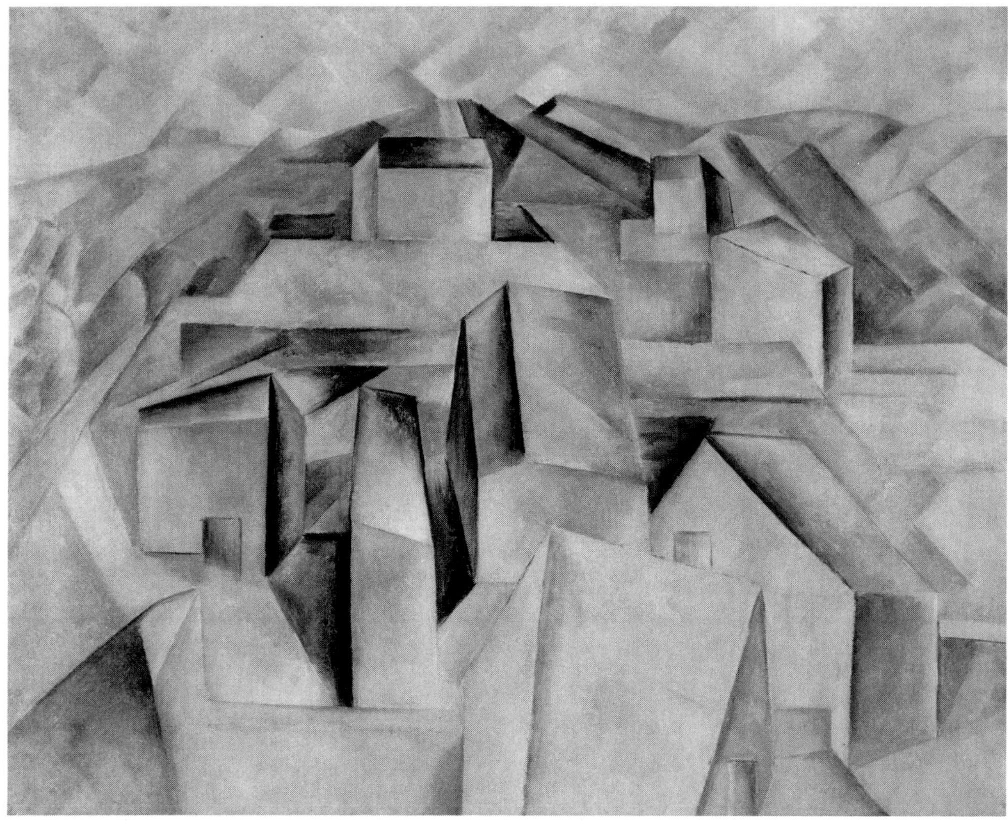

Pablo Picasso.
Houses on the Hill, Horta. 1909.
Oil on canvas, 25⅝ × 32 inches.
The Museum of Modern Art, New York.
Nelson A. Rockefeller Bequest

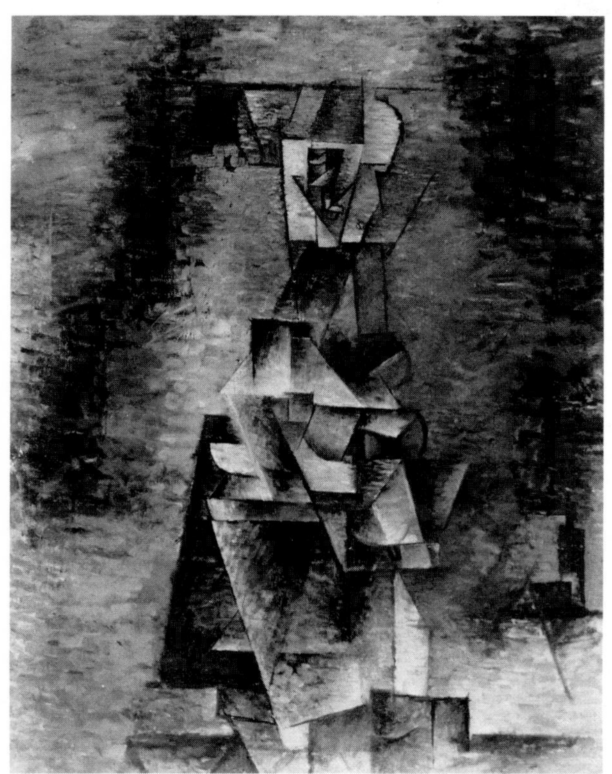

Pablo Picasso.
Female Nude. 1910–11.
Oil on canvas, 38¾ × 30⅜ inches.
Philadelphia Museum of Art.
The Louise and Walter Arensberg Collection

houses not following the landscape but cutting across and into the landscape, becoming indistinguishable in the landscape by cutting across the landscape. . . . The color too was characteristically Spanish, the pale silver yellow with the faintest suggestion of green, the color afterwards so well known in Picasso's cubist pictures. . . ."

Spain did something for Picasso: physically, in that he identified far more strongly with its spare, bleached landscapes than with the green distances of northern France, and morally, in that his ideas suddenly began to pull all the same way and with redoubled force. Nothing in earlier painting quite prepares us for the pounce on the essentials of form which Picasso achieved at Horta de San Juan. There was something in this of the sculptural interests which had come out so strongly in the *Demoiselles:* each form was given a specific vibration, a throb all its own, which would not have been found, or permitted, in the more conciliatory universe of Braque.

Georges Braque.
Man with a Guitar.
1911.
Oil on canvas,
45¾ × 31⅞ inches.
The Museum of Modern Art, New York.
Acquired through the Lillie P. Bliss Bequest

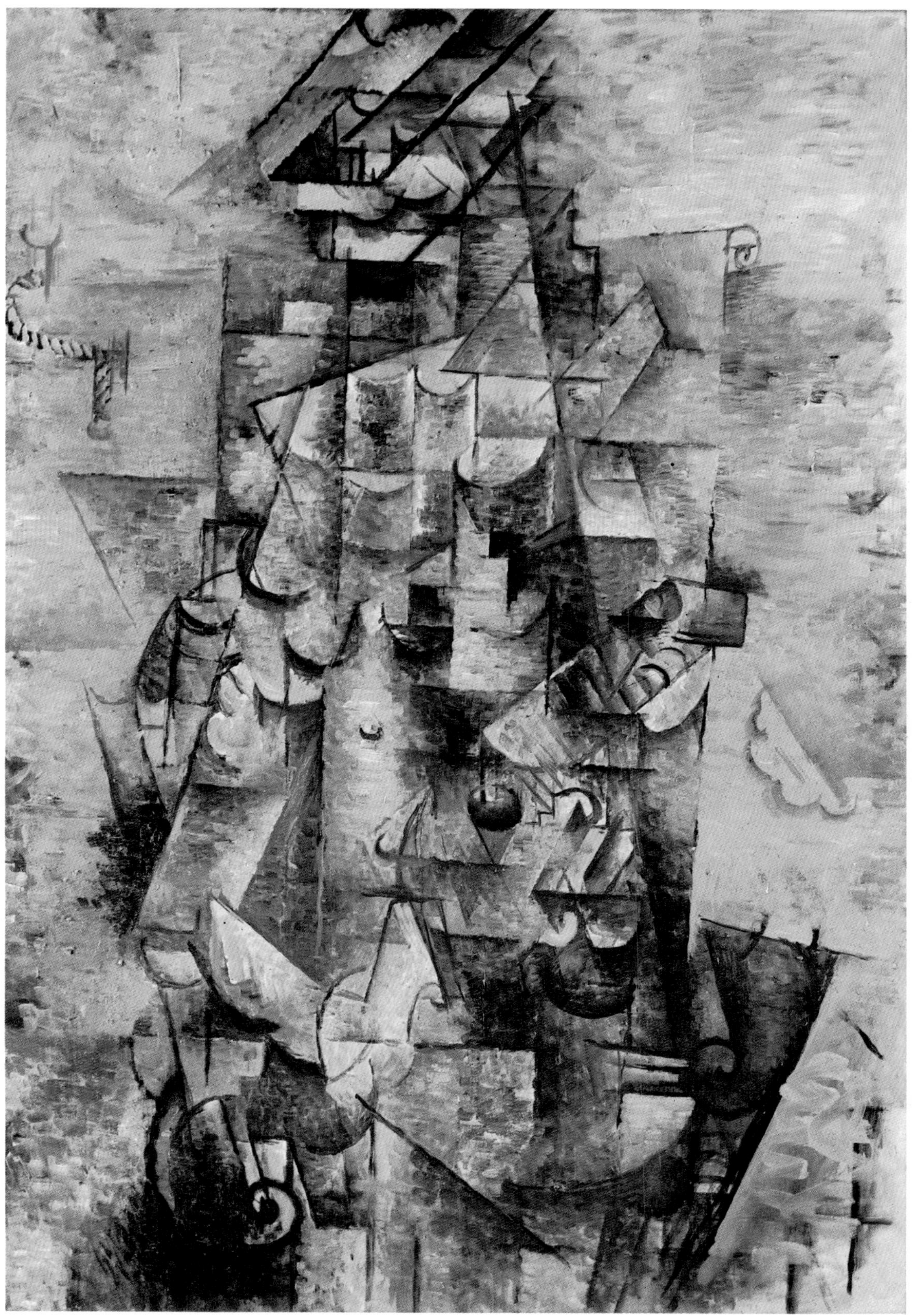

Picasso retained, however, his polyvalent curiosity. His work was still full of echoes and allusions, and full also of contradictory ambitions within one and the same picture. The *Girl with a Mandolin,* painted in Paris early in 1910, is in feeling a throwback to the elegiac figure painting of the Rose Period; parts of the body are modeled with a fullness and a tender simplicity which look back to the work of five years earlier, but at the same time Picasso has stamped the head flat on the picture plane. Picasso was still working from the model with the kind of tenacity which Cézanne had displayed in front of his sitters; and where the look of his sitters is known to us we can estimate how strong was the tension between the demands of the evolving picture language, on the one hand, and the demands of human particularity, on the other. A prize instance of this is the portrait of the dealer Ambroise Vollard, which Picasso painted in the winter of 1909–10. The surface of the painting is densely articulated in terms of a consistent, closely networked series of small, intersecting planes. This structure is independent of the contours of Vollard himself and of the still life which accompanies him; yet we have no difficulty in recognizing traits familiar to us from other likenesses of Vollard—the high-domed skull, the redoubtable knob of flesh at the end of the nose, the slight downward twist at the corner of the thin lips, and the deceptive air of being half asleep.

In the summer of 1910 Picasso once again returned to Spain, where he made another important step forward in his art. The basic element in the pictorial architecture was thereafter no longer the closed, sculptural form which had survived, in however multifaceted a manner, until then. It became something quite different: a linear framework made up, in the case of a figure painting, of the outlines or main directional lines of the body. This framework was used as the basis for a system of open, bladelike planes which intersected with one another, forming an autonomous structure that sometimes referred to the human figure and at other times went its own way. We can see from the *Female Nude* now in Philadelphia, done at Cadaquès in the crucial summer of 1910, that although these paintings are not easy to decipher they have a presence as formidable as anything in the *Demoiselles.*

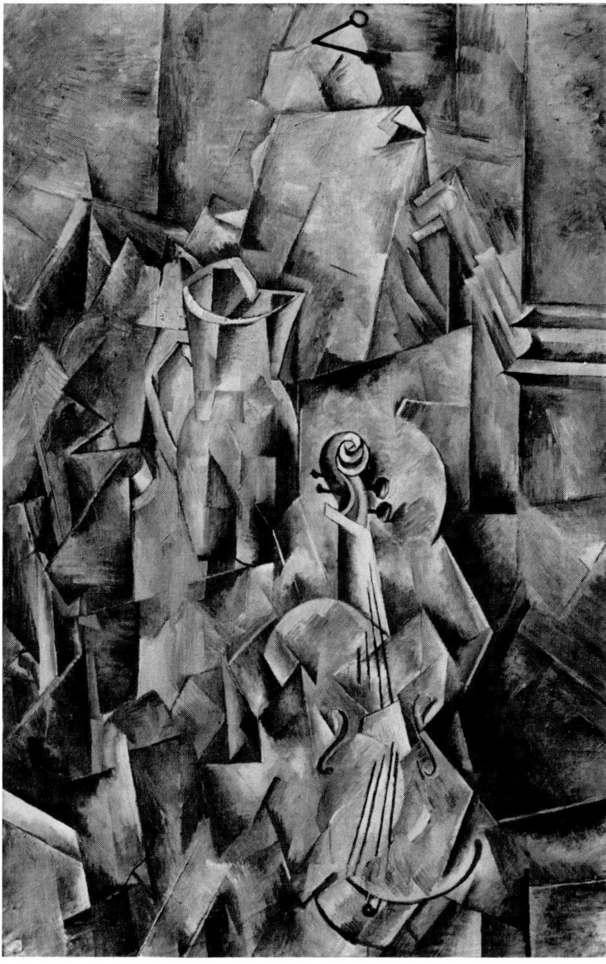

Georges Braque.
Still Life with Violin and Jug.
1909.
Oil on canvas,
46¾ × 29¼ inches.
Kunstmuseum, Basel

Picasso did not want to produce cult objects which would be accessible only to the few. Nor did he want to go over the edge and produce paintings which were purely abstract. He wanted to go on painting pictures which *presented* the visible world but did not *represent* it; he wanted to be sure that an intelligent person who looked at those pictures would know what he was looking at; at the same time he wanted to retain and enrich the new formal language which he and Braque had evolved. Between the autumn of 1910 and the spring of 1912 they worked on this problem.

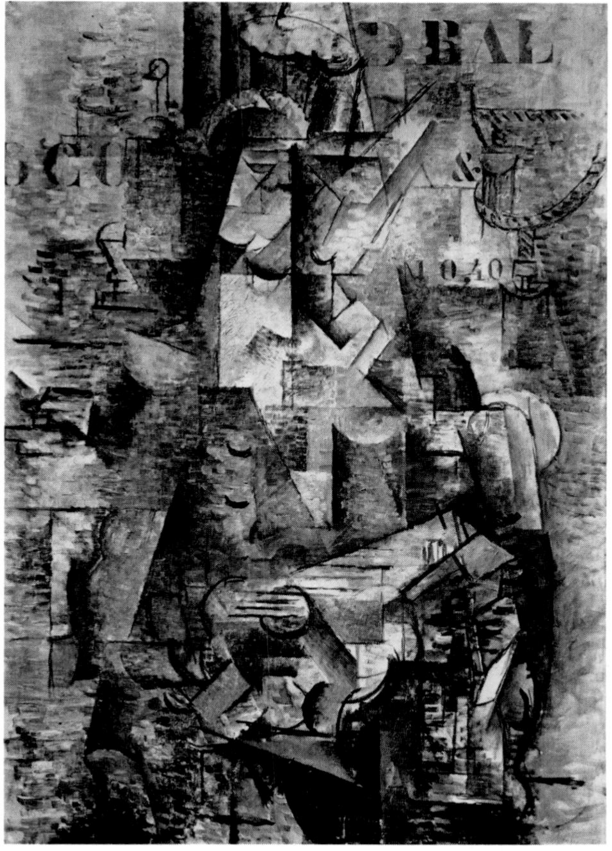

Georges Braque.
The Portuguese.
1911.
Oil on canvas,
46¾ × 32½ inches.
Kunstmuseum, Basel

Picasso solved it by introducing a system of visual cues which gave the observer a broad hint as to what was going on. Fragments of reality were imported complete into the picture—a watch chain, the name of a newspaper, a carpenter's T square, a calling card, the tassel from an upholstered armchair—with the object of forcing the observer to interpret the pictorial structure in terms of the known world and not merely as a structure which had its own internal consistency and existed in and for itself.

It was fundamental to Synthetic Cubism that color and form could act independently of one another. In other words, color was not required to describe, or even to identify form. In *Man with a Hat* there is a progression from light to dark as we read the head from right to left. The newsprint, now discolored with age, stands for the cheek which faces the light; the rich blue stands for the shadowed center of the face; the ink-black section to the left stands for those parts of the head which are in darkness and might not even be seen in normal conditions. Austere and summary as the drawing may be, there are signs that Picasso, the master portraitist, has been at work. Looks and character are defined in telegraphic form, and we can see that the derby hat has come from the best English makers. More than one scholar has lately pointed out that the printed matter was not chosen at random but includes apt references to tuberculosis, in the text that marks the location of the man's upper chest, and to nostrils and teeth in the text that runs vertically past his mouth and nose.

With Picasso these cues never quite lost the character of a challenge. It was man against man as he baited and needled the observer into identifying the subject of the picture. Braque was, as always, less combative in his approach. But he put the important questions all the same. Already in the winter of 1909–10 he inserted a perfectly legible illusionistic nail, complete with shadow, into the great still life called *Still Life with Violin and Jug.* The point of this was twofold. First, it took the picture out of the esoteric, fine-art world by suggesting that it had been nailed to the wall as a flat, painted surface of no particular consequence. Secondly, it was a reminder of the alternative convention: centuries-old picture-making methods, based on the imitation of everyday experience. Braque in this wonderful painting maneuvers back and forth between art and life. In life, the violin and the jug would have stood squarely on the table. But in Braque's picture, space is tipped up and forward, and everything in it—violin, jug, table, dado, angled wall, nail on that wall—is brought up close to us. Front, back and sides are seen simultaneously; and what in life would move sedately away from us comes alive in an elaborate system of hinges and flaps and diamond-edged facets that is nearer to El Greco's giddying *View of Toledo* than to the sobriety of conventional still life. Only the nail is true to everyday vision: partly in irony, partly to show that old ways of seeing can be combined with the new, and partly as a visual pun, to suggest that the picture itself is hung on that same wall.

In the spring of 1911 Braque introduced an idea of much wider and more lasting significance when he stenciled the letters BAL at the top of *The Portuguese,* a single-figure painting prompted by the memory of a musician he had seen in a Marseilles bar. Like the nail, the letters served to remind the observer of other and more familiar ways of conveying information. But, unlike the nail which had only one function, they were versatile adjuncts which could fulfill a wide variety of purposes. Weightless and incorporeal, they had a firm, exact, unalterable shape and substance; in this, they contrasted with the painted surface of the picture and made the observer conscious all over again both of the two-dimensional nature of the painted surface and of the three-dimensional forms which were being presented. And they could be read, finally, as they are read in life, for a specific message.

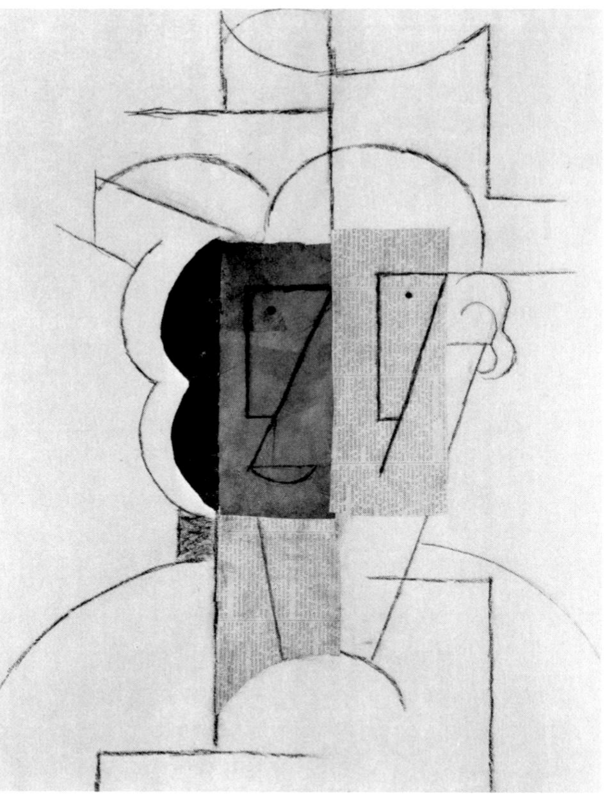

Pablo Picasso.
Man with a Hat.
1912.
Charcoal, ink and pasted paper, 24½ × 18⅝ inches.
The Museum of Modern Art, New York. Purchase

They signaled, in other words, a change of pace. A new kind of scrutiny was called for; and this at a time when the dosage of verifiable fact in Cubist painting was much diminished. "At the time," Picasso said to William Rubin, the art historian, when discussing a painting done in the spring of 1912, "everyone talked about how much reality there was in Cubism. But they didn't really understand. It's not a reality you can take in your hand. It's more like a perfume—in front of you, to the sides. The scent is everywhere, but you don't quite know where it comes from." Lettering introduced a new kind of specificity into painting; looking at Cubist painting in sequence, we realize that until that point it was deeply conservative in many of its aspects. The half-length seated figure, the neutral materials of still life, the landscape that kept close to the motif: all these were the classic constituents of European art. Cézanne, Corot and Chardin (above all with his *Attributes of the Arts*) stood godfathers to Cubist painting between 1908 and 1912. The paintings were real paintings, handmade with brush and pigment; and even at their most audacious they still have—or so it seems today—an Old Masterly echo. It is Rembrandt, against all expectation, who comes to mind when we look afresh at the tenebrous frontal *Female Nude* which Picasso painted in Cadaquès in that summer of 1910.

The importation of lettering, as a readymade, nonhandpainted element, was therefore a considerable step. With his craftsmanly upbringing and his extreme sensitivity to substance, Braque was anxious in 1912 to get away from the severe and all but monochromatic procedures which Cubism had developed since 1910. If not too much of life, then at any rate too much of language was excluded by those procedures. The new formal vocabulary could never have been developed if color had not been exiled; but the exile hurt, all the same. It is always a moving moment when we watch color being turned out of the studio, as it were, in the great still lifes which Braque painted in the winter of 1909–10; and now the delicate

Pablo Picasso.
Guitar and Wineglass. 1913.
Pasted paper and charcoal,
18⅞ × 14⅜ inches.
Marion Koogler McNay Art Institute, San Antonio

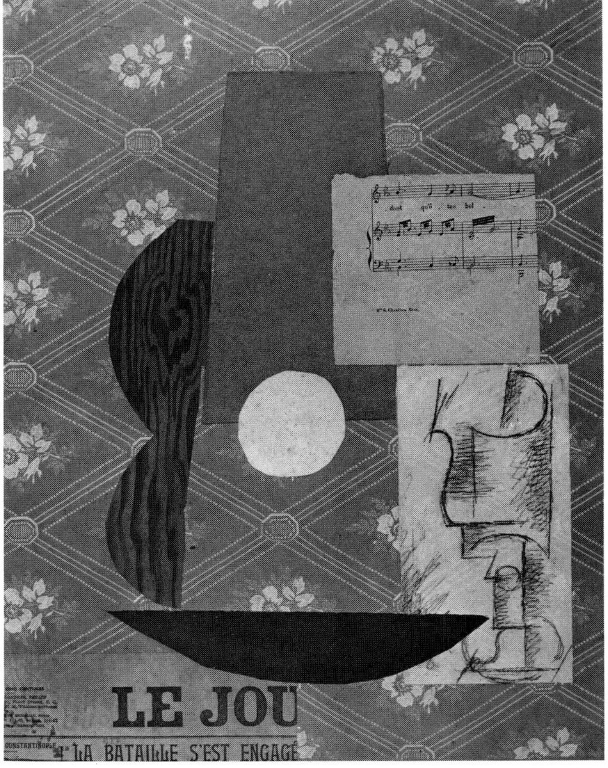

thing was to reintroduce it without allowing it to reintroduce illusionist space—for such is our conditioning that we simply cannot see two patches of colored pigment side by side without reading them in spatial terms. Somehow, color had to be brought back on quite another basis.

It was brought back toward the end of 1912 as part of a new development which was of enormous and lasting importance for 20th-century art. Braque and Picasso had been pondering for months whether it would be possible in future to *build* their pictures, as much as to paint them. Braque would seem to have been, in this, the logician who said, "If we want to show a man reading a newspaper, why do we have to fake it up with brushes and oil paint when we could just as well get the newspaper itself and stick a bit of it on the canvas?" This flouted both the Puritan ethic of hard work and the trade-unionism of the trained *artiste-peintre;* but it made good sense. Picasso tried something of the sort early in 1912, when he introduced into one of his still lifes a piece of oilcloth which had been overprinted to simulate chair caning; and in September, 1912, Braque went into a shop in Avignon, bought a length of artificially wood-grained wallpaper, and used it with perfect congruity to indicate the drawer and top of a wooden table on which were assembled the classic elements of Cubist still life: a glass, a fruit dish, a bunch of grapes, and the words BAR and ALE.

It was characteristic of the difference between the two men that Picasso's first steps in collage were direct and overtly subversive, as he thickly over-painted part of the oilcloth in order to lock it down into the substance of the painting. Braque by contrast introduced his strips of wood-grained paper in an exploratory way. Picasso's textures were so dense as to force the observer almost to rub his nose in the picture to find out what was going on; Braque's had plenty of air blowing through them. In a matter of months Picasso was using the new medium with a quite extraordinary freedom and élan, as if relishing every moment of the new and total liberty which he and Braque had brought into painting. For painters—"picture-builders" might be a better name—were now free to make their pictures from whatever materials took their fancy. They were also free to change the identity of those materials, and to use them literally, as themselves, or metaphorically, or in a purely formal compositional way and with no reference to their identity in the world from which they had been lifted.

In one and the same picture—the *Guitar and Wineglass* of 1913—Picasso would, for instance, use a piece of newspaper and a fragment of sheet music as themselves; he would indicate the outline and texture of a guitar with four pieces of pasted paper, one of which was wood-grained (and therefore suggestive of the guitar's appearance in life) whereas the other three were not; and he completed the picture with a drawing of a wineglass which was complete in itself, had been drawn on a separate piece of paper, dated from a year or two earlier, and was in short not so much a drawn glass

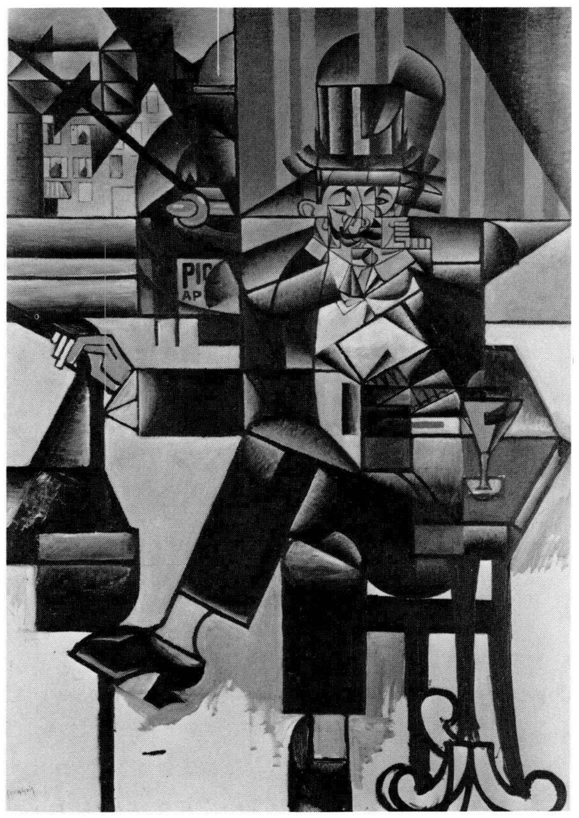

Juan Gris.
The Man in the Café. 1912.
Oil on canvas,
50½ × 34⅝ inches.
Philadelphia Museum of Art. The Louise and Walter Arensberg Collection

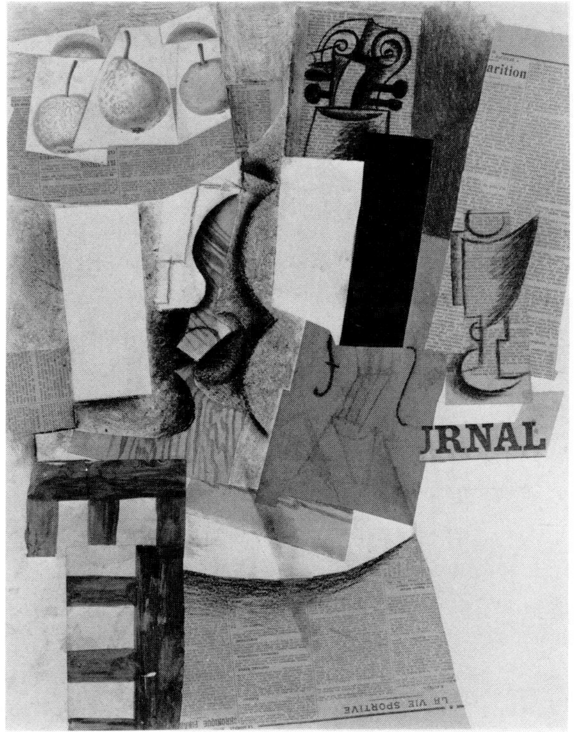

Pablo Picasso.
The Violin (Violin and Compote of Fruit). 1913.
Charcoal, colored papers, gouache and printed papers,
25¼ × 19½ inches.
Philadelphia Museum of Art. The A. E. Gallatin Collection

which was integral to the picture as a drawing of a glass which was also a historical object. In pictures of this sort identities were changed, ignored, borrowed or unexpectedly kept intact in ways which have never lost their capacity to surprise us. Color was employed as a free agent, without reference to modeling or light. The strips of colored paper were flat by their very essence—so much so that when they were drawn over, as they often were, there was no temptation to identify the drawn form with color beneath it. All this brought into painting a new kind of physicality: one that was clear, open and lean. Not only the painting itself but the act of looking at it was restructured; and there was as much an increase in the pleasure given, and in the kinds of pleasure involved, as there was in the material possibilities which were henceforward at the painter's disposal.

Picasso played in all this the more vigorous role. It amused him enormously, for example, to parody his own labors of a year or two before. Insolence (in Alfred Barr's term) was added to paradox when the subject matter of the *Fruit Dish,* done in early spring, 1909, turned up in his *Violin and Compote of Fruit* of 1913, in the form of some colored illustrations of apples and pears, cut out of a book, with newsprint and plain white paper to indicate the dish. Yet the new experience was as complete and enriching as the earlier one. And although Braque in general was not so aggressive in his use of the new medium, he did not disdain its opportunities for comedy. One of the grandest of his pasted-paper works is also one of the few in which no musical instrument appears. But what is it that anchors the whole composition in place? A rectangular strip of paper, cut from the title of a pulp novel, on which one word appears complete: VIOLON.

In 1912 Picasso and Braque were reinforced by the emergence of Juan Gris as a painter of real importance. Gris had been living in the same building as his compatriot Picasso since shortly after he arrived in Paris in 1906, at the age of 19. He had consequently been ideally placed to watch the progress of Cubism from the days of the *Demoiselles* onward. He had not presented himself as an aspiring painter but rather as a clever and attentive young man from out of town who lived by making illustrations for the humorous papers. His background was in the exact sciences—mathematics and engineering—and when he did begin to paint, in 1911, he tackled the problems one by one, in his own way, and made no attempt to rush the preliminaries. There was nothing fudged or approximate about his early paintings, and when he first showed his pictures, in October, 1912, they impressed at once by their almost military command of any given situation. In the portrait of Picasso, 1912, for instance, the fall of the light was plotted as if promotion at West Point depended upon it. In the second half of that year he developed a way of picture building in which the color was bright and high and a rigorous linear diagram parceled out the canvas; each particular parcel was then allotted to a sectional view of the subject matter. An instance of this is *The Man in the Café,* which was put on view in October, 1912, only a few months after Gris had made his debut as a painter, and which impressed at once by its size, its assurance and its schematic presentation of the given subject. The strict linear framework operated, in fact, as a kind of mincing and flattening machine from which nothing was allowed to escape.

Sometimes these sectional views were realistic, sometimes they weren't; Gris kept his options open. Trained as he was to keep a given subject in mind in all its mathematical aspects, he was able to plot his pictures in advance in a way that would never have appealed to the more intuitive Picasso and Braque. When he applied himself to extending the pasted-paper technique, in 1914, he did it with characteristic thoroughness. Instead of using the papers in a dispersed and intermittent way, he allowed them to cover the whole, or almost the whole, of the canvas in accordance with a preestablished formal idea. This idea often operated quite independently of the subject matter to be

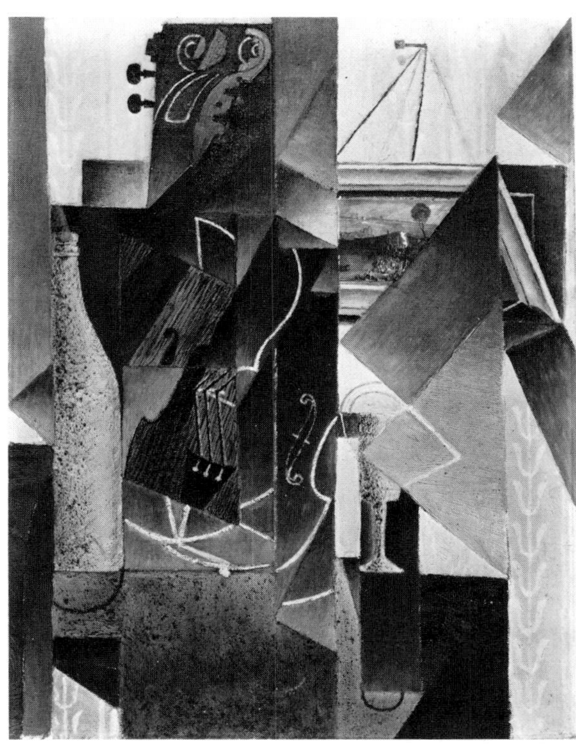

Juan Gris. *Violin and Engraving.* 1913. Oil and collage on canvas, 25⅝ × 19⅝ inches. The Museum of Modern Art, New York. Bequest of Anna Erickson Levene in memory of her husband, Dr. Phoebus Aaron Theodor Levene

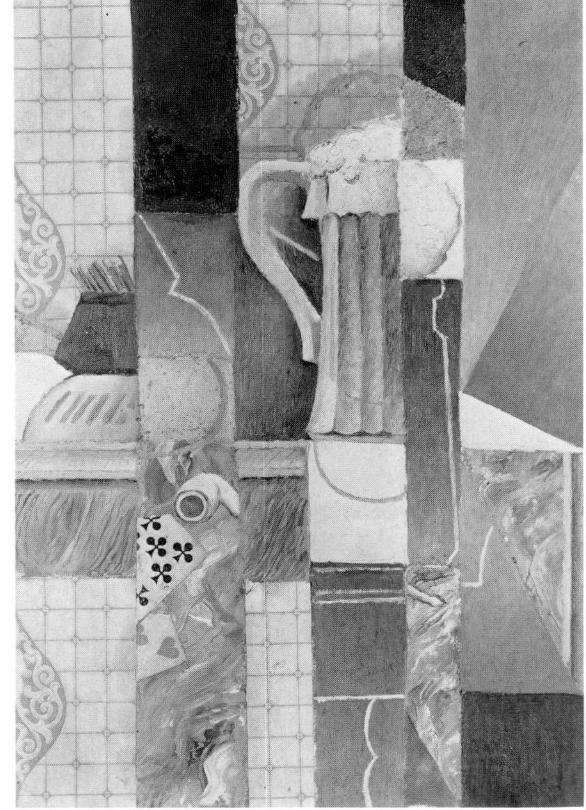

Juan Gris. *Playing Cards and Glass of Beer.* 1913. Oil on canvas with collage, 20⅝ × 14⅜ inches. The Columbus Gallery of Fine Arts, Columbus, Ohio. Ferdinand Howald Collection

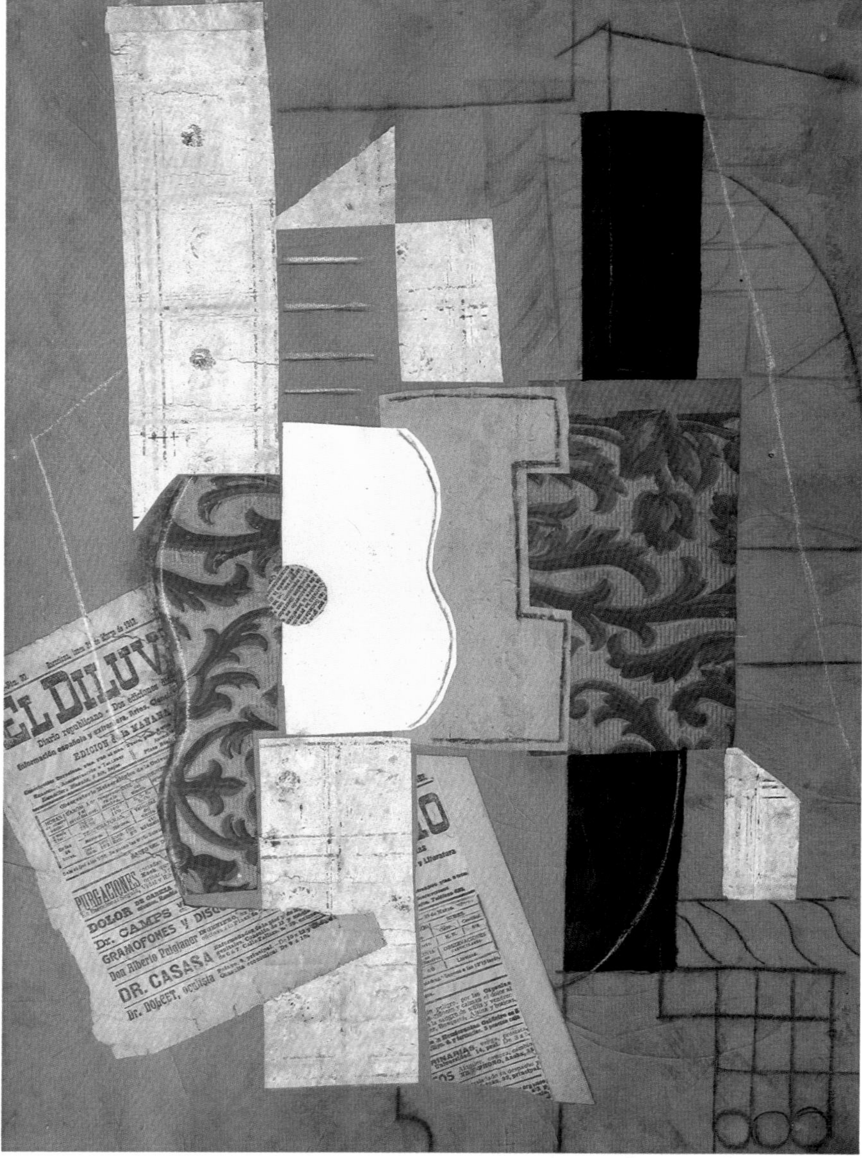

Pablo Picasso.
Guitar. 1913.
Charcoal, crayon, ink and pasted paper,
26⅛ × 19½ inches.
The Museum of Modern Art, New York. Nelson A. Rockefeller Bequest

presented; color was likewise left free and had not, as a rule, any descriptive function. From that point onward he allowed the subject matter to make its way into the picture, much as a latecomer in a crowded train finds a seat as best he can.

But just as there is usually someone who gets off the train at the next station, so Gris allowed for a give-and-take at this stage between the initial design and the nature of the subject matter. Gris by 1914 was a master organizer; there is creativity of a cool but quite special kind in the exactitude with which he would cut and trim his papers to the nearest fraction of an inch, and in the agility with which he would combine and recombine point after point of precise circumstantial detail. In the final product we see realized the dream of a world in which everything is ordered, everything is known, and everything finds expression in the clearest and most logical way. Once again, the act of looking is restructured as we realize with what a variety of lucid statement Juan Gris has presented the traditional still-life material.

Gris had made a very close study of Cubist painting as it was practiced by Picasso and Braque,

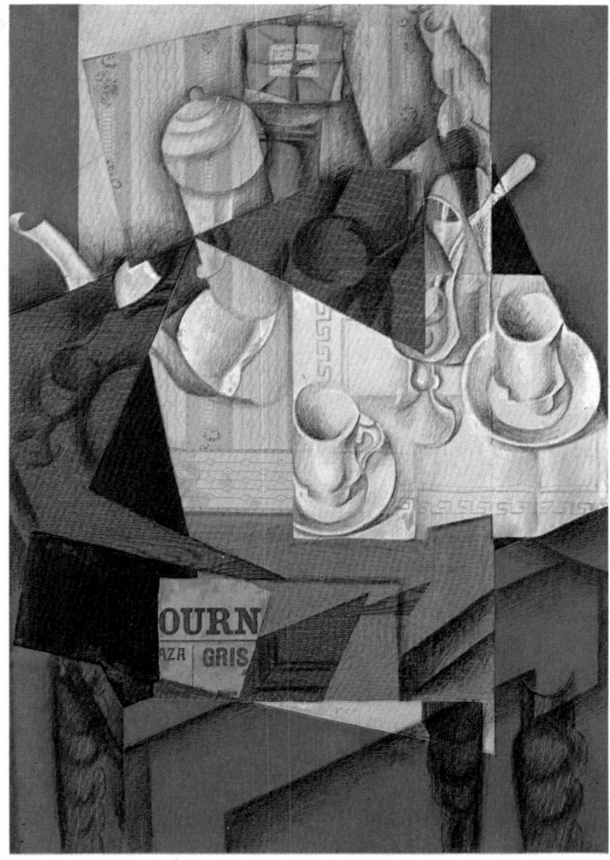

Juan Gris.
Breakfast. 1914.
Pasted paper over crayon and oil on canvas, 31⅞ × 23½ inches.
The Museum of Modern Art, New York.
Acquired through the Lillie P. Bliss Bequest

and he certainly knew the painting of 1909–10 in which Braque had introduced a *trompe-l'œil* nail in what was otherwise a purely Analytical Cubist picture. In *Violin and Engraving* Gris not only painted in a nail of this sort, but he pasted part of a real engraving into the frame in the upper right half of the picture. He also introduced Braque's favorite subject matter, the violin, while keeping to his own compositional device of building up the picture in terms of tall, vertical strips offset by sharply pointed triangular forms. In *The Man in the Café* the layout of the subject—its profile in space, in other words—was much as it is in life. But by 1913 Gris was dividing his canvas, as in *Playing Cards and Glass of Beer,* into vertical strips, within which the fragmented subject matter was allowed not only to slide up and down, as suited the composition best, but to be shown alternately in a naturalistic way and in notional form, as an outline drawn on a ground of flat color. Gris had also developed a voluptuous textural sense which delighted in the juxtaposition of many different kinds of surface, from simulated marble to the smoothness of a real playing card, and from patterned wallpaper to the rich, painterly substance of the foaming beer.

Nor is there any doubt that Gris was quite consciously defining the terms of an irreducible art, whose privileges could be neither withdrawn nor counterfeited. *"On ne truquera plus les œuvres d'art"* ("There will be no more faking of works of art") is one of the printed messages on a picture dated 1914; another pasted-paper of the same year makes a sly reference to a new law which forbade the pasting of bills on public buildings; and in case we should forget the name of the man who has brought the whole thing about, we are allowed to see just four letters of the main headline of the newspaper on the table in *Breakfast,* 1914: GRIS. What impresses in all this is the purity and coherence and consistency of Gris's ambitions and the strength of mind with which he carried them out. Psychologically his work does not have the layer upon layer of significance, and still less the ambiguity, which Picasso's never ceased to have. It would never have occurred to Gris, for instance, to combine two views of a guitar (as Picasso did in his *Guitar,* done in spring, 1913) in such a way as to make them into an emblem of a man and a woman making love; still less would he have allied this recondite image to a newspaper advertisement for "DR. CASASA, specialist in genital complaints." But there is a glorious openness and completeness about the way in which Gris had a specific idea of art and brought it to its point of maximum fulfillment.

Picasso loved the element of mischief that was inherent in the pasted-paper idiom. *Guitar* is on one level a formal statement marked by particularly strong contrasts of color and texture. It is also a storehouse of allusions, not all of them easily deciphered. Picasso has always been a master of the verbal joke that may or may not pass unnoticed, and those who can read the small print in

Guitar will find once again a wealth of sly insinuation. Even the round sound-hole of the guitar secretes a printed echo of the "lengthy ovations" which had been given to a speaker who upheld the "principles of liberty." Those principles are vindicated, in *Guitar,* by the freedom and assurance with which Picasso lays down a grand general design, on the one hand, and on the other hand pencils in such almost clandestine references as the fringed tassels which hang (bottom right) from the braided arm of a chair.

Picasso by 1914 was able to elaborate the surfaces of his pasted-paper works until the picture became a kind of total environment: an arena for wit and fancy of all kinds, in which Picasso would begin with a painted surround for the image proper, add a frame of his own invention and end with a simulated name-plate at the point where a proud collector might wish to put PICASSO in big letters. Gertrude Stein claimed later that for much of this there was a precedent in Picasso's native country: "In the shops in Barcelona instead of postcards they squared little frames and inside it [*sic*] was placed a cigar, a real one, a pipe, a bit of handkerchief, etcetera, all absolutely the arrangement of many a Cubist picture and helped out by cut paper representing other objects. That is the modern note that in Spain has been done for centuries."

As early as 1913 it was evident that the future of Cubism lay with the synthesization of objects: with the development, in other words, of a system of formal notation which would allow the painter to build a picture in terms of discrete elements and eventually to reassemble the subject matter in all its aspects. The pasted-papers did this with an effect of high-spirited sophistication; they offer us the chance of taking part in a play-structure as subtle and as complex as can be found in art. It was a structure in which the promptings of instinct could be satisfied immediately: a sharp pair of scissors, and the thing was done. Flatness was literal flatness, and obvious to all; it no longer had to be worked for, against the associations of a lifetime and several centuries of handcrafting. Gris did marvels with the enclosed world of the pasted-papers; but the system which he proposed was, even so, a finite and self-referring one. There was no room in it for the violent and unresolved emotional impulses which Picasso had often to commemorate; and no room, either, for the undertow of deep feeling which Braque could create just by laying one piece of colored paper beside another. Picasso repeatedly overran the emotional frontiers of the pasted-papers, as Gris had established them, now raiding the terrain of Expressionism, now racing ahead into what would later become the domains of Dada and Surrealism, now reinventing the whole notion of sculpture in pieces like the *Guitar* of 1912.

Picasso's earlier sculptures were conceived in traditional terms, as monolithic objects that could be seen from all sides. *Guitar* is meant to hang on the wall, like a relief, and it treats the subject matter primarily in terms of flat shapes cut out of sheet metal and allowed to overlap in a shallow space. In this way the component parts of the guitar are not so much represented as *listed,* and the final product is not so much "a sculpture," in the 19th-century sense, as (to quote William Rubin) "a sculptural painting"—and even an anticipation of such paintings as the *Guitar and Wineglass* of 1913. From the autumn of 1913 Picasso began to make relief constructions which are in effect three-dimensional extensions of the subject matter of his pasted-paper pictures. His *Still Life* is made of painted wood, and its subject matter includes a wineglass (opened down the front and flattened into the wall behind it), an open sandwich, a knife, the round table to be found in so many Cubist paintings, a fringed tablecloth with tassels, and a strip of wall complete with dado. As a sculpture it is *built,* rather than modeled. The two slices of sausage, the handle of the knife, and the dado have been particularized with Picasso's characteristic offhand wit; but the historical importance of this *Still Life* lies in the new notion of sculpture which it promulgates. Sculpture is here set free from the unity of material which had persisted even in the metal *Guitar* of 1912.

Even with so much happening, Picasso was bound to revert eventually to the heavier, slower and ultimately more consequential medium of oil paint on canvas. With Braque and Gris, he had shown that this was not the only medium in which serious pictures could be made; perhaps the time had come to carry over into the realm of oil paint the gains which had been made with collage and pasted-paper? For there is a moral quality about painting in oils. The marks on the canvas say something, in other words, about the person who makes them. The three Cubist masters knew this, and it was inevitable that they would turn back in the end to the medium in which they both challenged and continued the work of the Old Masters. What did Picasso say in 1923? "Drawing, design and color are understood and practiced in Cubism in the spirit and the manner in which they are understood and practiced in all other schools." What did Gris say in 1921? "In practice I cannot break away from the Louvre. Mine is the method of all times, the method used by the masters." As for Braque, when he was invalided out of the French Army in 1917 and set down some of his thoughts about painting, he echoed the disciplines inherent in the French classical tradition. "Nobility comes from contained emotion," he wrote; "progress in art consists not in going further but in the knowledge of art's limits."

When oil painting once again took over the responsibility for Cubism, it was in a form suggested and sanctioned by the success of the pasted-papers. It made use, that is to say, of paper-thin planes superimposed one upon the other. There was virtually no illusion of space; the forms were flattened as if with a roller. Their presentation was varied by accents of bright color which would not have been seen in Cubism before 1912, and by variations of texture which derived from pasted-paper practice and are sometimes so elaborate as to constitute, as William Rubin has pointed out, "a *trompe-l'œil* of collage." Between 1914 and 1916 Picasso was given to elucidating the position and extent of the overlapping planes with obtrusive patterning, with additions of sand to the paint and, on occasion, with verbal allusions of an esoteric sort. All these have their equivalent in the pasted-papers. Light and shadow did the rest.

This stage of Cubism was characterized by a certain evenmindedness of general effect. This was owed primarily to the ease and regularity with which the huge and readily distinguishable flat planes seem to interlock in space, sliding back and forth beneath one another without let or hindrance. It was not an idiom in which there could readily be expressed anything approaching the violence or the agitation of the *Demoiselles.* Braque was supremely at home with it, and we shall see later that Picasso in the summer of 1921 developed it still further in two festive masterpieces, versions I and II of the *Three Musicians.* But Picasso had not yet had the long experience of Diaghilev's Ballets Russes which went into the *Three Musicians;* nor was World War I the time at which to muster the all-pervading high spirits and the superabundant psychic energy which mark both variants of the work. More to the point, in the winter of 1915–16, was the gaunt figure of *Harlequin,* which Picasso set out against a void at a time of intense private emotional distress. In this painting he brought new starkness into Synthetic Cubism and reasserted, as so many times before and since, the element of the sardonic and the undeceived within his complex nature. With this life-sized figure he also took a first long stride in the direction of the epic representations of the human figure which were to abound in his paintings of the 1920s. And he went further than ever before in the systematic dislocation of the image of Harlequin—by giving us, for instance, two quite separate views of the head and by redistributing his arms, his trunk and his legs on many different levels and on planes sharply distinct from one another. In complete and obvious contrast to the sober monochrome of Analytical Cubism is the use in *Harlequin* of the whole gamut of tonal opposi-

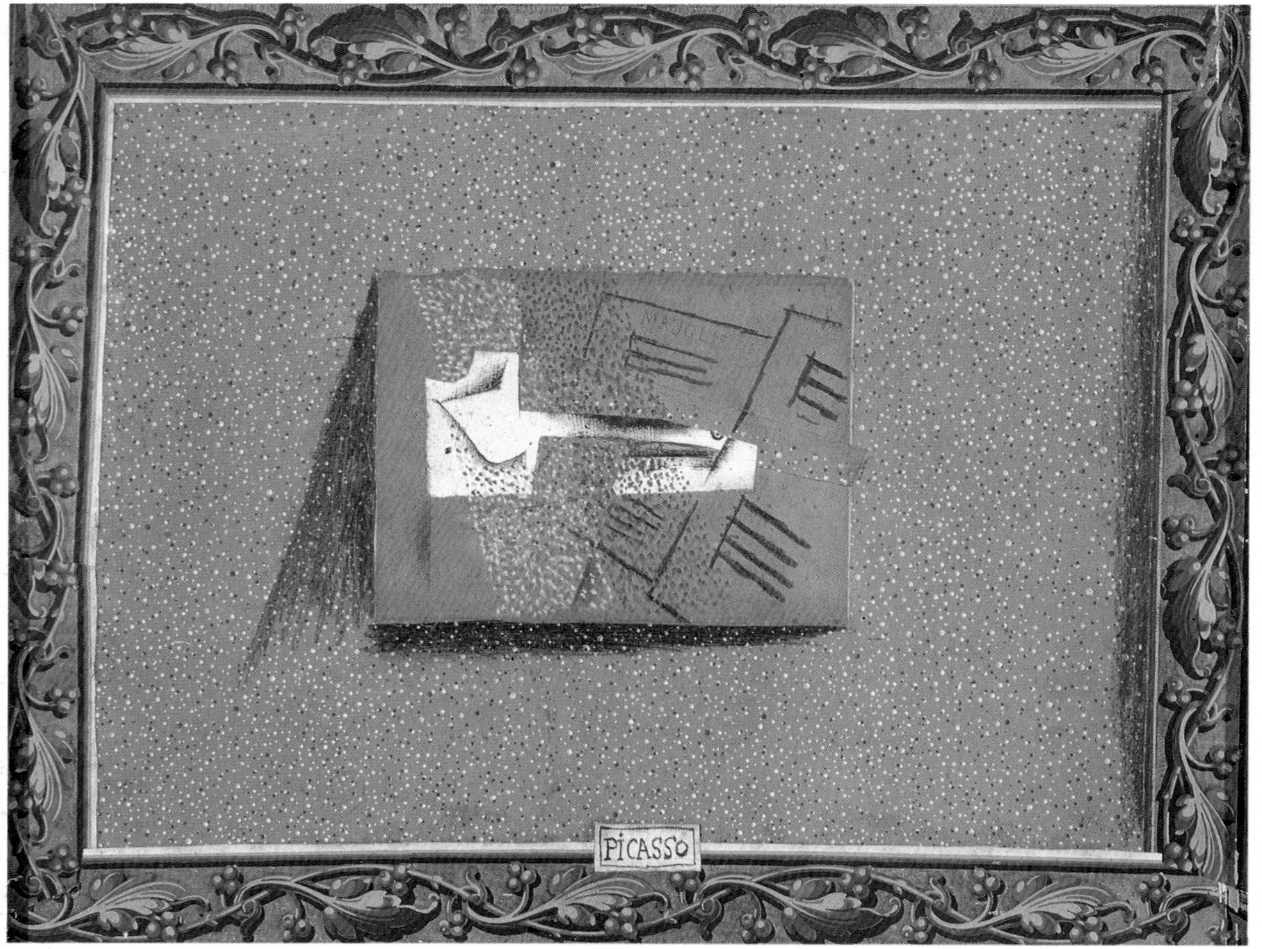

Pablo Picasso.
Pipe and Musical Score. 1914.
Pasted paper, charcoal, pencil and gouache on paper, 20¼ × 26¼ inches.
The Museum of Fine Arts, Houston.
Gift of Mr. and Mrs. S. M. McAshan, Jr.

tions, from bone-white to the deepest of blacks, and from the classic festivity and precision of Harlequin's costume to the enigma of the unfinished and barely brushed-in rectangular form—a playbill, perhaps, or a sheet of music—which he holds in his left hand.

I have in this chapter treated Cubism as the creation of three men only, and it is true that Picasso, Braque and Gris must jointly share the credit for what now seems to us one of the supreme moments in the history of art. But it is only fair to add that although Fernand Léger was not one of the founding fathers of Cubism, he was very much around at the time when Cubism came to fulfillment. With his tusky and thoroughgoing nature, he touched nothing that he did not in some way augment; and from 1907 onward he had something to say that was always relevant to the general direction of French painting. He was deeply impressed, for instance, by the Cézanne memorial exhibition of 1907. In no way an opportunist, he took a long time to adjust to the experience; but eventually, as in *Table and Fruit,* he began to work toward an emphatic personal statement of what it means to site fully realized forms in space. At this point he virtually abandoned color, the better to concentrate on the definition of form. In 1911 Léger showed at the Paris Salon a painting called *Nudes in a Landscape.* Unlike the masterpieces of Picasso and Braque, which were either addressed to a small gallery-public or never shown at all, this was a head-on confrontation with the big middlebrow public of the Salon. On that occasion, as on many others, Léger said what he had to say and didn't care who disliked it.

In 1913 he painted a series of pictures which

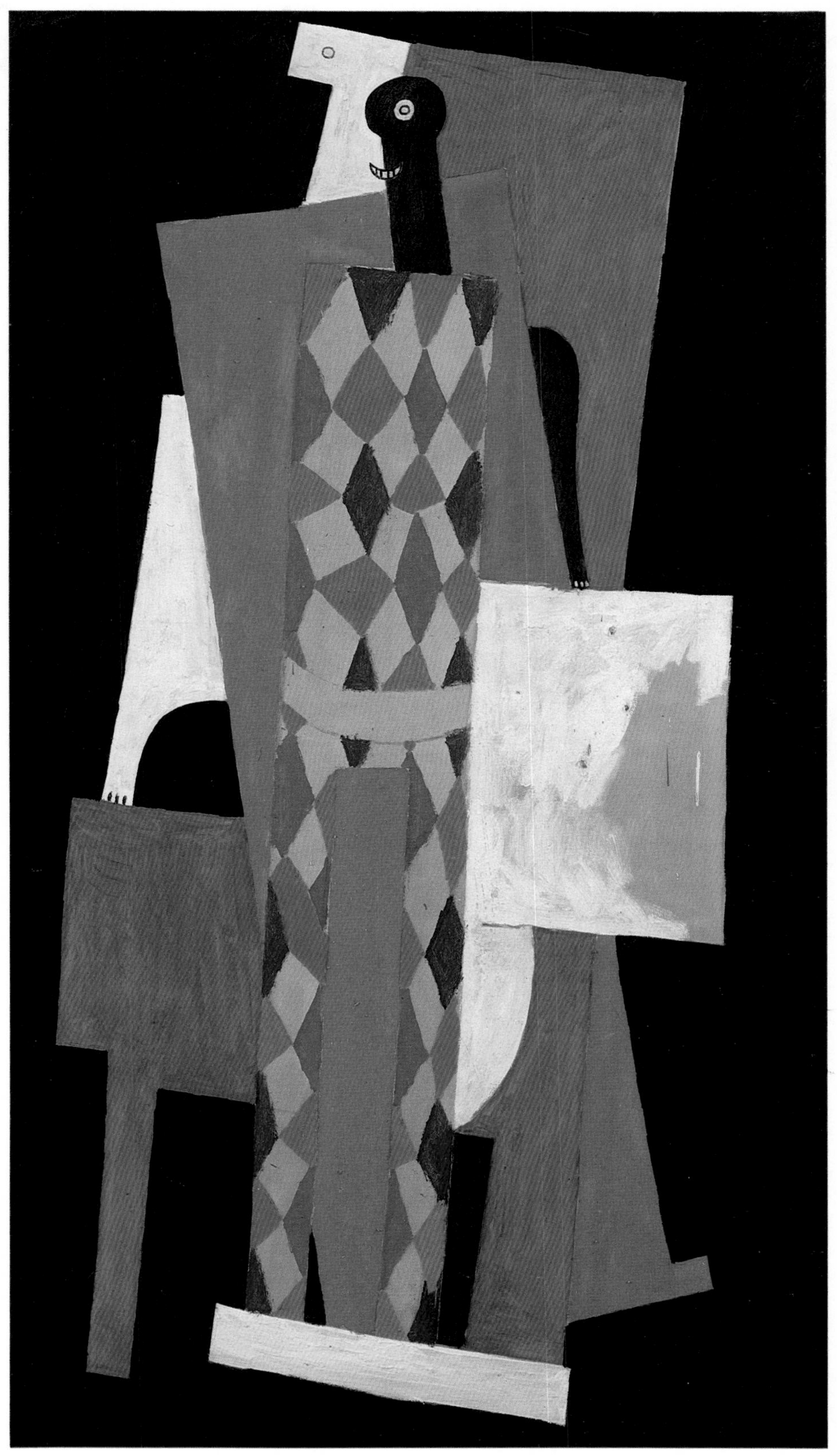

Pablo Picasso.
Harlequin. 1915.
Oil on canvas,
6 feet ¼ inch ×
41⅜ inches.
The Museum of
Modern Art, New
York.
Acquired through
the Lillie P. Bliss
Bequest

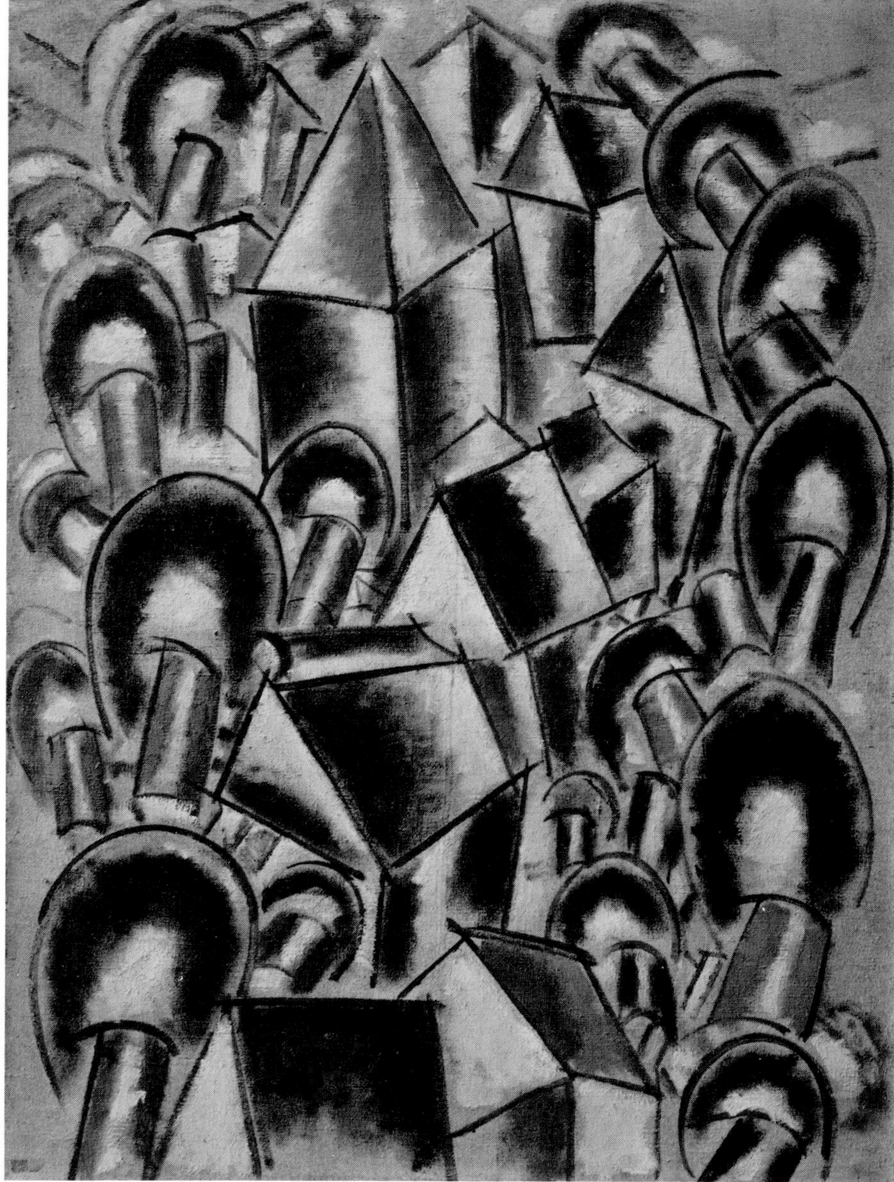

Fernand Léger.
Village in the Forest. 1914.
Oil on canvas,
52 × 38¾ inches.
Kunstmuseum, Basel

were exactly what their generic title suggests: contrasts of forms. The contrasts in question were as direct as possible—flat shapes set off by forms which were like sections cut from a drum. Léger drew them in outline with the unequivocal black line which was the mark of his open and candid nature; and he colored them with bright reds, blues and yellows. Léger prided himself on the punch which was packed by these alliances of simplified forms; but in a matter of months he decided to return to declarative statements which involved the traditional subject matter of French painting. Léger in *Village in the Forest* took a subject not unlike that of Braque's *La Roche-Guyon: The Château.* Braque muted the contrast between architecture and landscape and retained something of the feathery lightness with which Corot rendered nature in that same part of France. Léger, by contrast, gave an emphatic solidity to trees and houses alike, reducing the tree trunks to cylinders blocked out in a military red, foliage to a uniform, dark-shadowed egg shape,

Georges Braque.
La Roche-Guyon: The Château. 1909.
Oil on canvas, 31¾ × 23⅝ inches.
Moderna Museet, Stockholm

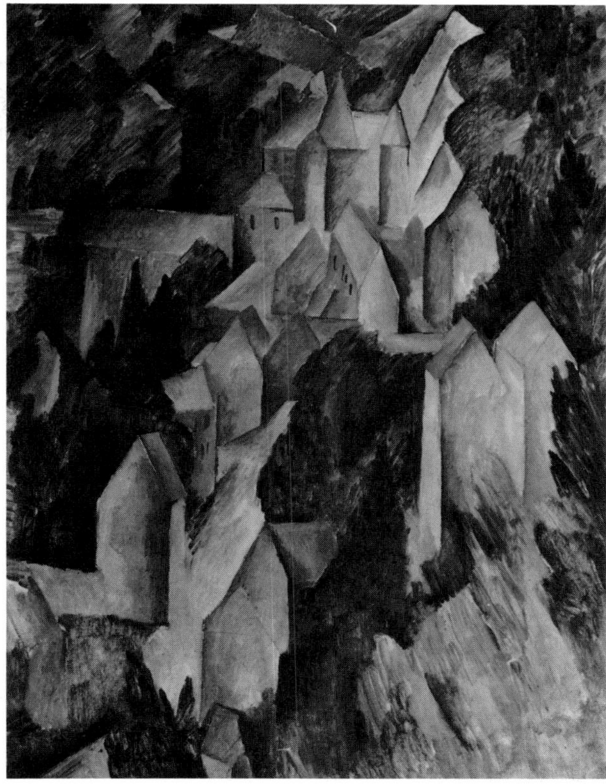

and houses to windowless canisters drawn in with an unwavering straight black line. The painting is as much a "contrast of forms" as any one of the paintings which actually bear that name, but the contrasts are tied to everyday reality.

Cubism as a joint effort came to an end with the outbreak of World War I in August, 1914. It was never reintegrated. The friendship between Picasso and Braque had been too intense, and had been lived through at too great an imaginative pressure, to be taken up again like a friendly game of chess. Phases in life cannot be relived, and when Braque came back from being trepanned in a military hospital his once-great strength had been diminished forever. But in his work of 1918–19 he produced what is in effect an elegy—and one of the most poignant things of its kind—for the lost oneness of the Cubist effort.

It was after a long and slow convalescence that Braque returned to painting toward the end of World War I. In *Café-Bar* 1919, he applied the methods of Synthetic or "late" Cubism to subject matter derived from popular life. The overlapping, flat planes defy conventional perspective and put us within touching distance of the basic elements of French café-life: the guitar, the sheet music, the white clay pipe on the table, the fruit in its dish, the diamond-patterned floor, the sharp-toothed decorative surround of door and window, the dado, the speckled wallpaper, the folded newspaper, the windowpane with its sprawly, outmoded lettering and the unpainted, rough-grained wood of the table. The lettering suggests that we are looking in from the street; but in reality we are neither inside nor out, but "in touch" with the scene in all its aspects. In its detail, the picture recalls the Cubist works of before 1914, with their stenciled letters and scraps of real newspaper; but in the majesty of its proportions, in the fullness and richness of its color, and in its ambitious and equivocal exploration of space, *Café-Bar* looks forward to the symphonic interiors of 1939–55 which were to be the crowning glory of Braque's long career.

Picasso likewise produced, at the very end of the decade, at least one major work in which the preoccupations of the previous ten years were given monumental and, in one way or another, definitive expression. The point of *Guitar,* 1919, lies not so much in the guitar, painted on torn paper, which is attached to the canvas by two real and all but invisible pins, as in the tall, thin diamond which lies behind it. William Rubin argued in 1972 that the subject of the picture is not "a guitar," but a guitarist. The diamond-shape represents, in other words, an immensely simplified human figure, with just one or two very discreet clues as to its pose and location. Thus read, the picture would constitute a late if not final contribution to Cubist iconography. The use of a paper nail with a simulated shadow at the top of the guitar is an echo, also, of the ways in which nails were used in Cubist painting to point the difference between depicted reality and "the real thing." Picasso in 1919 was able to use both of them simultaneously and in the same context.

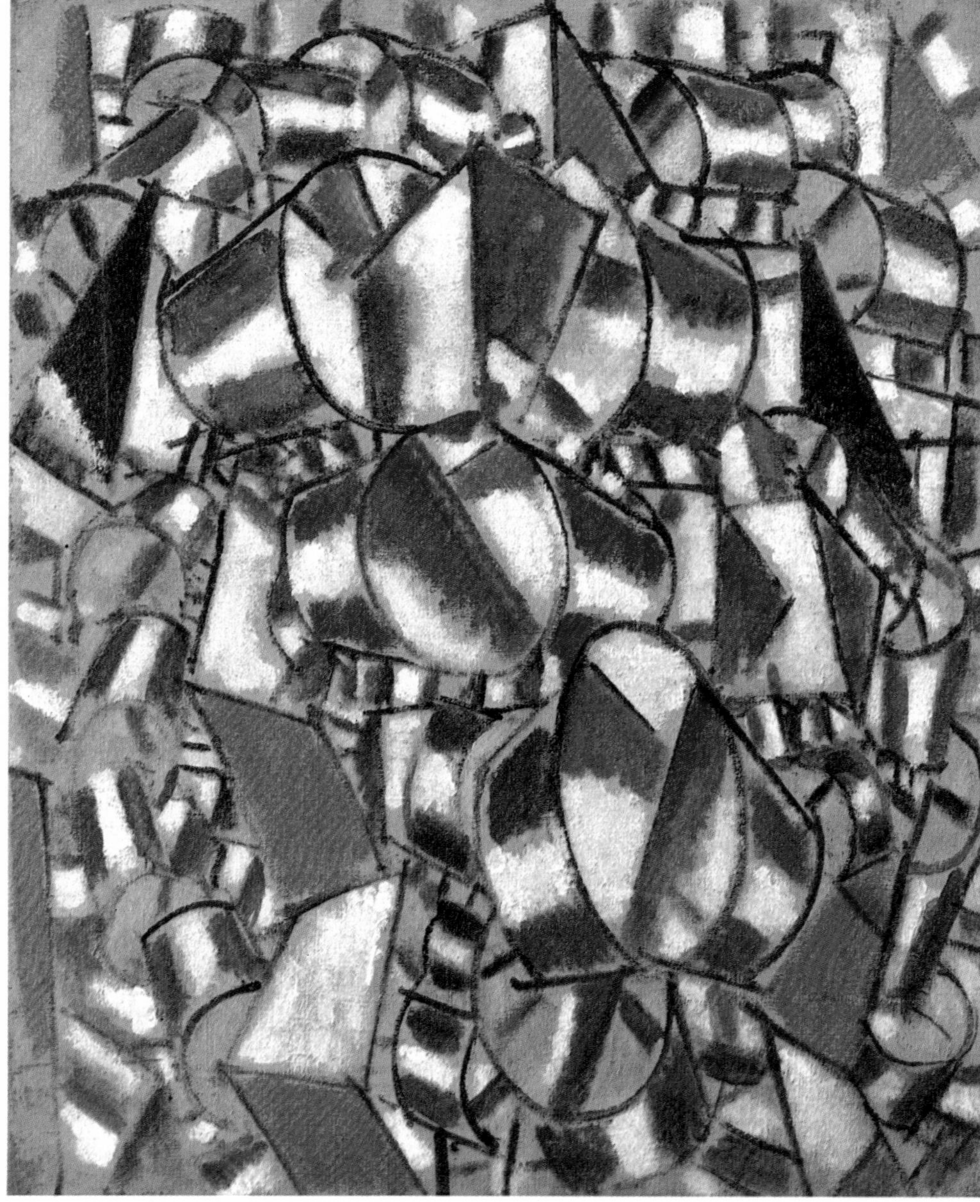

Fernand Léger.
Contrast of Forms.
1913.
Oil on canvas,
39½ × 32 inches.
The Museum of Modern Art, New York.
Philip L. Goodwin Collection

Picasso and Braque had not set out with any specific program in mind, and Picasso in 1923 rejected the idea of research in art with words which soon became famous: "To search is meaningless, in painting. To *find*—that is the thing." It will be clear by the end of this book that a very large proportion of what is best in this century's art has been predicated in one way or another on what Picasso and Braque "found" between 1907 and 1914. They had liquidated, one by one, the problems which had been left unsolved at the time of the death of Cézanne in 1906. They had given altogether new answers to the question, "What can a picture be?" They kept alive the idea of the masterpiece and on many occasions lived up to it. In 1914 their careers had still a long way to go, in that they were still giving new resonance to the idea of Cubism in the late 1940s and '50s; but it could be said that by the end of that fateful year there was already in existence what the art historian Edward Fry has rightly called the "greatest single aesthetic achievement of this century."

Georges Braque.
Café-Bar. 1919.
Oil on canvas,
64 × 32¾ inches.
Kunstmuseum, Basel

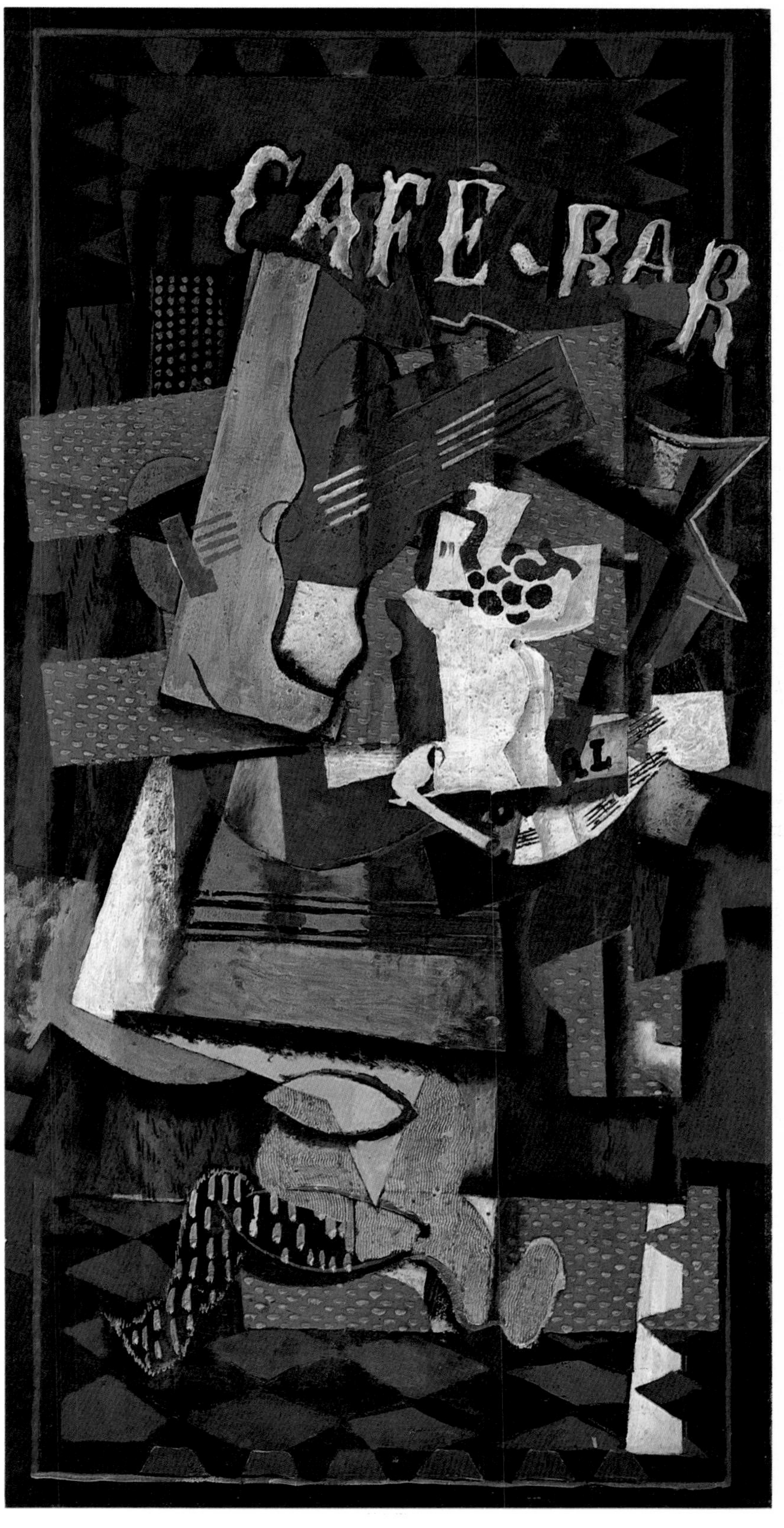

THE COSMOPOLITAN EYE

Shortly before 1914 modern art began to matter, all over Europe, in ways in which it had never mattered before.

No one date, no one place, no one name can be brought forward as proof of this; but there came about a general awareness that there was such a thing as a modern sensibility, and that that sensibility had the key to modern life. People were learning to live with the fact—well put by Fernand Léger in the summer of 1913—that "the modern conception of art is the total expression of a new generation, whose condition it shares and to whose aspirations it responds."

To be modern, in this sense, was to take due note of all the changes which were being brought about in the conditions of life. It involved an acceptance of the elements of the unconscious and the irrational in human affairs. It meant overturning the tyranny of high art and high culture, and realizing that great art was just as likely to arise from close scrutiny of other areas of human activity. It meant looking at the art of other times and other peoples than those of Athens and Florence, Venice and Rome. It meant believing, with Léger again, that a billboard stuck up in the middle of a field could enrich the landscape and not desecrate it. It meant accepting the airplane and the telephone and the steel-framed building as instruments of liberation. It meant seeing our human inheritance as a whole, without fear or prejudice.

Life in those years was dipped in the dyes of the new. After 1900, when Sigmund Freud published his *Interpretation of Dreams,* the role of the unconscious was bound to come sooner or later into the forefront of art. Between 1893 and 1914 museums in Leipzig, Brussels, Cologne, Stockholm, Paris, Frankfurt, Basel and Essen installed permanent exhibitions of primitive art. In each case a whole new vocabulary was made available to young artists. In 1910 Henri Matisse was one of many attentive visitors to the great exhibition of Islamic art in Munich. The Italian Futurist Umberto Boccioni spoke for a whole generation when he wrote in his diary in 1907 that "I want to paint

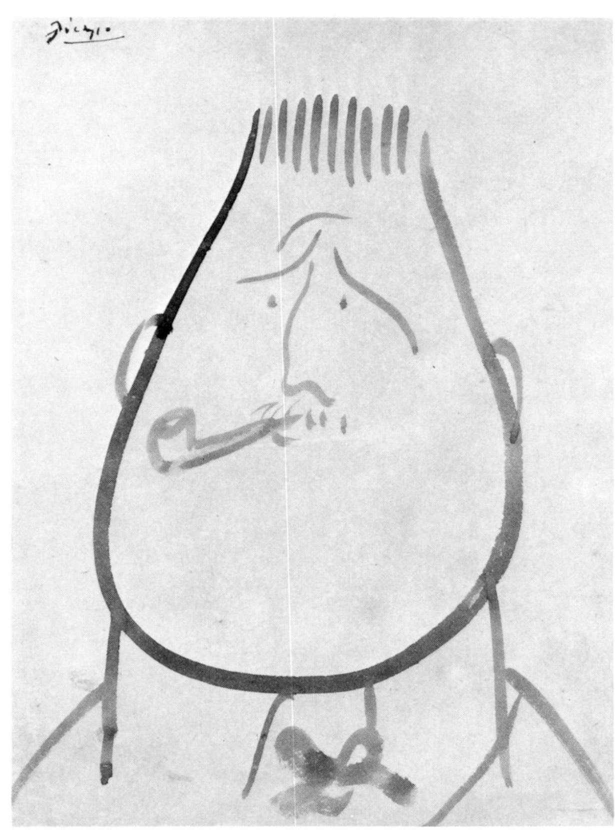

Pablo Picasso. *Portrait of Apollinaire.* 1905. Ink and wash, 12½ × 9¼ inches. Private collection, Washington

the new, the fruits of our industrial age. Old walls and old palaces, old motifs and old memories nauseate me. Our feverish era makes yesterday's productions obsolete and useless." The skirl and thump of Stravinsky's *The Rite of Spring* spoke in 1913 for elemental forces too long excluded from art. Radical changes were imminent—changes as radical as those set out in the Special Theory of Relativity, which Einstein had published in 1905, or in Rutherford's experiments with the atom in the years that followed.

News of these changes was carried, where art was concerned, by word of mouth, by the magazines, by one or two farsighted dealers and collectors, and by the huge conglomerate exhibitions in Paris, Berlin, London, Cologne, Munich and elsewhere, which operated before 1914 as a pacific International: a collective force which broke down national barriers, argued for a new openness of spirit, and exemplified a superabundant curiosity as to what was being done, anywhere and everywhere, in the name of the new. By 1913, when New York had a first taste of it, that pacific International had made itself felt all over Europe as the free expression of a genuinely modern sensibility.

The poet Guillaume Apollinaire (1880–1918) was, as much as anyone, the epitome of that sensibility. He had a position peculiar to himself, in that unlike most of the people who write or lecture about art he was in his own right a man of genius. In his poetry he made sense of modern life in a completely new way. Endowed with a lyrical gift of the rarest, most irresistible sort, he gave the new century the new tone for which it had been waiting; and his fragmented, unpunctuated, free-associating manner of speech became one of the basic elements in the creative practice of the 20th century. The closing section of *The Waste Land* could not have been written if T. S. Eliot had not read Apollinaire; Apollinaire stood, equally, as godfather to the best lyrics of Cole Porter and to the verbal agility which made the Beatles' song "Lucy in the Sky with Diamonds" so great a success in the late 1960s. It is well over 50 years since his two books of poems, *Alcools* and *Calligrammes,* were published; yet the poems still come across in a direct and confidential way which convinces us that Apollinaire is telling us the truth, without reserve or humbug.

In life, Apollinaire was never the high-collared Great Man. He was the involved, vulnerable, supremely human individual who got into scrapes because of the openhearted and guileless nature which made him everyone's favorite companion. When he was in love, he was unsuccessful as often as not. When society needed a scapegoat—as happened when two little statues were stolen from the Louvre—it was Apollinaire, the archetypal innocent, who was jailed on suspicion of the theft. Life made things difficult for him from the moment that he was born in Rome in 1880 of a young unmarried Polish lady and a well-connected but ne'er-do-well Italian officer, already in his middle 40s, who not long afterward disowned the relationship.

Reared first in Rome, then in Monte Carlo, and later in one or another of the towns by the Mediterranean where his mother hoped to find a protector, Apollinaire in first youth took the whole of Europe for his birthright. A natural cosmopolitan, he looked at every new place, every new book and every new person in terms of a potential adventure. If he found Nick Carter and Buffalo Bill more stimulating than Milton's *Paradise Lost*, he came straight out and said so. He was spontaneity personified: "Almost all my poems have been printed as they were first written down," he wrote to a friend in 1913. He was a natural identifier, and never happier than when instinct signaled to him —in a book or a picture or a human being—a genuine life force, or a perfection not paralleled elsewhere.

All this was invaluable to him when he was introduced to Picasso in 1904. From that day onward he saw more and more of painting and painters. From 1905 until his death in 1918, he spoke up in defense of just about everyone who was going to last on the European art scene. What he said was often rather silly; but there is no denying the record, which is that he was right in there in defense of Picasso (1905), Matisse (1907), Braque (1908), the Douanier Rousseau (1910), Robert Delaunay (1911), Kandinsky, Duchamp, Picabia, Gris and the Italian Futurists (1912), Chagall and Mondrian (1913), Larionov, Gontcharova and de Chirico (1914). Not all of them needed him; I have heard one protégé of Apollinaire say that he would write anything to fill up a page, and another that he could not tell Rubens from Rembrandt. But once again the record speaks for itself. Who introduced Picasso to Braque? Apollinaire. Who worked hardest to make Cubism acceptable to the general public? Apollinaire. Who was at the top of the visiting list for every informed foreigner who came to Paris? Apollinaire. The illustrated books on which Apollinaire worked with Derain in 1909 and with Dufy in 1911 are classics of their kind. Apollinaire gave Orphism its name in 1913. From February, 1912, onward he edited *Les Soirées de Paris,* as brilliant a review of art and literature as has ever existed. When he and Delaunay went to Germany in 1913 he made an unforgettable impression on the young Max Ernst. In 1917 he invented the word "Surrealism." When he got married in 1918 Picasso was a witness at the ceremony; and nothing in Picasso's work bespeaks a more heartfelt affection than the long series of portrait drawings of Apollinaire—Apollinaire plain, Apollinaire fantasized, Apollinaire in health and strength, and Apollinaire with the head wound he sustained as a willing soldier in 1916. Apollinaire was not always right about art—who ever was?—but one of the greatest periods of European art bears the mark of his passage over and over again.

He did more for art and for artists than just write about them. The conditions of his life had made him the most adroit of persuaders—who else has had a plaque put up in his honor on the wall of a hotel which he left without paying the bill?—and he never begrudged time spent on behalf of the new. When the minor or auxiliary Cubists (among them Gleizes, Metzinger, Delaunay, Léger and Le Fauconnier) determined to show together at the Salon des Indépendants in April, 1911, it was Apollinaire who acted as their champion. When they were invited to Brussels, again as a group, two months later, it was Apollinaire who prefaced the catalogue. What he said was not all true, but it did very clearly indicate what Gleizes, for one, was aiming to do. He was getting ready, Apollinaire said, to tackle "the vast subjects which yesterday's painters in their timidity had never dared to wrest from the presumptuous, outdated and tedious daubers of the official Salons." Today we know that "vast subjects" played no part in Cubist painting as it was brought to perfection by Picasso, Braque and Gris. Their subject matter was limited, concise, and most often emotionally neutral. Apollinaire unwittingly let slip the fact that Gleizes and Metzinger had no idea of what Cubism was really about and were using it simply as a way of giving a look of modernity to undertakings which funda-

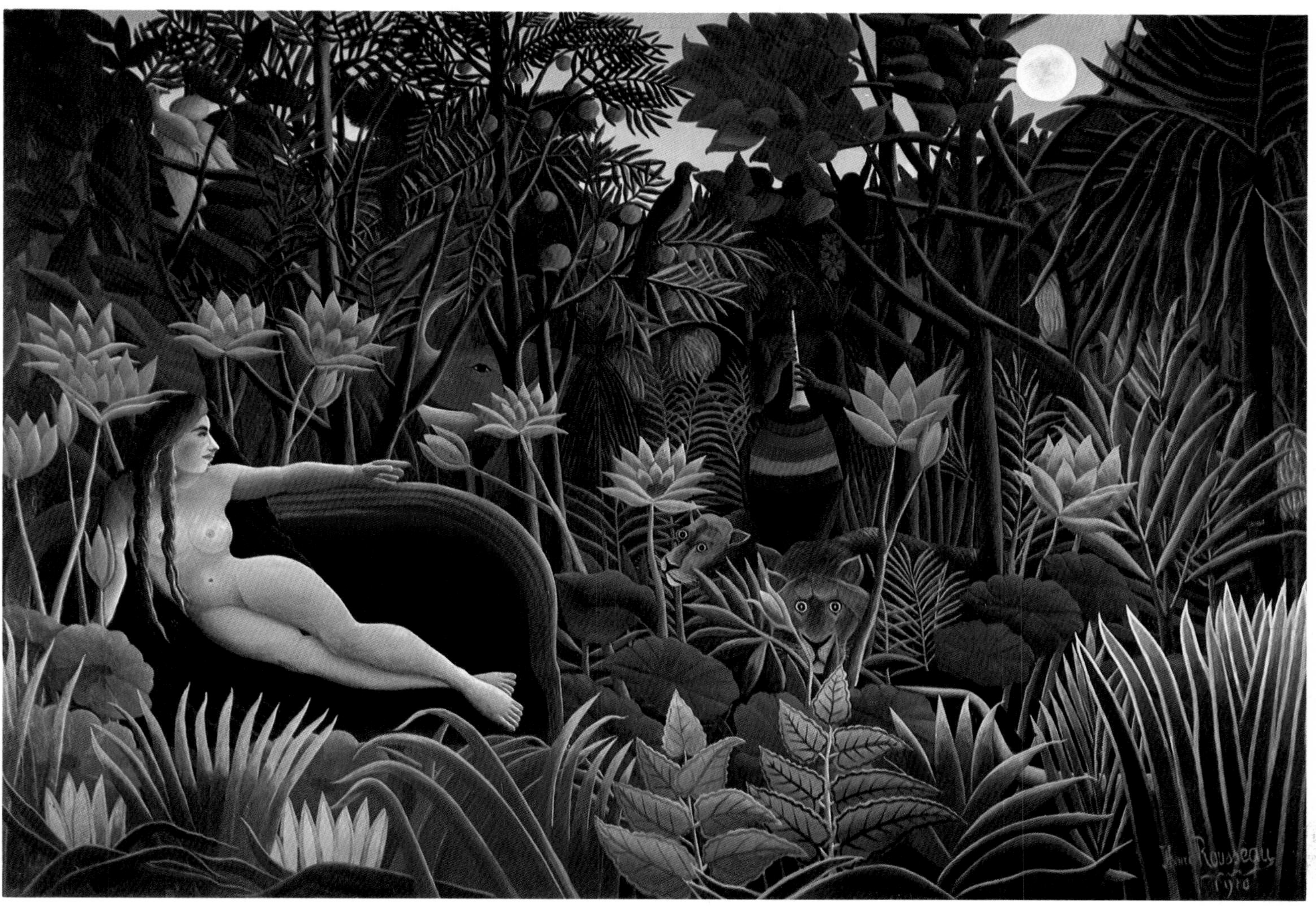

Henri Rousseau. *The Dream.* 1910. Oil on canvas, 6 feet 8½ inches × 9 feet 9½ inches. The Museum of Modern Art, New York. Gift of Nelson A. Rockefeller

mentally were pedestrian and conventional. When we have read his preface we see at once why Gleizes's huge *Harvest Threshing* had ended up looking like a Salon picture with the fidgets.

Sometimes Apollinaire was oddly slow off the mark. Henri Rousseau was, for instance, so fundamental to the evolution of a modern sensibility that Apollinaire might have been expected to get the point of him at once. (Rousseau's nickname, "le Douanier," was a friendly exaggeration, insofar as he was not a customs officer but simply a minor official—from 1871 to 1885—in the Paris municipal toll service.) A great part of European Surrealism is foreshadowed in Rousseau's matter-of-fact notation of the most startling and incongruous of images. There was nothing merely quaint or folksy, moreover, about Rousseau's handling of landscape; Picasso profited by his fearless conceptual approach in the paintings which he made in the autumn of 1908, and by 1909 it was common ground with many serious artists that Rousseau personified that clear break with conventional, "educated" painting which was an important element in the modern sensibility.

Apollinaire wrote in 1908 that Rousseau "does not know either what he wants or where he is going. . . . He should have stayed an artisan." However, in 1909 he came to know Rousseau well, and sat for him for his portrait. From his friend Delaunay, and doubtless from Picasso too, he learned that Rousseau was a key figure in living art. When

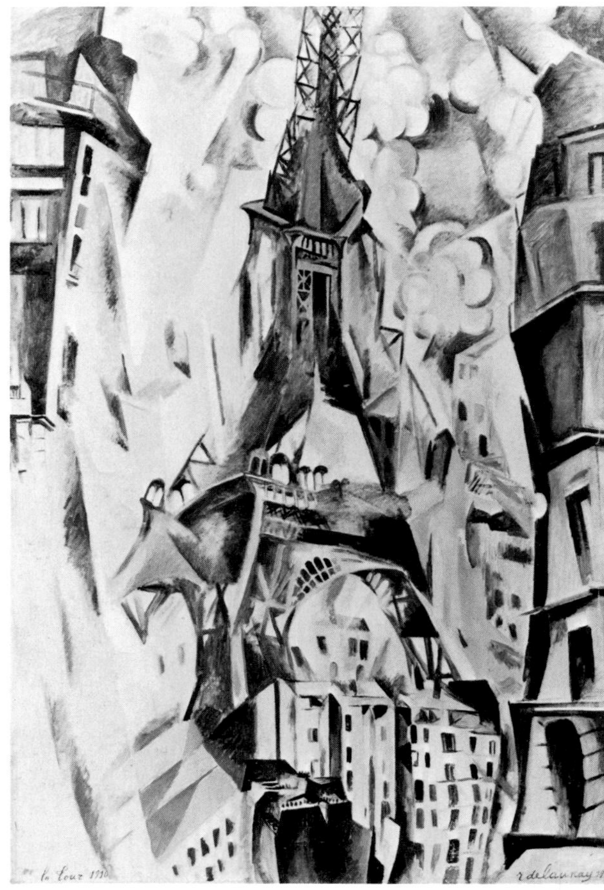

Robert Delaunay.
The Eiffel Tower.
1910.
Oil on canvas,
6 feet 7¾ inches × 54⅝ inches.
The Solomon R. Guggenheim Museum, New York

Rousseau showed *The Dream* in 1910, Apollinaire seized the chance not only to make amends on his own account but to emphasize that Rousseau had just about every good artist in Paris behind him. Here is his classic account of *The Dream:* "On an 1830-style sofa, a naked woman is asleep. All around her is a tropical forest swarming with monkeys and birds of paradise. A lion and a lioness pass calmly by, while a mysterious Negro plays on his pipe. No one can deny that this is a very beautiful painting. . . . This year nobody, I think, will dare to laugh at Rousseau. . . . Ask the painters. They are unanimous in their admiration. They admire everything in *The Dream,* let me tell you—yes, even the Louis-Philippe sofa lost in the primeval forest—and they are right."

The Dream was in point of fact the continuation of something that predated *The Interpretation of Dreams.* Already in the 1890s art had tackled the secret life of the unconscious. Gauguin for one, and Rousseau for another, had shown how sleep brings us face to face with fears and temptations and repressed wishes which we prefer not to acknowledge in our waking lives. In Gauguin's *Loss of Virginity* the young girl is innocence personified, in waking terms, and a sacred circle of fire is there to protect her; but that does not prevent the fox, symbol of insidious sexuality, from laying his paw on her breast while she is sleeping. (Nor does it prevent her from giving him the most trustful of welcomes.) In Rousseau's *The Sleeping Gypsy* the conventional patterns of savagery, fear and danger are suspended; the dream takes precedence over the conditions of everyday and a strange immunity envelops the sleeping woman.

"I, too, am a painter" was one of Apollinaire's working titles for his *Calligrammes;* and although it was not true in any literal sense, there was nothing that he liked better than to identify with his friends' intentions. Not all of them encouraged this—it is very unlikely that either Picasso or Braque confided in Apollinaire during the great years of Cubism—but Apollinaire found that Delaunay, for one, was delighted to do so. He was close to the Delaunays—he moved in with them for two months in the fall of 1912, at a time of intense private distress for himself, and he spent the summer of 1913 with them in a house party which also included Marc Chagall, the poet Blaise Cendrars, and the American painter Patrick Henry Bruce—and it must have been of Delaunay that he was thinking when he wrote in the winter of 1911–12 that "the secret ambition of the advanced young painters is to create a form of pure painting. This completely new kind of plastic expression is still in its infancy and is not yet as abstract as it aspires to be."

The new painting had nothing to do with the Cubism of Picasso, Braque and Gris, which was fundamentally a down-to-earth activity; but it did make sense in the context of the evolution of Delaunay, with which Apollinaire was intimately familiar. Delaunay in 1909 had been deeply in-

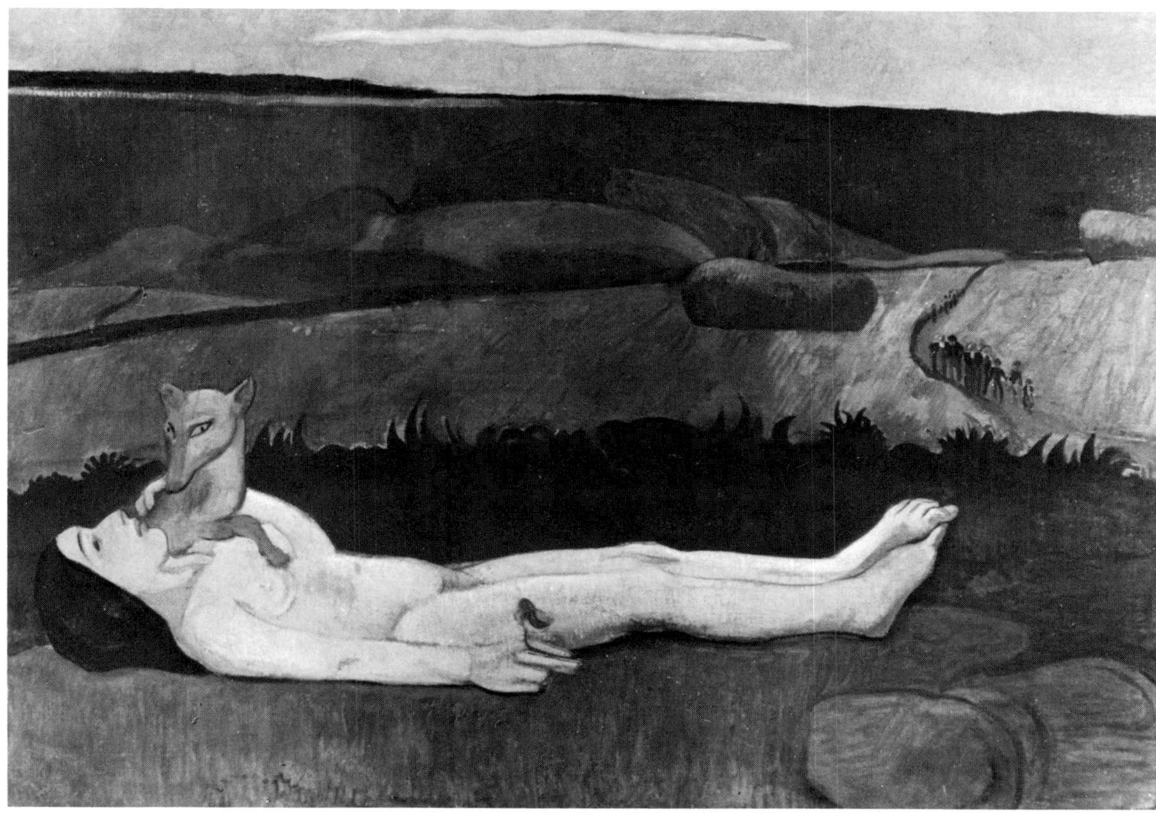

Paul Gauguin.
The Loss of Virginity. 1890–91.
Oil on canvas, 34 × 50 inches.
Chrysler Museum at Norfolk, Virginia.
Gift of Walter P. Chrysler, Jr.

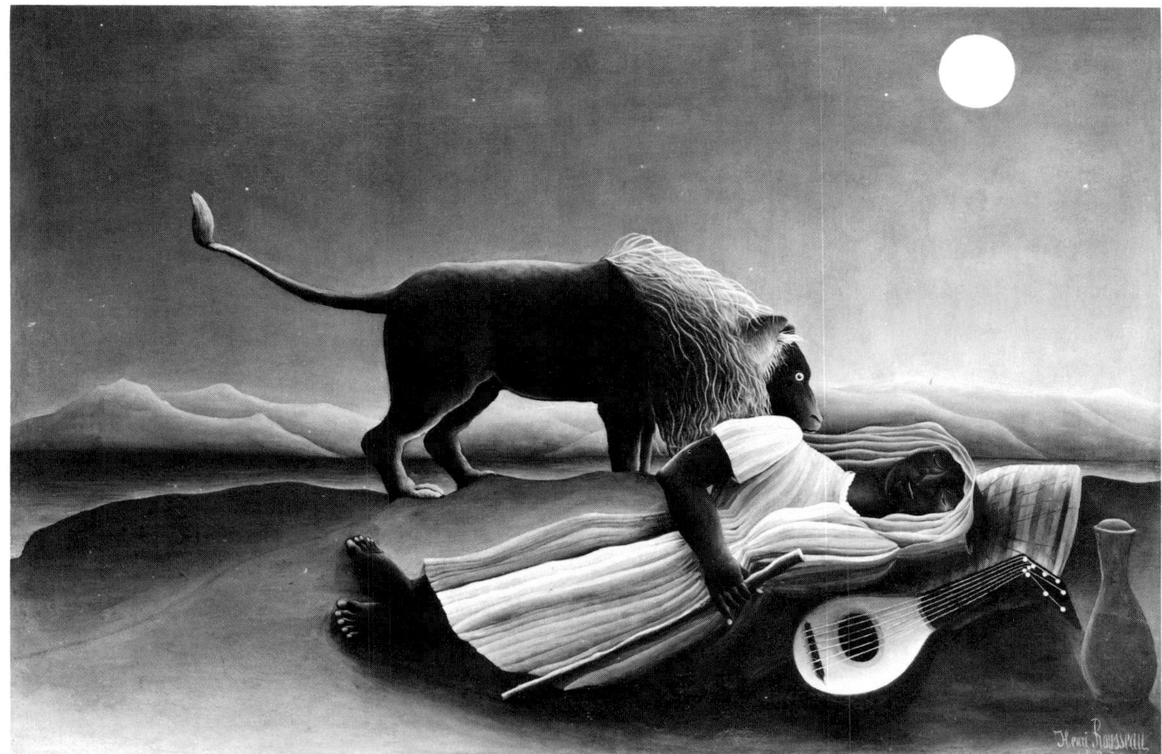

Henri Rousseau.
The Sleeping Gypsy. 1897.
Oil on canvas, 51 inches × 6 feet 7 inches.
The Museum of Modern Art, New York.
Gift of Mrs. Simon Guggenheim

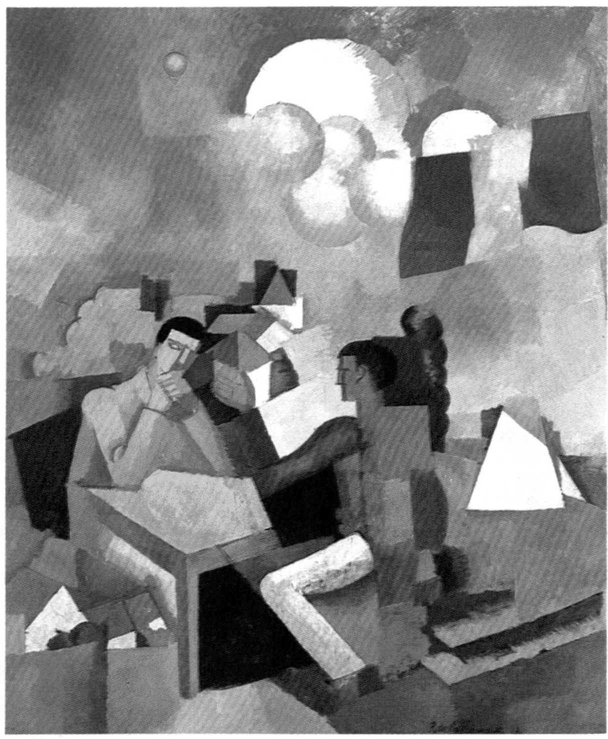

Roger de La Fresnaye. *The Conquest of the Air.* 1913. Oil on canvas, 7 feet 8⅞ inches × 6 feet 5 inches. The Museum of Modern Art, New York. Mrs. Simon Guggenheim Fund

fluenced by Cézanne, but like his friend Léger he wanted to get more of the throb and bluster of modern life into his work than Cézanne had ever aimed for. In fact he was altogether too boisterous, in 1910–11, to keep in line with the principles of pure Cubism: "But they're painting with *cobwebs*, these people!" was his first reaction when he saw Cubist paintings by Picasso and Braque which were virtually monochromatic. He liked strong contrasts of color and spectacular dislocations of form; and—above all in the Eiffel Tower series—he liked subject matter which had alrady an epic resonance.

He was not alone in this. For Roger de La Fresnaye, likewise, the world in 1913 was a place in which all changes were for the better—and the invention of the airplane, for instance, was something from which nothing but good could come. (La Fresnaye had, admittedly, a special reason to believe this, in that his brother was director of a firm which manufactured airplanes.) The airplane stood for a definitive triumph over gravity; and that in its turn stood—or so it then seemed—for a new freedom from stress and anxiety. *The Conquest of the Air* is the complete expression of all this; it was a great favorite of Apollinaire.

Like many artists who fall just short of greatness, Robert Delaunay was not at all shy of making big claims for himself later in life. "We, the first Cubists" was one phrase in his notebooks, and he also felt that he had a great impact on Expressionism, on films like *The Cabinet of Dr. Caligari* (1919), and on postrevolutionary Russian theater. But where he did undeniably exert an influence was with the series of paintings which was made during the period of his closest friendship with Apollinaire. These were what Apollinaire called his Orphic paintings, and they were begun at Louveciennes, on the outskirts of Paris, in the first half of 1913. Delaunay had always hoped to effect the free interaction of color, and he felt that the Cubist system of interlocking planes was as injurious to this free interaction as was the niggly microscopic structuring of pointillist painting. He wanted to banish Cubist faceting, and he also wanted to banish the gradations of color which had previously facilitated a smooth transition from one color area to another. Finally he decided that color was best handled in the form of round, unmodulated discs of pure color, initially prompted by celestial bodies but now freed from all figurative intention.

Delaunay's work had had since 1909 a direct emotional vibration which was independent of any systematic intellectual structuring and made it particularly attractive to painters in other countries. Perhaps some of them sensed—especially in Germany—that of all the French painters he was the most likely to lift off into the kind of pure painting, unballasted by any figurative concerns, which seemed likely on philosophico-mystical grounds to turn up sooner or later. Certainly Delaunay was courted from 1911 onward by the small group of Russo-German painters in Munich who had just decided to band together under the name of Der Blaue Reiter (The Blue Rider).

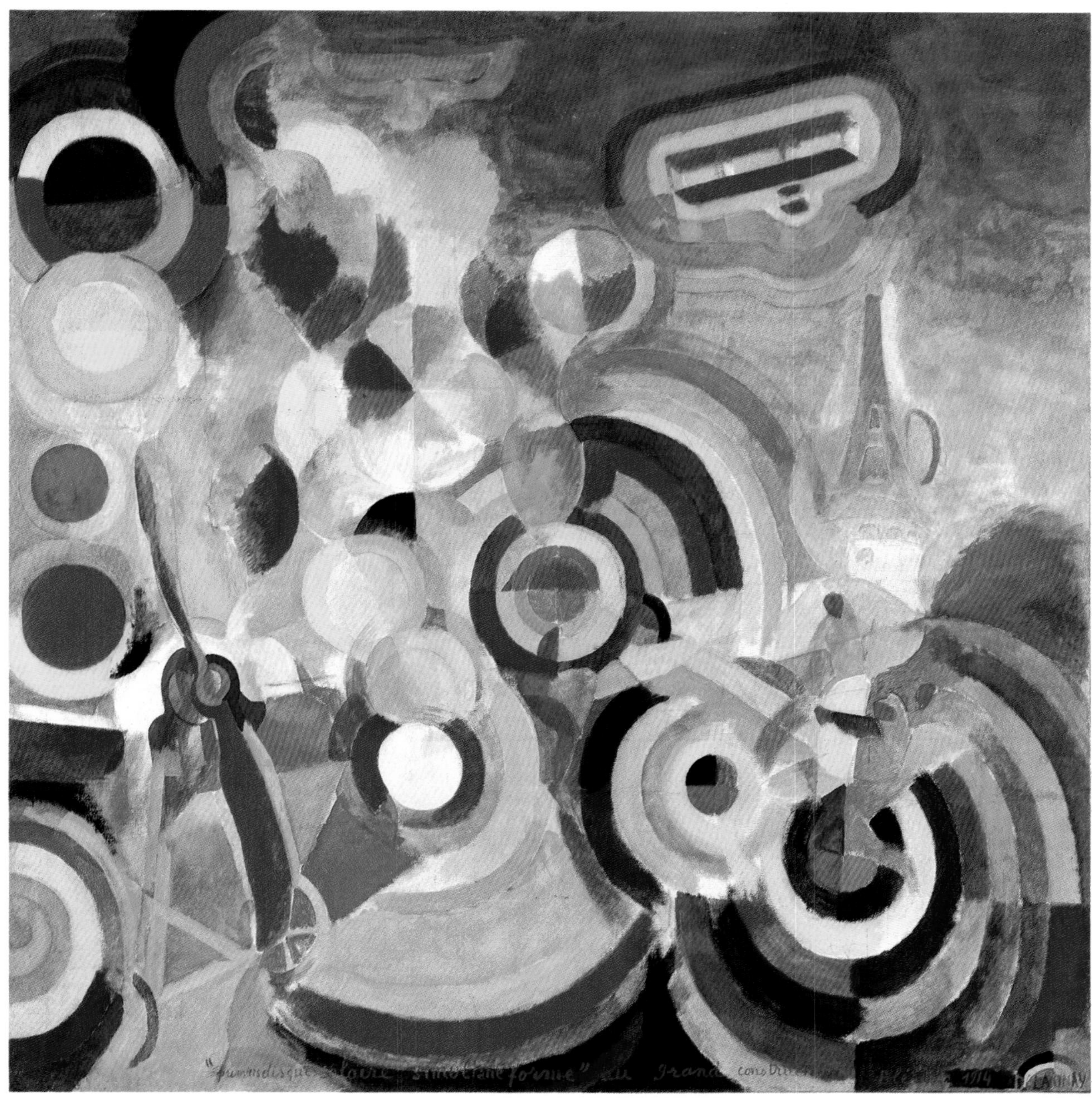

Robert Delaunay.
Homage to Blériot.
1914.
Distemper on canvas, 8 feet 4 inches × 8 feet 4½ inches.
Kunstmuseum, Basel

Munich before 1914 was a stronghold of the pacific International. It had always been a city open to great ideas and eager, often in a deadpan, literal way, to annex them. Visitors found echoes of Athens and Florence in its architecture and of English landscape gardening in the huge park which came right into the middle of the city. There was a tradition of the new in Munich, also. Wagner had been performed there when theaters elsewhere were closed to him. In 1893, the year in which Thomas Mann settled in Munich, a new exhibiting society called the Munich Secession brought together Franz von Stuck, Arnold Böcklin, Lovis Corinth, Max Liebermann, Max Slevogt and others who were then regarded as advanced artists. In 1895–96 three important magazines were founded there: *Pan, Jugend* and *Simplicissimus.* Art Nouveau produced one of its most celebrated triumphs in the façade which August Endell designed for a Munich photographer's studio in 1898. Good acting has always been treasured in Munich, and in 1901 the new Schauspielhaus set a new standard for theater architecture.

All this attracted foreigners; and the Munich art world was remarkable above all for its large Russian contingent. This was made up for the most part not of beginners but of mature men and women who had had experience of other cities and had finally fixed on Munich as the most stimulating place in which to live. The leader of this large group was Wassily Kandinsky, who had arrived in Munich in 1897 at the age of 30. He had not always meant to be an artist; only a few months before he arrived in Munich he had been offered a professorship in law at a Russian university, and whereas his fellow Russians in Munich had mostly been art students in Moscow or St. Petersburg, Kandinsky had followed a wide range of interdisciplinary interests before settling for painting as his main activity. He was, for instance, something of an amateur ethnographer, and he had traveled in parts of Russia in which a timeless folk-world was still intact. In those remote provinces, color was everywhere: houses were painted inside and out with a richness, a power of invention, and a spiritual energy which were deeply impressive to Kandinsky. He felt while there as if he were living in a world that was all art; and when he became an artist himself his ambition was not to produce beautiful and lucrative objects but to communicate something that was of vital importance to the spiritual well-being of mankind.

Kandinsky's maternal grandmother had come from the Baltic provinces of Russia, where the traditional culture was markedly Germanic, and from her he had learned not only the German language but the elaborate mythic structures of German folklore. This predisposed him to feel at home in Munich, which had the further advantage of having, in those days, a great deal of the emblematic color—canary-yellow mailboxes, bright blue streetcars, apricot-yellow baroque façades and burnished gold cupolas—which Kandinsky had prized in Moscow. Fixed, recurrent color was

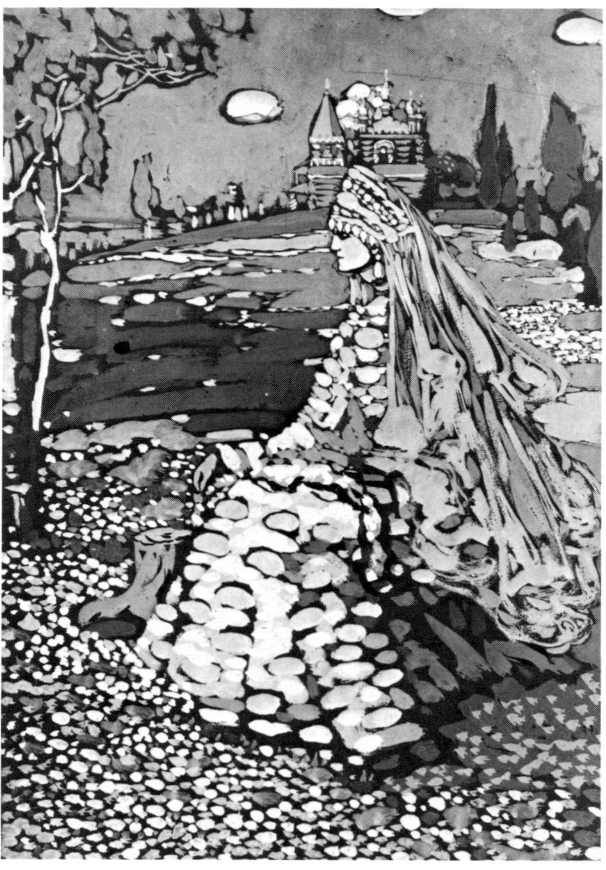

Wassily Kandinsky. *Russian Beauty in a Landscape.* 1905. Tempera on black paper, 16½ × 11¼ inches. Städtische Galerie im Lenbachhaus, Munich

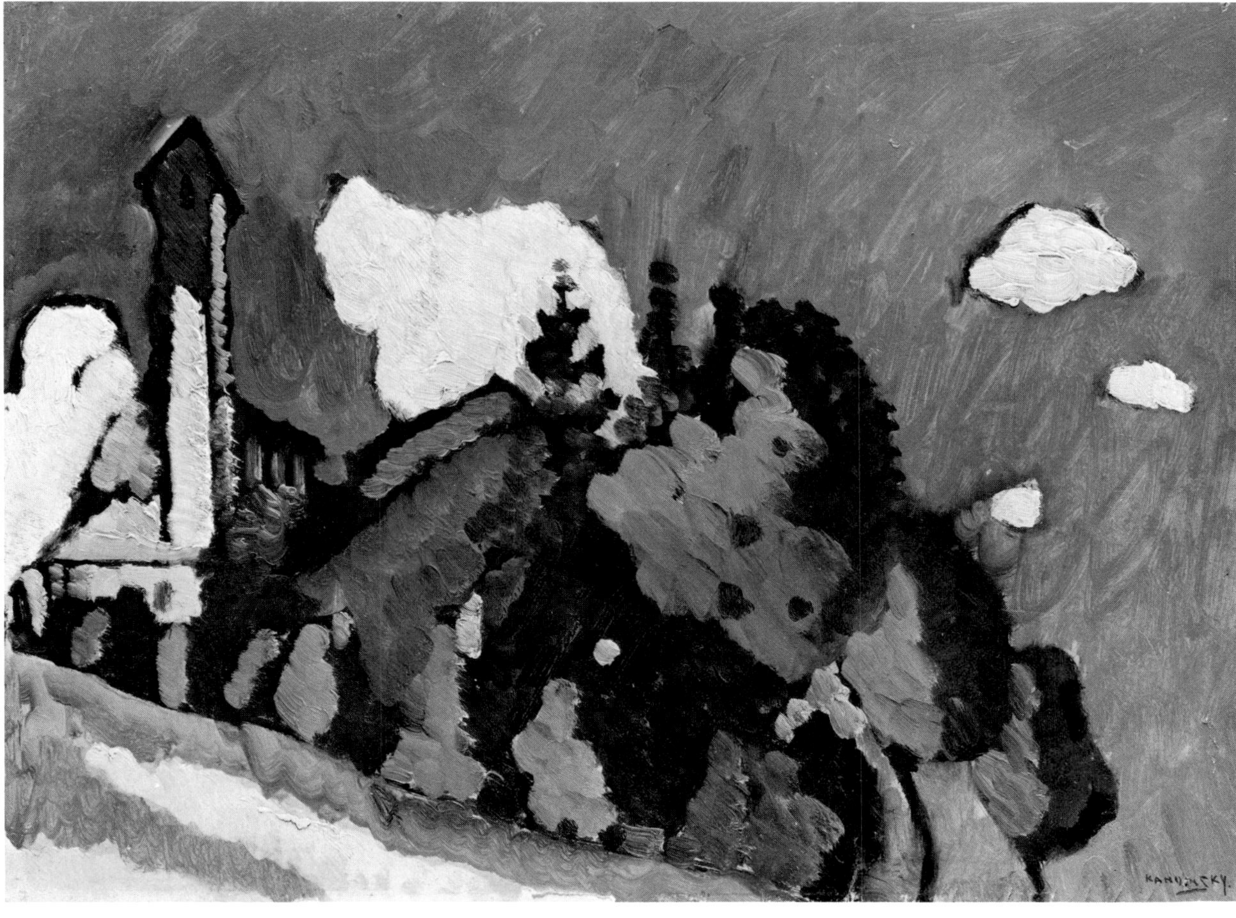

Wassily Kandinsky. *Study for "Landscape with a Tower."* 1908. Oil on board, 13 × 17⅝ inches. The Solomon R. Guggenheim Museum, New York

a necessity of life to him; from his childhood in Moscow he needed to be assured that at a certain time, every day, certain colors would be on hand. He found all this in Munich; and from Bavaria in general he got a parallel reassurance: the knowledge that certain ancient crafts—painting on glass, above all—were still being carried on with undiminished poetry. Munich was absolutely right for Kandinsky, and he lost no time in making an impression there.

He had, among other things, a very good sense of timing. He knew when situations were ripe for himself, and he knew when they were ripe for others. He knew when to start a liberal art school in Munich called the "Phalanx," just after the turn of the century, and he knew when to close it up (in 1902) and go on his travels. He knew when to start an association of artists in Munich (the Neue Künstlervereinigung, in 1909), and he knew when to secede from it (two years later) and found The Blue Rider. He was ideally open-minded—in its second exhibition, in the winter of 1910–11, the Neue Künstlervereinigung gave Picasso, Braque, Derain, Rouault, Vlaminck and van Dongen the freedom of its walls—and when The Blue Rider came to publish its *Almanac,* in December, 1912, the table of contents read like an index to modern sensibility. Everything was there: the perfected internationalism, the cross-references to theater and music, the sharp focus on primitive art, the total rejection of cultural hierarchies, the belief that much could be learned from children's art, and from peasant crafts, and indeed from anything at all that was done without thought of academic sanction.

Kandinsky was alive to all this, but he was also alive to his own particular needs. Even the name of The Blue Rider corresponded to them; he said later that "Franz Marc loved horses, and I loved riders, and we both loved blue. It was as simple as that." Kandinsky wrote later in his fragmentary memoirs: "The horse carries the rider with strength and speed, but it is the rider who guides the horse. Talent can bring an artist to great heights, again with strength and speed, but it is for the artist to direct his talent." Timing was vital: "There comes a predestined hour," he wrote in The Blue Rider *Almanac*, "when the time is ripe for decisions." What Kandinsky was waiting for in the first years of this century was the moment at which new values could be promulgated and mankind set on the path toward redemption.

It was in the course of this, and not as an aesthetic exercise, that Kandinsky came to paint abstract pictures. Such is our historical conditioning that for years it was very difficult to think of abstract painting as dictated rather by inner necessity than by one episode or another in a holy war between abstraction and figuration. Abstract painting was something that people had to be for or against, as they were for or against corporal punishment or universal free trade. To have "painted the first abstract picture" became a brevet of honor, like being the first man to step onto the moon. Even Kandinsky in later years staked out his claim, for fear that someone would boast of having beaten him to it.

But there was nothing willed or doctrinaire about Kandinksy's abstract paintings. Nor was there a Monday on which he was painting representational pictures and a Tuesday on which he gave them up forever. His development is vastly more complicated than that, and not the least of its complications is the fact that Kandinsky actually desiderated an element of mystery in the whole matter. In the winter of 1911–12 he defined

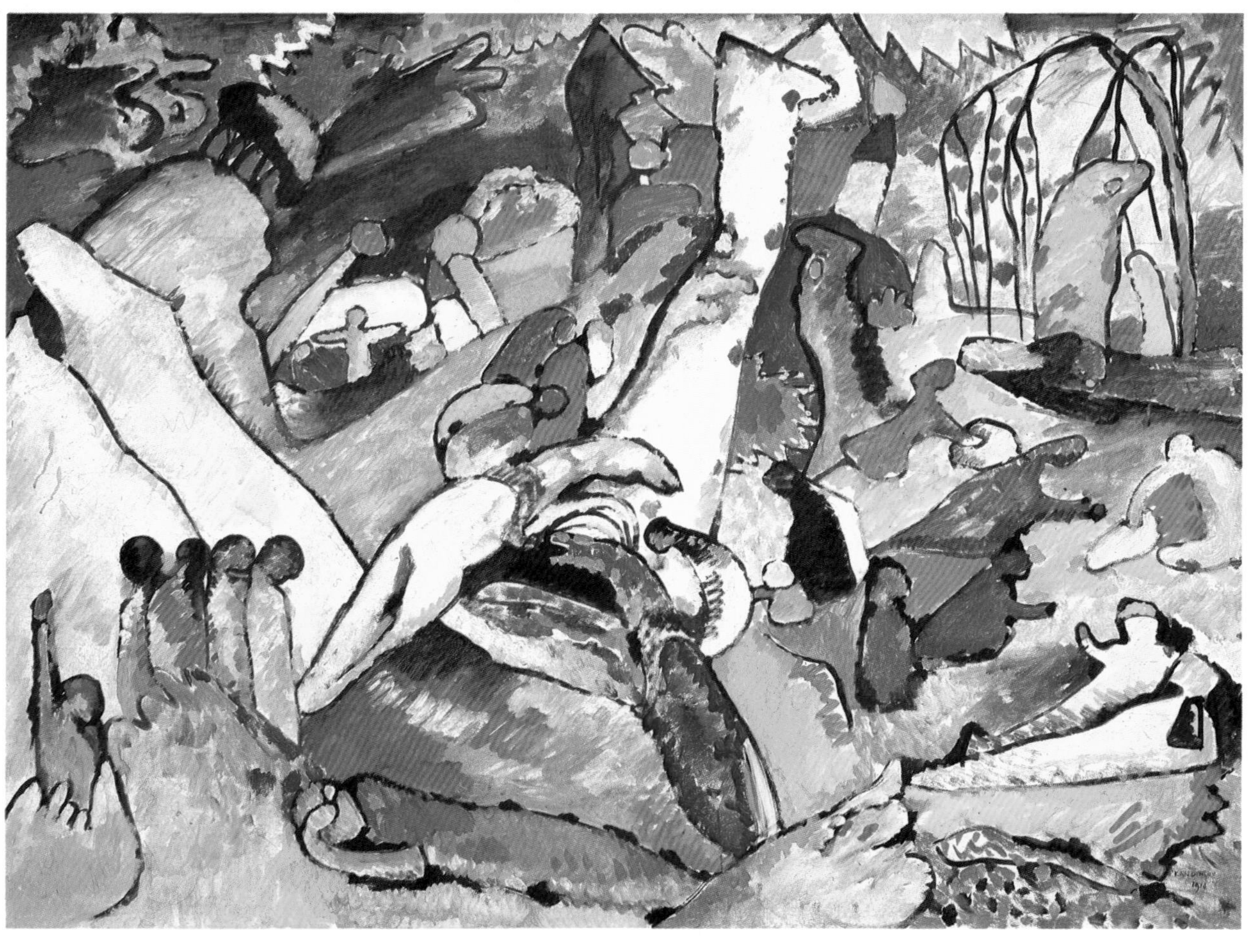

Wassily Kandinsky. *Study for "Composition II."* 1909–10. Oil on canvas, 38⅜ × 51⅝ inches. The Solomon R. Guggenheim Museum, New York

Wassily Kandinsky. *Landscape near Murnau.* 1909. Oil on board, 19⅞ × 25⅝ inches. The Solomon R. Guggenheim Museum, New York

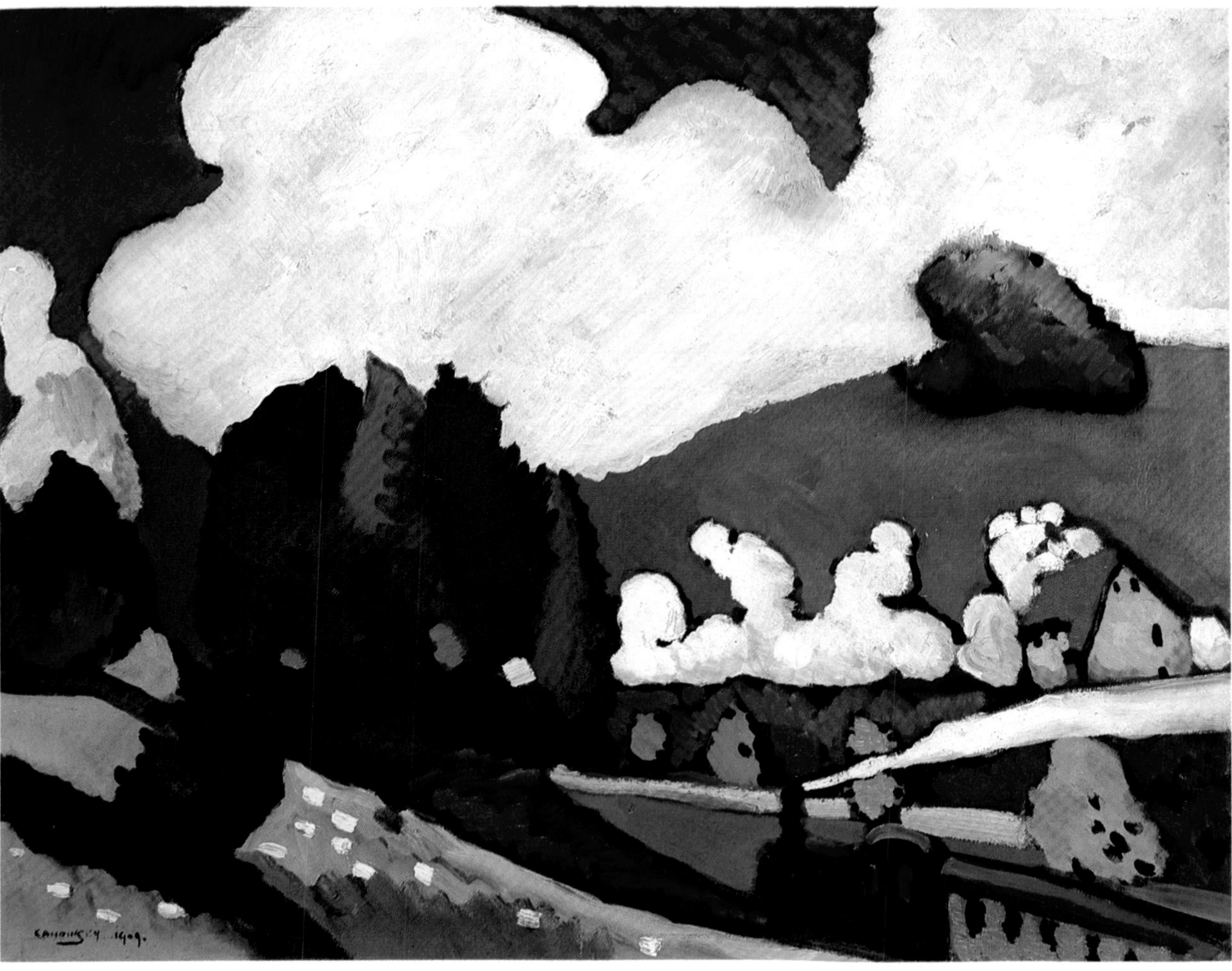

the content of his art as "the communication of what is secret by what is secret"; and it is on his terms, and not on those of the internal polemics of art, that we should look at the pictures.

It is relevant, for instance, that by 1909 Kandinsky had seen enough of Fauve painting to know what was likely to happen when, in his own words, he "let himself go" before nature. "Not worrying about houses or trees," he wrote, "I spread strips and dots of paint on the canvas with my palette knife and let them sing out as loudly as I could." French painting had given the green light for this in the fall of 1905; Kandinsky had been in Paris for much of the following year. But we must also consider what can be called the Central European element. The need to identify with strong, unbroken color was fundamental to the new, unshackled spiritual life as it was imagined by poets and novelists and painters alike. Looking at Kandinsky's *Landscape near Murnau* of 1909, where clouds and blossom are almost interchangeable and the rearing irregular forms careen this way and that, we might well remember the painter-hero of Hermann Hesse's long story *Klingsor's Last Summer.* That story was written in 1919–20 as an elegy for the lost hopes and betrayed ambitions of the world before 1914; and there is something of Kandinsky in the paintings which Hesse sets before us—"those free paraphrases on the world of phenomena, those strange, glowing, and yet dreamily tranquil pictures with their twisted trees and plantlike houses." Hesse goes on, "At the time his palette had been reduced to a few extremely vivid colors—cadmium yellow and red,

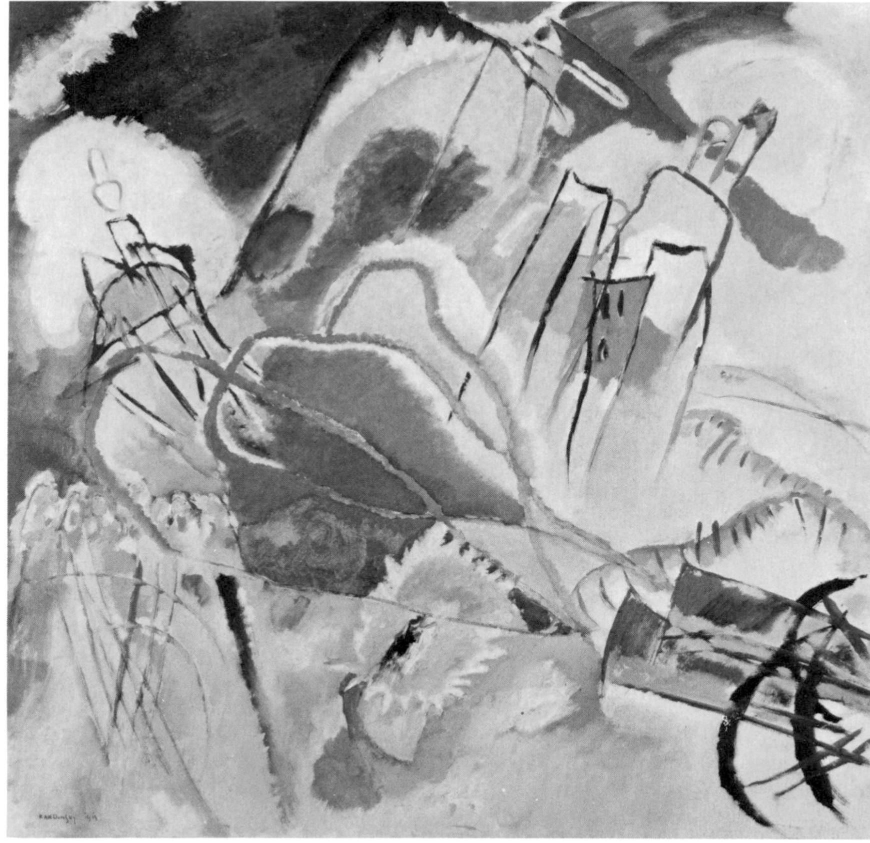

Wassily Kandinsky.
Improvisation No. 30. 1913.
Oil on canvas,
43¼ × 43¾ inches.
The Art Institute of Chicago.
Arthur Jerome Eddy Memorial Collection

Veronese green, emerald, cobalt, cobalt violet, French vermilion and crimson lake."

Beyond this, there is the fact that the subject matter of Kandinsky's Murnau landscapes meant more to him, in a concrete symbolical way, than the little French fishing village of Collioure meant to Matisse or L'Estaque to Derain. For Kandinsky, the church, the mountain, the still waters of the Staffelsee, and the horse and its rider were the forerunners of a vision of the Apocalypse; and when that vision finally presented itself the church, the mountain, the lake and the rider were all still there. Agents of the Apocalypse, they signaled the extent to which everyday vision had been overthrown and revelation had taken its place. Subject matter might be "a hindrance," as Kandinsky said later; but it was a necessary hindrance, in that without it the observer might lapse into mere passive aesthetic enjoyment. The purpose of art was to prepare the observer for the new realm of the spirit which was about to begin; only if enough people became aware of its possibilities would Madame Blavatsky's prophecy be fulfilled and the earth become, in the 21st century, "a heaven by comparison with what it is now."

Madame Blavatsky (1831–1891) spoke for occultist and theosophical beliefs which to most people, now as then, seem windy and unfounded. But in the pacific International there were many intelligent people who took her, and her fellow-theosophist Rudolf Steiner, quite seriously. Kandinsky, for one, saluted Madame Blavatsky for having been the first person (as he saw it) to see that what were then called "savages" could have valuable lessons for the European. And he seems to have believed, with Steiner, that the Revelation of St. John foreshadowed an era in which great catastrophes, then already imminent, would be followed by the attainment of an undreamed-of spirituality and the rebirth of mankind. Kandinsky saw it as his duty to make this known through his paintings: not in an obvious, literal, echoless way,

August Macke. *Making Fun of The Blue Rider.* 1913. Watercolor, 9¾ × 13¾ inches. Städtische Galerie im Lenbachhaus, Munich

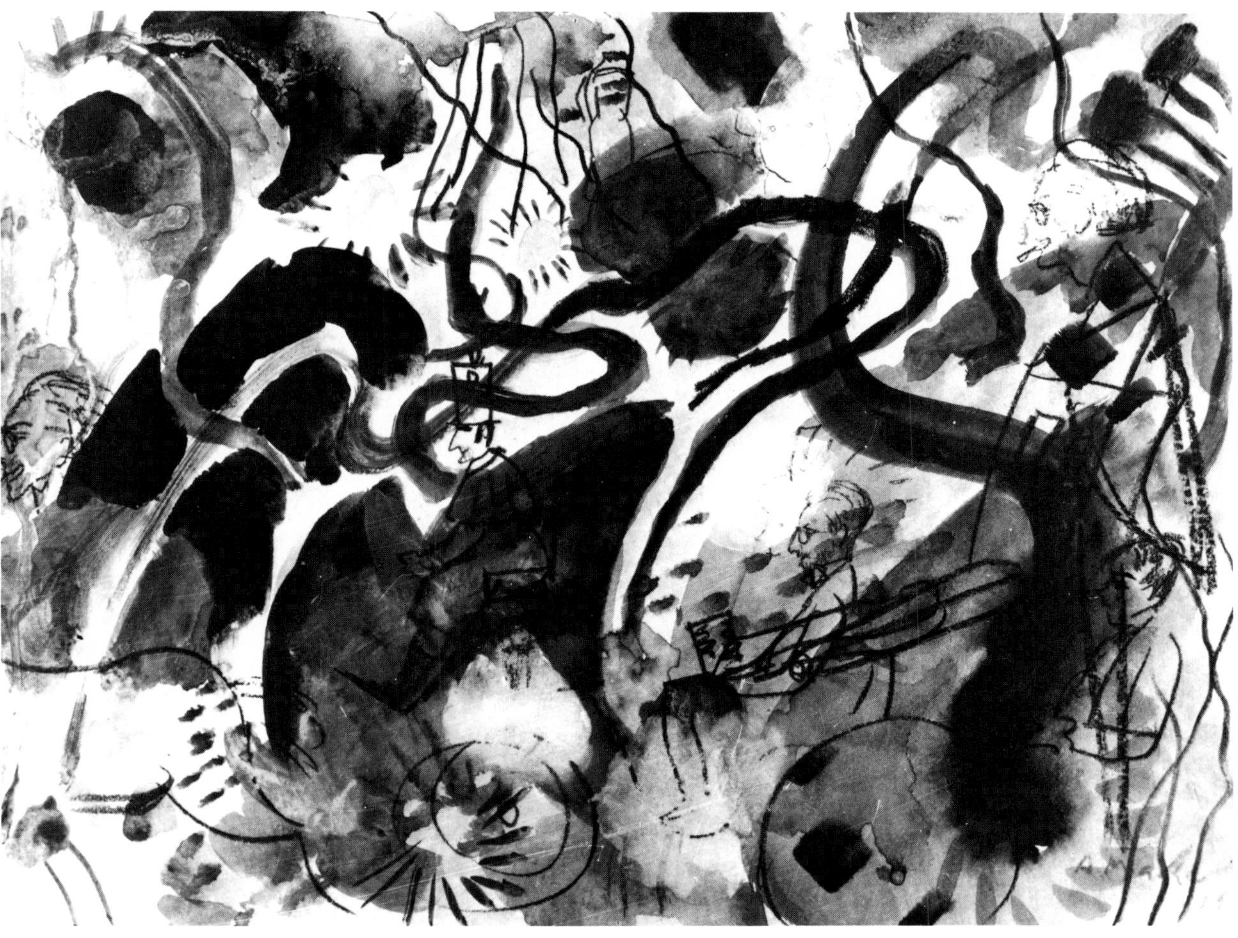

but not in a totally enigmatic way either. The vibration had to get through to those who were ready to receive it.

That is the background to the paintings of 1909–14 which have too often been looked at primarily in the context of whether or not they can be called "abstract." Kandinsky in these paintings was concerned to give something away, but not too much, of his secret intentions. His pyramidal *Mountain,* 1909, should for instance be read in terms of Rudolf Steiner's belief that the fulfilled artist, "immersed in the hidden, internal treasures of his art," was "a fellow-worker much to be envied for his part in building the spiritual pyramid which will reach to heaven." Steiner lived in Munich, and Kandinsky very probably had personal contact with him. He is said to have heard him lecture on Goethe's *Faust;* several of his friends and colleagues were wholehearted Steinerians; Kandinsky's theatrical experiments run close to Steiner's. Kandinsky's work from 1909 to 1914 can best be read, in short, as a personal commentary, idiosyncratic but nonetheless perfectly coherent, on Steiner's convictions. Kandinsky was by nature a mystic; not only did Steiner give him subject matter that called for the scale of epic, but he suggested a parallel between that subject matter and the creative process as Kandinsky had come to understand it. Making art, Kandinsky had decided, was like making the world in miniature: "painting is like a violent and thunder-wracked collision between different worlds that are destined to create a new world by fighting one another. . . . Every work of art comes into being in the way that the universe came into being—as a result of catastrophes in which all the instruments play out of tune until finally there sings out what we call 'the music of the spheres.'" What he

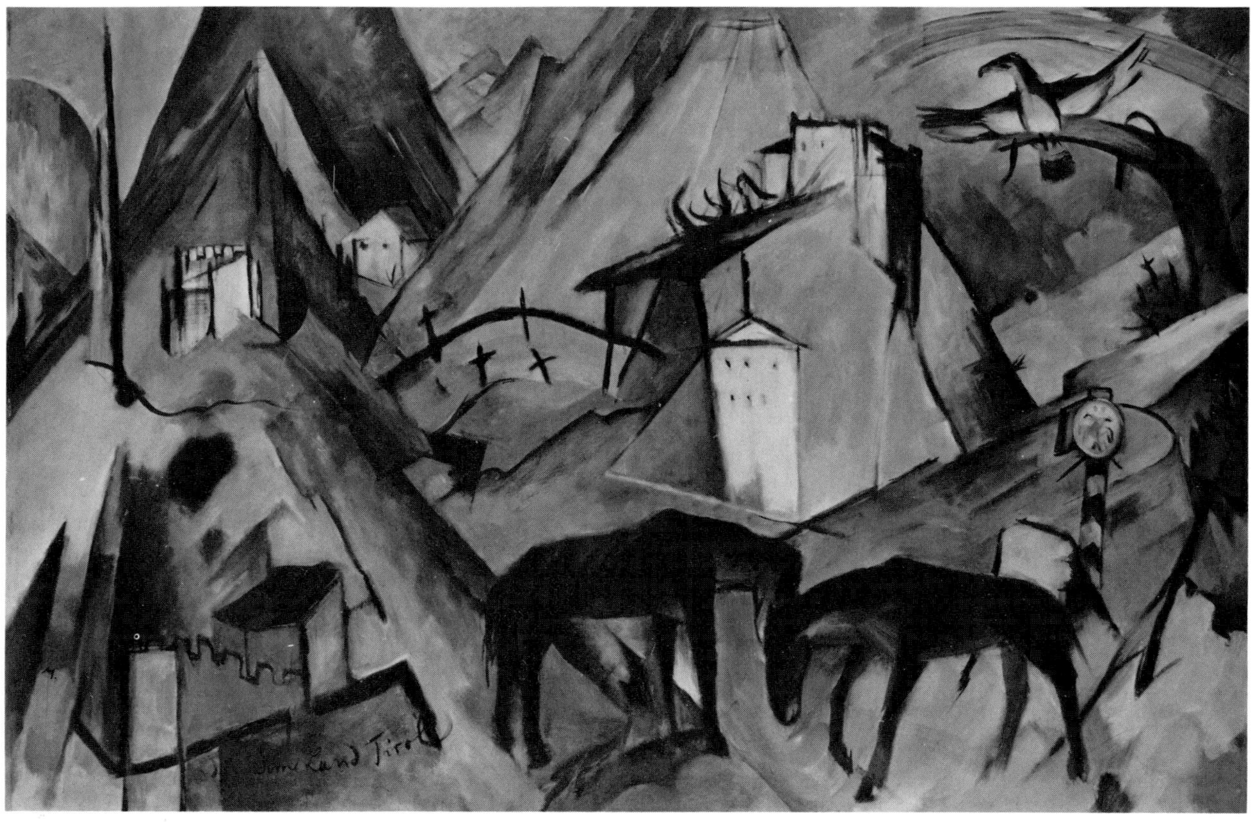

Franz Marc.
The Unfortunate Land of Tyrol.
1913.
Oil on canvas, 52 inches × 6 feet 7 inches.
The Solomon R. Guggenheim Museum, New York

painted under the impulse of these beliefs was not so much "abstract paintings" as images whose implications were coded to a greater or a lesser degree.

These images did, however, spring in part from ideas which predated Kandinsky's acquaintance with Steiner. Ever since his childhood in Moscow he had believed that colors had an autonomous life of their own. In his book *On the Spiritual in Art,* written in 1910, he said, for instance, that a strong yellow stood for aggression, that orange rang out like a church bell, and that green stood for smugness and passivity. Ever since he had seen one of Monet's Haystacks in Russia and had not at first been able to decipher it, he had believed that a painting can have an impact on the observer which is quite independent of its subject matter. To that extent he thought of an abstract, nonreferential art as the ideal art of the future. But he also foresaw that it could easily lapse into something of merely decorative interest, "like a necktie or a carpet"; for this reason he continued to secrete coded messages within what might have been taken for abstract paintings. From the fall of 1911 these paintings were much talked about in his circle, and Paul Klee, for one, wrote in his diary that "they appear to have no subject. Very strange paintings, they are." But even more relevant to this context is the little painting called *Making Fun of The Blue Rider,* which was produced in 1913 by a much closer associate of Kandinsky's, August Macke. The activities of The Blue Rider were in general unremittingly earnest. But that they had a lighter side is clear from this sketch, which includes recognizable portraits of Kandinsky, Marc, Gabriele Münter, August and Marie Macke and Herwarth Walden, editor of the magazine *Der Sturm* and director of the gallery which was associated with it.

The Blue Rider was not an association of equals, like the Impressionists, but a dictatorship in which Kandinsky and Franz Marc showed whatever

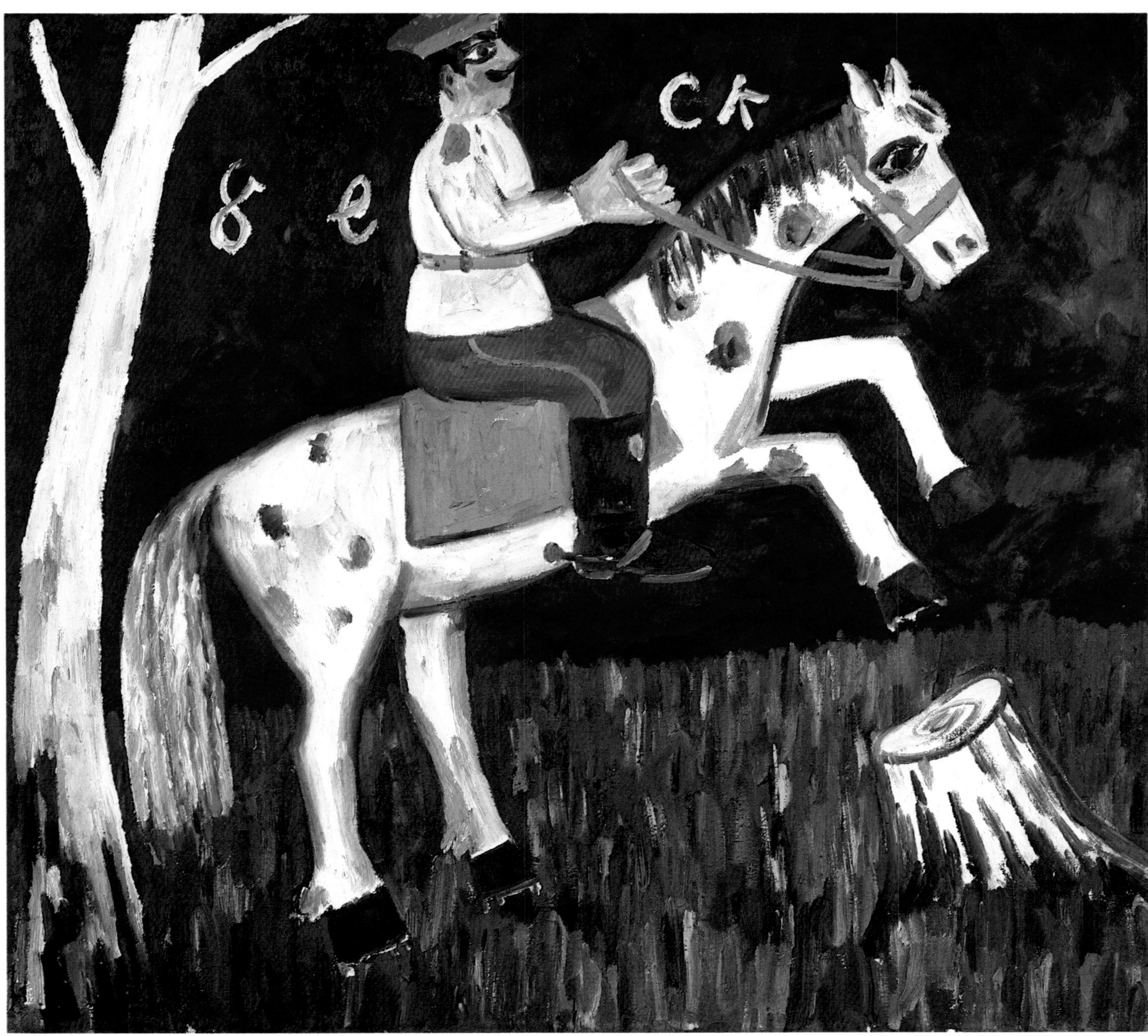

Mikhail Larionov.
Soldier on a Horse.
c. 1908–11.
Oil on canvas,
34¼ × 39 inches.
The Tate Gallery,
London

seemed to them to be right, without bothering about anyone else's opinions or wishes. Marc was a man of considerable intellectual powers; he had a wide-ranging curiosity, and although he did not share Kandinsky's theosophical beliefs he was convinced that his generation stood at a hingepoint in the history of the world. In paintings like *The Blue Horse,* 1911, he used color in a free and arbitrary manner, so that familiar images would vanish from view (like a water hen, as he himself put it) only to surface in a new guise and a new place.

"He lived on an alp," someone once said of Marc, "with sheep and cows and a couple of good books." And for several years Marc made a paradise on earth from these simple elements. But in 1913 Marc began to paint pictures which were haunted by loss and alienation. *The Unfortunate Land of Tyrol* prefigures a scene of desolation such as was to be found on every European battlefront between 1914 and 1918. Its broken, jagged and inconclusive formal structure is the complete antithesis of all that Marc had previously stood for: positive color, unlimited energy, formal rhythms strongly carried through, and a sense of limitless well-being in the presence of the animal world. "It is logical," he wrote, "to paint such pictures before a war, as a constructive act which makes the future visible."

Kandinsky, in all this, moved with the ordered assurance of one who was not so much "an artist" in the precarious or bohemian sense as a member of the professional classes who had turned to art and was doing uncommonly well at it. There is no reason to disbelieve what he wrote in his memoirs —that before perfecting a new idea he was in a state of extreme inner tension, and that the sense of inner necessity which was fundamental to all such advances had to be stalked through days filled with restless anxiety and nights haunted by "fantastic dreams full of terror and delight." But none of this showed in his public persona, which could have been that of a military man (two of his Russian colleagues in Munich were retired army officers) or a doctor in a very good way of business. In particular, he was completely at ease with his Russian inheritance. That inheritance was all gain,

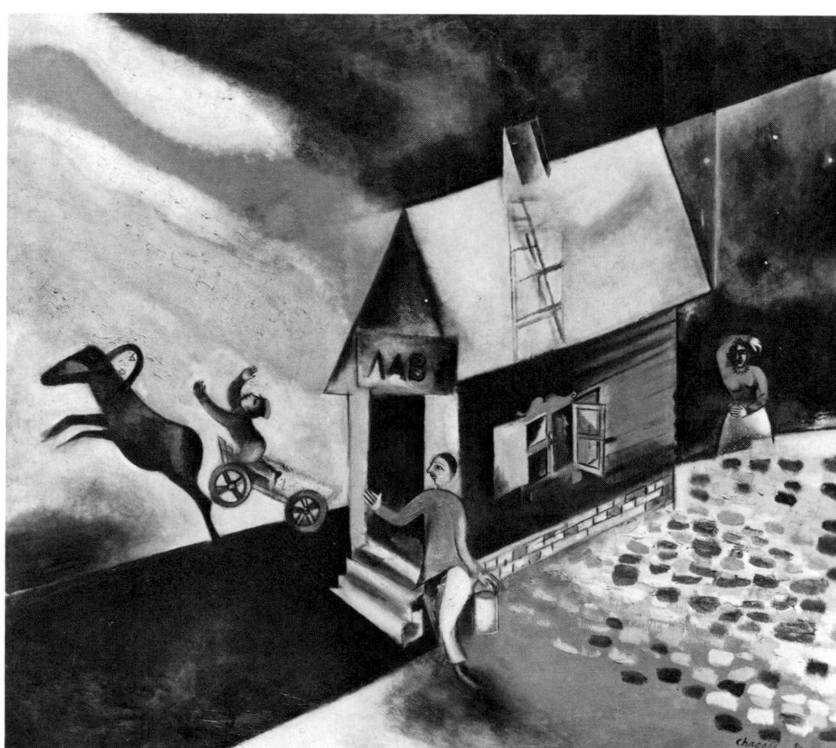

Marc Chagall.
Burning House.
1913.
Oil on canvas,
41⅞ × 47¼ inches.
The Solomon R. Guggenheim Museum, New York

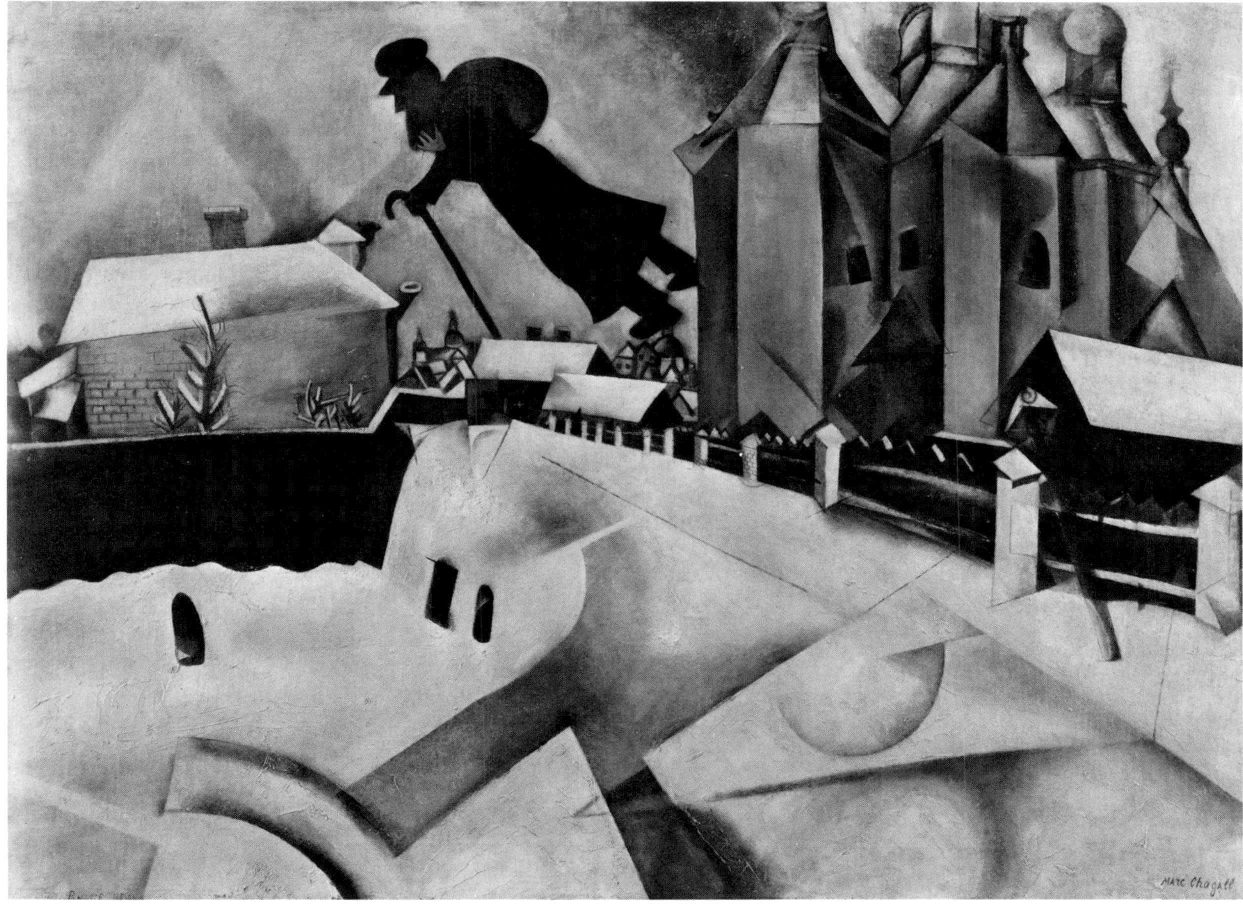

Marc Chagall.
Over Vitebsk (after a painting of 1914). 1915–20.
Oil on canvas, 26⅜ × 36½ inches.
The Museum of Modern Art, New York.
Acquired through the Lillie P. Bliss Bequest

as far as he was concerned; and he certainly had no reason to feel that conditions in Russia had been hostile to his personal development.

In this, he was in striking contrast to Marc Chagall, who arrived in Paris from Russia in 1910 and in time became a friend of both Apollinaire and Delaunay. The pacific International was very much in operation at this time in Franco-Russian artistic relations; by 1914 a young painter in Moscow, in particular, had easy access to the great paintings by Matisse and Picasso which two Russian collectors, Shchukin and Morosov, had brought together, and there had been loan shows of recent French painting which have never been surpassed for quality and discernment. For the well-bred, well-fed, much-traveled and personally not seldom irresistible aesthetes who made up the art world of Moscow and St. Petersburg, life had just about every advantage. It was very pleasant before 1914 to go to Paris as the countryman of Diaghilev, who had given Western Europe a new idea of what the ballet could be, and of Chaliapin, who was acclaimed as the greatest singer-actor in history, and of Scriabin, who had given a new dimension to concert life. (Scriabin's tone-poem *Prometheus* was the subject of a close and eulogious analysis in The Blue Rider *Almanac*.)

Among the Russians who visited Paris at that time were Mikhail Larionov and Nathalie Gontcharova, who between them were about to set Russian painting on a new path. They would have found it much harder to do so without the enlightened patronage of Diaghilev, who sent them to Paris in 1906—and, in a more general way, without the atmosphere of informed curiosity which the pacific International had created in Moscow. That curiosity was ubiquitous at that time, and

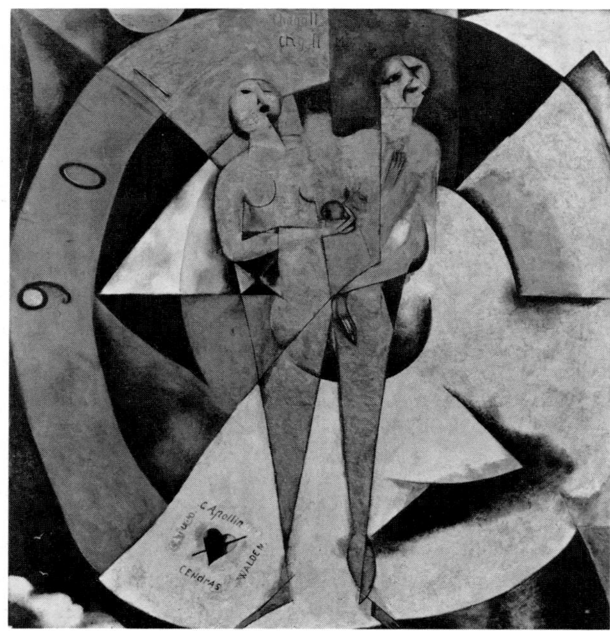

Marc Chagall. *Homage to Apollinaire.* 1911–12. Oil on canvas, 6 feet 10 inches × 6 feet 6 inches. Stedelijk van Abbe Museum, Eindhoven

when Larionov and Gontcharova came to live in Paris in 1914 Apollinaire wrote about them in *Les Soirées de Paris* as established and substantial figures, partners in the creation of "a universal art in which painting, sculpture, poetry, music and even science in all its manifold aspects will be combined." To be a gifted young artist in such conditions was to be one of a privileged brotherhood for whom national frontiers had no meaning.

Diaghilev almost always chose well. He knew for instance that Rimsky-Korsakov was a master of spangled and glittering orchestral timbres; and in her designs for his opera *Le Coq d'or* Nathalie Gontcharova found a precise visual equivalent for the intoxicating sounds which carried all before them when they were heard for the first time in Western Europe. It was to be quite sure of this kind of authenticity that Diaghilev had invited Larionov and Gontcharova to Paris. Nor did Larionov fail him, as a painter. At a crucial stage in his career Larionov had to spend nine months (1908–09) in the Russian army. From this he derived a wealth of new subject matter which was ideally suited to what he wanted to achieve: the mingling of Russian folk art with sophisticated European attitudes to color and form.

Things did not however look quite so well if, like Chagall, you were Jewish, came from a town in the sticks, and could not even get permission to live in St. Petersburg, much less to study there, unless you were registered as a domestic servant. Chagall survived all this, but he survived by using his art as a charm against alienation. In other words, he kept sane by painting an alternative world. It was in some respects a world of the most faithful realism; the township in *Over Vitebsk* is "true to life" in a way that strikes us at once as authentic, and the wooden house in *Burning House* could not sit more squarely on the canvas. Chagall in first youth had a way of hugging fact—of holding it ever more closely to him—as if by hugging it tight enough he could remake the world. He was a wonderful storyteller—later he became one of the great book illustrators—but his first purpose was to heal the hurt of living in a society which denied him certain fundamental human rights.

He did this in two ways. First, he used color to say to the observer, "This is not the world as you know it." Second, he used fantasy to show that at a given moment the events portrayed on the canvas became a revision of the known life and an emblem of a better one. The Jew in life, in the little town of Vitebsk, was a tethered man. He had none of the mobility, social and geographical, which was the birthright of the European Gentile before 1914. He was not precisely a captive, but he was not a free man either. Chagall dealt with this by positing an alternative world in which the Jew had supernatural powers. He could soar above the rooftops like a Montgolfier balloon, he could cross the town in one easy stride, he could make life dance to the tunes which he drew from his green violin, and when he met the girl of his dreams he could put the whole of Vitebsk to sleep as he and she whirled around it and above it as prince and princess. Imagination was the outcast's revenge in Vitebsk; and the paintings came from an inner necessity as strong as Kandinsky's and a good deal more immediate in its action. Later—much later—Chagall fell back on winsome repli-

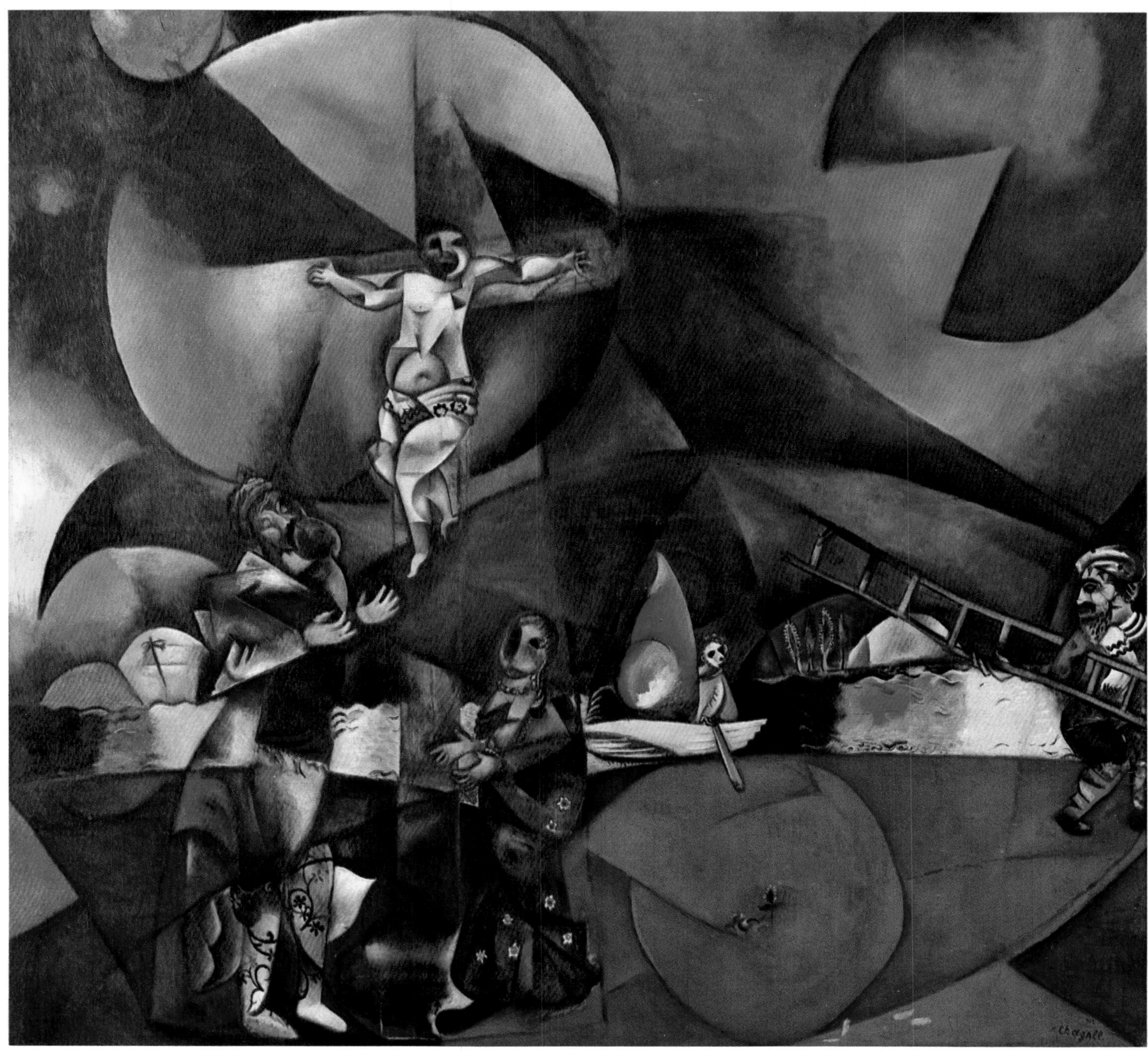

Marc Chagall.
Calvary. 1912.
Oil on canvas,
68¾ × 6 feet 3¾
inches.
The Museum of
Modern Art, New
York.
Acquired through
the Lillie P. Bliss
Bequest

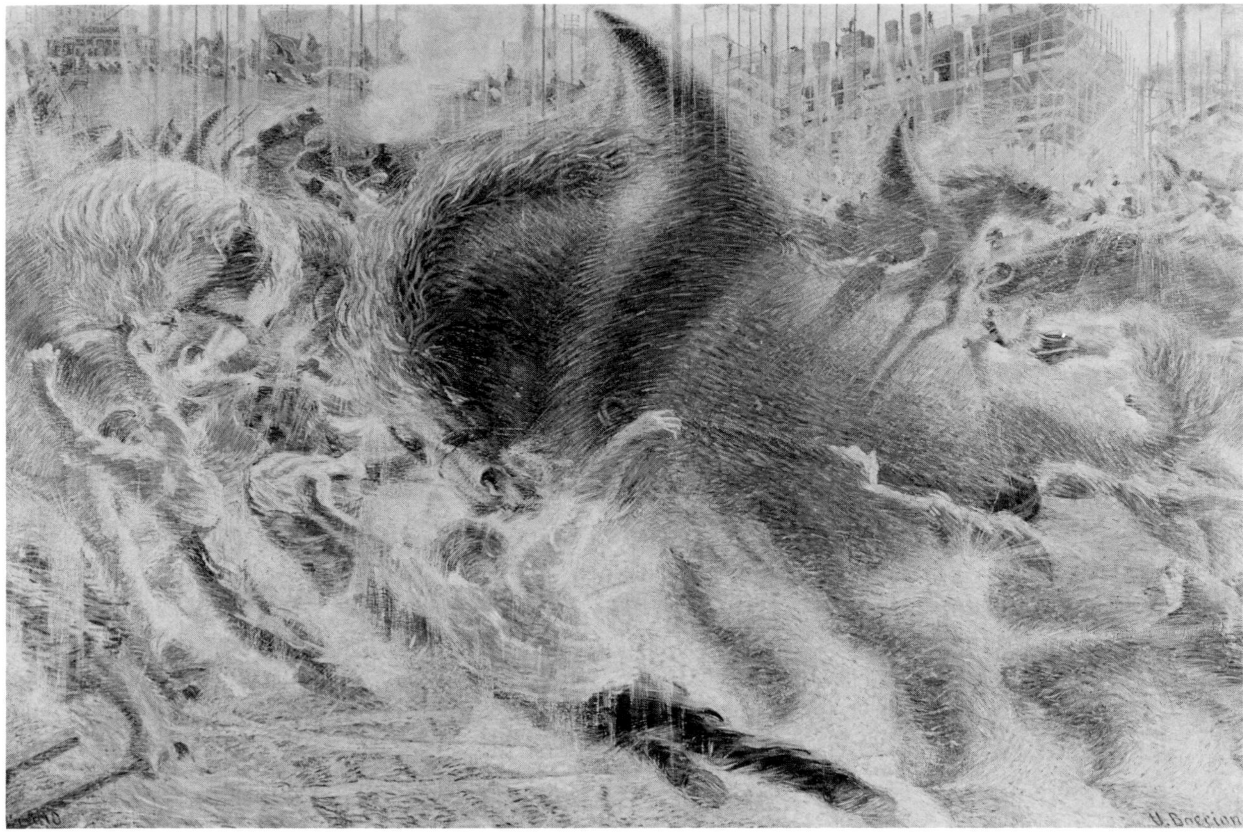

Umberto Boccioni. *The City Rises.* 1910. Oil on canvas, 6 feet 6½ inches × 9 feet 10½ inches. The Museum of Modern Art, New York. Mrs. Simon Guggenheim Fund

cation; but in the first years his was a healing art, and the interaction of personalities between him and Apollinaire was predictably vivid. Chagall's *Homage to Apollinaire* is one of the most successful of his early Parisian paintings; and Apollinaire in *Calligrammes* dedicated a poem called "A travers l'Europe" to Chagall.

Homage to Apollinaire is, by the way, a condensed version of the story of Adam and Eve. In a single image we see Eve, sprung from Adam's rib but still a part of him, in the act of offering Adam the apple of knowledge which will cause them to be expelled from Paradise. The pierced heart which stands for friendship is surrounded by the names of four close friends: Apollinaire, the poet Blaise Cendrars, Herwarth Walden, and Ricciotto Canudo, friend of the Futurist leader F. T. Marinetti and editor of the avant-garde review *Montjoie.*

Chagall impressed his friends in Paris by the immediacy, and the sense of total involvement, with which he re-created the facts of his childhood and first youth in Russia. Those memories were not "recollected in tranquillity"; they were relived. And when Chagall turned, as in *Calvary,* to a New Testament subject he still worked with the materials that lay nearest to hand: his own experience of suffering in a particular place at a particular time. In October, 1913, Blaise Cendrars, poet and globe-trotter, wrote of Chagall that "because he had spent his whole childhood on the Cross and was astonished that he was still alive," it was as natural for him to paint the figure of Christ as it was to paint his betrothed, or the district nurse, or the grocer on the corner.

Apollinaire had no trouble with Chagall, but he was distinctly more wary of a young Italian painter who called on him in October, 1911. Umberto Boccioni was just 29 years old, and in three months' time he and his friends of the Italian Futurist group were to have an exhibition at Bern-

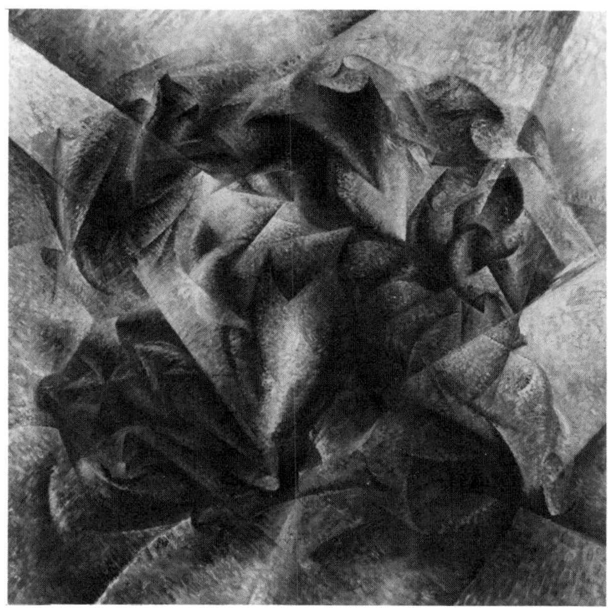

Umberto Boccioni. *Dynamism of a Soccer Player.* 1913. Oil on canvas, 6 feet 4⅛ inches × 6 feet 7⅛ inches. The Museum of Modern Art, New York. The Sidney and Harriet Janis Collection

heim-Jeune, one of the foremost dealers' galleries in Paris; Apollinaire was known to have considerable influence, and Boccioni was there to soften him up.

It is unlikely that Apollinaire had ever seen a painting by Boccioni, but like many other people in Paris he had read the "Futurist Manifesto" when it was published on the first page of *Le Figaro* on February 20, 1909. This "foundation manifesto" was the work of the poet and publicist F. T. Marinetti, and it was addressed not specifically to painters and sculptors but to every Italian who believed in the possibility of what was later called "a third great Italy." Italy was being buried alive—so the argument ran—beneath the weight of its past. Between them the Roman Emperors and the Popes of the Renaissance were imposing a mandatory secondhandedness on every detail of Italian life. Only when the libraries had been burned down and the museums flooded out could Italians live in the here-and-now. Once delivered from their past, they would see what an unprecedented beauty was all around them. They would acknowledge, in other words, that a racing car with its "machinegun-like" action was more beautiful than that pride of the Louvre, the Winged Victory of Samothrace.

Marinetti was by all accounts persuasive enough when he got on his feet, and undeniably he was dealing with real problems in a potentially decisive way. It is not wholly his fault that his speeches in translation sound like Disneyland's idea of Walt Whitman; Italy in 1909 was stagnant enough, in cultural terms, for there to be a genuine novelty about his "We shall sing of great crowds in the excitement of labor, relaxation and rebellion; of the many-colored and polyphonic wave-break of revolution in modern cities; of the vibration by night of arsenals and factories beneath their violent electric moons; of bridges leaping like gymnasts and barrel-chested locomotives prancing on the rails like gigantic steel horses." It was quite true that Italy had been for too long the preserve of professors and librarians and dealers in antiques. But there were disquieting overtones to the overdressed little demagogue with his popping eyes, his two protruding inches of stiff white shirt-cuff, his upturned mustaches and his English-style derby hat askew on his head. We have seen enough of "violence, cruelty and injustice" since Marinetti was around to resent the enthusiasm with which he preached that they should be the only subject matter of art. We don't want to hear from him or from anyone else that "war is the only health-giving thing in the world," or that women are by definition despicable, or that the burning of books is one of the highest forms of patriotism.

But when all that is said, it remains true that Marinetti was acting in the best interests of Italy. Futurism, in the sense of an unmixed belief in the future, was more promising than a backward glance misted over with awe. If we can speak of the Italian achievement in design since 1950 as something that has set high standards in every department of consumption, Marinetti and the Futurists are somewhere at the back of it. But for them, Fiat Motors might be copying the chariot in Piero della Francesca's *Triumph of the Duke and Duchess of Urbino,* and Olivetti might be prowling around the Vatican for a table to go with their smallest computer. It was thanks to Marinetti that

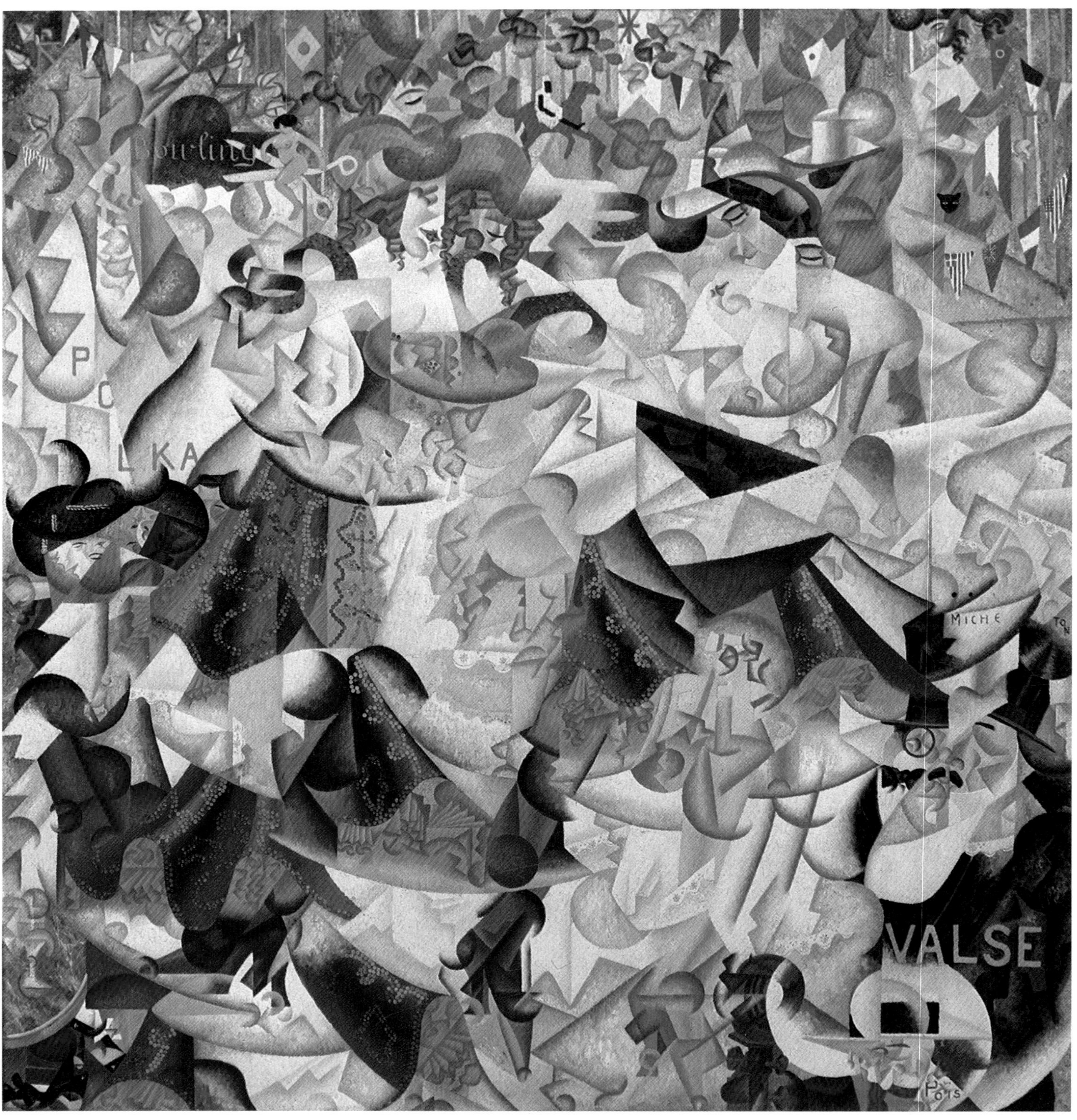
Bowling
P
O
LKA
MICHE
TON
VALSE

Gino Severini. *Dynamic Hieroglyph of the Bal Tabarin.* 1912. Oil on canvas with sequins, 63⅝ × 61½ inches. The Museum of Modern Art, New York. Acquired through the Lillie P. Bliss Bequest

the here-and-now got through in Italy and a re-thought and radical approach to design was adopted not long after Mussolini (much admired by Marinetti, by the way) had brought the country near to ruin and been hung up by a meathook for his pains.

In the spring of 1910 five Italian painters made common cause with Marinetti. The painters concerned were Umberto Boccioni, Carlo Carrà, Giacomo Balla, Gino Severini and Luigi Russolo. Severini lived in Paris and knew what was going on there; he had seen, therefore, with what a delicate and continuous historical awareness French painting had been brought into the 20th century. He must have known also that it was one thing for his colleagues to stand up and talk their heads off on the stage of a theater in Turin, and quite another for them to come across with paintings that would hold their own in the context of what was being done in Paris. It was for this reason, and at Severini's suggestion, that Marinetti sent Boccioni and Carrà to Paris, at his own expense, in October, 1911.

Once again, Marinetti was quite right. It would not do at all for the Futurist painters to make fools of themselves in Paris; there was far too great a gap between their ambitions, as set out in March–April, 1910, and their performance. From our point of view, however, the interesting thing is not that they should have fallen short of their aims, but that those aims should have been so concisely and so cogently formulated. A great part of modern sensibility is foreshadowed in the "Technical Manifesto of Futurist Painting," to which Boccioni, Carrà, Balla, Severini and Russolo put their names in April, 1910. Before long there was a large international audience for what they had to say: notably for such pugnacious opinions as that "all forms of imitation are to be despised," that "all subjects previously used must be discarded," and that "what was truth for the painters of yesterday is falsehood for the painters of today." It was the power of these ideas, and not the degree of their fulfillment, which spread the name of Futurism all over Europe and made it a constructive force even after Marinetti himself had been discredited.

What Boccioni and his friends had to say was comparatively free from the militaristic verbiage with which Marinetti seasoned his public appearances. It had affinities of a more exalted sort: with Henri Bergson, for instance, and especially with his *Matter and Memory.* Bergson believed that there was something ridiculous in the idea—fundamental to most pre-Futurist painting—of an object stilled and isolated. Not only was the interpenetration of past and present one of the cornerstones of his philosophy, but he believed that an object owes its essence and existence to its environment and could not possibly exist by itself. A fixed object in a fixed space was an academic fiction, therefore. Boccioni and his friends were saying meanwhile that "space no longer exists. . . . Our bodies penetrate the sofas on which we sit, and those sofas penetrate our bodies. The motorbus rushes into the houses which it passes, and the houses in turn throw themselves on the motorbus and mingle with it." Insofar as previous art had concerned itself with the "universal dynamism" which seemed to the Futurists the basic principle of life, it had focused on a notional fixed moment within it. Futurism aimed to set down on the canvas "the dynamic sensation itself, eternalized." Previous art had given a restricted and pedestrian account of man's potential; now that the full extent of that potential had been revealed by science, it was for art to catch up. The material nature of bodies had been revealed by science as no more than a convenient figure of speech; art should forthwith admit that, in the words of the Technical Manifesto, "movement and light destroy the materiality of bodies."

To all this there had seemed to be no natural Italian ancestor. At most the sculptor Medardo Rosso could be advanced as having once said that "in space, nothing is material." Rosso was reported in 1909 as having made mock of conventional sculpture, in which "forms are shaved off from the whirling center of universal life, remaining there

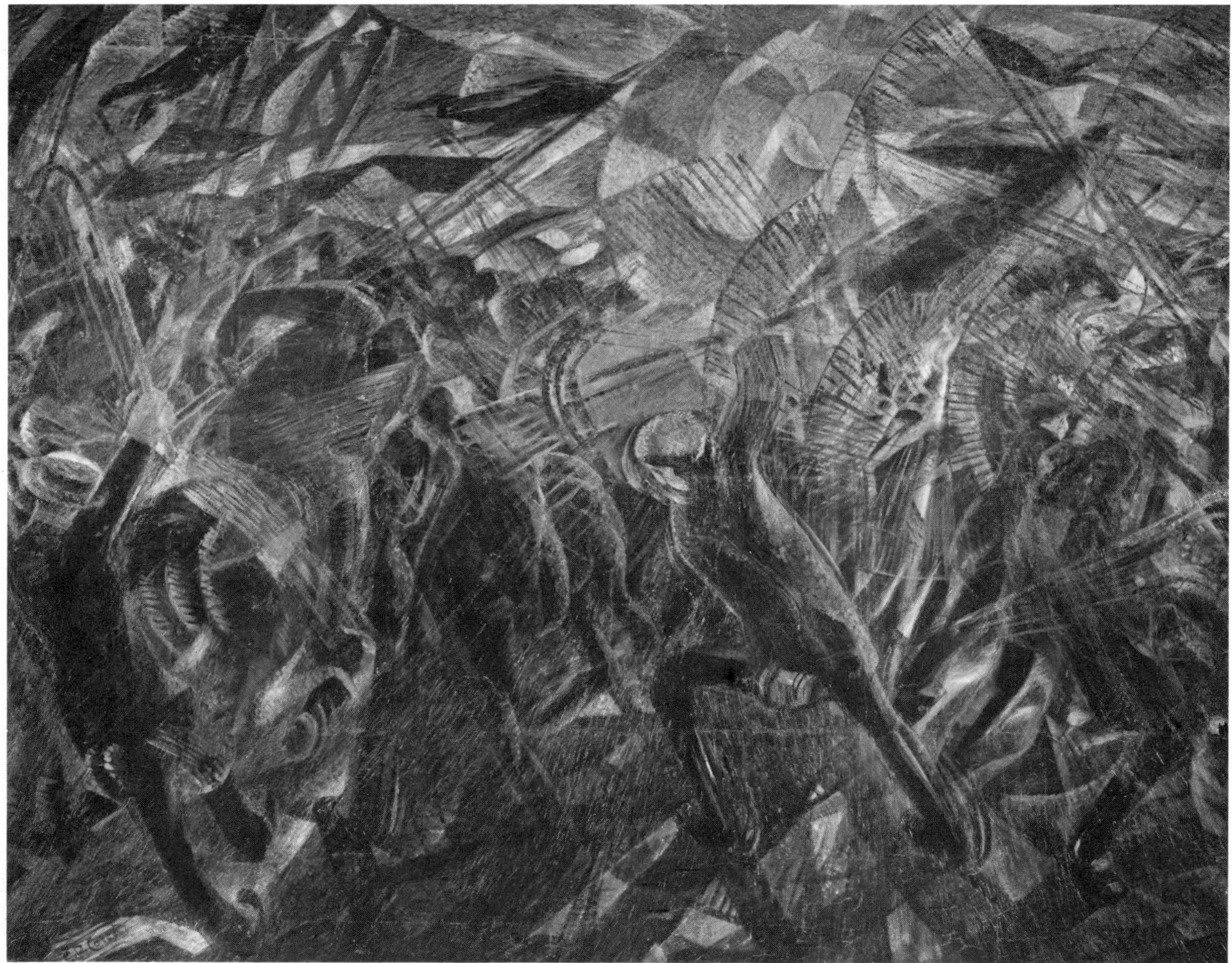

Carlo Carrà.
Funeral of the Anarchist Galli.
1911.
Oil on canvas,
6 feet 6¼ inches ×
8 feet 6 inches.
The Museum of Modern Art, New York.
Acquired through the Lillie P. Bliss Bequest

stiff and still, to be gaped at by the inquisitive spectator." Far better, he said, that the intensity of feeling in a work should "impel it out into space, radiating out to infinity in the way that an electric wave flies out to rejoin the eternal force of the universe." Rosso was, therefore, on the Futurists' side; but Rosso lived in Paris and was in virtual retirement. The Futurists had said what they were going to do; now they had to go out and do it, on their own.

If Paris gave them a rough ride at the first exhibition of Futurist painting in February, 1912, it was partly because they attempted to prejudge their own exhibition by saying that it established them as "the leaders of the European movement in painting." In particular, they derided Cubism for its reliance on the idea of the motionless object. Now, it is perfectly true that Cubism is an art of equilibrium, and that in the hands of second-rate artists an art of equilibrium becomes an art of stasis. It was not only the Italian Futurists who were to complain in time of the restrictions of the Cubist grid. But in several of the paintings which he showed in Paris, Boccioni, for one, borrowed heavily from the Cubist paintings by Gleizes and Metzinger which he had seen in the Salon d'Automne a month or two before; this was not quite, therefore, the moment at which to make fun of them.

"Sheer idiocy" was how Apollinaire summed up the Futurists' pretensions; and there were others in Paris who said that if the Futurists wanted to burn down the Italian museums it was because they couldn't stand the competition. And of course many of the key works of Italian Futurism

do look both inept and graceless. But they don't look negligible, even so; somewhere within them there is an authenticity of effort which keeps them alive. And if Futurism in general never ceased to needle the Parisian—Apollinaire almost had to fight a duel in March, 1914, when Robert Delaunay and others thought he had become too much in its favor—it was because the Futurists were at grips with modernity in a way which could not quite be dismissed. Their paintings got on the mat with modern life in situations where the French had preferred to watch from the sidelines. Their paintings were awkward, but it was a necessary awkwardness. "It is an appalling burden," Boccioni wrote later, "to have to elaborate within oneself a whole lost century of painting."

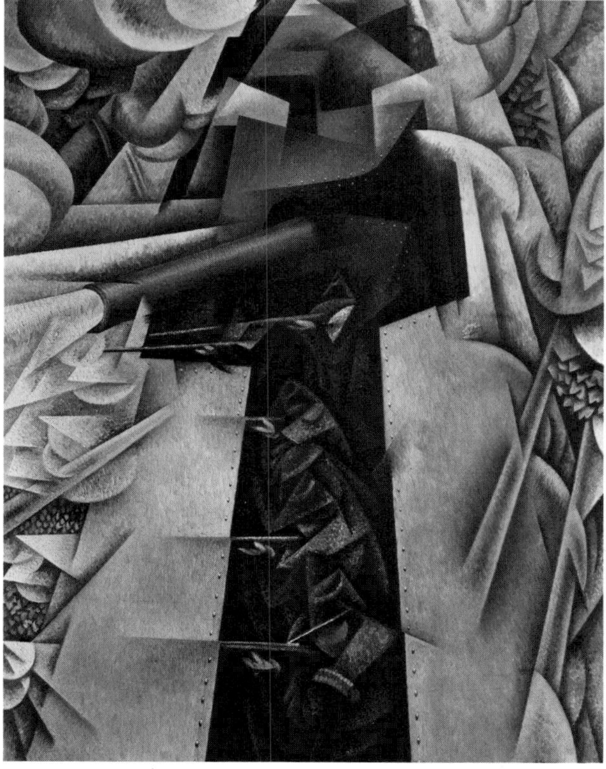

Gino Severini.
The Armored Train.
1915.
Oil on canvas,
46 × 34½ inches.
Richard S. Zeisler,
New York

When Severini wrote his own "Futurist Manifesto" in 1913, he said among much else that "objects no longer exist." The notion of the integrality of matter had been utterly destroyed in the sciences, and it was time for it to be utterly destroyed in art also. When Severini took that classic Parisian subject, the dance hall, he restated it in a new and complex picture language derived in part from his fellow Futurists, from odds and ends of Cubist practice (the use, for example, of words, whole or fragmented), from the color theories of Robert Delaunay, and from a flickering, allover animation of the surface which did not exclude a certain amount of realistic anatomical detail. The method was a mess, dialectically speaking; but in this big painting it worked, thanks to the overriding physical energy of the conception and to a superabundance of gossipy detail.

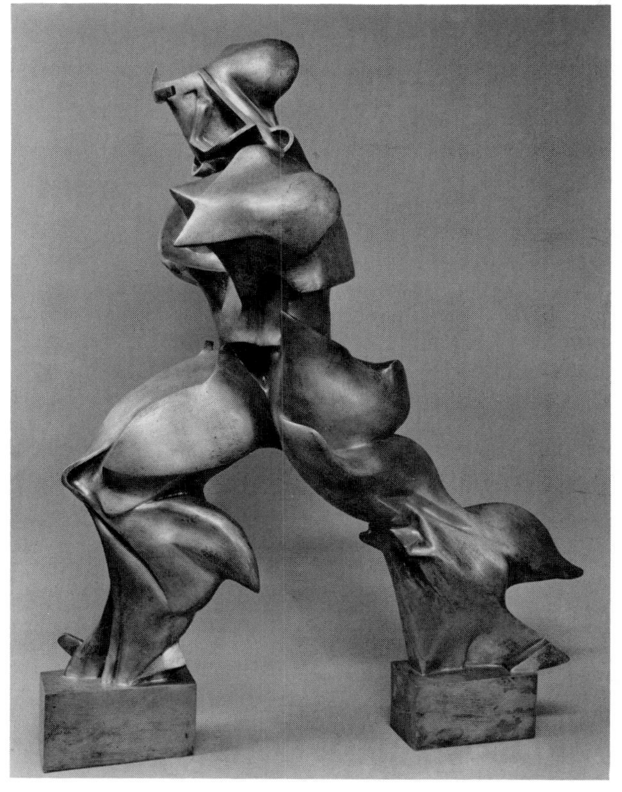

Umberto Boccioni.
Unique Forms of Continuity in Space.
1913.
Bronze,
43⅞ × 34⅞ × 15¾ inches.
The Museum of Modern Art, New York. Acquired through the Lillie P. Bliss Bequest

It was not only to easel painting that Boccioni and his friends directed their attention. Russolo moved into music and by 1914 was anticipating the notion of John Cage that all noise is music if you know how to listen to it. Balla and Boccioni moved into sculpture, and by 1914–15 Balla had pioneered many ideas that were to be fundamental to later practice: that physical mass was not essential to sculptural form, for instance, and that sculpture could be transparent, highly colored, lu-

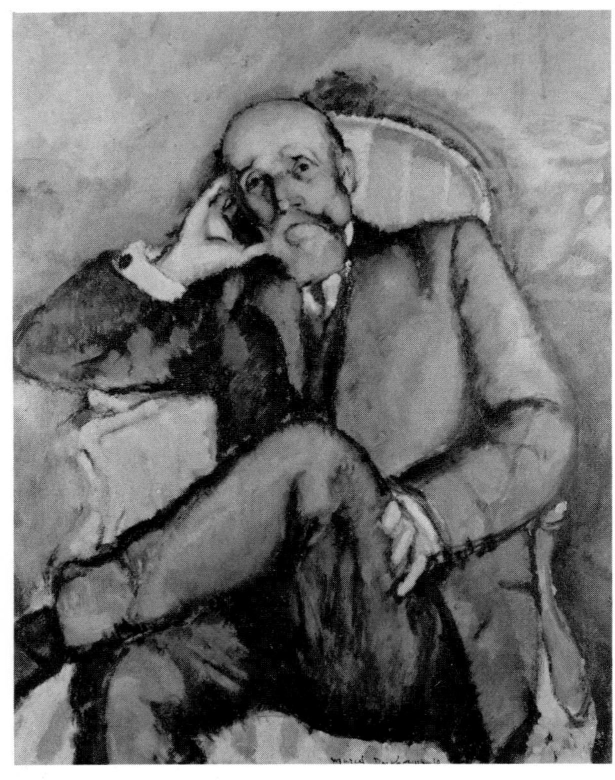

Marcel Duchamp. *The Artist's Father.* 1910. Oil on canvas, 36⅜ × 28⅞ inches. Philadelphia Museum of Art. The Louise and Walter Arensberg Collection

minous and virtually incorporeal. Boccioni, above all, went on spawning ideas until he died in 1916 after falling from a horse. As had happened with his paintings, he issued his program first and then had to make the work to fit it. Already in April, 1912, he was writing that the figure in sculpture should be broken open in such a way that its environment became a part of it; that the "wonderful mathematical and geometrical elements" which science had lately put before us should be brought into sculpture and "embedded in the muscular lines of the body"; and that a sculpture need not be in one material only but could incorporate whatever could contribute most vividly to its emotional impact—"glass, wood, cardboard, iron, cement, horsehair, leather, cloth, mirrors, electric light, etc."

It is one of the ironies of art history that the finest of Boccioni's few surviving sculptures should remind us not so much of that stirring passage as of the masterpiece of antiquity which Marinetti had outlawed in 1909: the Winged Victory of Samothrace. *Unique Forms of Continuity in Space* can, in fact, be read as much in terms of windblown draperies as of the lines of force which Boccioni had had in mind. But, once again, Boccioni's monument consists not so much in the surviving works as in the climate of total liberty which he promoted. Insofar as that total liberty is an integral part of the modern sensibility, Futurism initiated it. Its influence in that regard is still very far from exhausted: the notion of a disposable art—one that can be chalked on the floor or sent by telegram—has its origins in Marinetti. And if one day we settle for the state of affairs, long envisaged by R. Buckminster Fuller, in which buildings can be erected just for one season and thrown away at the end of it like paper handkerchiefs, that too will be the consummation of a Futurist attitude. ("It will be for each generation," the writ ran in 1911, "to build its own city.")

Apollinaire was sufficiently in tune with the times to know that Futurism had something real to offer. But he didn't care for the portentous tone,

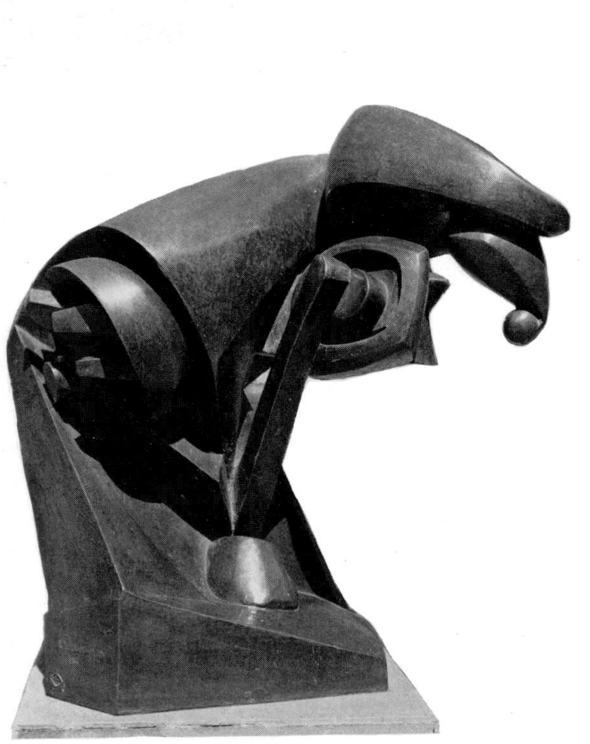

Raymond Duchamp-Villon. *The Horse.* 1914. Bronze (cast 1930–31), 40 × 39½ × 22⅜ inches. The Museum of Modern Art, New York. Van Gogh Purchase Fund

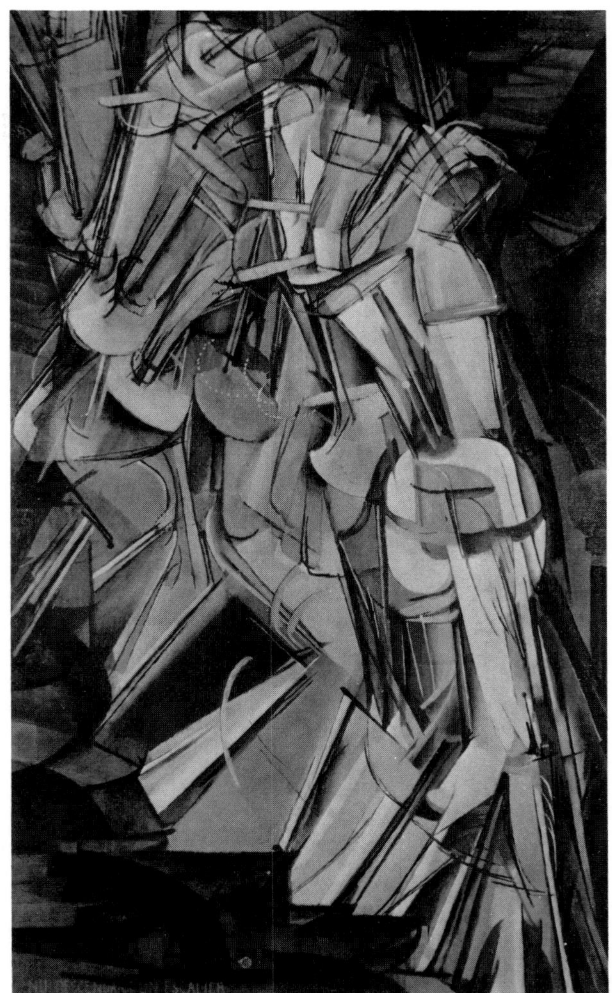

Marcel Duchamp. *Nude Descending a Staircase, No. 2.* 1912. Oil on canvas, 58 × 35 inches. Philadelphia Museum of Art. The Louise and Walter Arensberg Collection

or for the seething inner hatred, or for the delight in physical assault; and although he responded to anything that stressed the newness and the idiosyncrasy of modern life, he was really much happier with the unquestioning and beatific attitude of Roger de La Fresnaye in his *The Conquest of the Air,* or of Robert Delaunay in his *Homage to Blériot.* Quite apart from that, he responded best on a basis of personal contact; and during the period immediately before 1914 he was introduced to a completely new set of attitudes to art by his friendship with Marcel Duchamp and Francis Picabia.

It was by no means clear at that time that Marcel Duchamp was one of the most remarkable men of the 20th century and that Francis Picabia would turn out to have so many new ideas that he could never be bothered to follow any of them up very far. Duchamp in January, 1911, was simply the youngest and quite possibly the least gifted of the three sons of a provincial lawyer who were making a name for themselves in Paris as artists, certainly, but also as talkers and negotiators and spreaders of ideas. The oldest brother had taken the working name of Jacques Villon and was doing his best to graft a systematic and mathematical turn of mind onto the basically intuitive and pragmatical character of Cubism as it was practiced by Picasso and Braque. The second brother, Raymond Duchamp-Villon, was known to be tacking this way and that in the general direction of Cubist sculpture. Duchamp-Villon had been a partisan of the age of steel since 1889, when he was taken to an industrial exhibition at the age of 13. In *The Horse* he took a subject from a preindustrial phase of civilization and combined it with the "superior dynamism" which he believed to be characteristic of the machine age. The horse is unmistakably a horse, and yet it bears out what Duchamp-Villon once wrote: "The power of the machine imposes itself upon us to such an extent that we can scarcely imagine living bodies without it."

As for Marcel Duchamp, he was 23 when he painted a relatively conservative portrait of his father, 24 when he painted the *Portrait of Chess Players* and still not yet 25 when he painted one of the most famous pictures of this century, the *Nude Descending a Staircase, No. 2.* He was, in other words, outstandingly precocious in an age when, more and more, the big men tended to mature slowly. When the Armory Show opened in New York on February 19, 1913, it was Duchamp, at 26, who touched the nerve of popular interest with the *Nude Descending a Staircase,* even though there were masterpieces on hand by men 10 and 20 years older than he.

Popular interest often goes astray, but in this case New Yorkers were more discerning than those of Duchamp's colleagues who railed against

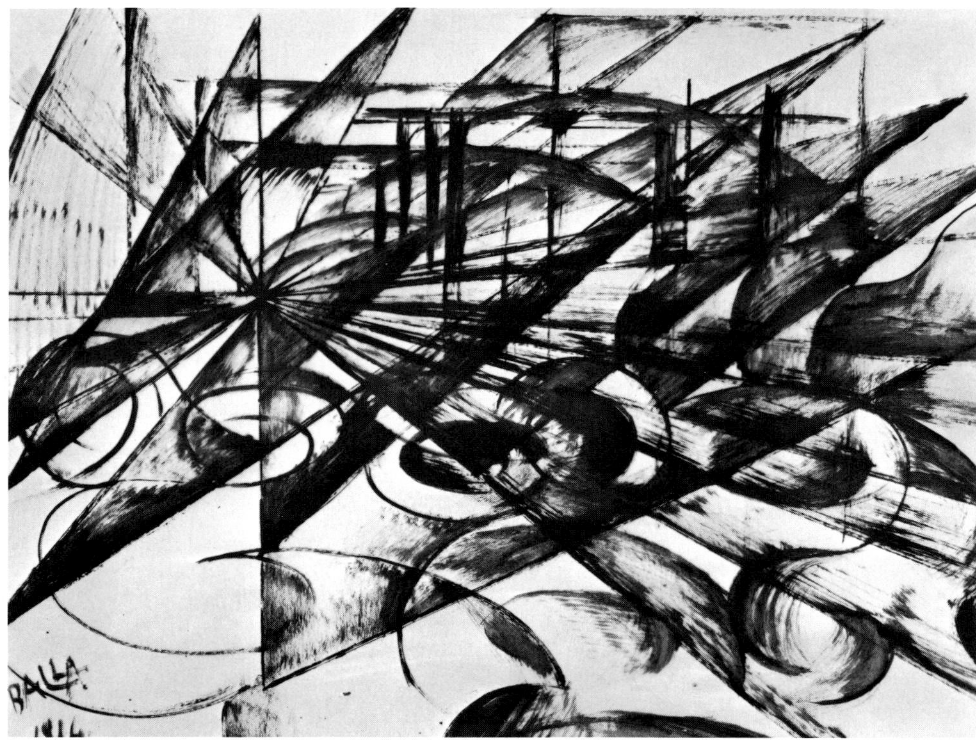

Giacomo Balla.
Car in a Race. 1914.
Brush, tempera and ink on paper mounted on canvas, 21¼ × 28⅞ inches.
Art Gallery of Ontario, Toronto.
Gift of Sam and Ayala Zacks

the *Nude Descending a Staircase* when he thought of showing it in the Salon des Indépendants in Paris in 1912. Duchamp's fellow Frenchmen regarded it as not authentically Cubist (in which they were quite right) and as a sellout to Italian Futurism (in which they were quite wrong, in that the picture was completed by January, 1912, and at a time when no examples of Italian Futurist painting had been seen in Paris). Duchamp had been close enough to the auxiliary Cubists for them to read the picture as in some way a defection from their beliefs; and the issues raised by the Futurists were hot enough, in February and March, 1912, for certain people to lose their heads when presented with what was a demonstration of, among much else, the Futurist thesis that "on account of the persistence of an image upon the retina, moving objects constantly multiply and become deformed as they succeed one another like vibrations hurled into the space which they traverse." Notations of that are fundamental to such classics of Futurism as Balla's *Dog on a Leash* and *Girl Running along a Balcony.*

But both these pictures by Balla were painted after the *Nude Descending a Staircase.* Duchamp got the point all by himself, just as he got the point of chronophotography (the recording of human beings or animals in motion by means of successive photographic exposures) in the form in which it first came to notice late in the 19th century. Indeed, he brought about a coherent if temporary alliance between these ideas and the practice of Analytical Cubism; and this he did in that spirit of detached and mischievous inquiry which was to characterize so much of his later work. Duchamp was one of the quickest learners in the history of art, but what he had learned was never presented in an unaltered, frontal way. It was angled: aligned, in other words, to certain steadfast preoccupations of his own.

The fascination of the *Nude Descending* does not derive from the successful crossbreeding of two idioms which were then much in the air. It has a more complex origin. Duchamp had been drawing and painting the female nude in one way or another since the beginning of 1910 (and in defiance, by the way, of the Futurists' ten-year veto on the painting of the nude). Few men have been more sensitive than he to the beauty of women, or more adroit in their acts of homage to it; but Duchamp was also very much aware both of the elements of comedy and indignity which beset all sexual relationships and of the absurdities inherent in the apparatus which Nature has provided for their fulfillment. Comparisons in this context with machinery, real or imagined, are sometimes to our advantage, sometimes not; either way, the subject in 1912 was wide open for treatment.

Duchamp never liked to "explain" his work, in an everyday sense; but he never deliberately concealed its meanings, either, and when he said that he owed a great deal to Odilon Redon he meant, I think, that like Redon he enjoyed secreting one mystery within another. When Redon made his illustrations for Flaubert and for Edgar Allan Poe, he never produced a one-to-one realization of ideas already explicit in the text. Duchamp, in the two versions of the *Nude Descending*, was starting from an idea suggested to him in a poem by Jules Laforgue; and the inner subject of the two paintings may well be the notion that even an ideal re-creation of feminine beauty, a machine freed from the imperfections of our real-life anatomy, would nonetheless end up looking much like the clanking, ungainly and fallible bag of bones that is familiar to us. No fulfilled work of art has any one definitive explanation; but it is because this idea is one of many that can be put forward and not laughed out of existence that the *Nude Descending* still bears endless discussion.

The Armory Show was not the last manifestation of the pacific International. Nor was it even the grandest thing of its sort; that title should go to the Autumn Salon of 1913 in Berlin, where virtually everything that has been discussed here was represented in an ideally ample way, together with the debuts of Americans like Marsden Hartley and Germans like Max Ernst. But the Armory Show has a special significance for us here, in that thereafter America was wide open to the new; and with the arrival in New York of Francis Picabia in 1913, and of Marcel Duchamp in 1915, there occurred a significant addition to the geography of modern art.

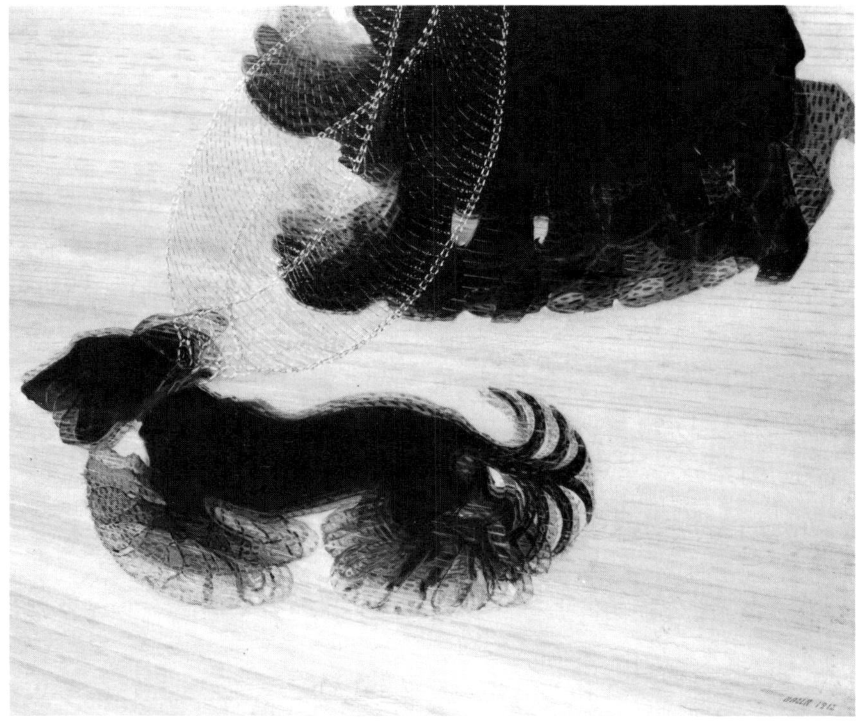

Giacomo Balla.
Dog on a Leash.
1912.
Oil on canvas,
35⅜ × 43¼ inches.
Bequest of
A. Conger Goodyear
to George F.
Goodyear,
life interest, and
Albright-Knox Art
Gallery, Buffalo

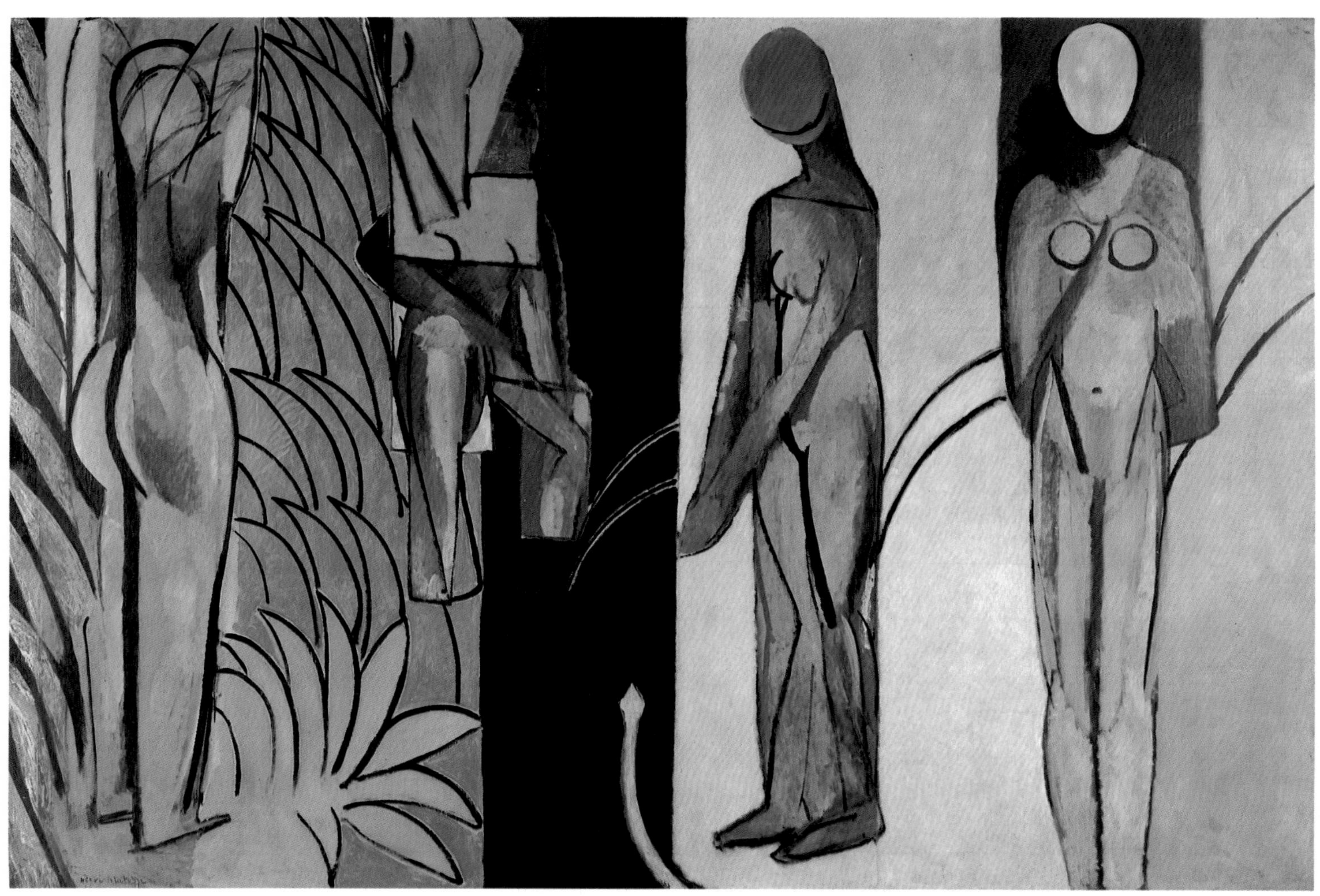

Henri Matisse.
Bathers by a River.
1916–17.
Oil on canvas,
8 feet 7 inches ×
12 feet 10 inches.
The Art Institute of
Chicago.
Charles H. and
Mary F. S.
Worcester
Collection

AN ALTERNATIVE ART

The old order fell apart in Europe in August, 1914; and art fell apart with it.

It didn't show all at once. Some people went on making art; some other people went on looking at it. Museums stayed open, exhibitions were held, magazines came out on time. But something had gone down forever: the unity, the stability, the perfected internationalism of the European art scene before 1914. How could it be otherwise, when Braque, Derain, Léger and Apollinaire were in the army on one side and Kirchner, Marc, Macke and Ernst were in the army on the other? What continuity of contact could there be when Mikhail Larionov was wounded in East Prussia while serving with the Russian Army and the heavy-shouldered, self-confident Max Beckmann was broken in mind by his experiences as a German hospital orderly?

One or two people held out. Matisse had so prodigious a power of concentration, and was so armored against outside interference, that he was able to go on producing masterpieces—few, but telling—throughout World War I. "A man who is not at the front feels good for nothing," he wrote in 1916; but a Matisse like the *Bathers by a River* of 1916–17 is an emblem of sublime determination, rather than of privileged inactivity.

There was also one major painter who was actually changed for the better by the war. Fernand Léger found in his service with the French artillery a degree of social and artistic fulfillment which had never come his way before. He loved the look of the guns and their immaculate functioning. He loved his comrades-in-arms for their offhand courage and their frank and incisive manner of speech. For the first time he felt himself a completely integrated member of society. "It was in wartime," he said later, "that I really got my feet on the ground." His paintings in 1913–14 had been concerned mainly with contrasts of abstract form; but life at the front soon put an end to that, and in paintings like *The Card Players* he tried to bring out the lessons of wartime—the oneness of man and machine, the total democracy of the con-

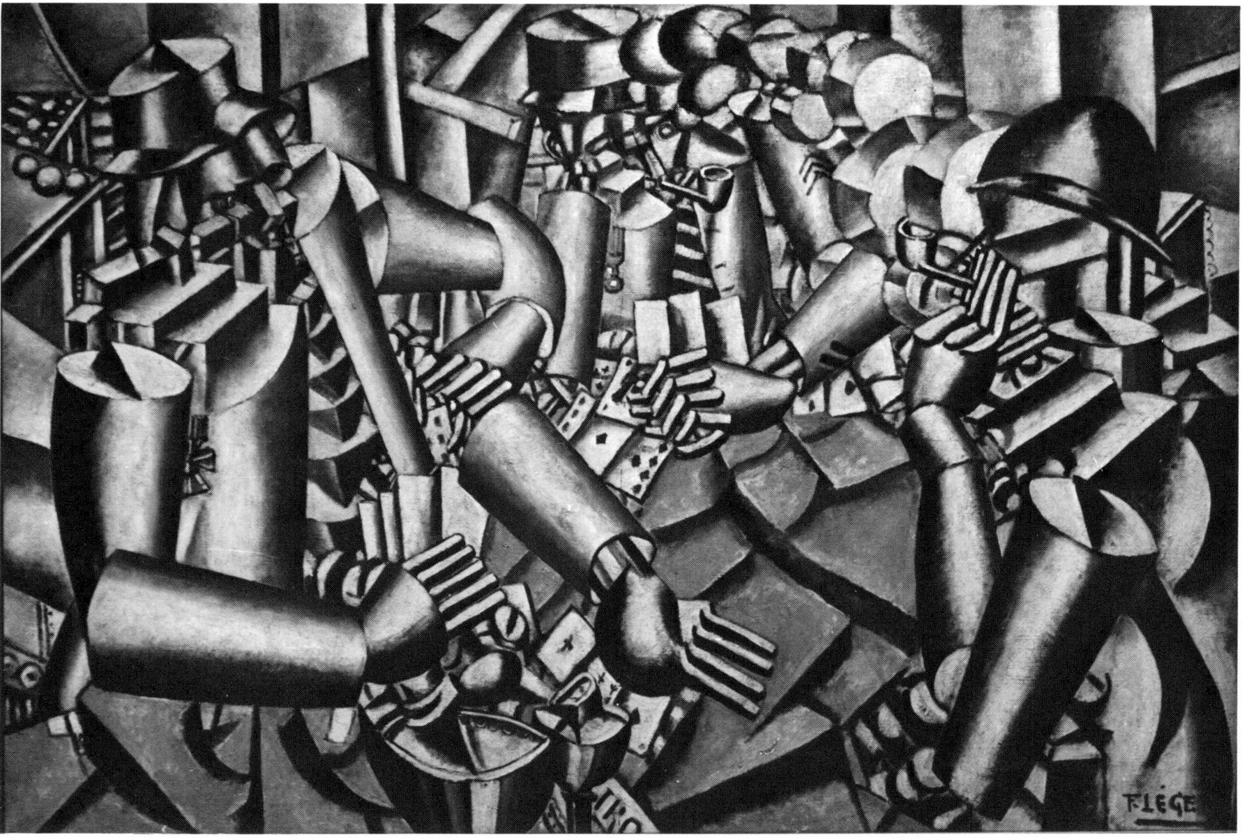

Fernand Léger.
The Card Players.
1917.
Oil on canvas,
50⅞ inches × 6
feet 4 inches.
Rijksmuseum
Kröller-Müller,
Otterlo, Netherlands

tacts between one enlisted man and another, and the satisfactions of a life lived for one thing and one only.

But in general the effects of World War I were wholly negative. People got out of it, if they got out at all, as damaged human beings—Braque was trepanned in 1915 after being temporarily blinded, Léger was badly gassed in 1917, Macke was killed in 1914, Marc was killed in 1916. Kirchner went into a long depression. ("Before the war so healthy," Kirchner wrote in the year before his suicide, "and since then nothing but sickness.")

World War I was no time, therefore, for the traditional "career in art." Between 1914 and 1918 it was indecent even to think of the long haul from canvas to canvas, exhibition to exhibition, patron to patron, book to eulogious book. Such things were part of a social structure that had been called in question by the extent, and by the horror, of its breakdown. Who would want to show their work in an official exhibition when that same officialdom had prompted the iniquities so vividly described not long after by Winston Churchill in his *World Crisis:* "No truce or parley mitigated the strife of the armies. The wounded died between the lines; the dead mouldered into the soil. Poison gas in many forms stifled or seared the soldiers. Liquid fire was projected upon their bodies. Men fell from the air in flames, or were smothered, often slowly, in the dark recesses of the sea."

The times called for an alternative art—something that would allow the creative instinct to come through at full strength and yet have none of the social or financial connotations of "fine art." Such an art would be a matter of ideas cut to the bone; it would travel light; it might have only a short life and a distribution among half a dozen people. It must be ready for an irreversible break with the past, and it must set no store by location. The artist could not depend on a certain light, a certain rhythm of life, a certain circumambient culture; himself and one suitcase would have to be enough.

Such an art did come about, from 1915 onward. It came about in New York, initially, and it came about later in Zurich, in Cologne, in Hanover, in Berlin and, eventually, in Paris. It was an odd, extreme and sometimes desperate art; but then those were odd, extreme and desperate times. It was not at all unified; its attitudes ranged from a wholehearted political commitment to a dandified rejection of the outer world *in toto.* There were people who risked lynching for their beliefs, and there were others who thought, with Picabia, that they should change their ideas as often as they changed their shirts. The art in question produced, in Marcel Duchamp's *Large Glass,* what has rightly been called "the most elaborately fabricated art object of this century"; it also produced at least one periodical of which no copy survives and art objects which the observer was invited to destroy. Tempers can still run hot when this alternative art is under discussion; but if any one thing about it is beyond dispute it is the fact that for a year or two, from 1915 onward, its headquarters was in New York.

Three things made this possible: the presence in New York of Marcel Duchamp and, intermittently, of Francis Picabia, the emergence of a new kind of American artist (Man Ray, above all), and the enthusiasm of a small group of new-style American collectors. (There was also, of course, the fact that until April, 1917, the United States remained neutral in World War I.) Collecting modern art in North America was pioneered at just this time by John Quinn, the beaky, pertinacious lawyer who had been one of the prime movers of the Armory Show; by Walter Arensberg, eventually to have a wing of his own at the Philadelphia Museum; by Arthur Jerome Eddy, one of the great benefactors of The Art Institute of Chicago; by the bizarre and redoubtable Dr. Alfred Barnes, founder of the Barnes Collection in Merion, Pa.; and by Miss Lillie P. Bliss, one of the founders of The Museum of Modern Art in New York. Add to these Miss Katherine Dreier, who, with Marcel Duchamp's help and support, formed the avant-garde collection which is now at Yale, and it becomes clear that New York from 1915 was exceptionally alert to the new.

The Armory Show traditionally gets the credit for this, and it is perfectly true that in 1913 it assembled in record time a panorama that on the European side ran from Ingres and Delacroix to Kandinsky's *Improvisation No. 27* and Brancusi's *The Kiss.* It updated enthusiasms, all around. The Metropolitan Museum of Art bought its first Cézanne from the Armory Show, for instance, and there was not an American artist of any quality who did not find it in one way or another a tremendous experience. But it should also be said that the bulk of the Armory Show represented a solid, safe taste. If the "new" was naturalized in New York by 1915, Alfred Stieglitz deserves much of the credit. An artist in his own right—with the camera—he had, since 1905, been running a little gallery at the top of a brownstone house at 291 Fifth Avenue. By 1913 regular visitors would have seen sizable shows by Rodin, Toulouse-Lautrec, Matisse (twice) and Picasso. Stieglitz had a nose for the new in American art, too, and he sponsored the debuts of John Marin, Max Weber, Arthur Dove and Georgia O'Keeffe (whom he married). "I am trying," he once said, "to establish an America in which I can breathe as a free man." He believed that America would not always be one of the outer provinces of art: a place from which moneyed people journeyed to France to buy Degas and Renoir. Out of America, something great would come. Stieglitz would have agreed in that context with Ezra Pound, who wrote to a friend in August, 1912, that the American awakening, when it finally came, would "make the Italian Renaissance look like a tempest in a teapot."

Intimations of this awakening were many, both in Paris and New York, in the years of Stieglitz's activity. In Paris before 1914 Patrick Henry Bruce

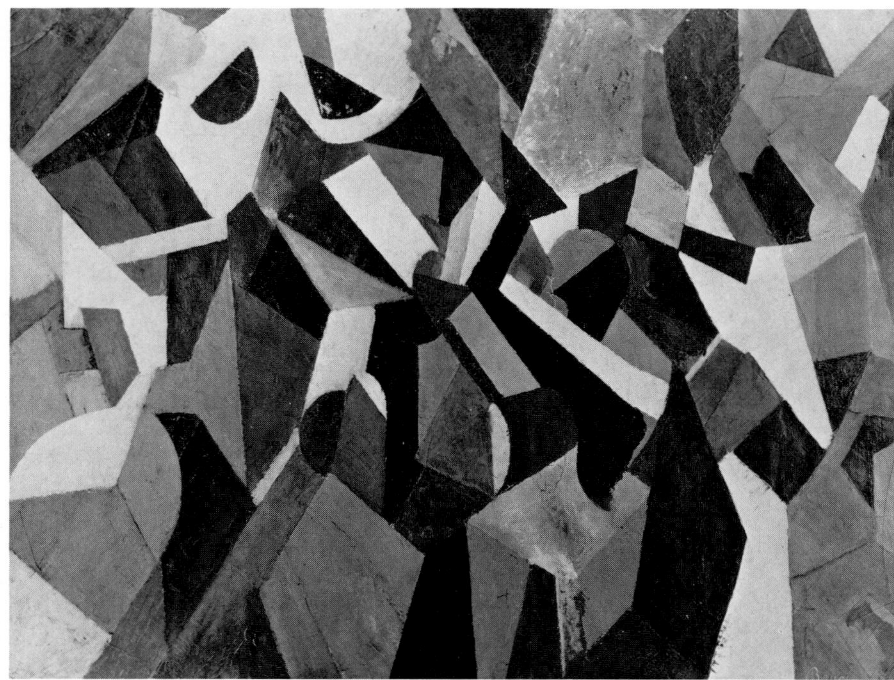

Patrick Henry Bruce.
Composition II.
c. 1916–17.
Oil on canvas,
38¼ × 51 inches.
Yale University Art Gallery, New Haven.
Gift of Collection Société Anonyme

was a student of Matisse and a friend of Robert Delaunay. As much as any American of his generation, he understood what had happened to painting, and more especially to color, in the 20th century. With his intelligence, his carefully nurtured gifts, and his close personal contacts in Paris, he could have been one of the leaders of a new American art; but he preferred to remain in Paris, where he pursued an increasingly isolated course. In 1932 he gave up painting and destroyed all but a few of his canvases; in 1937 he committed suicide.

Among the young American painters who abounded in Paris before 1914, Stanton Macdonald-Wright was outstanding for the energy with which he adapted to the theories of color which were propagated by Robert Delaunay. He brought to the exploitation of Delaunay's theories a largeness of feeling which can truly be called American; and after years of careful study he was able to use color, in itself and by itself, to blast off into an empyrean of his own devising. While still adhering to what he called "the fundamental laws of composition (placements and displacements of mass as in the human body in movement)" he avoided all direct reference to identifiable forms; the soft voluptuous shapes floated freely, defining and redefining themselves in terms of pure color.

There were also gifted Americans who had been to Paris and come back again. Max Weber, an American born in Russia, had studied painting in Paris, where he became engrossed with Cubism. But he also prized very highly the brilliant and unequivocal coloring of American Indian dolls, quilts and blankets; and when he took, as in his *Chinese Restaurant,* a subject from everyday life in Manhattan, he gave it a crisp, allover sparkle which derived as much from American sources as from the graver, more slow-moving procedures of Cubism.

Paris was not the only European city to tempt the American avant-garde. In his middle 30s Marsden Hartley spent much of his time in Germany. Stieglitz paid for him to go to Paris in 1912, but in 1913–14 he was in Munich and came to know Kandinsky and his colleagues in the Blue Rider group. Having seen the German military machine at close quarters, he was able in his *Portrait of a German Officer* to suggest to what an extent the uniform was the man. The little picture also dem-

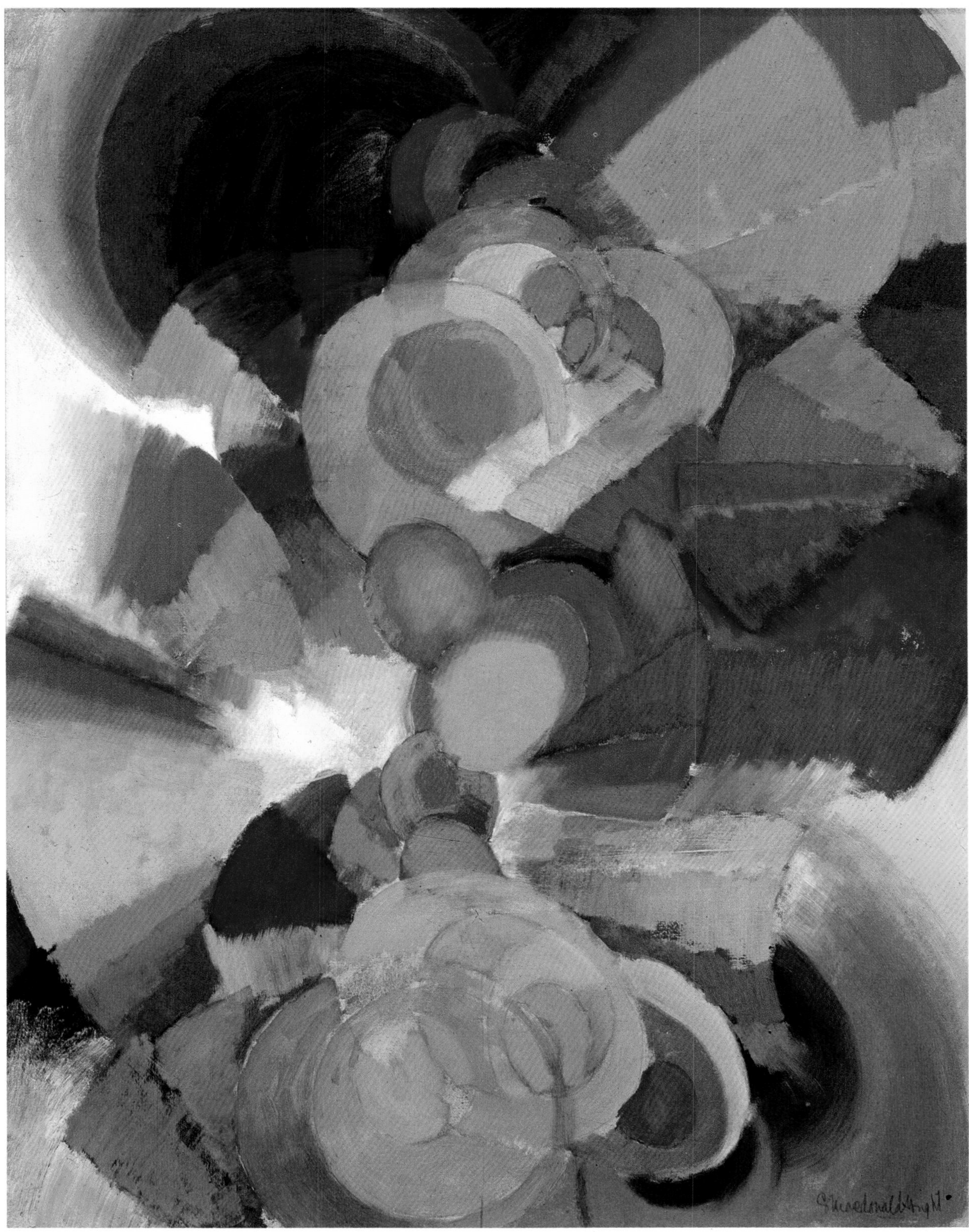

Stanton Macdonald-Wright. *Abstraction on Spectrum (Organization 5).* 1914. Oil on canvas, 30 × 24 inches. Des Moines Art Center. Nathan Emory Coffin Memorial Collection

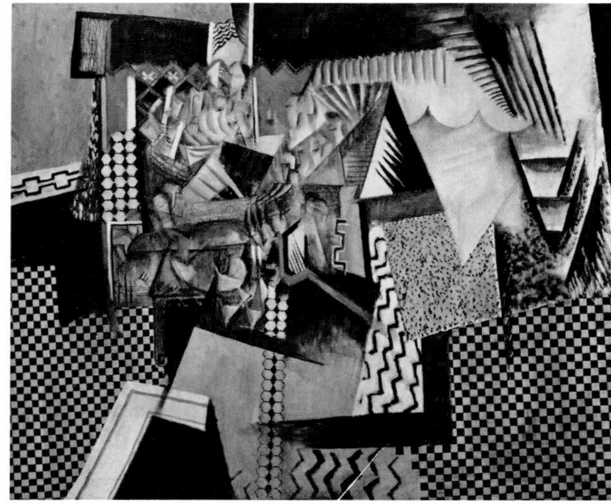

Max Weber.
Chinese Restaurant.
1915.
Oil on canvas,
40 × 48 inches.
Whitney Museum of American Art, New York

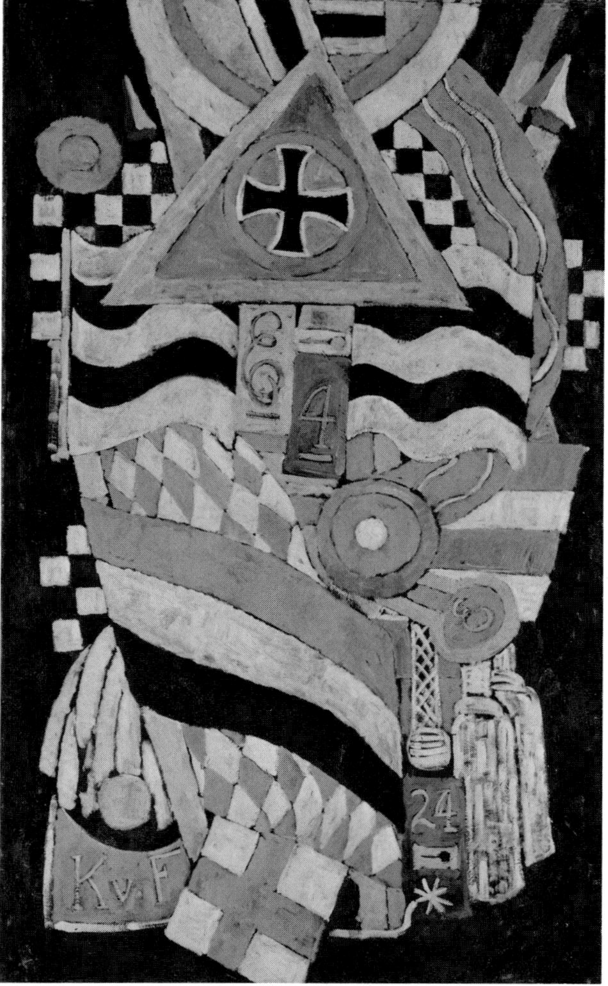

Marsden Hartley.
Portrait of a German Officer.
1914.
Oil on canvas,
68¼ × 41⅜ inches.
The Metropolitan Museum of Art, New York.
The Alfred Stieglitz Collection

onstrates the uses of a pictorial shorthand in which shapes are abstracted from nature and fitted together in such a way as to make an image as striking as it is concise.

But in point of fact an American artist at that time did not have to go anywhere to sense what was going on, both in art and in a more general sense. Man Ray was not the only artist to be haunted in 1914 by the notion of an army on the move; but there is something particularly vivid about the faceless and monolithic horde that obeys the order to march in his *A.D. MCMXIV.* As for *The Rope Dancer* of 1916, it could be called the last in the canon of circus paintings which began with Degas, Seurat and Toulouse-Lautrec. What Man Ray did was to chart the dancer's progress along the rope in terms of the different shadows that she cast from her lofty perch. By rendering the shadows in terms of flat panels of pure color he was able to divide up the canvas in a way that can be read either as abstract painting of an incisive and astringent sort or as a veracious portrait of the dancer's unsteady progress.

Sometimes the transmission of ideas from one continent was as mysterious to the layman as is the pollination that results from transoceanic winds. For instance, Arthur Dove was neither learned nor widely traveled, but by 1911 he was able to symbolize the forces of Nature as vividly as any of his contemporaries in Germany or elsewhere. With highly energized tusk-and-comma forms he could epitomize the look of an upland landscape traversed by high winds, marked out alternately by sun and shadow, sharply accented by hillock and tall tree.

New York by 1916 was the kind of forcing-house, in a smaller and more intimate way, that Paris and Munich had been before 1914. At the time of her New York debut in that year, Georgia O'Keeffe already had at her command a highly simplified vocabulary of form. With just one or two shapes, sumptuous in color and dreamlike in the way that they oozed slowly across the paper, she produced images which were peculiar to herself.

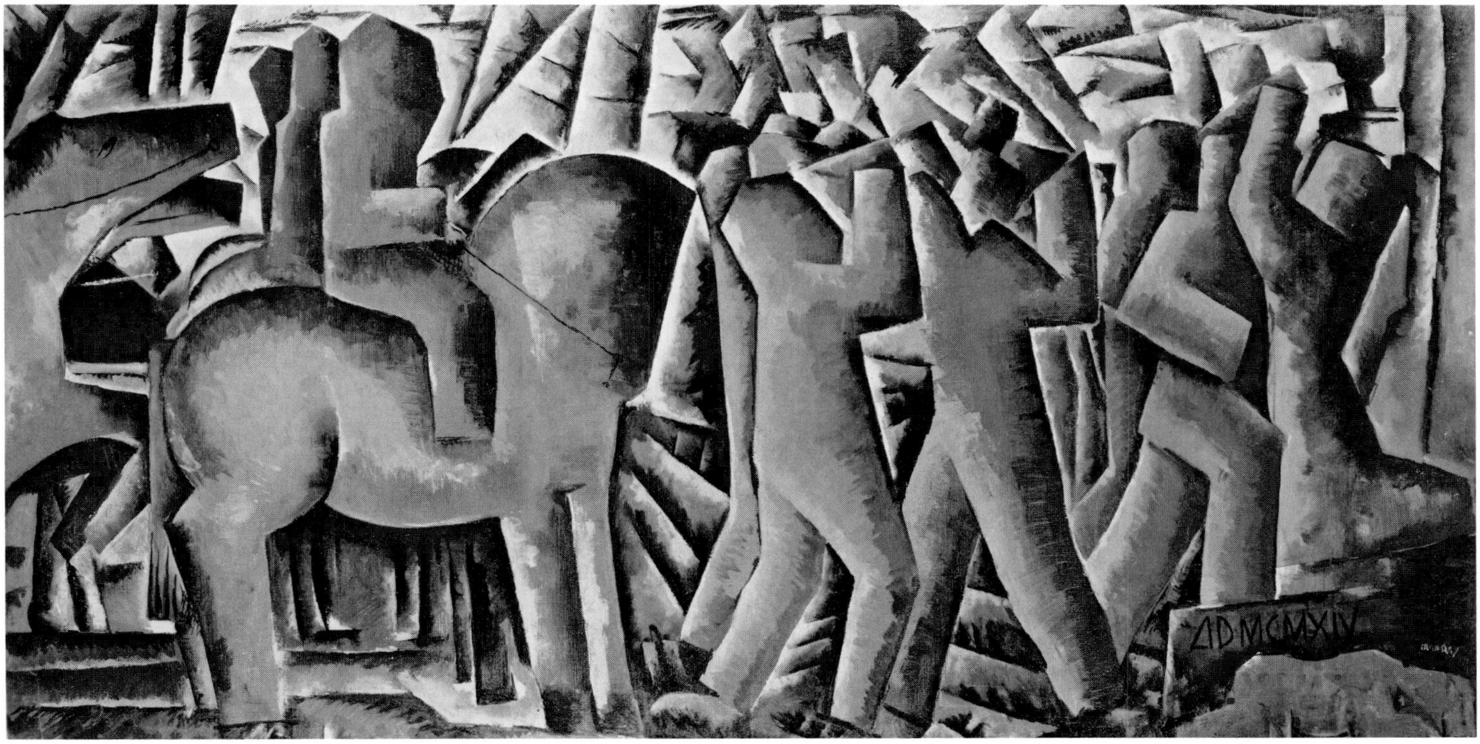

Man Ray.
A.D. MCMXIV.
1914.
Oil on canvas,
37 × 69½ inches.
Philadelphia Museum of Art.
The A. E. Gallatin Collection

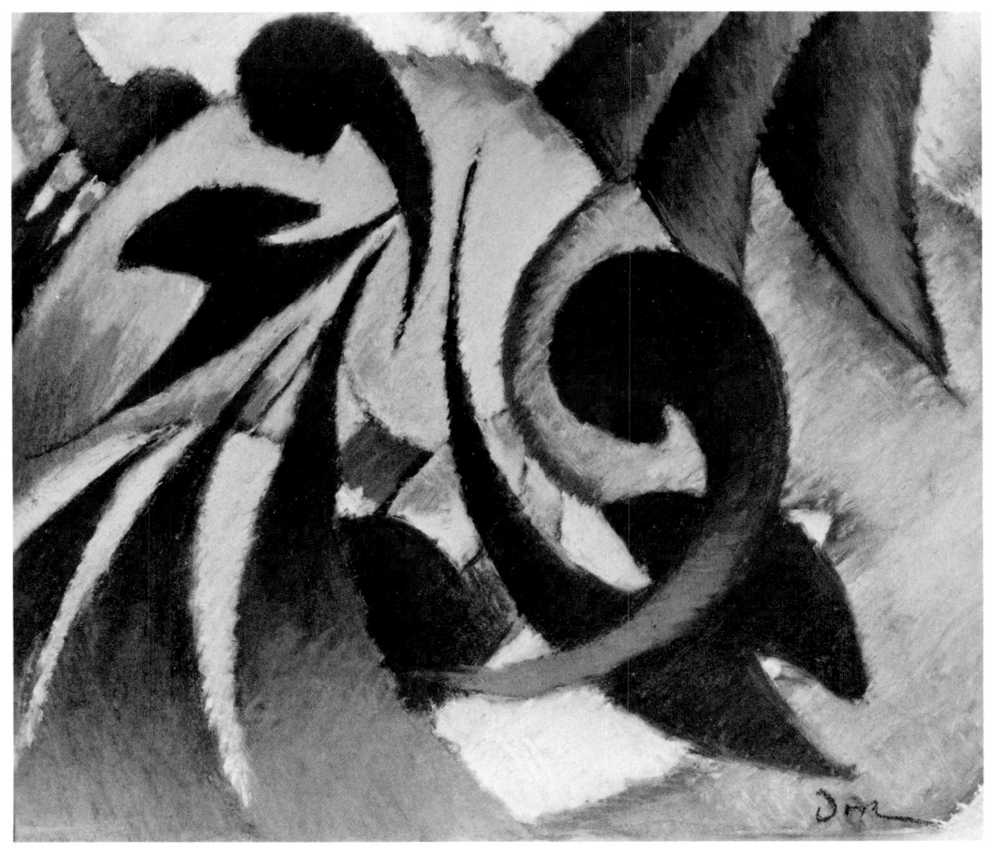

Arthur G. Dove.
Nature Symbolized, No. 2. 1911.
Pastel, 17⅞ × 21½ inches.
The Art Institute of Chicago.
The Alfred Stieglitz Collection

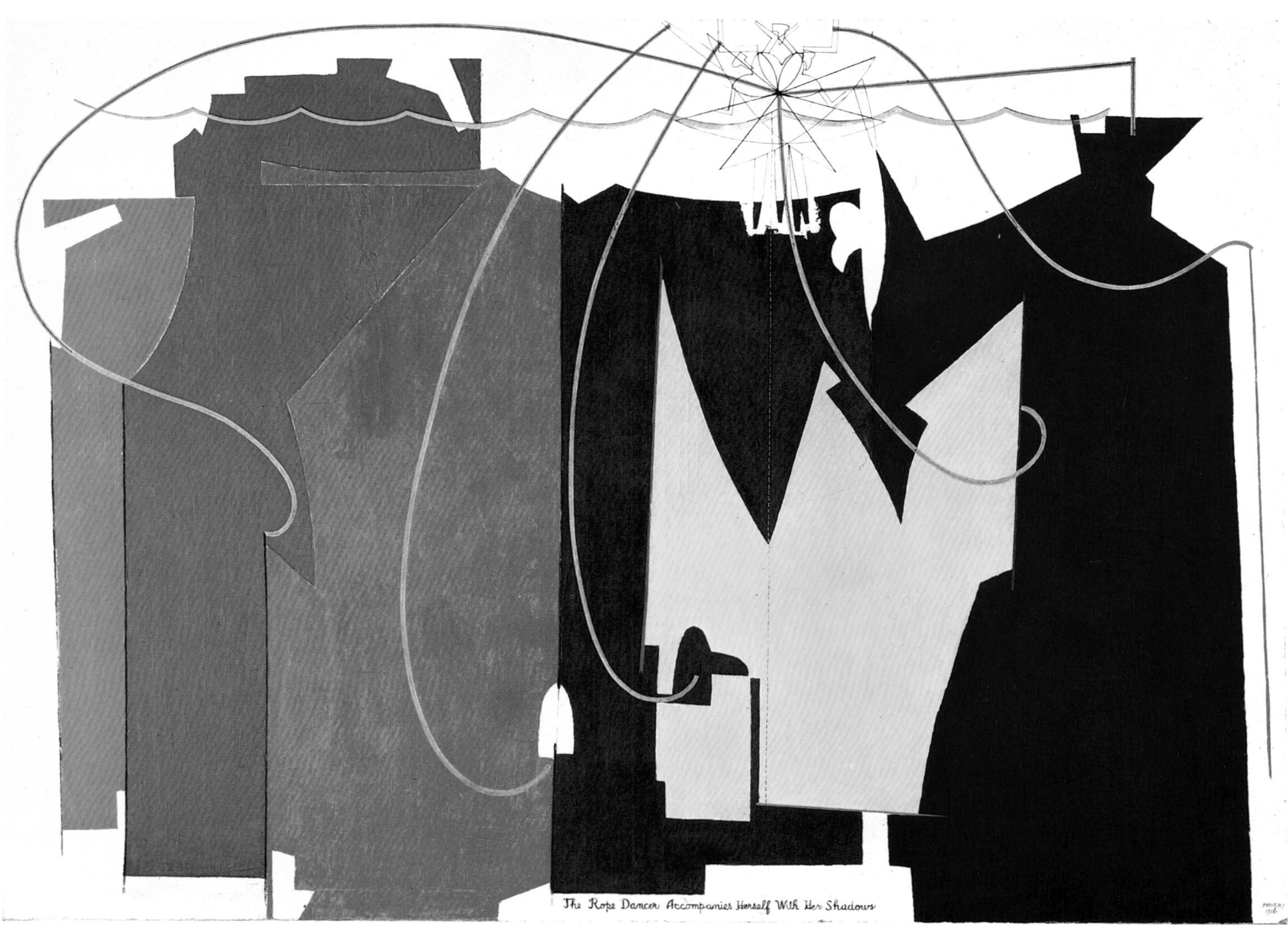

Man Ray.
The Rope Dancer Accompanies Herself with Her Shadows.
1916.
Oil on canvas, 52 inches × 6 feet 1⅜ inches.
The Museum of Modern Art, New York. Gift of G. David Thompson

Francis Picabia.
I See Again in Memory My Dear Udnie. 1914.
Oil on canvas, 8 feet 2½ inches × 6 feet 6¼ inches.
The Museum of Modern Art, New York.
Hillman Periodicals Fund

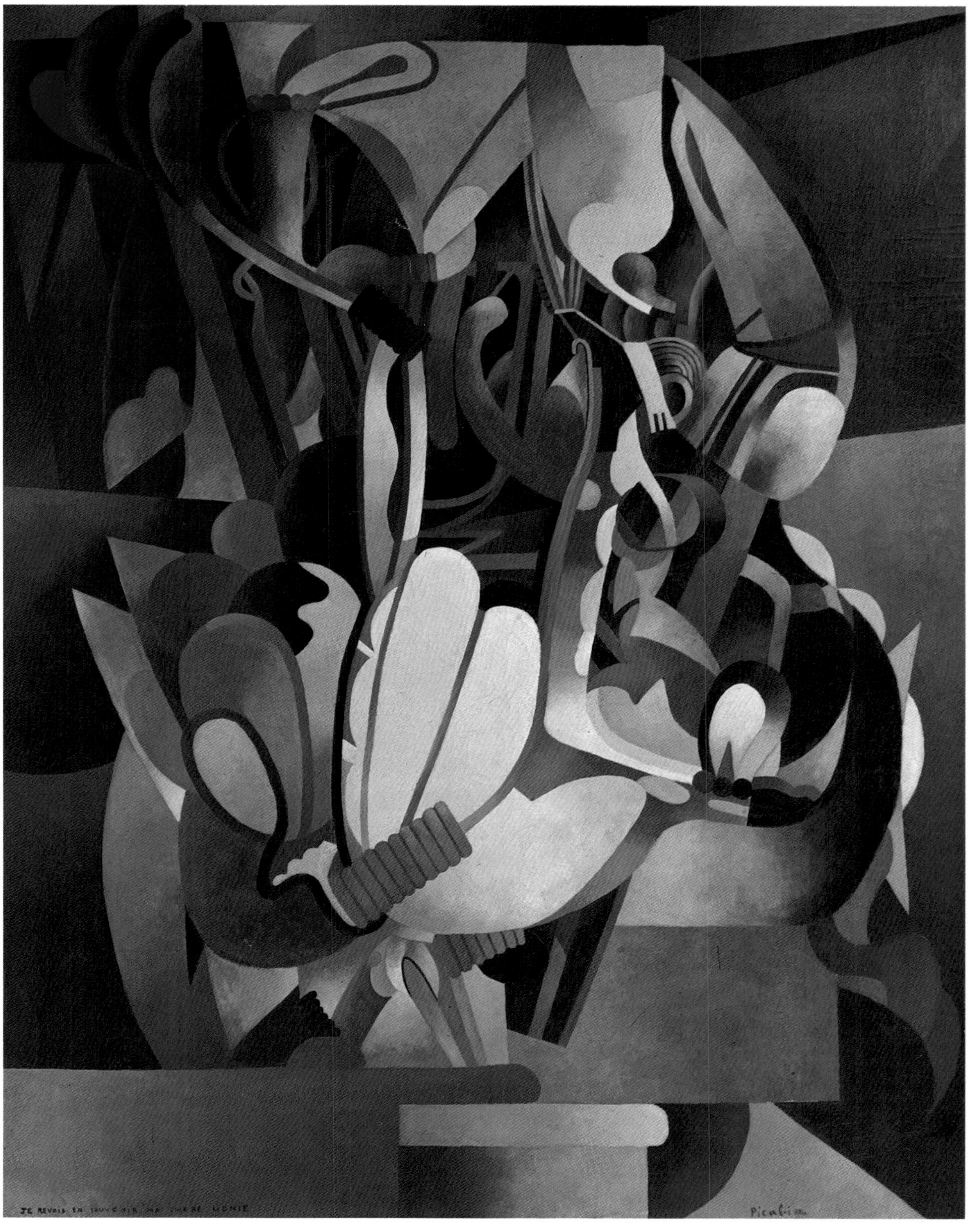

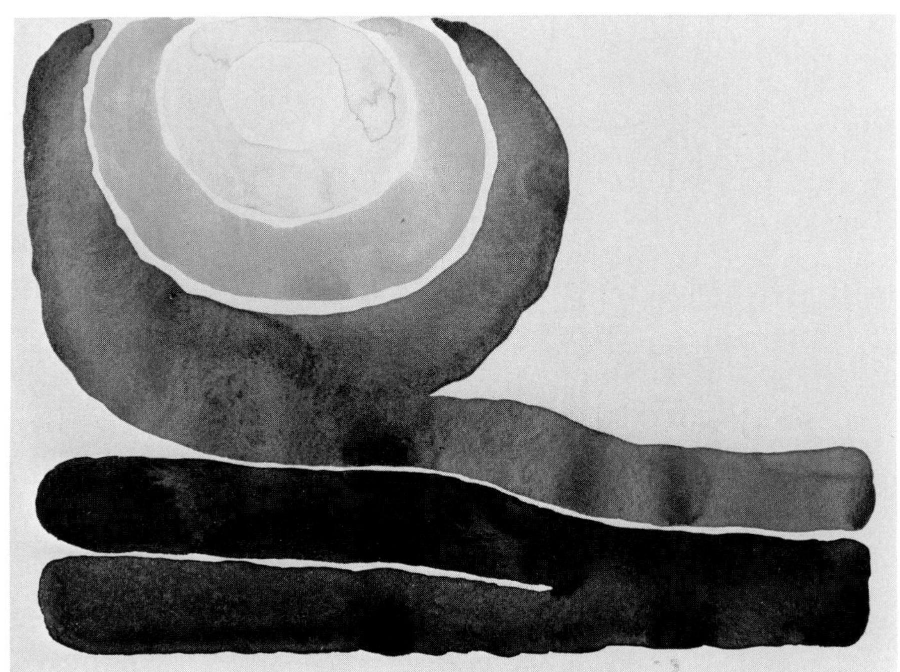

Georgia O'Keeffe.
Evening Star III.
1917.
Watercolor,
9 × 11⅞ inches.
The Museum of Modern Art, New York.
Mr. and Mrs. Donald B. Straus Fund

They might be a portrait of Nature at her most hushed and velvety; but they were also fragments of autobiography that stood, as she said herself, for "things that I had no words for."

Meanwhile the great American public was quite correct in sensing at the Armory Show that Duchamp and Picabia were modern in a sense that Matisse and Picasso and Braque were not. It was not their ambition to become part of the continuum of serious art which in Europe had stretched, unbroken, for eight centuries. In fact they thought that that continuum might just as well come to an end. Matisse and Braque were content to work 12 or 14 hours a day in the hope of ending up in the Louvre; but Duchamp had come to believe by 1915 that the role of the artist was to do things perfectly and do them once only. As for Picabia, he had been in New York at the time of the Armory Show; and he had very much made himself felt, with his swarthy good looks, his flamboyant manner and his readiness to be distracted from the studio by a fast car, a pretty woman or a first-rate bottle of wine. He was rich —his grandfather had pioneered the construction of a railroad from Madrid to Corunna—and he openly ridiculed the honest-workman approach to art which was common among the French painters of his acquaintance. In 1909 he was having every possible success in France as a late-Impressionist painter, only to decide from one day to the next that he couldn't be bothered to go on with it. *French Impetuosity* was the title he gave to one of his later paintings, and in New York he lived up to it. New Yorkers took to him at once, and they were relieved to find at the Armory Show that in his hands even Cubism took on a jazzy, accessible character. He identified very strongly with America, and he was serious enough to realize from his daily contacts with the Stieglitz circle that New York would soon have an avant-garde that would not have to depend on injections of new blood from abroad.

Duchamp had always liked and admired Picabia. As the youngest son of a French provincial lawyer, Duchamp had been reared in a tradition of thrift, hard work and systematic consolidation. Picabia had a recklessness, a wide and exotic social acquaintance and an iconoclastic, spendthrift turn of mind which were a revelation to Duchamp when the two first became friends in the fall of 1911. He just hadn't thought it possible that such people existed. Picabia by the spring of 1913 had become so much a New Yorker by adoption that Duchamp was beyond doubt wide open to suggestion when Walter Pach, coorganizer of the Armory Show, declared in the winter of 1914–15 that he, too, should cross the Atlantic. Duchamp had been excused from military service because of a weak heart. He was bored by the seedy, depleted, unsmiling character of Parisian art life in wartime. He took the boat for New York in June, 1915, and he lived there, on and off, until his death in 1968.

Duchamp at that time was known to thousands of Americans as "the man who painted the *Nude Descending a Staircase.*" That painting had been beyond question the great success of the Armory Show. It had been lampooned and caricatured day after day in the newspapers; it had been bought, sight unseen, by telegram from Albuquerque; at the Armory itself the crowd around it was so thick that many visitors never got to see it at all. Duchamp in 1915 had a celebrity in North America which he was never to acquire in the country of his birth. Walter Pach was at the dock when he arrived. They went straight to Walter Arensberg's apartment at 33 West 67th Street, and Duchamp stayed there not for an afternoon but for a month. Unlike Picabia, he had no visible needs, was not interested in possessions, and never put himself forward. But when it became clear that he had no new paintings to sell and that even to breathe the air of New York cost money, it was John Quinn above all who came to the rescue. Quinn was not rich by the standards of a Mellon or a Morgan, but when it came to man-to-man patronage he did more for art and literature in our century than anyone, anywhere. If it had not been for John Quinn, it is quite possible that T. S. Eliot would never have completed *The Waste Land* nor James Joyce seen *Ulysses* in the bookstores. Ezra Pound and Joseph Conrad were among the others who had reason to be grateful to Quinn; and when Quinn sensed that Marcel Duchamp could use a little money he hired him, part-time and with all possible discretion, to look after his French correspondence for an honorarium of $100 a month. With this, Duchamp could live as he liked to live and get on with his work.

What work? Duchamp in that respect was the opposite of his close friend Picabia. Picabia had the instincts of a top-class vaudeville performer. He liked to "make it new" continually, and he liked his ideas to get across on the instant. Like Duchamp, he liked to think of the human anatomy in terms of emblematic machinery. But whereas Duchamp took great care to cover his tracks and to present his findings in terms that were close to abstraction, Picabia came out into the open. *I See Again in Memory My Dear Udnie* was prompted by Picabia's admiration for a dancer whom he had met on the boat on his way to New York in 1913. Petal shapes, clearly expressive of uplifted skirts, open themselves to nozzle-like forms, no less clearly expressive of the male sexual organ at a moment of strenuous activity. Picabia at that time owned Duchamp's *The Bride* of 1912, and there are evident affinities between the two, but Picabia was explicit by nature and was determined to remain so.

Where living was concerned, Duchamp learned a great deal from Picabia, but in his work he was indifferent to direct contact with the public. If anything, he disliked the idea of the work of art as something that could be comprehended directly and instantaneously. He was insistent that the enormous work on which he had been engaged since 1912 was not "a picture" in the traditional sense and that immediate retinal effect was not its aim. Painting since Courbet had gone steadily downhill, in his view, by substituting retinal satisfaction—the "pleasures of the eye"—for the more complex mingling of image and idea, delectation and close study, which gives true dignity to art.

Duchamp acted on this belief with characteristic pertinacity. In his progress from conventional painting to something more like map- or diagram-making an important part was played by a choco-

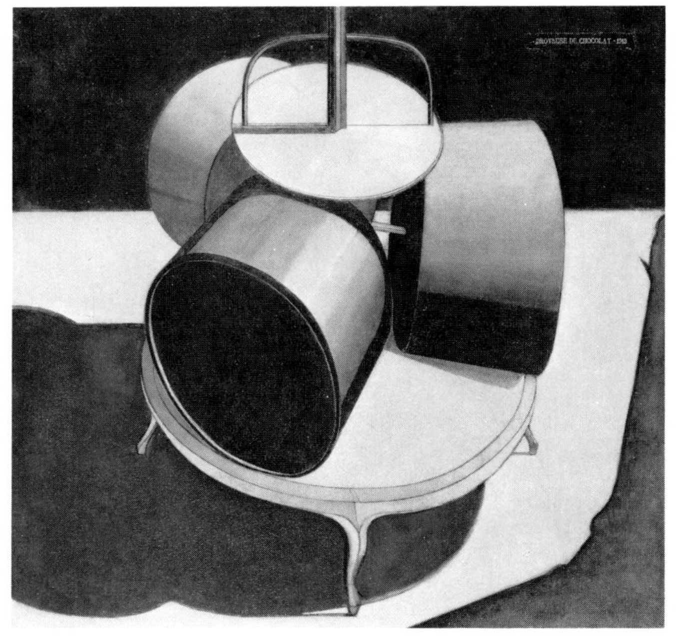

Marcel Duchamp.
Chocolate Grinder, No. 1. 1913.
Oil on canvas, 24⅜ × 25½ inches.
Philadelphia Museum of Art. The Louise and Walter Arensberg Collection

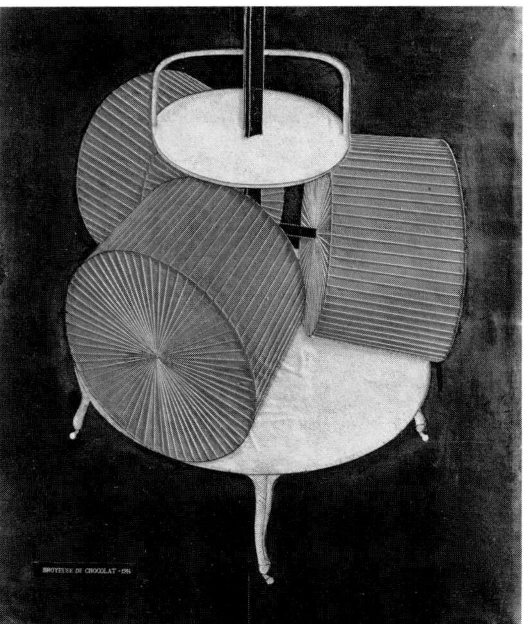

Marcel Duchamp.
Chocolate Grinder, No. 2. 1914.
Oil, thread and pencil on canvas, 25½ × 21¼ inches.
Philadelphia Museum of Art. The Louise and Walter Arensberg Collection

late grinder which he had seen in the window of the best confectioner in Rouen. Initially in 1913 he produced a traditional still-life painting *(No. 1)* varied only by the application of a leather label in the upper right-hand corner. Then in 1914 he produced an entirely different version *(No. 2)* in which the image was built rather than painted—and built quite frankly in three dimensions, with an emphatic use of glued string to make it clear that this was not "a painting," in the standard sense, but a constructed object of a new kind.

The Duchamp who disembarked in New York in June, 1915, was no longer, in any but a historical sense, "the man who painted the *Nude Descending.*" He had decided to demystify the act of painting, with its patient handcrafting, its pervasive smell of turpentine, and its courtship of the eye. New ways of conjugating experience were at hand, and it was for the artist to make use of them. A work of art was not simply something to look at; it was also, and much more, something to think about. And the way to force people to think about it was to take it out of the traditional contexts of art.

All this meant a break with art, as it was then understood (and nowhere more so than in Duchamp's family circle, where just about everyone was an artist and the theory, practice and politics of art were continually to the fore). Whether or not the break was prompted in part by a period of intense private emotion is a matter over which controversy has waxed hot and shows no signs of waning. But in any case Duchamp was, like everyone else, a product of his time. He grew up at a time when there seemed to be no limit to the number of ways in which machines could change life for the better. Machines made fresh miracles every day. And it seemed to Duchamp that the taut, impersonal procedures of the machine could also be carried over into art, and above all into the archaic procedures of freehand drawing. ("An absolutely precise coordinate drawing, with no relation to arty handwork," was his own description of what he was after at that time.)

In the late fall of 1911 Duchamp had been with Apollinaire and Picabia to see a stage production in Paris of Raymond Roussel's *Impressions of Africa;* in October, 1912, he made a motor trip from Paris to the Jura mountains, again with Apollinaire and Picabia. These were two capital experiences for him. From the Roussel he got a reinforced delight in the possibilities of the pun as a poetic instrument; he also got the notion, mooted in passing by Roussel, of a painting-machine which would put the honest workmen of the Salons out of business. During the journey to the Jura it undoubtedly became clear to him that Picabia fantasized about the motorcar-as-sexual-partner in ways now familiar to the point of tedium but then quite new; and from the notes which he later published we know that Duchamp took his habitual, detached but very incisive interest in the metaphoric possibilities of every aspect of the automobile, from the imperious silver-mounted headlamp to the lowly and fallible intestinal piping. Machines of one sort or another were to form the basic set on which many of his ideas would be structured. The machine did not serve him as a metaphor for limitless power and impeccable functioning. He saw it, rather, as a metaphor for frustration, discomfiture, pointless effort, self-deception and the failure to communicate. Duchamp was both skeptic and ironist; it was not in his nature to bow down to the machine. But from the time (November–December, 1911) when he painted a little picture of a coffee mill for his brother's kitchen, he was always aware of the machine's implications. The coffee mill in question had the unassuming look of a household pet, and it was still very painterly in its execution. But it stood for the analysis of a machine in movement; it stood for the diagram as opposed to the freehand drawing; and in a very discreet way it stood for the compulsive grinding which precedes the sexual climax. And it hung, like a ticking bomb, in one of the headquarters of Parisian retinal painting.

Duchamp was a child of his time in other ways too. His favorite books were the ones which had come out just before he himself was born, in July, 1887. "Rimbaud and Lautréamont seemed too old for me," he said later. "I wanted something younger." "Something younger" meant the Symbolist poet Jules Laforgue, whose two books of poems came out in 1885 and 1886; from Laforgue, Duchamp got the initial motif for his *Nude Descending.* (At a time when the traditional myths have lost most of their interest for artists and nonartists alike, the mythology of sexual pursuit and conquest has retained its fascination intact.) It also meant Mallarmé: the Spanish-language poet Octavio Paz is certainly right in associating the downward march of Duchamp's *Nude* to "the solemn moment" at which "Mallarmé's Igitur abandons his room forever and goes step by step down the stairs which lead to the crypt of his ancestors." "Something younger" meant finally Villiers de l'Isle-Adam's novel *Eve of the Future* (1886). It could be a coincidence, but it would be a pretty big one, that Duchamp worked for 12 years—1912–23—on his *Large Glass,* which, like *Eve of the Future,* has to do with the subjection of the male to a female of more than normal authority and power. Duchamp was born in the heyday of Symbolism, and he remained a symbolist all his life: a poet, that is to say, who produced complex

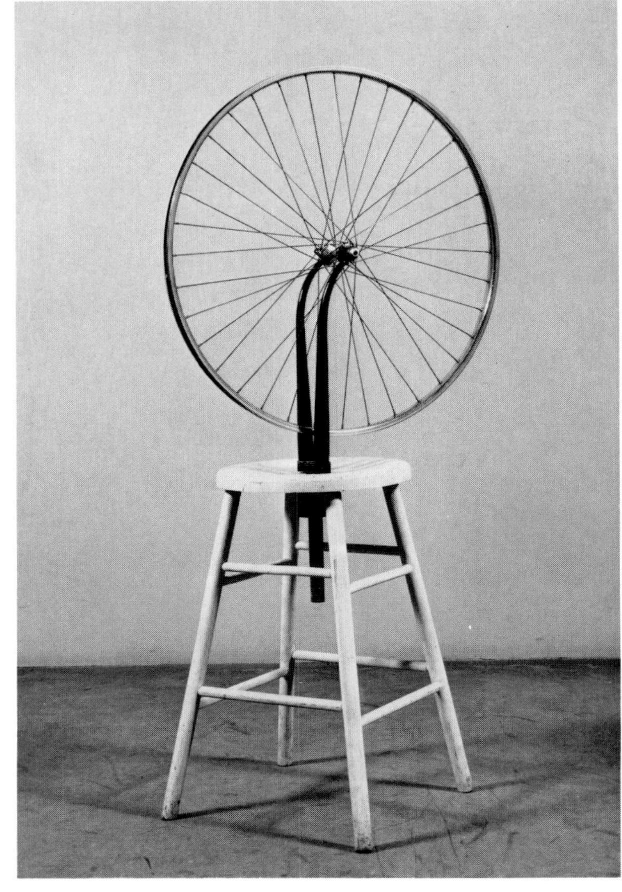

Marcel Duchamp. *Bicycle Wheel.* (1951; third version after lost original of 1913.) Readymade: bicycle wheel mounted on painted wooden stool, 50½ × 25½ × 16⅝ inches. The Museum of Modern Art, New York. The Sidney and Harriet Janis Collection

and evocative images which every generation reinterprets for itself.

That was the background of the man who, from 1912 onward, abandoned easel painting. Thereafter he produced, on the one hand, a small number of concise, irreducible, nonrepeatable statements; on the other, he made a sustained attempt, on the scale of epic, to reconcile image and idea. His immediate impact in New York was substantial, but it was not owed so much to individual works of art as to the elegance with which he questioned the hierarchies of art. Those hierarchies had to do, broadly speaking, with the mastery of two interdependent elements: emotive subject matter, to begin with, and a force of expression which could challenge comparison with the great achievements of the past. That was the basis on which Cézanne's *Grandes Baigneuses* and Matisse's *Joy of Life* and Picasso's *Les Demoiselles d'Avignon* were ranked where they were: at the top. They were "modern," but they also brought with them a long baggage-train of memory, and association, and affections asked for and readily granted.

When Duchamp began to produce what were later called his "readymades," he didn't want anything like that. He went to great pains to nominate objects to which it was impossible to have an aesthetic reaction: a bottle rack, for instance. "My choice," he said later, "was always based on visual indifference and a total absence of taste, either bad or good." In the precursor of the readymades, the *Bicycle Wheel* of 1913, he took a bicycle wheel and put it, fork upward, on top of a stool. The wheel still spins, but it has been taken out of the context in which we normally expect to see it. The same thing happened with the snow shovel which was the first readymade to be produced in New York, and with the comb, the urinal, the typewriter cover, the hat rack and the coat rack, which in the same way were nominated as readymades during Duchamp's first years there.

People have for so long been conditioned to think of new art in terms of scandal that it is worth saying here that Duchamp did not do these things to shock, or to annoy, but simply to investigate the nature of art and of our responses to it. He did not bring the bicycle wheel into the living room in order to be provocative but because he liked it. "To see that wheel turning," he said to the art dealer Arturo Schwarz, "was very soothing, very comforting, a sort of opening of avenues onto other things than the material life of every day. . . . I enjoyed looking at it, just as I enjoy looking at the flames dancing in a fireplace." This was, quite genuinely and without affectation of any sort, the alternative art for which the times were calling; and it reminds us of something soon forgotten when the routines of taste take over—that art does not lie only in the object perceived but also in the way we think of it. Duchamp liked to prove this by taking an object that was beyond the pale of established art and making it jump out of its class, as it were, either unaltered or with minimal interference from himself. Duchamp also delighted in what he called "corrected readymades": objects which he could transform with a minimum of embellishment. In the case of *Apolinère Enameled (Girl with Bedstead)*, a reference to the poet Apollinaire was grafted onto an advertisement for Sapolin Enamel. It is typical of Duchamp's delicate fancy that the grafting might seem to have been done by the little girl in the advertisement itself before she moved on to enamel the bedstead in the picture below.

Once he himself had opted out of the fine-art context, Duchamp found that ideas came to him as fast as he could note them down. He became, in fact, a kind of reception center for notions outlawed by the conventions of modernist art. Among those which he put down on paper but never followed up are questions which half a century later were to preoccupy a whole generation of intelligent young people. What is the irreducible element in language? What would constitute a truly modern dictionary? How should an index of all knowledge be organized? To what extent can chance be given its freedom in the arts? Other ideas remained peculiar to himself. What are the verbal equivalents of colors that cannot be seen? Should not every government have its Ministry of Coincidences? On a more practical level, how can we replace oil paint on canvas as a way of producing images? Couldn't we use toothpaste on glass? Or brilliantine? Or cold cream? How would they last? (Not too well, apparently: Duchamp scrawled the words "not solid" at the bottom of that page.)

It was one of the many contradictory things about Duchamp that although he enjoyed making fun of the traditional solemnities of art, he also occupied himself twice over—from 1912 to 1923, and again from 1946 to 1966—with works of art as ambitious, and as elaborate, as any that we have seen in this century. But he produced them on his own terms, and in the case of the *Large Glass* he had in mind what he called "a marriage of mental and visual reactions." It was not enough to look at the *Large Glass* as one looks at a Titian or a Vermeer; the *Large Glass* was there to be *consulted,* rather as one consults an atlas: as a sign-system incomplete in itself. "The ideas in the *Glass,*" he said in 1959, "are more important than the visual realization"; and the ideas were contained on the 94 unnumbered pages of notes which were first published in 1934.

The *Large Glass* belongs, beyond question, to that select and daunting company of major works of art as to the understanding of which there can be no shortcut. No other single work of art produced in this century has been so closely studied or commented on at so great a length. None has prompted so wide a variety of interpretations, nearly all of them valid in some degree yet none of them definitive. What follows cannot pretend, therefore, to replace the extended studies of André Breton, Robert Lebel, Richard Hamilton, Octavio Paz and John Golding.

The full title of the *Large Glass* is *The Bride Stripped Bare by Her Bachelors, Even.* Like most of Duchamp's titles it has mischief in it. But it does, even so, hint at the fundamental subject matter of the work, which is the possession of one human being by another. Every society, and within our own society every generation, has its own way of ritualizing the robings and disrobings which this involves. (The *Large Glass* had, for instance, a particularly brilliant and hilarious contemporary in Stravinsky's *Les Noces,* which occupied the composer over exactly the same 12-year period, off and on, and takes us to the point at which, in classic accounts of matrimony, all is presumed to go well.)

By choosing as his subject the overture to what is the most decisive single moment in most people's experience, Duchamp made sure that he would never lack an audience. From that point onward, however, he made things just about as difficult as he could, both for himself and for us. To the extent that he was a child of his time—a Frenchman born in 1887—he inherited a view of sexual activity which was pragmatic, ironical, uninhibited and dis-idealized. Among the Frenchmen of his age group, sex was a matter not of unfocused yearning but of fact: fact reconnoitered, fact evaluated, fact acted upon. All this lent itself very well to the mechanistic illustration, and Duchamp was by no means alone in seeing the machine both as an extension of human powers and as a commentary upon their shortcomings. Thus far, he ran with the winds then prevailing.

Duchamp in life laughed readily and with a most infectious enjoyment; and the subject of the *Large Glass* could be broken down in terms of a farce by Georges Feydeau (1862–1921), as great a master of theatrical contrivance as ever lived. We have only to think of the initial idea—nine bachelors in pursuit of the same pretty girl—to see Feydeau's mind begin to race. No less provocative to Feydeau would have been the fact that the bachelors are distinguished only by the molds into which the essence of their masculinity is to be poured. The uniform was the man, in each case, and the bachelors were not seen as individuals but as archetypes of the Policeman, the Undertaker, the Priest, the Delivery Boy, the Station Master.

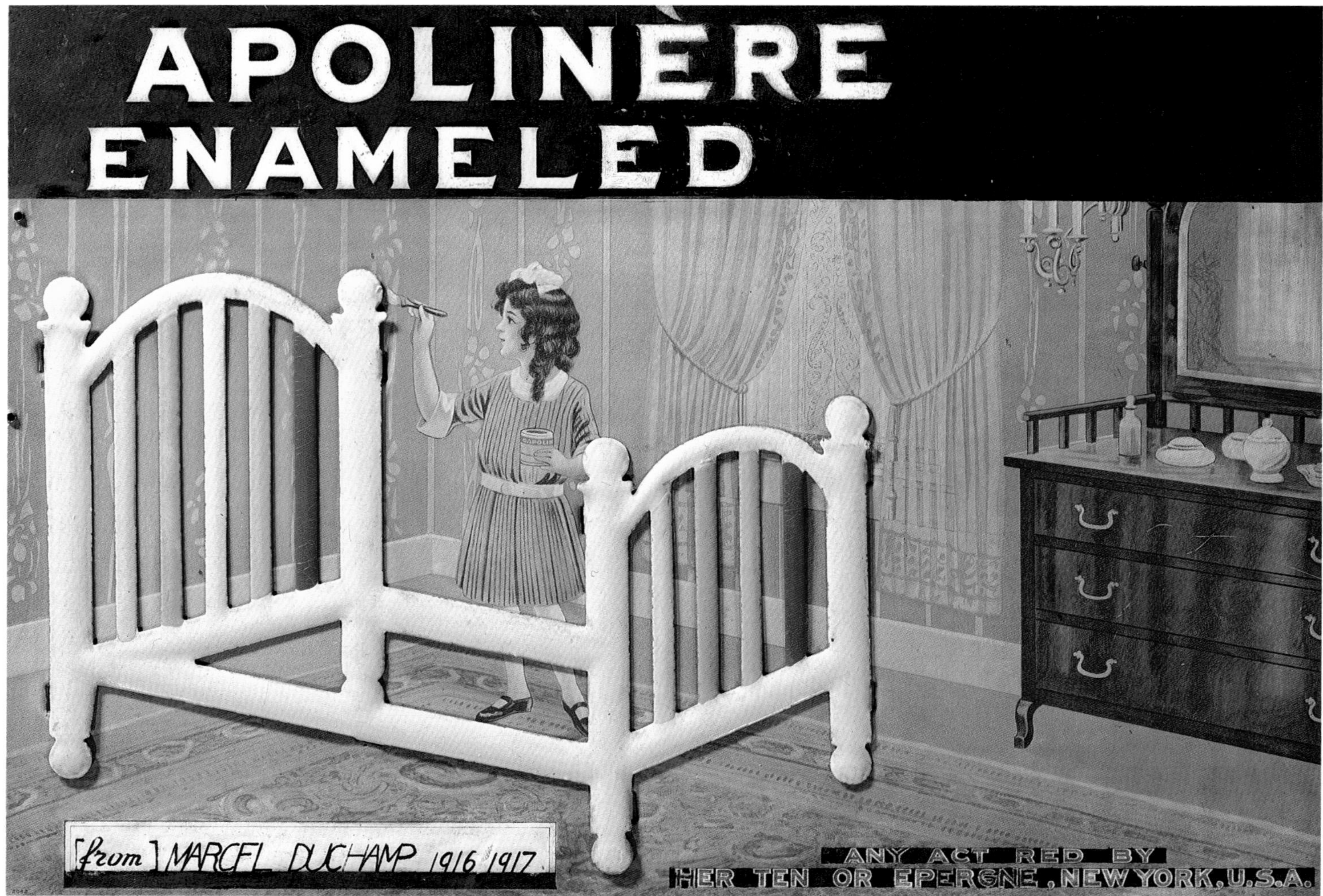

Marcel Duchamp. *Apolinère Enameled (Girl with Bedstead).* 1916–17. Painted tin advertisement for Sapolin Enamel, altered and added to by the artist, 9¼ × 13¼ inches. Philadelphia Museum of Art. The Louise and Walter Arensberg Collection

Marcel Duchamp.
The Bride Stripped Bare by Her Bachelors, Even (The Large Glass).
1915–23.
Oil, lead wire and foil, dust and varnish on glass (in two parts), 9 feet 1¼ inches × 69⅛ inches.
Philadelphia Museum of Art. Bequest of Katherine S. Dreier

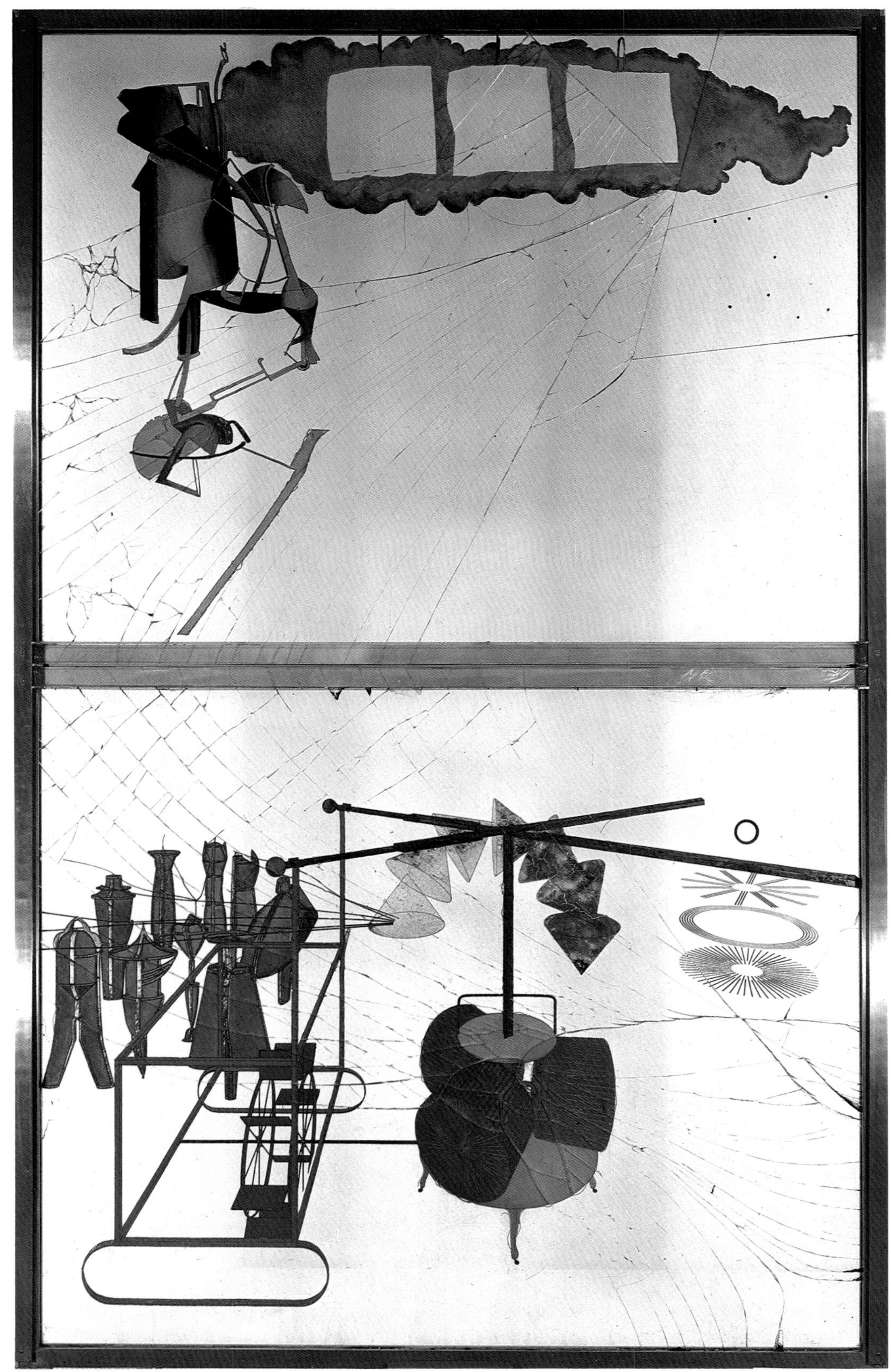

Feydeau would have left us weak with laughter; but although there are some very funny things about the *Large Glass* it is a great deal more than a metaphor, however ingenious, for the discomfitures which come about when young men pursue a pretty girl and don't quite get her. There is something awesome about the *Large Glass,* and that awesomeness does not relate only to its prodigious complication. The *Large Glass* has something to tell us, but to take possession of that something is almost as difficult as for the Bachelors to take possession of the Bride. The *Glass* works on many levels, and to concentrate on any one of them is to let the others slip out of focus. To see the truth of this, we have only to look at one of the many pictures by Picabia which, between 1915 and 1919, ran parallel to one or another of Duchamp's preoccupations. A Picabia of that date works perfectly, on the scale of epigram and on one level at a time. Himself a satyr in the prime of life, Picabia was both funny and direct in his treatment of sexual subjects. He stands before us as a practiced man of the world who is intelligent enough to abstract just one element at a time from what Duchamp is doing, and he brings that one element into sharp focus, on its own.

But with Duchamp nothing is ever quite, or ever only, what it seems. It is possible, for instance, to read the general layout of the *Large Glass* in terms of Christian iconography; the upper half then becomes a variant of the Apotheosis of the Virgin, while the lower half is given over to terrestrial concerns. But Duchamp also sanctioned a purely secular reading in which the theme of the Bride was prompted by the memory of the fairgrounds of his youth, where the public was invited to throw wooden balls at a pair of dolls which represented a bride and groom. In that case, according to Octavio Paz, "the Bride is a doll; the people who throw the balls are her Bachelors; the Oculist Witnesses are the public; the top inscription is the scoreboard." In the isolation of the Bride and in the fact that the Bachelors are seen to huddle together, set apart in their turn by the fact of being in uniform, there can equally well be seen an appeal to ancestral memory: to the cult of an unattainable womanhood, and to the mingling of terror and excitement with which the male animal stands on the threshold of manhood.

In these matters we all of us negotiate from strength in some areas and from weakness in others; that is one reason for the fascination of the *Glass.* But what if it secretes yet other levels of meaning? What if it is a metaphor for the renewal of language and for the possibility of completely new modes of communication? What if even the curiously dry, impersonal, nonassociative color had a meaning beyond the fact that Duchamp wanted to avoid the color structures of conventional art?

In his rejection of conventional art Duchamp did, in effect, impose upon himself year upon year of technical experimentation. He wanted to invent methods of image-making to which the concept of taste could not apply, any more than it applied to engineering drawings or to the color of the liquids in a drugstore window. (It took many months, for instance, to decide exactly how dust could be incorporated into the *Large Glass* as a material like any other.) In its use of lead, lead wire, silver foil, and perspective drawing of a minutely scientific sort, the *Large Glass* is not in the least like any other work of art. Yet the virtuosity is never there for its own sake: it is fundamental both to the thing seen and the thing thought about.

There are many aspects of the *Glass* over which controversy is still very much alive. We have to consider, for instance, the extent to which Duchamp meant to introduce into the *Glass* the concept of the fourth dimension, so much talked of in Paris at that time. He had been at great pains to reinvent, almost, the idea of the third dimension as it was elucidated by classical perspective. Was it because he believed that, as John Golding has put it, "three-dimensional objects could be considered as the flat shadows or reflections of the fourth dimension, invisible because it could never be seen by the human eye"? Was the *Large Glass* a projection of a four-dimensional object: "the apparition of an appearance"? On that reading, the ostensible subject of the *Glass*, with its bawdy, turn-of-the-century implications, would be no more than a bait to draw us into an adventure of quite another kind.

The exact nature of the mechanical implications of the *Glass* is also very far from having been decided once and for all. During a visit to Munich in July–August, 1912, Duchamp made a drawing which he later identified as the "first sketch for 'The Bride Stripped Bare by the Bachelors.' " He also painted *The Passage from the Virgin to the Bride*, which, as its title indicates, has likewise a hymeneal subject. That subject is treated, however, in a way which is partly mechanical and partly metaphysical. In other words the "passage" in question can be found in the female anatomy, and it is here shown in terms of machinery; but it also refers to the change of status which is implied in the condition of matrimony. The painting also has in it elements of the serial representation for which Duchamp became notorious at the time of his *Nude Descending a Staircase, No. 2.* In *The Bride* Duchamp carried the depersonalization of the human body just one stage further. Like *The Passage* it was painted in Munich, at a time when the idea of the *Large Glass* was in full germination. The female body is seen here both as a machine and as a vessel; the bride as engine room is its true subject, and there is no longer any trace of the hesitations and uncertainties which are traditionally associated with virginity.

Undeniably Duchamp was much impressed by the motor trip which he and Apollinaire took with Picabia in October, 1912; and when they all got back from the Jura mountains, Duchamp projected a large-scale work in which the protagonist would be an automobile: "the machine with 5 hearts, the pure child of nickel and platinum which must dominate the Paris–Jura road." The motorcar was personified in all this as "the girl born without a mother." It had a father-inventor, or an inventor-father, but it was generated independently of the female womb; there was an echo in this of the ancient alchemists' belief that when the alchemical formula was put into action a motherless child could be created.

Duchamp himself said that if he referred to alchemy in the *Glass*, it was "in the only way in which one can use alchemy nowadays—without knowing it." But there are many arcane references in the *Glass* which may or may not be there by accident. The subject itself, to begin with, can be interpreted in alchemical terms. In 1968 Pontus Hulten, then head of the Moderna Museet in Stockholm, took up a point first made by his compatriot Ulf Linde: that the disrobing of the bride was likened by the philosopher Solidonius to the way in which the material used by the alchemists lost all its color in the process of liquefaction and transmutation.

The *Large Glass* can be read, therefore, in terms of the "philosophical marriage" through which the alchemist aimed to produce gold. The marriage in question involved "the baser, dry, male element, sulphur" and "the volatile female element, mercury." Hulten goes on, "The generative operation took place within a 'cosmic oven,' whose lower and upper parts were respectively male and female; the mercury was contained in a vessel of pure glass—a metaphor often applied to the Virgin. It seems likely that the upper part of Duchamp's *Large Glass* relates to the philosopher's mercury, which is the principle both of the universal love of nature and of redemption through work; while the lower part, the Bachelor's apparatus, is connected with the alchemical concept of sulphur."

Duchamp's notional Minister of Coincidences might intervene at this point and say that when Duchamp was first working seriously on the *Glass*, in Munich in 1912, he had at hand one of the world's great alchemical libraries. Whether or not he ever went there, the alchemical interpretation of the *Glass* should be taken seriously, along with the automobilist interpretation, the symbolist in-

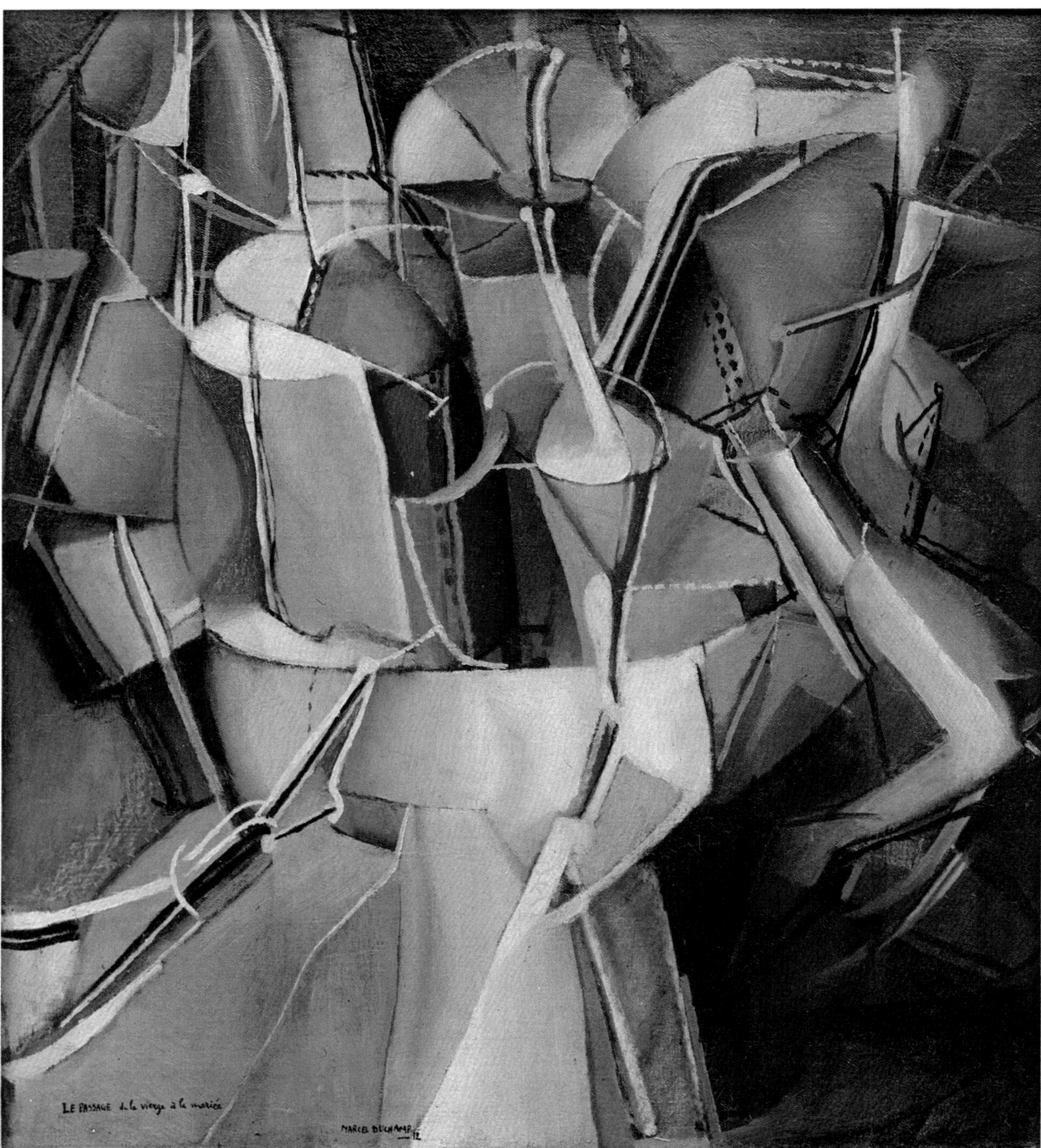

Marcel Duchamp. *The Passage from the Virgin to the Bride.* 1912. Oil on canvas, 23⅜ × 21¼ inches. The Museum of Modern Art, New York. Purchase

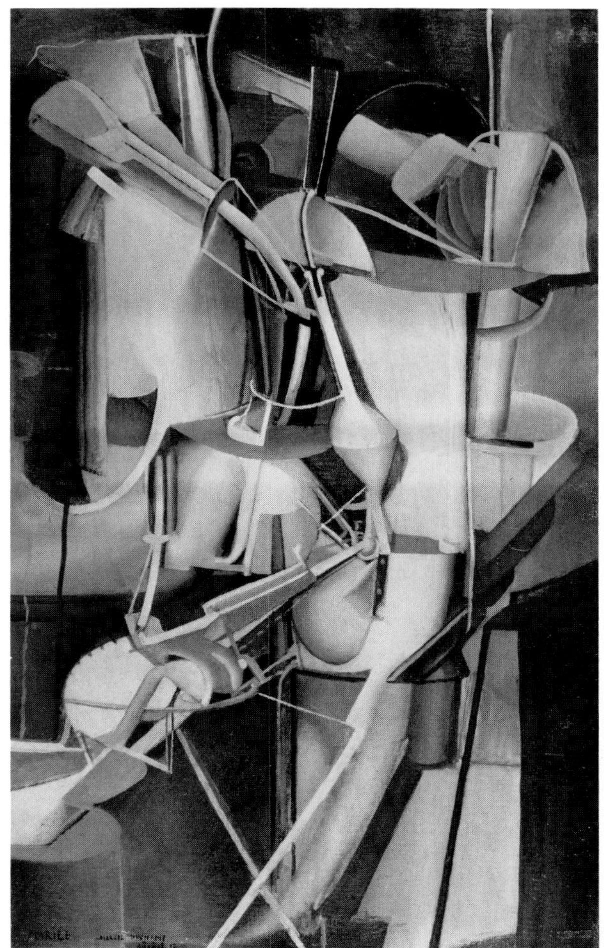

Marcel Duchamp. *The Bride.* 1912. Oil on canvas, 35⅛ × 21¾ inches. Philadelphia Museum of Art. The Louise and Walter Arensberg Collection

terpretation, the interpretation from speculative geometry, and half a dozen others. If there is in more than one of them an element of lunatic proliferation, that is in the nature of the game that the *Glass* plays with us. The stakes are high, and the wins and losses absolute.

The *Glass* is quintessentially modern, in that Duchamp is both the protagonist, the man who charts the work's progress in a spirit of total commitment, and the ironical spectator who continually asks himself, "What is a picture really for? What are we doing here that could not be done elsewhere? What are the new kinds of involvement that art has yet to bestow upon us?" Octavio Paz put this point to perfection when he wrote in 1969 that the *Glass* is both a contribution to mythology and a criticism of it. "I am reminded," he said, "of *Don Quixote,* which is both an epic novel and a criticism of the epic. It is with creations such as *Don Quixote* that modern irony was born; with Duchamp, and with other poets of the 20th century such as Joyce and Kafka, the irony turns against itself. The circle closes; it is the end of one epoch and the beginning of another." Once again it turns out that the *Glass* is always up-to-date. Where other classics of the early 20th century are already set fast in history, the *Glass* presents itself over and over again as the newest thing. Our own time is likely, for instance, to appear to posterity as the heyday of methodology: the moment at which method was accepted as the key to all things. If this is so, posterity will also remember what Octavio Paz said of the *Glass,* that "what it gives us is the *spirit of the age:* Method, the critical Idea at the moment when it is meditating on itself, and when it reflects itself in the transparent nothingness of a pane of glass."

The *Large Glass* is the masterpiece of alternative art. And it puts forward a true alternative: one which remakes the experience of art. But it was not at all typical of alternative art. Duchamp never tangled with Authority, for example. He worked slowly and tenaciously, and in conditions of security. He had no thought of sounding an alarm or setting the world to rights. His work was rarely seen and almost never written about. (The first serious study of the *Large Glass,* by André Breton, was not published till 1935.) Though outwardly a big-city man, and everywhere the most welcome of guests, he worked like a hermit in the desert: apart and alone.

By contrast, alternative art in Europe was often in trouble with the law: exhibitions were shut down, meetings ended in disorder, magazines were suppressed, prosecutions were initiated. The new art was improvised in times of national emergency and had, quite naturally, a frantic last-minute look. The economics of starvation dictated its materials, as often as not. Much of it was backed by a rudimentary but untiring publicity machine of a kind from which Duchamp held aloof. Under

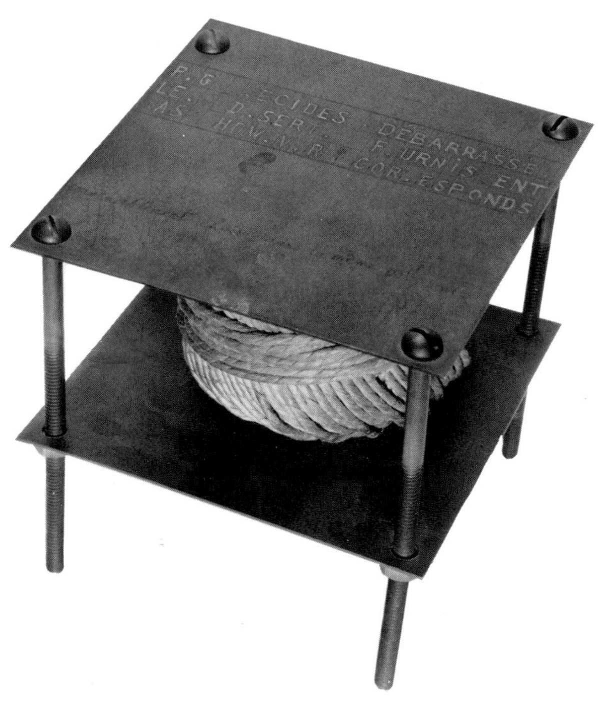

Marcel Duchamp. *With Hidden Noise.* 1916. Ball of twine, two brass plates and four long bolts, "assisted" by the artist, 5 × 5 × 5 inches. Philadelphia Museum of Art. The Louise and Walter Arensberg Collection

the generic name of Dada it was a rackety, pugnacious, many-sided and almost entirely subversive activity. And yet Duchamp turns out to have been perpetual president of the whole adventure, in ways which are still being deciphered. European Dada arose from a specific historical and geographical situation; and Duchamp for most of its life was 3,000 and more miles away. But it now seems as if the Dada group, like the Bachelors in the *Large Glass,* were poured into molds of Duchamp's devising.

Duchamp has many another claim to our attention. In his *With Hidden Noise* he pioneered, as early as 1916, the notion of the poetic object, which was to play an important role in Surrealist activity in the 1920s and '30s. He also pioneered the idea of participation by others (in this case, his patron Walter Arensberg) in ways unknown to the initiator of the piece. Here a ball of twine is held firmly between two brass plates, which in their turn are kept in place by four long bolts. Inside the twine is a small object, chosen and placed by Arensberg, which makes a mysterious noise when the piece is shaken. Objects of everyday use are combined in a completely irrational or nonutilitarian way to produce something that we recognize as having a strange power and a presence all its own. That strangeness is compounded by the addition of a further, hidden element: a secret from which even the artist himself is excluded.

For multiple incongruity, his *Why Not Sneeze* has few rivals in the history of the Surrealist object. Not only are its ingredients dreamlike in their improbability but in one important case their physical appearance is deceptive. (What we take to be lumps of sugar are, in fact, lumps of marble, so the piece is much heavier than it looks.) Throughout the 1920s and early '30s imaginations were put to work to invent disquieting conjunctions of everyday objects; but first prize still goes to Duchamp's bird cage, with its cargo of marble sugar, thermometer and cuttlefish bone.

Duchamp also loved puns, both verbal and vi-

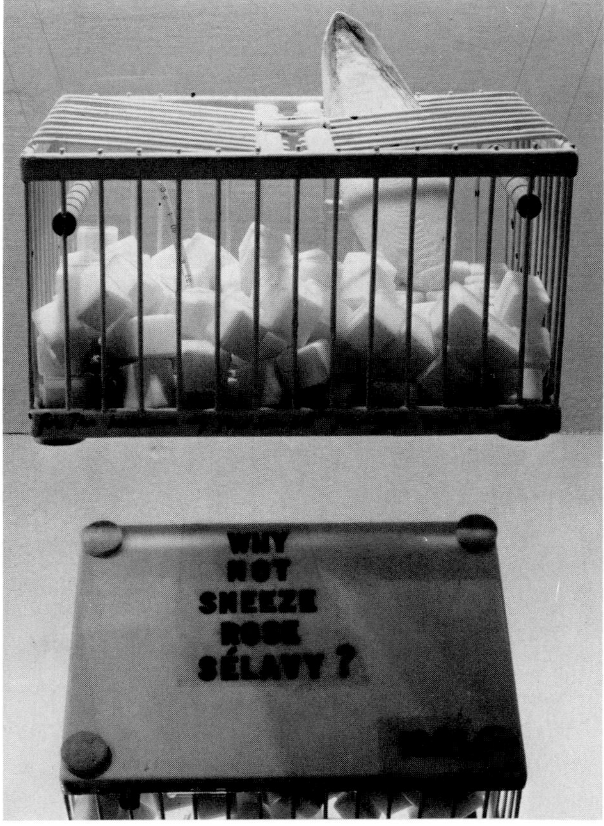

Marcel Duchamp. *Why Not Sneeze, Rose Sélavy?* (1964; replica of original of 1921.) Assisted readymade: marble blocks (in the shape of lumps of sugar), thermometer, wood and cuttlefish bone in birdcage, 4⅞ × 8¾ × 6⅜ inches. The Museum of Modern Art, New York. Gift of Galleria Schwarz

Marcel Duchamp. *Fresh Widow.* 1920. Miniature French window: painted wood frame with 8 panes of glass covered with black leather, 30½ × 17⅝ inches. The Museum of Modern Art, New York. Katherine S. Dreier Bequest

sual. The title of *Fresh Widow* combines the notions of (i) a French window, (ii) a woman recently and still deeply bereft and (iii) a widow already eager for masculine attentions. "Fresh," "French," "widow" and "window" form, that is to say, a kind of verbal conglomerate, which we may assemble as we think fit. In visual terms, what we see is a window in mourning: a standard French frame in which eight panels of polished black leather have been substituted for clear glass. The black has obvious overtones of widowhood—the "panes" could be there to protect the mourner from the curiosity of passers-by—but Duchamp wanted a high polish on the black leather, so that it could also seem that we are looking out, as we look out in times of mourning, upon nothingness.

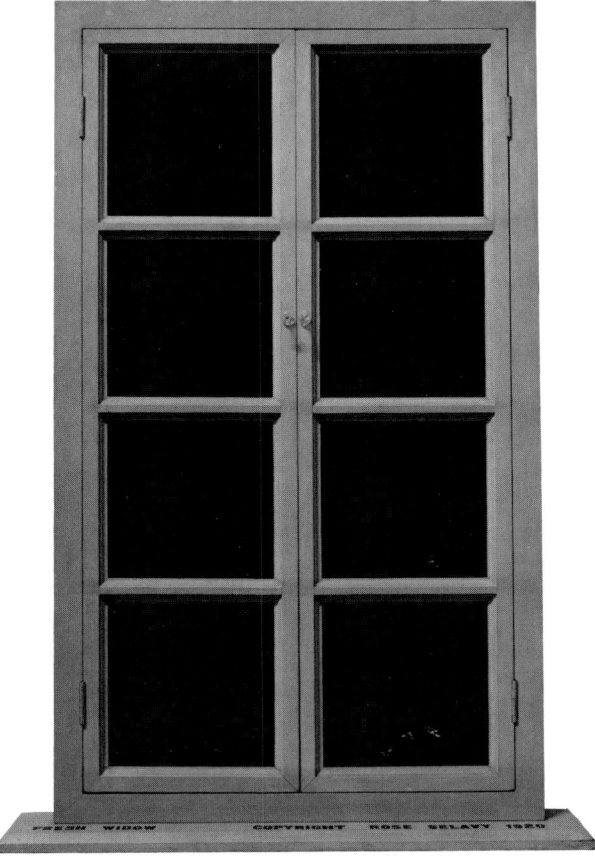

Duchamp was fascinated by chance. As much as any of his works, he liked the *Three Standard Stoppages* of 1913–14, which was based on a chance operation: the outline of three threads, each one meter long, dropped from a height of one meter onto a canvas painted Prussian blue. It amused him very much to build an elaborate structure around these random marks, just as it also amused him to start from a ready-made verbal statement and gently take it apart, as happened in the piece called *Apolinère Enameled* of 1916–17. He gave such things an overlay of meaning upon meaning that was all his own, but the basic ambition had a wide currency at the time. In Zurich, it was taken for granted among the writers and artists who formed from 1916 onward the Dada group that the liberation of chance was one of the best things that had come out of the new century. "Chance appeared to us as a magical procedure by which we could transcend the barriers of causality and conscious volition, and by which the inner ear and eye became more acute. . . . For us, chance was the 'unconscious mind,' which Freud had discovered in 1900." The voice here is that of Hans Richter, painter, collagist, photographer and filmmaker, but the opinions are those of the Zurich Dada group as a whole. Dada was not, strictly speaking, an art movement—in fact, it stood for the repudiation and abolition of art—and its energies related for the most part to poetry, typography, public relations and an idiosyncratic subspecies of the performing arts. Nurtured in a neutral country and galvanized by occasional visits by Picabia, Zurich Dada established prototypes of avant-garde activity which have still to be superseded: among them café-theater, the mixed-media happening, concrete poetry, automatic writing and the use of aleatory procedures in art, poetry and music. When the Rumanian poet Tristan Tzara composed a Dada poem he would cut up newspaper articles into tiny fragments, shake them up in a bag, and scatter them across the table. As they fell, they made the poem; little further work was called for. When Jean Arp, the German-born sculptor-poet, tore up a drawing in despair and threw it on the studio floor he realized after a time that that, too, was a perfectly valid way to start a picture. And in

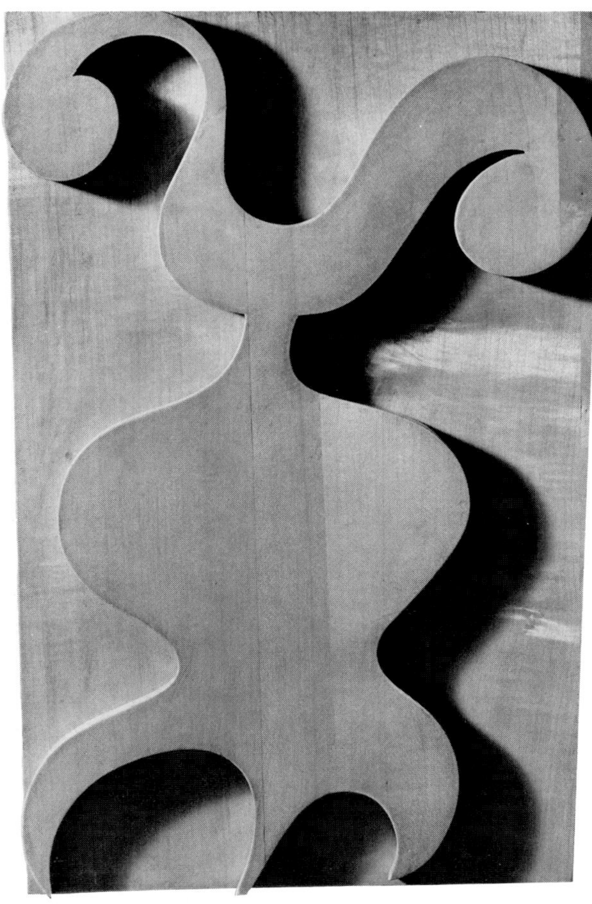

Jean (Hans) Arp. *Madame Torso with a Wavy Hat.* 1916. Wood relief, 16 × 10 inches. Kunstmuseum, Bern. Hermann and Margrit Rupf Foundation

1917 Arp got into the habit of closing his eyes, underlining words or sentences in the newspaper with a pencil, and going on from there to write a complete poem. "A sentence from a newspaper gripped us as much as one from a prince among poets," he wrote in 1953.

Implicit in all this was contempt for the discredited bourgeois society which had allowed language to be debased by the mendacities of wartime and art to become a matter of routine. "In that wonderful Dada time," Arp wrote later, "we hated and despised finicky, laborious habits of work. We couldn't stand the otherworldly look of the 'titans' as they wrestled with problems of the spirit." Oil painting, in particular, had a rough ride with Dada. "When closely and sharply examined, the most perfect picture"—Arp is again the speaker—"is a warty, threadbare approximation, a dry porridge, a dismal moon-crater landscape."

History has not always been kind to the Dadaists, and much of what they did now looks what they least wanted it to be: arty. In Zurich particularly the fact of Swiss neutrality makes the big talkers seem, in retrospect, both sheltered and effete. What still commands our respect is the constructive element; and that was provided by artists who would have come through in any case. Arp spoke for them when he said later that "we were looking for an art based on fundamentals, one which would cure the madness of the age. We wanted a new order of things to restore the balance between heaven and hell. Something told us that power-crazed gangsters would one day use art itself as a way of deadening men's minds."

It was a formidable program. Arp's work has survived not so much for its specifically Dada qualities as because he was equipped by his heredity, and by several years of intensive solitary effort, to decide for himself in which directions art needed to go. Born and reared in Strasbourg, he had, like Strasbourg itself, a dual nationality. (Strasbourg, by turns French and German for centuries, was German till 1919, French thereafter.) Arp for years called himself Hans Arp when in Germany and Jean Arp when in France; and in all his activities there was a mingling of German lyricism with down-to-earth French logical analysis. This paladin of modernity never lost the hot line to the German Middle Ages which he had acquired in first youth from a prolonged study of *Des Knaben Wunderhorn,* the anthology of German folksongs which had been published by Brentano and von Arnim in 1805–08. But at a very early age Arp became acquainted with Robert and Sonia Delaunay in Paris, and with Kandinsky and his friends in Munich, and with Herwarth Walden, the editor of *Der Sturm* in Berlin. By 1914 he was a valued though still youthful member of the pacific International: the gifted group who believed that creativity made nonsense of nationalism. And what he did under the aegis of Dada was, largely, to go on as before. There is an obvious contradiction between the grandiose program of Dada and the sweet good taste which is uppermost in the so-called Dada collages of Arp. In his painted wooden reliefs of the same period he indulged a play instinct which, once again, has nothing to do with an aesthetic of desperation. But the point of these beguiling little works is that they reintroduce into serious art a repertory of forms for which Cubism had had no place. Whimsy of a superior kind stood behind the shorthand ideograms for "bird," "forest," "water" and "human being"; and the shorthand in question was expressed in biomorphic terms. Arp's floppy, joky, wayward, curvilinear forms took the stress out of art at a time when the major Cubists were mostly off duty and it had become clear that art was in need of an alternative formal alphabet. In his case, that alphabet was in the service of a relaxed humor; but over the next 50 or 60 years it was destined to run the whole gamut of human expression.

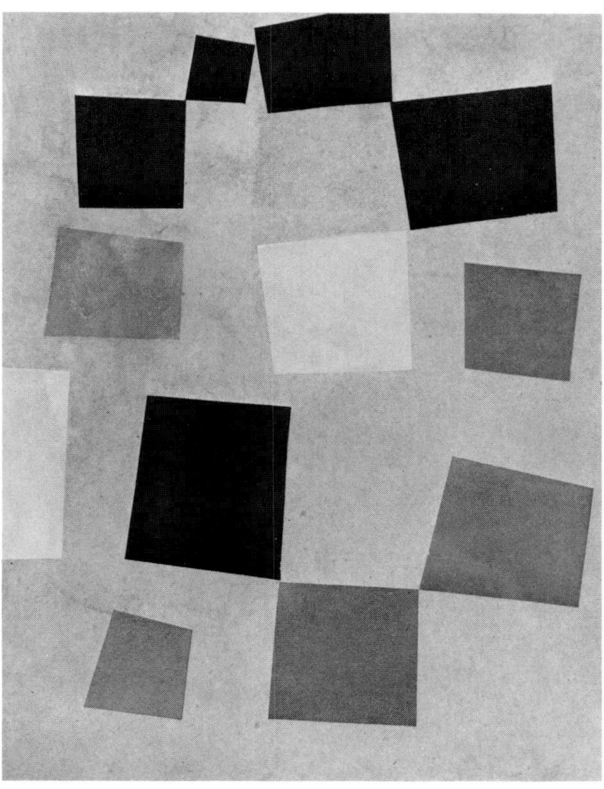

Jean (Hans) Arp. *Squares Arranged According to the Laws of Chance.* 1917. Collage of cut and pasted papers, gouache, ink and bronze paint, 13⅛ × 10¼ inches. The Museum of Modern Art, New York. Gift of Philip Johnson

It was fundamental to an alternative art that magic could be made from the humblest of materials. "We 'painted,'" said one of the pioneers of Zurich Dada, "with scissors, adhesive plaster, sacking, paper." In Zurich this sprang from a conscious polemical preference; but the time was approaching when art would simply be compelled, in a defeated Germany, to work from an aesthetic of scarcity—in other words, with just about anything that came to hand. This applied as much to artists like Kurt Schwitters, who stood aloof from politics, as to those who stood for a committed point of view. If magic was made in Cologne, in Hanover and in Berlin, it was because artists were able to release the buried life within disregarded materials, just as Duchamp had released the buried life within the bicycle wheel.

As with Duchamp, language played its part in all this: sometimes in caption form, sometimes by unexpected conjugations of printed matter which made the observer jump back and forth between the act of looking and the act of reading. Duchamp had raided both domains in a spirit of detached inquiry; but German Dada was carried on in a society that was teetering toward total collapse. It was the work of men with nothing to lose, and its notional trajectory was not at all that of the traditional work of art: dealer → collector → museum. Its life span was estimated as nearer to that of the newspaper, or the public meeting, or the telegram marked "Urgent." Its function was to negotiate with chaos for terms of truce. It borrowed from the techniques of the handbill and the poster, and it counted on the cooperation of observers whose situation was so desperate that they just couldn't afford not to understand. We should remember this when we try to imagine how the steeplechase of image and idea must have looked to those who had run it in the heyday (1919–22) of German Dada.

German Dada had nothing but the name in common with Zurich Dada. Fundamentally, Zurich Dada was a sub-department of the entertainment industry. Genuine revolution was not to be expected from evenings on which the young Arthur Rubinstein played the piano music of Saint-Saëns and other performers evoked the Parisian

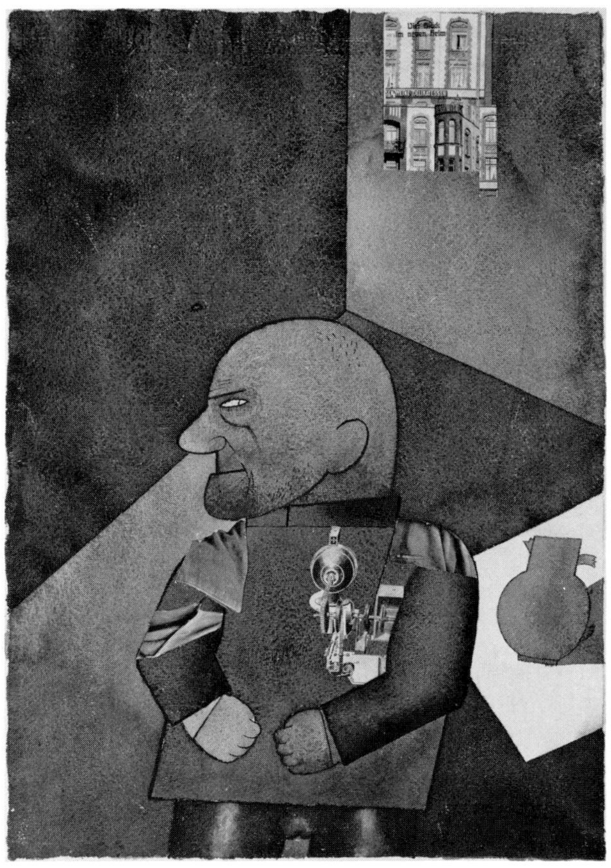

George Grosz. *The Engineer Heartfield.* 1920. Watercolor and collage, 16½ × 12 inches. The Museum of Modern Art, New York. Gift of A. Conger Goodyear

café-chantant as it had been in the lifetime of Toulouse-Lautrec. "In Zurich," Richard Hülsenbeck wrote later, "people lived as they would have lived in a health resort, running after women and longing for the coming of night that brought with it pleasure barges, colored lights and music by Verdi." Hülsenbeck had arrived in Zurich from Berlin in the winter of 1915–16 as a 23-year-old medical student to whom the war was abhorrent. He was a versatile young man with a talent for insolence, and he turned out to play a leader's role in Zurich Dada. He was poet, performer, coeditor with Hugo Ball of the Dada periodical *Cabaret Voltaire,* and a most ferocious champion of what in Switzerland passed for jazz. He fancied himself as a writer of nonsense verse ("The whole Monist Club is gathered on the steamship Meyerbeer," one passage ran, "but only the pilot has any conception of high C"), but he did not agree with another Dadaist, Tristan Tzara, that "Dada means nothing." And when he got back to Berlin in January, 1917, he saw to it that, as he said, "in Germany Dada lost its art-for-art's-sake character with its very first move."

Evenings at the Galerie Dada in Zurich were frankly eclectic: new music by Arnold Schoenberg and Alban Berg took its turn with readings from Jules Laforgue and Guillaume Apollinaire, demonstrations of "Negro dancing" and a new play by the Expressionist painter and playwright Oskar Kokoschka. Hülsenbeck would have none of that in Berlin. The Expressionists, in particular, seemed to him like "those famous medical quacks who promise that 'everything will soon be back to normal.' " He goes on, "Under the pretext of turning inward, the Expressionist painters and writers have banded together into a generation which already looks forward to honorable mention in the history books and a chestful of civic distinctions." The Expressionists stood for subjectivity, for the spiritual life, for the old-German Gothic world; to that extent they backed up the status quo. "Dada was not a 'made' movement," George Grosz wrote; "it was an organic product, which began as a reaction against the head-in-the-clouds attitudes of so-called high art, whose disciples brooded over cubes, and over Gothic art, while the generals were painting in blood."

This was the state of mind in which Hülsenbeck and Raoul Hausmann wrote their Dada manifesto in Berlin in April, 1918. It called for an international revolutionary union of all creative men and women; for progressive unemployment through the mechanization of all fields of activity; for the abolition of private property; for the provision of free daily meals for creative people and intellectuals; for the remodeling of big-city life by a Dadaist advisory council; and for the regulation of all sexual activity under the supervision of a Dadaist sexual center. These proposals were put forward at what George Grosz called "the time of the turnip": a period in which it was nothing unusual for the supply of potatoes to give out and be replaced by turnips normally used as cattle fodder. The Allied blockade brought starvation daily nearer; the German Army was getting more and more demoralized; there had been the beginnings of mutiny in the German Navy as early as July, 1917; 400,000 munition workers had been on strike in Berlin. It was, if ever, a time for desperate measures; and we cannot blame the Berliners who thought of Zurich as a city not so much neutral as neutered.

Much of Berlin Dada is a matter of legend. There were bold single acts which nobody followed up, as when Johannes Baader climbed up to the pulpit in Berlin Cathedral and treated the congregation to a Dadaist harangue. There were projects well over the frontiers of fantasy, as when that same Baader planned a five-story-high "Dio-Dada-Drama" which was to encapsulate "The Greatness and the Fall of Germany." There were prosecutions for antimilitarist activity. There were publications which have clung to history as burrs cling to the jacket of a hunter. Alternative art reached its point of maximum immediacy in the Berlin of 1918–20; and though not much of it survived as museum material something of its quintessence can be seen in the photomontages which were produced by John Heartfield, George Grosz, Johannes Baader, Raoul Hausmann and Hannah Höch. (In his witty little portrait of Heartfield, Grosz used some of the techniques that Heartfield had perfected. The printed message on the cut-out section of a Berlin street reads, "The best of luck in your new home"; but the new home in question is clearly a prison cell. Heartfield at that time was constantly in danger of arrest for subversive activities.) Berlin is a quick-witted, skeptical city in which a certain lapidary derision stands high among conversational qualities; and in the photomontages in question that trait is carried over into art.

In any account of international Dada an invidious distinction must be made between the people who went on to be major artists of a more general sort and the people whose association with Dada is really their only claim upon us. Cologne Dada, like Berlin Dada, had its full share of glorious human oddities; but it is on Max Ernst, finally, that our attention rests. When Ernst returned to Cologne as a demobilized soldier in 1918 he sized up the situation not as a social revolutionary, like his friend Johannes Baargeld, but as an artist who had proved himself a considerable painter as early as 1906. He had been a member of August Macke's

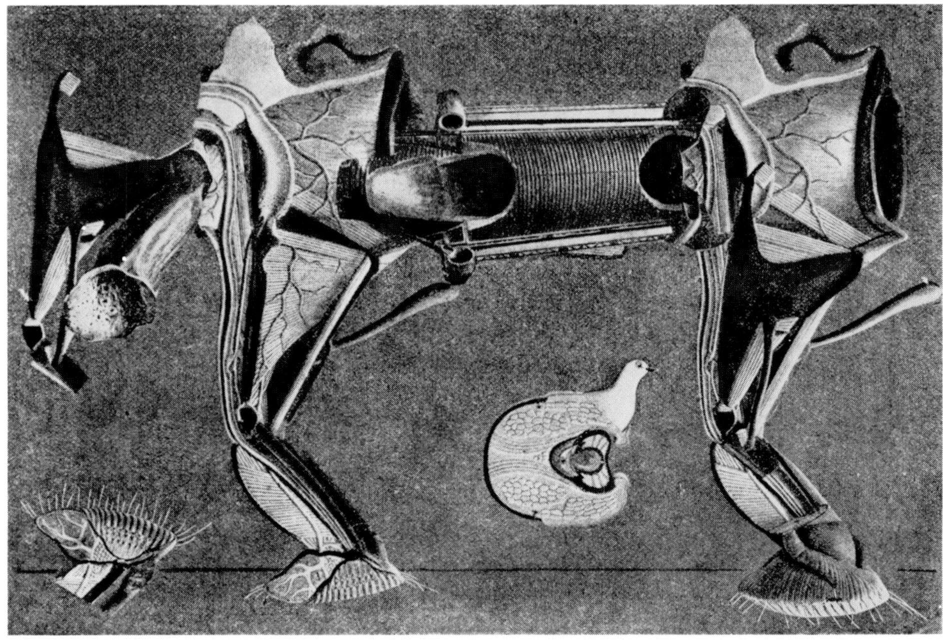

Max Ernst.
The Horse, He's Sick.
1920.
Pasted papers, pencil and ink, 5¾ × 8½ inches.
The Museum of Modern Art, New York. Purchase

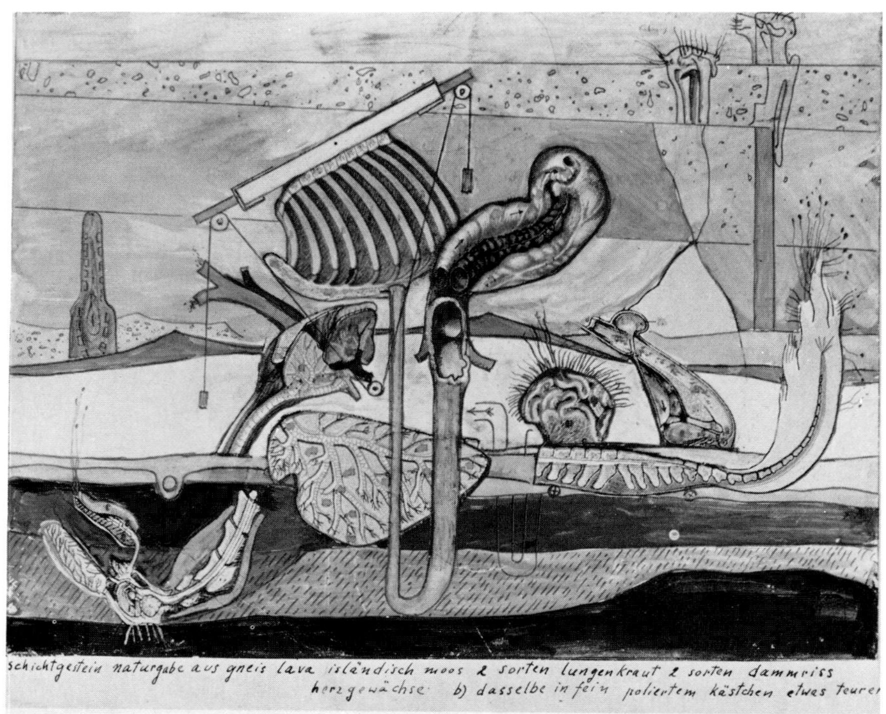

Max Ernst. *Stratified Rocks, Nature's Gift of Gneiss Lava Iceland Moss 2 Kinds of Lungwort 2 Kinds of Ruptures of the Perineum Growths of the Heart (b) The Same Thing in a Well-Polished Box Somewhat More Expensive.* 1920. Anatomical engraving altered with gouache and pencil, 6 × 8⅛ inches. The Museum of Modern Art, New York. Purchase

Young Rhineland group in Bonn before the war, he had known Jean Arp since 1914 and he had made himself familiar with the prewar art scene in Paris, Cologne and Berlin. Already as a student he had realized that the untaught scribblings of children, mad people, obsessives of all kinds might have more to contribute to modern art than anything that was taught in the academies. So it was by extension of a long-held opinion that Max Ernst spoke out in 1919 against "Everyman," who "loves Everyman's expressionists but turns away in disgust from the graffiti in public lavatories."

He was still only 28 in that year, and he had arrears of experience to make up. Until he and Baargeld went to Munich on a visit, he had no idea of the role that Arp had played in Zurich Dada; and it was from a magazine picked up by chance in a Munich bookshop that he learned what Carlo Carrà and Giorgio de Chirico had been doing in Italy. He was a convinced Dada member, who enjoyed the nickname of "Dadamax," was co-founder with Baargeld of the Rhineland branch of Dadaism (address: W/3 West Stupidia), edited its Dadaist review, *Die Schammade,* and took a leading role in the Dada exhibition which opened in Cologne in April, 1920, and was almost immediately shut down by the police. Dada owed a great deal to Max Ernst by the time he left Germany for Paris in 1921; but he owed something to Dada, too, and to the notion of a general strike for art which Dada had been mooting since 1916. He spoke of himself in November, 1918, as "a young man who aspired to find the myth of his own time"; he had studied abnormal psychology at an early age, and he knew that what had applied to individuals before 1914 might well apply to whole societies when World War I at last came to an end. In life he was antipaternalism personified and had an especial horror of the word "duty"; if Dada could do away with the structures of obedience which had for so long been mandatory among Germans, so much the better.

Max Ernst was not so anxious to do away with art as to extend full membership to forms of statement which had previously been denied admission. This was, of course, typical of Dada; but he brought to his Dada works a steely determination, a malicious humor with overtones of intellectual

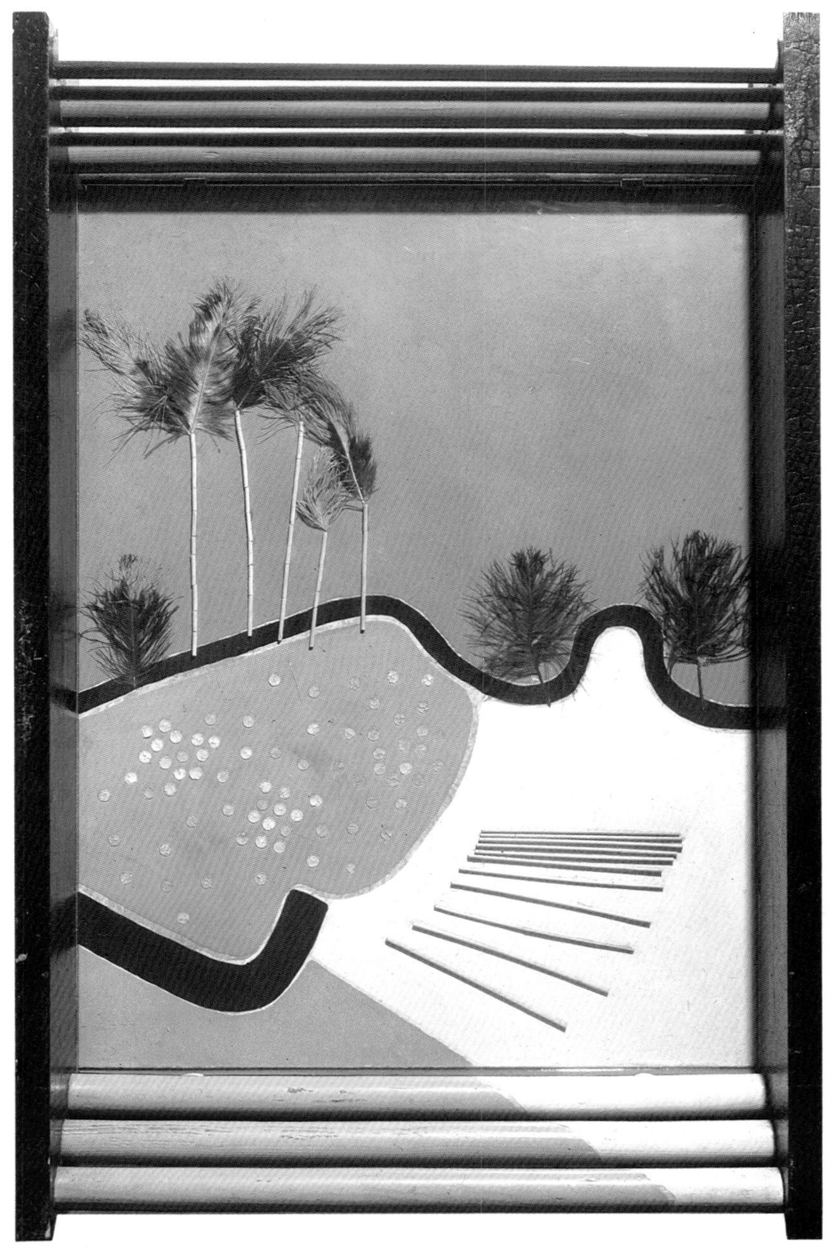

Francis Picabia.
Plumes.
c. 1923–27(?).
Ripolin, feathers, macaroni, cane and corn plasters on canvas in a doweled frame, 46⅞ × 30⅞ inches.
Private collection

terrorism, and a gift for verbal embellishment which was quite the equal of anything that had been done in that line elsewhere. At the same time he had an existence of his own outside of Dada, and interests which were independent of it. As much as Duchamp, he had that flair for irreverent conjunction which had been pioneered by Lautréamont and carried onward by Jules Laforgue, Alfred Jarry and Guillaume Apollinaire. Above all, his work was quintessentially modern in that he used, to still unsurpassed effect, the device of the quick cut.

The quick cut was a combination of ellipsis, on the one hand, and a well-calculated jump in the dark, on the other. Fernand Léger was quite right when he said in 1914 that modern man could be distinguished from earlier man by the fact that the number of impressions with which he had to deal was a thousand times greater. Léger himself tackled this problem both by rigorous selection and by the fragmentation or overlapping of images which would formerly have been shown complete. But only after a complete break with previous pictorial tradition could the kind of quick cutting which was perfected by Max Ernst become incorporated in the act of reading a picture. To that extent, and by making a certain nimbleness of mind mandatory among those who looked at new art, Dada created a climate in which Max Ernst could go to work.

It was in art that the quick cut and the well-calculated jump imposed themselves most vividly at this time. Anyone who looked at Max Ernst's *Here Everything Is Still Floating* had to adjust to an underwater scene in which a steamship was fathered by an anatomical drawing of a beetle seen upside down; above and to the right was a fish, seen as if in an X-ray photograph, which could also be read as a primitive airship. Air and water, soaring and swimming, anatomy and engineering —all exchanged roles in this tiny and mysterious picture, and yet all were still present as themselves. In such pictures as these Max Ernst restructured the act of reading a work of art. He was not alone in doing it—it could be said to have begun, like so much else, with Cubism—and the acts both of reading and of looking were, of course, being restructured in other forms of human activity also.

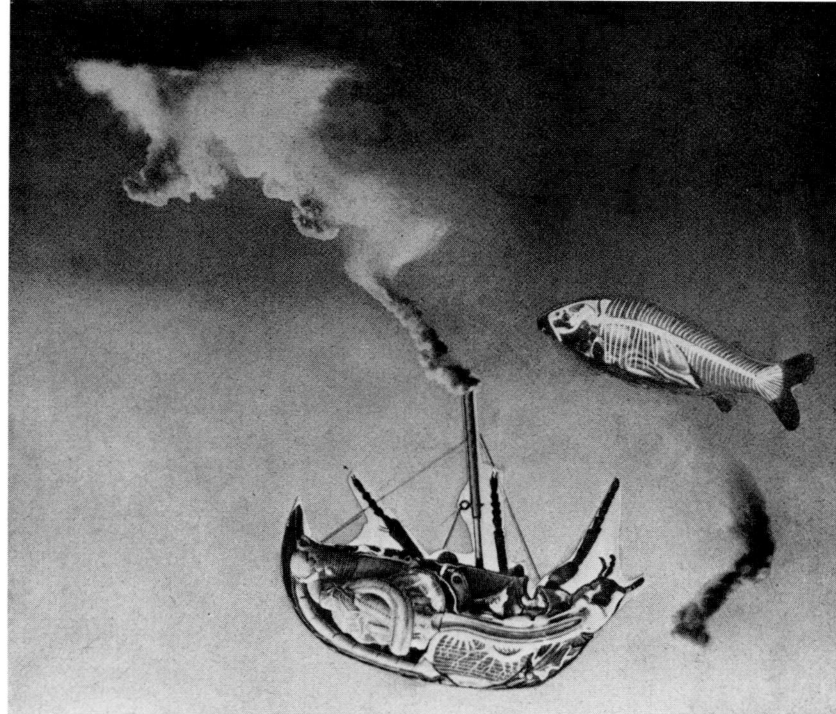

Max Ernst.
Here Everything Is Still Floating. 1920. Pasted photoengravings, 4⅛ × 4⅞ inches. The Museum of Modern Art, New York. Purchase

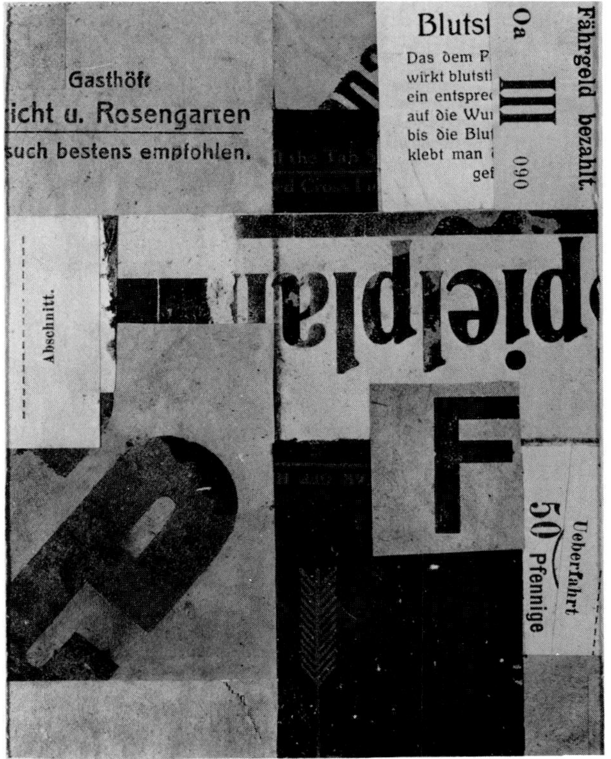

Kurt Schwitters.
Merz 83: Drawing F.
1920.
Collage of cut paper wrappers, announcements and tickets, 5¾ × 4½ inches.
The Museum of Modern Art, New York. Katherine S. Dreier Bequest

At its most inventive, the silent cinema of the 1920s demanded of its audiences such acrobatics of attention as had never been performed before. Max Ernst knew when to tease, when to present an image directly, and when to spike the whole adventure with a long caption that darted in and out of common sense as a lizard darts in and out of the shade. What he made was not "a Dada picture" but an accelerated statement for which Dada had given the go-ahead.

Max Ernst was against Authority, as such, and it never worried him that Cologne Dada was more than once in trouble with the police. But he was not a political activist. He stood somewhat apart, therefore, from the Berlin Dadaists when they took (often from the most innocent of motives) a straight Communist line. He was his own man.

Kurt Schwitters in Hanover was his own man, too, much to the exasperation of Hülsenbeck, who called him "a highly talented petit-bourgeois." One of Schwitters' closest friends was nearer to the point when she said that he "simply didn't have a conventional bone in his body." But he did, admittedly, sit out the vicissitudes of postwar Germany in his house in Hanover, unaffected by the commitments of Dadaists elsewhere. This was the more enraging to the activists in that Schwitters was in many ways the ideal (and potentially the supreme) Dadaist. Others got up on platforms and made fools of themselves, more or less. Schwitters survives, through a gramophone recording, as one of the most extraordinary performers of the century. When he read his "Primeval Sonata"—a long poem made up entirely of wordless sounds—it was as if there had come into existence a completely new mode of human expression, by turns hilarious and terrifying, elemental and precisely engineered. Others dreamed of reconciling art and language, music and speech, the living room and the cathedral, the stage and the unspoiled forest. Schwitters had the sweep of mind not only to dream of these things but to carry them out, within the physical limits available to him. All this he did in the name of an invented concept which he called "Merz."

Merz (derived from the second syllable of the German word *Kommerz*) was a working name which Schwitters used to identify all his activities (and himself, also, at times: one of his publications was signed Kurt Merz Schwitters). "Everything had broken down," Schwitters wrote of the beginnings of Merz, "and new things had to be made out of fragments. It was like an image of the revolution within me—not as it was, but as it might have been." Schwitters was a one-man encyclopedia of Dada preoccupations. He was painter, collagist, sculptor, poet, performer, typographer, visionary architect. He was the consummation of Dada. As much as anyone, he completed the union of art and nonart which had always been fundamental to Dada. In intention he was one of our century's great reconcilers: as a roller-back of boundaries he has still to be surpassed. It was never easy, and it is now impossible, to see his achievement in its totality. That achievement was summed up in the union of the arts which he

Kurt Schwitters.
Merz 19. 1920.
Collage,
7¼ × 5⅞ inches.
Yale University Art Gallery, New Haven.
Gift of Collection Société Anonyme

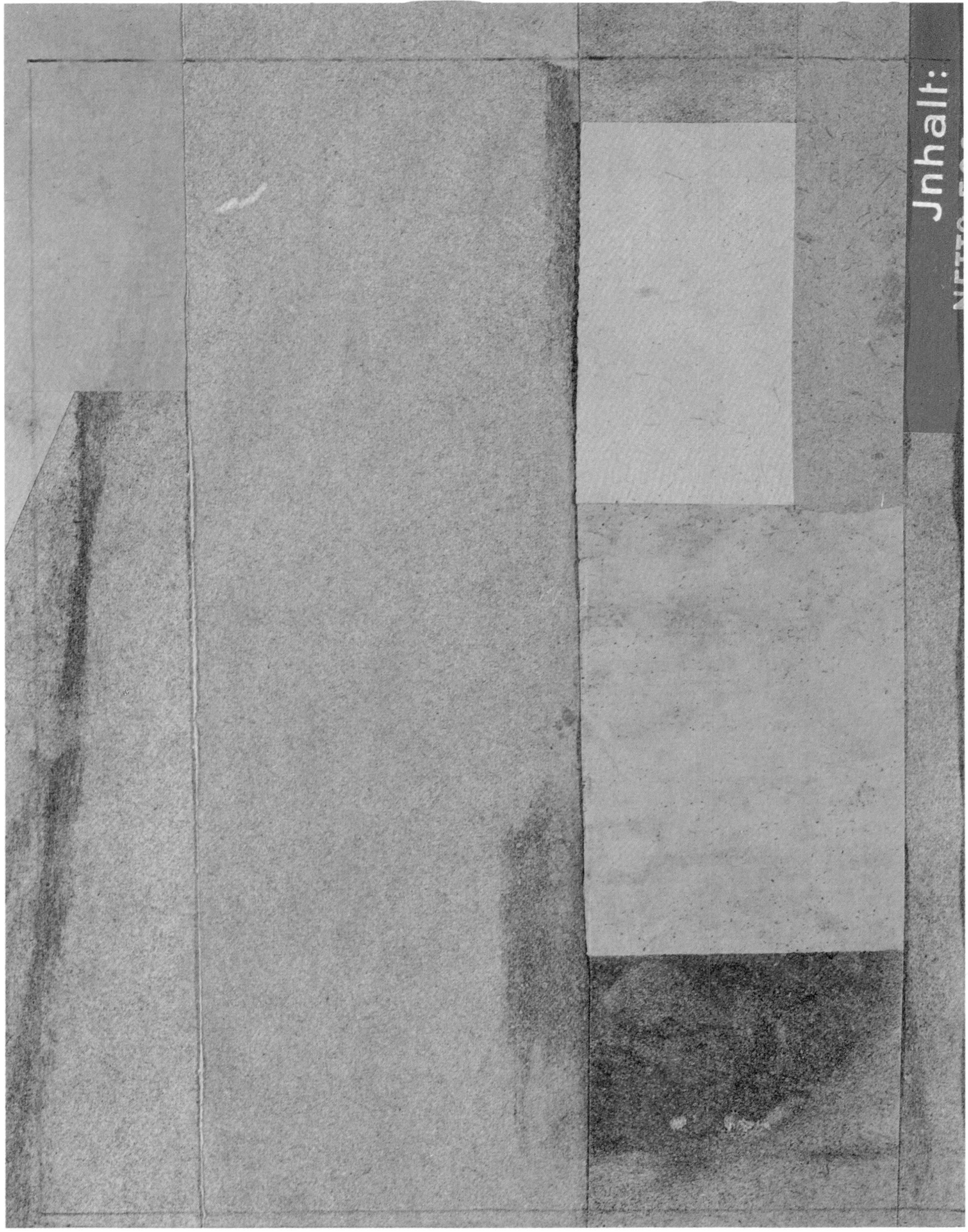

Kurt Schwitters. *Merz 380: Schlotheim.* 1922. Collage, 7½ × 5¼ inches. Yale University Art Gallery, New Haven. Gift of Collection Société Anonyme

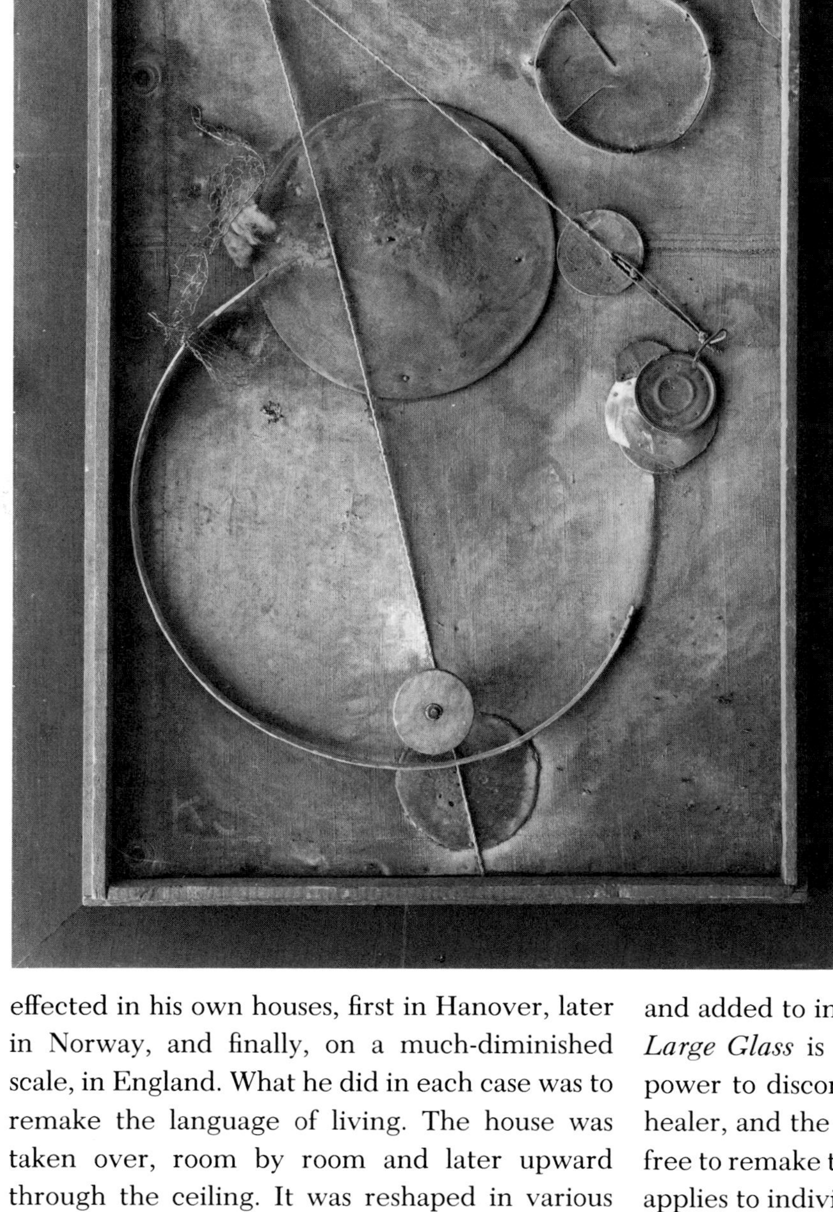

Kurt Schwitters. *Revolving.* 1919. Wood, metal, cord, cardboard, wool, wire, leather and oil on canvas, 48⅜ × 35 inches (sight). The Museum of Modern Art, New York. Advisory Committee Fund

effected in his own houses, first in Hanover, later in Norway, and finally, on a much-diminished scale, in England. What he did in each case was to remake the language of living. The house was taken over, room by room and later upward through the ceiling. It was reshaped in various radical ways and filled slowly and consistently with material objects which were neither architecture, nor painting, nor sculpture, nor reading matter, but an as-yet-unnamed amalgam and crossbreeding of all four of them. Like Duchamp's *Large Glass,* the first Merz building (in Hanover) had an elaborate program which was conceived and added to in a spirit of irony; but whereas the *Large Glass* is Voltairean in its mockery and its power to disconcert, Schwitters was by nature a healer, and the lesson of his work is that men are free to remake the world from its beginnings. This applies to individual elements within the world—the theater, for instance: every experimental theater owes something to Schwitters—and it applies to our environment in its totality.

Schwitters' paintings and collages can be read as an effort of reconciliation, insofar as they often draw upon the achievement of others, notably on the constructed objects produced by Picasso and, more generally, on Synthetic Cubism, with its overlapping flat planes and its mainly rectilinear structure. Sometimes they stand for the antiaesthetic attitudes of Dada—as, for instance, in *Revolving,* where the materials used are as brutish as they could be. Yet the effect of *Revolving* is to create from those materials a reminder that our much-battered world is part of a planetary system which goes on revolving no matter how grievously we misgovern ourselves. Sometimes, equally, they elaborate ideas explored elsewhere by Dada: the strange power which resides in printed matter that has been removed from its original context, for instance. And sometimes they draw on other forms of art: on the color theories of Robert Delaunay, or the affinities with nature of Franz Marc, or the collapsing cosmos of Kandinsky. But Schwitters was not "a borrower," in any disparaging sense. His borrowings were metamorphosed by a poetry that was entirely his own.

Nor did he have the apocalyptic ambitions that Dada had sometimes claimed for itself. He was for an alternative art; and he produced it, as well as anyone. But he knew that an alternative is not necessarily a substitute. "I never meant," he wrote in 1926, "to demonstrate that henceforward pictures could only be made out of junk. I believe that if my paintings are at all successful I have somewhat enlarged the domains of art, without thereby endangering the standing of great works of art in any age." Remarks of this kind reveal the angelic modesty which so vexed the big talkers of full-time Dada; and as most of Schwitters' collages will go comfortably into an overcoat pocket, there is a risk of their being discounted as charm-school work of only marginal importance. Delicious they are, but their small size should not deceive us. It is only very rarely that we find in art a body of work that so tenaciously persuades us to look more closely, and to look in a new way.

Dada as a collective adventure did not take over the world, as had been hoped by some of its more extravagant supporters. And by 1922 it had evolved—in Paris, above all—into a primarily literary movement that was marked over and over again by spectacular clashes of temperament. But it is to the credit of Dada that it acted as the lever on which whole new departments of modernity swung into view. Perhaps Richard Hülsenbeck spoke truer than he knew when he said in 1919 that "Dada is the only savings bank that pays interest in eternity."

THE DOMINION OF THE DREAM

Dreams and dreaming are fundamental to human life; and in just about every work of art that is worth discussing a dream has somewhere been caught and completed. The impossible has been made to happen: we are face to face with what is, and yet is not; with what is not there, and yet is most vividly present to us.

This applies as much to the cooking pots and the half-peeled lemon in a still life by Chardin as it does to the stately forward march of Plato and Aristotle in Raphael's *School of Athens.* Such paintings perpetuate something that comes to the rest of us only momentarily, when the dream makes poets of us all.

Since 1900 it has become clear to us that we dream because we need to dream. We do not dream at random, but in ways dictated by our own inmost nature. Rightly interpreted, the dream will reveal that inmost nature to us. The key event in this development was the publication in 1900 of Sigmund Freud's *The Interpretation of Dreams,* in which a central status was claimed for something that had until then been regarded as marginal to the serious business of life. "He is a dreamer. Let us leave him," says one character to another in Shakespeare's *Julius Caesar;* and the dreamer is by tradition someone of whom no effective action can be expected. But after 1900 people began to realize that the dream was the one department of life in which nobody fakes. In the dream, and there only, do we have direct access to the unconscious. "The dream," C. G. Jung wrote many years later, "is a little hidden door into the innermost and most secret recesses of the psyche." In the dream we lead a supplementary life: as Jorge Luis Borges puts it in his *Labyrinths,* "While we are asleep in this world, we are awake in another one; in this way, every man is two men."

In the novels and plays and poems by which our imagination is nourished, the dream operates for the most part as an early warning system. It brings an urgent, uncensored message from the unconscious. No matter how firmly we repress that mes-

Giorgio de Chirico.
Song of Love. 1914.
Oil on canvas,
$28\frac{3}{4} \times 23\frac{1}{2}$ inches.
The Museum of
Modern Art, New
York. Nelson A.
Rockefeller Bequest

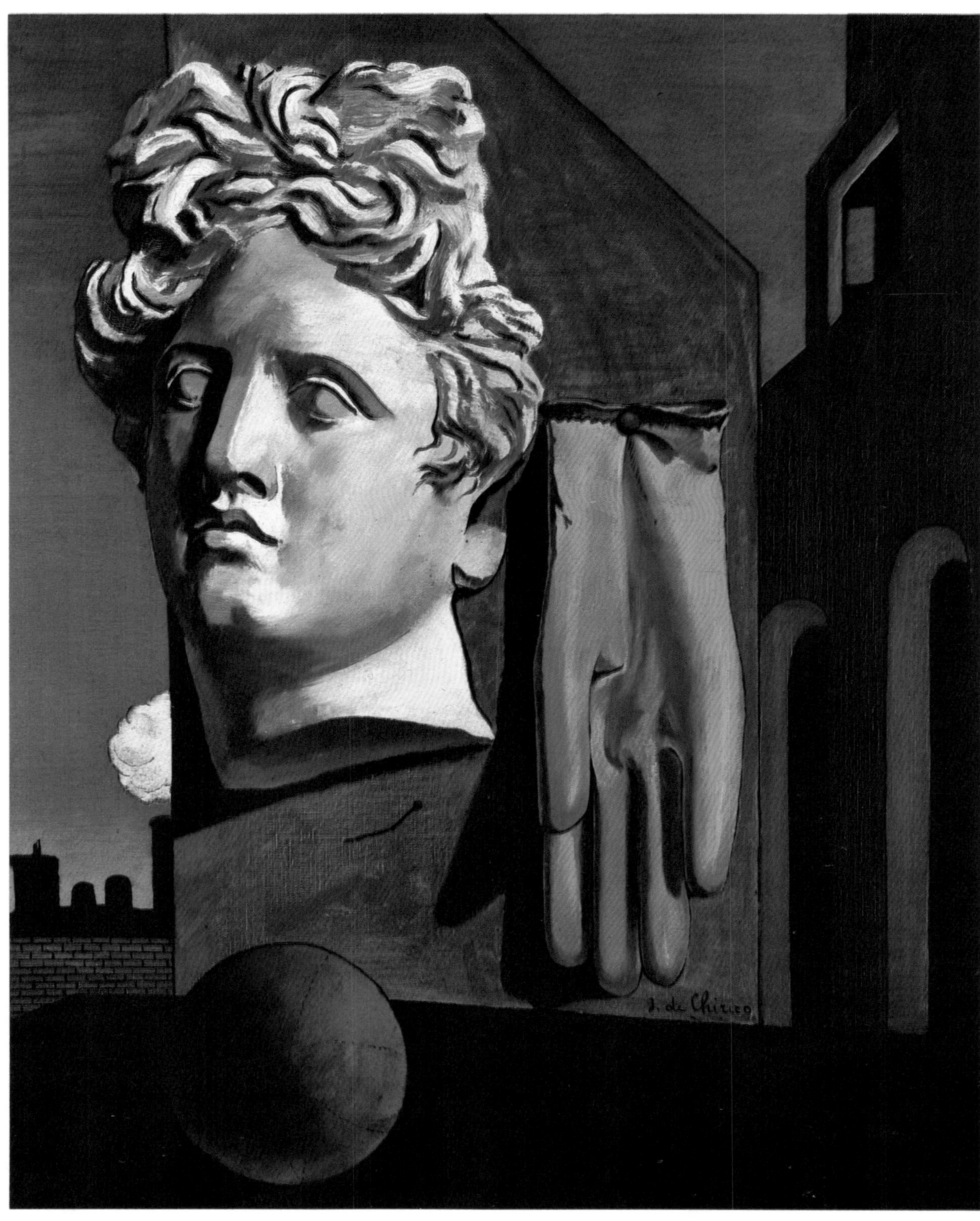

sage in our waking hours, it will steal upon us in our sleep. It is not always explicit. It is likely, in fact, to come upon us as an enigma. Sometimes we can unriddle it, sometimes not. And a comparable strangeness characterizes some of the very greatest works of art. In Giorgione's *The Tempest,* in Rembrandt's *Polish Rider,* in *The Fortune Teller* by Georges de La Tour, life is stilled and suspended. Learned people can tell us that in the Giorgione an emblem of martial valor, on the left, is balanced by an emblem of womanly abandon on the right; that in the *Polish Rider* there is an echo of the skeleton horse and its skeleton rider which Rembrandt had seen in an anatomy theater in Leyden; and that the Georges de La Tour is not about fortune-telling at all, but about the gulling of a rich and inexperienced young traveler. But none of this will explain the particular spell of these pictures or the belief, common to all of us, that in looking at them we have access to a privileged state of mind. There is a literal explanation, but there is also something else: and that something else is the dream. At such times we are at one with Edgar Allan Poe, who wrote:

All that we see or seem
Is but a dream within a dream.

But Poe died in 1849; and from his position in time he could write those lines with an unselfconsciousness which would be impossible today. He could not have foreseen to what extent the dream would be upgraded in our century. In Poe's day it was the prerogative of the artist to make sense of his dreams; the dreams of other people were thought of as either a suburb of Spooksville or a wishful incident in an otherwise pedestrian existence. Today people go to their dreams as in ancient Greece they went to Delphi: to consult the oracle. It was Jung's belief that "all consciousness separates": that from the first moment of self-awareness man begins to stand apart from other men, and from such elements in his own nature as he finds shameful or inconvenient. It is by censoring ourselves that we build an acceptable social nature; "but in dreams," Jung went on, "we put on the likeness of that more universal, truer, more eternal man who dwells in the darkness of primordial night. Out of these all-uniting depths there arises the dream—infantile, grotesque, or immoral as it may be."

So radical a shift in human attitudes was bound to be reflected in painting. In such matters the arts sometimes race ahead of the sciences, much as a solitary horseman could once race ahead of a covered wagon. For an image of Jung's "all-uniting depths" nothing could be more telling than the vast rumination on the triad of E-flat major with which Wagner begins *The Ring;* yet Jung published that remark in 1934, while Wagner wrote in 1853. In literature there was gradually constituted throughout the 19th century an international confederation of the dream. Its founder-members included an Englishman, Thomas De Quincey; a German, E. T. A. Hoffmann; an American, Edgar Allan Poe; and a Frenchman, Charles Baudelaire. Another Englishman, Lewis Carroll, proved with *Alice's Adventures in Wonderland* (1865) that it was not only to a heavyweight adult literature that Jung's "little hidden door" would swing open. The dominion of the dream had been staked out in literature (and incidentally in art by Max Klinger, Odilon Redon, the Douanier Rousseau and others) long before Freud gave it clinical sanction.

All this corresponded to deep-lying needs that were peculiar to their time. The French poet and dramatist Victor Hugo put that very well when he wrote of the 19th century as "the daughter of a religious past who sees in herself the mother of an industrial future." This dual, transitional nature expressed itself in a whole literature of adventure, natural and supernatural, in which a quasi-religious enthusiasm was applied to the results of modern technology. From Jules Verne's *20,000 Leagues under the Sea* (1870) to H. G. Wells's *The First Men in the Moon* (1901), pre-Freudian fancies allied the technical agility of Victor Hugo's "industrial future" to a depth and assurance of belief which were the equivalent of his "religious past."

Art was slower to adapt itself, and for a good reason. In an age of great storytellers—perhaps the last great age, in fact, of the printed narrative—there was not much for art to do in that domain. Art's traditional subjects were far from exhausted when Jules Verne was at the height of his powers. Between 1880 and 1914 the waking life provided quite enough material for the constructive imagination of a Cézanne or a Matisse to get to work on. But when life began to patch itself together again after the end of World War I there was a case for saying that new art must fulfill new needs, and that the most urgent of new needs was to find ways of dealing with the liberated unconscious.

It was in response to this imperative that Surrealism came into being. The role of the Surrealists was to go where almost no one had gone before: to disentangle the dream and to present it—"infantile, grotesque or immoral as it may be"—complete and unaltered. The spokesmen for Surrealism were frankly and markedly imperialistic, in that they annexed terrain to which they had no exclusive right and dismissed, unheard, arguments of great weight and cogency. Paintings and sculptures which were not Surrealist in their allegiance were derided as sterile, outmoded, timid and effete. The dream was *everything* at that time. After 50 years we can see that a bathroom scene by Bonnard or an abstract painting by Mondrian was every bit as much of an imaginative achievement as any of the masterpieces of Surrealism. But at the time preconscious fancies stood on their own as the new subject matter of art, and he who was not with the Surrealists was against them. The dream *was* the imagination: or was at any rate the imagination's only rightful outlet. The sense of life stilled and suspended had always been present in art, and sometimes it had come out with a particular radiant gravity in parts of the world which could strictly have been called provincial—what better example than the *Mourning Picture* which was painted in the late 1880s by a little-known American, Edwin Romanzo Elmer?—but in the 1920s a small group of gifted people suddenly put forward the idea that this was the thing, and the only thing, on which the dignity of art would thereafter depend.

Like the earlier confederation of the dream of which I have just spoken, this one was international. Its most conspicuous members were Max Ernst, a German; Jean Arp, an Alsatian; Joan Miró, a Spaniard; André Masson, a Frenchman; René Magritte, a Belgian; Man Ray, an American; Alberto Giacometti, a Swiss; and Salvador Dali, another Spaniard. Insofar as they had a joint ancestor, he was Giorgio de Chirico, an Italian born in Greece. Most of the masterpieces of Surrealism were made in Paris, but the Surrealists did not rely, as Cézanne and Matisse had relied, on the almost unbroken evolutionary thrust of French painting as it had existed for several hundreds of years. Their allegiances derived from literature, from medicine, from psychoanalysis, and from the ideology of political revolution. "Beauty must be convulsive," wrote their chief spokesman, poet and critic André Breton, "or it will cease to be."

Because Surrealism overlapped with the last days of Dada, and because some of the same people took part in both, it is convenient to treat the one as the outcome of the other. But the truth is that they have almost nothing in common. In the First Surrealist Manifesto as it was published by Breton in 1924 there was none of that hostility to the past, that wish to ignore or abolish "art" and "literature" as they had previously existed, which was basic to Dada. Surrealism was fundamentally the continuation by other means of activities which could be traced back to the late 18th century. In 1936, when Breton was invited to introduce Surrealism to an English audience, he traced its origins to the summer of 1764, when Horace Walpole wrote his novel, *The Castle of Otranto,* under the influence of a dream in which he found himself on the great staircase of an ancient castle and saw on the topmost banister "a gigantic hand in armor." Walpole went on, "In the evening I sat down and began to write, without knowing in the least what I wanted to say or relate." In this way there was initiated the idea that Surrealism had one foot in automatism and the other in the dream.

Another English novel, Charles Maturin's *Melmoth the Wanderer* (1820), was among the ancestors of the book which is most often quoted in connection with the methodology of Surrealism. Maturin's demonic adventurer found his French counterpart in *Les Chants de Maldoror,* which was written in Paris in 1868 by the 22-year-old Isidore Ducasse, self-styled Comte de Lautréamont. The key passage in this context is one in which Lautréamont speaks of an English boy as being "as beautiful as the chance meeting on a dissecting table of a sewing machine and an umbrella." The famous passage is very much stronger, in point of fact, if it is read in full. We need, for instance, the image of the deserted Paris street along which the boy is walking while overhead "a screech-owl with a broken leg flies dead straight above the Madeleine"; and we also need the crescendo of oddity by which the boy's beauty has already been likened to "the retractility of the claws of birds of prey," to the specific effects of "wounds in the soft parts of the lower cervical region," and to the mechanism of a self-operating rat trap. But even in its diminished form the phrase upholds that fundamental principle of Surrealism by which seemingly unrelated objects turn out, when set side by side, to have an unexpected significance. The umbrella, the sewing machine and the dissecting table symbolize the improbable encounters in inappropriate places that can play so decisive a role in human life; and when André Breton wanted to justify the picturing of such encounters it was Edgar Allan Poe whom he called in as chief witness. Poe had written in his *Marginalia* that "the pure imagination chooses from either Beauty or Deformity only the most combinable things hitherto uncombined." He went on, "As so often happens in physical chemistry, so not unfrequently does it occur in the chemistry of the intellect that the admixture of two elements results in something that has nothing of the qualities of one of them, or even nothing of the qualities of either."

Reactions of this kind had been set up in painting since 1911 by Giorgio de Chirico. The paintings in question were first exhibited in Paris before 1914, and Apollinaire for one got the point of them immediately. De Chirico became a familiar though quietly mutinous attender at Apollinaire's weekly receptions, and before long he assumed a place which he has never lost: that of the acknowledged forerunner of the new visionary painting. There was something almost supernatural about the initiatory powers which his work seemed to possess, and about the seemingly accidental ways in which it imposed itself on those who were predestined to make use of it. Breton first saw it in a shop window, Max Ernst in a bookshop in Munich, Yves Tanguy from the top of a bus, René Magritte when a friend chanced to show him a reproduction of the *Song of Love.* These were "chance encounters," but each came at a moment of maximum need for the artists in question.

We can still see why this was. A de Chirico of the period 1911–17 gives classic and definitive expression to anxieties characteristic of our century. With its unexpected jumps in scale, its backward glance at antiquity, its unfathomable architecture, its locomotive with a head of steam up and its bizarre conjunction of unrelated objects, de Chirico's *Song of Love* is a painting that took its time by the throat. Such has been the proliferation of the image over the last 80 years that we have to apply to every new work of art a terrible question: "Who needs it?" Only if the answer is "Everybody" do we accept the work unreservedly; and I hope to make it clear that in the case of a de Chirico of those years we can still return that answer.

If these pictures make so much of Surrealism look feeble, contrived, or superfluous it is partly because de Chirico set himself so stringent a criterion. It was that the basic idea of each painting must give the painter "such joy or such pain that he has no alternative but to paint it and is driven on by a force greater even than that which drives a starving man to bite into the first piece of bread that comes his way." The observer must identify, equally, with the first man in the world, "who must have seen auguries everywhere, and trembled with every step that he took."

De Chirico had a very low opinion of the accredited Surrealists when they eventually materialized, and there is nothing in his work of the invalidish imaginings which run wild in Lautréamont. His compound images derive from identifiable elements in his own life, even if they have been edited and recombined in ways for which "dreamlike" is as good a word as any. He had also looked with great intelligence both at the union of disparate elements in the pasted-paper works of Picasso and Braque and at the use of flat silhouette in Synthetic Cubism; these helped him to present his ideas with measured coherence and a logic that was not of the waking world.

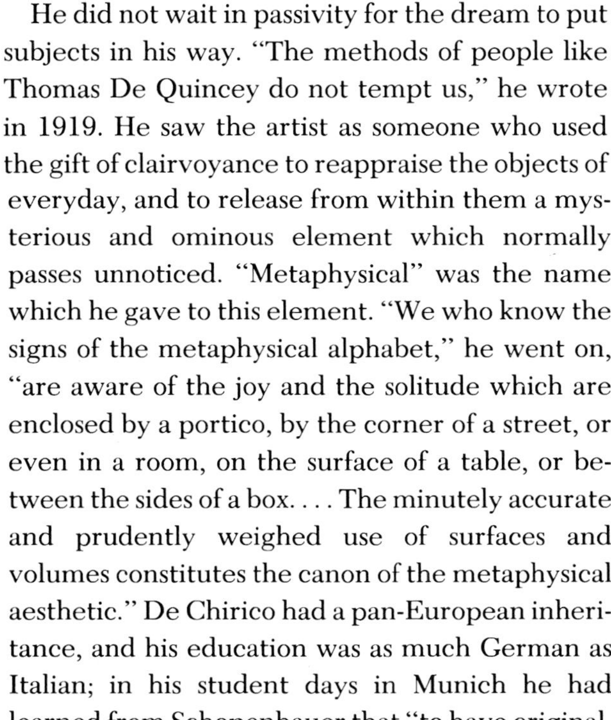

He did not wait in passivity for the dream to put subjects in his way. "The methods of people like Thomas De Quincey do not tempt us," he wrote in 1919. He saw the artist as someone who used the gift of clairvoyance to reappraise the objects of everyday, and to release from within them a mysterious and ominous element which normally passes unnoticed. "Metaphysical" was the name which he gave to this element. "We who know the signs of the metaphysical alphabet," he went on, "are aware of the joy and the solitude which are enclosed by a portico, by the corner of a street, or even in a room, on the surface of a table, or between the sides of a box. . . . The minutely accurate and prudently weighed use of surfaces and volumes constitutes the canon of the metaphysical aesthetic." De Chirico had a pan-European inheritance, and his education was as much German as Italian; in his student days in Munich he had learned from Schopenhauer that "to have original, extraordinary and perhaps even immortal ideas one has only to isolate oneself from the world for a few moments in such a way that even the most commonplace happenings seem new and unfamiliar, and so reveal their true essence."

He remained loyal to this idea: "The daemon in everything must be discovered." Sometimes it was enough simply to displace an object from the environment in which we expect to see it, "like an armchair, a divan and some chairs, grouped together on the traditionless prairies of distant America." Sometimes a change of scale did the trick, as when he noticed how, outside a little workshop in a Parisian side street, "a huge glove made of painted zinc, with terrible gilded nails, was pointing with its index finger at the stones of the sidewalk." Sometimes the image was carried forward like a mascot from his childhood: a huge and archaic cannon, for instance, which he remembered from the harbor in Volos, the Greek seaport where he had first been brought up. Sometimes he stayed even nearer to the facts of his youth. His father had been a railway engineer; and

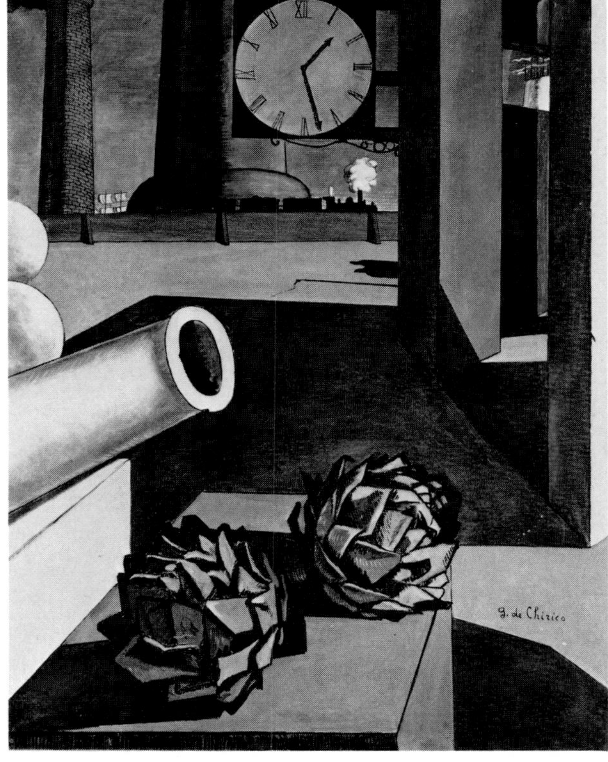

Giorgio de Chirico. *The Philosopher's Conquest.* 1914. Oil on canvas, 49½ × 39¼ inches. The Art Institute of Chicago. The Joseph Winterbotham Collection

the town terminal, the station clock and the locomotive with its plumes of steam were early members of the "metaphysical alphabet." Sometimes he drew upon the grander, more spacious elements of Greek or Italian town planning, sometimes on specific works of ancient art (notably an antique statue of Ariadne), sometimes on fragments of the Italian industrial scene: factory chimneys above all. A tireless window shopper, he found metaphysics in the shapes of the biscuits put out by specialized pastry cooks and metaphysics again in the relief maps of Europe which were in vogue after the outbreak of World War I.

The belching factory chimney, the symbols of imminent departure (locomotive and sailing ship), the phallic artillery with its accompaniment of two huge balls, the mysterious cowled figures whose shadows appear beneath the clock—all these make *The Philosopher's Conquest* one of the most dense, as well as one of the most cryptic, of de Chirico's paintings. Where other painters strove for infinity with pictures of mountain ranges and distant horizons, de Chirico from 1914 onward aimed to induce in the observer a systematic disorientation. He did nothing that was not personal to himself; yet the result has a universal resonance, and we can agree with what de Chirico said of it in 1919—that it arose from "a fatality of the human spirit which is governed by fixed mathematical laws. It ebbs, flows, departs, returns and is reborn like everything else on our planet." He was to turn up everywhere. Something of his vocabulary—his menacing way with architecture, his delight in relief maps, his ability to see the human body half as a lay figure, half as automaton—was taken up in 1917 by the Futurist painter Carlo Carrà in his *Metaphysical Muse.* The painting is, moreover, an anthology of themes which were to preoccupy other artists many years later: the target (Kenneth Noland and Jasper Johns), the map (Johns, once again) and the summary, schematic automaton (Oskar Schlemmer in the 1920s). After World War I George Grosz exploited elements from de Chirico's vocabulary to press home a satirical point about the people who had served like robots in the German Army and lost no time in adapting to a change of political regime.

Giorgio de Chirico invented as valid a metaphor as painting has to show for the anxiety, the sense of unfocused guilt and dread, which has been common to almost every thinking individual throughout the 20th century. In his world nothing is what it seems; our relationship to our environment is warped at every turn; normal life is suspended. Omens are everywhere: we cannot see the little girl bowling her hoop in *The Mystery and Melancholy of a Street* without being reminded by her two-dimensional silhouette of how running figures were turned into flattened and calcinated profiles when Dresden was destroyed by fire in 1945.

What de Chirico did, between 1911 and 1917, was to create a modern mythology—a compound of private guilt and the externals of big-city life—which has never been superseded. Proud and re-

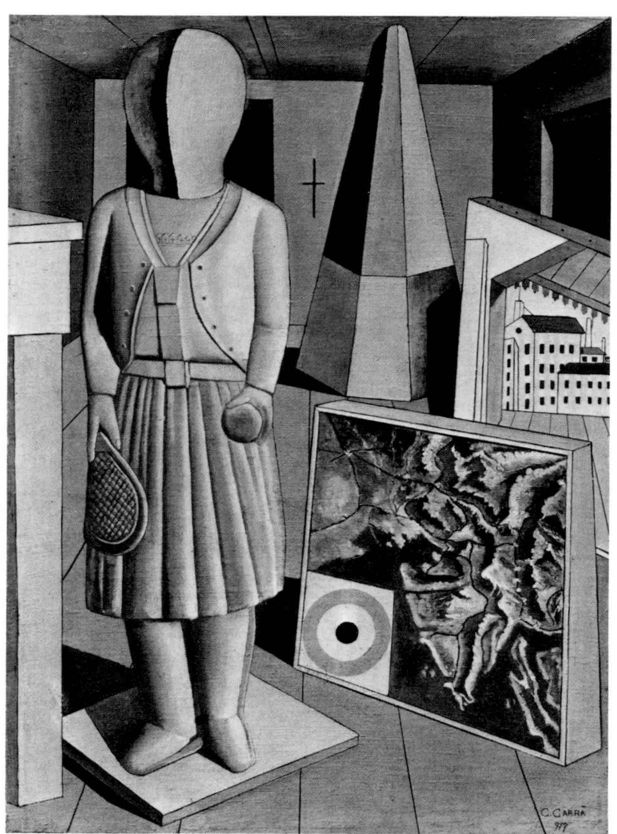

Carlo Carrà.
Metaphysical Muse.
1917.
Oil on canvas,
36 × 26¼ inches.
Emilio Jesi, Milan

sentful by nature, he did not at all care for the interpretation which was put upon his work in Paris from 1914 onward. First Apollinaire, and in later years André Breton, had major paintings by de Chirico in their apartments; in both cases the pictures were used as a point of departure for the poetics of free association. But whereas de Chirico distinguished sharply between the climate of the dream and the dream itself, Breton and his friends identified the cult of the dream with the cult of psychic automatism. "I define Surrealism once and for all," Breton wrote in the First Surrealist Manifesto, "as that pure psychic automatism by which we propose to express, whether in speech, on the printed page, or by any other means, the true functioning of thought. Whatever thought dictates to us is to be immune from conscious control by our reason and shall be set down without regard either for aesthetics or for morality. Surrealism is based on a belief in the superior reality of certain hitherto neglected forms of association, in the supreme authority of the dream, and in the disinterested play of the thought processes."

It sounded categorical enough. And it did, in point of fact, apply to the experiments in automatic writing which Breton and his friends had been making. Other, earlier precedents in literature were adduced by Breton: the state of "supernaturalist reverie," for instance, in which the poet Gérard de Nerval (1808–1855) claimed to have written a series of sonnets. If no such precedents were brought forward in art it was because art had, in Breton's view, lagged behind. "It is preposterous," he wrote some years later, "that drawing and painting should still stand today at the point at which writing stood before Gutenberg." But there was not in 1924 a body of work which could be discussed in terms of the "internal model" which was to apotheosize the role of the dream in human affairs. By 1928, when Breton for the first time wrote specifically on Surrealism and painting, he was able to present not only de Chirico but Max Ernst, Joan Miró, André Masson and Yves Tanguy as committed Surrealists. Over the next year or two René Magritte, Salvador Dali and Alberto Giacometti came along to complete what was by any count a body of very substantial artists. But in 1924 Max Ernst was the only person who had consistently followed de Chirico's lead in producing images which effected "a meeting of two distant realities on a plane foreign to them both"; and as he made many of these under the aegis of Dada (and at times under the name of "Dadamax") it got to be taken for granted that Dada overlapped into Surrealism and had much the same base.

This is true on a personal level, and it was partly true on the level of literature. Breton was anxious to annex for Surrealism the things that he admired in Dada; when outflanked in that intention he put it about that Dada had died in the spring of 1921, in any case, and that "for a long time now, the risks have been taken elsewhere." The fact that many people concerned remained the same made it even more natural to smudge history; but the differences between Dada art and Surrealist art are fundamental enough to be worth defining here.

Dada was an emergency operation. Based on an economy of starvation and on the total rejection of the past, it was international and even intercontinental in its development. It responded to a situation in which the end of the world as it had previously existed for art could reasonably be regarded as imminent. In such a situation, ad hoc materials alone were appropriate. Surrealism was hardly less radical in its program; but, in spite of that, Surrealist art was largely a matter of old-style paintings on canvas which were put on offer in old-style galleries in a world bent on "going back to normal." It is also pertinent that Dada was opposed to the very idea of "a career in art" and that with one or two exceptions the Dadaists were not people whose gifts would support a long lifetime of continuous effort. With Miró, Ernst, Magritte and Giacometti—to name four only—the case was quite different; and during the years from 1917 to 1921 Miró as a very young man was painting pictures of a fulfilled and completely energized sort which were the antithesis of Dada and could be said to have guaranteed, on their own, a great future for painting.

André Breton was by origin a man of letters, and in 1921 he was still fundamentally the young man who had come to Paris on leave from the French Army in 1916 and made a name for himself by reason of his extreme beauty of person ("archangelical" was the adjective most in favor for this), his precocious gifts as a poet, and the frenzy of excitement and awe in which he presented himself to the writers whom he most admired. Breton had that same effect upon others in later life; but it came to be overlooked that at the age of 18 he had written a sonnet which drew from Paul Valéry, a great poet 25 years his senior, the rueful admission that in Breton's lines he heard a language which he himself no longer knew how to speak.

Breton always remembered the exact moment at which the image began to rank equal, in his eyes, with the written word. It was early in 1921, at Picabia's house in Paris. Breton was there with the poet and novelist Louis Aragon, the poet Philippe Soupault and Tristan Tzara, the veteran of international Dada, when the mailman delivered a package from Cologne. Inside it were the collages which Max Ernst was to show in Paris. "They introduced," Breton wrote, "an entirely original scheme of visual structure; yet they corresponded exactly to the intentions of Lautréamont and Rimbaud in poetry. . . . We were all filled immediately with unparalleled admiration. The external object had broken free from its normal environment, and its component parts had become emancipated from it in such a way as to maintain entirely new relationships with other elements in the collages."

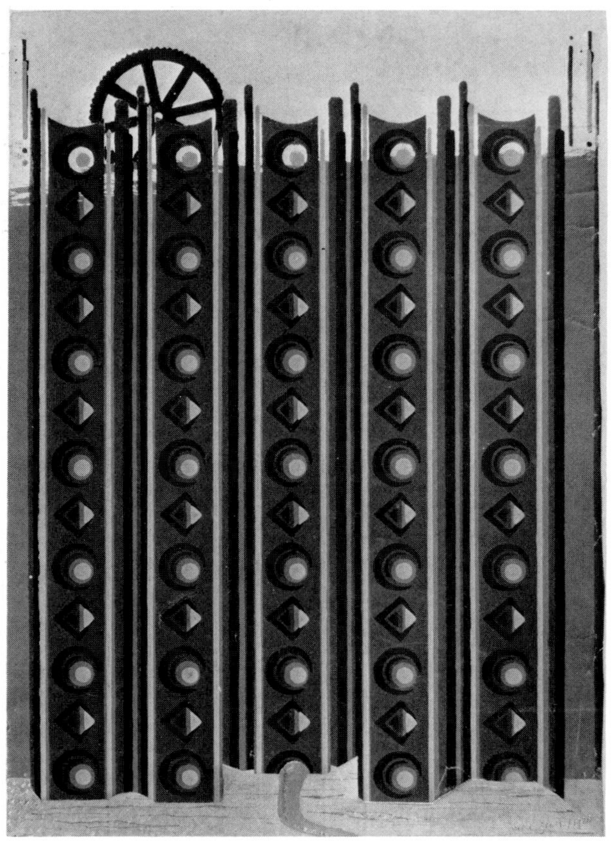

Max Ernst. *The Little Tear Gland That Says Tic Tac.* 1920. Wallpaper borders altered with gouache, 14¼ × 10 inches. The Museum of Modern Art, New York. Purchase

Thereafter, Max Ernst was the test case, the exception to the rule, the man from out of town (he moved to Paris in 1922) who was manifestly as much at home in literature as he was in art. He was a poet among the poets, a painter among the painters, a prehensile many-sided inventor who gave art, in the eyes of the Surrealist writers, a fresh start and a prestige without precedent. There was nothing in Ernst's works, Breton said, which could not be found in the observer's own experience; yet they invalidated all our systems of reference, so that we could no longer find our way among our own memories. In the work which Max Ernst showed in Paris in May, 1921, speed of wit was allied to speed of manufacture. He racked up in double time a whole dictionary of new technical possibilities for art. With a piece of wallpaper, a cogwheel from a manual of engineering and a hand-painted flow of heavy, viscous liquid, he produced in *The Little Tear Gland* what is both an odd image in itself and a sly commentary on the machinery by which our inmost feelings make themselves visible. He was not "a natural painter," in the sense that Chardin or Manet or Braque was a natural painter. If he could elide, abbreviate, or with impunity miss ten turns in the long manual process of "painting a picture," he did so; what

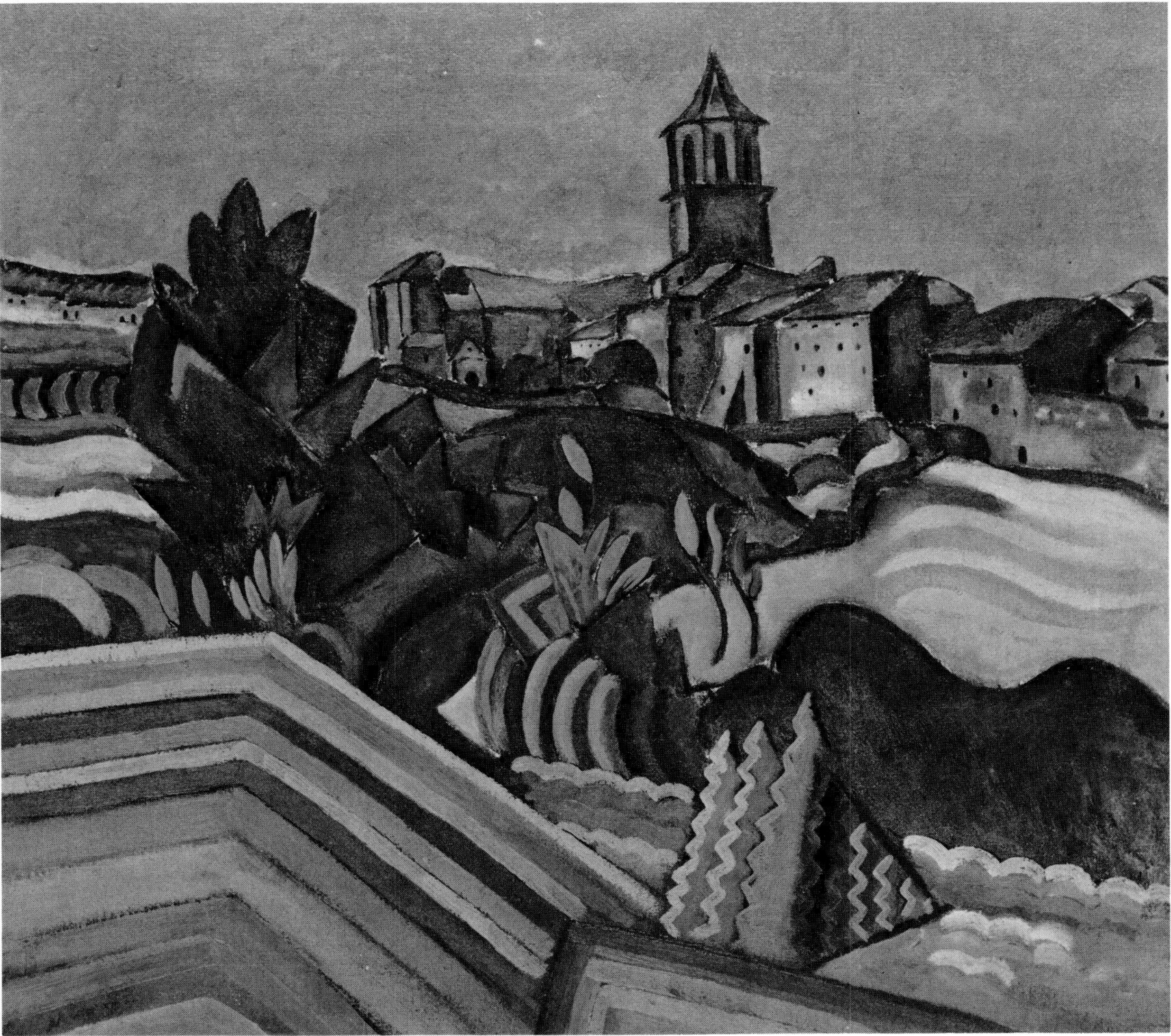

Joan Miró.
View of Montroig.
1917.
Oil on canvas,
26⅛ × 29 inches.
The Solomon R. Guggenheim Museum, New York

mattered was not the physical beauty of the thing done but the readiness—as Breton had noticed at once—to put our experience at risk.

Joan Miró did not in 1921 seem likely to rival Max Ernst in his mastery of dislocation. The son and grandson of Catalan craftsmen, Miró had had none of the intensive literary education which was common to both Ernst and Breton. Nor was he familiar, as they were, with the development of abnormal psychology. But as a student in Barcelona during World War I he had seen a majestic survey of recent French painting which had been chosen by Ambroise Vollard and sent to Barcelona. Among wartime visitors to that delectable city he had met Picabia in 1917 and the French poet Pierre Reverdy, who was a lifelong friend of Braque. He had also seen the Ballets Russes which Diaghilev had brought to Barcelona. All this had helped to de-provincialize him; and as he combined an appetite for the new with an inherited command of robust craftsmanship, it came about between 1917 and 1921 that without ever having been to Paris he produced painting after painting which amounted to, in effect, an inspired critique of the state of French art.

His *Portrait of E. C. Ricart,* 1917, was, for instance, an appendix to the enthusiasm for the Japanese print which infected one major artist after

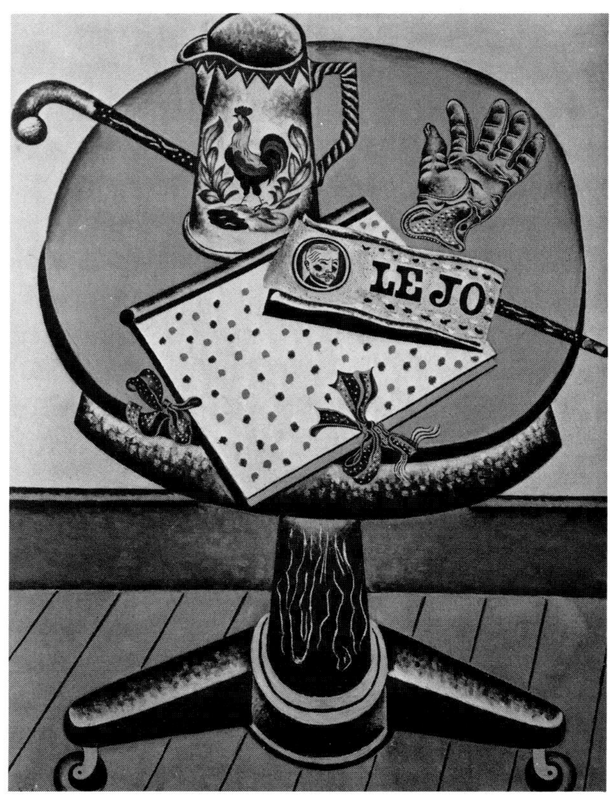

Joan Miró.
Table with Glove.
1921.
Oil on canvas,
46 × 35¼ inches.
The Museum of Modern Art, New York.
Gift of Armand G. Erpf

another from van Gogh to Bonnard. His *Portrait of a Woman* of 1918, in the Art Institute of Chicago, came near to Matisse in its presentation of a firmly modeled human body against a background and floor-ground of vivid allover patterning. No account of Fauvism is complete without some reference to the riot of color which characterizes the landscapes which Miró painted at Montroig, not far from Barcelona, in 1919. *Table with Glove* of 1921 is as remarkable as Picasso's great *Still Life with Bread and Fruit Dish* of 1909 for its mingling of up-to-date formal devices with the extreme solidity of traditional Spanish still life. This was painting of a class which did not need to look beyond itself for its justification. Still less did it need to sign a treaty of alliance with the printed word. An extreme particularity of vision—the power to identify strongly and in turn with every object in the picture—is allied in paintings like *Table with Glove* to rock-steady compositional powers; the result is an icon of stability.

Yet within a year of his first sojourn in Paris Miró was painting in a completely different and new way. Familiar images, released from the solid architectural schema of the earlier paintings, raced helter-skelter across the canvas; concurrently, a free-running fantasy brought with it an atmosphere of carnival in which it seemed quite natural for a lizard in a wizard's cap to break off his reading of the newspaper to start a conversation with a snail. Whereas in 1917 Miró tilled every inch of the picture as carefully as the Catalan farmer tills his red earth, by 1923 he was treating the canvas as a blank space on which to rough out his thoughts in diagrammatic style and according to a shorthand of his own devising. Heads in that shorthand were transparent and triangular; hearts were shown as ticking bombs; and a rifle at the ready became a tall thin black cone with a flame at the top of it. Where Matisse in his *Joy of Life* had included a faithful representation of a Catalan round dance called the *sardana,* Miró in his *The Hunter (Catalan Landscape)* of 1923–24 simply wrote in the first four letters of its name in the corner. He then left it to us to work out whether he was thinking of the SARDana or, no less plausibly, about the SARDine which, fresh and lightly grilled, is a great delicacy in that part of Spain.

Miró from his beginnings had subjected every object in his paintings to that penetrating scrutiny which is traditional to the Spanish *bodegón,* or still life. He could not paint so much as a watering can or a pair of steps, let alone a dead rabbit, without giving it an animistic intensity; and as early as 1917 he had invented an ideogram of brightly colored stripes to stand for a ploughed field. In the early 1920s he went one step further—just one, but a big one—in the direction of a purely poetic evocation. He still regarded his landscapes as realistic—"more essentially Montroig," he said later, "than if they had been painted from nature"—but he no longer thought of painting as an ambition complete in itself. His new friends in Paris, and above all his neighbor André Masson, taught him to think of the act of representing the everyday world as something subordinate and transitional;

the role of the true artist was to go beyond painting. ("Beyond Painting" is, by the way, the title of an important essay by Max Ernst.) The artist's activity should be what we now call trans- or interdisciplinary; he was there not to *represent* the ideas that came to him but to *list* them, uncensored. By bringing into the open what is most often bundled out of the way he would resite the locus of human uncertainty and put it where it belonged: in the unconscious.

One of the things that Miró did was to carry over into painting the idea of automatic writing. Many of his paintings from 1923 onward were as much written as painted: sometimes literally, in that handwritten texts were an important part of the picture's formal constituents, and sometimes metaphorically, in that the forms in a picture like his *Carnival of Harlequin* were noted down individually and in terms of condensed biomorphic symbols. (Something in those lollopy biomorphic signs was owed to Arp, who lived in the same house as Miró at the time.) Miró said in 1933 that his work was "always born in a state of hallucination due to a shock of some kind—subjective or objective—for which I bear no responsibility." In other words, he switched off the conscious mind and just let the images come: initially under the pressures of hunger, later as the result of a faculty by then well developed.

This is of course a grossly simplified account of a complex, intermittent and often self-contradictory process. It takes time to make a picture, even if the means employed are as summary as those of the *Spanish Dancer* of 1928; and although the notion of total automatism can be upheld as a philosophical position it is difficult not to believe that automatism is more effective when used as a booster, or as a form of overdrive, than when the artist allows it complete command of his actions. What passes for successful automatism may result from a dis-inhibited fancy, an original gift for metaphor, and the ability to move forward from

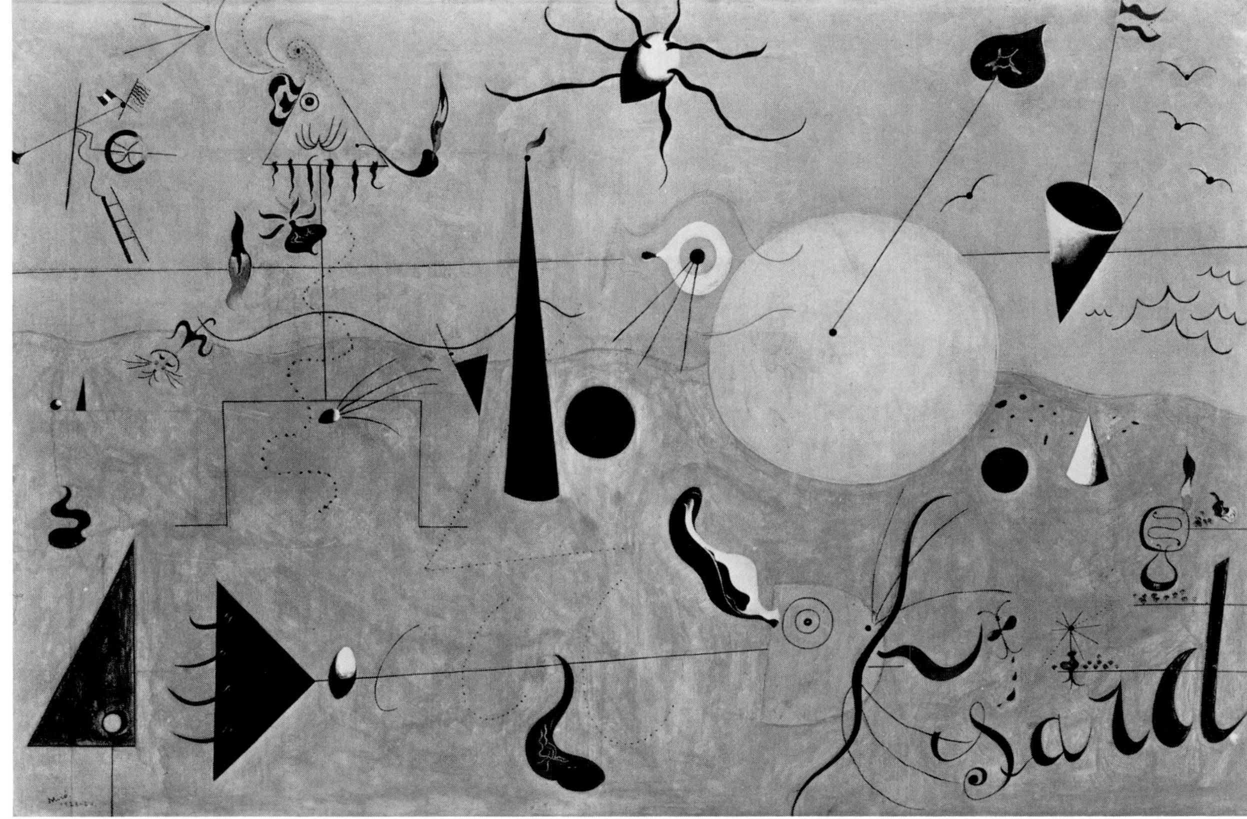

Joan Miró. *The Hunter (Catalan Landscape).* 1923–24. Oil on canvas, 25½ × 39½ inches. The Museum of Modern Art, New York. Purchase

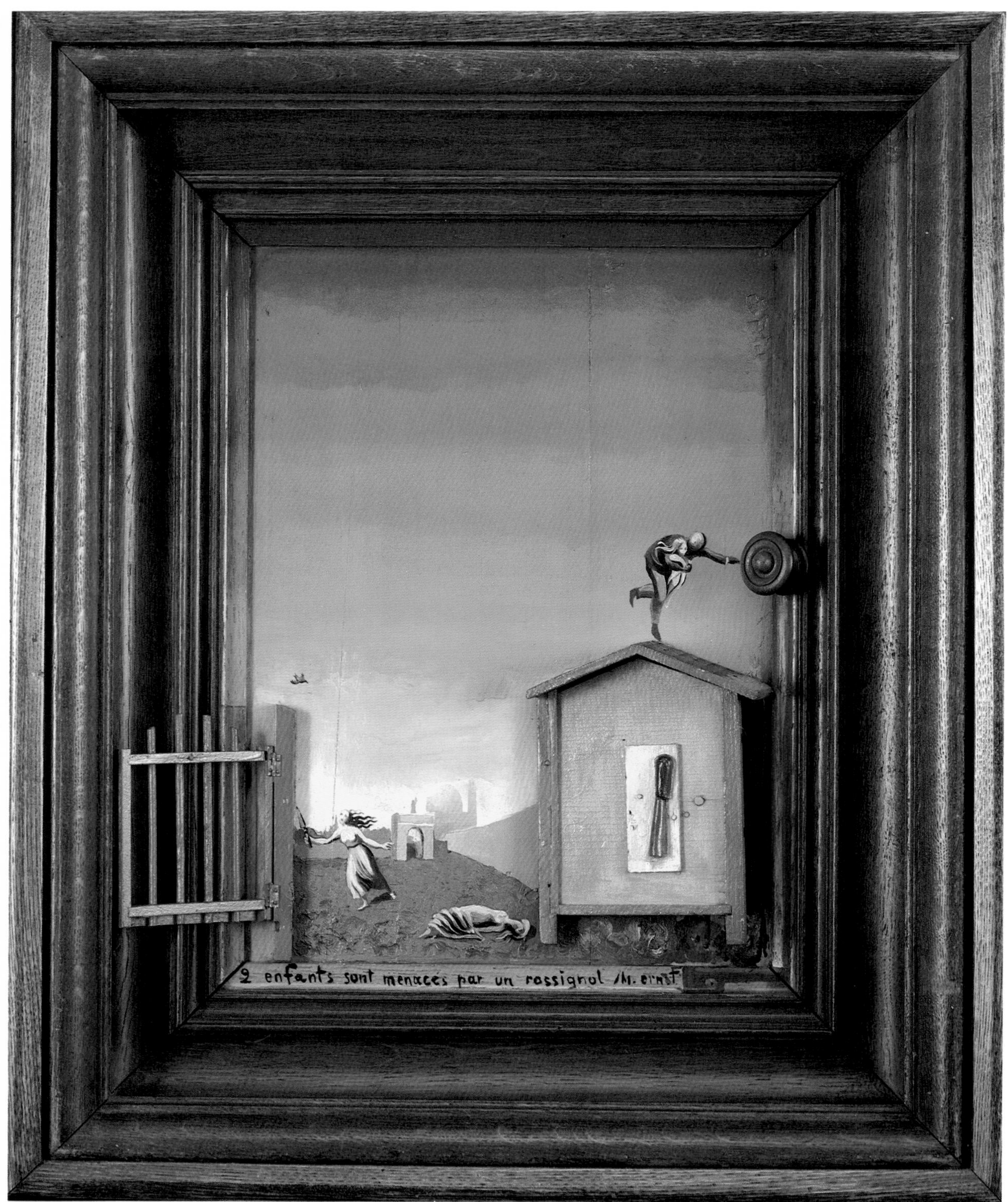

Max Ernst.
Two Children Are Threatened by a Nightingale. 1924.
Oil on wood with wood construction, 27½ × 22½ × 4½ inches.
The Museum of Modern Art, New York. Purchase

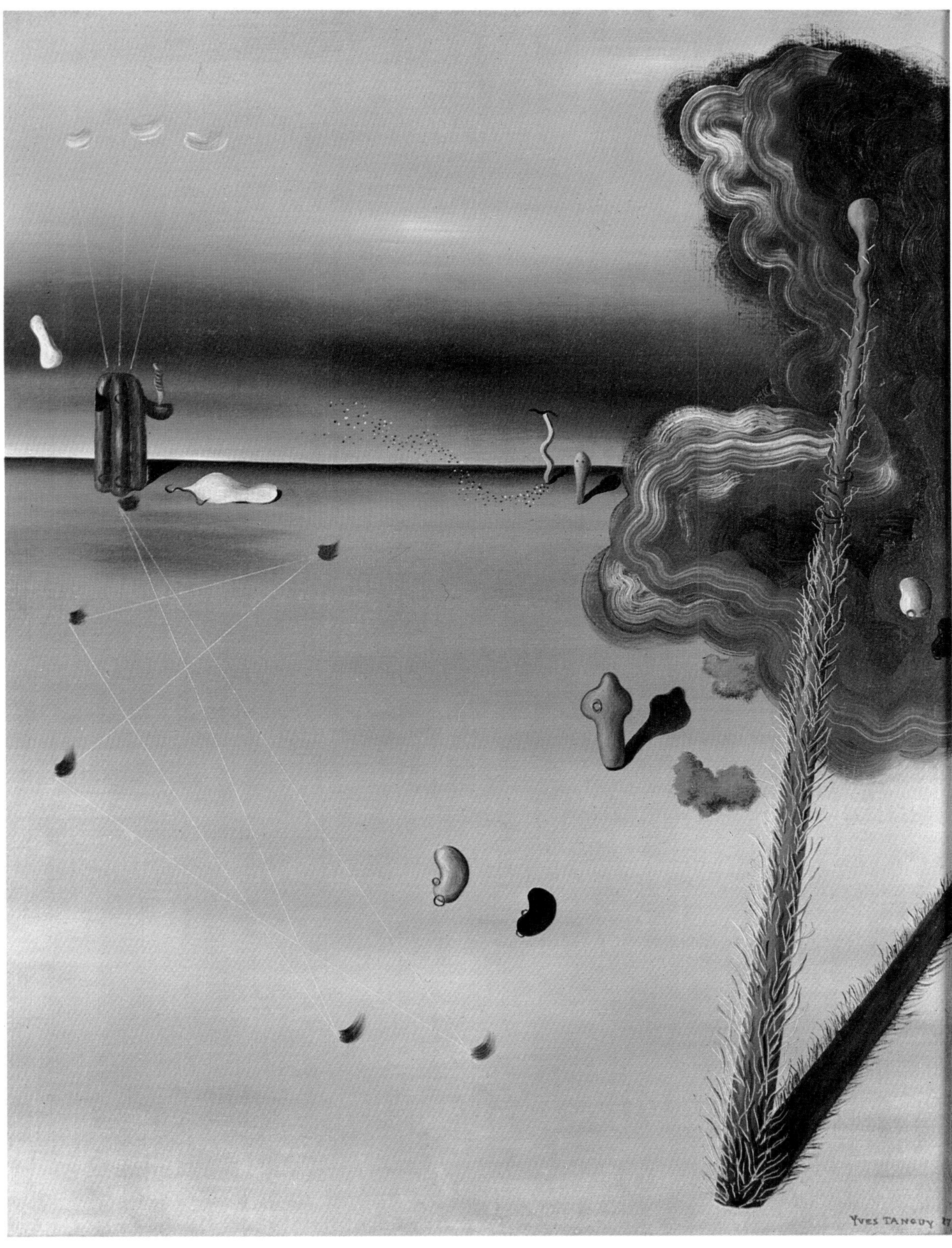

Yves Tanguy. *Mama, Papa Is Wounded!* 1927. Oil on canvas, 36¼ × 28¾ inches. The Museum of Modern Art, New York. Purchase

"painting," as hitherto understood, to an amalgam of painting and object making. A signal instance of this is Miró's *The Writer*, which dates from the crucial year 1924 and is at once a portrait (of Apollinaire, according to the interpretation of Margit Rowell), a list of the writer's materials, a list of the vowels at his disposal, and (by virtue of the two postage stamps in the upper right corner) a demonstration of what it can all amount to: a letter ready for mailing. Hallucinatory it may have been, in its origins; but there is too much in the way of wit and allusion (to Apollinaire's play *Les Mamelles de Tirésias*, in particular) to make us accept it as an unaltered message from the unconscious.

When André Masson took André Breton to Miró's studio in 1924, Breton dismissed Miró's work as altogether too childlike. The pictures were daring, but they were not seen to be daring in terms of the iconography of panic which Breton was promoting. To the extent that the unconscious does not usually bring us good news, and that what we repress is hatred more often than love, Breton was right to prefer the dislocated images of Max Ernst (or, for that matter, the arrowy, allover, seemingly improvised drawings and paintings of Masson). Miró in 1924 still stuck to the traditions of easel painting, and to the logic of pictorial statement that he had learned from Cubism. Moreover, he was interested in consolidating rather than destroying the world in which he had come to manhood. He had always drawn his inspiration from the landscape, the people, the climate and the produce of his native Catalonia. He was still doing it in the at first sight cryptic painting called *The Hunter.* William Rubin has identified no fewer than 58 specific local references in what is basically "an image of a peasant hunting in the Catalan countryside." It is, however, a deft mingling of factual references (the hunter has a mustache and a beard, smokes a pipe and wears an identifiable kind of local cap) with elements of pure fantasy: "monstrous animals and angelic animals," as Miró wrote at the time, "and trees with ears and eyes."

It was Max Ernst, in 1924, who best fulfilled the Surrealists' mandate. Ernst did it above all in the construction called *Two Children Are Threatened by a Nightingale,* which starts from one of those instincts of irrational panic which we suppress in our waking lives. Only in dreams can a diminutive songbird scare the daylights out of us; only in dreams can the button of an alarm bell swell to the size of a beach ball and yet remain just out of our reach. *Two Children* incorporates elements from traditional European painting: perspectives that give an illusion of depth, a subtly atmospheric sky, formalized poses that come straight from the Old Masters, a distant architecture of dome and tower and triumphal arch. But it also breaks out of the frame, in literal terms: the alarm or doorbell, the swinging gate on its hinge and the blind-walled house are three-dimensional constructions, physical objects in the real world. We are both in, and out of, painting; in, and out of, art; in, and out of, a world subject to rational interpretation. Where traditional painting subdues disbelief by presenting us with a world unified on its own terms, Max Ernst in the *Two Children* breaks the contract over and over again. We have reason to disbelieve the plight of his two children. Implausible in itself, it is set out in terms which eddy between those of fine art and those of the toyshop. Nothing "makes sense" in the picture. Yet the total experience is undeniably meaningful; Ernst has re-created a sensation painfully familiar to us from our dreams but never before quite recaptured in art—that of total disorientation in a world where nothing keeps to its expected scale or fulfills its expected function.

In principle, the entire terrain of human experience was open to the Surrealists, yet what actually happened was far more restricted in its implications. Surrealism as sponsored by André Breton was predominantly Freudian in its allegiances; and like much of what Freud wrote it was founded on a patient replay of childhood experience. Above all, Surrealism was about the overthrow of authority, and more especially about the overthrow of authority as represented by the father. De Chirico was haunted by the withdrawn, authoritarian figure of his father. Max Ernst was marked for life by the imperious rhythm of childbearing which his father imposed on his mother, and by the hallucinatory intimations of this which came to him in dreams. Fathers in general stood for authority, for repression, for conjugal rights exercised with a brutish regularity; and the Surrealists turned with a particular ferocity on public men whose activity seemed to them to be paternalist in character. One such was Paul Claudel, the playwright and poet who for many years held high rank in the French diplomatic service. Claudel was strong on duty, strong on obedience, strong on the letter of the law. He would have been anathema to the Surrealists even if in 1925 he had not been imprudent enough to say that "neither Dada nor Surrealism can lead to anything new; they are for pederasts only." The Surrealists replied with a long collective letter that ended, "We ask for ourselves the 'dishonor' of having treated you once and for all as the trash that you are." Claudel deserved it; but the riposte was addressed as much to the institution of fatherhood as to the prepotent rhetorician, then in the prime of life, who was the French ambassador in Tokyo.

In such contexts, art was the best possible way of paying off old scores. Oedipal feelings ran berserk throughout the 1920s. Imaginary misfortunes were constantly being wished on the representatives of fatherhood, and not least on God the Father himself. The prototypical Surrealist title is *Mama, Papa Is Wounded!* and it would stick in our minds even if the painting in question (by Yves Tanguy) were not one of the finest of its date. Salvador Dali returned over and over again to the image of the son castrated by his father. The father, everywhere, was seen as having done his son an irreparable mischief; and his presence, whether in de Chirico's *The Child's Brain* or in Max Ernst's *Pietà or Revolution by Night* or in one of their many derivatives, was seen as granitic, oppressive, unyielding.

As a comment on intergenerational hostility, these things were memorably vivid. Insofar as several of the artists concerned did genuinely still bear the wounds of childhood, the works in question had an immediacy which can no longer be recaptured. The mid-1920s were the first moment in time at which it was possible for an artist to interpret his early experience in the light of psychoanalysis: they were also the last moment in time at which this could count as authentic pioneering. On a more general and less private level many taboos which now seem to us impossibly archaic were then still taken for granted.

Surrealism stood in all this for the restatement of the rights of man. Breton had always in his mind what he called "the future continent": a landmass, as yet unlocated, on which all men would tread freely and as equals. All women, too: many years before Women's Liberation was heard of, Breton laid it down as an integral part of Surrealism that "not only must we put an end to the exploitation of men by other men, but we must review—from top to bottom, in a totally unhypocritical spirit and as a matter of the first urgency—the problem of men's relations with women." In this, the Surrealists ranged themselves behind Charles Fourier (1772–1837), the Utopian socialist, who said that the essential prerequisite for social change was that women should be free to dispose of themselves as independent human beings.

The masterpieces of Surrealism have long ago been tamed and ticketed. But it is still very well worthwhile to look at them in the light of what the English historian G. M. Young once had to say about the writing of history. "The real central theme of history," he said, "is not what happened but what people felt about it when it was happening." Time and the museums combine to flatten what was for the artist and his contemporaries the most urgent aspect of his work: its either/or quality. For those who live by them, beliefs are nonetheless tenacious for being unfounded. It seemed to the Surrealists that there was, for instance, a straight choice, a clear-cut either/or, be-

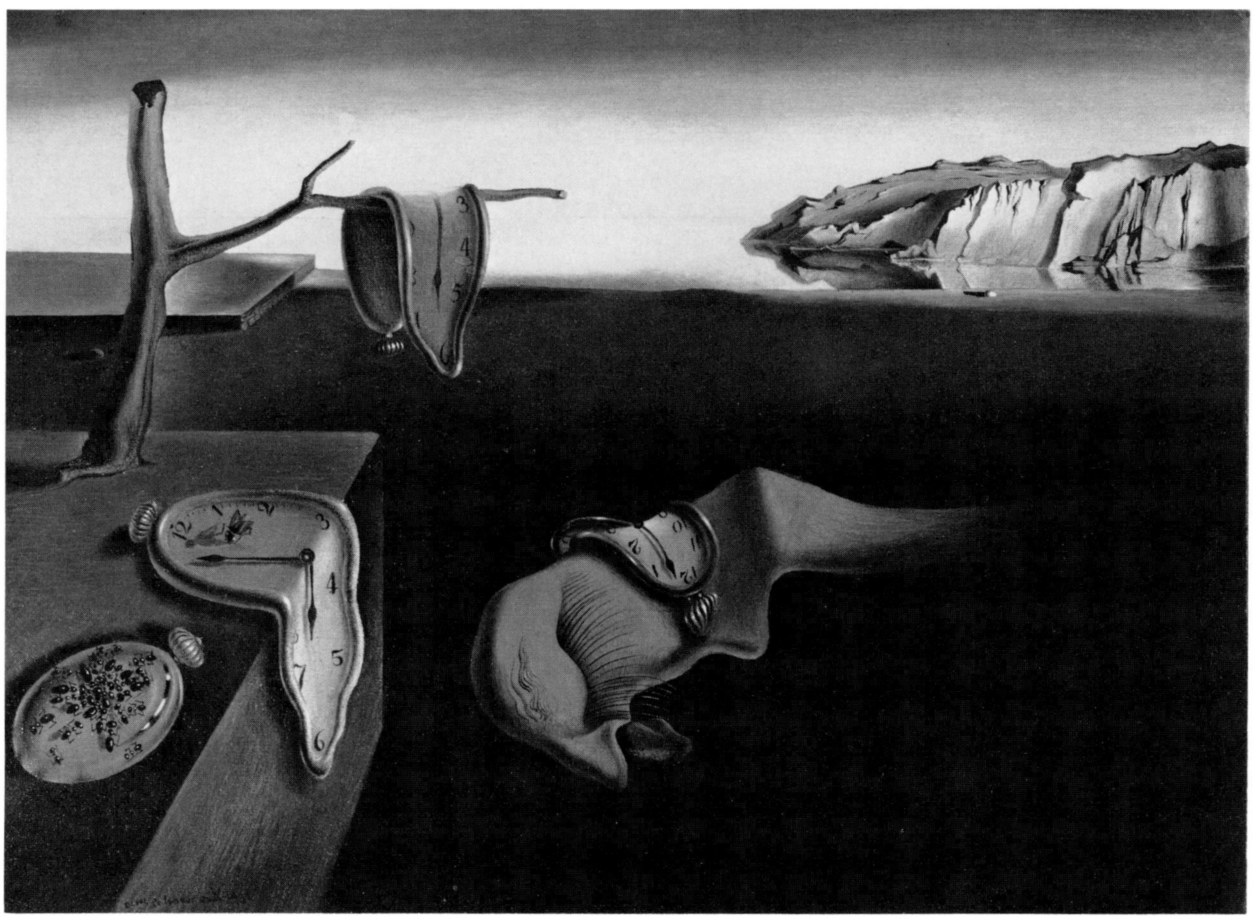

Salvador Dali. *The Persistence of Memory.* 1931. Oil on canvas, 9½ × 13 inches. The Museum of Modern Art, New York. Given anonymously

tween the liberated imagination and the drudgery of copying appearances; a straight choice between liberated sexuality and the shams and compromises authorized by society; and a straight choice between the steeplechase of image and idea which the Surrealists had in mind and the predictable manufacturing of standard subject paintings which was to turn much of French painting into a subdepartment of the souvenir trade.

In all this the truth was bent, much as it is bent in time of war when the overriding consideration is to keep the reader, or the listener, in good heart. Time sorts all things out: and time has already told us that the dosage of poetic imagination in a great Matisse is as high as in the finest of Surrealist paintings; that the sexual content of Ingres and Courbet has as much weight and resource as can be found anywhere in Surrealism; and that it was not the Surrealists but Mondrian, with his search for a constructive and immutable truth, who put forward the most audacious alternative to traditional painting in the 1920s. But this is quite immaterial: artists believe what they have to believe, and in the 1920s and '30s this was as true in the private domain—the management of their own gifts, that is to say—as it was in matters of universal principle. Max Ernst had so strong a creative identity that whatever he did was distinctly his own, even if it began from the automatic imprint of a piece of graining on the floorboards of a country hotel. What resulted was specifically, unmistakably, peremptorily his own. But when he was asked to define Surrealism in 1934 he said that there was no such thing as individual talent, and that the legend of individual creativity was one of the last and most ridiculous of the superstitions with which the civilization of the Occident was encumbered. The active, constructive, initiatory role of the artist was a myth; all that he had to do in reality was to open the doors of the unconscious and play host to the inexhaustible stock of images which would come flooding in.

That was, and is still, the dialectical position of the Surrealists. Talented people can afford to place a taboo on the name of talent, since they know perfectly well that under one name or another their gifts will be acknowledged. But since the Surrealists were also very strong on the destruction of taboos it may well seem to us paradoxical that in this one context they were all for their re-erection. Apart from anything else it is simply not true that the stock of images which came flooding in from the liberated unconscious was inexhaustible. On the contrary: the repertory of images which each of the Surrealists had at his command is fundamentally quite small. What makes their work remarkable is the resource, the energy, the deep feeling with which they deployed these images. The triumphs of individual talent are as clear, in Surrealism, as they are anywhere else; what is peculiar to Surrealism is the cruelty with which it points to individual shortcomings. Even inanimate objects suffered from this cruelty. When Dali took over from de Chirico the notion of mechanized timekeeping, he showed the watch as softened (and by implication, as emasculated). He hung it from the tree like laundry. He allowed it to hang down from the tablecloth like a used napkin. He draped it across the back of a nonexistent sea creature like a saddle that will never be needed.

Surrealism always tended toward an iconography of disquiet. An art which is expressly anticonformist makes its point by sabotaging the existing order of things; and a free and open sexuality was intended to be the model, in this instance, for a free and open society. But the view of sexuality which actually came out in the work was, as often as not, pessimistic and incomplete, crippled and fearful. Breton wanted women to be in charge of their own destinies; but that same Breton was obsessed with the praying mantis—a species of insect where the female eats the male after he has satisfied her desires—to the point of rearing them in his own house and keeping them as pets. The image of Woman in Surrealism is predominantly that of a ravening monster: we need think only of the war dance of Ernst's *The Angel of Hearth and Home;* of Dali's vision of sex appeal as an amalgam of terror and abnormality; of André Masson's *Landscape with Mantis* and Hans Bellmer's *Machine Gun*—from which we can only infer that anyone who approaches the female sex is likely to be gobbled up or shot down as soon as he gets within reach. Fear dominated in all this; access to the unconscious has been bought at a very high price. In Picasso's *Seated Bather,* 1930, the image is specifically Surrealist in the freedom with which Picasso puts forward the notion of woman as a devouring animal. The watchful, waiting bather is the personification of the female praying mantis.

An iconography of disquiet, then; almost an iconography of doom. There were good reasons for this, both private and public. But there was also a generic reason: one which had been set out quite

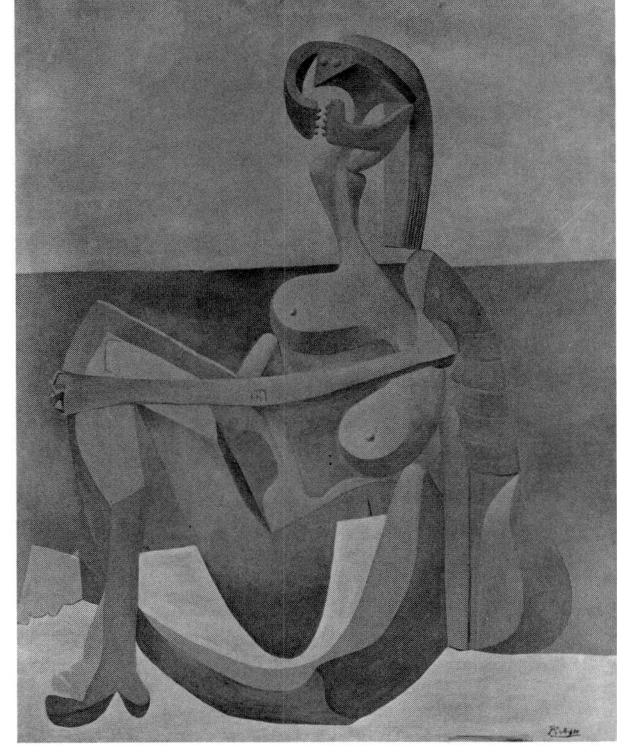

Pablo Picasso.
Seated Bather. 1930.
Oil on canvas,
64¼ × 51 inches.
The Museum of Modern Art, New York.
Mrs. Simon Guggenheim Fund

clearly many years before by Gustave Flaubert, the author of *Madame Bovary*, when he wrote that "the mental vision of the artist should not be regarded as equivalent to that of a man laboring under a hallucination. I know all that there is to know about both states, and an abyss separates one from the other. In hallucination, strictly so called, there is always an element of fear. You feel that you are losing your own personality and that you are on the point of death."

Flaubert could not have foreseen how amply his opinion would be borne out by Surrealism. The Surrealists claimed for themselves a freedom of reference which had neither limit nor precedent.

Sometimes they used that freedom in ways that leave us amused and exhilarated. In the heyday of Surrealism the picture postcard was treasured by poets and painters alike for its direct and unsophisticated expression of popular feeling. At the end of the 1920s Max Ernst began to introduce postcards into collages both as themselves and as formal elements in a design whose intention was to please, to amuse, and sometimes to dismay. *The Postman Cheval* is named after a postman who had lately come to notice for the contribution which he had made to naive or self-taught art; and, sure enough, the postcard in the lower right-hand corner comes in an envelope such as Cheval the postman must have carried every day on his rounds. But the point of the picture lies also in the contrast between the pretty but undeniably fallen women on the postcard and the conventional attributes of youth and innocence which abound elsewhere. Apart from the variations of space and texture which further thicken the plot, Ernst has penciled in beneath the largest rectangular form in the picture a pair of stylized feet which suggest that somewhere behind the main image is a sandwich man for whom the day's task has been altogether too much.

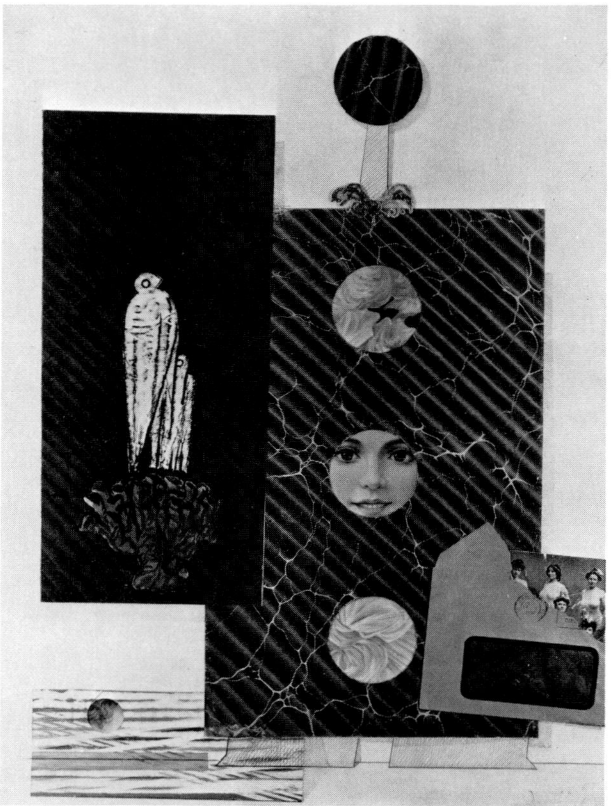

Max Ernst. *The Postman Cheval.* 1929–30. Collage on pasteboard, 25¼ × 18⅞ inches. Peggy Guggenheim Foundation, Venice

Miró is another case in point. In the summer of 1933 he busied himself with a series of "drawing-collages" that can be related to comparable works by Ernst. A particular one with three postcards has a covert mathematical basis in the relation of the postcards to the collaged piece of sandpaper, and of the sandpaper in its turn to the format of the work as a whole. The three postcards are used half in mischief and half in wonder, as indications of popular feeling. Miró then comments on their idealized account of sexuality by adding four quite different images, each of which has a more down-to-earth implication. Finally, he linked these disparate images with a freehand drawing that touches discreetly on the facts of the female body and on the potential of its involvement with the male.

Miró liked to hazard himself on completely unfamiliar terrain. At first glance his *Object* of 1936, for instance, may seem purely nonsensical. But in point of fact everything in it relates to a logical sequence of associations. The hat stands for the archetypal dreamer, the red plastic fish for the uncharted deeps which are the domain of the unconscious, and the map for the universe through

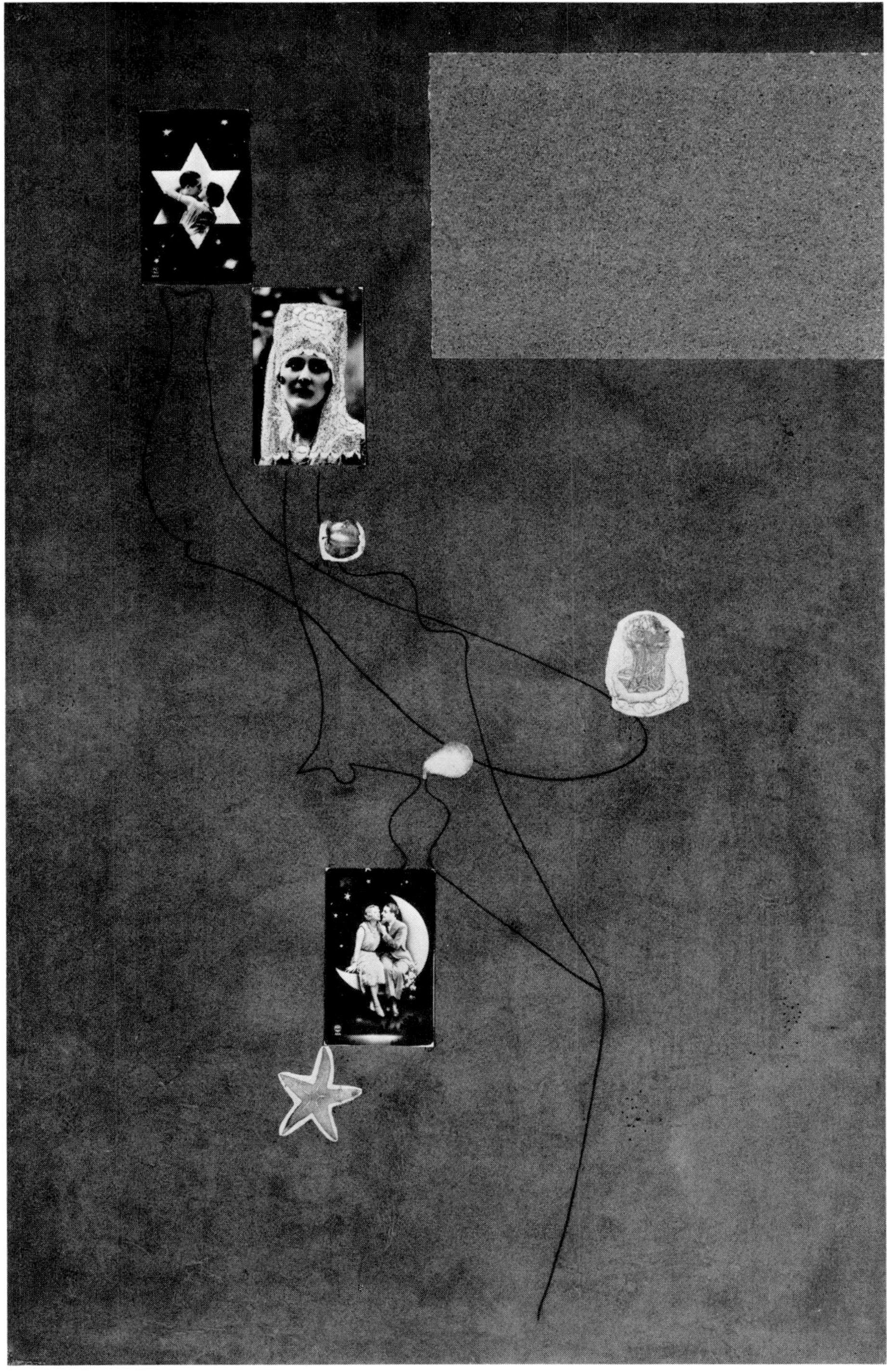

Joan Miró.
Drawing-Collage.
1933.
Collage and charcoal drawing on green paper with three postcards, sandpaper and four engravings, 42½ × 28⅜ inches.
The Museum of Modern Art, New York. Kay Sage Tanguy Bequest

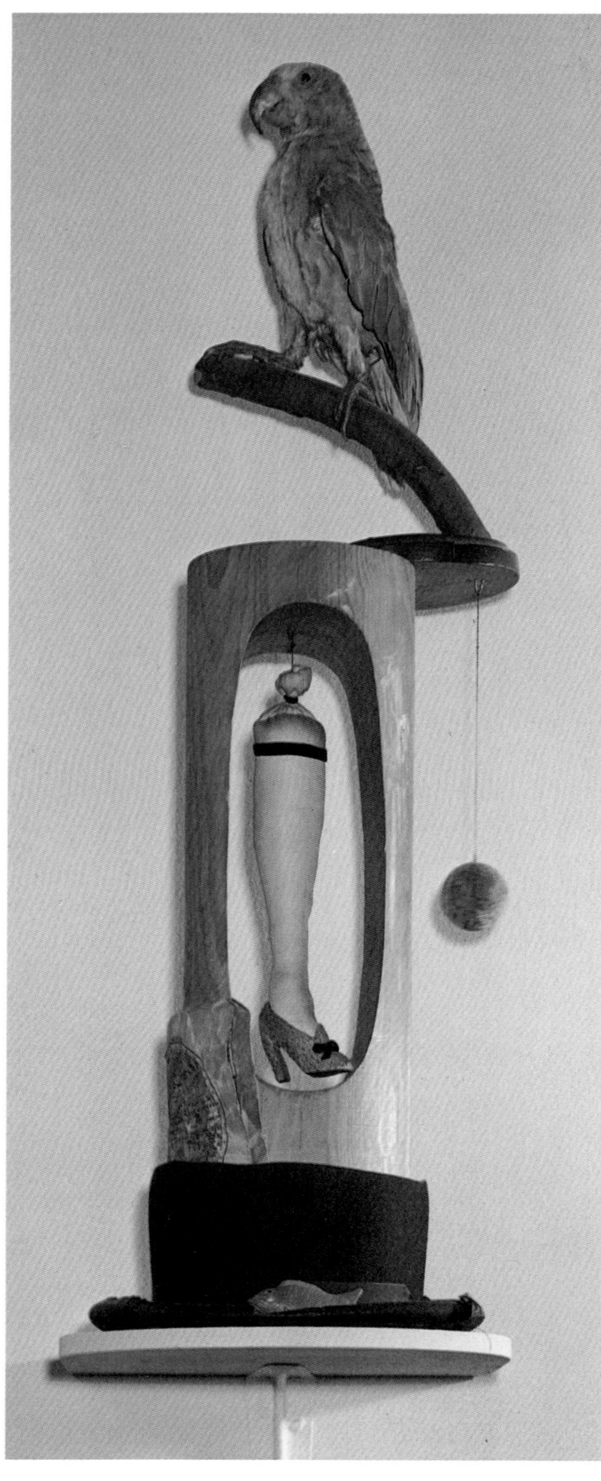

Joan Miró.
Object. 1936.
Assemblage: stuffed parrot on wood perch, stuffed silk stocking with velvet garter and doll's paper shoe suspended in a hollowed post, derby hat, hanging cork ball, celluloid fish, and engraved map, 31⅞ × 11⅞ × 10¼ inches.
The Museum of Modern Art, New York. Gift of Mr. and Mrs. Pierre Matisse

which the mind ranges freely. The heightened sexuality which is fundamental to Surrealism is symbolized by the gartered female leg in its high-heeled shoe. The parrot is, in this context, the bird of love. The ball which hangs from a piece of string is, once again, a familiar Surrealist symbol; pioneered by Giacometti in a sculpture well known to Miró, it stands for masculinity. *Object* is therefore a poem about love: and one soon unriddled once we know how to read Miró's work.

Meanwhile the notional unity of the Surrealist group was growing more precarious as year followed year. When Max Ernst produced his *Loplop Introduces Members of the Surrealist Group* in 1931, he assembled an impressive collection of active members of the group, among them Tristan Tzara, Paul Eluard, Salvador Dali, Alberto Giacometti, Man Ray, Yves Tanguy and Ernst himself. (Newcomers include film director Luis Buñuel.) The general environment is, however, distinctly somber: the masked figure at the top could be an executioner, and at the bottom on the left André Breton, self-appointed dictator of the group, is seen swimming—perhaps for his life—beside what might well be a sinking ship.

For there was as often as not something of defeatism in their stance before life, and of helplessness in the way in which they sent out some grim new report on the facts about human existence. No doubt it could be said that this was merely a transitional stage on the way to a freer, more open, less compromised life structure; only when all the monsters have been stared down can men and women begin to live in the light. It can also be stated, as Breton said in 1945, that Surrealism was specifically an interwar movement: a miming, between one world war and another, of tensions which we should otherwise have been happy to overlook. The early warning system had implications which went far beyond private life; and it is certainly true that many of the masterpieces of Surrealism make perfect sense when read in this way. Giacometti's *Woman with Her Throat Cut* of 1932 becomes a portrait of Europe,

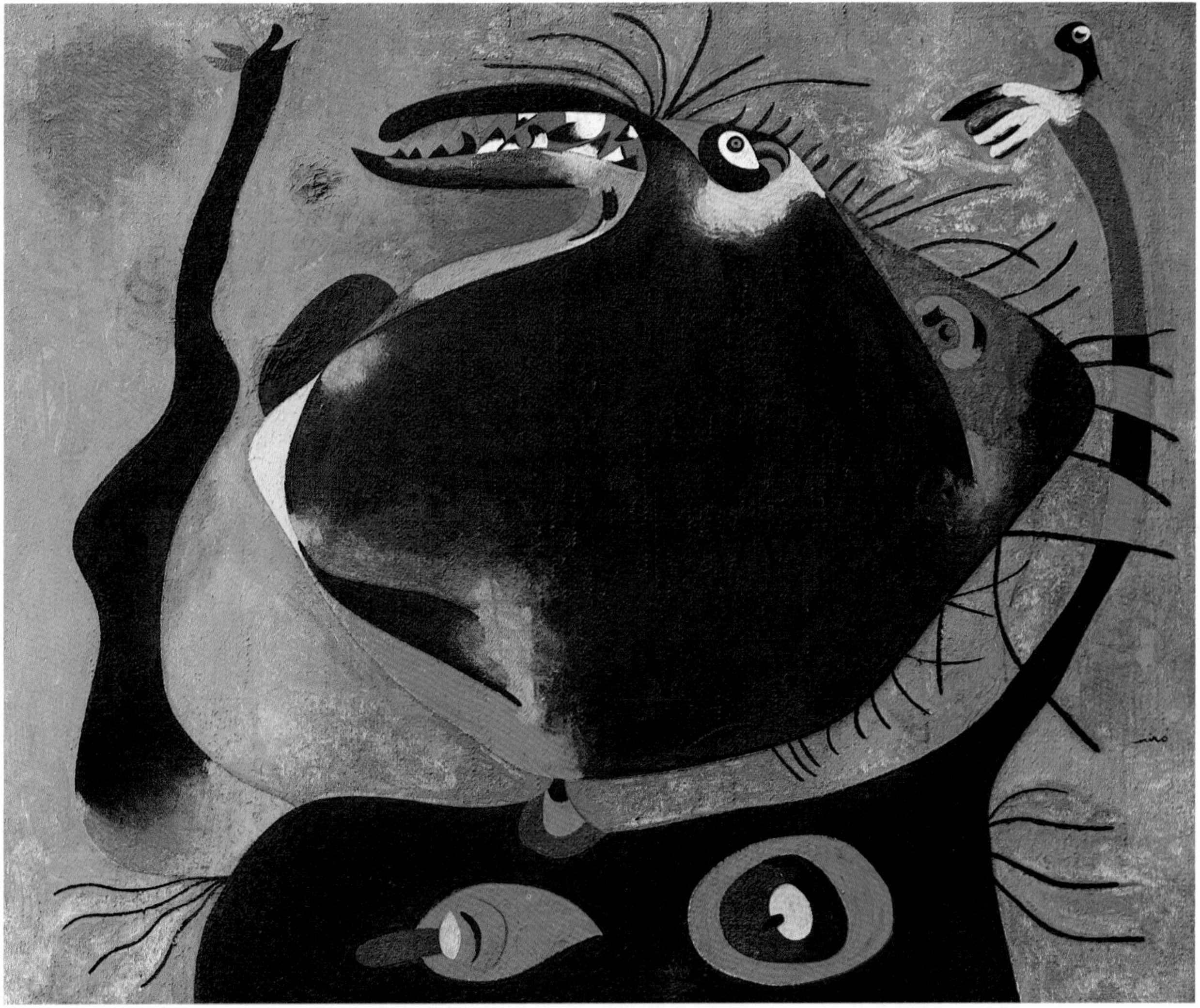

Joan Miró.
Head of a Woman.
1938.
Oil on canvas,
18 × 21⅝ inches.
The Minneapolis Institute of Arts.
Gift of Mr. and Mrs. Donald Winston

laid flat on her back and summarily done to death. Max Ernst's *The Horde* of 1927 becomes even more explicit in the light of Hitler's coming to power in 1933. Miró's *Head of a Woman* of 1938 has an aggressivity which would verge on dementia if we did not associate it with the civil war which had broken out in Miró's own country. Thus seen, it deserves its place in any illustrated history of outrage. Nobody would call Dali a profound political thinker, but his *Soft Construction with Boiled Beans: Premonition of Civil War,* 1936, gives us an unforgettable image of how society can tear itself apart in a specific landscape and under a specific sun.

There would be no difficulty, therefore, in presenting Surrealism in terms of premonitory illustration. The mid-1930s were a time of anguish for all thinking Europeans. Miró got something of this into *Rope and People* by implying that the man on the left was not just "biting his nails" in anxiety, but on the edge of biting his whole hand off. Miró confirmed many years later that he imagined the twisted skein of rope as "binding and torturing" the three human beings in the picture; and he carried over into the two women on the right the sensations of helpless disarray with which people waited for the worst and knew that it could not be long delayed. A panorama like Max Ernst's *Europe after the Rain,* 1940–42, offers few problems in that context, since history caught up with it before

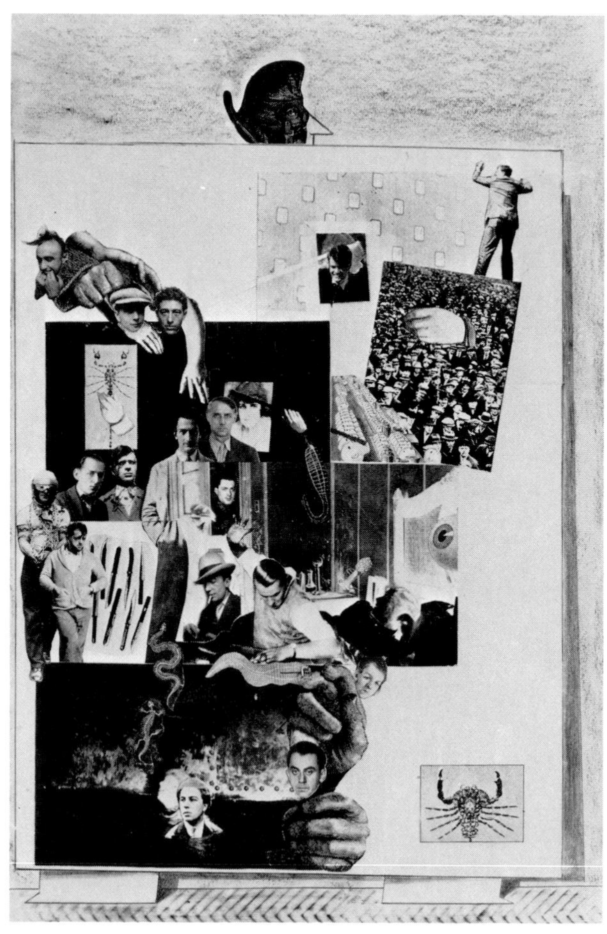

Max Ernst.
Loplop Introduces Members of the Surrealist Group.
1931.
Pasted photographs and pencil,
19¾ × 13¼ inches.
The Museum of Modern Art, New York. Purchase

the paint was dry. One of the most prescient and dismaying of 20th-century images, it was smuggled out of Europe and completed in the United States. It has to do with a Europe overwhelmed by catastrophe, in which all distinctions between animal, vegetable and mineral are abolished and a universal desolation reigns.

There is a distinction, of course, between someone like Ernst, who lived in his own person the dramas of Europe between 1918 and 1945, or like Joan Miró, who even in his late 70s was willing to undergo real physical discomfort in order to demonstrate against social injustice, and those whose activity was primarily parasitic: parasitic on the horrors of war, and parasitic on the psychiatric case histories which still made novel reading in the 1920s and '30s. Miró and Ernst were not "history painters" in the conventional sense; but they functioned as irreplaceable witnesses to a crucial moment in European history.

Yet the final, decisive, irreversible claim of the major Surrealists upon us does not derive from their stature as poetical commentators on a Europe far gone toward self-destruction. Nor does it derive from their skill at mapping the interior landscapes which had previously been kept hidden from sight: the glassy, detailed and hypnotic arenas to which Dali and Tanguy, above all, had access. What puts them in the Pantheon is the scale of their contribution to something quite different: the science of signs.

By "the science of signs" I mean the wordless communication system by which we agree to receive messages from one another. The science of signs is about the things in that system which can be taken for granted. The hunter goes along with it when he puts on the red shirt which saves him from getting shot. The pirate went along with it when he hoisted the black flag at sea. Hospitals count on it when they paint a red cross on their roofs in time of war.

Art is the most highly evolved manifestation of the science of signs. Were it to stagnate in that respect it would forfeit its claim upon us; and it is because the Surrealists did not allow it to stagnate in the 1920s and early '30s that people today go along with visual acrobatics that would have been way beyond their capacity 50 years ago. Surrealism taught us, for instance, that the step-by-step narrative systems of the 19th century were not the only ones. It taught us that surprise may be the beginnings of wisdom. It taught us to deal simultaneously with pieces of information that zero in on us at differing levels and in differing guises. It taught us that what "doesn't make sense" may sometimes make the best sense of all. It taught us to watch out in everyday life for the poetic and mysterious connections for which one or two men of genius had noted the prototypes. It taught us, finally, that there is no pattern of life so pedestrian that it cannot be transformed by poetic principle, nor any combination of objects so pointless that a valid connection cannot be made between them. (Picasso made this last point once and for all when he made a most lifelike head of a bull from the saddle and the handlebars of a bicycle.)

Surrealism has long ago broken out of those areas of human activity which we label "art" and "literature." It is present in design, in film, in advertising, in humor, in dress—in the form of a general acceptance of incongruities which would once have been dismissed as meaningless nonsense. Sometimes one and the same man is still doing it: Luis Buñuel, for one, whose movies of the 1970s have fundamentally the same allegiances as they had in 1930, when Max Ernst played a bit part for him in *L'Age d'or.* But most often Surrealism has simply passed into the bloodstream of modern life like a benign virus, leaving the collective imagination by just that much the more liberated. Its ciphers have been cracked, and it is by now an instrument in everyday use; it does not, for instance, occur to the stand-up comic to call himself a Surrealist when he uses the quick cut and the one-line gag in ways perfected by Surrealist writ-

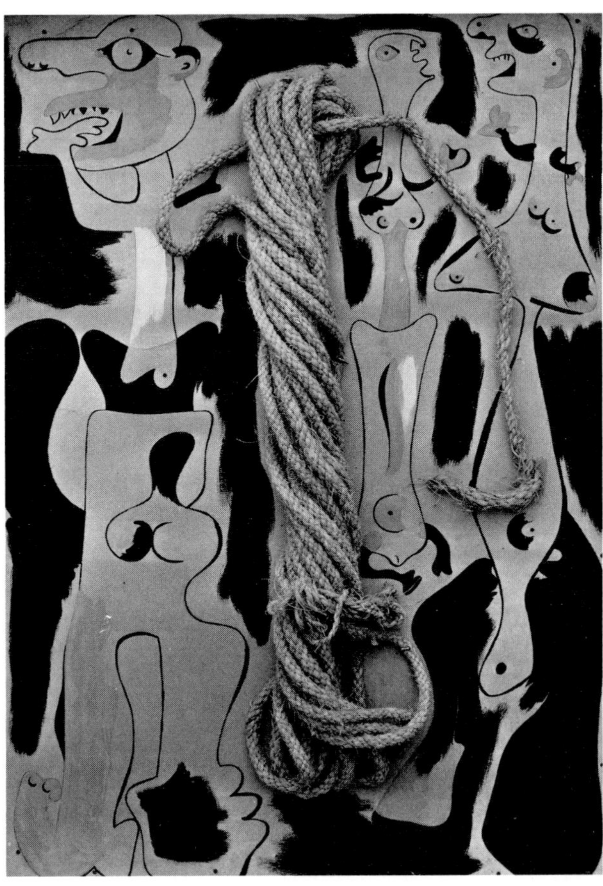

Joan Miró. *Rope and People I.* 1935. Oil on cardboard with coil of rope, 41¼ × 29⅜ inches. The Museum of Modern Art, New York. Given anonymously

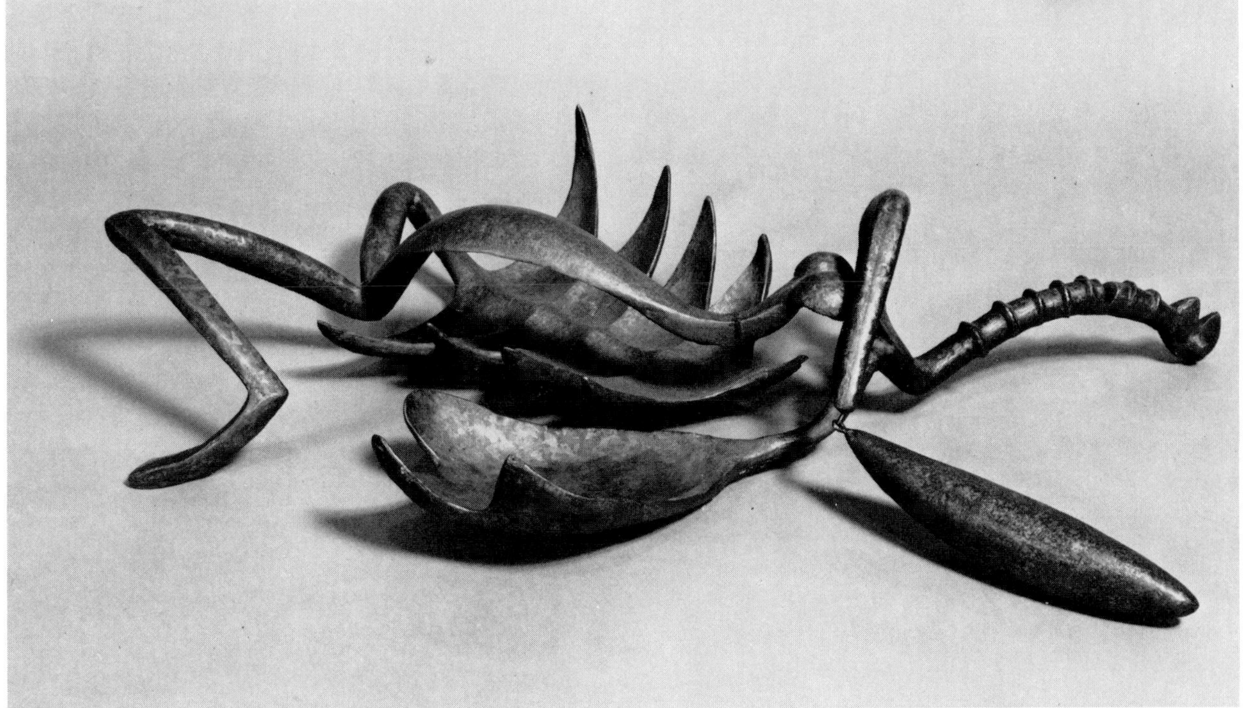

Alberto Giacometti. *Woman with Her Throat Cut.* 1932. Bronze (cast 1949), 8 × 34½ × 25 inches. The Museum of Modern Art, New York. Purchase

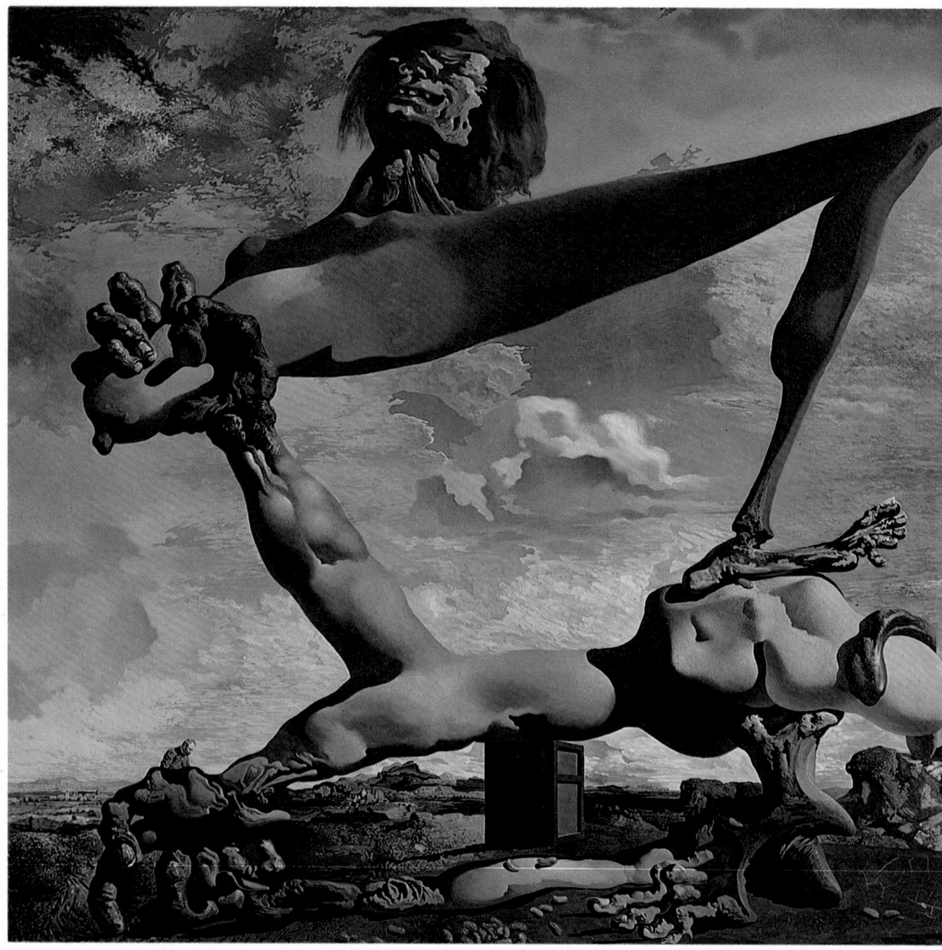

Salvador Dali.
Soft Construction with Boiled Beans: Premonition of Civil War. 1936.
Oil on canvas, 39½ × 39½ inches.
Philadelphia Museum of Art. The Louise and Walter Arensberg Collection

ers in the 1920s, any more than the automobile manufacturer claims the title when someone points out to him that his new season's models are being publicized in ways lifted straight from the paintings of Magritte.

The initial statements retain their magic, even so. The moment at which something new was added to the science of signs is as significant as ever it was. The additions are of many kinds, but dreams and the dreamer are somewhere at the back of most of them. In 1929, for instance, a long series of poetical objects by Giacometti was prefaced by his *Reclining Woman Who Dreams.* In that series, Giacometti never repeated himself. Each idea was used once and for all, and the function of the dream was to let fresh air into the problem, "How can sculpture continue?" From 1925 to 1933 he probed and reprobed the poetics of art to see just what kind of magic could be made with objects that were unlike anything that had borne the name of art before. Sometimes they came in cages, in ways that were taken up in later years by artists of quite other persuasions. In the summer of 1932, for instance, Giacometti built and rebuilt, every night, a palace of matchsticks. From this there came in time one of the most haunting and influential of modern sculptures: *The Palace at 4 A.M.* It is haunting for its uncanny mingling of practicality and the dream. It has been influential because it exemplifies the idea that sculpture can be open, skeletal and all but incorporeal, rather than solid, weighty and self-consciously monumental. The roofless and wall-less palace is open to inspection from every angle. The spinal column in the cage on the right stands for the woman with whom the nights in question

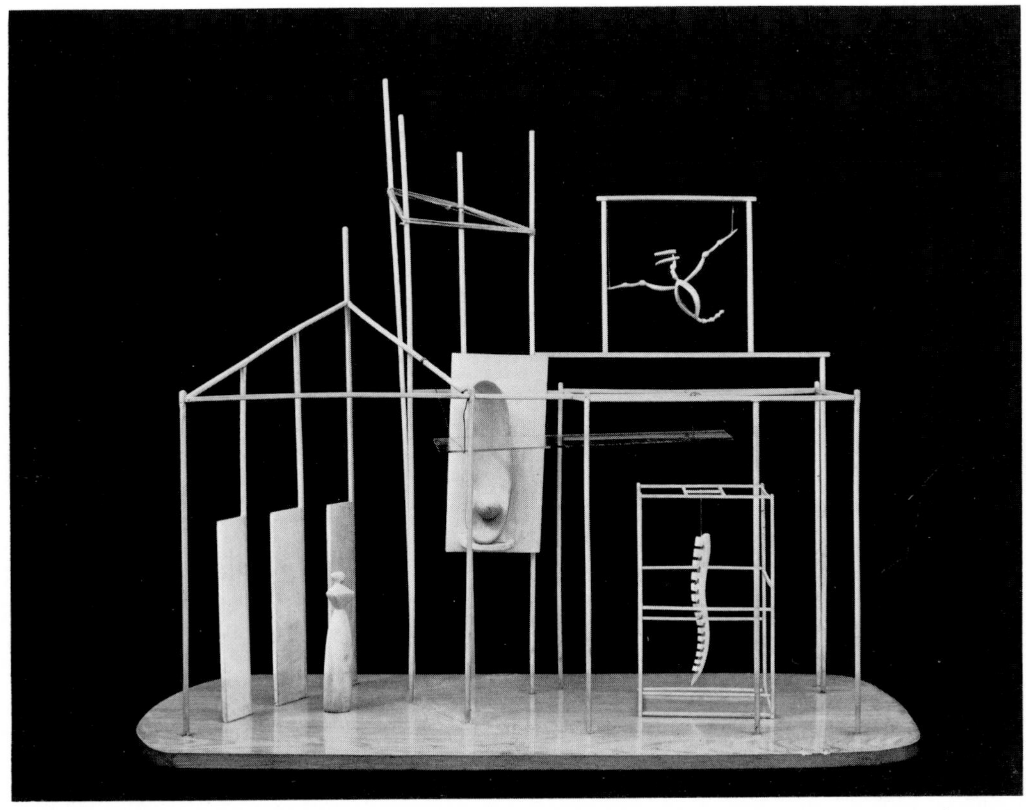

Alberto Giacometti.
The Palace at 4 A.M.
1932–33.
Construction in wood, glass, wire and string, 25 × 28¼ × 15¾ inches. The Museum of Modern Art, New York. Purchase

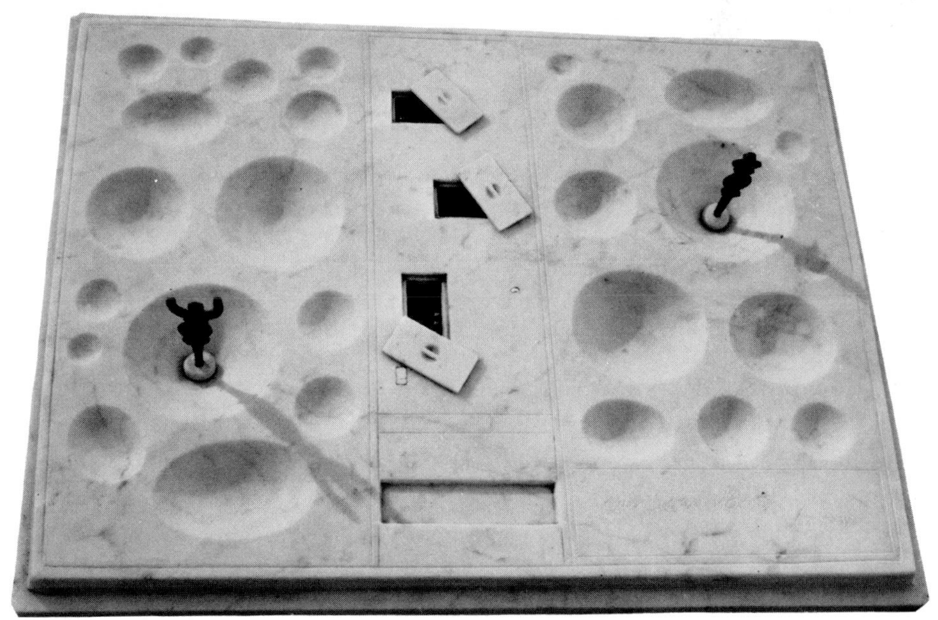

Alberto Giacometti.
No More Play. 1933.
Marble, wood and bronze, 23 × 17⅝ inches. Collection Julien Levy, Bridgewater, Conn.

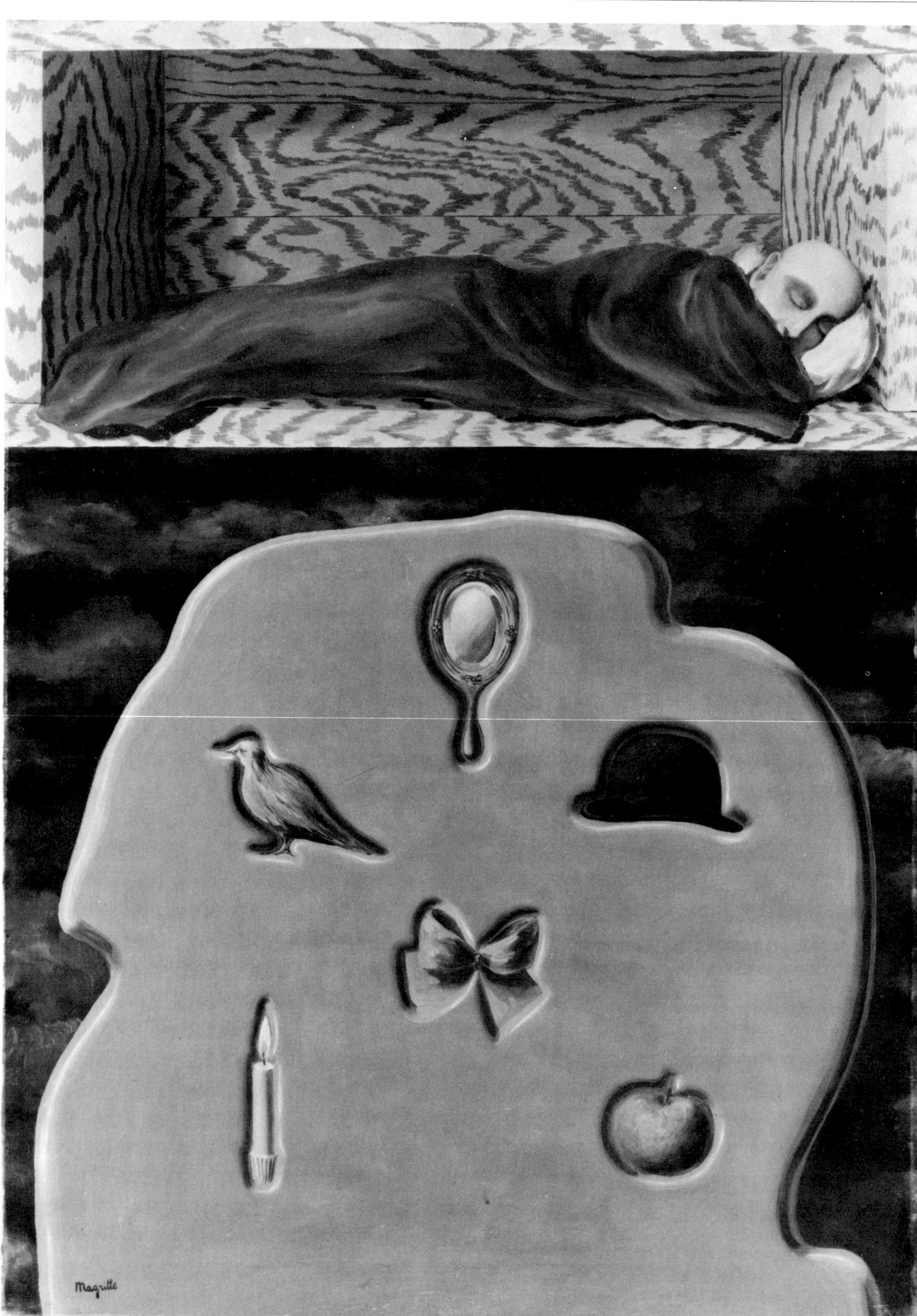

René Magritte.
The Reckless Sleeper. 1927.
Oil on canvas,
45¼ × 31¼ inches.
The Tate Gallery,
London

were spent. The figure on the left in a floor-length skirt represents Giacometti's mother, "just as she appears," he wrote, "in my earliest memories." The thrice-repeated curtain on the left is "the very curtain I saw when I opened my eyes for the first time." The skeleton bird (above right) stands for the birds which signaled the approach of a new day at 4 A.M. that summer, and in particular "the very night before the morning in which our life together collapsed." As for the object halfway up the broken tower in the middle, we remember that in 1926 Giacometti made a sculpture called *Spoon Woman;* and here, six years later, is a spoon man, the sculptor himself, close to and yet apart from the two women who meant most to him.

Sometimes these sculptures were like freakish kitchen utensils; sometimes, like scale models of the terrain on which some new kind of ball game would one day be played. Among symbolical objects in everyday use the game board (chess, checkers, backgammon) stands high. In 1933 Giacometti invented, in *No More Play,* a game board of his own: a mysterious terrain, a matter of deep hollows and coffinlike indentations on which the door could be shut tight. In the midst of this were human figures that were left stranded at the end of the game, with nowhere to go. Giacometti made no claims for these sculptures—to the point of naming some of them as "disagreeable objects of no value which should be thrown away." But they turned out, all the same, to enlarge the science of signs.

"Surrealist" is too narrow a word for the best of what has been discussed here. It resulted, that is

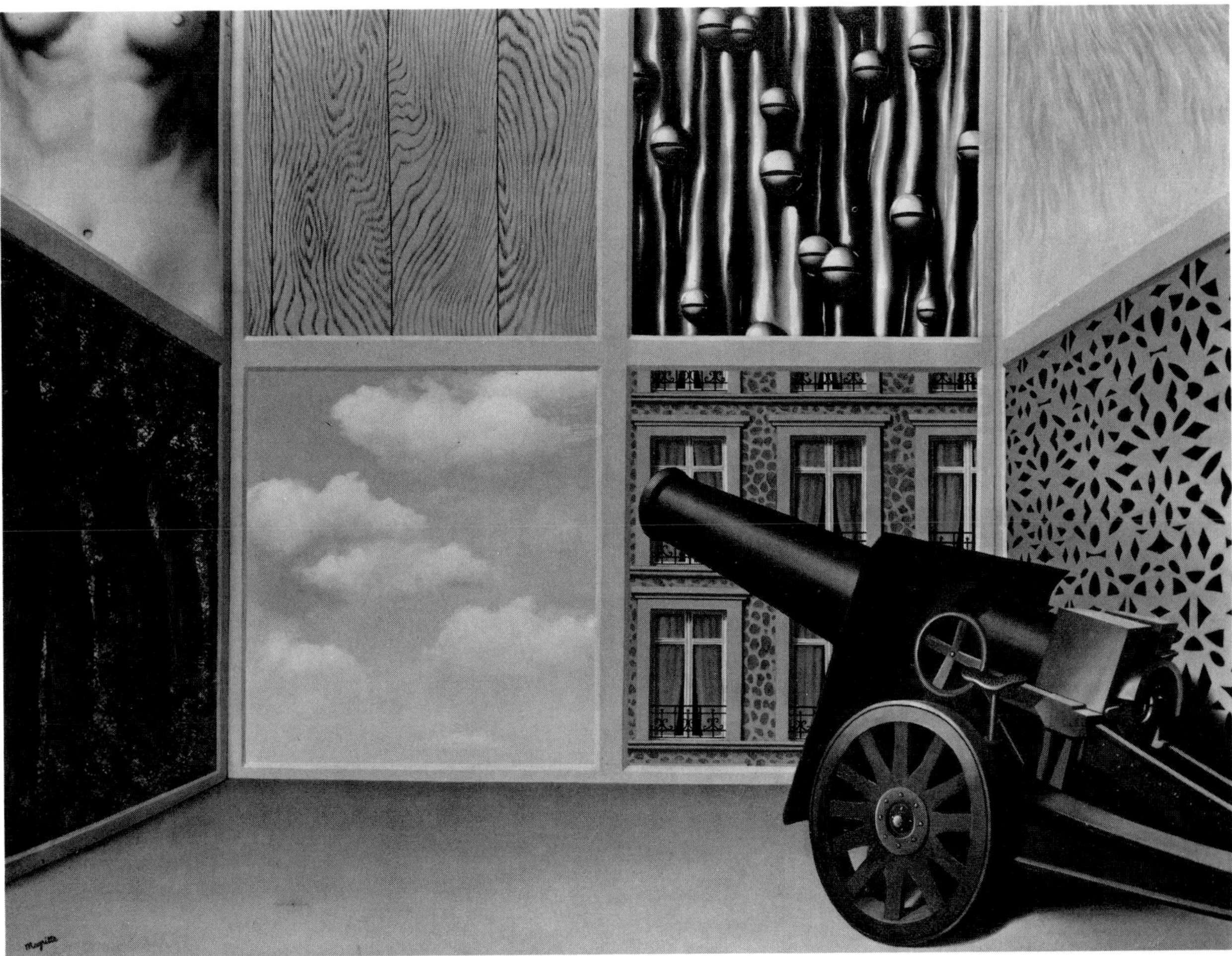

René Magritte. *On the Threshold of Liberty.* 1929. Oil on canvas, 45⅜ × 57⅞ inches. Museum Boymans–van Beuningen, Rotterdam

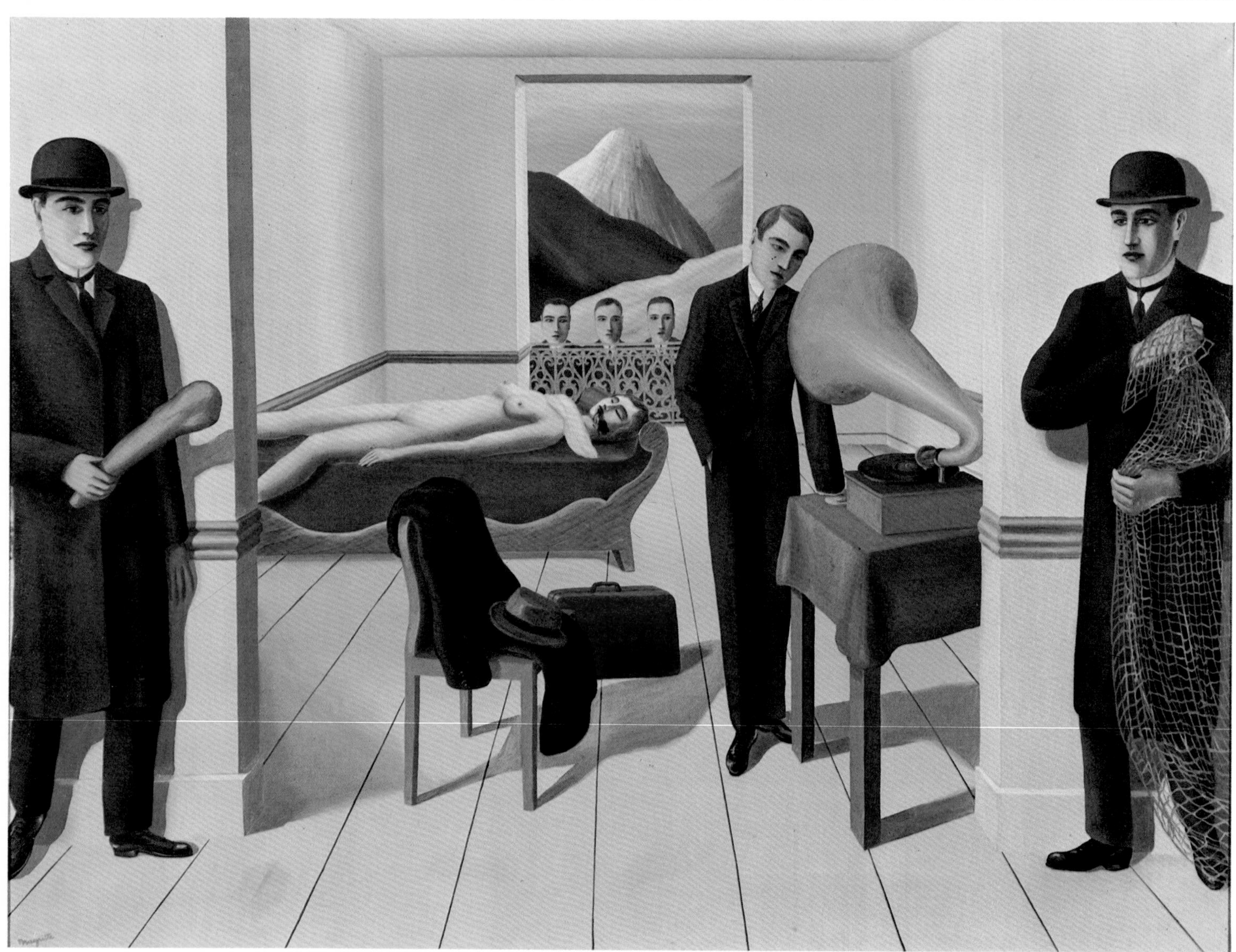

René Magritte. *The Menaced Assassin.* 1926. Oil on canvas, 59¼ inches × 6 feet 5 inches. The Museum of Modern Art, New York. Kay Sage Tanguy Fund

to say, from Surrealism and *from something else:* from a thoughtful scrutiny of Cubism, in Giacometti's case; from an interaction with the distant past of German art in the case of Max Ernst; from an atavistic tradition of Roman *gravitas* in the case of Giorgio de Chirico. Surrealism in such instances was the leaven, or the well-timed explosive, or even at times the latecomer who tidied things up and demanded all the credit. "If it's good, annex it" was the order of the day among the official Surrealists.

A case in point is that of the Belgian painter René Magritte. Magritte at one time lived in Paris, but he was never quite accepted by the Parisian Surrealists, who thought of him, alike in his work and in his habits of life, as altogether too prosaic. And it is true that we never get from Magritte what we get from a Miró of the late 1920s—the sense of the painting as an arena in which literally any combination of signs can be accepted as valid. Magritte had certain specifically Belgian traits, and his procedures were slow-moving, workmanlike, and unfailingly regular in the beat of their pulse. Sometimes, as in *The Reckless Sleeper* of 1927, he showed a dreamer walled up with the matter of his dreams. Sometimes he mated material private to himself with themes familiar from earlier years in our century. For instance, the cannon as instrument of aggression and the cannon as phallic symbol had been familiar in Surrealist painting since the early days of de Chirico. It presides, in *On the Threshold of Liberty,* over an anthology of Magritte's favorite subjects—among them the straight-faced townhouses of suburban Brussels, the bells that pick up the slightest breeze, the detail of a particularly handsome female torso and the forest through which Magritte's horsemen will shortly come at a canter.

The unconscious did not present itself to him as a dancing dervish. Yet when it came to restating the science of signs no one was more radical than he. He did it under auspices with which the reader will by now be familiar. Nowhere is the dreamer more vividly portrayed or more bizarrely accompanied. The spirit of Edgar Allan Poe hovers over and over again, with *The Narrative of Arthur Gordon Pym* conspicuous in one painting and the whole of another one devoted to Poe's *Domain of Arnheim.* Magritte realized, too, that the mass-audience thriller (see his *The Menaced Assassin*) was one of our century's new sources of myth. He had a delight in word games which had been the mark of the Surrealists since long before the name of Surrealism was first invented; and he knew that when language is subverted the whole of life is subverted with it. He was interested in the word *as sign*—and as a sign that should not be taken for granted. When he wrote "This is not a pipe" beneath a painted image of a pipe, people took it at first as a harmless little joke; but as time went on it turned out that the joke was not so harmless after all, and that Magritte had questioned the whole nature of acceptance where the science of signs was concerned. "Go back and start again" is the message which he relays to those who look at his pictures; and by looking again, and looking again, and looking more closely, we arrive at a new understanding of the role of the sign in human life. Magritte, in this sense, can be related to linguistic philosophy as other Surrealists can be related to the psychopathology of the individual, or to the state of the European collective unconscious at a particular moment in time, or to the liberation of the play instinct in everyday life, or to one of the many other preoccupations of the 1920s and '30s which found their highest and most telling expression in art. Looking back on the two decades in question, we may well be reminded of what the British scientist J. Z. Young wrote in his *Introduction to the Study of Man* (1971): "There is a case for saying that the creation of new aesthetic forms has been the most fundamentally productive of all forms of human activity. Whoever creates new artistic conventions has found methods of interchange between people about matters which were incommunicable before. The capacity to do this has been the basis of the whole of human history."

A WORLD REMODELED

It is one of the most resilient of human illusions that some day, somewhere, we shall be granted a fresh start in life.

To what else, after all, do we owe the vast, unreasoning and contagious euphoria which traverses the world every New Year's Eve? Or the sympathetic excitement with which we greet the news of a fundamental change in the lives of our friends? A change of partner, a change of occupation, a change of habits, even a change of scene can precipitate against all odds the feeling that henceforth all must go well for the person in question.

This is not the easiest of things to convey in pictorial terms, but I am put in mind of it most vividly by a watercolor which Chagall painted in 1917. He did it more than once, and it is variously titled *The Bridegroom, The Traveler, Forward!* and *Upward and Onward Forever!* It seems to have served as the curtain for a short play by Gogol called *The Wedding,* and Chagall in 1918 planned to use the image on a large scale, out-of-doors, as part of the decorations for the first anniversary of the Russian Revolution in his native town of Vitebsk. So its associations are with adventure and festivity and fulfillment. I know of few pictures which give us so convincingly the sensation of a fresh start in life.

In painting this picture Chagall doubtless had in mind his own situation, which had changed radically since he first came to St. Petersburg in 1907 as a member of a despised minority. At that time and as a Jew he could not even enter the city without a special pass; but by the winter of 1917–18 he was a successful painter with admirers in Paris, in Berlin and in Moscow. He was also a full citizen of his country, and had not long before married a particularly beautiful girl. By the end of 1918 the new regime had installed him as director of the art school in Vitebsk, with jurisdiction over the art life, such as it then was, of the entire province. A year or two later he was painting murals for the Jewish Theater in Moscow. Not only he himself but the whole Jewish community had a fresh start in the new Russia; and he must truly have felt, as the young man in the picture feels, that with one elastic stride he could step over the rooftops and be off and away.

The young man in the picture may of course have expected far too much of a momentary exhilaration. Certainly Chagall's career during the years from 1917 onward was by no means a story of uninterrupted success. In Vitebsk he was outmaneuvered and forced to resign after less than a year in office. Anti-Semitism in Russia was not so much abolished as in abeyance. By 1922 he had given up and gone back to Western Europe with 50 years and more of exile before him. His little painting might now seem to stand for an overconfidence more ludicrous than poignant—a last match struck in a hurricane. What was there to be so cheerful about in 1917, with Russia on the edge of famine and civil war, with nearly a million men, French and German, lately killed around Verdun, and with the United States newly committed to a European war?

And yet Chagall's spring-heeled young man really does stand for something that can be traced to the year 1917: the beginnings of a reconciliation between art and society. After about a hundred years in which the two had pulled different ways there was a real chance of their reintegration. Initially the idea of the artist as builder and healer must have seemed ridiculous to those who remembered how for generations art had only to come up with new ideas for society to turn them down flat. (We think of Courbet in jail, Cézanne walled up within his own thoughts, Matisse among the cackling crowds at the Salon d'Automne.) If the people whom Ibsen called "pillars of society" looked to art for confirmation of their importance, they too could count on a rebuff; from Honoré Daumier to George Grosz, art made mock of them. Art and society were in a state of war, declared or undeclared; and even the supposedly safe men, the bemedaled architects and the official portraitists, could not be relied on.

There were exceptions, of course—times when the arts and society worked well together. But it was not through governmental foresight that Henry Hobson Richardson gave a marvelous plain grandeur to the Marshall Field Wholesale Store in Chicago, and when *Harper's Weekly* commissioned wood engravings from Winslow Homer no one at the office knew that they would perpetuate the quintessence of rural America. When Hector Guimard designed entrances for the Paris subway in 1900 the result was art; but that was not because the city fathers had had art in mind. The posters designed in England in the 1890s by James Pryde and William Nicholson were also art—more so, in fact, than most English paintings of their date—but once again it would be too much to say that the advertisers had planned on getting museum material for their money. What happened from 1917 onward was something quite different—a systematic attempt, all over Europe, to reconcile art with society.

Such things do not happen overnight. The time and the man have to be in collusion, for one thing, and meanwhile the points of departure may pass almost unnoticed. Who would have thought in 1917 that the look of the world would be changed in the end by the publication in neutral Holland, a country then almost phantomatic in its isolation, of a little magazine called *De Stijl*? What possible importance could have been placed on the arrival in Paris of a Swiss architect called Charles-Edouard Jeanneret who had not yet taken the name of Le Corbusier? A notional union of the arts had been much talked about in Germany before 1914; but with defeat drawing steadily nearer it was hardly likely that the aristocratic patrons of the original idea would be in a position to go on with it. Russia was known to have some gifted painters with a firm grasp of general ideas; but at the moment in November, 1917, when Lenin got control of the entire country, it must have seemed the merest fantasy that the new government would have time for such people.

A partisan of the new might, in fact, have made a two-word note in his diary—"conditions hope-

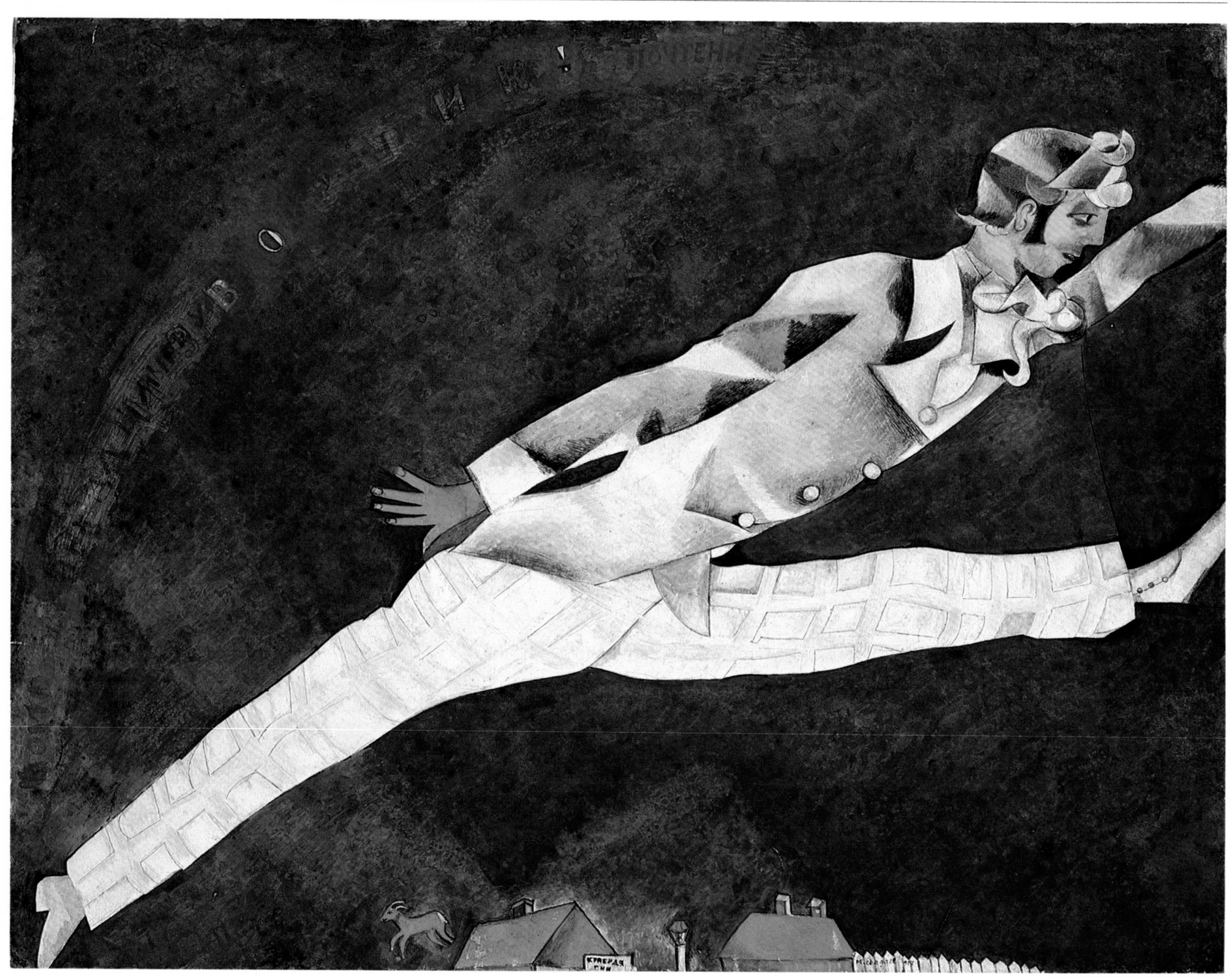

Marc Chagall.
Forward! 1917.
Gouache,
15 × 9¼ inches.
Art Gallery of
Ontario, Toronto.
Gift of Sam and
Ayala Zacks

less"—at any time, and at almost any place, in the year 1917. But he might also have taken comfort from something said many years earlier by Victor Hugo and almost too often repeated since: "No army in the world can hold out against the strength of an idea whose time has come." When the idea is right, and the man is right, though political and social upheavals do their worst, the idea will make its way. That was what Hugo believed, and history from 1917 on bore him out.

Nothing great can be done in a hurry, and almost all the people who concern us here had gone through a slow and thorough seasoning by 1917. The magazine *De Stijl* had been thought of as early as August, 1914, by a many-sided near-genius, Theo van Doesburg, who was its animator and ideas man. Already in 1912, at the age of 29, van Doesburg had defined one of the governing principles of De Stijl: "Disengage form from Nature," he wrote, "and what remains is style." What he meant was that the artist should not aim to reproduce—and still less should he aim to rival—the wayward, luxuriant, ever-varying charms of Nature. He should think his way through to the simplest, the fundamental, the irreducible elements of form. Having found them, he should stick with them. It was not his business to imitate, or to ornament, or to tell stories. The question to be asked of his work was not "Is it beautiful?" but "Is it true?"

This was an aesthetic question. Where architecture and design were involved it was also a practical question; but above all it was a moral question. Truth and falsehood, not beauty and ugliness, were the criteria to bear in mind. Truth in architecture meant a style purified of ornament and idiosyncrasy, and one which declared its function from the outset and used new materials and new building techniques quite openly. Truth in painting meant the end of painting as it had previously existed and the substitution of an art based on equilibrated relationships which owed nothing to Nature.

Van Doesburg shared this point of view with his colleagues of De Stijl: the painters Piet Mondrian and Bart van der Leck; the architects J. J. P. Oud, Gerrit Rietveld and Jan Wils; the sculptor Georges Vantongerloo; the designer Vilmos Huszár. It was fundamental to all their activity. But it was not a point of view that they had invented. Already in the 1890s the Belgian painter, architect and designer Henry van de Velde had said that the architecture then in favor was "a lie; all posturing and no truth." The Dutch architect H. P. Berlage, who built the revolutionary Stock Exchange building in Amsterdam in 1898–1903, said much the same thing: the prevailing style was "sham architecture—i.e. imitation, i.e. lying." Berlage went on, "Lying is the rule, and truth the exception. That is why our parents, our grandparents and we ourselves have had to live in surroundings more hideous than any that human beings have known before."

Lying in architecture is the same as lying in life—it means covering up, faking motives, evading, pretending, misleading. As to what form a truthful architecture should take, much was owed before 1914 both to the writings and to the exemplary finished work of an American, Frank Lloyd Wright. As they walked through Paris and Brussels, Berlin and London, European architects could turn in loathing from the fidgety, overblown office buildings that had sprung up on every hand and console themselves with what Wright had had to say: "Simplicity and repose are the qualities that measure the true value of any work of art." Confronted in Wright's own country with the New York Racquet and Tennis Club (an imitation Italian palazzo) or with the domineering portico of the Metropolitan Museum, they could remember what Wright had said in 1910: "The old structural forms, which up to the present time have been called architecture, are decayed. Their life went from them long ago and new conditions industrially—steel and concrete, in particular—are prophesying a more plastic art." The United States had what Europe had not: a plainspoken tradition in architecture and design. If there was such a thing as a North American norm, a common standard to which American design should revert instinctively, it was the tradition of Pennsylvania Dutch barns and Shaker furniture. Such things were truth made visible; and it should be remembered that when a new magazine called *House Beautiful* began publication in Chicago in 1896 it stood for an honest simplification in matters of decoration and design.

But if there was a moral imperative behind all this, there was also—from 1914 onward, especially—a practical one as well. Le Corbusier was a Swiss, and he grew up in La Chaux-de-Fonds in the Jura, which from a cosmopolitan point of view was a long way from anything that mattered. But he had traveled; he had made it his business to get to know the most inventive of living European architects—Josef Hoffmann in Vienna, Auguste Perret in Paris, Peter Behrens in Berlin— and he had taught himself to respond to any given situation by asking himself, "What can architecture do?" As early as 1910 he set down on paper his plans for a new kind of art school: a school strikingly similar, as it turned out, to the one which still had the force of novelty when it was set up by Walter Gropius in Weimar in 1919 and christened the Bauhaus. In the fall of 1914, when most people were still wringing their hands in despair at the destruction to which World War I had already given rise in Flanders, Le Corbusier came up with an idea which, if adopted, would have cut reconstruction time by nine-tenths.

He devised a standard two-story framework, independent of any floor plan, which carried both floors and staircases. Truth, in this context, lay with the methods of the assembly line, the standardized design ingredient, and the mass-produced prefabricated living unit. The architect was no longer restricted to forms that huddled together as if for warmth, or propped one another up in ways that had hardly varied since the building of Stonehenge. The monolithic, earth-oriented forms of earlier architecture could be discarded, just as single-point perspective was being discarded in painting; as early as 1909 Frank Lloyd Wright's Robie House in Chicago had shown how cantilevering made it possible for forms to fly outward and onward without visible support. Nothing but neurosis could justify continued subjection to such fundamentals of old-style architectural practice as the load-bearing wall, the small fixed window, or the design that was thickest and fattest at the point of its junction with the earth. The time was approaching when houses could be flown in the air on stilts; when inner space could be adjusted at will; when houses need have no front and no back but could be experienced from every point of the compass as fully energized living spaces.

Le Corbusier behaved all his life as if this could be taken for granted. Circumstances did not always run his way, but—to take one example only—his Villa Savoye of 1929–31 is on more than one count a classic of modern architecture. Where earlier houses sat heavily on the ground, this one stood on legs slender as a gazelle's. Where earlier houses had a front and a back, this one presented itself with equal eloquence in all four directions. Where earlier houses had gardens attached to them at ground level, this one had its garden slung above the living area. The conditions of building and the conditions of living were alike turned upside down.

The fundamental prerequisite for buildings such as this was that people acknowledge the truth: that architecture had changed as radically as painting and sculpture, that new materials and new methods of construction should serve new ideas and not old ones, and that the pioneer moves in these directions were manifestations of a collective will to make the world a better, simpler and more rewarding place to live in. It was the De Stijl group who got closest, fastest, to this general idea. They knew that painting and building could have a great deal in common, and that a house could be very like a sculpture and all the better for it. Theirs was an art of first principles; Mondrian

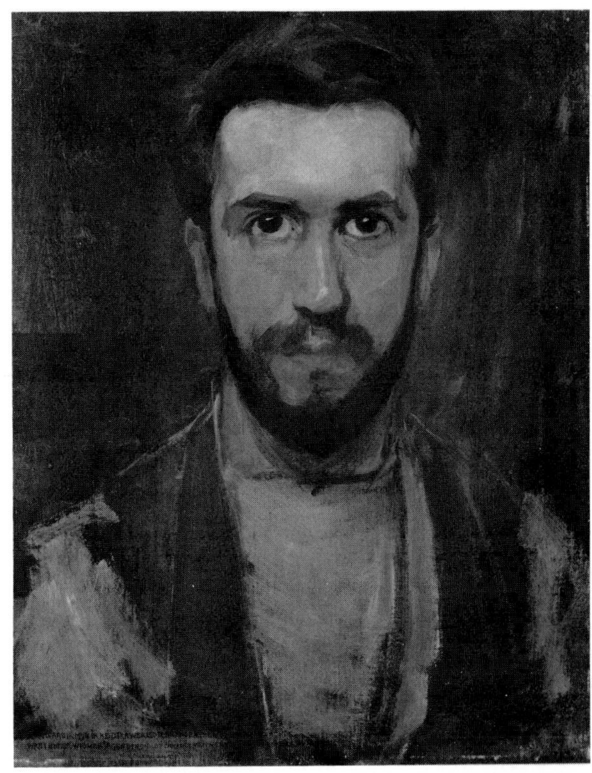

Piet Mondrian.
Self-Portrait.
c. 1900.
Oil on canvas mounted on composition board, 19⅞ × 15½ inches.
The Phillips Collection, Washington

wrote in 1922 that "Theo van Doesburg brought *De Stijl* into being not to 'impose a style,' but to discover and disseminate in collaboration what in the future will be *universally valid.*" Mondrian at that time and later very much disliked what he called "art as ego expression"; his ambition was to break through to a kind of painting which would make known to everyone the fundamental characteristics of the cosmos. His subject matter was the workings of the universe, not the workings of his own temperament.

This was not an idea that he took up from one day to the next, in a doctrinaire way. He was driven to it in part by the results of his 20 years' investigation of the modes of art—from Symbolism to Cubism—that were current in his youth, and in part by the conversation of the Dutch philosopher M. H. J. Schoenmaekers, whom he met in Holland in 1914.

In looking at a Mondrian of no matter what period it is important to remember that he was a man of almost angelic purity, a high-souled mystic who put up uncomplainingly with a long lifetime of isolation and near-penury. (Something of this comes out in the self-portrait now in the Phillips Collection in Washington, which dates from his late 20s.) In the work of the young Mondrian there were echoes of the Symbolist movement and, also, of van Gogh's sometimes sententious way with still life. A dying sunflower would be turned, for instance, into an image of insistent poignancy. But there were also times when, as in *Red Amaryllis,* Nature looks her finest and firmest; and if the lofty, cruciform image of the lily has mystical overtones it also has affinities with the forms of Art Nouveau glass as it was brought to its point of maximum fulfillment by Louis Comfort Tiffany and others.

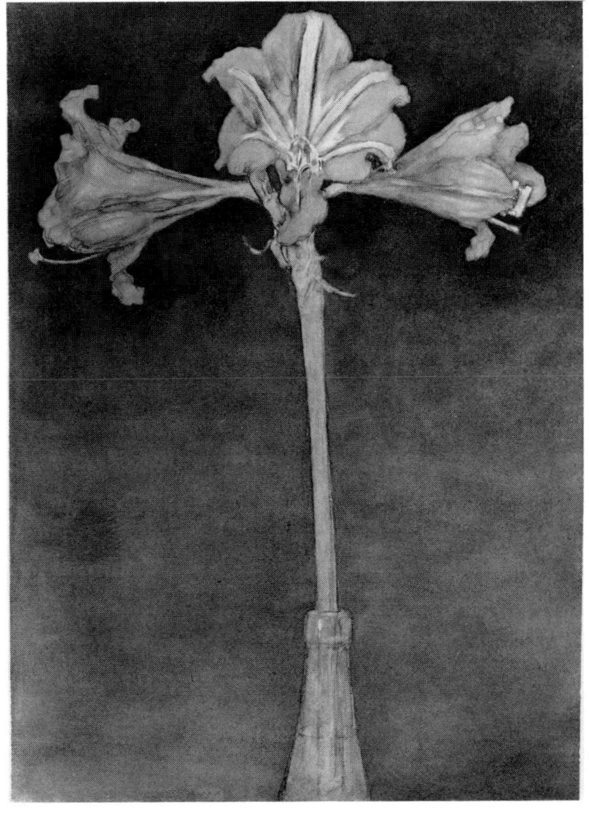

Piet Mondrian.
Red Amaryllis with Blue Background.
c. 1907.
Watercolor, 18⅜ × 13 inches.
The Museum of Modern Art, New York.
The Sidney and Harriet Janis Collection

As much as Edvard Munch, and as much as van Gogh in his more somber moments, Mondrian in his early years would call upon Nature to abet him in the portrayal of states of turbulent emotion. His *Woods near Oele* of 1908 may well remind us of those Scandinavian forests, lit by the unearthly glow of a northern night, into which Munch sent

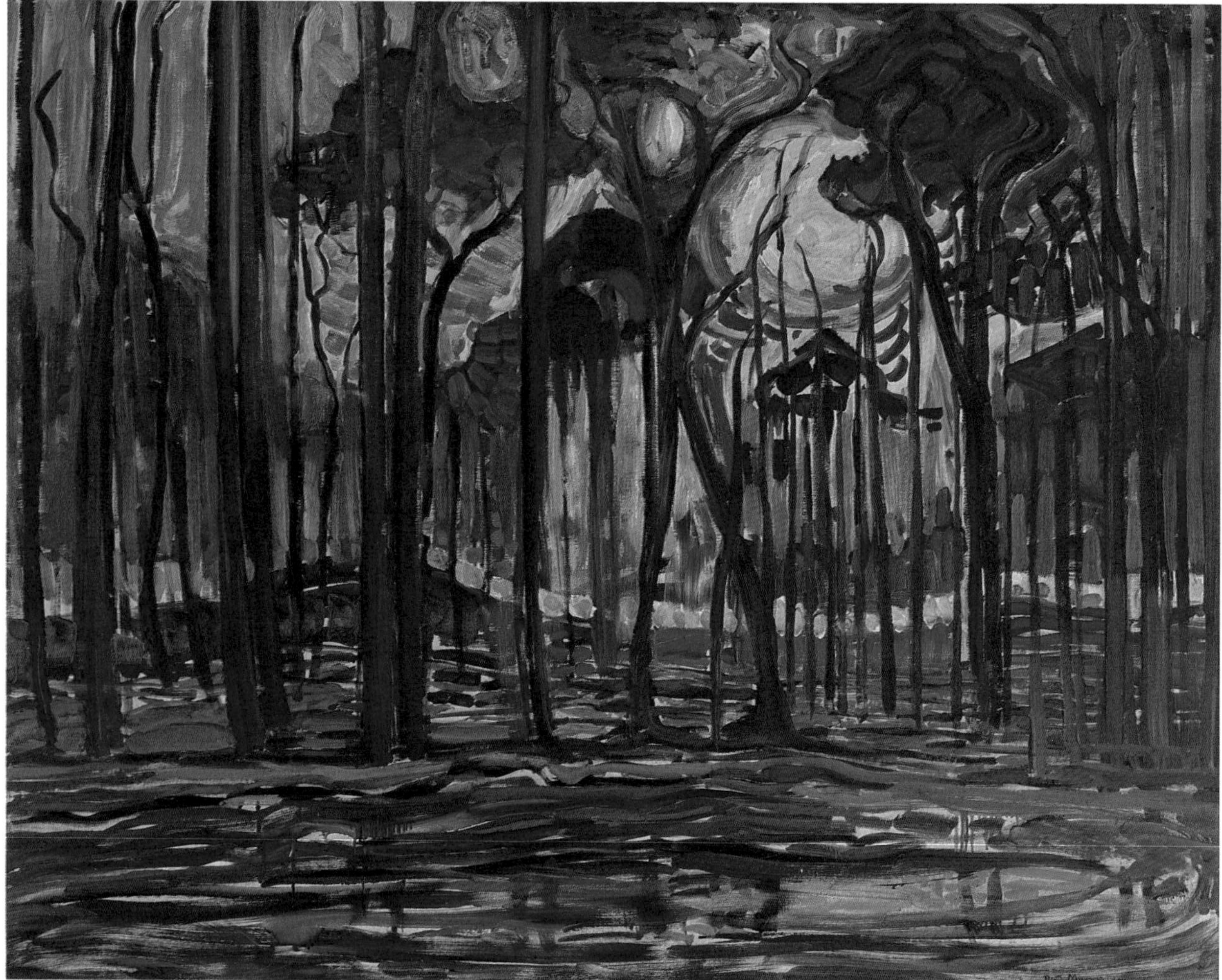

Piet Mondrian.
Woods near Oele.
1908.
Oil on canvas,
51 × 63 inches.
Gemeentemuseum,
The Hague

men and women in search of their destiny. It is, moreover, in a wood such as Mondrian sets before us that the woman in Arnold Schoenberg's opera *Erwartung* stumbles upon the body of her dead lover. What we have here is not the peaceable Dutch countryside but a primeval forest ringed with an unnatural fire: a place of trial and torment, in which a whole generation lived out an important part of its emotional life.

It was in the fall of 1911 that Mondrian first saw Cubist paintings by Picasso and Braque. In May, 1912, he went to live in Paris and set himself to relive, in his own work, the evolution of French painting since Cézanne. (The motif that dominates Mondrian's *Still Life with Ginger Pot* was a favorite theme of Cézanne's.) Four years after the frantic emotionalism of his *Woods near Oele,* Mondrian was concerned with something entirely different: the reduction of still-life material to severe, blocklike forms, with echoes here and there of architecture (see the majestic, portal-like forms to the right of the ginger pot) and of Cézanne's preoccupation with the cube, the cylinder and the cone.

Living in the Montparnasse district of Paris, and scrutinizing day after day the battered gray façades of the buildings adjacent to his own, Mondrian gradually extracted from them what he needed: a motif in which both verticals and horizontals presented themselves quite naturally, with occasional notes of blue, in the rounded forms of chimney pots, to offset flat, pigeon-gray walls and

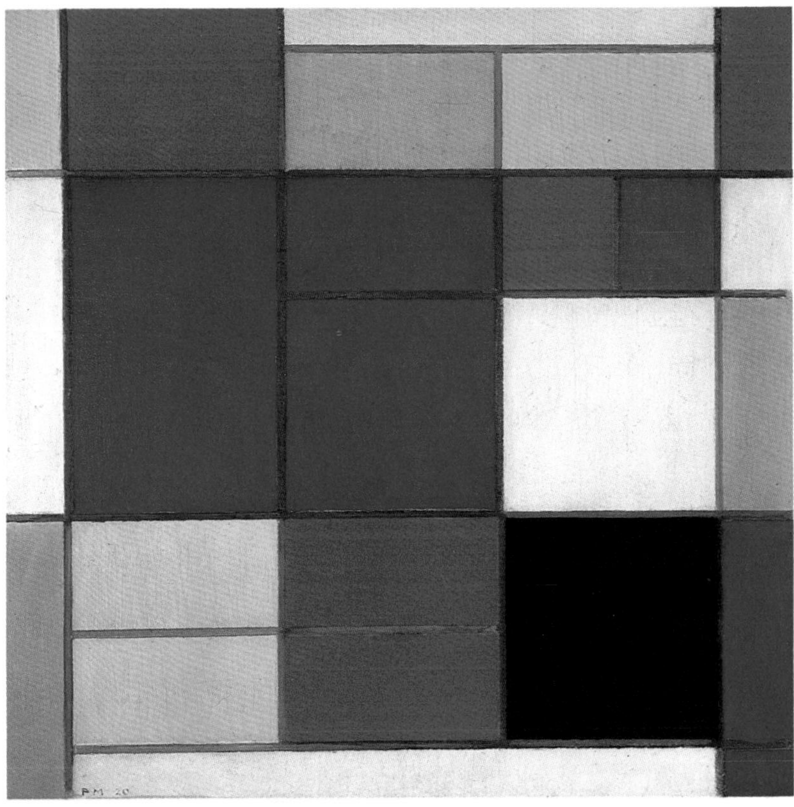

Piet Mondrian.
Composition C.
1920.
Oil on canvas,
23¾ × 24 inches.
The Museum of Modern Art, New York.
Acquired through the Lillie P. Bliss Bequest

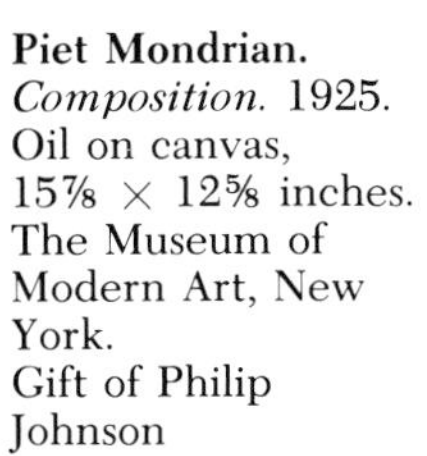

Piet Mondrian.
Composition. 1925.
Oil on canvas,
15⅞ × 12⅝ inches.
The Museum of Modern Art, New York.
Gift of Philip Johnson

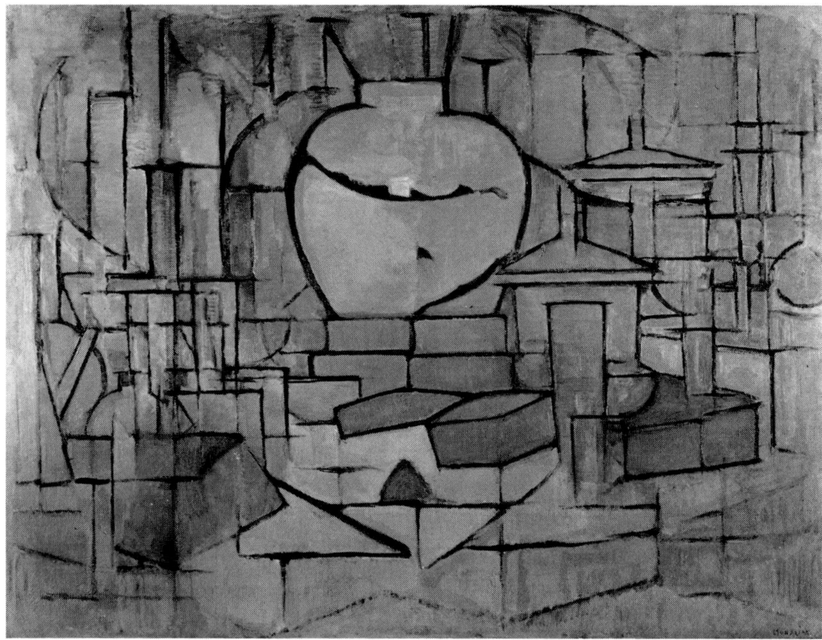

Piet Mondrian. *Still Life with Ginger Pot.* 1912. Oil on canvas, 36 × 47¼ inches. Gemeentemuseum, The Hague

the bright, light-reflecting rectangle of a studio window. The result may look near to abstraction, but everything was drawn from direct and day-long observation. He had in fact made careful notes of the look of the street in which he lived: the street lamp, the jut and thrust of walls and windows and chimney stacks, and the eye-catching advertisements for KUB and CUSENIER.

At the outbreak of World War I, Mondrian was momentarily in Holland, where circumstances forced him to remain until July, 1919. Looking around for a motif which would allow him to portray visual experience in terms of straight lines that crisscrossed at right angles, he fixed on the look of the North Sea as it lapped against the pier at a neighboring seaside resort. An oval format echoed the Cubist paintings produced by Picasso and Braque in 1912. Except for the firm vertical accent of the pier itself (in the center of the lower edge of the canvas) the painting is dominated by the regular, even, unaccented movement of the sea as it chops back and forth; Mondrian had always enjoyed painting the Dutch coast, and in this case he went beyond the particular to produce a universal image of an enveloping Nature.

In the Pier and Ocean series both pier and ocean were still present, in however skeletal a form; but there was no pretext in Nature for the pale forms which float in total freedom (so much so that at the top and bottom of the canvas they seem about to move out of sight) in the *Composition with Color Planes V* of 1917. By 1918 Mondrian was to enclose his rectangles in the thick and usually black lines which were to mark his mature style for many years; but in 1917 he emphasized the centrifugal, de-focused nature of his composition by allowing them a complete liberty. In this seraphic painting he put forward for the first time in his career an alternative to the taut, focused, centripetal practices of Cubism.

Later, these rectangles became locked into a mathematical grid and were separated from one another by thick straight lines. The year 1919 saw them set fast in a checkerboard pattern. After his return to Paris in July, 1919, Mondrian allowed himself, as in *Composition C,* both a greater variety in the shapes and sizes of the interlocking rectangles and a new complexity of color: intermediary hues were admitted, where red, blue and yellow had once ruled in their simplest and most uncompromising form.

No group holds together forever, and Mondrian

withdrew from De Stijl when Theo van Doesburg insisted on reintroducing diagonal elements into his paintings. Possibly it was by way of a reaction to this episode that Mondrian himself was at his crispest in paintings like the *Composition* of 1925 in The Museum of Modern Art. With red, blue, black and white, and with no concessions to the complex and relatively suave color structures which he had used a few years earlier, he produced an effect of imperious brilliance.

Mondrian's development has been no more than sampled in these pages. But it will have been clear, even so, that in his reactions to what had been done by others in living art he was both persevering and adroit. But no mere stylist could have painted his pictures. They had another dimension, and much in that dimension was owed to his friend Schoenmaekers. Schoenmaekers was both mystic and mathematician, and he believed that it was possible, by a process of inner concentration, to arrive at a mathematical understanding of how the universe works. The principles thus established were universally valid and would equip the believer to live in harmony with the universe, with his fellow men and with himself. The truths of art and architecture were intimations of these more general truths. The straight line, the right angle, the alliance of the three primary colors—red, yellow and blue—resulted on this reading from an inspired insight into the nature of the universe. "When beauty was the criterion," van Doesburg wrote, "the undulating line was to the fore. But when truth was the criterion the line simplified itself and will in the end be quite straight."

What Mondrian called "equilibrated relationships" were as fundamental to architecture, in the view of the De Stijl group, as to everything else in life. "Once we realize," Mondrian wrote in 1919, "that equilibrated relationships in society signify what is just, then we shall realize that in art, likewise, the demands of life press forward when the spirit of the age is ready." Balance was all-important: van Doesburg and his colleagues believed that a house should be capable of being scrutinized from no matter how unexpected an angle

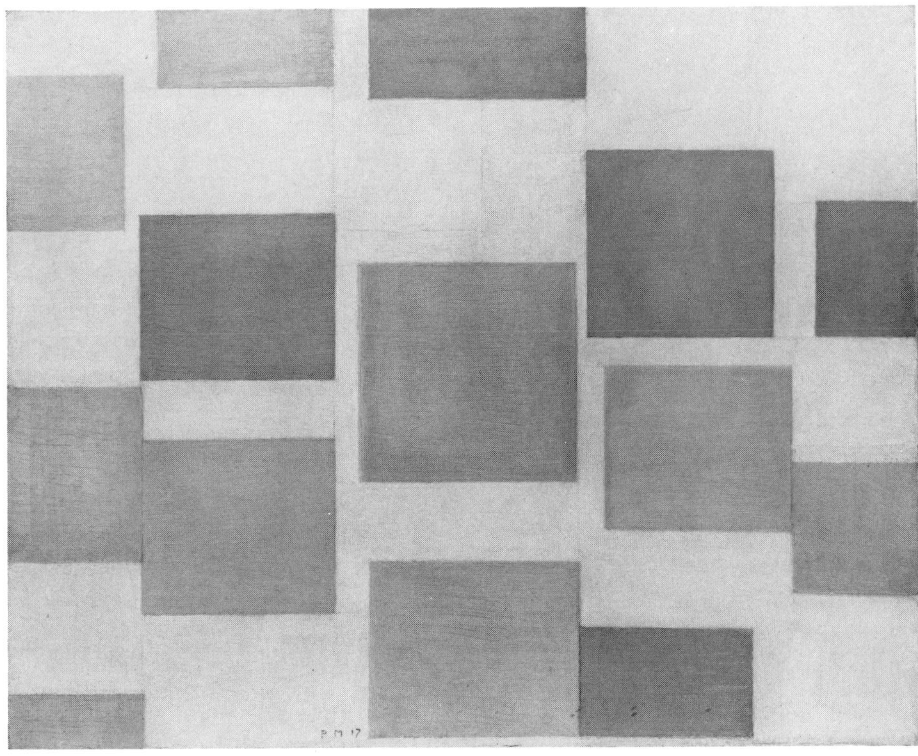

Piet Mondrian.
Composition with Color Planes V.
1917.
Oil on canvas,
19⅜ × 24⅛ inches.
The Museum of Modern Art, New York. The Sidney and Harriet Janis Collection

Piet Mondrian.
Painting I. 1926.
Oil on canvas, diagonal 44¾ × 44 inches.
The Museum of Modern Art, New York. Katherine S. Dreier Bequest

without being caught out in a disequilibrated relationship. They kept, also, to the primary colors, which were in favor with Mondrian.

Cranky as this may have seemed at a time when many laymen still associated good architecture with a superabundance of decoration, it was an idea which soon made its way. For the next 50 years and more the "quite straight" line was the quintessence of modernity. It dominated in architecture, in town planning, in almost every aspect of design. It was accepted as "modern" by people who had never heard of van Doesburg or of De Stijl. No one name was attached to it. Insofar as it made its way in painting, however, it was attributed, and quite rightly, to the man who pioneered it and stayed with it: Piet Mondrian.

Mondrian's was, as we have already seen, an exemplary career on more than one level. In his art, as in his life, he stood for the cutting away of inessentials. Frugal, solitary and undemanding in his ways, he exemplified one of the key propositions of modern art. In his view, painting should concern itself only with the things that were specifically its own: flat planes laid parallel to the two-dimensional surface of the canvas. His first sojourn in Paris (December, 1911–July, 1914) convinced him that "Cubism failed to accept the logical consequences of its own discoveries; it failed to develop toward the fulfillment of its own ambition, the expression of *pure plasticity.*" (By *plasticity* Mondrian meant a picture language which operated on its own, as a closed system, without any descriptive intention.)

He was quite right, of course. Cubism did not develop into abstract art; nor did its founders wish it to do so. It was left to Mondrian to personify the reductive principle: straightening his lines; cutting down his palette to the primary colors; avoiding even the remotest allusion to volume or recession. He did this not in a dull or doctrinaire way, but at the prompting of an exceptionally full and resonant emotional nature. His pictures were never the same from one canvas to the next. With means which looked meager he produced a body of work which is rich, strange and surprising beyond all expectation; and he went on developing, as we shall see, until the day of his death.

Straight line and right angle are fundamental to Mondrian's mature work, though no one in our century has used the curved line to more rampageous emotional effect than Mondrian as a young man. Straight line and right angle are the basis, in Holland, of an agriculture which would otherwise soon be under water. They also stand for that element of unyielding puritanism which is basic to the Dutch character; geometry was the basis after all of the ethical system which was erected in the 17th century by the Dutch philosopher Spinoza. It was natural that during World War I, when Holland was isolated by her neutral status, the brightest and most ambitious Dutch minds should remain loyal to the traditional armature of Dutch thought. Any student of architecture who has seen a building by Rietveld in Holland will have recognized a reintegration of art and society—the thing needed and the thing done are one. But how much in this success is owed to the clearly defined and sharply characterized nature of the society in question, and to a shrewd assessment of local needs? Would the same principles apply in an unsettled and backward society? Or in quite different climatic conditions? Or in an area which varied enormously in its ethnic ingredients and extended over hundreds of thousands of square miles?

These questions are relevant to the situation as it presented itself to the new rulers of Russia in the winter of 1917–18. It is one thing to seize power, and quite another to know what to do with it. Lenin and his colleagues had got the power, beyond a doubt; but now they had to build, organize and administer a completely new society. Over the next three years they would be faced with famine, with a particularly savage and unsparing civil war, and with bumbling but vindictive interventions by more than one foreign power. This being so, it is really rather remarkable that from

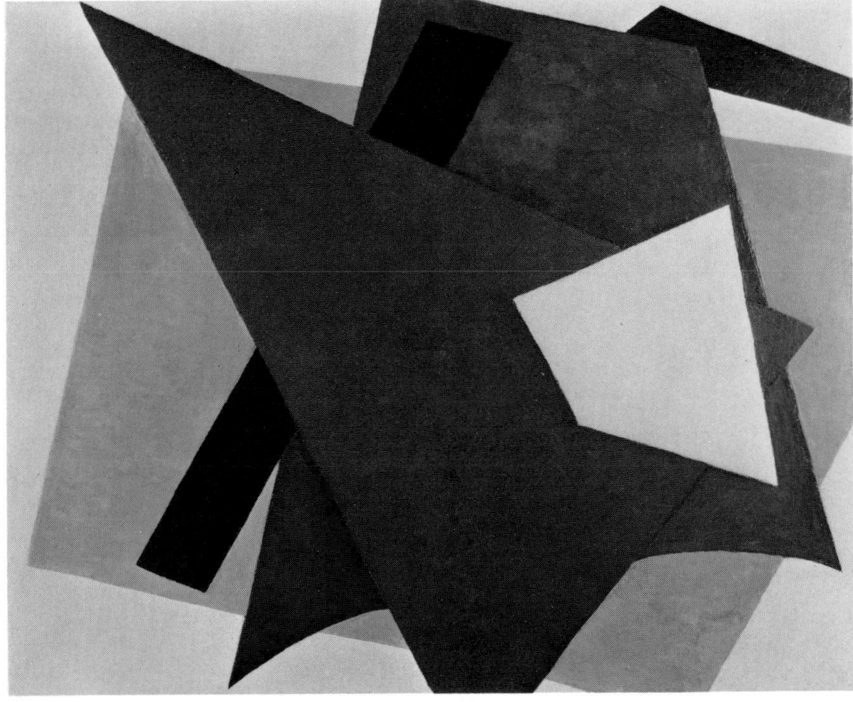

Liubov Popova. *Architectonic Painting.* 1917. Oil on canvas, 31½ × 38⅝ inches. The Museum of Modern Art, New York. Philip Johnson Fund

the very day—November 7, 1917—on which Lenin formed his first government an official role was allotted to the art of the avant-garde.

A. V. Lunacharsky, himself a poet, a philosopher and a playwright, was put in charge of education and the arts. He had spent much of his adult life in exile in Western Europe; he had a good working knowledge of the modern movement in France and elsewhere; above all, he was an enthusiast who saw it as his duty to make the totality of human achievement freely available to everyone. "Lunacharsky is drawn toward the future with his whole being," Lenin said of him. "That is why there is such joy and laughter in him, and why he is eager to pass on that joy and laughter to others."

In choosing his collaborators Lunacharsky largely disregarded political allegiance and went all out for quality. This was not an outlook which commended itself to the hard-liners in the Communist Party, and Lunacharsky often had to compromise, to shift his ground, to say one thing one day and another the next. But for three full years, at a time of appalling and ever-worsening tribulations for Russia and her peoples, he made sure that anyone with something important to offer could count on official backing. This applied to theater, literature, music, the fine arts and architecture; for the first and last time the Russian people were to have free access to the work of their most gifted members. Lunacharsky sensed quite rightly that something of the dauntless energy of the age got into works like Liubov Popova's *Architectonic Painting,* above all in the sharp-pointed arrowlike form that reaches out toward the top left-hand corner of the canvas. In no other country at that time was there a woman painter with quite such a dynamic approach to painting.

In matters of art, Lunacharsky could take his pick of a particularly brilliant list of men and women. Some of them had returned to Russia at the outbreak of World War I. Nothing in the world is more tenacious than Russian patriotism; and it was this which had brought Kandinsky back from Munich, Chagall back from Paris, and the young

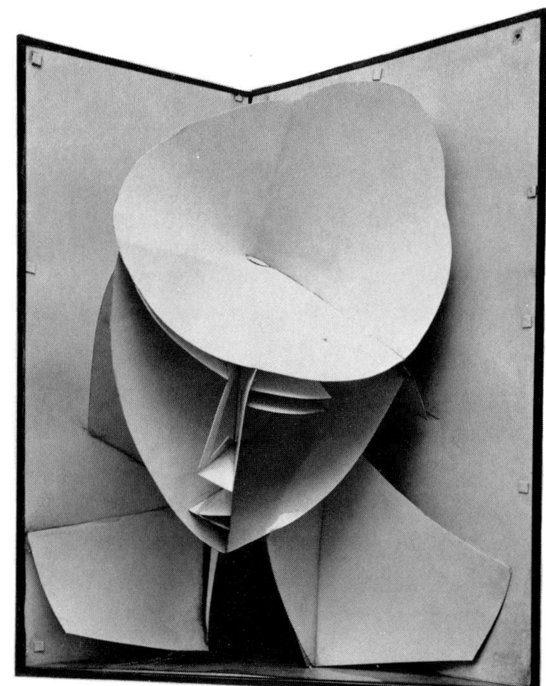

Naum Gabo.
Head of a Woman.
c. 1917–20.
Construction in celluloid and metal, 24½ × 19¼ inches.
The Museum of Modern Art, New York. Purchase

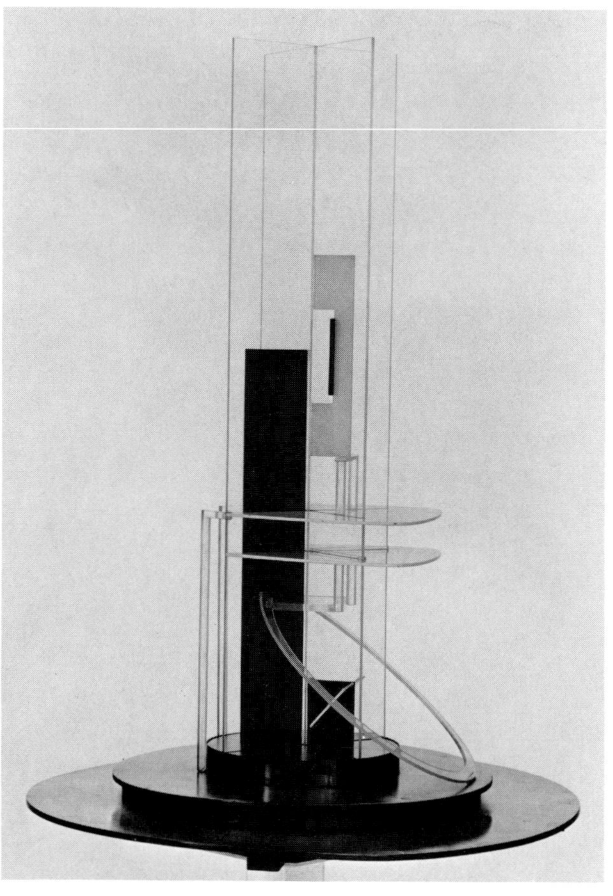

Naum Gabo.
Column. 1923.
Plastic, wood and metal, 41 inches high.
The Solomon R. Guggenheim Museum, New York

sculptor Naum Gabo back from Norway. Others could well have been mentioned earlier in this volume as part-time members of the pacific International and long-distance adherents of the cosmopolitan eye. For instance, Vladimir Tatlin had called on Picasso in Paris in 1913 and had been deeply impressed by Picasso's constructions in metal; Kasimir Malevich had exhibited with the Blue Rider group in Munich in 1912; El Lissitzky had lived in Darmstadt (at that time one of the liveliest art centers in Europe), had talked with Henry van de Velde in Brussels, and had walked the length and breadth of Paris in search of what he called "architecture—that is to say, art in its highest sense: mathematical order." As for Gabo, it was in 1915–16, when he was living in Norway after several years in Munich and some crucial visits to Paris, that he began to sculpt (or, as he put it, to construct) the human head in terms of opened-out and interpenetrating volumes. What is normally the exposed surface of the head was cut away, in other words, and the head was realized with the use of planes of wood or metal which pushed outward into space. Back in his native Russia he adapted the same principles to transparent materials which made the idea doubly clear. He was convinced that time, as much as space, would play its due part in the art of the future. Kinetic rhythm, he said, was the basic form in which we perceive what he called "real time"; and in 1920 he attempted to make duration visible in his motorized *Kinetic Construction,* where a metal rod was made to vibrate in such a way as to create an illusion of volume. Later he decided that comparable rhythms would be set up with the use of static materials only; an outstanding instance of this is his *Column,* first mooted in the winter of 1920–21 and later shown all over Europe as a key work in the modern movement. Gabo believed that its principles could be applied not only to works of art but to public buildings; and he made projects of this kind for a radio station, an observatory, an airport and an institute or physics and mathematics. Russia was ready for such ideas. Even before the Revolution, alert Muscovites had responded to the erection in Lubyansky Square of a five-story department store, designed by the three Vesnin brothers, in which a reinforced concrete frame did away with the necessity of structural walls.

It is with human material of this order that Lunacharsky proposed to institutionalize the avant-garde. In normal times this would have been a contradiction in terms, in that the avant-garde is by definition outside and ahead of officialdom. But one of the central facts about Lunacharsky's position in 1917–18 was that the natural enemies of the avant-garde had simply melted away, leaving the chairmanships and the professorships and the headmasterships all empty. "They didn't like us," Naum Gabo said 50 years later, "but they had to put up with us because there wasn't anybody else." The titles were in any case mainly honorific at that time: "Being a profes-

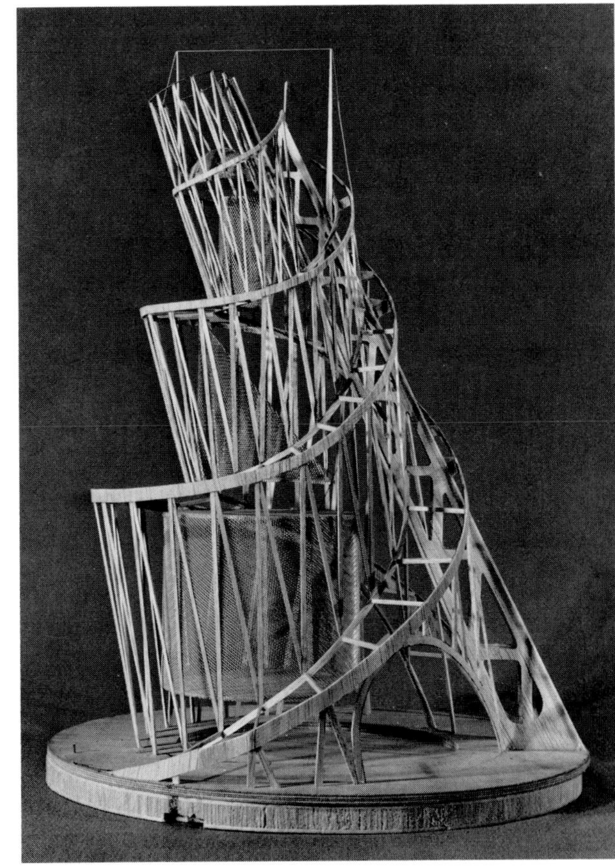

Vladimir Tatlin. *Project for the Monument to the Third International.* 1919–20. Reconstruction. Photograph courtesy the Arts Council of Great Britain

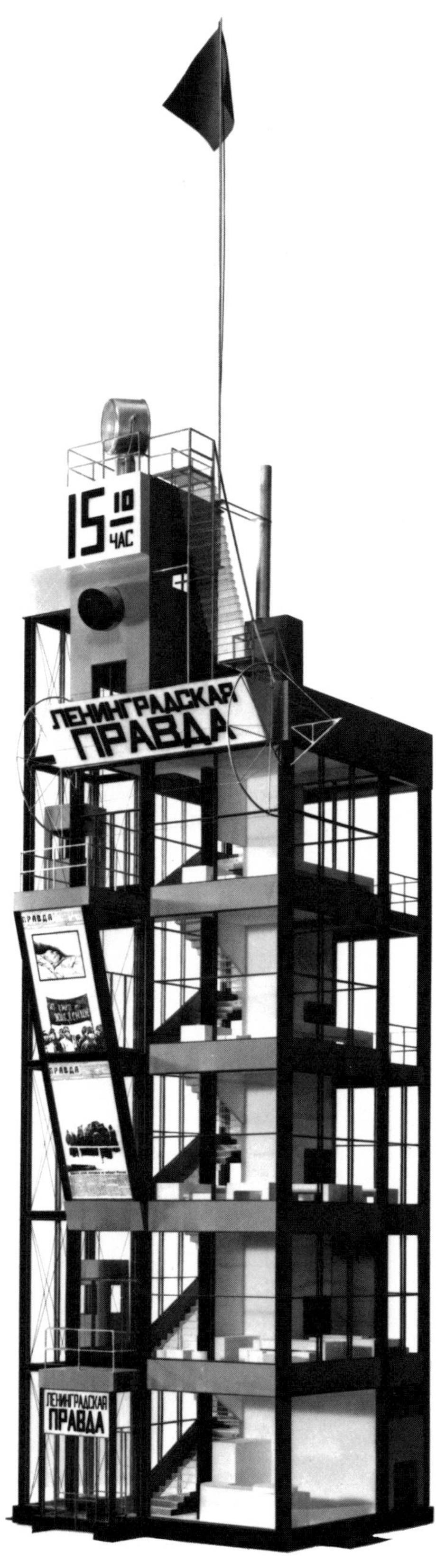

Victor and Alexander Vesnin. *Project for the Leningrad "Pravda" Building. 1923–24. Reconstruction. Photograph courtesy the Arts Council of Great Britain*

sor," said Gabo, "simply meant that you got a little more bread and herring."

Thus it was that Chagall got an important post, and that Kandinsky was given carte blanche in 1920 to redraft the structure of art education throughout the country, and that Lissitzky got to design the flag which was carried across Red Square on May Day, 1918. The right flag in the right place is, as we all know, a very stirring thing; Lissitzky was only one of the artists who made good use of the new, brief rapprochement between art and society. Interdisciplinary activity flourished in Russia, between 1917 and 1921, in ways not quite paralleled before or since. It is difficult for us to imagine Manet designing a radio station, or Cézanne making sets for a completely mechanized theater-in-the-round; but to Lunacharsky's protégés it seemed perfectly natural that the architect Alexander Vesnin should devise a transparent scaffolding which could be used in a dozen different ways for a production of G. K. Chesterton's *The Man Who Was Thursday,* and that Naum Gabo should take the delicate colorless membranes which made up his abstract sculptures and transform them into the outline of a radio station which would serve its purpose perfectly.

By no means all of these projects got beyond the stage of the sketch or the model. Building materials were scarce at that time, and skilled labor scarcer still, so that many of the more visionary notions of the Lunacharsky regime had only a faint chance of realization. The most famous casualty of the period is the *Monument to the Third International* on which Vladimir Tatlin worked in 1919–20. As planned, this would have been approximately the height of the Empire State Building. Within a spiral framework of iron three huge and inhabitable glass forms were to revolve at varying speeds. The first, a cylinder, would complete its revolution once a year; the second, a cone, once a month; the third, a cube, once a day. The three glass forms were to be hung on a dynamic asymmetrical axis in such a way that the building as a whole would seem to be accelerating into space, moving faster and faster as the eye followed it upward. The monument was intended to make visible to everyone, on the largest imaginable scale and with all possible versatility, the reintegration of art and society. Quite apart from the inventive magic of the building itself, its functioning would serve as an encyclopedia of the ways in which the poetic imagination of the artist could enrich the life of everyday. Tatlin envisaged the use of giant loudspeakers, for instance, and messages beamed onto the clouds when the weather was bad, and a gigantic cinema screen, clearly visible from below, on which the news of the day would be available to all.

Some of these notions were carried over into the design for the *Pravda* building in Moscow, which was prepared by the Vesnin brothers in 1923–24. They had what may now seem to us an unfounded belief in the impartiality and total openness of the Soviet news services; the *Pravda* building is, in effect, a hymn to transparency. It suggests by implication that *Pravda* has nothing to hide; the elegant inner workings of the Vesnin brothers' design are as open to us as the workings of a specimen watch in a Swiss shop window; the entire building functions as an instrument of communication. Eye, ear and mind were to be seduced in turn; what the Vesnins had on the drawing board was an architecture which would serve up "the truth, and nothing but the truth."

Pravda did not turn out to be that kind of newspaper; nor did the Vesnins' building get built. But if projects like these still haunt our imagination it is because they stand for the hope of a better world in which all the news will be good news and the last of the tyrants will have been shipped off to some maximum-security playpen. Not to have shared at least momentarily in that hope is to have fallen short of our potential as human beings, and it is not surprising that Tatlin's monument has so often been built and rebuilt in scale-model form by architectural students. It symbolizes the fulfillment of the aim which Lunacharsky once set himself—the acceptance at government level of a cultural policy in which everything was possible.

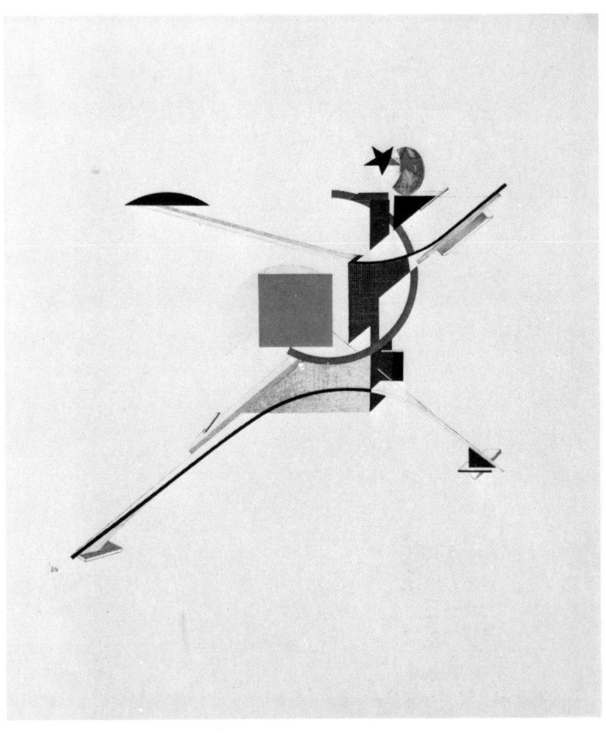

El Lissitzky. "The New One" from the portfolio *Victory over the Sun.* 1923. Lithograph, 21 × 13¾ inches. The Museum of Modern Art, New York. Purchase

In the conditions then prevailing in Russia it would have been out of the question to initiate an avant-garde of the kind which was already in existence. It was Lunacharsky's good fortune that the people in question not only knew what they wanted to do but in most cases had already been doing it for years. One of the most controversial achievements of the pre-Revolutionary avant-garde in Russia was for instance the opera *Victory over the Sun,* which was produced in St. Petersburg in 1913. The text, music and scenery (the last by Malevich) were all equally daunting to conventional taste; the theme had a prophetic interest in that it described how technology would change the conditions of life by discovering new sources of energy. After the Revolution Lissitzky adapted this same theme for what he called an "electro-mechanical peepshow" or mechanized puppet theater. A portfolio of prints on the same subject, published in 1923, included a classic image of man as he might one day be: alert and indestructible, a mechanized version, in fact, of the young man in Chagall's *Forward!*

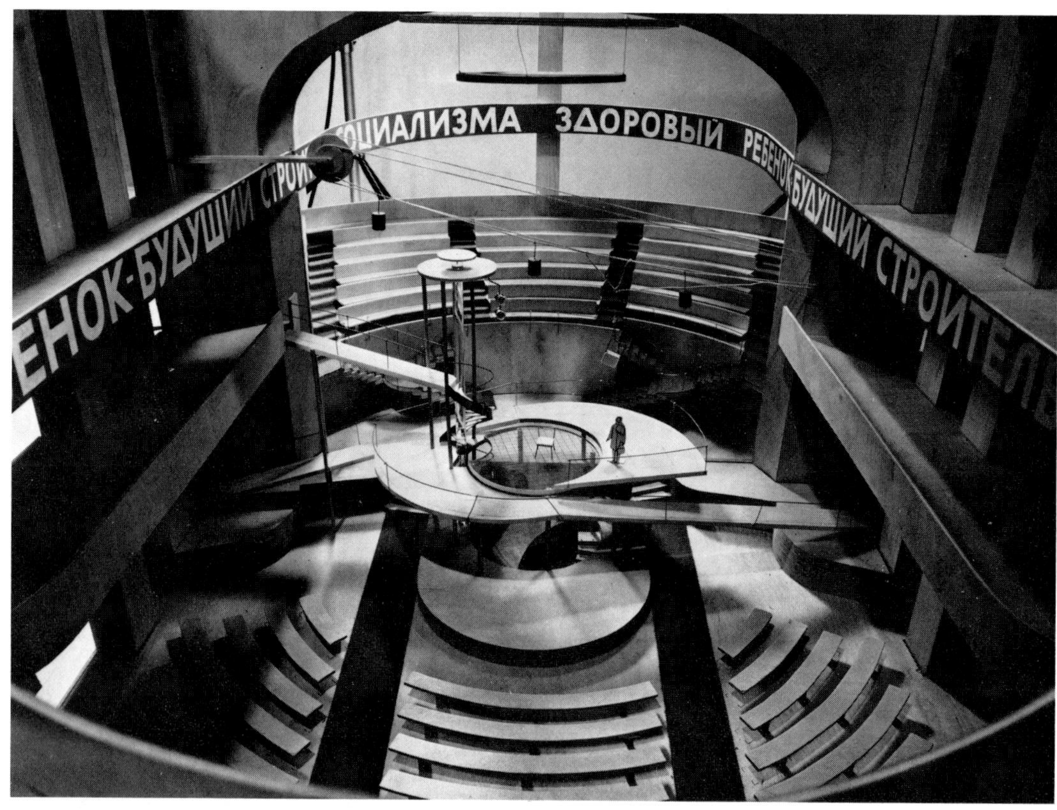

El Lissitzky. Model of the set for *I Want a Child* (by Sergei Tretyakov), commissioned by Meyerhold for production at his Moscow theater. 1926–29. Photograph courtesy the Arts Council of Great Britain

If the political revolution and the aesthetic revolution could work together very closely, for just a year or two, it was not because the one brought the other about. It was because the political revolution had no aesthetic identity and was prepared to settle for whatever lay within reach, just as a man in a hurry to leave for the tropics will buy the featherweight suit that hangs nearest on the rack. There were artists like Tatlin, who genuinely identified himself with Communism and did all that he could to foster its advance; but there were others —Kandinsky, Gabo, Chagall—who were completely apolitical. It is part of the mythology of the period that Lunacharsky's protégés worked together as a band of brothers; but the truth is that if they were brothers it was in the way that Cain and Abel were brothers. Tatlin and Malevich had literally come to blows already in 1915 and never ceased to represent antithetical points of view. Malevich did not scruple to intrigue against Chagall in Vitebsk at a time when Chagall was away in Moscow. Kandinsky's draft plans for the remodeling of art education in Russia were turned down by a majority vote of his colleagues in 1920. Art life in Czarist Russia had always been a ferocious affair, with faction pitted against faction, and all this was if anything intensified after 1917. It was to Lunacharsky's credit that he made no attempt to produce a homogenized official line in such matters, but maintained a watchful impartiality throughout what Naum Gabo has called "the oral period"—the years 1917–20 during which open forums and seminars were available in Moscow to an audience totaling in all several thousand. It was in these discussions, rather than in any formal teaching sessions, that ideas were hammered out and tested in debate.

If these things are still worth talking about, it is because so much of what still passes for the latest thing in the arts was pioneered in Russia at that time. The internal situation of the country was so desperate between 1917 and 1921 that literally anything could be tried out on the assumption that Authority was far too busy to object. If someone wanted to stand on top of the highest building in the town and conduct a symphony of factory sirens, he was allowed to do it. If someone wanted to mark a special occasion by painting not just one big canvas but the whole town, the project went through unopposed. If street theater with "a cast of thousands" seemed more the thing, the thousands in question were drafted. If people in the theater itself—the indoor one—were bored with the proscenium arch and with the studied naturalism of plays like Chekhov's *The Cherry Orchard,* they were encouraged to leave the stage open to the brick wall at the back of the theater, or to use what Lissitzky called "alogical language" and cast their dialogue in the form of phonetic poems.

Vsevolod Meyerhold, for many years a commanding figure in the world of Russian theater, had it in mind in the 1920s to open the theater to new social ideas. Not only would these be acted out on the stage, but the audience would be free to interrupt the action if they wished, and turn the performance into an open forum. For this, a new conception of stage design was needed; and Lissitzky provided this in the context of a play, *I Want a Child,* which dealt with the problems of a woman agronomist who was bent on having a child out of wedlock. The text did not find favor with the Soviet authorities and the production was never realized, but Lissitzky's design remains a pioneer work in the domain of "total theater." One of Meyerhold's most dynamic productions in the early 1920s was a farce by the Belgian playwright Fernand Crommelynck. Set in a windmill and dealing in the broadest possible way with the discomfiture of a husband who believes his wife to be irresistible, *The Magnanimous Cuckold* had a transparent, mechanized set by the painter Liubov Popova, which left the back wall of the theater in full view of the audience. The wheels, the disk bearing a version of the author's name, and

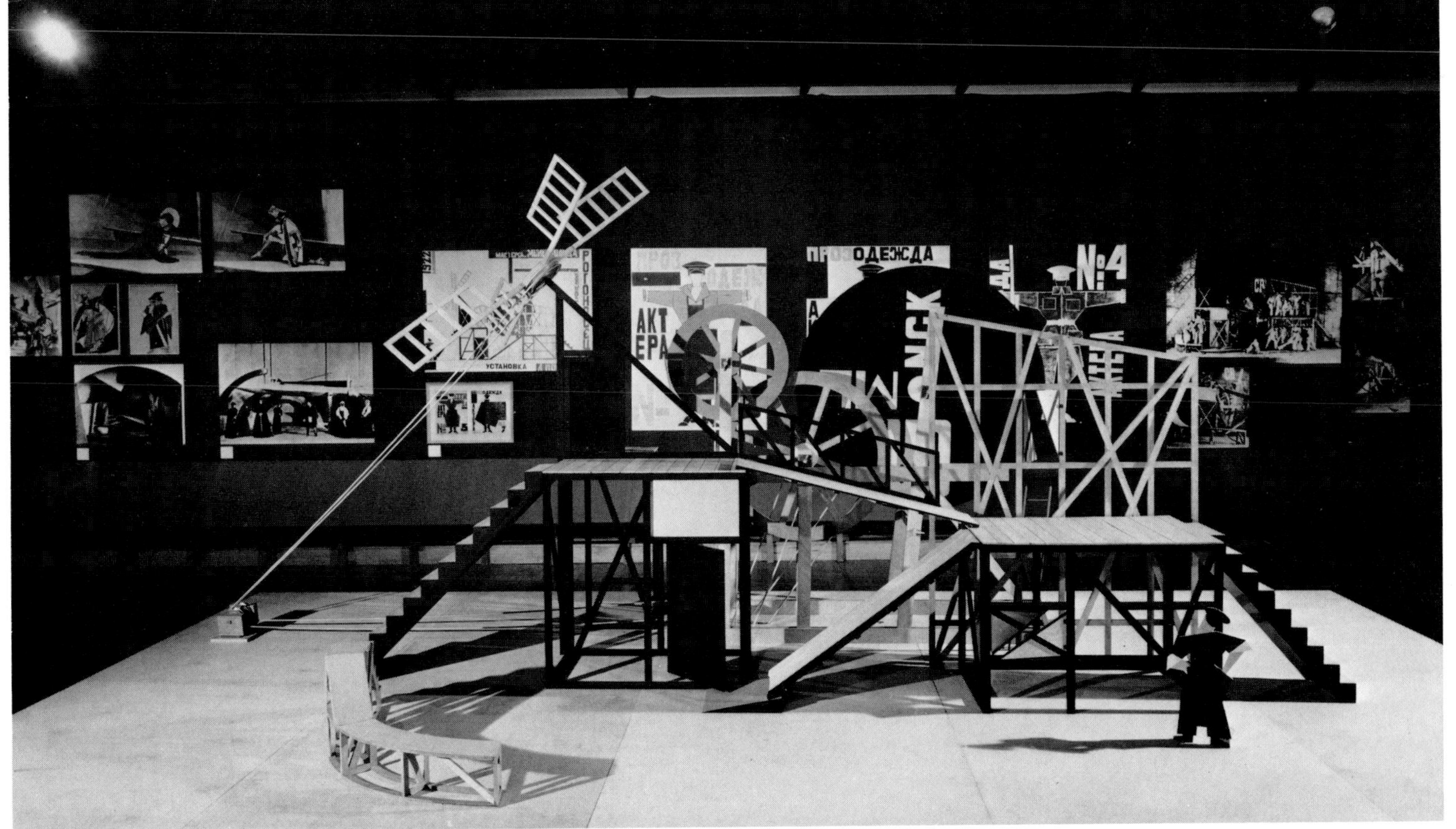

Liubov Popova. Model of the set for *The Magnanimous Cuckold* (by Fernand Crommelynck), produced by Meyerhold at the Nezlobin Theater, Moscow. 1922. Photograph courtesy the Arts Council of Great Britain

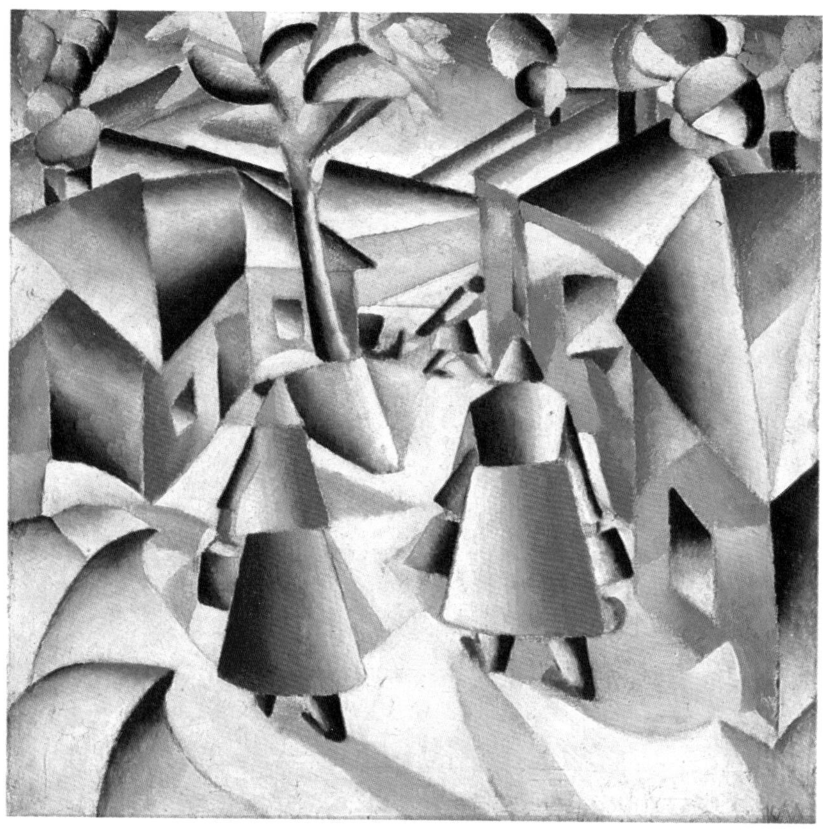

Kasimir Malevich. *Morning in the Village after Snowfall.* 1912. Oil on canvas, 31½ × 31⅜ inches. The Solomon R. Guggenheim Museum, New York

the windmill sails all revolved at speeds adjusted to the action of the play. In skeletal form, the set became in turn a bedroom, a balcony, a machine for grinding flour, and a chute through which sacks of flour could be discharged.

This new brief freedom made itself felt everywhere. If people wanted to paint the trees beneath the Kremlin walls blue and orange, Lunacharsky let them do it (though Lenin was not at all amused). If technology put new marvels at the disposal of the artist, there was no hint of bureaucratic delays; what Lissitzky called a "radio-megaphone" was brought into the theater, for instance, to allow the audience to be engulfed in "the deafening noise of railway stations, the rushing of Niagara Falls, the hammering of a rolling mill." Nothing was allowed to obstruct the integration of art and society.

And not only could artists do anything, in that brief period of tolerance and liberty, they could do *everything* as well. Tatlin could design anything from an exceptionally economical stove to an all-purpose suit of clothing. Malevich took formal elements from his paintings and transformed them into the basis of a new architecture. Alexander Rodchenko was as ready to design a tubular steel chair as to paint an abstract painting—more so, indeed, after 1921, when in common with a number of other painters he moved away from anything that could be called "fine art" and toward the direct service of the proletariat.

Much of all this arose, as I said earlier, from ideas that were in the air all over Europe. But there was also something specifically Russian about it—in the political situation, to begin with, but no less effectively in what can only be called the Russian nature. That nature is distinguished, in a particular context, by a readiness to deal in absolutes of a kind that in most other countries are subject to irony and doubt, an embattled common sense and a readiness to "see both sides." In particular, Russians can move from the everyday to the mystical

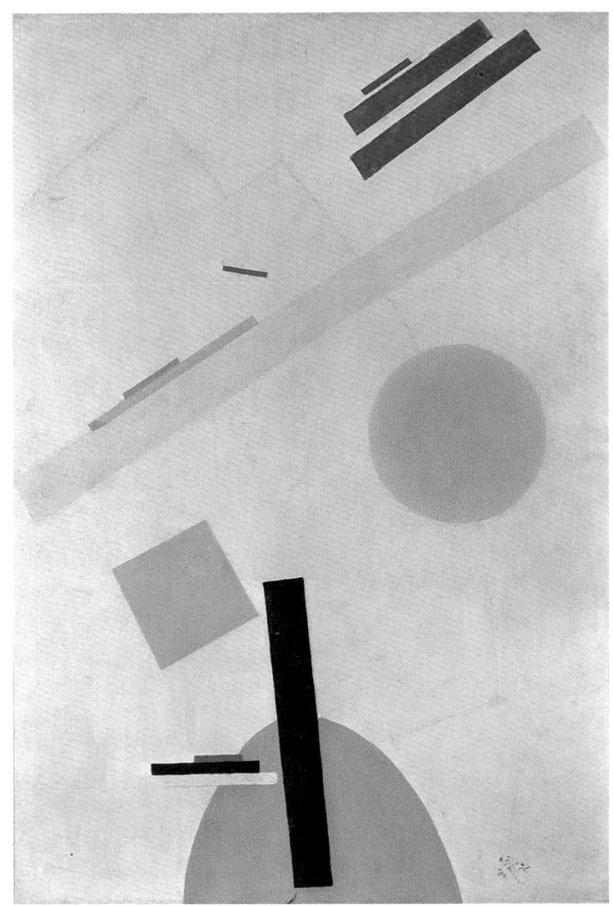

Kasimir Malevich. *Suprematist Composition.* 1916–17(?). Oil on canvas, 38½ × 26⅛ inches. The Museum of Modern Art, New York

without so much as a conversational change of gear. Ultimate problems in most English-speaking countries are thought of as something to be discussed with circumspection and in private. Among Russians they are the staple of human exchange, no more to be skirted than we would expect our butcher to skirt the price of a leg of lamb. Nothing is kept back. Ideas, if held, are held with one's whole being.

All this has been said before by others, but certain things are nonetheless true for being familiar (not least in the novels of Dostoevsky). An individual human nature that is fundamentally oriented toward mysticism will find its way in that direction, no matter how discouraging the circumstances in which it finds itself.

The development of Kasimir Malevich, for one, bears this out. Malevich in 1910 was 32 years old. Unlike so many of his colleagues he had never been to Western Europe; but from the magazines, and from studying the great French pictures which were freely available to him in the collections of Shchukin and Morozov in Moscow, he knew more than most Frenchmen about what had lately happened in Paris. But when he came to paint the Russian peasant we see what might be called the pawmark of the Russian bear—the heavy, stamping, pounding rhythms that come through so memorably in the Russian dance in *Petrouchka,* which Stravinsky had composed in 1911. Such paintings have a double inspiration: on the one hand, the French Post-Impressionists' use of pure flat color and simplified drawing, on the other, the emphatic plain statement of the Russian *lubok,* or popular print.

Malevich's peasant subjects of 1911–12 should, in fact, be related to something that turned up all over the civilized world before 1914—the wish to reinvigorate painting by reference to primitive or demotic modes of expression. Malevich knew a great deal about older European art, but he agreed with the dissident group of painters in St. Petersburg who had said in 1905 that no art of general communication could be fashioned from what they called "a sauce of history." If primeval energies were to hand, they should be tapped; if popular imagery, popular songs, popular forms of narrative were valid for the whole community in ways denied to more sophisticated forms of statement, then they too should be annexed for art. That is what Charles Ives believed when he brought "America the Beautiful" into his Second Symphony, and what Ernst Ludwig Kirchner and his friends believed when they adapted to their own purposes the peremptory black-on-white of the old German woodcut. Malevich had looked closely at Fernand Léger before he painted his *Morning in the Village after Snowfall,* 1912; but the energizing influence, in formal terms, was that of the *lubok* and of the simplified forms of Russian peasant embroidery.

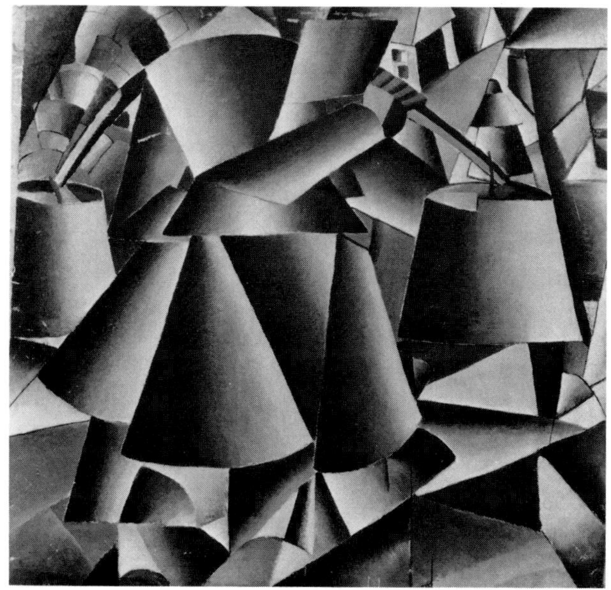

Malevich in this landscape stressed the look of a little country town after a storm: crisp, delicate, newborn. But he gave unity to his composition by using the same formal ingredient—a cross-section, cut to size, from a cone—for virtually everything in sight: the roofs of the houses, the foliage on the trees, the ups and downs of the village street, the broad back and even broader backside of the woman on the right. This common denominator, shaded in almost every case from left to right and from dark to light, gave an unfailing dynamism to every part of the picture. And eventually it took over from the ostensible subject of the painting to become its true subject—the pulsebeat by which all else was governed.

At a moment which it is now impossible to date, Malevich decided that the pulsebeat of abstract form should be not merely the underlying force within the picture but its only reason for existence. He got nearer to the fulfillment of this idea in a painting of 1912 called *Head of a Peasant Girl*, in which the parts of the head look like starched and folded napkins. Cézanne, a generation earlier, had made his tablecloths look like scaled-down mountain ranges; Malevich in 1912 took the human head—an object which we view with a much greater degree of protectiveness—and gave it, likewise, the stature of a pretext only. But that, too, was a transitional move. Malevich was marking time until he was ready, and until the world was ready, to dispense altogether with recognizable subject matter. In later years he could be very rough with people who still thought that subject matter was essential to art. Meanwhile he wanted to annex for himself the formal devices of Cubism, but it was not in his nature at that time to aim for the austere and lucid procedures of Braque and Picasso. He just put in everything—numbers, letters, collaged objects from real life, simulated graining, fragments of printed paper, overlapping flat planes—in the hope that something specifically modern would emerge. Like many another artist in 1914—not least, the American Marsden Hartley—he added some echoes of militarism to make sure that the picture would look well and truly up-to-date.

Malevich in 1914 also thought that the airplane had "awakened the soul from its long sleep in the catacombs of reason," and that a new life "somewhere between earth and sky" was waiting for us. Of this new life, the airplane was the true symbol. "Sail forth!" he wrote. "The white free chasm of infinity lies before us!" To make that visible, he allowed his forms to float freely in a dimensionless ether. His object was not to represent any specific airplane, but to confront the observer with an abstract idea of motion in space.

A painter who delighted in Nature as a subject for art was like a free man who delighted in handcuffs; that was Malevich's eventual point of view, and he went on to make his point with paintings like the famous *White on White* of 1918. After well over 50 years these paintings still startle by their total simplification; we have before us a statement that has been pushed as far as it can go by someone who would not settle for anything but the absolute. "In art," said Malevich in 1916, "we need *truth*, not sincerity." He did not mean by this that the artist should not be sincere, but that sincerity on its own could result simply in the perpetuation of obsolete modes of expression. The

Kasimir Malevich. *Woman with Water Pails: Dynamic Arrangement.* 1912. Oil on canvas, 31⅝ × 31⅝ inches. The Museum of Modern Art, New York

sympathetic observer was back with the notion of truth, just as he was back with it in Western Europe and back with it in the Chicago of Frank Lloyd Wright; truth meant defining the quintessence of the painting experience. When Malevich put a black square in the middle of a white canvas he meant the square to stand for sensation and the white surround to stand for the blank state of awareness and expectation on which sensation impresses itself. Even that came to seem to him too obvious, and in the *White on White* painting, first shown in 1919, color dropped out altogether; sensation and its surround merged into one another, distinguished only by a change of texture and by the spectral pivoting of a white square which hovered, weightless, within the confines of a larger square of its own color.

We may feel, in commonsense terms, that such paintings give us nothing to look at. But Malevich took exactly the opposite point of view. In his Suprematist pictures (as he called them) there is, for the first time in the history of art, nothing to distract or deceive. The experience comes to us pure and entire. The square on a square, thus interpreted, stands for primary, irreducible emotional structure: the power to set one element in our experience against another, and to define the relationship between them. These paintings provide, in other words, a schema or pilot system which helps us to find our way among our own feelings. Malevich and Kandinsky did not always see eye to eye; but fundamentally Malevich was carrying on with the mystic or intuitional line of thought which Kandinsky had pioneered in his book *On the Spiritual in Art.* Once again, and without falling back on any stereotyped view of the Russian nature, one could say that the speculations of both men had an all-or-nothing character, a compulsive inwardness and a disdain for ridicule which are not common in other countries. The square, the circle and, to a lesser degree, the triangle are fundamental to much of the abstract painting of the last 50 years; but nobody has quite felt about the square in the way that Malevich felt about it, any

Kasimir Malevich. *Suprematist Composition: White on White.* 1918(?). Oil on canvas, 31¼ × 31¼ inches. The Museum of Modern Art, New York

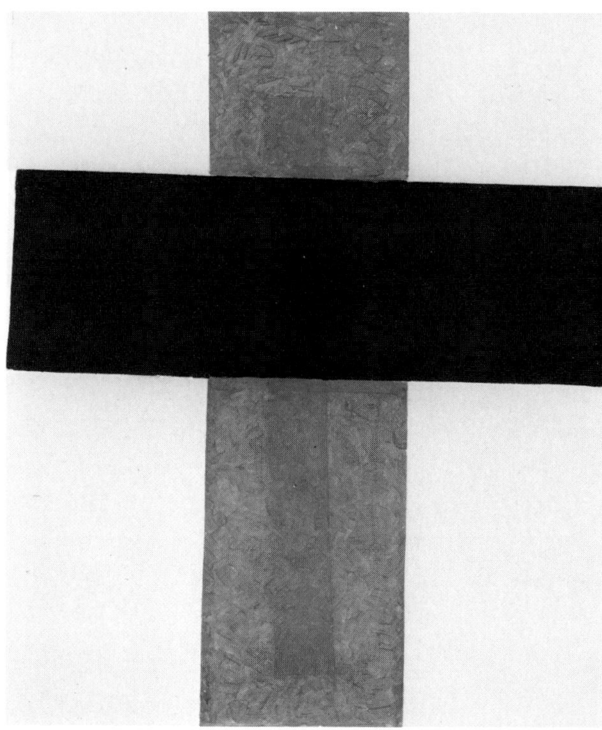

Kasimir Malevich. *Suprematist Painting.* After 1920.
Oil on canvas, 33½ × 27½ inches.
Stedelijk Museum, Amsterdam

more than anyone has felt about the circle in the way that Kandinsky did in the 1920s. ("If I have used the circle so often and so passionately in the last years," he wrote in 1929, "it is not because of the geometrical shape of the circle, or of its geometrical attributes, as because of my overwhelming recognition of its inner strength and its limitless variations.")

Malevich did not think of these paintings as objects of luxury to be sold to the highest bidder. Still less did he regard them as addressed to a cultivated elite. He thought of them as terminal statements. If they signaled the end of art as it had previously been known—if "art," thus understood, was a casualty of evolution—that seemed to him a perfectly fair exchange for the new spirituality which his paintings made available to everyone. Those simplified flat shapes afloat on a plain background stood, in his eyes, for the new life that was opening up for the human spirit. And the coming of that new life was overdue. "Their bodies may fly in airplanes," he said of his contemporaries, "but they live by the beauty of ages long past."

The Malevich who wrote those words was not a peripheral crank to whose ravings no importance was attached. He had established himself among his fellow artists as early as December, 1915, as a leader with whom it was rash to quarrel. Nor was he a man to put his head in the clouds by way of escape from the realities of life after 1917. He saw nothing contradictory in calling on the one hand for a new and exalted degree of spirituality and in promoting on the other a future bound up with automated, electrified and prefabricated housing. It may seem that at a time of extreme national emergency the one might have precluded the other. But that is to misunderstand what Edmund Wilson in *A Window on Russia* called "the Russian perception of time—a sense of things beginning, of things going on, of things to be completed not at the present moment but in the future, of things that have happened in the past all relegated to the same plane of pastness with no distinction between perfect and pluperfect: a sense, in short, entirely different from our Western clock time, which sets specific events with exactitude in relation to an established and unvarying chronology."

Our Western clock time did catch up, even so, both with Malevich and with Lunacharsky's regime as a whole. By the end of 1921 Lunacharsky's policy of humane tolerance had been dismantled in favor of a program which admitted only those forms of art which had an immediate social utility. A Russia in which anything was possible gave way, step by step, to a Russia in which nothing was possible. To have some idea of the personal suffering which was inflicted on people who had much to give to the world, the reader should turn to the poems of Anna Akhmatova and Nadezhda Mandelstam's two volumes of memoirs, or to those late compositions in which Shostakovich turns a bleak and unforgetting eye upon the ordeals of his generation. What we are concerned with here is something quite different: the continued existence in other countries, and into other decades, of that same pacific International which had been active before 1914, and of which the Lunacharsky regime was a distinguished and highly localized offshoot. It was thanks to this pacific International, and to the extreme receptivity of its most prominent members, that the contribution of Russia between 1917 and 1921 should be seen not as an isolated and foredoomed experiment, but rather as one episode in an ongoing process that made itself felt all over Europe in the 1920s and later spread to the United States.

As early as 1910, when he was in his late 20s, Walter Gropius was arguing that aesthetic creativity and industrial mass-production were perfectly compatible. Noting how in the United States Thomas Edison had made extensive use of poured concrete and standard components made of iron, he foresaw a time when the bricklayer and the carpenter would play no part in architecture. In 1911 his factory for the shoe-last firm of Fagus proved that exterior walls need no longer bear heavy loads and could, on the contrary, be no more than transparent shields against the weather. Even in the worst days of World War I Gropius went on planning for a school that would synthesize the arts and the crafts and see to it that the best ideas of the age were made available cheaply and to everyone. Himself a Berliner, he would have preferred to have a school in Berlin, one of the great capitals of the world, rather than in Weimar, a small country town best known for its associations with Goethe, Schiller, Liszt and Nietzsche. It is one of the ironies of history that the Bauhaus, which was finally dreamed up in a Berlin on the very edge of a proletarian revolution, should have its first home in a set of buildings designed in 1904 by Henry van de Velde at the request of the Grand Duke of Saxony. A comparable irony was built into the inaugural prospectus of the Bauhaus, which was written by Walter Gropius in April, 1919. "We must all return to the

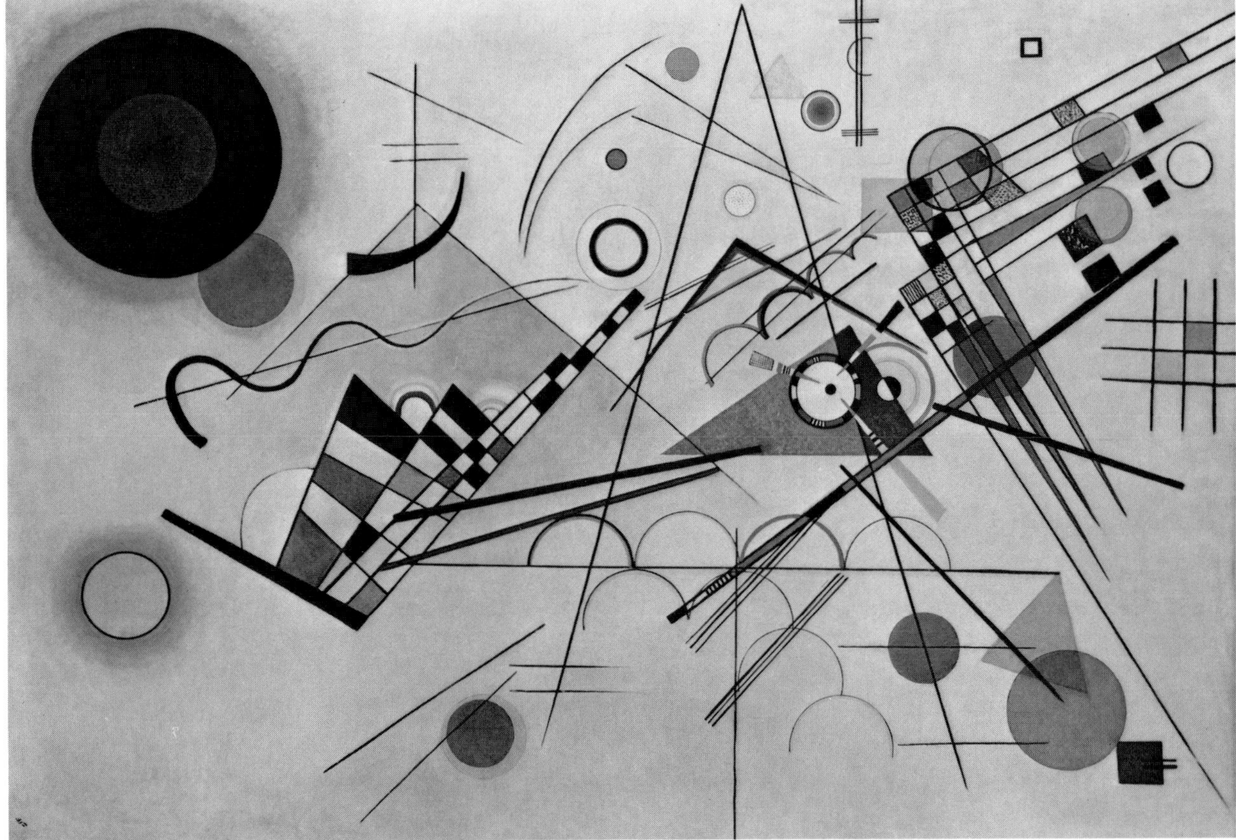

Wassily Kandinsky.
Composition 8.
1923.
Oil on canvas, 55½ inches × 6 feet 7⅛ inches.
The Solomon R. Guggenheim Museum, New York

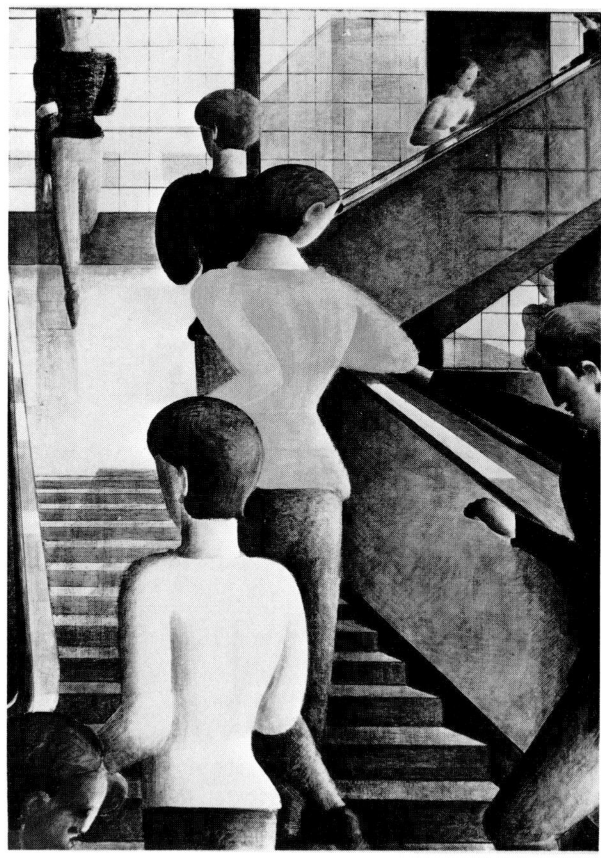

Oskar Schlemmer.
Bauhaus Stairway.
1932.
Oil on canvas,
63⅞ × 45 inches.
The Museum of
Modern Art, New
York. Gift of Philip
Johnson

crafts!" was its theme; and although Gropius looked forward to "the new structure of the future" which was to "rise toward heaven from the hands of a million workers like the crystal symbol of a new faith," the structure which appeared on the program itself was of purely medieval inspiration.

Between 1919 and 1933 the Bauhaus had on its staff, at one time or another, as brilliant a group of men as ever taught. The New Yorker who wishes to realize the extent of their radiation has only to walk around midtown Manhattan. The Seagram Building is by Mies van der Rohe (Bauhaus, 1930–33) and Philip Johnson; the Whitney Museum is by Marcel Breuer (Bauhaus, 1920–28); the Pan Am Building above the train shed at Grand Central Station is by Walter Gropius (Bauhaus, 1919–28) and his partners. The collection of the Solomon R. Guggenheim Museum is dominated by Wassily Kandinsky (Bauhaus, 1922–33).

It is difficult to go into an office that calls itself modern and not find chairs designed at the Bauhaus by either Breuer or Mies. In a more general way, Moholy-Nagy (Bauhaus, 1923–28) produced a revolution in communications techniques and Herbert Bayer (Bauhaus, 1921–28) a revolution in graphic design, which still influence every American who wants to get a message across. Generations of American students owe much to the painter Josef Albers (Bauhaus, 1920–33), who began teaching at Black Mountain College in 1933 and was teaching classes at Yale as recently as 1960. Not merely the example but the name of the Bauhaus crossed the Atlantic when, in 1937, Moholy-Nagy founded The New Bauhaus: American School of Design (since 1939 The Institute of Design) in Chicago. It would be fair to say that American life is permeated by the influence of the Bauhaus and that even those who have never heard of the original school have had reason to be grateful to it.

This is not to say that the history of the Bauhaus was either consistent or glorious. There were changes of internal policy, changes of personnel, changes of orientation. Though outwardly nonpolitical, the school depended for its existence on support from whatever party was in power; the times were turbulent, as often as not, and things were done which would not have been done had the school been functioning with ample funds in a stable society. Internal disputes set individual against individual, and discipline against discipline. Sometimes students complained that they did not see their famous teachers for months on end. A regime which aimed at the updating of the medieval guild system would be followed by one which crossbred lectures on Gestalt psychology with compulsory physical training. It is easy to speak ill of a school which aimed in 1919 to "build the cathedral of Socialism," only to peter out in August, 1933, with the announcement that it was closing down not because of any reluctance to make concessions to the Nazis but because it simply hadn't the money to go on.

Yet the indispensable thing in the 1920s was to keep the Bauhaus in being as a laboratory in which ideas of every kind could be tested in practice, from the prototype of a mass-produced house (summer, 1923) to the experimental ballets devised by Oskar Schlemmer (Bauhaus, 1920–29). Oskar Schlemmer's activity was fundamental both to the sculpture workshop at the Bauhaus and to its theatrical ventures. His experiments in the field of ballet can still be reconstructed with hallucinatory impact. Something of their effect—part sculptural, part humanized robot—can be judged from Schlemmer's paintings. In *Bauhaus Stairway*, the upward movement of students on the main staircase of the Bauhaus can be read symbolically: a new world lies on the next landing.

The Bauhaus propositioned the future continually. Already in the mid-20s Gropius was experimenting with new forms for architecture that would be seen to best advantage from the air; Ludwig Hirschfeld-Mack (Bauhaus, 1920–27) was encouraged to "make the immaterial visible" in his reflected-light compositions with musical accompaniment; on the level of the everyday, anyone who wanted a Bauhaus wardrobe, a Bauhaus letterhead, a length of Bauhaus fabric or a roll of Bauhaus wallpaper could count on finding one. The Bauhaus was meant to cover the whole spectrum of human activity, from the loftiest and most spiritual to the plain and down-to-earth, and from handcrafting and Oriental mysticism to electronic music and the six-screen cinema. It was for this reason that when the school was in danger in 1924, an international committee was formed to support it; science was represented on that committee by Albert Einstein, music by Arnold Schoenberg, painting by Marc Chagall and Oskar Kokoschka, architecture and design by the veteran pioneer Josef Hoffmann. These people knew that the Bauhaus was invaluable to a convalescent Europe, and that for all its internal divergences and contradictions it wanted to give everyone, everywhere, a better life.

As to just what that better life should be like, the version in favor varied from year to year. (It seems likely, for instance, that the Bauhaus authorities were none too pleased when Theo van Doesburg arrived in Weimar in 1921 and set up public classes of his own.) Johannes Itten (Bauhaus, 1919–23) was the author of the first version of the foundation course which all students had to take; but his mixture of esoteric wisdom with the wearing of specially designed robes and a mandatory Bauhaus diet with quadrupled garlic ration was too much for his colleagues, and Itten was replaced in 1923 by László Moholy-Nagy. Moholy-Nagy was a one-man compendium of the postwar pacific International. He had shared a studio with Kurt Schwitters, he had attended the Constructivist Conference which had been called by van Doesburg in Weimar in 1922, he knew Lissitzky, he was familiar with the achievement of Malevich. By the

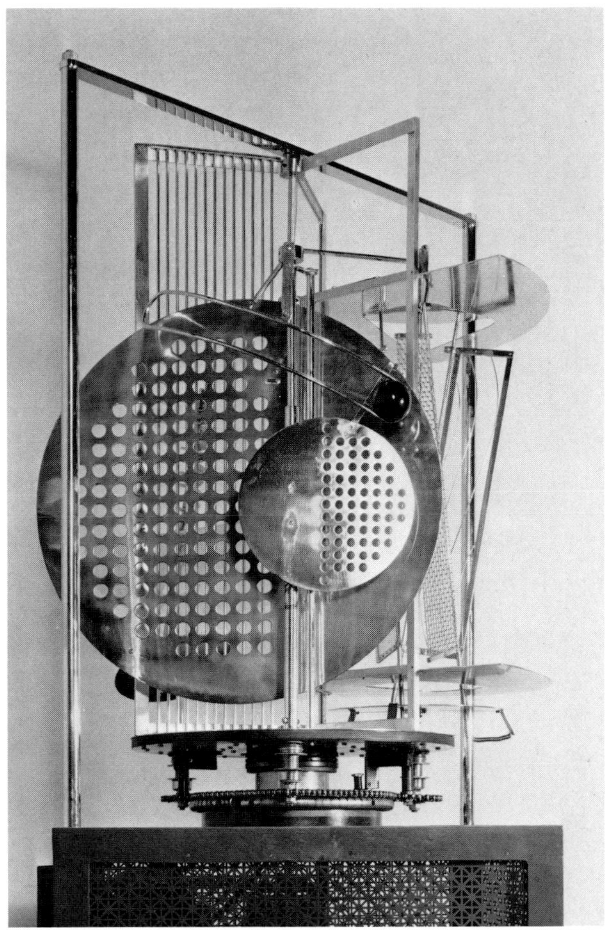

László Moholy-Nagy. *Light-Space Modulator.* 1923–30. Metal, glass and plastic, 59½ × 27½ × 27½ inches. Busch-Reisinger Museum, Harvard University, Cambridge, Mass.

time he arrived in Chicago as a refugee in 1937 he had distinguished himself as painter, filmmaker, stage designer, kinetic sculptor, photographer, editor, book designer, cultural historian, poster maker, interior designer and above all as one of this century's great teachers.

He believed that the manipulation of light would one day be one of the most eloquent of all the techniques which art has at its disposal. He envisaged projections onto clouds, three-dimensional displays of colored light through which the spectator was free to walk, and even more grandiose light spectacles which would be viewed from a seat in a specially chartered airplane. Light and color would not merely make use of space with a new freedom; they would remake and remodel space in ways never before dreamed of. His mobile *Light-Space Modulator* was a first start in these directions.

It may, in fact, be Moholy-Nagy in the end who most thoroughly validates the Bauhaus' reputation for modernity. By the second half of the 1920s people were already remarking on the fact that the school was dominated by people whose careers had begun before 1914, and that the arts-and-crafts element in the Bauhaus had always augured oddly for an institution which prided itself on being up-to-date. With Moholy-Nagy, no such complaints were possible. He, if anyone, was alert to all the possibilities of his time. (In 1922 he had painted a picture by telephone, giving orders so exact that they could be carried out by any skilled executant.) In his books *The New Vision: From Material to Architecture* and *Vision in Motion* an attentive reader will find a running fire of ideas and injunctions as to how best to bring about the reintegration of art and society.

Moholy-Nagy said in 1922 that "the art of our century, its mirror and its voice, is Constructivism." In this he followed Lissitzky, Gabo and Tatlin, all of whom were convinced that new materials called for a new art, and a new art which would above all be dynamic and kinetic in its allegiances; a clean break was to be made with the static apartness of older art, and with its traditional stance on wall or floor. There was inevitably some conflict of direction between the teaching which set out this point of view and the teaching of Wassily Kandinsky, Paul Klee (Bauhaus, 1920–31) and Lyonel Feininger (Bauhaus 1919–33); these three were "fine artists" in the traditional sense insofar as their end product was predominantly an oil painting on canvas. Kandinsky was still preoccupied with states of being rather than with the potential of technology; and as far as the Bauhaus was concerned he regarded the inclusion of his ideas as fundamental to the mix. Mies van der Rohe told Kandinsky in September, 1932, that as director of the Bauhaus he meant to curtail, if not actually abolish, the art classes in the school. Kandinsky wrote back that every student had the right to rediscover those inward links with Nature which had been lost for centuries. Dependence on the outward look of Nature was more and more a thing of the past in painting; what modern art called for, and what Kandinsky tried to provide, was the spiritual element: "Not the shell, but the nut," as he put it. The art classes were kept on.

With Paul Klee there was also no question of a blanket rejection of the past, or of a surrender to new materials from which new magic might or might not be conjured. "Klee taught us," one student wrote later, "to see the composition and structure of animal and vegetable life. Not only did he teach us to perceive it visually, but in his theory of forms he taught us the principles of creativity. He showed us the all-encompassing synthesis which embraces all life, whether organic or inorganic. Everything—zoology, biology, chemistry, physics, astronomy, literature, typography—helped us to understand how with every bit of our existence and every one of our activities we are part of humanity and part of the rhythm of the cosmos."

In his art, as in his teaching, Paul Klee let the whole world come in. When it was a matter of sorting out, he was the best man in the business. There was no such thing as a situation that he

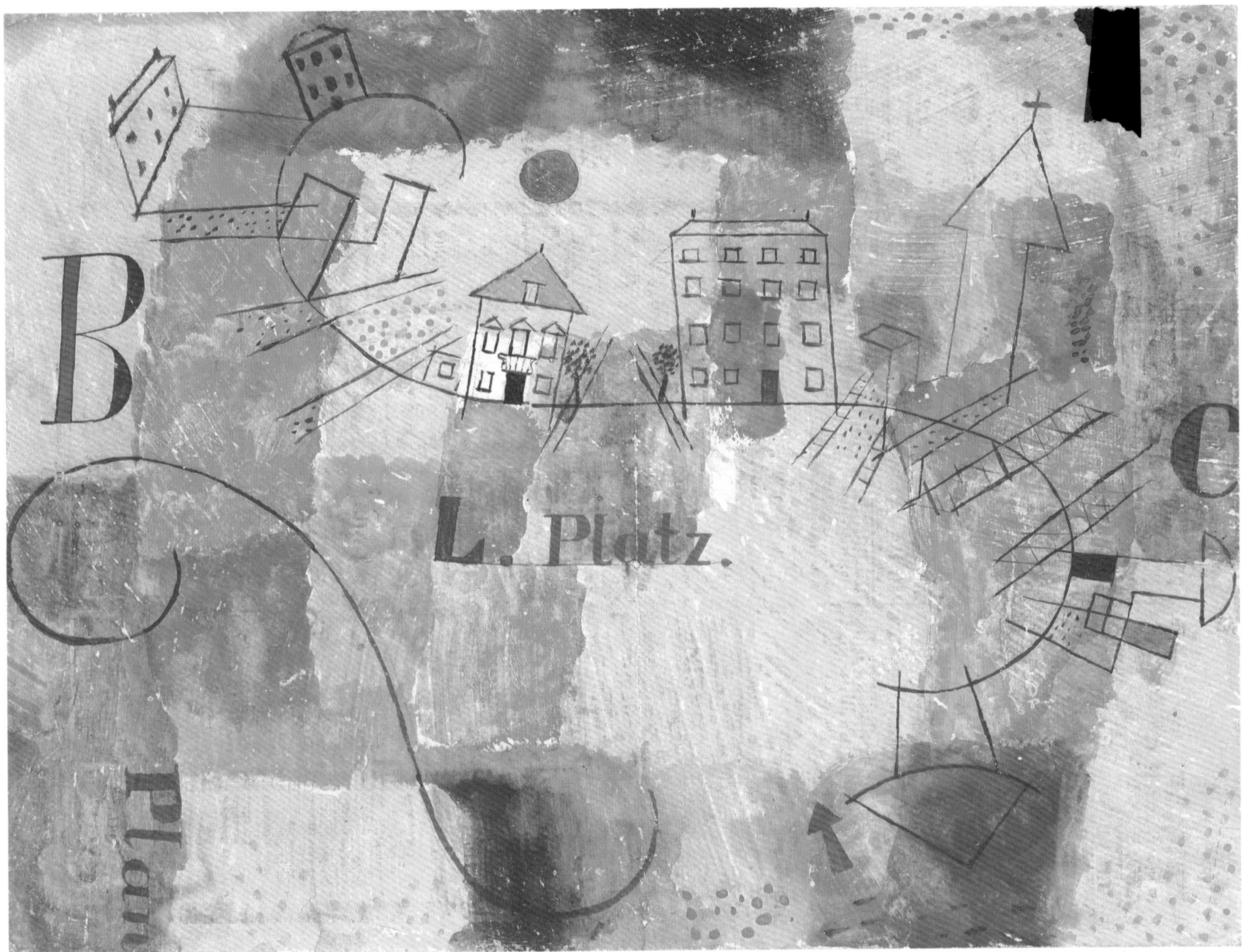

Paul Klee. *Building the L-Platz.* 1923. Watercolor, gouache, chalk and newsprint on cardboard, 15¾ × 20½ inches. Kunstsammlung Nordrhein-Westfalen, Düsseldorf

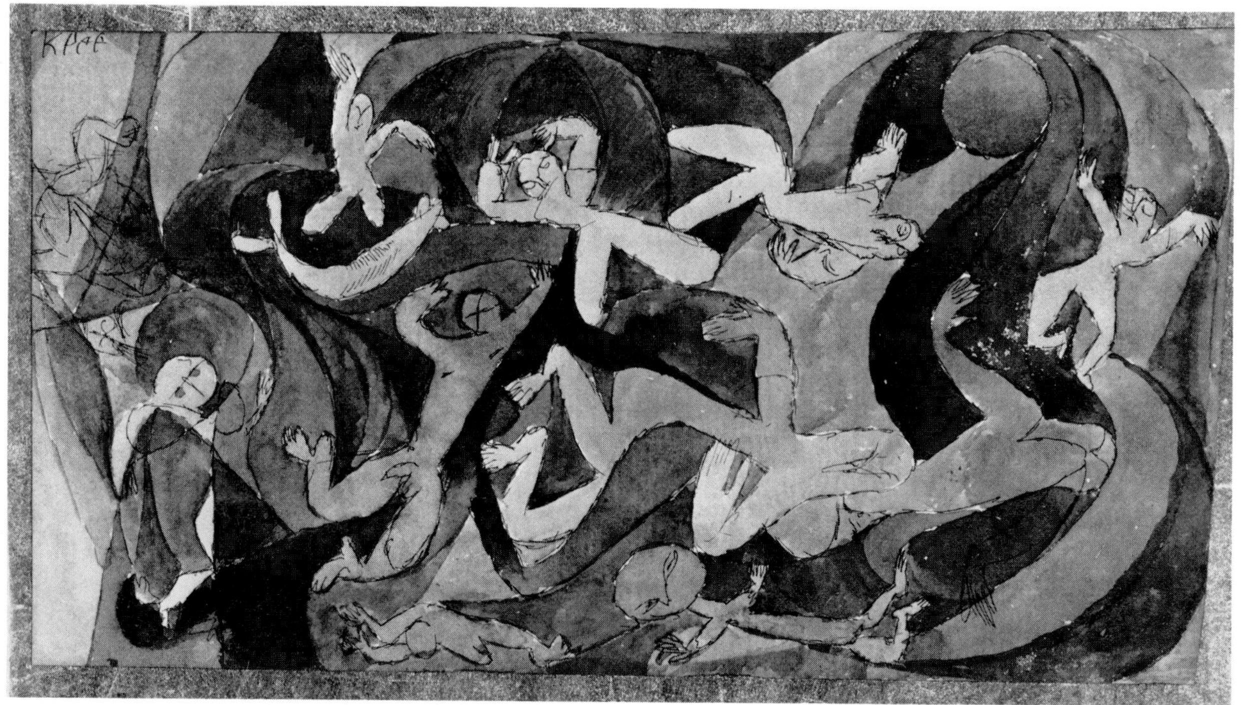

Paul Klee.
The Hopeless Ones.
1914.
Watercolor,
5 × 8½ inches.
Marian Willard
Johnson, New York

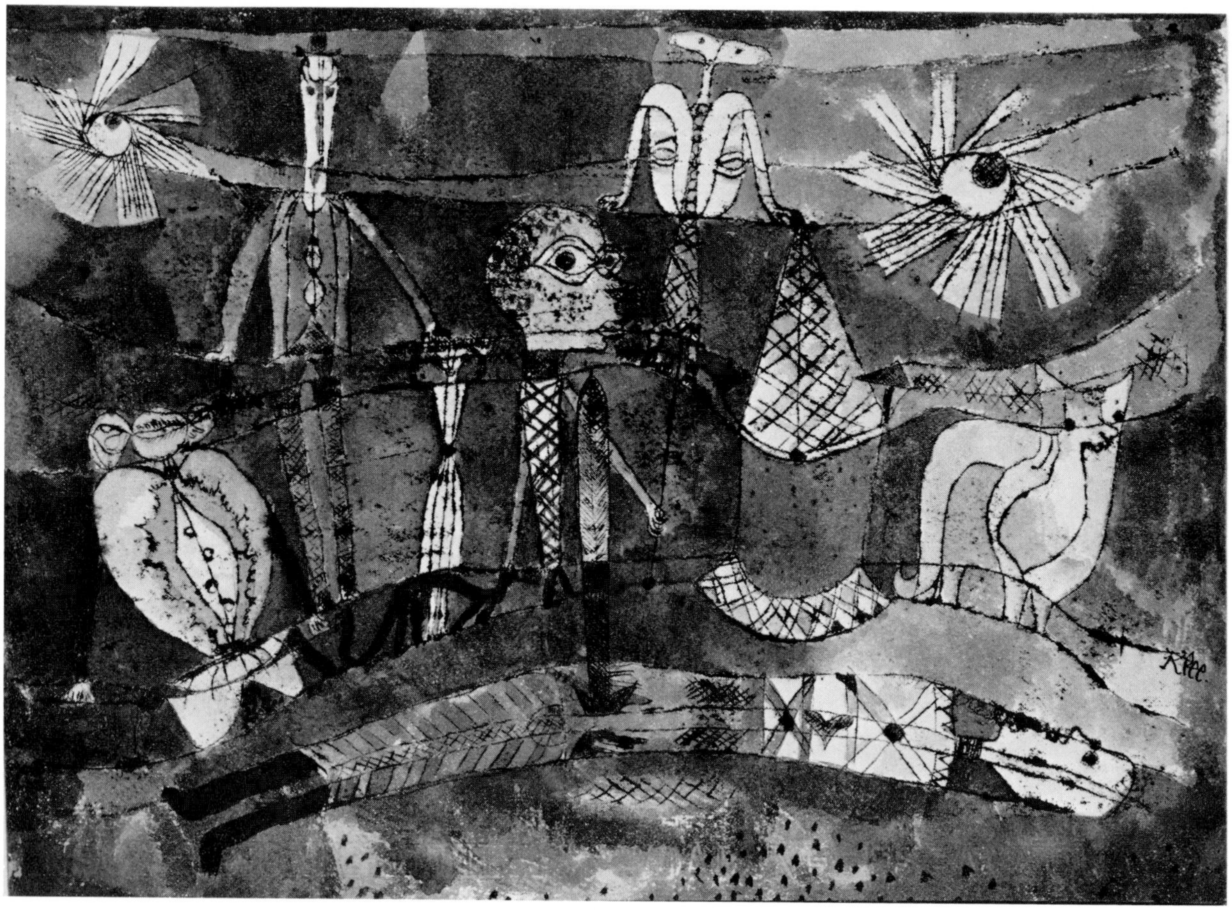

Paul Klee.
The End of the Last Act of a Drama.
1920.
Watercolor on
transfer drawing,
8⅛ × 11⅜ inches.
The Museum of
Modern Art, New
York. Gift of Dr.
and Mrs. Allan Roos

could not deal with in paintings—most of them quite small—whose delicacy belies the strength and the firmness of what he had to say. In 1914, for instance, he painted a little picture called *The Hopeless Ones.* Time was running out for the old order in Europe in 1914; and for all its characteristic modesty of scale *The Hopeless Ones* gives us most vividly a sense of civilization gone out of control, and of the incapacity of individual human beings to master destiny.

Klee's paintings are sometimes taken to be pure whimsy, but in fact they almost always have their point of departure in something that he had observed with particular precision in the world around him. He loved the theater in all its aspects, from the homemade marionettes which he once produced for his small son to the sweep and splendor of great actors at full stretch. He once likened the last scene of Mozart's opera *Don Giovanni* to "the moment after a thunderstorm when people look out of the window to see who's still alive"; and in *The End of the Last Act of a Drama* he portrays a moment of that sort, with the body of the main character laid out across the length of the foreground and the rest of the company standing silent and aghast. Only the cat (on the right) and the sun and the moon in the sky go about their business as usual.

By the time he was on the edge of middle life Klee knew everything there was to know about how to make a picture: what codes to use, how to combine them, when to surprise the observer and when to ease him back onto familiar ground. As a teacher at the Bauhaus he made all this available to his students. But there remained something that could be neither taught nor learnt: the imaginative energy which Klee possessed in the highest degree. *Building the L-Platz* is, on one level, as flat as the map which it pretends to be: "B" and "C" stand for adjacent areas on that map, the word "Plan" drives the message further home, and the designation "L-Platz" marks out a space on which nothing will be built. Klee has drawn in the roads which meet at the L-Platz, and the houses, the church and the railroad tracks which form part of the scene. Sometimes they are in diagram form; sometimes they are realized in depth, as happens with the tree-lined road in the center. The picture pulls several ways, and the wiry but strictly evocative drawing is offset by patches of color which harmonize in ways unrelated to the principal image.

Klee was not at all a globe-trotter by nature. But like many another hyperintelligent Swiss, he made the very most of such journeys as he actually made. Faced with a new kind of landscape, he at once wondered how best to code it. All systems of notation fascinated him. In *Pastorale* he mimicked the look of an incised tablet, covered it with forms of the kind that are universal among doodlers, and yet ended up with a painting that exactly evokes the open arches of North African architecture, the carefully cultivated strips of land that have to be coaxed into growing anything at all, the spiked forms of trees and (at the very top) a sliver of pale blue to stand for the sky.

When he went to Egypt in the winter of 1928–29 he was deeply impressed by the patterns of Egyptian agriculture: long strips of tilled land, precisely parallel to one another but varying in width, with here and there an irrigation channel to offer a contrast both of color and of texture. On his return to Europe he completed a series of pictures which derived from this experience. Some of them bore titles like *Upper Egypt,* or *Monument on the Edge of Fertile Country,* which made the reference doubly clear. Others "moved far from Nature"—in Klee's own words—"and found their way back to reality." Among the latter, *Fire in the Evening* is the finest. There is nothing directly illustrative about it, but the rectangle of brilliant red, just right of center, stands out as a fire would stand out in the far distances of the Nile Valley. In the foreground, below, are browns and greens, colors of earth and vegetation, hooded by the onset of the night; at the top, unbroken bands of pink and blue stand for the last flaring of the light. The point of departure was the stratified look of

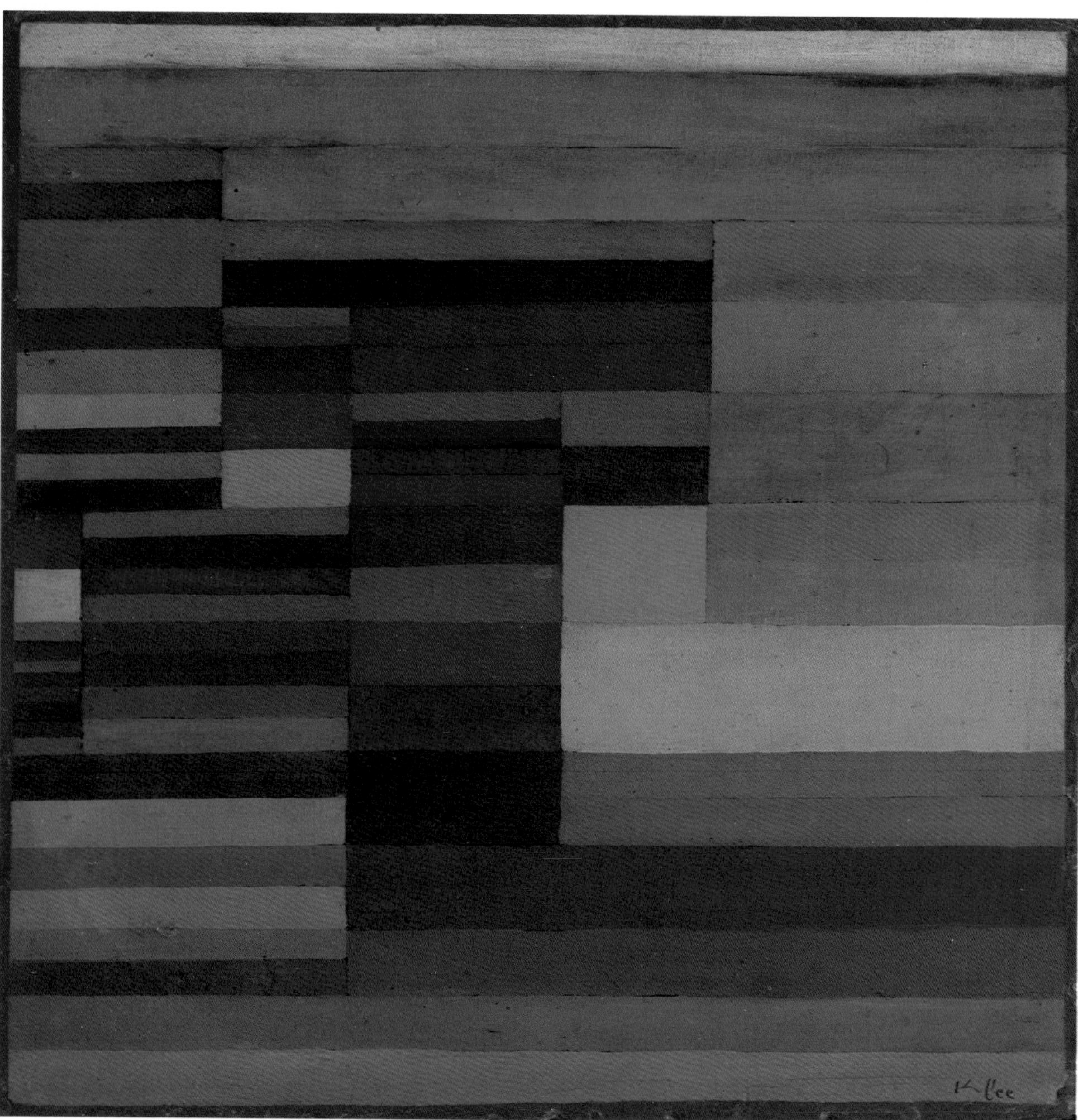

Paul Klee.
Fire in the Evening.
1929.
Oil on cardboard,
13⅜ × 13¼ inches.
The Museum of
Modern Art, New
York.
Mr. and Mrs.
Joachim Jean
Aberbach Fund

Egyptian agriculture; but from that point onward Klee felt free to find his own way back to reality.

It will by now be clear that the Bauhaus was too complex and too variable an institution to be epitomized in a few sentences. But at its best it was powered by the fresh-start syndrome to which I referred initially. Whether it was Gropius with the transparent, wraparound design for the new Bauhaus building in Dessau, or Moholy-Nagy with his plans for the projection of cinematic images onto clouds of tinted vapor, or Kandinsky and Klee rethinking the pictorial process from the first dot onward, there was a determination to begin again from the beginning. It was an international and collective adventure, which allied gifted Berliners, with their inborn sense of emergency and openness to ideas from all over, to a Russian, a Swiss, and a Hungarian, as well as to ideas first mooted by Dutchmen.

From this concert of the nations one great European voice was lacking, however; France contributed nothing to the Bauhaus, and the Bauhaus might as well have been in Kamchatka for all the impact that it made on French thinking and French life.

There were several good reasons for this. French life, unlike German life, had not been brought to a near standstill at the end of World War I. The fundamental re-analysis for which the Bauhaus stood had no appeal in France, where it was taken for granted that the best art had been made in Paris and would go on being made there until the end of time. The best and brightest natures in France were not, on the whole, preoccupied with the making of a new society; nor was the old society disposed to let them try. The French were complacent, but they had a great deal to be complacent about: not least, a life style which, as visiting Americans saw for themselves, was uniquely agreeable. Men and women were left alone to be themselves, in France in the 1920s, with a civilized discretion which it would be hard to parallel today.

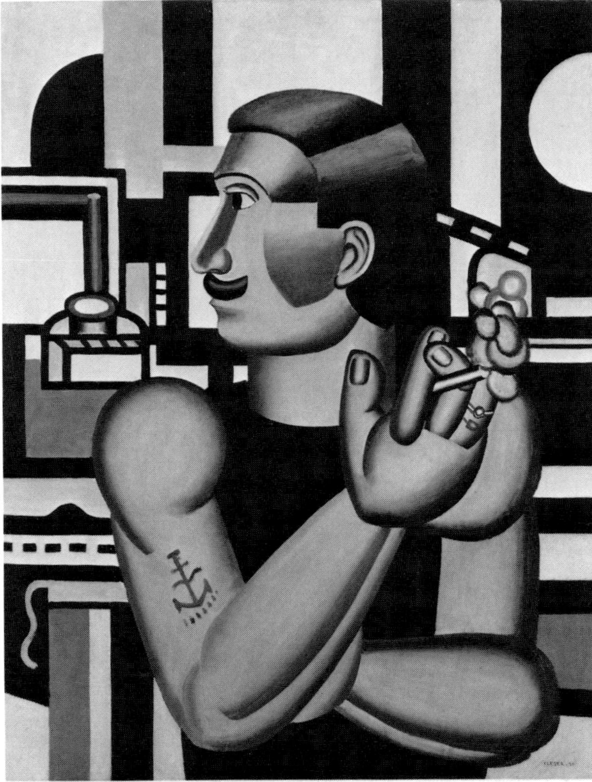

Fernand Léger. *The Mechanic.* 1920. Oil on canvas, 45½ × 34¾ inches. National Gallery of Canada, Ottawa

So the idea of the fresh start did not have too many attractions in France. At a time when Monet was still alive, and when Matisse, Braque, Picasso, Bonnard and Max Ernst were in full output, the case for starting again all over—in art, at any rate—was really very weak. But there was one major artist who did, even so, purpose to reformulate the relationship between art and society, and that artist was Fernand Léger. As we have already seen, Léger as a soldier in World War I formed social allegiances which were remote from those of the moneyed man of taste. There was nothing exclusive or doctrinaire about these allegiances—he was delighted, for instance, to make friends with the American expatriates Gerald and Sara Murphy, and through them to sample the world which was memorialized by F. Scott Fitzgerald in *Tender Is the Night;* but it seemed to him self-evident that a new kind of art and a new kind of man should go together. And in a painting called *The Mechanic* of 1920 Léger gave that new kind of man the treatment that painters reserved in earlier times for the great ones of the earth—he made him immortal, in other words.

The Mechanic is so compelling, so absolutely true to one particular moment in time, that it puts the social historian out of business. Here is the archetypal French working man for whom the machine might still prove to be an instrument of social liberation. He is seen in profile, like the kings and queens on their gold and silver coins. With his nautical tattoo, his sleeked-down hair and his heavy mustache, his cigarette in full combustion and a pair of rings on his well-fleshed third finger, he stands for the belief that the life of the industrial masses need not be without dignity, nor the individual mass-man become a disinherited cipher. He is neither heroicized nor sentimentalized, but seen for what he is: a man with a mind of his own, who is at one with his machines and could ask no greater fulfillment than to be in charge of them.

In this painting, and even more so in the panorama called *The City* of 1919, Léger presented the new metropolitan scene as an earthly paradise: a place of bright, flat color, simplified machine forms, and staircases that climbed straight into the sky. No such city existed, but Léger hoped that his paintings would help to bring one about. Nor did his optimism exceed the bounds of practicality. He never pretended, for instance, that the role of the human being in the new city would be anything but subordinate. The human being was shown as an object among other objects: a color note, or an abstract, simplified volume. He was not individualized—except when, as happens in *The*

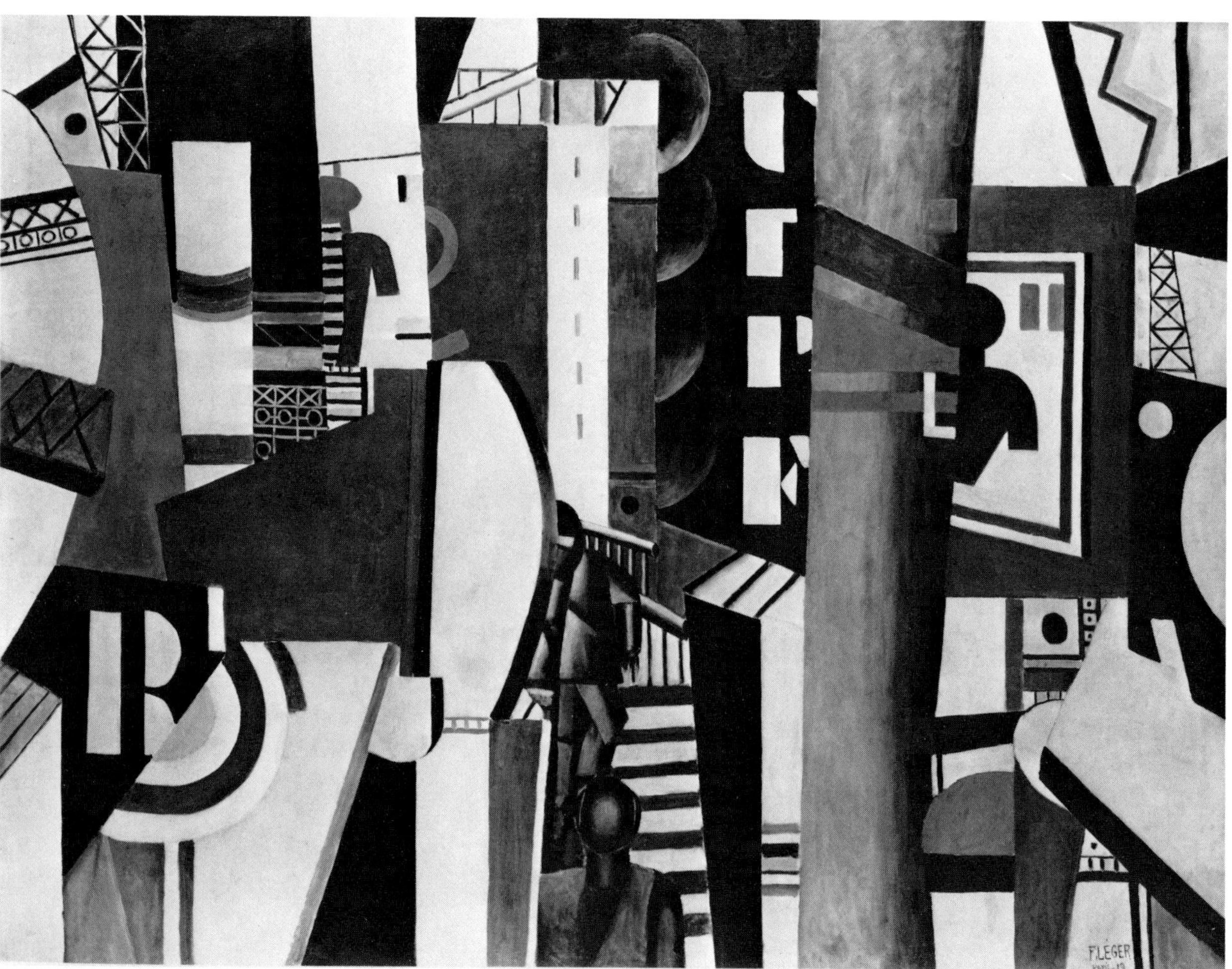

Fernand Léger.
The City. 1919.
Oil on canvas, 6 feet 6¾ inches × 9 feet 9¼ inches.
Philadelphia Museum of Art. The A. E. Gallatin Collection

Mechanic, he was off duty and could smoke a cigarette. But neither was he diminished by his objecthood: rather, it raised him to the level—that of a functional elegance, a stripped-down beauty independent of hierarchical precedent—that was the mark of every other element in the new metropolitan scene.

These were not undertakings in which Léger could hope for support from his French contemporaries; but they did commend themselves, very much indeed, to the members of the De Stijl group. Piet Mondrian was living in Paris from 1919 onward; he had written enthusiastically about Léger in an early issue of *De Stijl,* and it seems likely that the background of *The Mechanic* was prompted by van Doesburg's paintings and, even more, by Mondrian's insistence on the power of the straight line to equilibrate even the most complicated subject matter. In 1920 Léger also made friends with the architect who came nearest to realizing his dream of the new metropolis—Le Corbusier. Le Corbusier in 1925 gave Léger his first mural commission, and in 1928 Léger returned the compliment by giving a lecture on Le Corbusier in Berlin.

Léger also differed from Matisse and Braque in that he looked about him for aspects of modern communications systems which could be annexed for painting. *The City* is, for instance, on the scale of the movie screen; Léger had been keenly interested in the movies since Apollinaire took him to a Chaplin program in 1916, and in the year after he painted *The Mechanic* he collaborated on a film called *La Roue* with that pioneer of the epic film, Abel Gance. *The City* can be read as an anthology of cinematic method at the time, with its abrupt changes of scale and focus, its rapid crosscutting from one image to another, its purposeful singling out of incidents which in everyday life might seem trivial or escape notice altogether. (In 1924 Léger made a film of his own, the storyless *Ballet mécanique,* with the American cameraman Dudley Murphy. In this, as in his paintings of the same date, he took objects of everyday use, abstracted them from their normal contexts, and banished all attempts at "atmosphere" and all references to Nature or the human body, and by the skillful use of crosscutting, repetition and rhythmic emphasis was able to give the objects in question a planned and calculated identity of an entirely new sort.)

What Léger had in mind at this time was an aesthetic of concern: a scale of values which would admit to the canon of beauty such manifestations of the new age as the Motor Show, the Aviation Show, the Boat Show, the neon sign, the cross section of a spark plug and—yes, why not—the soda syphon. The ultimate ambition of the aesthetic of concern was that every man and every woman should feel part of "an unhurried, peaceful and well-regulated society, in which Beauty is in the natural order of things and need neither be gushed over nor romanticized."

In this, Léger was at one with his friend Le Corbusier, and at one with Amédée Ozenfant, the teacher and theorist with whom Léger was to set up a school in 1924. Le Corbusier had in many ways a middle-class orientation—"in a decent house," he wrote in 1926, "the servants' staircase does not go through the drawing room"—but he did nonetheless envisage a classless aesthetic of construction, in which houses would go up all in one piece, "assembled the way Henry Ford assembles cars," and "built like an aircraft, with the same structural methods, lightweight framing, metal bracers and tubular supports." In this, as in so many pronouncements of the period immediately after World War I, the syndrome of the fresh start is fundamental. And the best way to make a fresh start, so it then seemed, was to define the irreducible essentials and begin again from there.

Here the painter had the advantage over the architect. The architect needed a patron and could be betrayed by him not only while he was building the house but at any time after it was finished; the painter had complete control over his canvas. He could not compel anyone to look at it, but at least he alone was in charge. Le Corbusier had so many unhappy experiences in his architec-

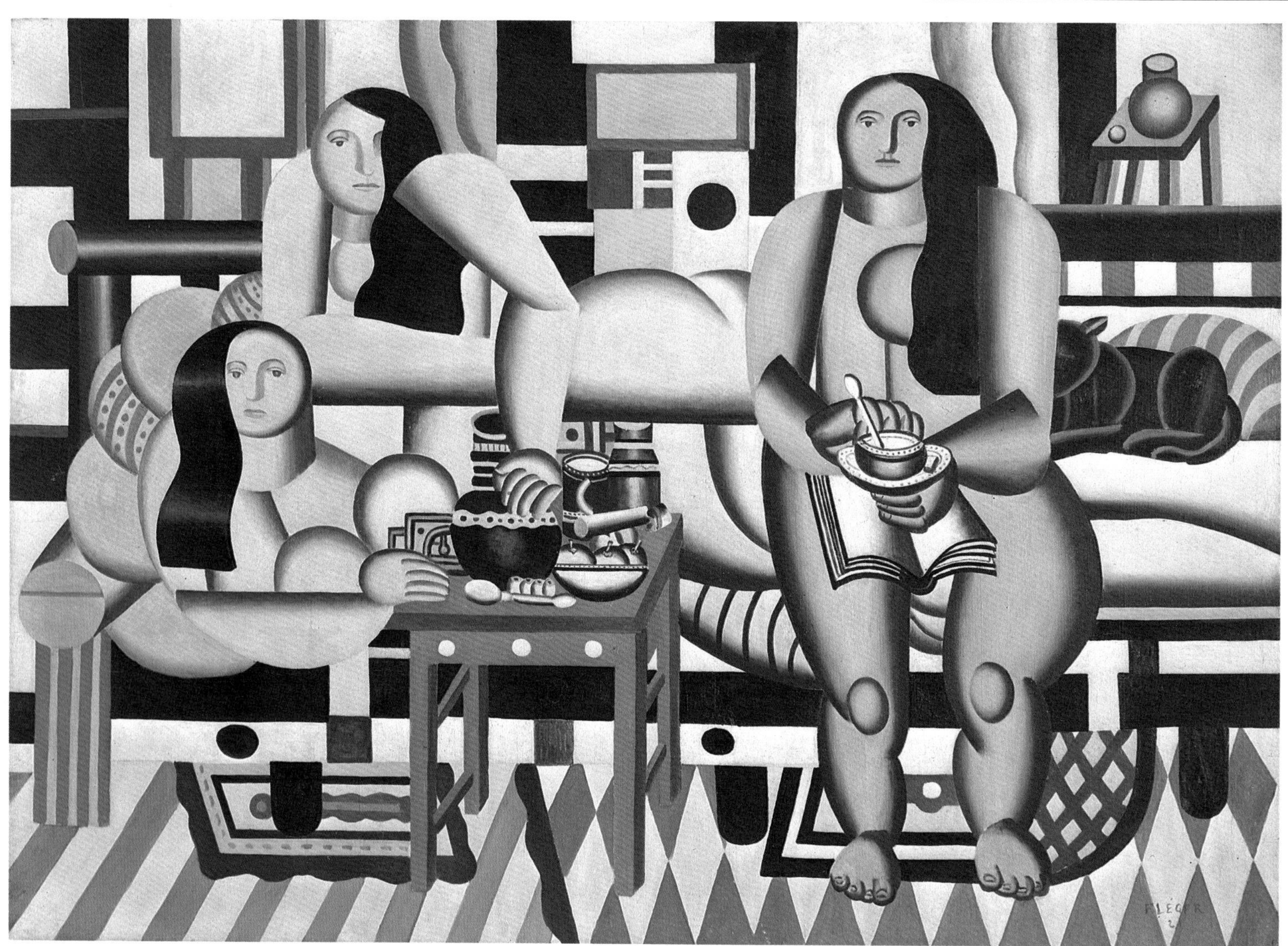

Fernand Léger. *Three Women (Le Grand Déjeuner).* 1921.
Oil on canvas, 6 feet ¼ inch × 8 feet 3 inches.
The Museum of Modern Art, New York. Mrs. Simon Guggenheim Fund

tural career—projects scorned and derided, projects acclaimed but unfulfilled, projects completed but later degraded by their inhabitants—that he set what often seemed an exaggerated value on his activity as a painter. Neither he nor Ozenfant wished to seduce in their paintings. "The aim of pure science," they wrote in 1919, "is to express natural laws through the search for constants. The aim of serious art is, likewise, the expression of invariants." The work of art thus arrived at should, in their view, be "generalized, static, and expressive of the invariant." An absolutist outlook of this sort is often modified in practice, but Ozenfant and Le Corbusier were not the men to waver; and their paintings had almost always, and not surprisingly, a look of the drawing board.

They are important to us, even so, and not least because we can learn from them how rich and various, by comparison, was Léger's creative nature. Beside the severe and careful distillations of Ozenfant and Le Corbusier, Léger's *Three Women* of 1921 is the work of a born painter who can re-create the monumental structures of the European past in terms of the new art, the new technology, and the new styles of living which the third decade of the 20th century had already brought into being. Léger liked to present himself as the spokesman of the industrial working man (though in point of fact he was the son of a prosperous cattle-breeder and had never done a day's work in a factory), and in his published writings he never stressed his knowledge of the French classical tradition. But, just as Naum Gabo said that "the history of Russian art had more influence on our generation than Cubism, Futurism and all the rest of the Western ideologies put together," so there is often behind Léger's most down-to-earth compositions a discreet echo of the brothers Le Nain, who proved with their still and reserved studies of peasant life in the 17th century that even the humblest among us can be the subject matter of great art.

Léger had worked in an architect's office, and he had a great architect, Le Corbusier, for his close friend and colleague. He liked to introduce into his paintings what was in effect an ideal architecture. This was a matter of forms reduced to an ultimate simplicity: a horizontal plane, or a vertical one, undecorated except by the application of a perfectly judged quantity of pure color. This architecture was intended neither to excite nor to distract. On the contrary, "in this new environment a man can be seen. Everything has been thought out. Against these big calm areas the human face assumes its rightful status. A nose, an eye, a foot, a hand or a jacket button becomes a precise reality." As with this imagined architecture, so with the paintings: an aesthetic of concern reinvented the notion of human dignity. This is something that every generation has to do for itself; but there are times when a shared concern has seemed to sweep across the civilized world, and the period which we have examined here was one of them.

A LOST LEADERSHIP

Something was lost to Europe in the first half of this century that can never be put back again.

This is not a matter of physical destruction—though nothing can restore the look of the European countryside before industrialization, or of Dresden and Warsaw, Rotterdam and the City of London, before World War II. It has nothing to do with economics: most people in most parts of Europe live better than ever before. It has nothing to do with world domination: not many young people mourn the days when Great Britain ruled India, when much of Africa was dominated by Germany and Italy and when France and Holland had fiefs in Southeast Asia. If Western Europe is moving toward federation, that is all to the good; we can only rejoice if a war between France and Germany now seems hardly more likely than a war between New Hampshire and Vermont. A great many exceptional individuals withdrew from Europe in the 1930s—among them Einstein, Mondrian, Schoenberg, Mies van der Rohe, Thomas Mann, Stravinsky—but the loss which I have in mind is not of them. It is of a more general and a more fundamental sort.

What was lost to Europe between 1900 and 1950, and above all between 1939 and 1945, was the sense of predestined leadership which had been taken for granted since the days of Plato and Virgil, Charlemagne and the builders of Chartres Cathedral. It was to everyone's advantage—or so it had seemed to those who had the power—that the world should be run by Europeans. European ethics, European systems of law, European science, European medicine, European organization and the European capacity for disinterested enquiry were self-evidently superior to all others; when a European of the class of 1880 read that God had created Man in His own image he put down the book and said, "He was thinking of ME —and He did a pretty good job."

In political and social terms this assurance was somewhat battered by the end of the 19th century. But in literature, music and the arts the heroic age of modernism—1905 to 1914, let us say—did much to confirm it. A minority of far-seeing natures had sensed that there might have to be, at the very least, some radical adjustments: what is put before us in Thomas Mann's *Death in Venice* (1912) is not the death of a middle-aged man of letters but the death of a certain idea of Europe. (Europe might not, that is to say, have all the answers. Beauty could destroy, as well as uplift, and plague could break out where nothing had been foreseen but exalted pleasure.) Nor could an intelligent reader of Joseph Conrad's *Heart of Darkness* (1902) fail to sense that the European domination of distant and alien peoples was entering upon its terminal phase. But the general tenor of life during the heroic age of modernism was affirmative: looking at Picasso's *Les Demoiselles d'Avignon* (1907), listening to Stravinsky's *The Rite of Spring* (1913), admiring the lucid disentanglements of human oddity in Sigmund Freud's *Totem and Taboo* (1913), feeling our way into the first volume (1913) of Marcel Proust's *Remembrance of Things Past,* we recognize in every case a determination to master the new dimensions of human nature and, by mastering them, to keep Europe on top.

Such was the density of European achievement before 1914, such the sense of shared energy, and such the imperiousness of the historical logic which prompted a breakthrough in one domain after another, that in comparison the achievement of the 1920s and '30s is bound to seem dispersed, occasional and unsystematic. A four years' war is destructive of moral energy; D. H. Lawrence put that point in *Aaron's Rod* (1922) when he said that after World War I Europe was like a soldier in shock, outwardly unhurt but in reality "wounded somewhere deeper than the brain." Before long, what the French thinker Julien Benda in 1927 called *La Trahison des clercs*—the betrayal of society by those best fitted to guide it—had come to characterize every department of European life; politically, morally, economically, Europe was decaying, hour by hour. It should not surprise us that at such a time the masters of the modern movement decided, one after another, to take stock of the European tradition and to see how much of it was worth preserving and restating and how much might as well be thrown away.

There was in all this an element of fastidious differentiation. If the proceedings had sometimes a touch of Savonarola—all fire, all ice, all righteous condemnation—there was much more of Montaigne, and of Montaigne's delight in turning over the facts one by one, at leisure and without prejudice. To painters like Bonnard and Braque, and to a sculptor like Brancusi, today's craving for instantaneous approval would have seemed both childish and self-defeating; one of the things that they had inherited from the centuries of European hegemony was the right to a privileged silence.

The Rumanian-born sculptor Constantin Brancusi is, in fact, a very good example of this. Brancusi was born in 1876 in the humblest of circumstances in a farming village in the foothills of the Transylvanian mountains. From the outset of his career he was clearly very gifted; but when he decided to go off to Paris in his middle 20s he was so poor that he had to walk almost all the way. He was quickly recognized—by Apollinaire, by Matisse, by Léger, by Marcel Duchamp—as someone quite out of the ordinary; but although Paris remained his base till his death in 1957 he never had a one-man exhibition there. His first one-man show was in New York in 1914. The photographer Edward Steichen installed it, the collector John Quinn took a great liking to his work, and in 1921 the *Little Review* ran a special Brancusi number with appreciations by Ezra Pound and others. None of this was allowed to interrupt the serene rhythms of Brancusi's working life. He would as soon keep his work as sell it; pieces like the 90-inch-high *Caryatid* stood around in his studio, unremarked and unrecorded, for 40 years; with his total immunity to fuss and flummery and his streak of peasant cunning, he was the epitome of anti-careerism. Only perfection would do; and if perfection took forever, that was all right with him.

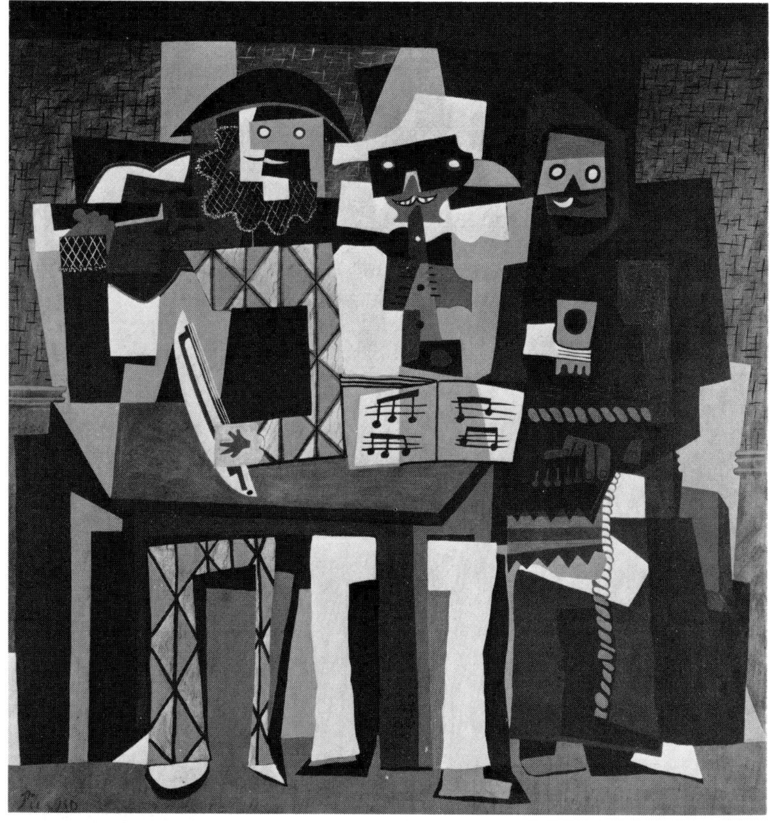

Pablo Picasso.
Three Musicians.
1921.
Oil on canvas, 6 feet 8 inches × 6 feet 2 inches.
Philadelphia Museum of Art.
The A. E. Gallatin Collection

In the 1920s there was no Apollinaire to act as the nerve center of a pacific International. The masters of the modern movement were moving into middle life; the urgencies of first youth were over. It was too late for a symbiotic alliance of the kind which had united Picasso and Braque until 1914; but effective working partnerships could still be formed, and one of the most fertile of these had been consolidated in Rome in the year 1917 between Pablo Picasso, painter, and Igor Stravinsky, composer. The intermediary in this was Sergei Diaghilev, who brought his Ballets Russes company to Paris in 1909 and had kept it in being ever since. Diaghilev had commissioned from Stravinsky the three great ballet scores for which Stravinsky is still best known: *The Firebird, Petrouchka* and *The Rite of Spring;* and Picasso was at that time a camp follower of the company, insofar as he was preparing the scenery and costumes for *Parade,* a ballet first produced in Paris in May, 1917, and was attracted to a member of the company, Olga Koklova, whom he subsequently married.

When they moved on to Naples Picasso and Stravinsky became fascinated by the commedia dell'arte, a form of street theater which had flourished in Italy for more than three hundred years. One of its main characters, Harlequin, was already a longtime favorite with Picasso and the subject of some of his most deeply felt paintings. But in Naples, where life is lived to a great extent in the street and every man learns in childhood to look after himself, the most important figure in the commedia dell'arte was Pulcinella, a hook-nosed, barrel-bodied intriguer with a talent for getting into scrapes and a genius for getting out of them.

Himself no slouch when it came to practical joking, Picasso came to see as much of himself in Pulcinella as he had formerly seen in Harlequin. But although the stock figures of the commedia dell'arte were in and out of his paintings and

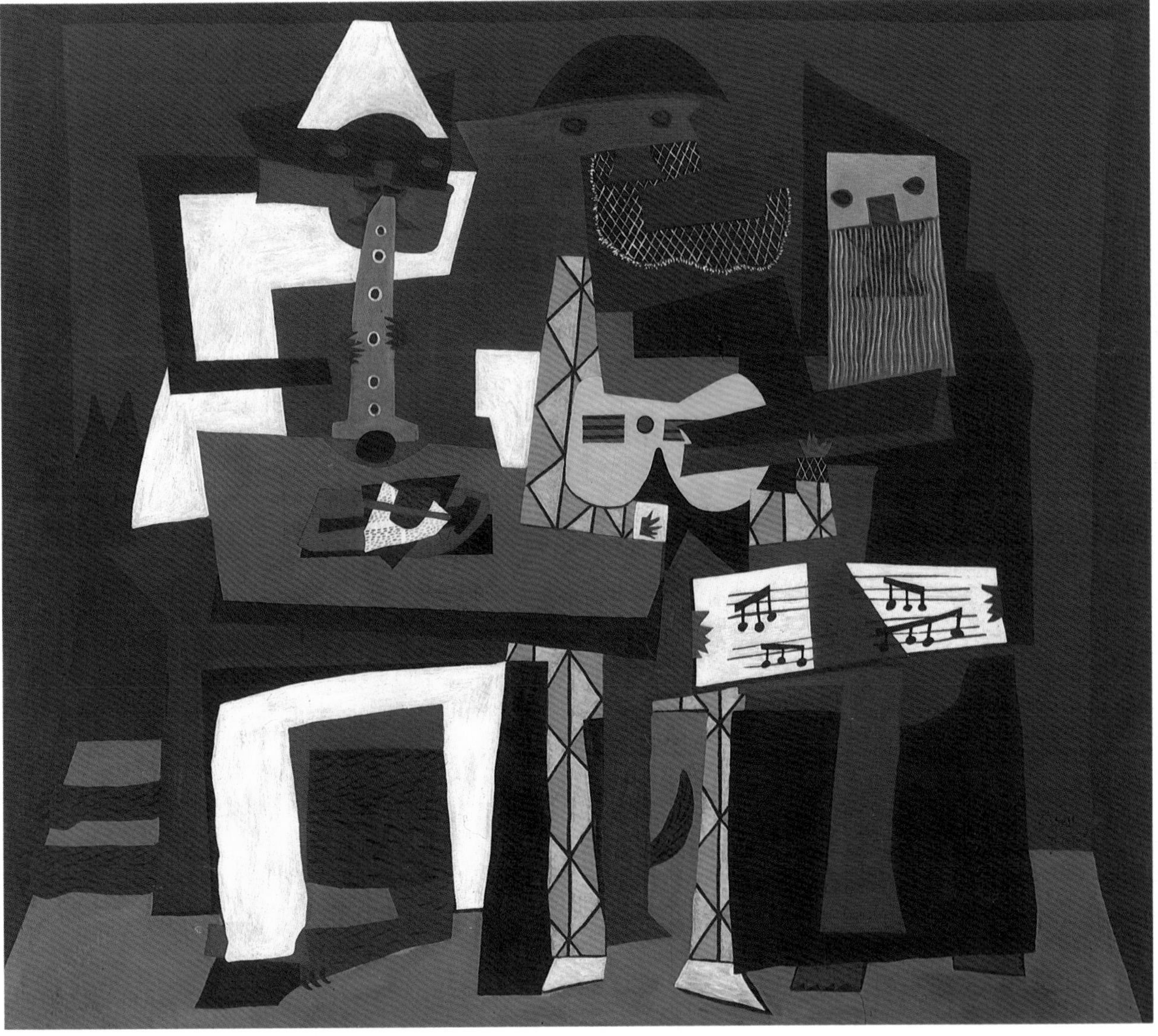

Pablo Picasso.
Three Musicians.
1921.
Oil on canvas, 6 feet 7 inches × 7 feet 3¾ inches.
The Museum of Modern Art, New York.
Mrs. Simon Guggenheim Fund

drawings throughout 1917 and 1918, the images in question were mostly elegiac in tone and had neither the insidious fun nor the potential for horseplay of the Neapolitan performers. Something in the total experience of the Neapolitan street theater had still to come out in Picasso's work; and in December, 1919, with a characteristic flash of inspiration, Diaghilev invited Picasso to join forces with Stravinsky and with the dancer and choreographer Léonide Massine in a ballet to be called *Pulcinella.*

It was difficult in later years to say who had enjoyed *Pulcinella* most: those who devised it, those who appeared in it, or those who just sat there and watched. But for Stravinsky and Picasso it was something more than an immensely successful entertainment which allowed them to quintessentialize a form of theater now extinct.

Stravinsky went so far as to say, in fact, that *Pulcinella* was "the epiphany through which the whole of my late work became possible." As for Picasso, he used the experience as the raw material for two of the most arresting of 20th-century paintings—the *Three Musicians, I* and *II,* which he painted in Fontainebleau in the summer of 1921. Something more had been at stake, for both of them, than the refashioning on the one hand of songs and instrumental pieces by the 18th-century Neapolitan composer Pergolesi and others, and the refashioning on the other of costumes long hallowed by tradition.

For Stravinsky, *Pulcinella* meant a decisive shift away from the barbaric energies of his native Russia. It inaugurated the 50 years' investigation of the Western European musical tradition which he was to continue in one form or another until the day of his death. There is nothing portentous about the music for *Pulcinella*, and least of all about the formalized ribaldry of the concert suite, which never fails to bring down the house with its buffoonish duet for trombone and double bass; but the decisive shift is there, nonetheless. Equally there are no signs of exceptional involvement in Picasso's working sketches, even if the stocky, belted, great-nosed figure of Pulcinella does have a look of Picasso himself in disguise. But in the one case, as in the other, what had been undertaken as a delightful collaboration turned out to have consequences of a larger and more momentous kind.

Pulcinella was first performed in Paris in May, 1920. As late as 1918 Picasso was still preoccupied with Pierrots and Harlequins of a withdrawn and woebegone sort; but from the moment that *Pulcinella* got under way he took a completely new tack. The pictures might be no more than ten inches high, but the figures had the bulk, the aggressivity and the straightforward frontal stance which were needed to win over a difficult audience in the back streets of Naples. Where the *Pierrot* of 1918 had classical fine features and a look of introspection, the paired figures of 1920 were as much coded as portrayed. If Picasso wanted to emphasize the hooked nose of Pierrot's mask he would set it firmly in profile, for instance, against the white outline of a head seen from the front; and if Harlequin's right hand was drawn quite realistically, as it hung down from the far side of Pierrot's shoulder, his left one was indicated by four vertical nicks in the baton that Harlequin carried with him everywhere. The paired figures were seen as flat, cut-out giants who filled the whole of the picture space from top to bottom; in this, and in the rhythmic alternations of dark and light which gave vigor and animation to the whole surface of the picture, there were echoes of that most disquieting of earlier Harlequins, the lifesize painting done late in 1915.

The two versions of the *Three Musicians* (one is now in New York, the other in Philadelphia) are virtually identical in size: more than six feet high, more than seven feet wide. They are "life-size," therefore, with all that that implies in the way of heightened actuality. The three musicians themselves are both in life and apart from it, both real and fictitious. Festive in their costume, they nevertheless bring with them intimations of quite other states of mind. As they face us in their shallow, stagelike space the three musicians echo, for instance, the way in which the Holy Trinity form up in many a Renaissance painting. Equally, they may remind us of the trio of judges—robed, remote and yet with power over life and death—who gaze back at us in Daumier, and later in Rouault. The masker is traditionally a figure both hilarious and sinister. He is the pretender who speaks true. ("The maskers cover their faces," wrote John Lyly in 1580, "that they may open their affections.") By coding his own features the masker could be said to come halfway to meet Cubism. And Cubism, in the *Three Musicians*, comes halfway to meet the maskers, in that they represent between them an anthology of earlier Cubist subject matter: the clarinet, so great a favorite with Braque, the sheet music, the guitar, the sturdy wooden table with its upended top, and (in the Philadelphia version) the hint of a dado. The friar in that same version may remind us also of a famous photograph in which the young Braque is seen sitting down with a concertina on his knee.

Altogether, the two big paintings give us a sense of unfinished business completed once and for all. They have the sleight of hand of a picture like

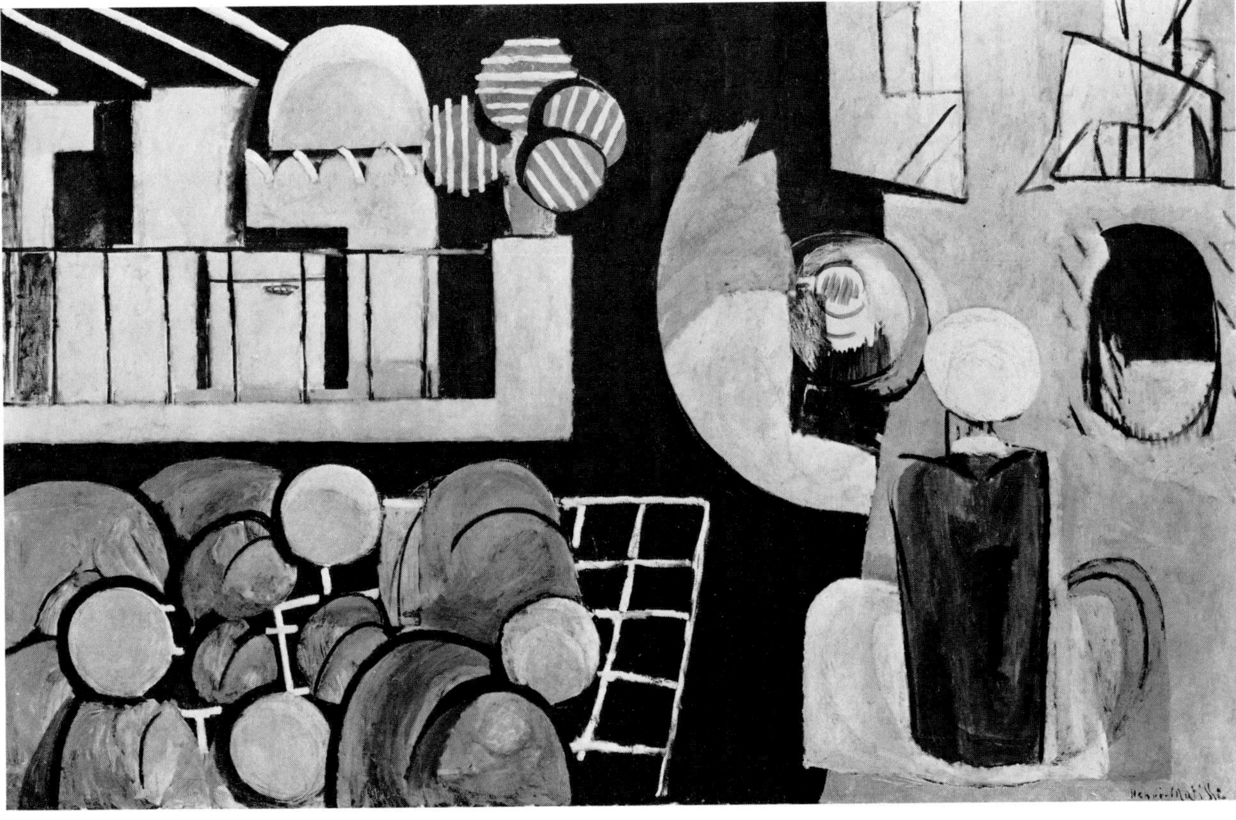

Henri Matisse.
The Moroccans.
1916.
Oil on canvas, 71⅜ inches × 9 feet 2 inches.
The Museum of Modern Art, New York.
Gift of Mr. and Mrs. Samuel A. Marx

Picasso's *Still Life with Fruit,* 1915, but with none of that painting's purely decorative aspect; and they have the grave monumental quality of earlier Cubist seated figures without being withdrawn from the hurly-burly of life on stage. They are very witty: note how in the New York version the hands of the cowled figure on the right are sketched in with just two specimens of paper-tearing in the sheet music. And they are minutely thought out: note how in the Philadelphia version Harlequin is not playing a violin, since a violin might not have quite the compositional weight that the picture requires, but the broader-bellied viola.

The two versions differ much more than appears at first sight; and just when we have decided that the New York version is altogether plainer and less "busy" we notice that Picasso has introduced a completely new formal element in the dog which lies beneath the table. Is it a real dog, a rug or a shadow? All three, one could say; and its tail has the further advantage of rhyming with the outline of Harlequin's hat. Fun is never far from the *Three Musicians;* but it does not exclude a most exact and peremptory marshaling of the flat color areas which make up the surface of the picture. In compositional terms the New York version has a severity which, as William Rubin says, "might seem more appropriate to a Byzantine *Maestà* than a group of maskers from the commedia dell'arte; but it is precisely this structuring that informs the monumentality of *Three Musicians* and endows it with a mysterious, otherworldly air."

The *Three Musicians* belongs to the European tradition of the outright masterpiece, in which the artist stands back and sums up what he has lately achieved. Picasso, like Braque, Bonnard and Matisse, had the 19th-century conviction that the duty of the artist was not just to do good work, as part of an ongoing process, but to concentrate his whole energies from time to time on something that could hang in the Louvre with Rembrandt's

Bathsheba and Poussin's *The Four Seasons* and not be discomfited. The achievement in question was to be deliberate, not accidental; and the process by which it came about was to be fundamentally consolidatory.

When Picasso painted these two pictures that particular ambition was not easily achieved. An aesthetic of immediate astonishment was coming into favor: the aftereffects of Dada and the current effects of Surrealism were all against the majestic, long-ruminated impact of paintings like these. An art of the here-and-now was coming up over the horizon, whereas the old-style masterpiece matures slowly and can with impunity be put aside for a generation. It was not, for instance, until 1927 that Matisse bestirred himself to show his *The Moroccans* of 1916 and his *Bathers by a River* of 1916–17. The dealer Paul Rosenberg bought the New York *Three Musicians* from Picasso in 1921 and kept it by him until 1949. It was not the current form in the 1920s for the major artist to get up in public every year and say, "This is where I'm at."

It was not, for instance, in the nature of Constantin Brancusi to act in that way. Brancusi was sly, devious and secretive. He was also endlessly patient. He didn't mind how long a sculpture took, or how long it stayed in the studio. It was an accident of taste, rather than a fact of chronology, that made him begin to be talked about very widely in the 1920s. His ideas were timeless and long-lasting, as was their execution.

His birds went on forever, in one guise or another. They had a complex derivation. The *Maiastra,* familiar to all Rumanians through their native folklore, was a golden-feathered bird with magical properties. It could cure the sick and the blind. It could outsing the nightingale. It could even bring back the dead to life. In this, it was the descendant of the solar birds which figure in many ancient cultures. Brancusi may well have been reminded of it, as the art historian Athena T. Spear has suggested, both by the publication of a long poem on the subject in Bucharest in 1909 and by the first

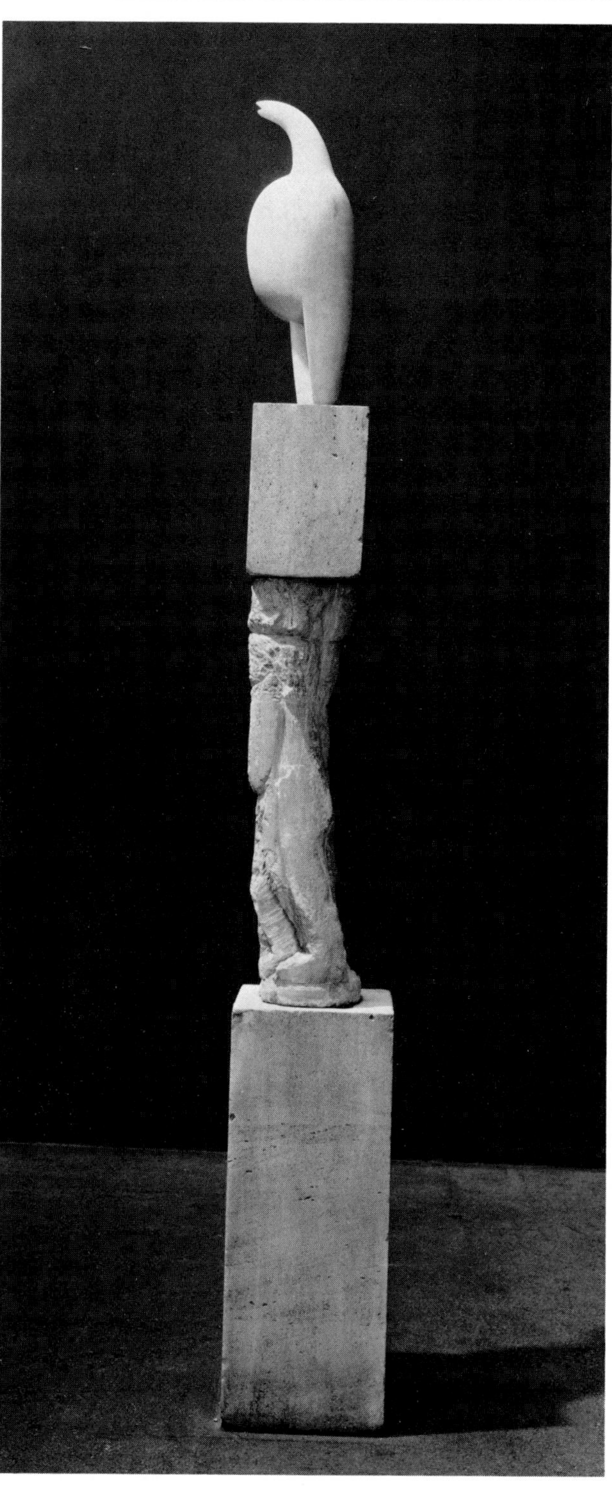

Constantin Brancusi. *Magic Bird.* Version I. 1910.
White marble, 22 inches high; limestone pedestal, in three sections, 70 inches high.
The Museum of Modern Art, New York. Katherine S. Dreier Bequest

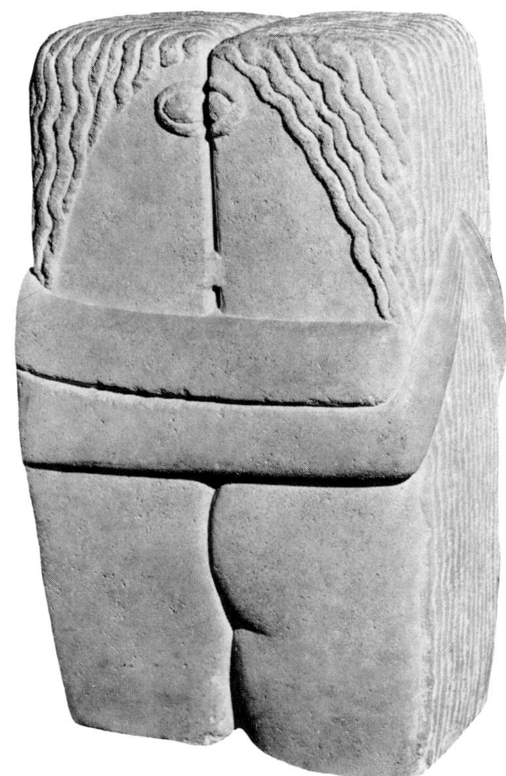

Constantin Brancusi. *The Kiss.* c. 1912. Limestone, 23 × 13 × 10 inches. Philadelphia Museum of Art. The Louise and Walter Arensberg Collection

performances in Paris in 1910 of Stravinsky's ballet *The Firebird,* which has a related subject. But in any case he went on perfecting the idea of the bird for many years, and in his many versions of the *Bird in Space* he intended to evoke both the effortless upward movement of the bird and the trajectory of its flight. The bird can also be seen as a metaphor for the poetic imagination as it blasts off, unencumbered, into the empyrean.

Himself an archetypal satyr, Brancusi produced before 1914 an image that gradually earned for itself a universal celebrity. In portraying the embraces of his well-mated if undeniably paunchy pair of lovers, Brancusi presented an ever more stylized variant of the idea that in the act of love man and woman become one flesh. In this version, the confrontation is literally "eyeball to eyeball." The woman's breasts, stomach and knee-length hair are delicately suggested, but the emphasis is on the completeness of the union—whence the locked lips, the identical blocklike form of the heads, and the paired and flattened arms which encircle the central mass as straps encircle an old-fashioned suitcase.

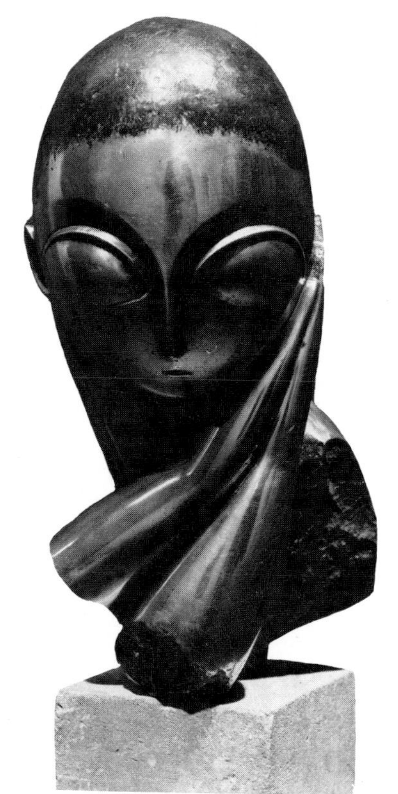

Constantin Brancusi. *Mlle Pogany.* Version I. 1913. Bronze (after a marble of 1912), 17¼ inches high. The Museum of Modern Art, New York. Acquired through the Lillie P. Bliss Bequest

Brancusi was also preoccupied with the idea of a reinvented portrait sculpture. In the summer of 1910 Margit Pogany sat for Brancusi a number of times. She was a young Hungarian painter studying in Paris, and he especially admired the way in which her head nestled over a strikingly elegant pair of wrists and hands. He went on working from her, or from memories of her, until 1933, and the portraits which resulted are probably the most sustained and celebrated attempt at personification which modern art has to show. Sometimes her huge bulging eyes, her finely drawn nose and her diminutive mouth were portrayed quite naturalistically; sometimes they served primarily to trap the dazzle of light as it fell on an artfully chosen material. Her distinctive and lyrical personality is everywhere present; but sometimes the portrait has the concision of epigram, whereas at other times it appears to us as (to quote Jean Arp—sculptor, poet, pioneer of Dada and Surrealism) "the

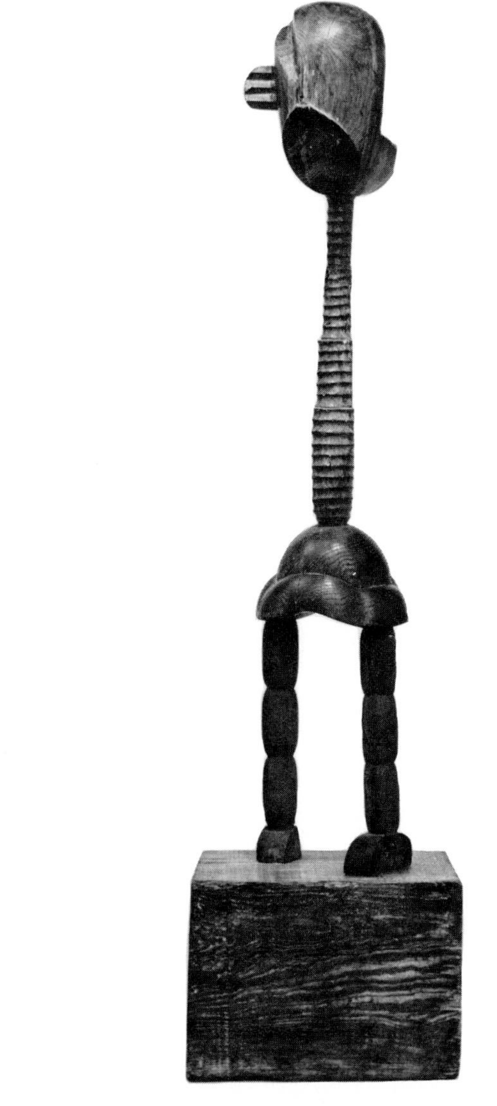

Constantin Brancusi. *Figure (Little French Girl.* 1914–18(?). Wood, 49 × 8¾ × 8½ inches. The Solomon R. Guggenheim Museum, New York

fairy godmother of abstract sculpture."

In 1913 Brancusi's innate elegance was disturbed by the experience of African tribal sculpture. He began to build up his images, as in his *Little French Girl,* by the addition of one cryptic element to another. Vestiges of naturalism remain: Brancusi always started from an exact observation of human idiosyncrasy, and in this case the spindly legs, the slightly turned-in feet and the tall, thin, as yet unrounded torso suggest a particular little girl at a particular stage in her life. Like many another artist at that time, he was bent on annexing for European art some of the energies that were inherent in so-called "primitive" art.

Around the turn of the century Auguste Rodin had introduced the idea that a fragmentary sculpture could be exhibited as such, and that its incompleteness might even give it a heightened emotional force. Brancusi was one of the many sculptors—others were Matisse, Boccioni and Duchamp-Villon—who took the hint. In his *Torso* he reduced the basic facts about the male torso to three gleaming columnar elements. In its rejection of all descriptive or anecdotal matter, and in the candor of its erotic allusion, the work retains, as Sidney Geist has remarked, "a quintessential modernity that must have been the more dazzling when it was created, more than half a century ago."

Brancusi's natural cunning paid off, all his life long. From 1922 onward he tried again and again to make a sculpture which would show not the physical appearance of any given fish but, as he himself said, "the flash of its spirit." Such a sculpture would concentrate on the horizontality of all fish, their slithery and apparently weightless deportment under water, and the smooth and largely featureless nature of their bodies. He tried many materials, many forms of base, many solutions for the problem of how the sculpture itself was to relate to the base. In the Museum of Modern Art's version he concentrated on the idea of the fish as it lifted itself off the seabed with its mouth tilting ever so slightly upward.

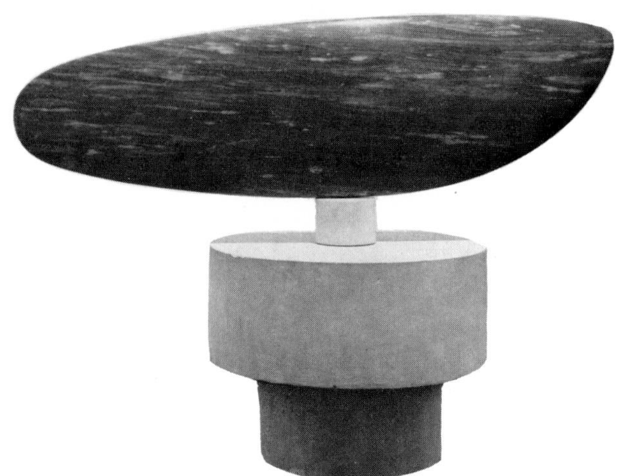

Constantin Brancusi. *Fish.* 1930. Marble, 21 × 71 inches. The Museum of Modern Art, New York. Acquired through the Lillie P. Bliss Bequest

Looking at Brancusi's achievement, and at that of many another major artist, we realize all over again that the 1920s had a double nature. There was the aspect of the decade which has become a part of folk memory. Quick returns and a horror of going on too long are common to many of its manifestations: the cocktail, the wisecrack, the jazz band, the Charleston, the encapsulations of *Time* magazine, the songs of George Gershwin and Noel Coward and Kurt Weill, the contribution of Art Deco to dress and design, the laconic first stories of Ernest Hemingway. Limits were set to scale, to ambition, and above all to the intrusion upon others' time: "An hour is enough of anything," said the American novelist Edith Wharton, one of the most redoubtable hostesses of the day. (A classic of the period is Paul Hindemith's opera *There and Back Again* [1927] in which the action is played twice over, forward and backward, and the audience still gets out in under 20 minutes.)

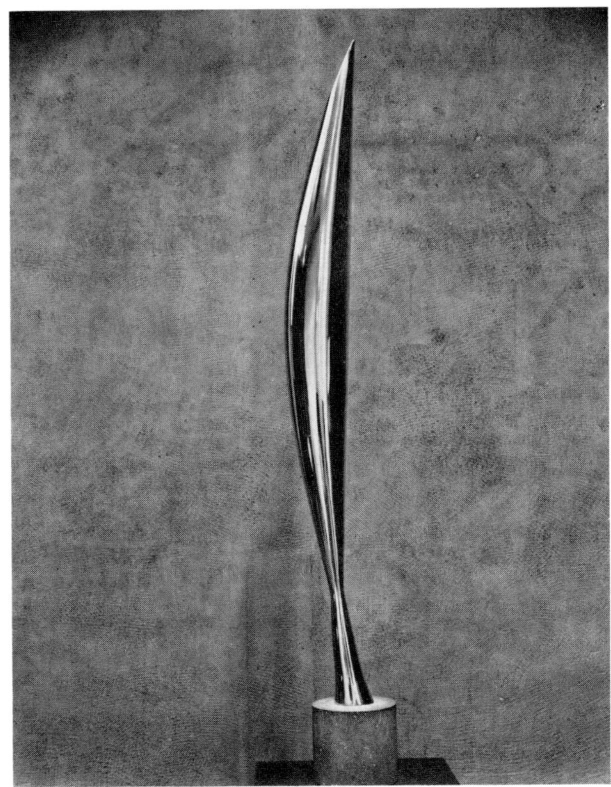

Constantin Brancusi. *Bird in Space.* 1928(?). Bronze, 54 inches high. The Museum of Modern Art, New York. Given anonymously

Folk memory errs, however, in leaving out precisely those vast and pertinent enterprises for which the 1920s will be longest remembered. If we stick to the conventional view of the decade we may find these ventures anachronistic in their amplitude, foredoomed in the impossible scale of their ambitions, and in more than one case inevitably and predictably unfinished. But we may equally well see them as majestic delaying actions in which were reviewed, almost for the last time, the full resources of the European tradition. Not for them the closed forms and the finite perfection of earlier ages; Ezra Pound made that distinction very clear when he wrote that "art very possibly *ought* to be the supreme achievement, the 'accomplished'; but there is the other satisfactory effect, that of a man hurling himself at an indomitable chaos and yanking and hauling as much of it as possible into some sort of order (or beauty), aware of it both as chaos and potential."

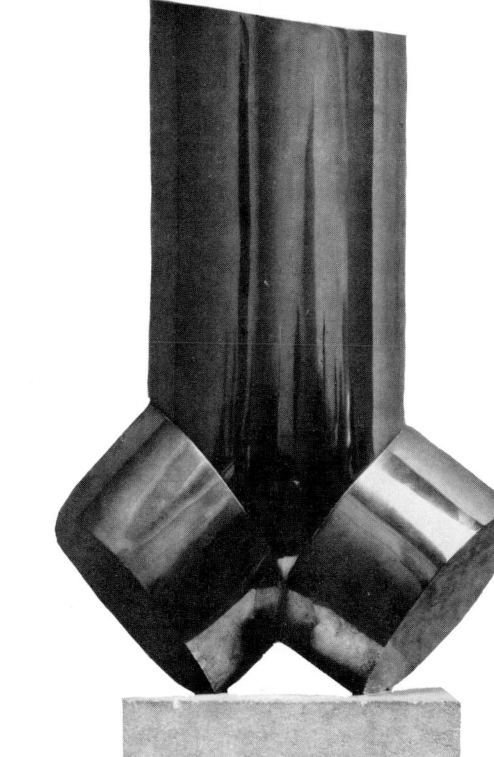

Constantin Brancusi. *Torso.* 1917. Brass, 18⅜ × 12 × 6⅝ inches. The Cleveland Museum of Art. Hinman B. Hurlbut Collection

It is exactly this twofold awareness—of an ever-encroaching chaos, on the one hand, and on the other of its unprecedented and unmanageable potential for art—which comes out so strongly in certain voluminous masterworks of the 1920s and '30s. Examples are James Joyce's *Ulysses* (1922); the novel series of Marcel Proust, who died in 1922 with his manuscript still not completely revised; *The Magic Mountain* (1924) by Thomas Mann; Arnold Schoenberg's unfinished opera *Moses and Aaron* (1930–32); Robert Musil's *The Man without Qualities,* begun in 1930; the *Cantos* of Ezra Pound, begun in 1915 and unfinished even at the time of Pound's death in 1972. There are too many points of kinship between these comprehensive summations for us to dismiss the matter as one of coincidence. There is about every one of them something valedictory, as if the end of the recording would signal the end of the thing recorded.

And where did art stand in all this? Betwixt and between. Cubism had been, apart from so much else, a school of concision: no waste, no fat, no rhapsodizing. Insofar as *The Magic Mountain* and *Moses and Aaron* had their equivalents in art, they were in existence already before 1914, in the panoramas of convulsion to which Kandinsky gave the impassive name of Compositions; but when Kandinsky returned to Western Europe in the 1920s he turned to a less headlong mode of expression. Between 1918 and the day of his death in 1940, Paul Klee had a delicate and unerring intuition as to what was happening to Europe: but he was not going to launch out on the scale of the Sistine Chapel when he could say all that he had to say on the scale of a pocket handkerchief. Léger had, as we have seen, as keen an eye as anyone for the potential of the 1920s; but when chaos began to get the upper hand of that potential he could offer only a robust irrelevance. (To the end of his days, he believed in the hard-hat as the hope of the world.) The early warning systems of the Surrealists led in more than one case to what can be called a masterpiece. One such was Dali's *Soft Construction with Boiled Beans: Premonition of Civil War,* 1936, and another Ernst's *The Horde,* 1927. But the accolade was won involuntarily and in breach, almost, of the Surrealists' charter. (The traditional notion of a masterpiece implied, for one thing, a belief in sober effort.)

On reflection, it seemed most likely that if masterpieces were going to be made in the 1920s and '30s, they would be made in Paris, where the continuum of major art was most strongly in evidence, and made by people brought up in the 19th-century tradition. Who were these people? Matisse, Picasso, Bonnard and Braque. What was so special about Paris? Simply the fact that, as the critic Clement Greenberg said as late as 1946, "Paris remains the fountainhead of modern art. Other places (Berlin at the time of the Weimar Republic, for example) may have shown more sensitivity to immediate history, but it is Paris over the last hundred years that has most faithfully conveyed the historical essence of our civilization." As to the effect of Paris upon those who lived there in the 1920s, James Joyce for one said: "There is an atmosphere of spiritual effort here. No other city is quite like it. It is a racecourse tension. I wake early, often at five o'clock, and start writing at once."

In ways that we recognize but cannot always account for, great art keeps something in reserve for each successive generation. The *Three Musicians* once had a look of pure festivity: but observers from a later generation may be in some doubt as to what would happen if the masks were to be laid down. We know more today about the function of role-playing in human affairs. We may have seen Jean Genet's play *The Balcony* (1956), in which a false judge, a false general and a false bishop act out the roles which their costumes impose upon them. What if Picasso's harlequinade should be headed for a sinister ending? We shall never know the answer, but there is something minatory about the *Three Musicians* which plays directly on the nerves of a generation which was not even born when it was painted.

In formal terms, some of the works which we are considering here are sedate by comparison with their predecessors in the heroic period. But a particular weight and assurance may turn out to

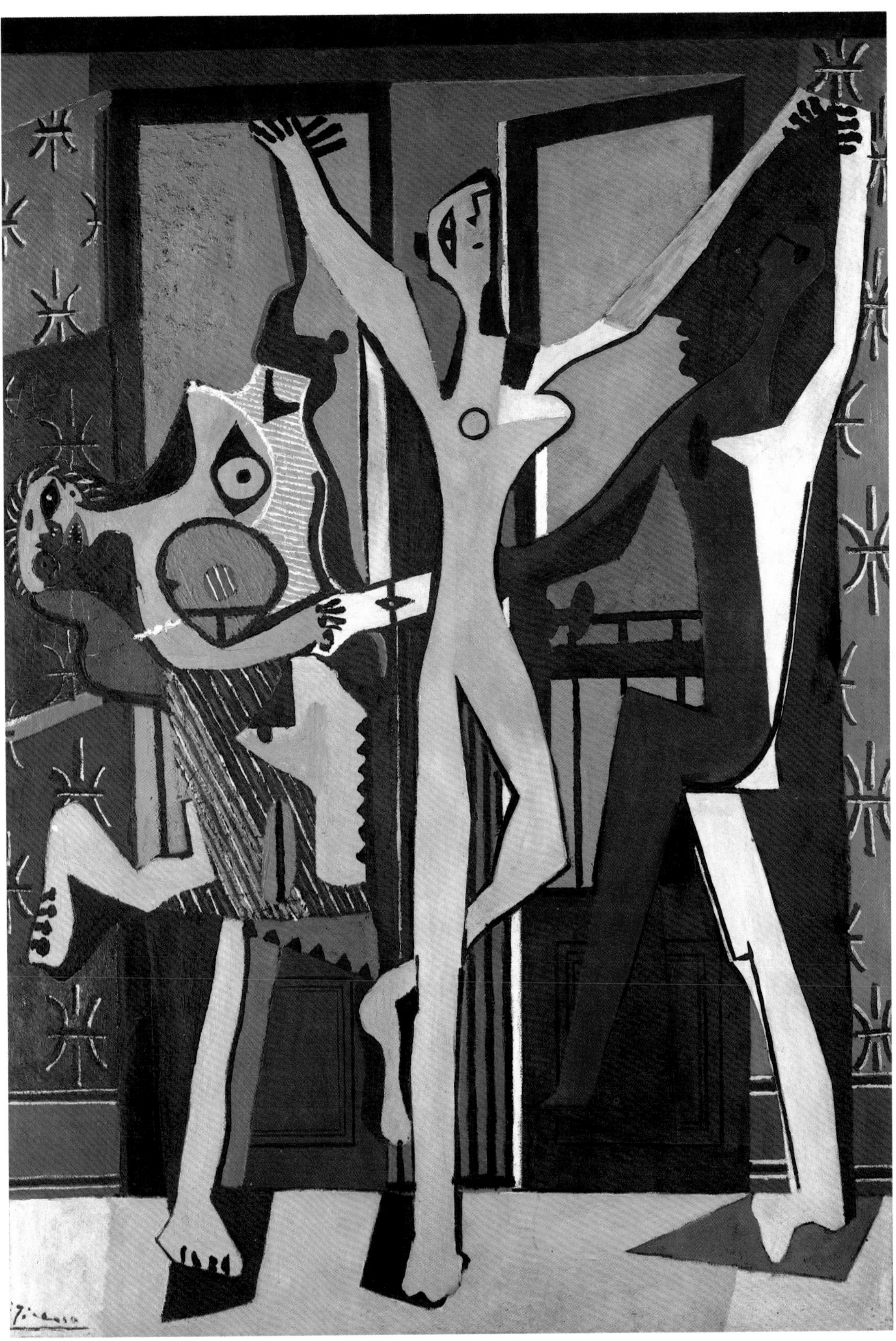

Pablo Picasso.
The Three Dancers.
1925.
Oil on canvas, 7 feet ¾ inch × 56 inches.
The Tate Gallery, London

reside in that very steadiness, that air of acquiescence in procedures which were already a part of history. I can best demonstrate this by examining two paintings which Picasso completed in the spring and summer, respectively, of 1925. They could not be less alike. *The Three Dancers* speaks for a grief that is violent, destructive and disorderly. *Studio with Plaster Head* is outstanding for its vivacity, its contrapuntal control and its wide range of perfectly adjusted allusion. *The Three Dancers* could be called the last masterpiece of European Expressionism, just as the *Studio with Plaster Head* could be related to the French still-life tradition. Both readings would be correct. Expressionism—the use, that is to say, of distortion in the interests of a greater intensity of feeling—can show nothing more telling than the strange antics, halfway to hysteria, which unite Picasso's dancers. The order, the balance, the sense of organization that characterize French still life in the 17th and 18th centuries find their consummation in the *Studio with Plaster Head,* where Picasso includes several of the properties most favored by Chardin when he painted his *Attributes of the Arts:* a plaster cast from the antique, a scroll of drawing paper, a geometrical instrument and a book.

Yet how much is still unsaid! *The Three Dancers* represents, in a context of private desolation, a number of motifs that we associate with a civilized well-being: the patterned wallpaper familiar from Cézanne onward, the tall window open to a southern sea, the unflawed blue of the sky, and the shaped energies of the dance. The subject of the picture is the transformation of this scene by the intrusion of grief in its most extravagant and implacable form. The picture was prompted by the death of a Spanish friend of Picasso's, a fellow painter who had been close to him in his youth; the dead man's profile can be seen beneath the left arm of the central figure in the painting. Picasso was not the man to render grief in terms of genteel resignation. His instinct was rather—in the words of Dylan Thomas's lines to his father—to "rage, rage against the dying of the light." But by the time that the picture was bought for the Tate Gallery in London in 1965, history had caught up with it on two important counts. One of these was first identified by André Malraux in 1947 in *Museum without Walls,* volume 1 of his book *The Psychology of Art.* André Malraux was then at the height of his fame as a novelist, as a resistance leader, and as potentially one of the most eminent of men in a resuscitated France. His stature as a philosopher of history has been called in question since then; but there has been the most widespread practical assent, even among those who have never heard his name, to the basic idea of the *Museum without Walls,* which is that we are no longer tied to any one style as representative of our age, but are free to anthologize as seems to us best. Malraux made, in 1947, his own personal anthology among the art works of the past; in doing so he authorized for the general public a practice which had been common form among men of genius for the best part of half a century.

In the 1920s and '30s words like "eclectic" and "opportunistic" had been used of the foreign language quotations which bring *The Waste Land* to a close, and of Stravinsky's use of the Latin language—"a medium not dead," he said, "but turned to stone"—in *Oedipus Rex;* it was common form, equally, to speak of Picasso's borrowings from the past in terms of pastiche. But in time it became clear that what was important in such borrowings, whether by Eliot or Stravinsky or Picasso, was the degree of their reinvention. Something about the left-hand figure in *The Three Dancers* was mysterious to many people when the picture first came to London; then the painter and art historian Lawrence Gowing identified her as a derivative of the Maenad as Bacchante, a motif first known to us in Greek reliefs and later taken up by Donatello when he grouped the three Marys at the foot of the cross. The Maenad in question was a dancing figure who had a tambourine crooked under her right arm. Picasso had a great deal of trouble to get her right; but, as Gowing says, "the figure that emerged was the same figure that had been drawn from antiquity five hundred years earlier for the same purpose. . . . It was re-created in *The Three Dancers* to fill the same need, to epitomize the agonizing incongruity between death and sensual life, which is the source of grief."

History had also caught up with *The Three Dancers* by the late 1960s, insofar as we had had continual reminders from news photography of the way in which people react in real life to unexpected and appalling situations. In the light of such reminders the left-hand figure in Picasso's painting is not at all histrionic in her bodily contortions, in the disorder of her dress, or in the grimace which tears her face in two. This is what grief does to people. We had seen it in art before —in Gothic sculpture, for instance, where the sculptor spares us nothing of the physical impact of mourning—but before we could *feel* it again someone had to reinterpret it.

To say the last word about a great painting is always a vain endeavour; it will look different, in any case, to those who come after us. *The Three Dancers* is about the dance, but the dance seen as convulsion. It is about the crucifixion image—a tall thin figure with upstretched arms, outlined against a T-shaped cross. It is about mourning and about the aggressivity, the wish to take Destiny by the throat, to which mourning notoriously gives rise. It is about Cubism, and about the way in which Cubism can operate within a complex system of allusion. And it is about the painter's job, part of which is to bear witness to the worst that can happen to human beings.

The *Studio with Plaster Head* at first sight seems much less complex in its implications. Its subject matter is straightforward enough—the table itself (cut foursquare to steady the composition); the tumbled cloth, a triangular fold of which reappears beneath the table to balance the many triangular forms in the upper half of the canvas; the insistent, repeated pattern of the wallpaper; the mass-produced woodwork, here given a most powerful thrust and counterthrust; the Chardinesque group of evocative objects. The only thing that speaks loud and clear for the 1920s is, in fact, the toy theater—a precise rendering of a recent gift from Picasso to his four-year-old son—which makes us wonder if we are indoors or out-of-doors as we explore the top left quarter of the painting. (Even the sky looks like a painted sky and seems to be both outside the window and inside the theater.)

A tour de force, therefore, of ingenuity and high spirits: a working model of a world in which reality and make-believe change places and nothing can ever go wrong. But something more than that, as well. Those severed arms and hands, for instance, and the big sculptured head which we see three times (in shadow, in profile and in a half-hidden frontal view): are they just decorative additions to an already crowded scene? Certainly the hand meant enough to Picasso for him to remake it on its own many years later, in sculpture, and with an effect of peculiar poignancy. And what about that sprig of laurel, soon to wither? Picasso in the summer of 1925 was living quietly in a still unspoiled Juan-les-Pins, and as he was not at all a political person nothing is less likely than that he consciously foresaw the downfall of Europe. But there is in great art a clairvoyance for which we have not yet found a name, and still less an explanation; and there is no doubt that in the *Studio with Plaster Head* Picasso was making ready the language which he would need both for *Guernica*, 1937, and for the expression of more private exasperations in years to come. More exactly, as William Rubin has pointed out, the look of the plaster head in the painting of 1925 forecasts the rictus of dismay which we see on the severed head of the soldier in *Guernica*. And the severed arm reappears, holding a broken spear, in that same formidable picture. The *Studio with Plaster Head* looks brisk enough, open enough, pellucid enough; but it runs a gamut of experience that ranges from civilized recreation (reading, drawing, the stage) to pre-echoes of *The Charnel House* of 1944–45. But then Picasso was someone who could keep a

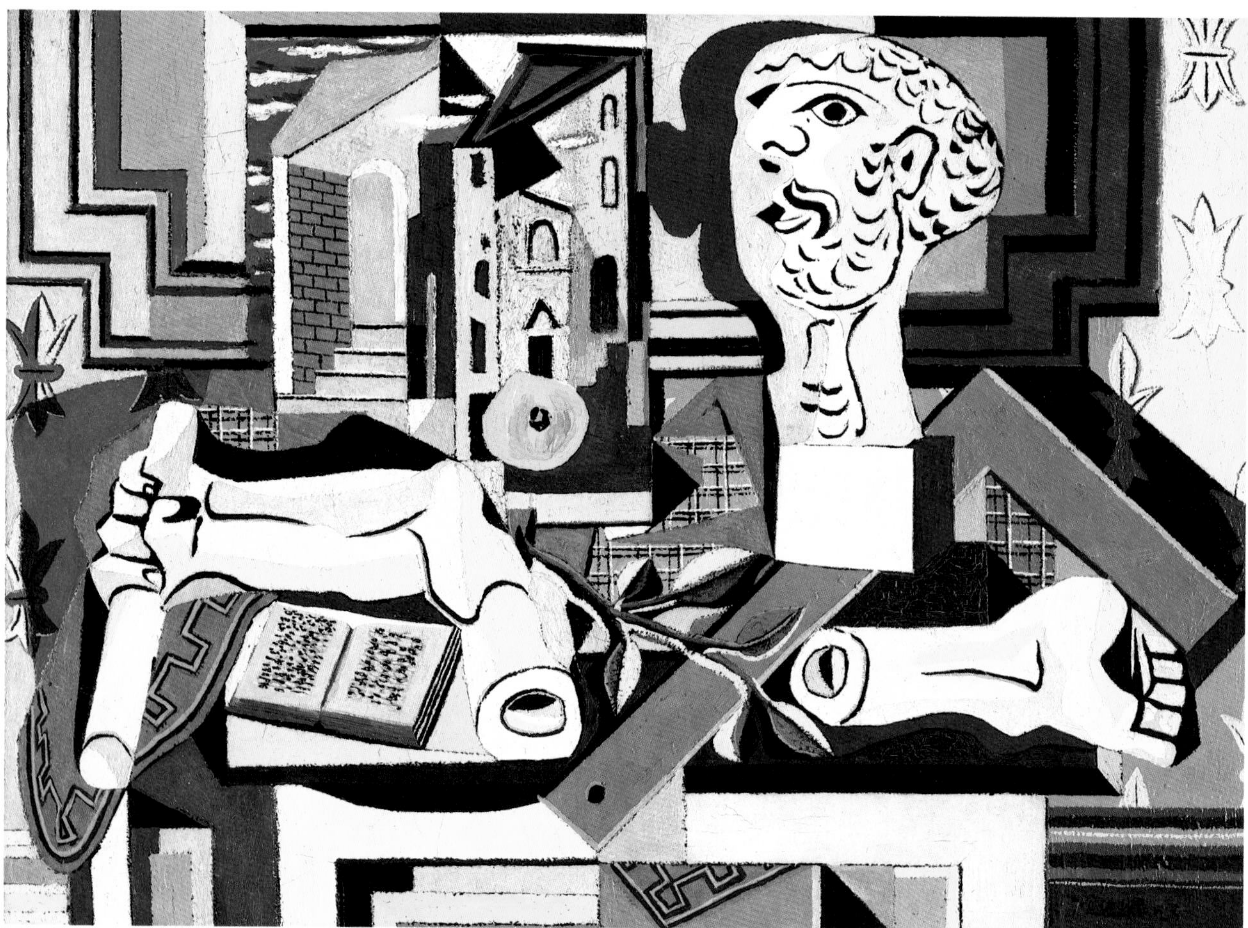

Pablo Picasso.
Studio with Plaster Head. 1925.
Oil on canvas, 38⅝ × 51⅝ inches.
The Museum of Modern Art, New York. Purchase

dozen ideas going at a time. In *Painter and Model* he showed his awareness of Matisse in the patterning (white on yellow) of the painter's chair in the lower right-hand corner. He remembered the ferocious reworking of the human face in Oceanic art when it came to his presentation both of the painter's own face and of the face of his model. Reversing the traditional procedures of modern art, he metamorphosed the head of the model into a naturalistic profile on the canvas. He also remembered the decorative flat patterning of Art Deco (then at its height) when he came to organize the picture in terms of interlocking flat planes. These planes rhymed with the natural flatness of the chair back, the chair's tasseled fringe, the picture on the wall, the wall itself, and the stylized dado which traverses the wall at shoulder height. The use of bright flat color relates, also, to current practice in architecture (see, for this, the workings of De Stijl; Chapter 8). When we are faced with paintings such as this, which can be thought over for a lifetime, it is more than ever difficult to see the 1920s as a period of secondary achievement in art.

If the 1920s have that reputation it is because the best work of the period so often turns up in isolation, with none of the armature of chronology with which we can find our way, week by week, through the heroic age of modernism. Even the best artists have dry periods: no one can make history every day of his life. A long patience and a strategy of withdrawal or concealment may be the best way of coping with these periods. The great Europeans with whom we are dealing were prepared to lie low, or to shift their ground, or to withhold all news of their activity in ways that would now be taken as evidence of instability or decay. They were forgetful, too: Matisse did not even remember whether there were three pieces or four in the series of Backs which was fundamental to his activity as a sculptor. Everything would come out, sooner or later; meanwhile there was the day's work to be got on with.

For reasons which have never ceased to be valid, Pierre Bonnard gets away to a very good start in the history books. From 1888 he was part of the new painting as it was being formulated under the influence of Gauguin. He knew the new novelists, the new composers and the new poets. He sat in on rehearsals at the Théâtre de l'Oeuvre, at that time the most adventurous theater in Europe. He was admired by Félix Fénéon, the most discerning critic of the day, and he was taken up by Ambroise Vollard, who for all his half-awake ways was in a class by himself as a dealer. It is difficult, as we have seen, to find a comment on human affairs that is stronger or more candid than Bonnard's *Man and Woman,* 1900.

Then two things happened. One was that Bonnard found himself walled up alive with the woman who shared his life from 1894 onward and eventually, in 1925, became his wife. When Bonnard first met her, she was only 16 and had the quality, irresistible at that time, of a lost child; the 1890s were the heyday of Maeterlinck's *Pelléas et Mélisande,* and Bonnard may well have felt that he had come upon Marthe as Golaud, in act 1,

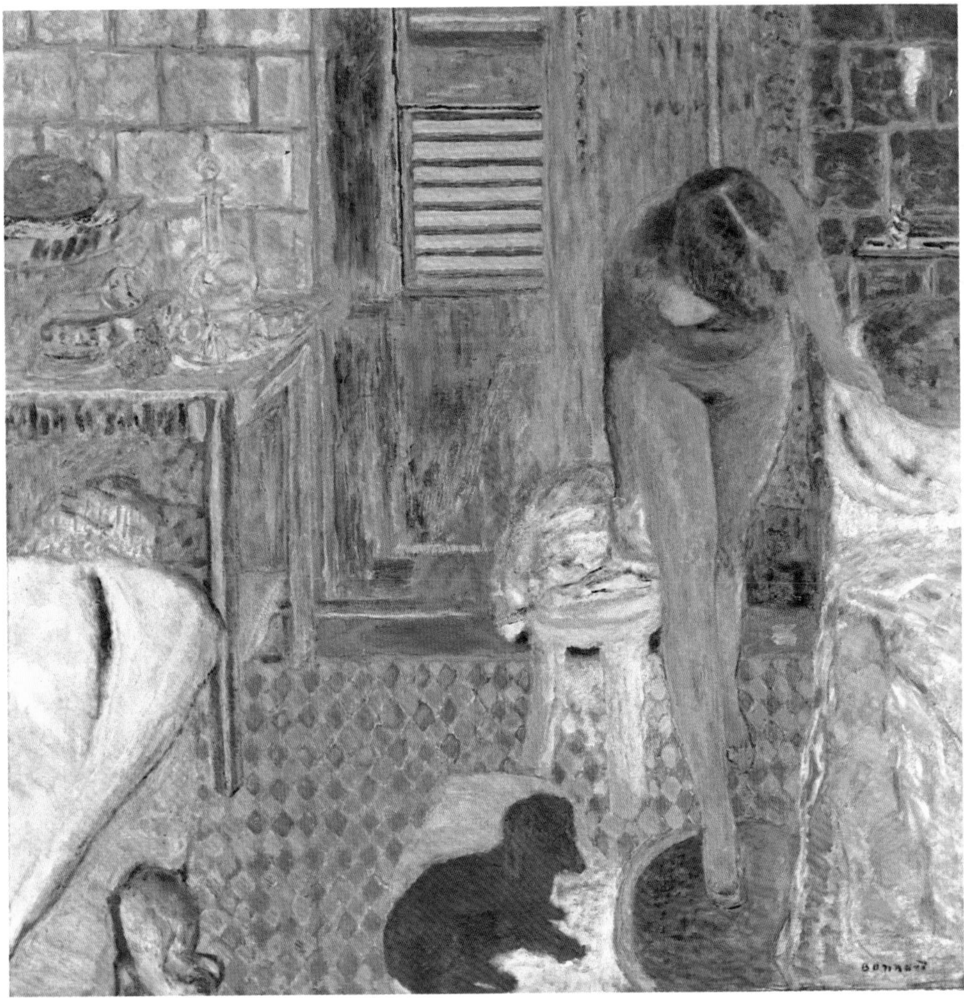

Pierre Bonnard. *Nude in Bathroom.* 1932. Oil on canvas, 47½ × 46¼ inches. The Florene May Schoenborn and Samuel A. Marx Collection, New York

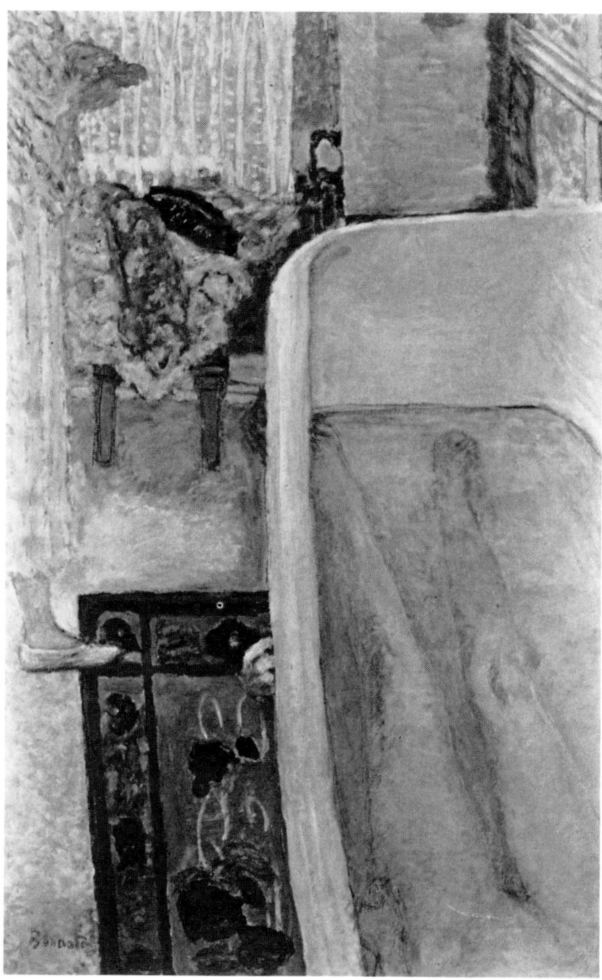

Pierre Bonnard.
Nude in Bath.
c. 1935.
Oil on canvas,
40 × 25 inches.
Private collection

scene 1 of the play, comes upon Mélisande. But as she grew older Marthe Bonnard came to have a horror of society, and Bonnard for a great part of his life was compelled to live quite alone with her. Old friends were unwelcome, new ones unthinkable; the sociable, quick-witted Bonnard of the 1890s dropped out of sight.

It also happened that Bonnard and his friend Vuillard were no longer in the foreground of the modern movement. Other people and other ways were talked about from 1905 onward with a vivacity and a commitment which were not in evidence when Bonnard showed, year by year, at the Bernheim-Jeune gallery. Bonnard went to all the galleries and he looked carefully at the Fauve paintings in 1905, and the first Cubist paintings in 1908, and the pasted-papers of Picasso and Braque in 1913. He particularly liked the way the collaged parts of the pasted-papers introduce an element of physical reality which heightens our awareness of the parts that are drawn or painted. But his personal contacts at that time were with older artists: Claude Monet, who lived not far from Bonnard's house in the Seine Valley, and Auguste Renoir, whom he saw constantly when wintering in the south of France; and it bothered him to foresee—quite rightly—that people would think of him primarily as a belated Impressionist: someone who came along when the real work had already been done.

"We were left hanging in the air," Bonnard said later of the situation of himself and his friends in 1914. "We had wanted to take the same direction as the Impressionists, but to go further than they did in the rendering of color as it actually exists in Nature. But art and Nature are two different things. . . . And then progress came upon us faster than anyone expected, and the public was ready for Cubism, and even for Surrealism, before we had realized our intentions completely."

In the heyday of Surealism Bonnard was often written off as an earthbound artisan, overconcerned with subjects that by their very nature were sedate and repetitious. But in pictures like the *Nude in Bath*, Bonnard showed qualities of daring and invention which make most of the Surrealists' fancies look both labored and gratuitous. In the reinvention of color he goes far beyond the Fauves. In the use of multiple viewpoints he makes most Cubist painting look dull and regimented. He also introduces an element of psychological ambiguity which is neither forced nor overexplicit. The picture contradicts all our expectations. Who else would have made the far end of the bath look like the blank wall of a reservoir, or contrasted the demure, lace-ridden figure on the left with a pair of legs that look as if they might have come straight from a slaughterhouse?

"A picture," Bonnard said, "must be a little world sufficient unto itself." With the green of fresh almonds, with an orangey yellow and with the deep violet that stood midway between them, he had his way with Nature. Tyrannizing his subject matter, bending space to his will, he in later life allowed himself a total liberty where color was concerned. And when it seemed likely that all this would result in something luscious but formless, daring but fundamentally illegible, it turned out that Bonnard had remembered the lessons not only of the "advanced" painting of his own day but of a master not usually mentioned in this context: Vermeer.

Bonnard had, pinned up in his studio, a postcard of Vermeer's *The Little Street.* It might have seemed irrelevant to his own work; but if we look closely at a masterpiece of Bonnard's middle 60s, the *Nude in Bathroom,* 1932, certain shared preoccupations will appear. Vermeer's *Street* is remarkable for the ingenuity with which he has patterned almost the entire surface of the canvas with rectangles of one kind or another: the brickwork, the lattice of the windows, the doorways, the shutters (both open and closed), the cut of the benches on the street, the deeply indented roof. Vermeer also included in the upper left-hand area some contrasted diagonals; and all this gives a particular poignancy and an unforced naturalness to the figures of the four human beings, young or old, as they go about their business. We realize, finally, that there is something unexpectedly modern about the way in which Vermeer has parceled out the picture surface and conferred upon almost two-thirds of it a literal flatness: one backed up, that is to say, by the nature of the things portrayed.

Bonnard's picture is set, as were so many of his later paintings, in the bathroom in which his wife spent a disproportionately large amount of her time. Like the Vermeer it has been given a tectonic quality by the division of a great part of the canvas into rectangles, large or small. The vertical lines of table, window frame and what looks to be a curtain are balanced by the fat blue line which runs across the canvas between the edge of the tiled floor and the foot of the wall. All this brings out the flatness of the picture surface in ways not often equaled since Matisse, in 1911, would organize almost the whole of a picture in terms of a continuous repeated arabesque on an uninflected red ground and yet make the whole scene read quite clearly.

Where Bonnard went beyond Matisse was in his entirely arbitrary use of color—switching tiles from blue and white to blue and yellow, for instance, and getting his planes to overlap and intermingle, clear at one point and opaque at another, in ways that are nearer to Synthetic Cubism than to Impressionism. Like Vermeer, he introduced a diagonal, just below the slatted shutter. This prevented the composition from getting too stiff (it also balances the parting in Madame Bonnard's hair). And, again like Vermeer, he gave the human figure an unaffectedly touching and vulnerable look by setting off its rounded forms and air of preoccupation against the rigorous marshaling of flat forms in all the rest of the picture. Bonnard did, on the other hand, take liberties with the human body which would never have occurred to Vermeer: the forward movement of his wife's right leg in the *Nude in Bathroom* could have been painted only by someone who had seen how Cézanne, in his *Grandes Baigneuses,* had let feeling take precedence over exactitude. In this inexhaustible picture the dog is a survivor from the world of Manet's *Olympia,* where it was taken for granted that every pretty woman had an animal of some sort as witness to the secret rituals of beauty. As for Marthe Bonnard herself, Bonnard was too chivalrous to monitor the inevitable decay of the compact little body which he had recorded so often and, at the outset, so faithfully. I suspect, in fact, that he drew upon the memory of that antique marble whose photograph was pinned up on the studio wall beside the Vermeer.

Bonnard in this painting borrows from the antique world not only the forms of the body, but also the sacrificial manner in which Madame Bonnard addresses herself to what is in itself quite a commonplace action. There is something in this of that backward glance toward happier days which we find in the marble grave reliefs which proliferated in ancient Greece after the end of the Peloponnesian War. It was in just such terms that the Greeks commemorated the dead mistress of the house at a time of national misgiving. I have suggested that in the 1920s and early '30s the arts in Europe had in common a wish to reexamine the achievements of the past in ways which might yield strength where strength was much needed. If we accept that idea, there can be included among the rewards of this great and complex painting an echo of that earlier time when art had "kept its calm even in the midst of catastrophe."

All this takes us a long way from the Bonnard whose landscapes and still lifes can be read in terms of pure seduction. But then Bonnard is not the only major artist who is too often associated primarily with the amiabilities of life. Matisse for many years was regarded as not quite serious, on the basis of those many paintings from his years in Nice which appeared to ignore both the chaos of which Ezra Pound wrote and, more especially, its potential for art. It was at the cost of a continual struggle, both with the subject matter and with himself, that he painted pictures like *The Moorish Screen,* 1922, but it was a matter of pride with him to conceal that struggle from the public. The end result was curiously neutral, in emotional terms, as if the people portrayed had come to exist only as captives of Matisse's will. The work was perfect, within its own terms: no one has ever reordered the world with greater dexterity. But something of human involvement was lost—as we may see if we compare *The Moorish Screen* with the picture called *Two Friends* which Matisse's close friend Albert Marquet painted in 1912.

Picasso and Matisse, Braque and Bonnard were never allies, in the sense that Picasso and Braque were allies before 1914; but ideas passed from one to the other, back and forth and irresistibly, to the day of their deaths. Picasso in 1915 had the idea of the mantelpiece—tall, flat, with a shelf at the top—as an ideal subject for paintings that would combine elements of architecture with elements of

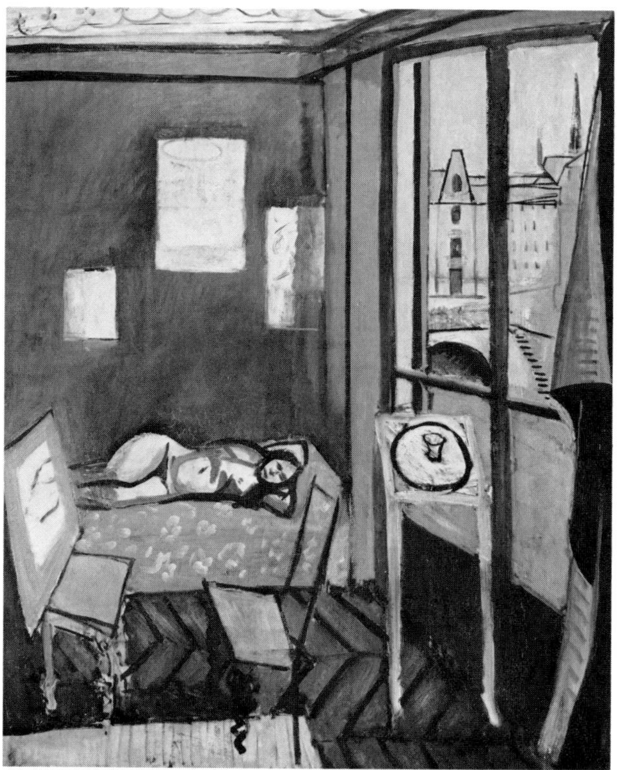

Henri Matisse. *Studio, Quai St-Michel.* 1916. Oil on canvas, 57½ × 45¾ inches. The Phillips Collection, Washington

still life. After his demobilization from the army Braque was to take up this idea and bring to it an unmatched command of texture and a stately grandeur of tone. Matisse in 1916 used that staple ingredient of French interior decoration, the splay-footed table, as the animating feature of *The Window;* in a composition where so much depends on tall straight vertical lines, he used the feet of the table to persuade us to circle round from one part of the picture to another. Just such a splay-footed table was to be taken up by Braque a decade later; and Braque made something special of the symphonic interior from a standard French middle-class living room.

Matisse between 1918 and 1925 was like a sundial that marks only the unclouded hours. There is a most evident contrast, for example, between the Paris studio scenes of 1916–17 and the Nice version (1919) of the same subject. But then the years 1916–17 were crucial to the survival of France as a free nation, and something of the times got into these paintings. In the earlier of the two, the stu-

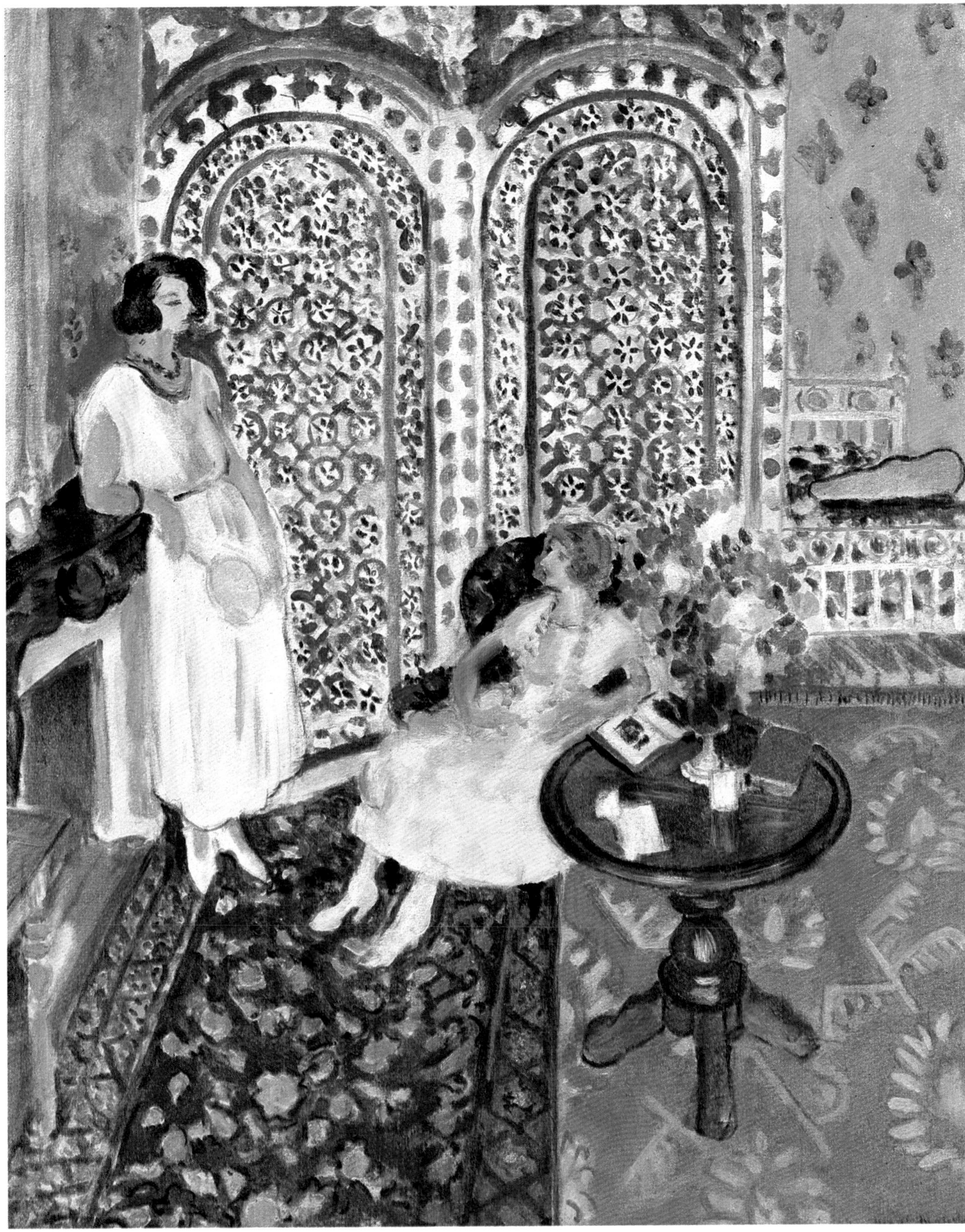

Henri Matisse.
The Moorish Screen.
1922.
Oil on canvas,
36¼ × 29¼ inches.
Philadelphia
Museum of Art.
Bequest of Lisa
Norris Elkins

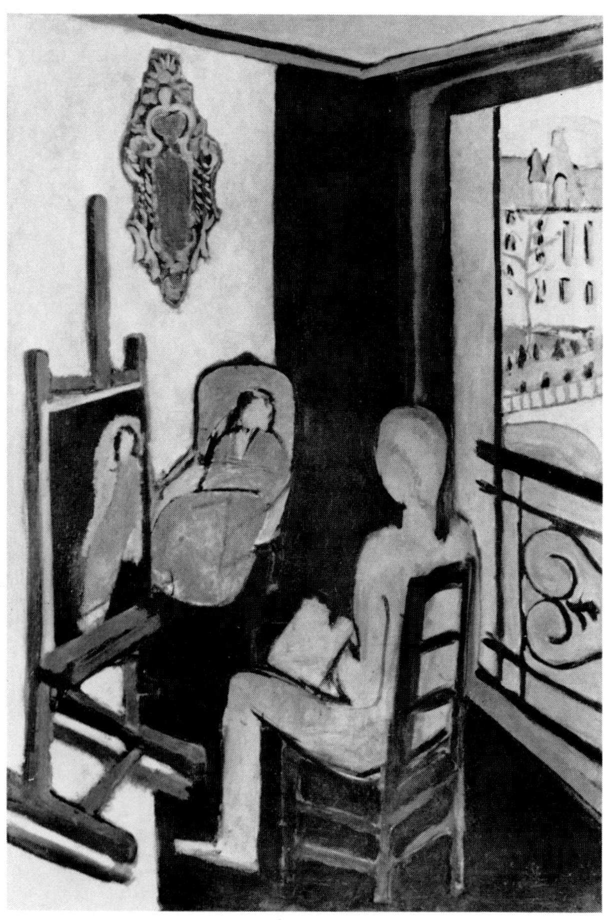

Henri Matisse.
The Painter and His Model. 1917.
Oil on canvas,
57⅞ × 38¼ inches.
Musée National
d'Art Moderne,
Paris

dio is half condemned cell and half operating room: all is bare, sparse, severe (not least, the house fronts across the Seine and the staircase that leads down from the bridge to the quayside), and the painter himself is not even present. In the second, the baroque looking-glass and the classic Parisian balcony rail alone relieve the plainness of the scene; and the artist is seen as a kind of generalized bolster, engaged on a task that drains away his individuality as a social being. It is one of the lessons of this painting that art demands the whole self: nothing less will do.

Matisse in 1919 had not gone soft. He was applying the pressure elsewhere. Not many people know, even today, the strenuous little sculptures with which Matisse came to terms in 1918–19 with quite another side of his nature. In the Nice *Artist and His Model* of 1919, we glimpse the long slender brush with which Matisse, in a distillation of delight, would feather his subject matter from the overcrowded little room onto the canvas. The sculptures come from something quite different: what the art historian Albert Elsen has called "the desire to shape and feel the literal fullness of a woman's body." Matisse was furthered in that desire by close study both of Michelangelo (in particular the famous figure of *Night* in the Medici Chapel in Florence) and of antique sculpture. Like Bonnard, he responded to the beauty and poignancy of those young female torsos that have come down to us from the Hellenistic world. In fact he owned a Roman copy of a Greek torso of the 4th century B.C.; and whereas in his paintings and drawings of the 1920s he allowed himself merely to dominate the naked female figure from a distance, he took quite a different liberty when sculpting in private and on the scale of his ever-intrusive thumb.

Matisse was a man of many guises. Unsurpassed as the poet laureate of indolence, he also kept into old age the ability to tackle a completely new task, no matter how arduous it might be. Timing played a great part in this: for Matisse knew just when to stay where he was and when to cut and run. His decisions were predicated in part on the wish to retain his powers in their totality until extreme old age. But there also entered into them something that has now vanished: a belief in serious European art as a continuum. "An artist of talent cannot do what he pleases," he said in 1936. "We are not the masters of what we produce. It is imposed upon us." Matisse saw himself as part of an organic process in which his role, as a gifted individual, was to remain alert to what needed to be done at any given time.

In this context, Matisse also saw himself—and quite rightly—as the complete artist: the man who could do anything. He could paint, he could sculpt, he could draw, he could make prints, he could illustrate on the grand scale, he could design scenery and costumes for the stage. At every turn he was conscious of the European tradition which

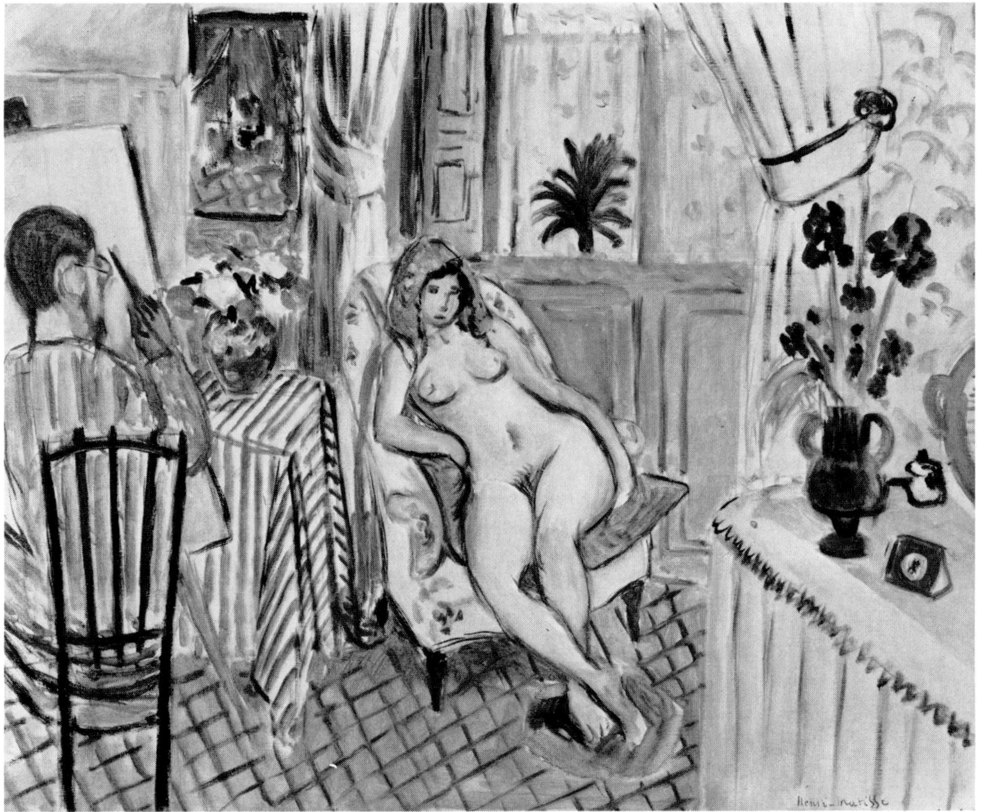

Henri Matisse. *Artist and His Model.* 1919. Oil on canvas, 25⅝ × 28¾ inches. Ruth Bakwin, New York

lay behind him. There was no reason to suppose that that tradition would be interrupted, or that artists of comparable accomplishment would not go on feeling that Matisse was in back of them, just as the Greeks, the Italians of the Renaissance, the Dutch painters of the 17th century, and the unfaltering relay team of the French School had been in back of Matisse since he first picked up his brushes in 1890.

He did not, however, see the limits of art as having been established once and for all. Himself the author of some of the most covetable of all easel paintings, he was nonetheless convinced that "one day easel painting will cease to exist. Things are changing all round us, and eventually mural painting will take over." When easel painting gave him only intermittent satisfaction, as was the case in the 1920s and '30s, he would embark on a series of prints: a long-meditated construct. It was as if he carried within himself not only the past of European art, but its future as well; and never more so than in the enormous commission which he completed in 1930–33 for the Barnes Foundation in Pennsylvania.

Matisse knew that the only department in which modern art had yet to excel was that of the alliance between painting and architecture. The modern movement had reached its highest point in the self-sufficing, autonomous, portable statement. Only once or twice had a Rousseau, a Kandinsky, a Bonnard, a Léger or a Delaunay worked on the scale which Tintoretto and Rubens had taken for granted. Matisse with *Dance* and *Music* in 1909–10 had a chance of that sort; and now, in 1930, he had it again.

It was not an easy task. Dr. Albert C. Barnes, the Argyrol millionaire, had built in Merion, a suburb of Philadelphia, a sizable mansion in the French style with stone brought from château country in the center of France. This he had filled with a collection primarily of major French painting, in which Cézanne, Seurat, Renoir and Matisse

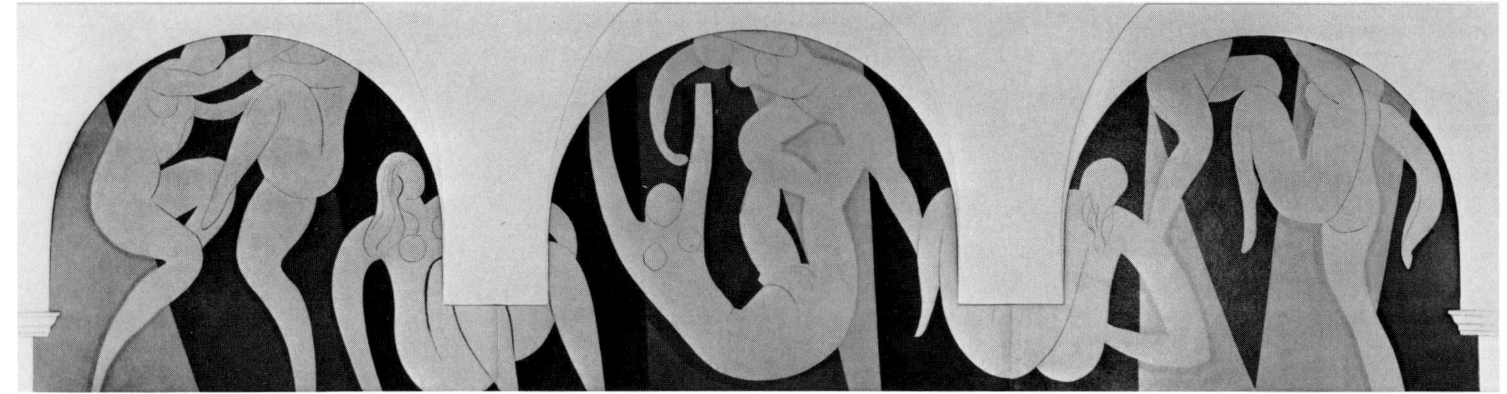

Henri Matisse.
Dance II. 1932–33.
Oil, 11 feet 8½ inches × approximately 47 feet.

himself predominated. The room which Matisse was to decorate was already hung with easel paintings of such quality that, as Matisse said himself, "another painting would simply have been out of place." Extending above the masterpieces in question was a row of windows, each 18 feet high, which looked out onto tall trees. Higher still were the three lunettes, nearly 12 feet in height at their highest point and in all nearly 16 yards across, which Matisse was to fill as he thought best. Between these lunettes were two pendentives which came down so low that the visitor has almost to bend double, in his imagination, to get from one lunette to the next. Three self-contained images would have filled the space acceptably; but Matisse was determined to overcome the awkwardness of the site. He wanted a dynamic image; one that would make the visitor forget that in relation to the room as a whole the lunettes were just three dumpy little spaces between the windows and the roof.

Most of the terms of Matisse's contract with himself were negative, therefore. The mural was not to be "another painting": there was to be no rivalry with the easel pictures below. The mural also had to stand up for itself at two completely different levels. From the floor it was to function as a substitute for the sky, which could not be seen through the windows. But from the balcony level, to which every visitor climbs in the course of his visit, the mural had to read as a statement on its own. A double play of perspective was added, in this way, to problems which were already thorny enough. Matisse also took due account both of the color of the stone and of the fact that the only source of light was from below.

In his preliminary sketches Matisse made use of his recent sculptural experience to produce group after group of athletic Amazons, each one superbly realized in the round and set against the dense and vibrant color which Matisse had perfected during his many years at the easel. But they were rejected, in turn, when Matisse found that they were forming up *as pictures* and not as an integrated mural. What he made in the end was fundamentally a huge drawing, carried out by himself with the help of a long pole. So far from giving in to the stunted conditions which were imposed by the architecture, Matisse presented his figures as giantesses who were far too tall to fit into the threefold frame. This allowed him to generate a degree of physical excitement which takes the visitor by surprise. It is as if the stone had spawned human figures many times larger than life and was no longer able to restrain them.

Not everyone can get to see the Barnes mural. It remains one of the more secret of this century's enterprises. (Matisse did it twice over, in point of fact, since Dr. Barnes gave him the wrong dimensions the first time round; the earlier version is now in the Musée d'Art Moderne de la Ville de Paris.) The mural is important not only for itself but because Matisse pioneered in it a notion which was of great importance to art after World War II: that of the painting as arena, and of the final result as something owed to a physical encounter be-

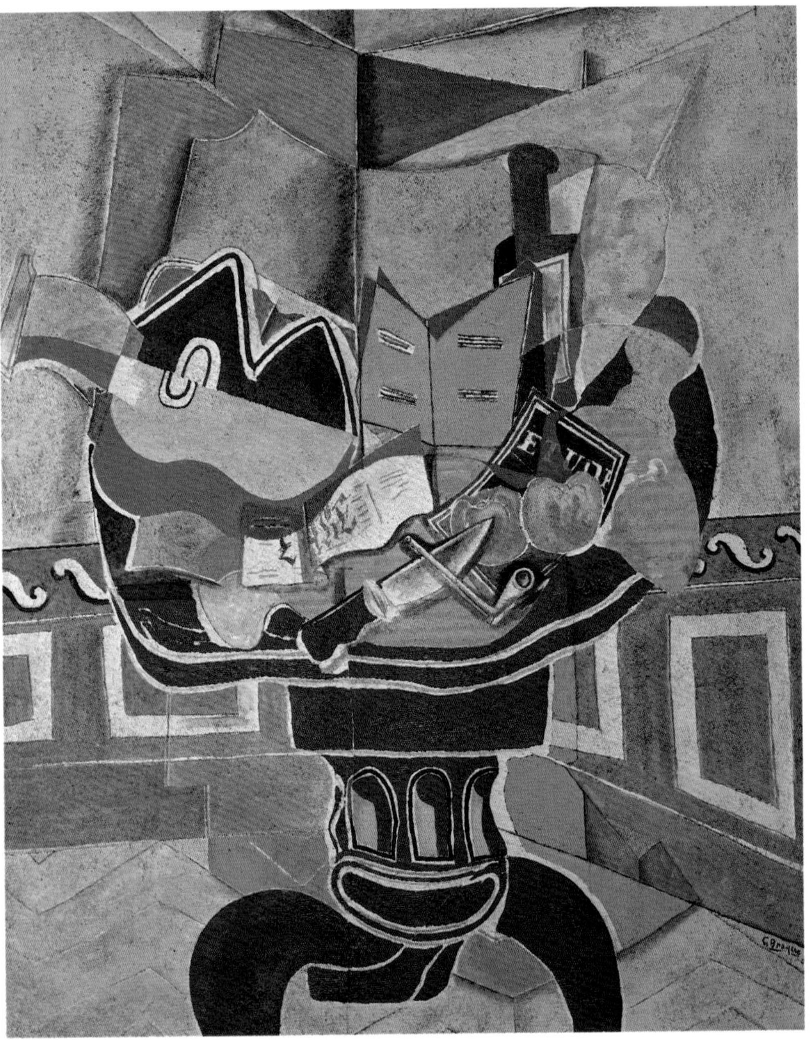

Georges Braque. *Le Guéridon (The Round Table).* 1929. Oil on canvas, 58 × 45 inches. The Phillips Collection, Washington

tween the painter and a given number of square feet of space. If Matisse was "born to simplify painting," as his teacher had told him in the 1890s, this was one of the ways in which he passed on his mandate to posterity. He was to do it to even more spectacular effect at the very end of his life in big cut-paper decorations where painting was dematerialized and color was as near as not made incorporeal. Meanwhile the Barnes mural set an august precedent.

Matisse went on renewing himself, even into the 1950s, by finding new solutions for new tasks. This was never the case with Braque. Everything that Braque did in middle and later life turned out in the end to be a way of nursing painting along; and as he grew older and frailer his studio became the whole world for him and he reacted hardly or not at all to the outside involvements—exhibitions, major commissions, polemics in print—on which art history battens. He painted for himself, not for the historian. Interpretation of his work seemed to him at best superfluous, at worst actively harmful. "The only valid thing in art is the one thing that cannot be explained," he once wrote; and in the 1950s he said that "to explain away the mystery of a great painting would do irreparable harm, for whenever you explain or define something you substitute the explanation or the definition for the real thing."

It takes a rash man to ignore a warning of that sort. But it ought to be said that these remarks apply above all to Braque's paintings of the 1940s and '50s, in which he went all out for what he called a metamorphic ambiguity; in other words, he blurred the distinction between the real and the imaginary, the literal and the metaphorical, the named and the unnamed. In those late paintings identities melt like butter in the pan; where ambiguity is fundamental to the picture it is reasonable enough that the artist should resent any attempt to explain it away. Even in a relatively early painting like the *Café-Bar* of 1919 there are passages where the images overlap in such a way that we are hard put to disentangle them. Braque at that time prepared his canvases with what the art critic John Richardson calls "a thickish sandy layer of matt black paint, which Braque compared to coffee grounds or tea leaves because, like a fortune teller, 'he can divine there things which others cannot see.' " This dense black foundation conferred upon his images a kind of immunity: press them too hard to declare their identity and they vanish.

But, like the other great Frenchmen of his generation, Braque was a strategist. It was not at all his style to peak in his 20s or 30s and thereafter go into a long decline. He was also anxious to nurse painting, as I said earlier, through a difficult period in its evolution. What Léger aimed to do by close attention to the Aviation Show, and what Matisse hoped to do by a sage diversification of his activities, Braque did by staying still in one place and counting up the things that he could do better than anyone else. He had the true French feeling for continuity; he would never have talked as Arnold Schoenberg talked when he said to a visitor in 1922 that he had "discovered something that will guarantee the supremacy of German music for the next one hundred years." But he did undoubtedly intend to put French painting beyond the reach of rivalry. *Le Guéridon (The Round Table)*, 1929, is one of the grandest and most completely realized paintings of our century. In it, Braque summed up once and for all the traditional preoccupations of Cubism: the splay-footed table with its arcaded support, the piece of sheet music, the pipe, the musical instrument, the labeled bottle, the scrolled dado, the still life of fruit. He also introduced the knife which from Edouard Manet onward had been an important element in still life. And at the top of the canvas, where the con-

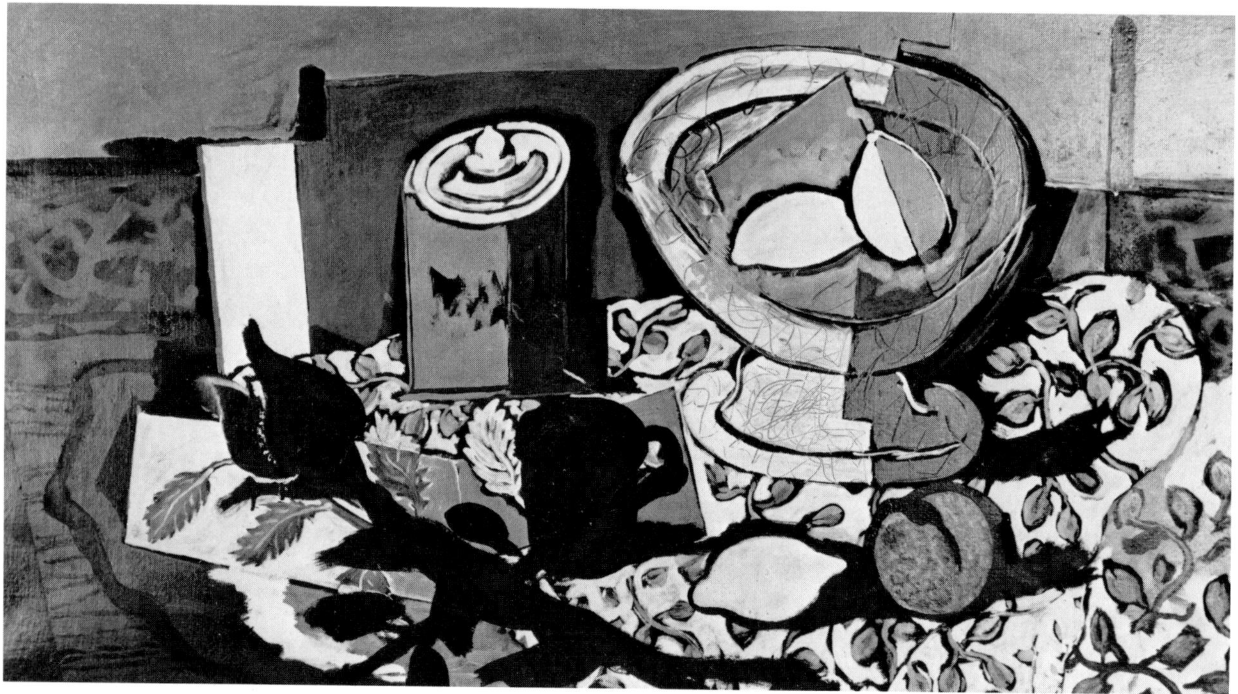

Georges Braque.
The Black Rose.
1927.
Oil on canvas,
20 × 37 inches.
Mr. and Mrs. Burton Tremaine, Meriden, Conn.

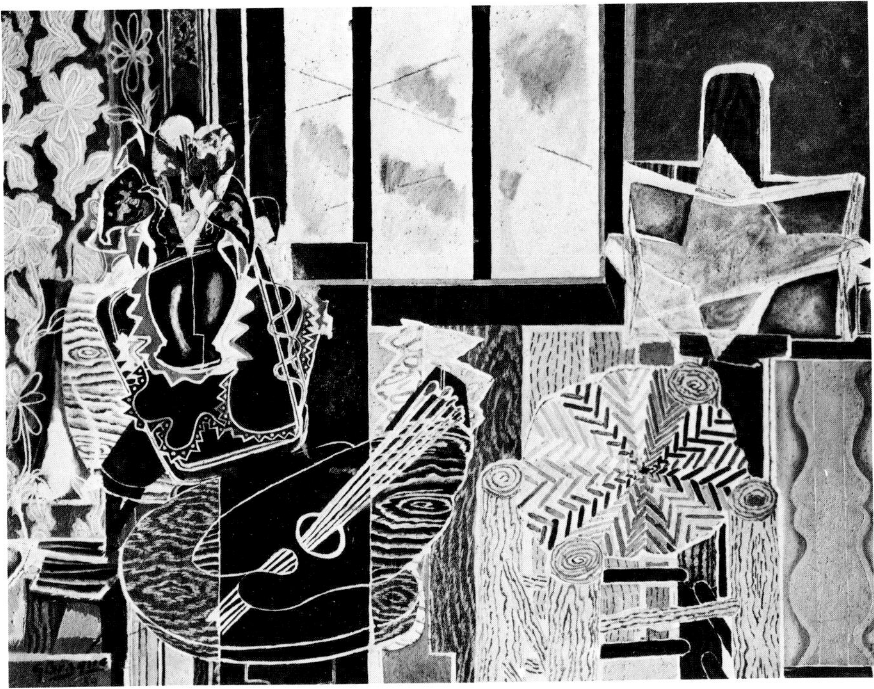

Georges Braque. *Studio (with Wooden Stool).* 1939. Oil on canvas, 45½ × 58¼ inches. Lucille Simon, Los Angeles

vergence of walls and ceiling can make for dullness, he brought the whole matter down to within an inch or two of the observer's nose and animated it with shifts of perspective and changes of color.

Braque had an unequaled sense of touch. No one has ever put on canvas a more varied or more consistently delectable substance than he. Next, he had a sense of the space in his paintings as being infinitely adjustable: something that could be bent back, folded over, hinged, cut into slivers and made transparent or opaque as suited him best. In particular, he learned to maximize the impact of his sense of touch by bringing the objects in his still lifes within reach, one and all. He carried over from Synthetic Cubism the practice of distributing color without regard for its local allegiances, and he felt at liberty to reorder the shapes of things in the interest of a majestic harmony of his own devising.

All this went in tandem, throughout his career, with a total appreciation of the still uncorrupted countryside of France, and of the things which it could produce for the still-life table top. Looking at a picture like his *The Black Rose,* 1927, we remember what the Goncourt brothers said of Chardin: that he could reproduce for us "the shaggy velvet of the peach, the amber transparency of the white grape, the sugary rime of the plum, the moist crimson of strawberries, the hardy berry of the muscatel and its smoke-blue film, the wrinkles and tubercles of an orange skin, the embroidered guipure of melons and the copperas of old apples. . . ." But when we look more closely it turns out that what Braque sets before us is an equivalent, not an imitation; in this context Braque evokes, but does not specify. As he grew older, indeed, Braque began to pit the identities of art against the identities of everyday life. In a painting like the *Studio Interior with Black Vase* of 1938, everything has equal status: the paneled wall, the grained wood of the easel, the vivid wallpaper, the palette with dabs of paint still wet, the canvas on the easel and the framed canvas on the wall. Braque practiced, as between each and every one of these surfaces, a perfect equality: none had precedence over the others. Each form, each plane, each texture, each nicely contrasted patch of color slid into its place.

When ruminating on the nature of art, and on the tasks which art could still validly undertake,

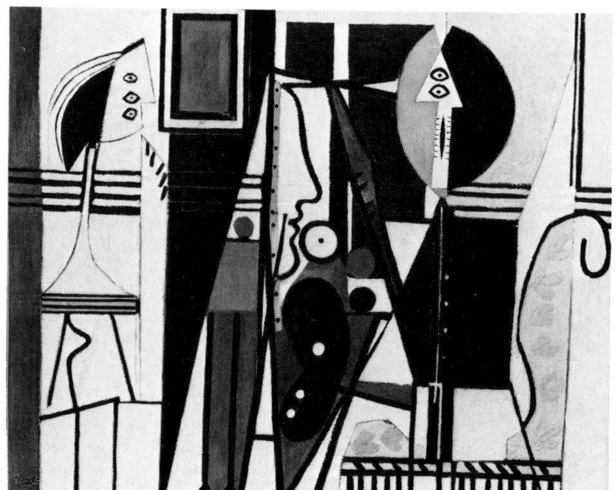

Pablo Picasso.
Painter and Model.
1928.
Oil on canvas,
51⅛ × 64¼ inches.
The Museum of
Modern Art, New
York. The Sidney
and Harriet Janis
Collection

Braque was at one with Matisse and Picasso in that he turned again and again to the studio itself for his subject matter. The best way to think about art was to see what actually happened when someone was making it. The act of painting was a metaphor for creativity in its purest, most absolute form, and a lot of irrelevance could be avoided if the scrutinies of art were turned inward, upon art itself; that was the idea, and it lent itself to the widest possible range of statement. Picasso in the late 1920s most often took an aggressive and schematic point of view, emphasizing the polarization of artist and sitter and the ways in which the information given by the sitter's appearance is censored (or added to, or transformed) by the time it reaches the canvas. Matisse enjoyed playing with our expectations in such a way that we are never for instance quite sure (as in *The Artist and His Model,* 1936) whether we are looking out of a window onto a real landscape or whether we are looking at a picture that has been hung on the wall in just the right place. (In this case it's a picture: a cartoon for a tapestry in which Matisse drew on his memories of a visit to Tahiti.) Braque did not align himself with either, but went quietly ahead with his own inquiries, which were about the extent to which objects can lose their identities and yet retain them. He wanted to find out how many kinds of reality could live together within a single picture and in ways that only painting could bring about.

All this took him a long way from the Cubism of 1910–12, which was fundamentally an art of plain statement about a small number of identifiable facts. But Braque in the 1930s was a very different person from the enormously strong young man who before 1914 could overturn a carnival float with his own two shoulders. There is in great art an element of historical fatality; but something is also owed to the private evolution of an individual human being. Braque's health never recovered from the wounds which he sustained in 1915, and in middle life he had none of the power of attack which made Picasso react instantaneously to whatever happened around him. "A picture is not a snapshot," Braque said in 1939; and in the late 1930s he began to treat the world in terms of a consciousness which took as much account of what was not as of what was. He was still interested in fact, and was as ready as ever to evoke a specific kind of graining in wood or the precise outline of a bottom-heavy jug. But if mystery entered into his experience—if there was a bird on the canvas on the easel, for instance, and if that bird seemed to take off and fly around the room—Braque did not demur. Nor did it at all disturb him if objects went adrift from their presumed positions in space and floated around the room in a state of transparency. This vision of a world in a state of perpetual flux, motion and change was, after all, no more unreal than the traditional picture image of a world artificially stilled and categorized according to a single unvarying canon.

These late Braques are philosophical paintings, even if the manner of their presentation is irresistibly voluptuous. Such a gamut of sanded tans, so close a conjunction of purple and violet had rarely been seen before. As surely as the Surrealists, but with none of their sensational or pathological subject matter, Braque in the 1930s reintroduced the irrational into painting. (In 1935 he said that "writing a poem, painting a picture, carving a stone—all three of them are irrational acts.") What he wanted at that time was to achieve an equipoise, peculiar to himself, between logic and the free

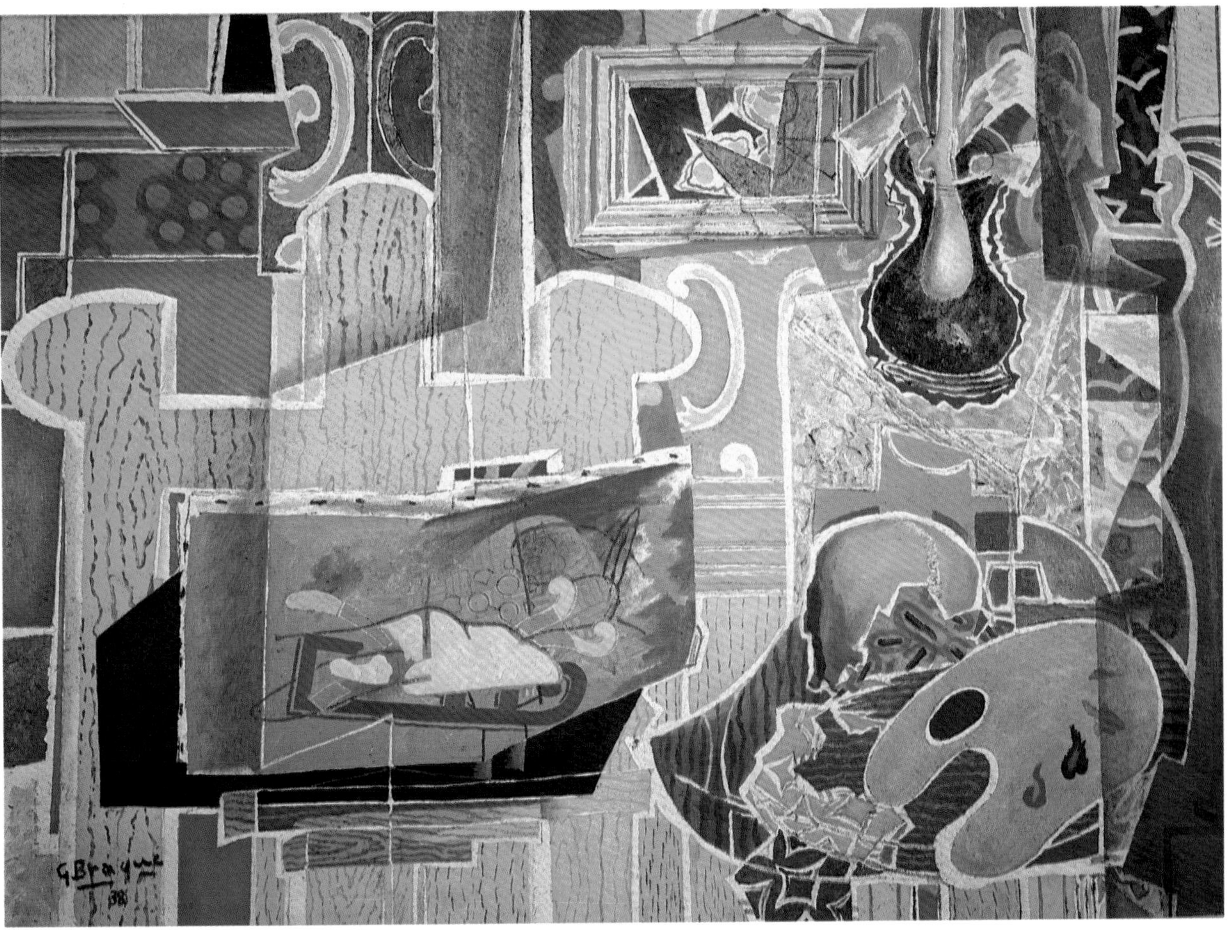

Georges Braque. *Studio Interior with Black Vase.* 1938. Oil and sand on canvas, 38¼ × 51 inches. Mr. and Mrs. David Lloyd Kreeger, Washington

play of instinct—and between the strict scaffolding of Cubism as it had evolved before 1914 and the fluidity and irrationality of life as it actually presents itself.

As in Picasso's *Painter and Model* of 1928, the studio in Braque's *Studio (with Wooden Stool)* of 1939 is represented mainly in terms of tall flat rectangular panels. But Braque allowed himself an infinitely greater license in the matter of textures, in the scale on which individual objects are presented and in the way in which space is reordered. Objects move forward and back, turn opaque or transparent, at the painter's whim. Real flowers are set off against simulated ones; imitation wood is set off against the real thing. As with the splay-footed table in Matisse's *The Window* of 1916, the spokelike interweaving of the seat of the stool on the right is used to guide us gently from one point of the compass to the next. As for the bird on the easel, it is the forerunner of many others in Braque's later work. Is it a picture of a bird? Or is it a real bird that has flown into the studio from outside and is posing in front of the easel? Or is it a painted bird that has "chosen liberty" and refused to stay on the canvas? Braque isn't telling: this is just the kind of poetic ambiguity which he most enjoyed.

It could be argued from 1933 onward that philosophical inquiry might well be suspended, in deference to the steadily worsening condition of Europe. Braque did not agree. "We must insist," he said in 1939, "on a categorical distinction between act and actuality." This belief has sometimes got him into trouble with self-appointed moralists, most of whom have never seen a shot fired in anger, let alone fought as gallantly as

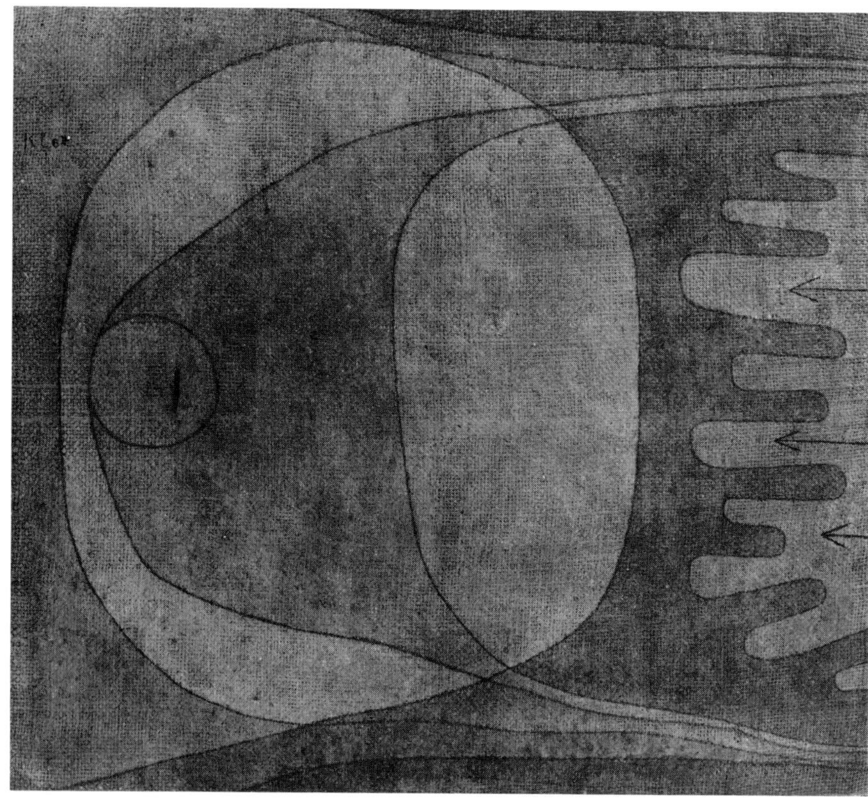

Paul Klee.
Fear (Angst). 1934.
Oil on burlap,
20 × 21⅞ inches.
The Museum of
Modern Art, New
York. Gift of Nelson
A. Rockefeller

Braque. Where the future of Europe was concerned Braque saw as clearly, and felt as deeply, as any other intelligent and humane observer. But in his art he was an armored man, and the pictures went their own way without interruption until France herself was brought almost to a standstill during the later stages of the German occupation.

Throughout the 1930s Braque was free, moreover, to wall himself up in his studio if he so wished. The case was very different for Paul Klee, who in 1933 was deprived of the right to teach in Germany and in 1934 learned that the Nazis had ordered the confiscation of a book on his work which had been written by his old friend Will Grohmann. Switzerland was the country of Klee's birth, and to that extent his misfortunes were mitigated; but he felt them acutely, nonetheless, and his son Felix has described how one of his first actions on arriving in Switzerland as a refugee was to make a little picture called *Struck off the List.* Klee was sensitive to every vibration of the world around him—after the outbreak of World War I in 1914 he wrote in his diary, "For a long time I have carried this war within me"—and between 1933 and his death in June, 1940, he referred over and over again in his work to the all-encompassing persecution which was the lot of so many of his friends and colleagues.

He never did this in a literal or a descriptive way. It was not his role to duplicate what could be seen on the newsreels or read about in those newspapers which could still report freely. He was there to find what he had so often found before in happier contexts: the perfect metaphor for what everyone was feeling but no one knew as well as he how to express. He set before us the idea of fear, at a time when virtually every European had fear as his daily companion. Klee saw fear in terms of an inescapable intrusion. In an oblique but unforgettable image, he made us feel that a man was trying to escape from his terrors in sleep, only to find that fear had impregnated the very blankets that he tries to pull up to his chin. Klee imagined his *Letter Ghost* at a time when not to get a letter

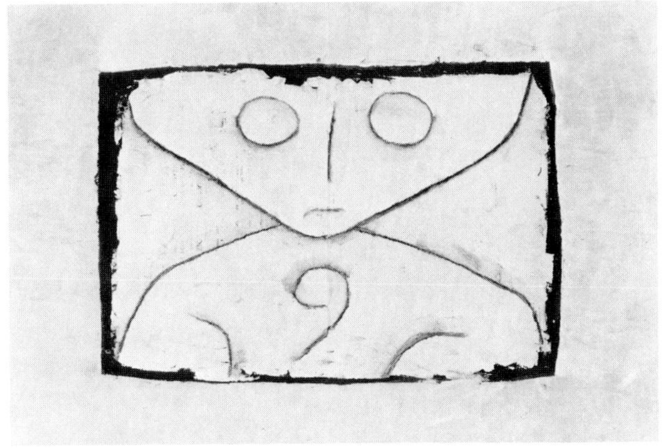

Paul Klee.
Letter Ghost. 1937.
Gouache, watercolor and ink on newspaper, 13 × 19¼ inches. The Museum of Modern Art, New York. Purchase

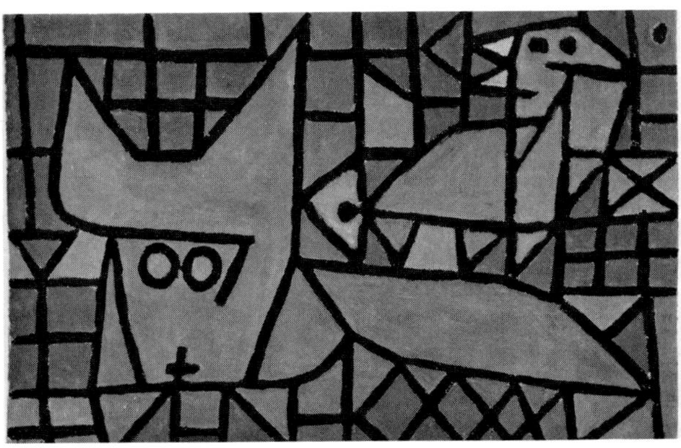

Paul Klee.
Imprisoned Animal. 1940.
Gouache on paper, 12¼ × 19¼ inches. Private collection, Switzerland

often meant the arrest, if not the death, of the person who had gone to the mailbox as a free human being the week before. Waiting for a letter that does not come is torture, as we all know. What could be more natural, to Klee's way of thinking, than that letters should have ghosts—white-faced presences that take on the look of a human head and a pair of shoulders? The image of an imprisoned animal in 1940 was as poignant to Klee, and therefore to ourselves, as was the image of the imprisoned unicorn to the people who made *The Hunt of the Unicorn* tapestries in the 15th century. Klee did not apply himself in literal terms to the history of his own times. But we know, all the same, that this imprisoned animal with its huge staring eyes is a metaphor for the millions of people who were to experience imprisonment in one form or another in the 1940s. It is thanks to people like him, as much as to commentators of a more straightforward kind, that posterity knows what it was like to live in Europe at that time.

Yet there is a case for saying that in terms of immediate public impact Picasso's *Guernica* was a greater service to humanity, at the time it was painted, than any other single painting of the period. It was in April, 1937, that the Spanish city of Guernica was destroyed by German aircraft under the order of General Franco. The world has seen many such things since, and seen them on a bigger scale and with more calamitous weapons. But at the time there was something uniquely chilling about the deliberate obliteration of a historic city. Six days later Picasso began work on the huge monochromatic painting which bears the name *Guernica.* This painting was shown from July, 1937, onward in the Spanish Pavilion at the Paris International Exhibition; and as a contribution to the poetics of outrage it had a colossal effect.

It is a tribute to the power of *Guernica*—and a comment, also, on the confusion of the times—that we still find it difficult to place the picture once and for all in the context of Picasso's output. He himself said in 1965 that as between *Guernica* and *The Three Dancers* of 1925, "I much prefer *The Three Dancers.* It's more a real painting—a painting in itself without any outside considerations." And there is in *Guernica* something descriptive—something of the "Agit-prop" wall-newspaper raised to the scale of epic—which lays it open to comprehensive explanation in just the way that Braque regarded as unworthy of high art. But there are moments in history at which it is more important to strike hard and strike soon than to aim at the privileged status of high art, and the summer of 1937 was one of them.

In painting *Guernica* Picasso took up a challenge—that of the specific event from recent history—which for one reason and another is now often regarded as being outside the province of serious art. Its affinities in that respect are with the 19th century: with Goya's *The Third of May, 1808,*

Delacroix's *Liberty Leading the People,* Manet's *The Execution of the Emperor Maximilian.* Beyond these it looked back to a classic figure subject from still earlier days—the Massacre of the Innocents. At the same time it has characteristics which relate it to our own era: the image is put before us in the blacks and whites of the 1930s newsreel, and the scale and format foreshadow the sprawling animation of the wide-screen movies of the 1960s. There is something of everything in *Guernica,* from the tabloid headline to distant echoes of 11th-century Spanish illuminated manuscripts. On one level the imagery is as explicit as that of a news photograph; on another it secretes layer upon layer of recondite allusion, some of it conscious, some of it most probably not.

There are in existence 45 preliminary studies for *Guernica,* all but one of them dated. There are also seven photographs of successive phases during the painting of the picture itself. We know a great deal about *Guernica,* therefore. We know that the figure of the wounded horse derives from a drawing made by Picasso in 1917, and that the striped skirt and flung-back head of the woman on the left derive from the mourning Maenad in *The Three Dancers* of 1925. The broken spear and the head of the dead soldier in *Guernica* hark back, as we also know, to the *Studio with Plaster Head,* again of 1925. There are many pre-echoes in Picasso's work for the figure of the bull, bemused and stationary despite all the tumult around him. If the arm that holds the lamp seems to be 15 feet long, and if the necks of the four women seem to be made of elastic, these elongations were initiated in the 1920s, when Picasso spent a lot of time at the seaside and noticed how people seem to deny their normal dimensions when they get to run and jump around the beach.

Every great artist carries much of the past of art within him, and when he is under exceptional pressure the past is likely to break in, unbidden, in ways not to be foreseen. When the English art historian Anthony Blunt published a book on *Guernica* in 1969 he had no difficulty in tracing the formalized masks of Picasso's women to massacre subjects painted in the 17th century by Guido Reni and Nicolas Poussin. But along with identifiable borrowings of this kind there came allusions of an oblique and perhaps involuntary sort. On the ground in the middle of the picture, beneath the forefeet of the horse, there is for instance a flower for which no logical reason can be adduced in a purely metropolitan scene. "Is it permissible," Blunt asked, "to see in this an allusion to the anemone which sprang from the blood of Adonis and became a symbol of his resurrection?"

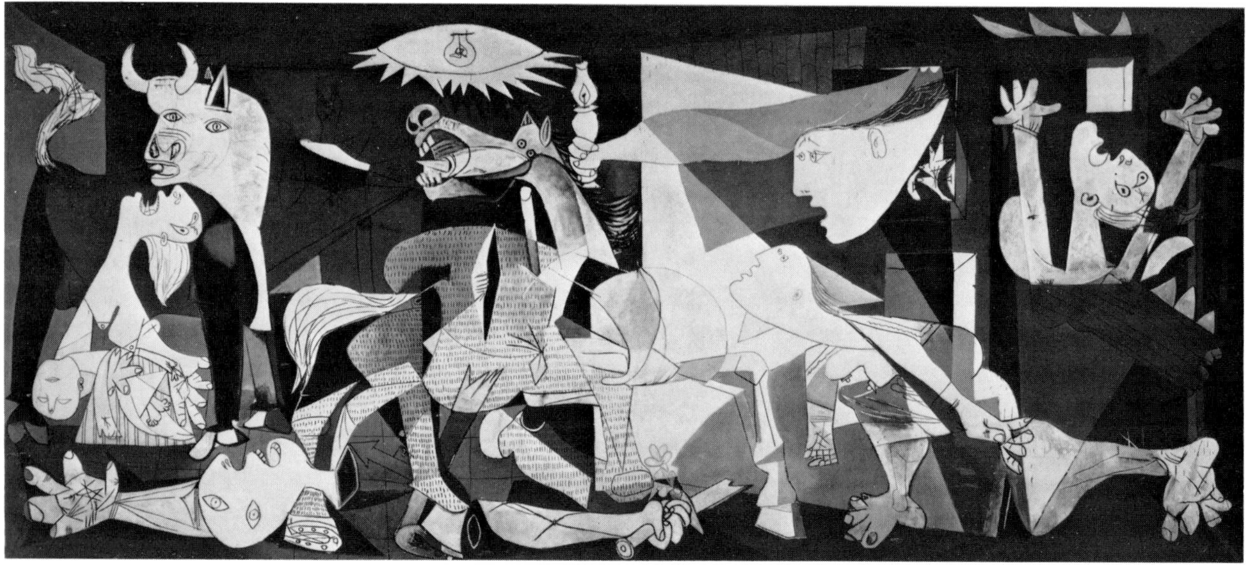

Pablo Picasso. *Guernica.* 1937. Oil on canvas, 11 feet 6 inches × 25 feet 8 inches. The Museum of Modern Art, New York. On extended loan

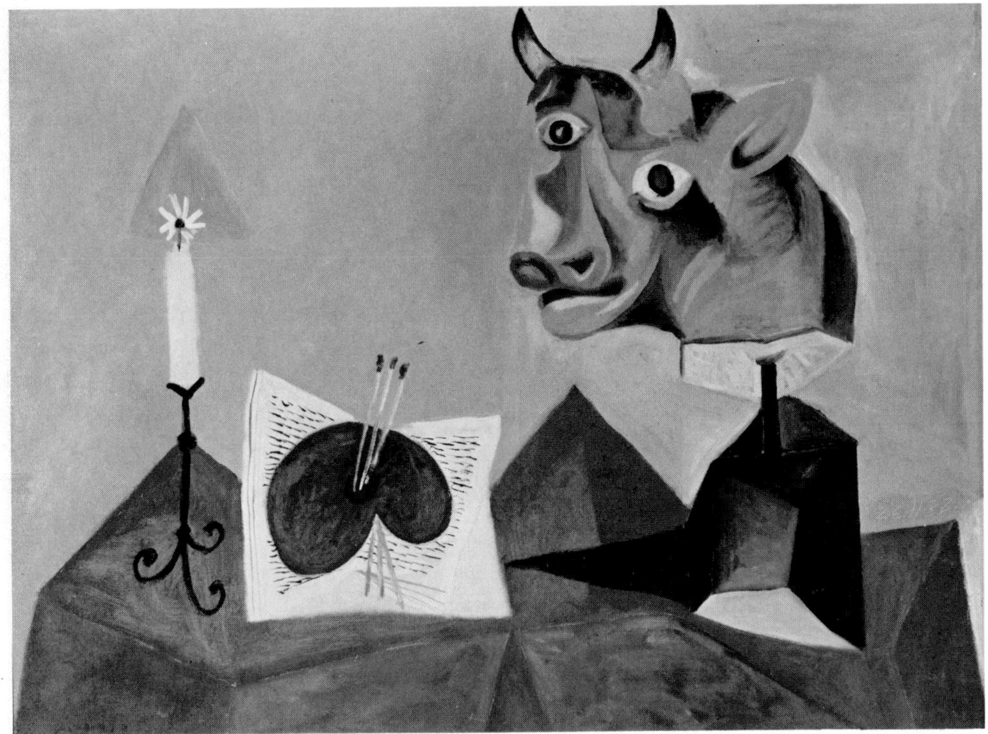

Pablo Picasso. *Still Life with Red Bull's Head.* 1938. Oil on canvas, 38⅛ × 51 inches. The Museum of Modern Art, New York. Promised gift of Mr. and Mrs. William A. M. Burden, New York

Guernica is, therefore, on one level a polemical painting that goes all out for quick results. On another, it stands for that general mobilization of the European past which was art's last line of defense in the 1920s and '30s. It can be seen as a magniloquent patchwork, and it can also be seen as one of the instances in which a major modern artist has faced directly up to his responsibilities as a social being. As to precisely where the truth lies, opinions are likely to vary from one age to another. My own view is that as larger lunacies efface the memory of the destruction of Guernica, the picture is likely to look more and more like an isolated phenomenon in Picasso's work: one that by the standards of the highest art relies too much, as Picasso himself said, on "outside considerations." It stands out, all right; but does it quite stand up? Does it do something that could not be done in any other medium, or is there in the end too much of illustration in it?

When Picasso painted his *Still Life with Red Bull's Head* in November, 1938, he must have had this problem on his mind. For what he did was to carry over from *Guernica* the steady flame which stands for reason and truth; with it, he carried over the head of the bull. Between the two are a palette and a book, symbols of the power to make truth visible. There are changes, since *Guernica.* Not only has the bull's head been skinned, but it has taken on an unmistakable look of Picasso himself. The huge helpless head glares across at the flame; the painter's tools lie to hand; the picture has a message: it is that it is one thing to see the truth and quite another to know how to put it on canvas. Nothing in this picture is explicit; but like so much that we have considered here it is a delaying action on behalf of a European tradition far gone in decline.

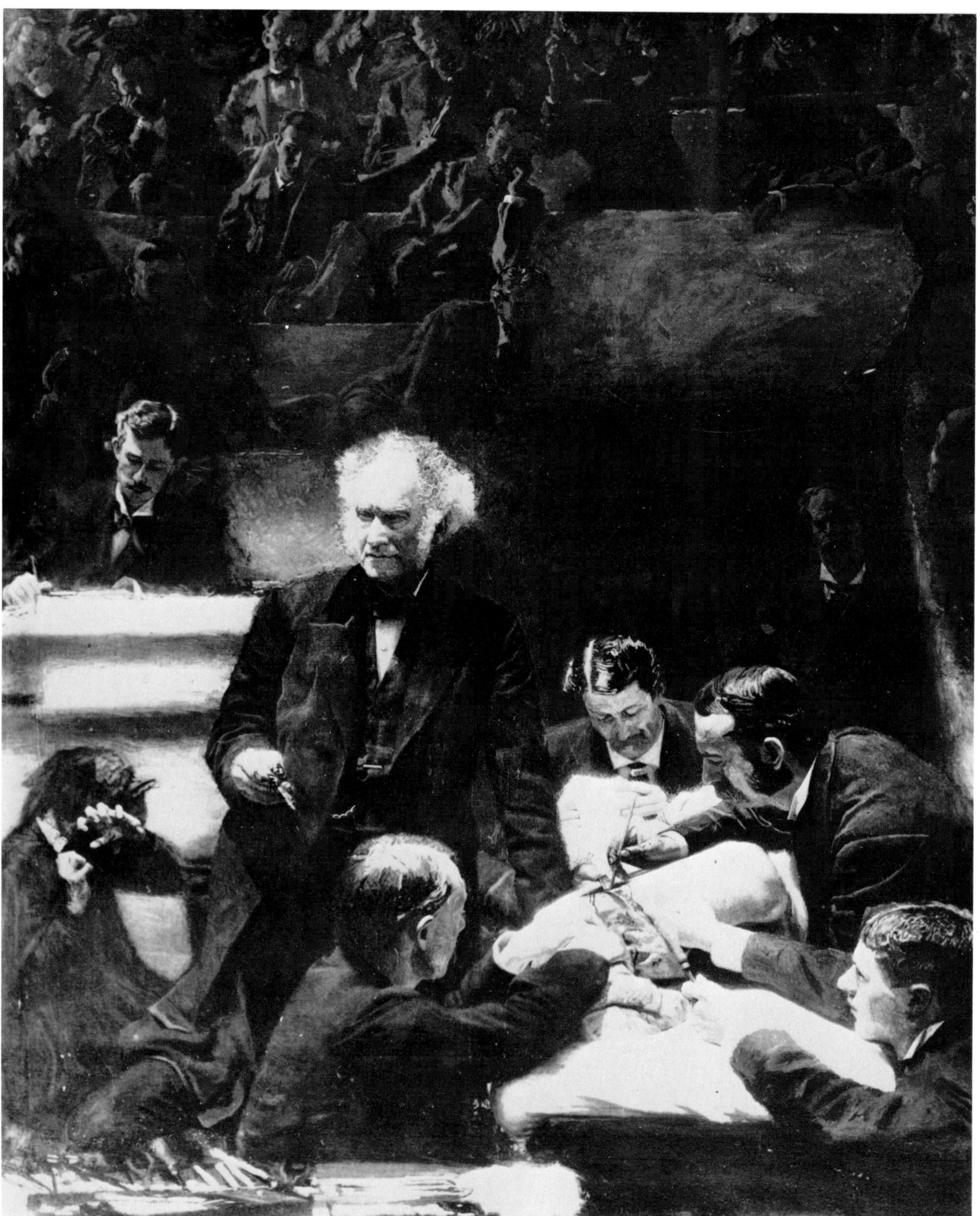

Thomas Eakins.
The Gross Clinic.
1875.
Oil on canvas,
8 feet × 6 feet
6 inches.
Jefferson Medical
College of
Philadelphia

AMERICA REDEFINED

Between 1945 and 1970 there was acted out in New York City a considerable human adventure: the emergence after nearly 300 years of an independent, self-generating and specifically American art.

Why *then*, and not before? Why *there*, and not somewhere else? These questions deserve an answer. For there had of course been art in America before, and some of it had been very good. But it had stood in the shadow of European art. Such independence as it had was owed sometimes to its American subject matter, sometimes to the American turn of mind which lay behind it, sometimes to the irresistible complicity which links a painter to his public. There had also, as we have seen, been instances in America from 1913 onward of an art which could be called "new." But these were phenomena without progeny; the artists in question did not, for one reason or another, produce that continuing body of distinctly new work which was the mark of the great Europeans. Sometimes they died young, sometimes they turned conservative, sometimes they gave up hope, sometimes they went so far as to destroy their earlier and more experimental work.

It is for these reasons that American painting remained until 1945 in what might be called a colonial situation. It was dominated, in other words, by the art of other times and older places. Thomas Eakins was a first-rate human being, but something in his art came to him at second hand —from Rembrandt, in the case of *The Gross Clinic*, from Gustave Courbet, from Thomas Couture. *The Gross Clinic* is one of the noblest pictures ever painted by an American. Though clearly based on Rembrandt's *Anatomy Lesson*, it is specifically of the American 19th century in its determination to get at the truth, no matter how awkwardly. Medical studies were not for the squeamish, as we can judge from the attitude of the man in the foreground on the left; and art was not for the squeamish either. It demanded the same degree of dedication and that same insensibility to ridicule which distinguished the great pioneers in other disciplines. Anatomy was as fundamental to art in Eakins's day as it was to medicine: whence the gravity with which he recorded the attitudes of those who, like himself, were looking for the truth at no matter what cost to themselves.

Eakins was probity personified; there are paintings by him which stand out as landmarks in the history of American self-awareness; nothing in his work is fudged or faked. But if we put an Eakins on the wall beside a great Courbet it ends by looking limited, local, and in the noblest sense provincial. We have to remind ourselves that for an American painter to come so far in the 1870s and '80s was already a prodigious achievement.

Yet America had already a literature of the kind, and of the stature, which stamps and defines a great nation at a crucial stage in its development. In the France of the 1850s Edgar Allan Poe was one of the most influential of all English-speaking writers; and a nation which had produced, in that same decade, Melville's *Moby Dick,* Whitman's *Leaves of Grass,* Thoreau's *Walden,* Hawthorne's *The Scarlet Letter,* Emerson's *Representative Men* and Motley's *The Rise of the Dutch Republic* did not have to bother about being called "provincial." Every one of these books was unmistakably and irreducibly American; and so firmly did Melville, Whitman and Hawthorne probe the sensitive places of American awareness that they can be said to have usurped the prerogatives, and to a real degree the idiom, of art. Clement Greenberg

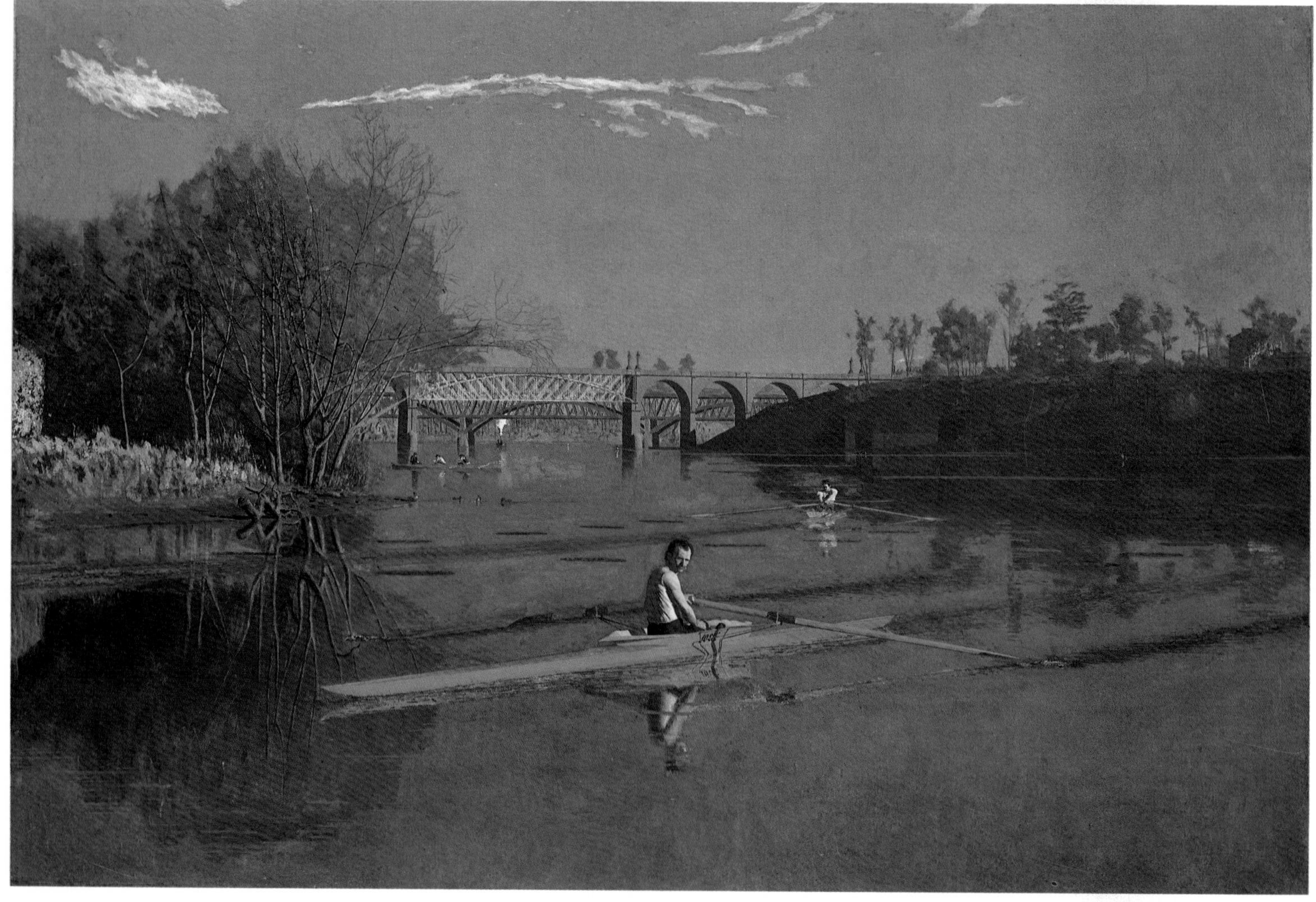

Thomas Eakins. *Max Schmitt in a Single Scull.* 1871. Oil on canvas, 32¼ × 46¼ inches. The Metropolitan Museum of Art, New York. Alfred N. Punnett Fund and gift of George D. Pratt

pointed this out as long ago as 1944 when he said that chiaroscuro, or the instinctive play of light against dark, was fundamental to *Moby Dick*, where "blackness and night are the dominants of the first chapters; the narrator stumbles through pitch darkness to find a Negro prayer meeting being held behind the first door from which a ray of light emerges; this prepares us at a long remove for the contrast of the evil whiteness of the whale."

It would have been difficult, in any case, for American painters to rival the epical assurance with which both Whitman and Melville addressed themselves to an expanding America. The language of painting was not in the American grain, as was the language of literature. It had to be learned, and learned in relation to alien examples from alien lands. It was all very well for Ralph Waldo Emerson to say to a Harvard audience in 1837 that "our day of dependence draws to a close. . . . We have listened too long to the courtly muses of Europe. . . . We will walk on our own feet; we will work with our own hands; we will speak our own minds." The American poet, novelist, philosopher, statesman or jurist did not need to look overseas; in his domain, and in the American life style as a whole, there was already a tradition to be proud of. If the American painter looked around him with an equivalent ambition he saw only what had been done better in Rome, in Venice, in Paris, in Düsseldorf, in Munich, even in London. It was a discouraging state of affairs; and there was no shortcut to its transformation.

The only thing to do was what the best American painters kept doing instinctively: plug away at the alliance of European styling with American subject matter until one day there would exist a native tradition with enough momentum to lift off onto a completely different level of achievement. In particular the steadfast contemplation of everyday fact might one day yield impressive results. Emerson defined this admirable and enduring American trait when he said at Thoreau's funeral in 1862 that "every property of matter is a school for the understanding—its solidity or resistance, its inertia, its extension, its figure, its divisibility. The understanding adds, divides, combines, measures, finds nutriment and room for activity in this worthy sense." It was this side of Thoreau—what Emerson called his "natural skill for mensuration" —which makes him so outstanding as an observer of Nature; and I owe to the art historian Barbara Novak the insight that this same skill underlies many of the finest of American 19th-century paintings. We could say of George Caleb Bingham in his Mississippi River scenes, of Winslow Homer in his *Dad's Coming*, and of Eakins in his minutely planned and replanned studies of sculling, what Emerson said of Thoreau, that "his power of observation seemed to indicate additional senses. He saw as with microscope, heard as with ear trumpet, and his memory was a photographic register of all that he saw and heard."

Implicit in all this was not only a care for exact statement but a determination to tell the truth. American painters had not the fluency of their contemporaries in France or England or Germany, but their very awkwardness makes us the more confident of what they have to tell us. When Henry James was writing regularly about new painting in the 1870s his idea of a good "modern" subject was something that reeked of the picturesque: local life in Capri or Tangier, for instance. For this reason he despised Winslow Homer for what he called his "blankness of fancy": his trust, in other words, in the meticulous measurement of the local scene. We can almost hear James grind his teeth as he lists Homer's subject matter: "his barren plank fences, his glaring, bald, blue skies, his big, dreary, vacant lots of meadows, his freckled, straight-haired Yankee urchins, his flat-breasted maidens, suggestive of a dish of rural doughnuts and pie, his calico sun-bonnets, his flannel shirts, his cowhide boots." But mensuration wins out: it would be hard to find anything painted in Capri or Tangier that is fit to hang in the same room with Homer's *The Nooning*.

A provinciality that is accepted and lived

through for what it is may have a dignity all its own. Listening to Dutch music, grappling with the Norwegian novel, sitting in the main square of a market town in the Balkans, we become aware of this. But American 19th-century painting does not come across to us as an art that is resigned to never getting any nearer to the mainstream. It has the quality of an art that one day will get, from the society which surrounds it, a charge so strong as to be almost without precedent. An imaginative American just *knew*, in the 1870s and '80s, that time was on his side. Eakins had been to Paris in the 1860s, and no American painter ever put the city to better use; but he told his students, all the same, that "if America is to produce great painters, and if young art students wish to assume a place in the history of art in their country, their first desire should be to remain in America, to peer deeper into the heart of American life."

And American life really did reward those artists who put their trust in it. This was particularly true of American landscape, and of the plain-spoken character of American country life. But there was still a European overlay to most 19th-century accounts of the American experience. Sometimes the artists had actually been born in Europe, like Albert Bierstadt. Often they went to Europe for a mandatory period of study and assimilation. Even if—like Fitz Hugh Lane—they had never left the United States there were still echoes, somewhere in back, of a European achievement. We cannot look at Lane's paintings of the New England seacoast without thinking of German Romantic painting, any more than we can look at an Asher Brown Durand without thinking of Claude Lorrain, or at the giddying panoramas of Frederic Edwin Church without thinking of how J. M. W. Turner had tackled the immensities of the Alps. What gives such paintings their singular beauty is precisely the tension between these echoed achievements and a specifically American subject matter. Henry James thought that Winslow Homer had taken "the least pictorial features of the least pictorial range of scenery and civilization"; but the vigor of Homer's *Snap the Whip* comes as much from the careful plotting of horizontals and diagonals—an echo, most probably, of Old Master painting—as from the linked energies of the nine little boys as they pull this way and that.

Toward the end of the 19th century, two things combined to disturb the equilibrium between Europe and America which had been achieved, however approximately, by the painters I have named. One was that the new European influences were of quite another kind; the other, that New York became what it has remained ever since—the effective capital of American creativity. These two factors in combination brought about the loss of the crystalline, hymnlike character which reached its apotheosis in the work of Fitz Hugh Lane and his fellow Luminists. They also meant that metropolitan imagery made its appearance, for the first time, in American art.

Sometimes this metropolitan imagery prompted an art of record: one which preserved the look of things in a specific place at a specific time. Eastman Johnson's New York interiors of the late 1860s and early '70s are examples of this. Johnson was as good a craftsman, in his way, as Léon Marcotte, the French decorator and cabinetmaker who was much in demand in New York at that time, and when he was commissioned to portray one of Marcotte's interiors the two men played ideally into each other's hands. But in such paintings the role of the artist did not really differ in kind from the role of the valet who saw to it that the master of the house had a clean shirt every day; these tightly packed pictures are fundamentally menial in their function.

New York had nothing of the exalted teaching tradition which had been initiated in Philadelphia by Eakins and was continued from 1877 onward by his successor, Thomas Pollock Anshutz. It was with Anshutz that there entered into American painting something that had never been there before: the completely realized perception of metro-

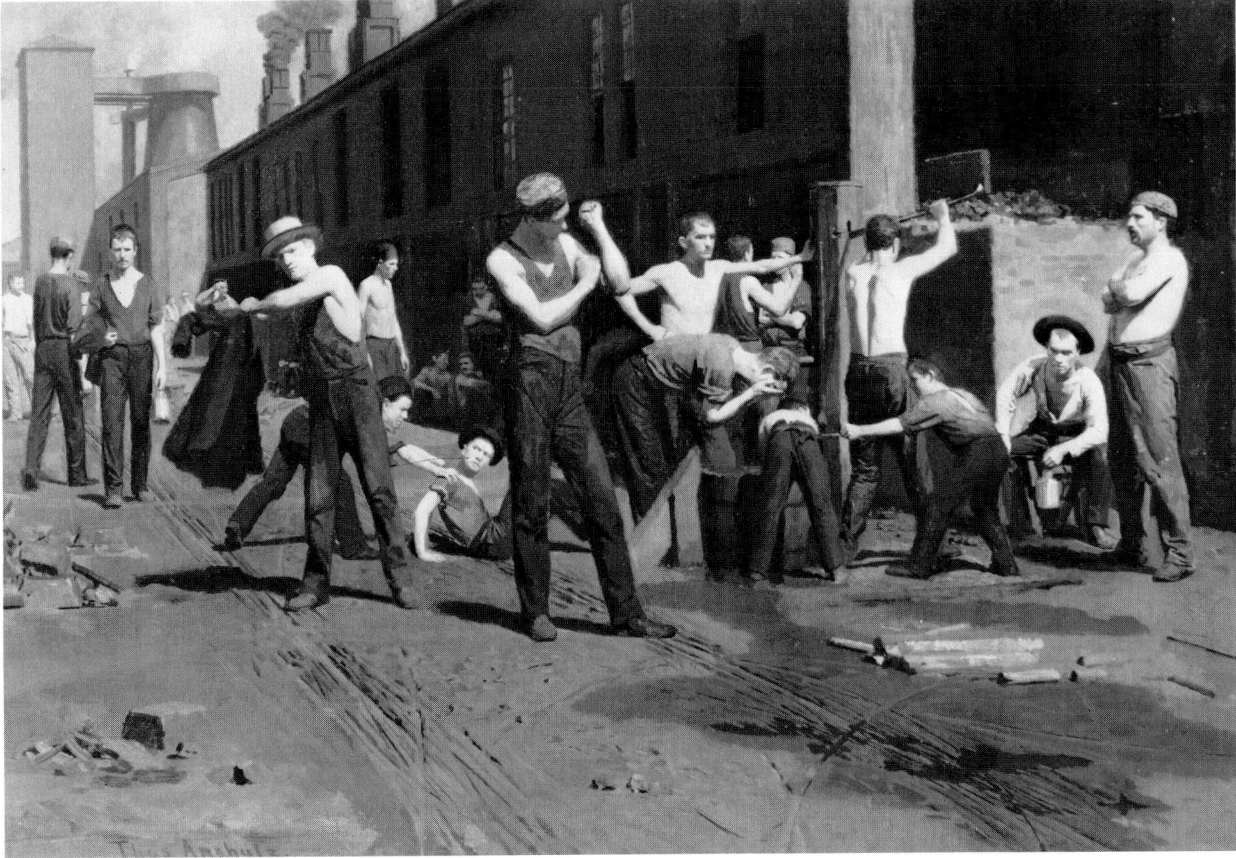

Thomas Anshutz.
Steelworkers—Noontime.
c. 1880–82.
Oil on canvas,
17 × 24 inches.
Private collection

politan life. In a painting like his *Steelworkers—Noontime* (first exhibited in 1883) the principle of mensuration still applies; it was certainly not of Anshutz that William Morris Hunt was thinking when he wrote in his influential *Talks on Art* that "people think it isn't smart to measure, and take pains. Well, let such draw fine things—if they can." We can see from *Steelworkers—Noontime* that Anshutz took enormous pains: measuring, plotting the fall of light, testing his long diagonal, balancing light against dark, making sure that the rutted tracks in the narrow street echoed the line of his roofs. Care of this order had been taken by William Sidney Mount, for one, in the 1840s. But whereas Mount quite consciously dealt in an unspoiled Arcadia which found a ready market among moneyed metropolitans, Anshutz annexed for art the new conditions of industrial society. Earlier even than Georges Seurat in Paris, he brought an echo of the ancient world to the day-to-day life of the factory worker. He was Eakins' assistant when he painted this picture, and it has something of Eakins' own moral grandeur.

Anshutz spent all his life in Philadelphia; but as his pupils there included Robert Henri, George Luks, William Glackens and John Sloan, he can be said to have formed at least four artists who went on to become prominent New Yorkers. New York lacked, as I said earlier, a teaching tradition; and it also lacked the tradition of patronage that had fostered the development of European painting. (Louis Palma di Cesnola, director of the Metropolitan Museum from 1879 to 1904, said categorically that New York artists were just not good enough for the Metropolitan.) To buy work by a New York artist was a faintly second-rate thing to do. Nor did New York have what Paris and London had had for generations: an officialdom which doled out the big commissions and dominated the taste of the well-to-do.

For this reason there was no settled Establishment to which an ambitious artist might hope to graduate. If you wanted to live like John Singer Sargent you had to go and do it where Sargent himself did it: in Europe. In New York there was journeyman art, and there was Bohemia, and there was nothing much in between: the artist was not a professional man. This could be galling; but it made for an open, unstuffy, precarious way of life which turned out in the end to be favorable to art.

It also demystified the act of painting. It is difficult in the United States of America to make a mystique of something that has neither social status nor academic status and doesn't make any money. When Anshutz's pupils got out into the world it seemed to them quite natural that the only demand for their work was from newspaper editors. (At one time Sloan, Luks, Glackens and Everett Shinn were all "artist-reporters" on the *Philadelphia Press;* and when Mark Tobey was growing up to be an artist he dreamed of being able to put the American girl of 1910 on canvas with the assured skill of Charles Dana Gibson.) In time, and because photography could do the job faster and more cheaply, newspaper editors stopped hiring young artists. Thereafter, the climate of New York art life was established: painting was an activity like any other, to be carried on in circumstances no matter how discouraging and in the knowledge that almost nobody would be interested.

There are, of course, as many New Yorks as there are New Yorkers. New York is a self-devouring, self-renewing city, with which we come to terms as best we can. It is one of the supreme subjects of our century: one for which we would wish Balzac, Dickens and Proust to have been born again. New York is never the same for ten days together. Every novel about it is a historical novel before it gets to the printer. The movies do better: but even there we notice a landmark lately torn down, a turn of speech now obsolete, an ethnic frontier since readjusted. Where literal evocation was concerned, art lost out to photography: Robert Henri and John Sloan tried hard to get the real rough life of everyday into their paintings, but even so they had to yield to the photographs of Jacob A. Riis when it came to the facts of immigration, just as their successors had to yield to Walker Evans and to Paul Strand when it came to the facts of a later age. To paint "the American scene" came to be regarded as almost a national duty; but where New York was concerned it now seems that a literal transcription was never enough, and that some kind of poetic ellipsis, some transfusion of high style, was indispensable. It is certain, at any rate, that when New York was painted by Joseph Stella in 1919–20, by John Marin in 1928, by Georgia O'Keeffe in 1928–29 and by Mark Tobey in 1936, over and over again, it took on a timeless and a paradoxical look. Tobey's *Broadway* is Broadway today, even if many of the buildings he painted have come down. The plunging view adumbrated by John Marin still holds true. We know just where we are with O'Keeffe. And although the Brooklyn Bridge is no longer the phenomenon that it was in Stella's day, it is vividly present to us in his big painting.

These artists had nothing in common with one another but a refusal to fall back into illustration. There was much to illustrate in the America of the 1920s and '30s, and there were good painters who saw it as their duty to illustrate it; but of a specifically modernist approach to painting there was very little. In the mid-1920s the conditions for modernism were wretched, by the standards of today: no Museum of Modern Art, almost no dealers for modern art, almost no collectors, almost nowhere to publish and almost nothing to read. Modernism was thought of as un-American: a word at first used in mockery but later to have a more sinister inflection. The critic Harold Rosenberg remembered the exhibitions of the 1930s: "Without an awareness," he said, "of that endless mass of mill runs, fields with scarecrows, white barns and distant windmills, railroad tracks, crowded evening streets, housewives undressed to the waist staring earnestly into the spectator's eyes, marble mother-and-child themes in cubistically simplified forms, it is impossible either to apprehend the burdensomeness of American painting and sculpture in those days or, what is much more important, to appreciate the desperate creative force that it took to break into new ground in the years that followed."

American art was at that time the poor relation of American literature. When Alfred Kazin published *On Native Grounds* in 1942 he could say without fear of ridicule that "the emergence of our modern American literature" was regarded as "the world's eighth wonder, a proof that America had at last 'come of age.' " If that now reads like a message of reassurance to an America newly at war, there is still a very great difference in range, in power, in depth of understanding and in agility of formal invention between even the best American painting in the 1920s and '30s and the novels of William Faulkner, the best stories of Ernest Hemingway and the poems of Marianne Moore.

But then major art does not come out of nothing, or out of the unsupported will to create. It comes out of tradition, and out of knowledge, and out of a developed understanding of just where art stands at the time in question. When T. S. Eliot published *The Waste Land* in 1922 it was neither a fluke nor a flash in the pan; Eliot had prepared himself as a poet, and as a man, in the only way that makes fine work possible. Already in September, 1914, when Eliot was 26, Ezra Pound wrote of him that "he is the only American I know of who has made what I can call adequate preparation for writing. He has actually trained himself *and* modernized himself *on his own.* It is such a comfort to meet a man and not have to tell him to wash his face, wipe his feet, and remember the date (1914) on the calendar."

Ezra Pound had many faults; but he knew what it was to be modern, and he knew how peculiarly difficult it was to be modern in America. At that time the question "What does it mean to be an American?" still called for an answer in terms of the known and the safe. "All right," he wrote to a young editor in 1932, "you want a *style* out of America. Stick at it. But when it comes it mayn't be where you are looking for it."

For a painter to "modernize himself," as Pound put it, he needs to know what is strongest in modern art. This means not so much seeing the work once—as it was seen for instance at the Armory Show in 1913—as having it to hand day after day, week after week, year after year. It also means talking about it with like-minded people: ideally, with those who made it. The impact of the Armory Show was enormous, as we have seen; but it was an impact that died away. What New York needed was the climate of the new; eventually, toward the end of the 1920s, New York began to get it.

It began quietly. Katherine Dreier and Marcel Duchamp had been introducing Miró and Klee, Kandinsky and Max Ernst and Mondrian, in the exhibitions which were held at 475 Fifth Avenue under the aegis of the Société Anonyme. A dealer called J. B. Neumann opened on Fifty-seventh Street in 1924; specializing in German Expressionism, he wrote above the gallery door, "To love art truly means to improve life." Something of this moralizing tack, this tendency toward uplift in its most exalted form, was to characterize the new American painting. Miró, Mondrian and Lissitzky had a place of honor in an international exhibition which was put on in 1926 at the Brooklyn Museum. From 1927 onward the collection of A. E. Gallatin was on view in the library of New York University, within walking distance of the section of the city which was most in favor with artists. To have work by Cézanne, Braque, Picasso, Mondrian, van Doesburg and others continuously on view was a long stride toward deprovincialization. In 1929 The Museum of Modern Art was opened, and Alfred H. Barr and his colleagues began to assemble a pioneer collection which has never been equaled. In 1936 the resources of abstract painting in New York were strengthened by the arrival of the Museum of Non-Objective Painting, which was particularly rich in Kandinsky and later formed the nucleus of the Solomon R. Guggenheim Museum.

This may sound like an orderly progress toward enlightenment; but in fact it was nothing of the kind. Modernism is not something that can be learned step by step, like bookkeeping. To come to terms with it means a many-years' struggle, in which faction is pitted against faction and the very basis of the enterprise is subject to calumny and recrimination. There were decent American artists in the 1920s and '30s who thought that modernism was a waste of time. Others associated it with the materialism of great cities and felt that the only salvation for Americans lay in what was the original strength of America: its vast and still largely uncorrupted landscape. There were also intelligent observers, like the Austrian-born architect and visionary Frederick Kiesler, who thought that Americans should concentrate on what we would now call mixed-media art, leaving the old, handcrafted, individualistic tradition to Europe. "The expression of America is the mass," Kiesler wrote in 1930, "and the expression of the mass, the machine." Throughout the years of the stock-market crash, the Depression and the New Deal these ideas were thrown back and forth like hand grenades; and the context in which they were thrown was one not of detached aesthetic enquiry but of an awesome self-questioning: Can America survive?

To piece this together after nearly half a century is the historian's privilege. Actually to live through it was something quite different; and, as in athletics, those who were out front at the beginning were not always out front at the end. Among those who figured in the first American Abstract Artists exhibition in 1937 there were many whose personalities, as artists, were already at their point of maximum development. The men who were going to produce the new American art in the late 1940s were at an earlier phase in their evolution. The vital thing at that moment was for them to keep open, as individual human beings, until American art began to do America a most signal service. After a long, dull patch in the 1920s, there were a few people around who were prepared to give unequivocal expression to that point of view. In 1937, for instance, the Russian-born artist and aesthetician John Graham said of Stuart Davis, Arshile Gorky, David Smith and Willem de Kooning that "some are just as good as, and some are better than, the leading artists of the same generation in Europe." It was a lot to say at the time, but luckily

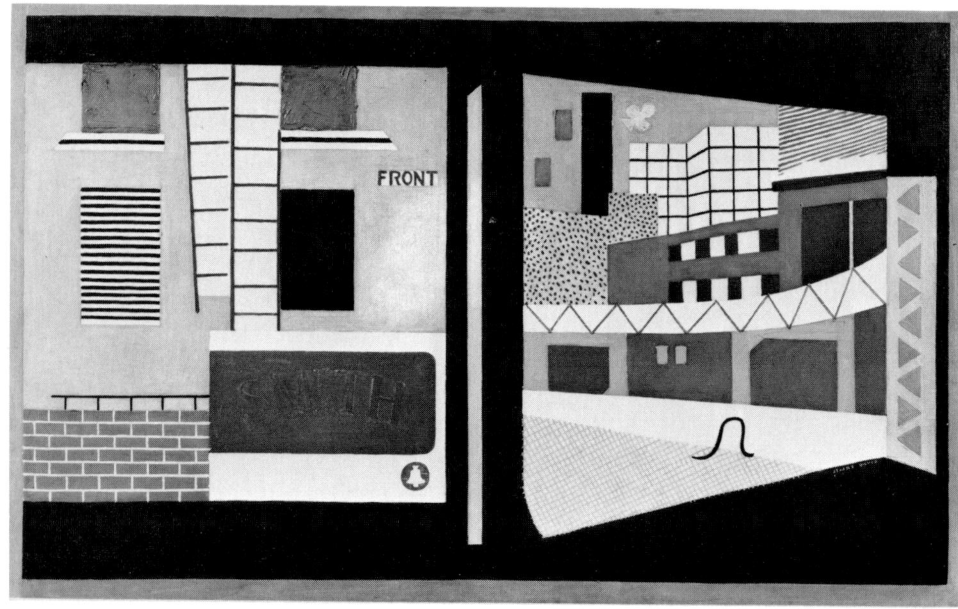

Stuart Davis.
House and Street.
1931.
Oil on canvas,
26 × 42¼ inches.
Whitney Museum of American Art, New York

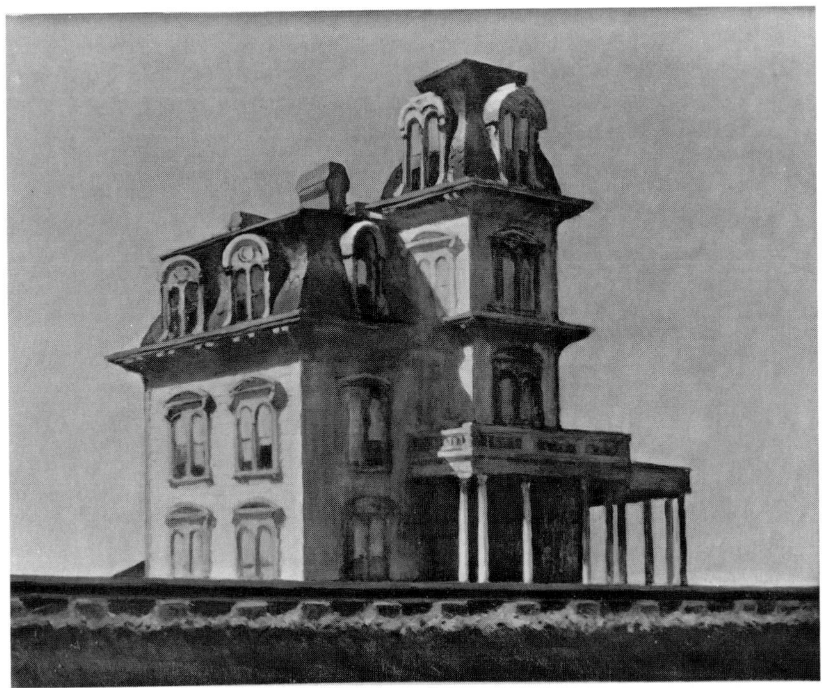

Edward Hopper. *House by the Railroad.* 1925. Oil on canvas, 24 × 29 inches. The Museum of Modern Art, New York. Given anonymously

it was true; for the future role of American art was nothing less than to redefine America.

There could be no more lofty ambition. It is given to few men to bring to their own countrymen a new degree of national self-awareness. This was the role of Shakespeare in England, of Pushkin in Russia, of Giuseppe Verdi in Italy, and of Nietzsche, for better or worse, in Germany. "Now I know who I am!" was the reaction of their first audiences; and it is still the reaction of their audiences today. It is the highest function of art to tell us who we are. That function is difficult to fulfill at any time and in any society; but when a society takes it for granted that its artists are second-rate it is more difficult than ever. There were exceptions, even then: when it comes to the distillation of those sensations of loneliness and disinheritance which play so large a part in American life, Edward Hopper has no equal. He is ahead of the novel, ahead of the movies, ahead even of Eugene O'Neill. Give him a deserted gas station, a half-empty cinema, or the terrace of a townhouse lit by the declining sun, and he will sum up a certain idea of America. But Hopper was a man on his own.

If American art overcame this handicap by the late 1940s some part of the credit must go to an administration which made American artists feel for the first time that they were part of a society which cared whether they were alive or dead. In 1935 the Roosevelt administration initiated a scheme by which, at a time of the direst national distress, thousands of artists came to receive a regular monthly subsidy from the government. Thanks to the WPA (Works Progress Administration) and to its director in matters of art, Holger Cahill, American art was freed from the depressive posture which had kept its line of sight so unduly low. As to what kind of art should come of it all, the dispute was as lively as ever; but something of moral apathy had been abolished.

Looking back at the 1930s and early '40s, and taking a long-term view, we may well regard them as a time at which the auguries for American art were good. Matisse in the 1920s and Léger in the '30s had forecast a great future for American art if Americans would only realize their full potential. And when wave after wave of gifted refugees began to arrive from Europe, American art had its full share of the reinvigoration which en-

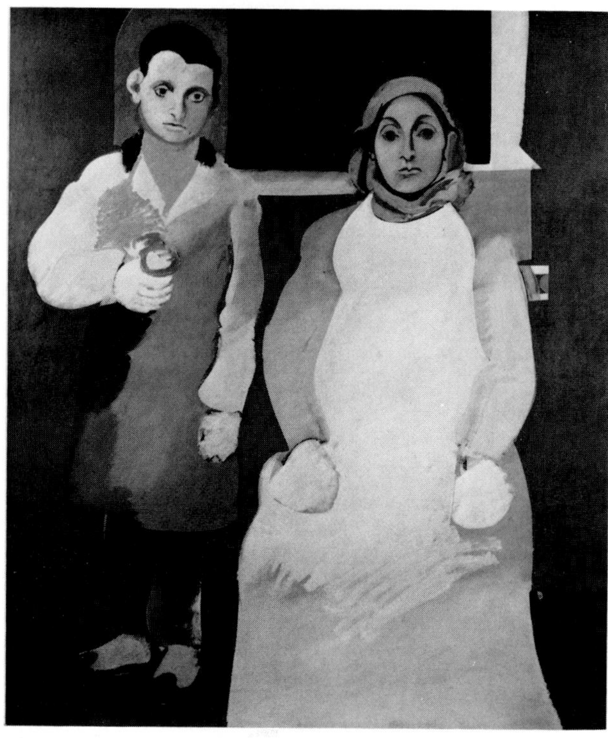

Arshile Gorky. *The Artist and His Mother.* 1926–29. Oil on canvas, 60 × 50 inches. Whitney Museum of American Art, New York. Gift of Julien Levy for Maro and Natasha Gorky in memory of their father

sued. "Reinvigoration" is not, in this context, a mere formal compliment. Europe had lost Albert Einstein among physicists, Thomas Mann and Vladimir Nabokov among novelists, Igor Stravinsky and Arnold Schoenberg among composers, and Mies van der Rohe and Marcel Breuer among architects. All had their peers in art, and an astonishingly high proportion of them came to the United States at some point between 1933 and 1942. The American poet John Peale Bishop once said that it was given to the United States at that time to prolong the past of Europe into the future; and nowhere was this more true than in art.

Not everyone came, of course. Matisse said "What will become of France if all the talented people leave?" Nor did it occur to Picasso to take the boat. But they were present in New York as the most vivid of influences: Matisse's *Bathers by a River* hung for years in the entrance to the Valentine Gallery, and the new American art battened especially on Picasso's *Girl before a Mirror* of 1932 which was given to The Museum of Modern Art in 1938. Léger in the 1930s visited New York more than once, before he arrived as an exile in 1940. Hans Hofmann opened a painting school in New York in 1936; and to many a thoughtful observer he was continuity personified. Here was a man who had been in touch with all that was best in European art since he had first gone to Munich in 1898. He had drawn alongside Matisse at the Grande Chaumière, most famous of the old-fashioned free art schools in Paris. He had known Picasso, Braque and Delaunay before 1914. In Munich during World War I he had stored many paintings by Kandinsky in his studio after Kandinsky himself had left for Russia. In his teaching, and later in his work, he looked forward to a fulfilled future in which Cubist structure and Fauvist color would somehow be allied to the rhapsodic outpourings which Kandinsky had brought to perfection in his Improvisations. In life, Hofmann was a very large man with a commanding manner; by the mid-1930s, 20 and more years as a teacher had reinforced his inborn powers of persuasion; artists and critics alike were deeply impressed when he got to his feet. What he had to offer then was not a set of predetermined lectures. It was a day-to-day account of his attempt to remake himself as a painter, in the light of all that he had known and seen and thought about; for the previous 15 years he had virtually abolished painting, feeling that until he had found out how to "sweat out Cubism" he had best stick to drawing.

Hofmann approached the problems of painting with an immediate physicality which was very attractive to his audiences in New York. The group known as the American Abstract Artists inclined toward a geometrical abstraction in which every straight line was trued and faired and the color was applied with a fastidious thinness; the results often looked, if not starched, then freshly laundered. Hofmann introduced an element of bodily involvement in which painting became "an affair of prodding and pushing, scoring and marking, rather than of simply inscribing and covering." Those words come from Clement Greenberg's essay of 1961 on Hofmann; and Greenberg is

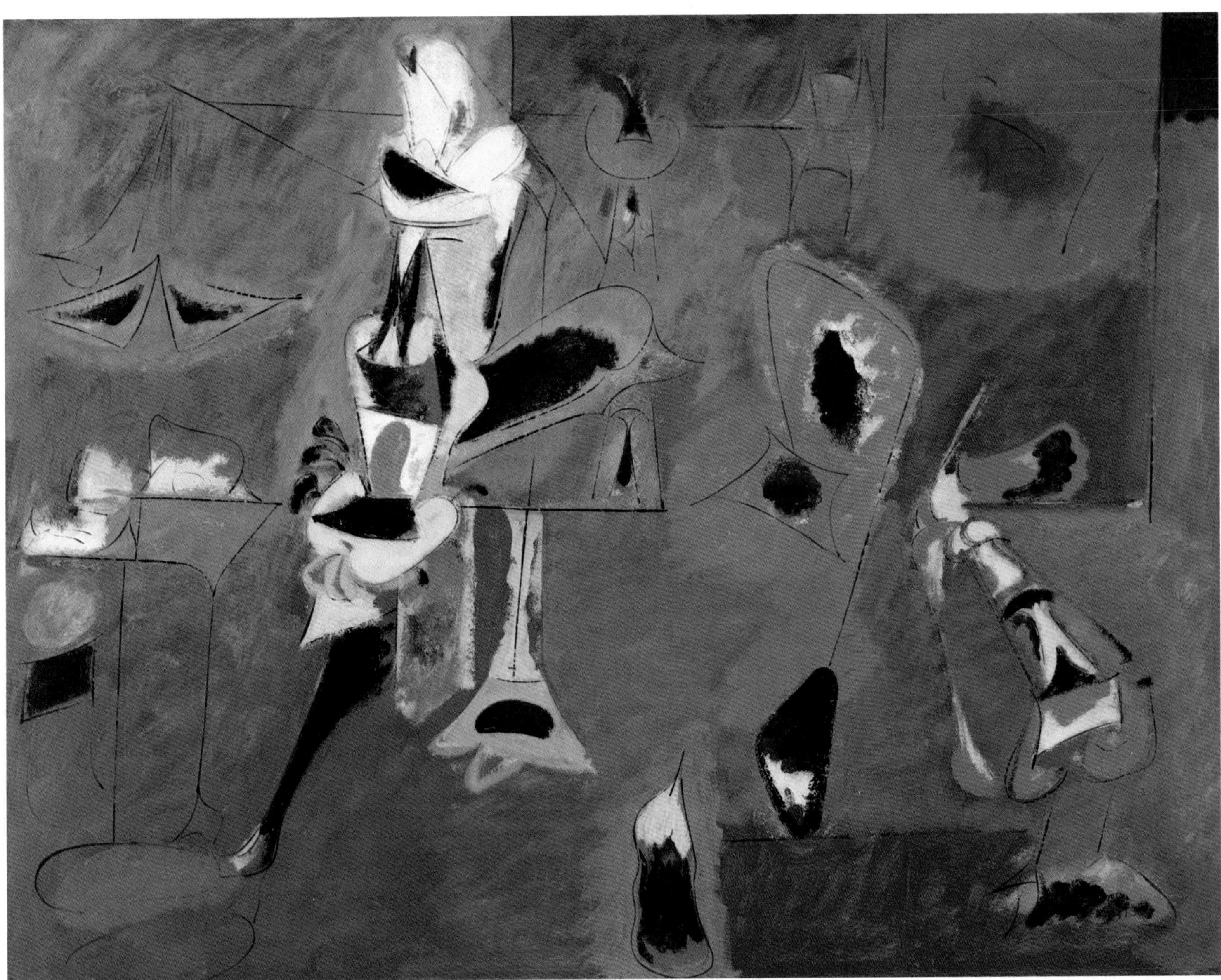

Arshile Gorky.
Agony. 1947.
Oil on canvas,
40 × 50½ inches.
The Museum of Modern Art, New York.
A. Conger Goodyear Fund

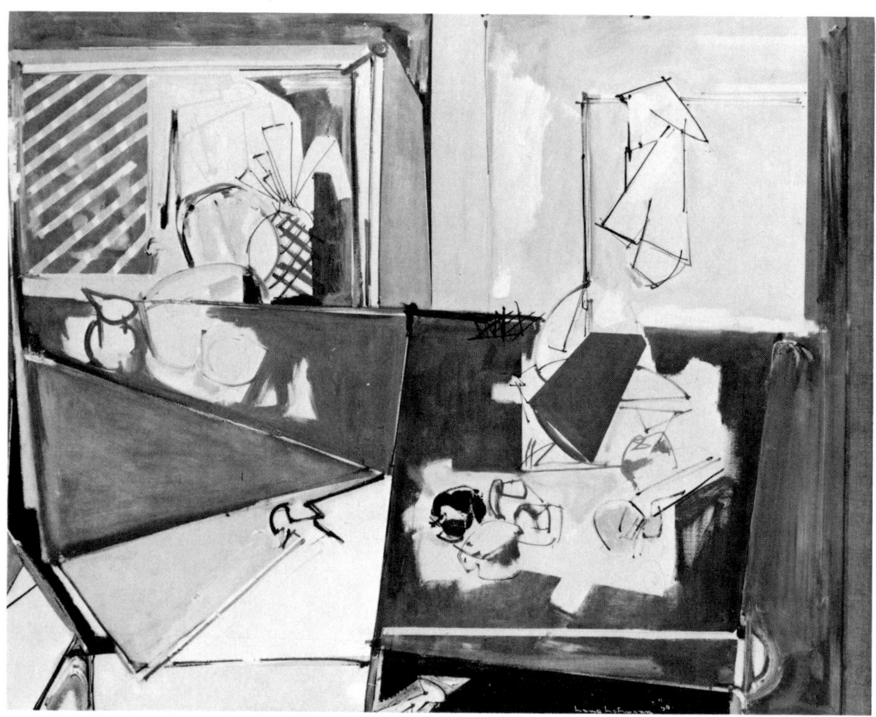

Hans Hofmann.
Magenta and Blue.
1950.
Oil on canvas,
48 × 58 inches.
Whitney Museum of American Art, New York

doubtless correct in citing Soutine—above all, Soutine's Céret landscapes—as the source of this element in Hofmann's teaching. In the landscapes which Soutine painted in Céret, in southern France, there is foreshadowed one of the chief characteristics of the First New York School: an intense nervous energy which communicated itself to the movement of the brush. Soutine painted what looks to us like a world in convulsion; but the convulsion in question was in his own fingers' ends, and in the rapid and purposeful to and fro of the brush. As much as in anything painted by Jackson Pollock, the canvas becomes what Harold Rosenberg in 1952 called "an arena in which to act, rather than a space in which to reproduce, redesign, analyze or 'express' an object, actual or imagined." Insofar as any one man could set up the conditions for the new American painting, that man was Hans Hofmann. He was the complete cosmopolitan; but whereas the cosmopolitan has often more knowledge than drive, Hofmann had in the highest possible degree the German's will to win. And he kept at it with the kind of big, square-built ambition that made it possible for him to peak toward the end of his long life, rather than 30 years earlier. *Magenta and Blue,* 1950, looks back to the classic French interiors which Matisse for one had brought to perfection; but it also looks forward to the day when Hofmann would be able to structure his paintings in terms of large flat rectangles of pure color.

Early in 1939 Picasso's *Guernica* arrived in New York. With the outbreak of World War II, and more especially with the fall of France in the summer of 1940, New York began to harbor not only the masterpieces of modern European art but quite a few of the men who had made them. The men in question included Piet Mondrian, Fernand Léger, Max Ernst, Yves Tanguy, László Moholy-Nagy, André Masson and the Chilean-born Sebastian Matta Echaurren. André Breton was there to assure the continuity of a certain idea of Surrealism, and Peggy Guggenheim was there to open, in 1942, a gallery called Art of This Century. In World War II, as in World War I, the European avant-garde was in and out of New York all the time.

Somewhere in the mid-1940s the notion of a

specifically American modern art began to be discussed, and what history calls the First New York School came into being. The name is unhistorical, in more ways than one. There was no one school, in the sense of a teaching institution, in the sense of an orthodoxy or shared body of beliefs, or in the sense of a group of artists who showed together, like the French Impressionists. There was not even the kind of unified activity which the word generally implies. The artists were as unlike one another, as human beings, as it is possible for artists to be. Yet the words "First New York School" stand for men who do undeniably belong together: Jackson Pollock, Arshile Gorky, Willem de Kooning, David Smith, Hans Hofmann, Franz Kline, Mark Rothko, Barnett Newman, Adolph Gottlieb, Philip Guston, Clyfford Still. It is thanks to them that feelings of wonder and acceptance took the place of the defeatism which had been so widespread among the public for American art in the 1920s and '30s.

These feelings were generated by men who were not young, at the critical moment, as Picasso and Braque were young when they broke through to Cubism. To one degree or another they had all taken a battering from life. Beyond that, what was there in common between Arshile Gorky, who was born in Turkish Armenia of a family of village tradesmen, and Clyfford Still, who was born in North Dakota of Scottish and Irish ancestry? Gorky learned the European masters by heart, the way an aspirant actor learns "To be or not to be"; Still thought of the Armory Show as "that ultimate in irony" which "had dumped upon us the combined and sterile conclusions of Western European decadence." There were close friendships among the artists concerned—Pollock and Guston, de Kooning and Gorky, Rothko and Gottlieb —but there were also divergences of experience and of origins, which were so extreme as to exclude anything more than a wry and intermittent admiration.

For instance, Willem de Kooning was born in Rotterdam, Holland, and he was going on 22 when he got into the United States with false papers at the third time of trying. He did not have, therefore, the sense of an American-ness within him that cried out for redefining. "It is a certain burden, this American-ness," he said in 1963. "If you come from a small nation, you don't have that. When I went to the Academy in Rotterdam and I was drawing from the nude, *I* was making the drawing, not Holland." In the 1930s and early '40s very dull things were done in the name of American-ness. ("Art in America today," Barnett Newman wrote in 1942, "stands at a point where anything that cannot fit into the American Scene label is doomed to be completely ignored"; de Kooning spoke of "making art out of John Brown's body." Just about the only artist who used specifically and unmistakably American subject matter without falling into an isolationist aesthetic was Stuart Davis, who loved France and French art and yet never reneged on his wiry, sinewy, plainspoken nature. He cut the descriptive element in painting to essentials that could be reduced no further; and then he put them together again in ways that owed much to French mentors but were also quintessentially American in their throwaway wit. It was Davis, as much as anyone, who deprovincialized American painting. This was acknowledged already in 1931 by Arshile Gorky, then 26 years old, when he paid tribute to Davis as "this man, this American, this pioneer, this modest painter, who never disarranges his age, who works to perfect his motives, who renders—clear, more definite, more and more decided—new forms and new objects." The phrase that matters here is that Davis "never disarranges his age"; the art and the age were one, in his work, and a painting like his *Lucky Strike* of 1921 has about it not only an after-echo of Fernand Léger but a specifically American form of plain statement.

To those who wondered if American painters would ever manage to modernize themselves in Ezra Pound's sense, Stuart Davis brought reassurance. But it was not enough for one man and one picture, here and there, to have exceptional status.

Clyfford Still.
Painting. 1951.
Oil on canvas,
7 feet 10 inches × 6 feet 10 inches.
The Museum of Modern Art, New York.
Blanchette Rockefeller Fund

Mark Rothko.
Number 10. 1950.
Oil on canvas,
7 feet 6⅜ inches ×
57⅛ inches.
The Museum of
Modern Art, New
York. Gift of Philip
Johnson

What was dreamed of in the 1930s, and what found all too little in the way to support it, was a state of affairs like the one described by Harold Rosenberg in an article first published in 1940. Inspired by the entry of the German armies into Paris, it began with the sentence: "The laboratory of the 20th century has been shut down." Rosenberg went on to look back to the period immediately before 1914, when "suddenly, almost in the span of a single generation, everything buried underground was brought to the surface. The perspective of the immediate was established—or rather, a multiple perspective, in which time no longer reared up like a gravestone or flourished like a tree but threw up a shower of wonders at the will of the onlooker."

That was exactly what people were beginning to ask of New York in the 1940s: a shower of wonders, in which everything buried underground was brought to the surface and a perspective of the immediate was established. This could not be one man's doing, any more than what happened in Paris before 1914 was one man's doing. Picasso and Matisse, Braque and Delaunay, Bonnard and Mondrian, late Cézanne and continuing Monet—all had contributed to Paris at that time, sometimes in the closest collaboration but most often with no interconnections whatever. Frenchmen like Braque played their part; but so did new arrivals from abroad, like Juan Gris and Constantin Brancusi, and visitors who stayed only a season, like Kandinsky. A bit of everything, in human terms, and all of it good: that was the idea.

And New York in the 1940s carried it through. Even more than St. Petersburg before 1917, or Paris in the 1920s, New York is the completely cosmopolitan city: the place in which no one need feel a complete outsider or despair of finding someone of his own race, color, tastes and beliefs with whom to strike up acquaintance. New York has something of Athens, something of Shanghai, something of Odessa, something of Dublin, something of Tel Aviv. It's all there: there is no tune that cannot be played on the human keyboard that this city provides.

New York is also very good at processing new arrivals and making them its own. First- and second-generation immigrants made up the greater part of the New York School, along with country boys from Wyoming (Jackson Pollock) or from the coal-mining part of Pennsylvania (Franz Kline). Willem de Kooning was born in Holland, Mark Rothko in Russia, Arshile Gorky in Armenia, Hans Hofmann in Bavaria, and Barnett Newman's parents came over from Polish Russia at the turn of the century; yet in the 1940s all these people were complete Americans. They were as committed to America as if their forefathers had come over with Columbus. What Thomas B. Hess had to say about Newman is true of all of them: that Newman was "a quintessential American. His passion to move with pragmatic curiosity and idealist self-confidence into the modern experience came not only from living an experience of freedom and independence in a new country, but also from an understanding of, and holding onto connections with, a European tradition."

Even so, major art can come about only when the tradition in question is the one that can most fruitfully be carried further. And there was no doubt in the 1940s that the future for art lay in a working alliance between the reasoned order of Cubist painting, with its emphasis on the virtues of equilibrium, and the demands of the liberated unconscious. Cubism in itself seemed to have nowhere to go (though Braque was to prove this mistaken); the heyday of European Surrealism seemed, equally, to be a thing of the past. Somehow the two might be made to work together by a mysterious multiplication. Hans Hofmann, for one, believed this: after spending years "sweating out Cubism," by his own account, he said in 1944 that "the highest in art is the irrational." The task of the irrational was to release "the potential inner life of a chosen medium, so that the final image resulting from it expresses the *all* of oneself."

As far as any one sentence could define the mandate of the New York School, that one does it: the task of the painter was to release the potential inner life of his chosen medium, and in so doing to produce a final image that expressed "the *all* of oneself," unprecedentedly. As to the who, the when and the how of all this, the historian is free to tidy the record as he pleases: or, as Hess once said, to "make a seamless web of process out of what had been a shambles of false moves, happy accidents, and precious insights gained through heartbreaking labors." The artists themselves knew better. Willem de Kooning said in 1949 that "it is impossible to find out how a style began. I think that it is the most bourgeois idea to think that one can make a style beforehand."

And it is of course true that every member of the New York School (and one or two other very fine painters who cannot be so categorized) negotiated quite freely in the late 1940s and early 1950s between the promptings of his own nature and his individual sense of what remained for painting to do. Like many another American artist of his generation, Mark Rothko came under the influence of European Surrealism in the 1940s. But even when he was using hybrid forms derived from that source he enveloped them in a fluid, dimensionless space of his own invention. By 1950 the hybrid forms had dropped out of sight and Rothko had arrived at the compositional device which he employed for the rest of his life: the juxtaposition of rectangular areas of paint in which color was allowed to bloom undisturbed either by drawing, by any suggestion of deep space, or by anything that could be called geometry. Within this basic schema, which might have appeared limited, he produced a huge and unexpectedly varied body of work. The enveloping poetry of his best paintings is owed not only to a superfine color sense but to shifts of emphasis, shifts of proportion, and a continual give and take between one floating shape and another.

Mark Rothko and Clyfford Still at that time were just about as unlike one another as it is possible for human beings to be: in looks, in their ethnic origin, in temperament and in their general experience of life. Still looked like what he was: an irreducible homegrown American. Rothko, too, looked like what he was: a transplanted Eastern European in whom the sense of loss was never quite subdued. But they did have one thing in common: a conviction that their paintings should keep no company but their own. There is about Still's vast fissured shapes, and also about his stark and intransigent writings, something that rejects absolutely the idea of art as a superior distraction. "This is the most serious thing there is," he seems to say. As the art historian Robert Rosenblum pointed out in 1961, there is in this an echo of that craving for the sublime which is perhaps the strongest of all motives for the making of art. There is also something of the archetypal American belief that no limits need be set to human ambition.

Nothing can replace the testimony, in such matters, of the painters. But it is also worthwhile to listen to a very intelligent observer who was around at the time. Thomas B. Hess set out the general position as follows: "Like all artists in the decade 1935–45, the New York painters were faced by a crisis in modernism that took the dramatic form of a clamping down on art—the Paris masters had stamped each approach with so personal a style that it seemed impossible to grow around, much less to move beyond them. . . . The Americans, like their contemporaries in Europe, faced what one artist has called a hotel full of rooms each marked 'Occupied.' "

Hess went on to say that "the solution that de Kooning and his colleagues (including such artists as Pollock, Motherwell, Newman, Kline, Rothko, Still, Gottlieb) attempted was to confront the European masters on their own ground and to work through their styles by changing the hypotheses. A shorthand way of expressing it would be to say that the Americans would base their art on ethical rather than aesthetic pressures. They would turn their concentration inward, focus on the personal experience, express it as forcefully as possible and as efficiently as possible in pictorial

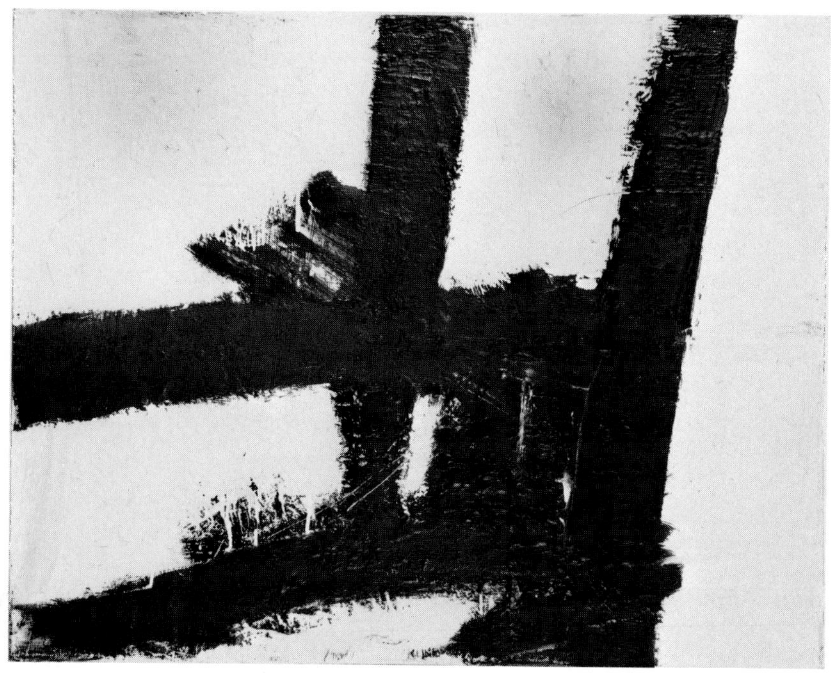

Franz Kline.
Two Horizontals.
1954.
Oil on canvas,
31⅛ × 39¼ inches.
The Museum of
Modern Art, New
York. The Sidney
and Harriet Janis
Collection

terms." The question to be answered was "What can a man still do, with paints and canvas, to express the *all* of himself?"

As to the results of this, a large and ferocious literature is already in being. In situations of this kind the best thing is always to look at the work; for it was the work that made its way from 1943 onward. Between 1943 and 1950 there were substantial one-man shows in New York by Hofmann, Pollock, Gorky, Rothko, Still, Kline, Gottlieb, Newman, de Kooning and David Smith. What matters is to examine major works by these artists in the context of their first appearance.

Even the look of the city at a given time can be important in this context. Franz Kline knew New York when the elevated railway was still a fact of everyday life and the crisscross of black girders high above a construction site was just beginning to replace the terraced houses of the last century. His mature paintings were in no sense portraits of that city; but in paintings like *Two Horizontals,* 1954, the headlong power of the slashed black-on-white derived from a townscape in which ruthless change was beginning to be taken for granted.

"I think," de Kooning once wrote, "that innovators come at the end of a period. Cézanne gave the finishing touches to Impressionism before he came face to face with his 'little sensation.' " De Kooning was 44 when he wrote that, and 45 when he painted his *Excavation* in 1950. He had at that time been concerned with art, part-time or full-time, for 33 years. His first one-man show had been in April, 1948; and as a man in his 40s he had had plenty of time to put the "finishing touches" to the art of the immediate past. Now, with *Excavation,* he was completely himself. The painting is already set fast in history, but it is worthwhile to try to see it as it looked in 1950: a picture unlike any other.

It is a big picture, by the standards of its day. It came immediately after a long series of paintings in which de Kooning had expressly avoided the emotional associations of color. He had used these black-and-white paintings as a way of crossing over, as it were, from drawing to painting. De Kooning is one of the great draftsmen of this century, with a variety of attack and a range of subject matter which are almost beyond comparison. He can do anything that he wants with line; and the line in question can be as thin as a silk thread or

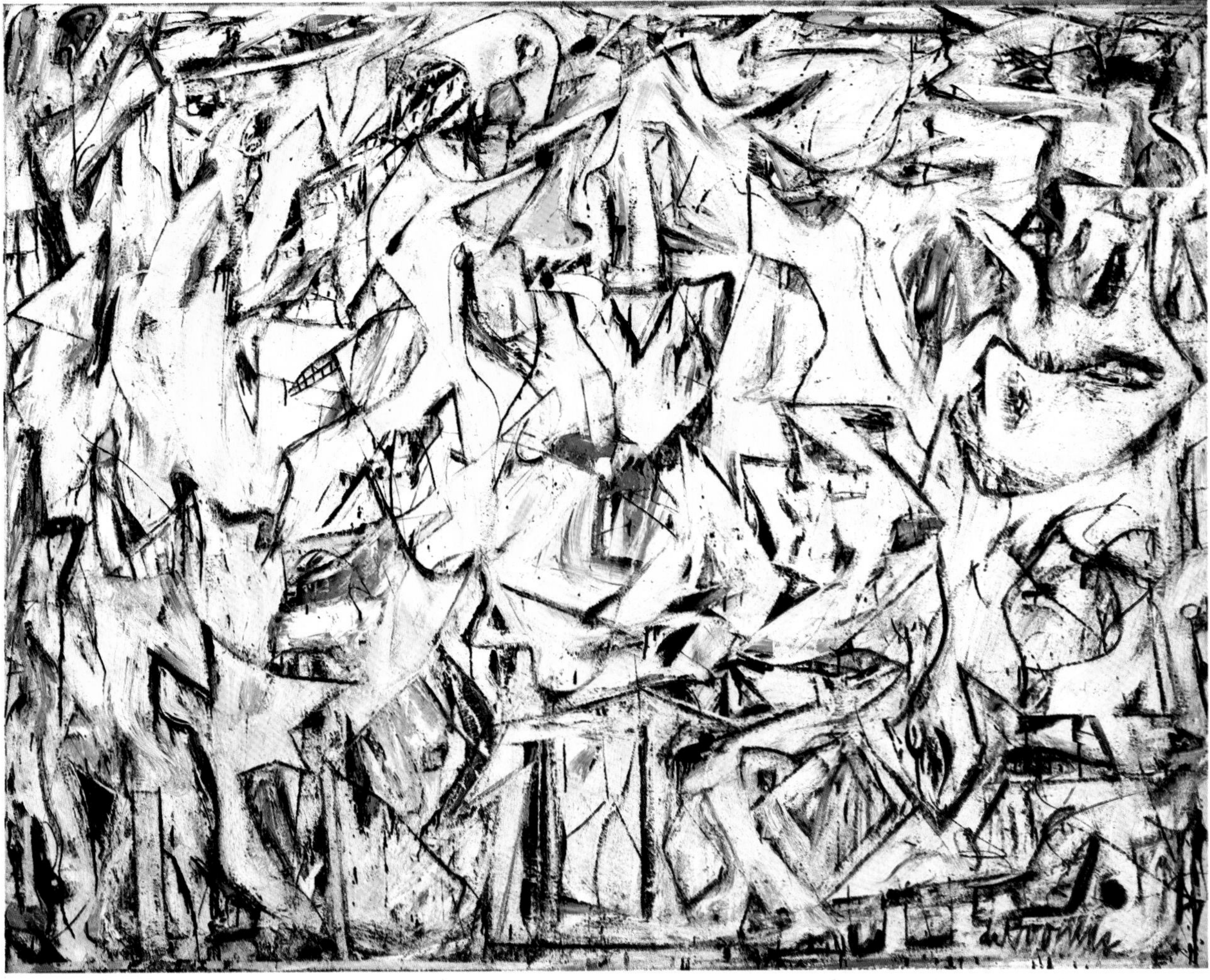

Willem de Kooning. *Excavation.* 1950. Oil on canvas, 6 feet 8 inches × 8 feet 4 inches. The Art Institute of Chicago. Mr. and Mrs. Frank G. Logan Purchase Prize, gift of Mr. Edgar Kaufmann, Jr., and Mr. and Mrs. Noah Goldowsky

as broad as the nose of an orangutan. And when he crossed over from drawing to painting at the end of the 1940s he used zinc white and a house-painter's black enamel to make forms which were completely flat, like the forms in late Cubism. They were not so much painted as *laid on;* and they related to the signs which had been devised by Arp and Miró to echo the human body without actually naming it. "Even abstract shapes must have a likeness," de Kooning once said. And in pictures like his *Painting,* 1948, every shape has its likeness: its familiar companion, which stays within hailing distance but does not come forward to be identified.

As Hess has remarked, the black-and-white paintings are "packed to bursting with shapes metamorphosed from drawings of women which have been cut apart, transposed, intermixed until they were abstract, but always with a 'likeness' and a memory of their source and its emotive charge." (I should add that among the sources in question was the energy with which the Cubist masters had raided the outlines of guitar and violin for their affinities with the female body.)

After these black-and-white de Koonings, *Excavation* impresses at once by the overall fleshiness of its tonality. Color has come back into painting with an echo that is perfectly distinct: that of the pink and white and yellow of well-remembered Dutch womanhood. Color speaks, also, for something even more directly erotic: the red of human vents and orifices which have been taken by as-

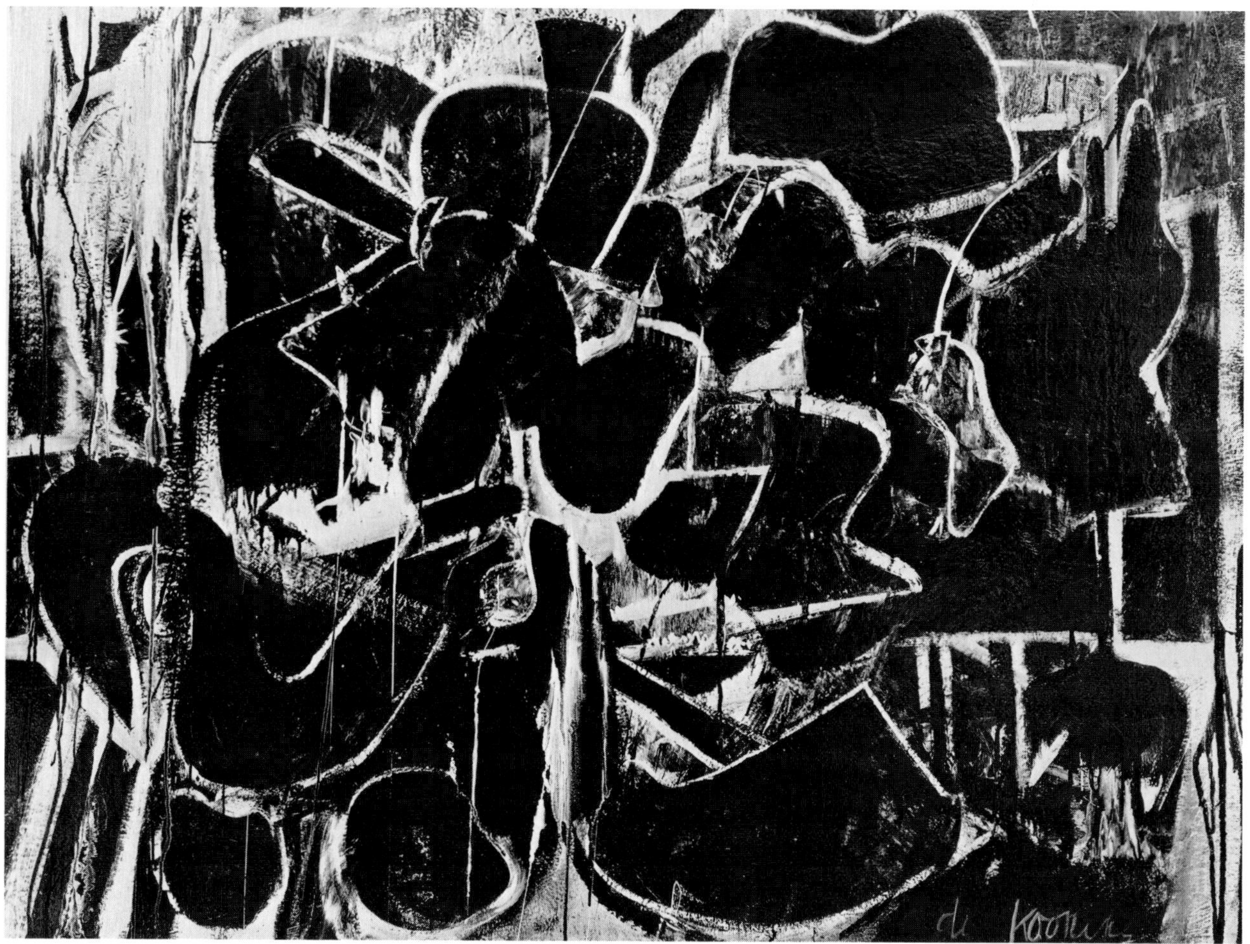

Willem de Kooning. *Painting.* 1948. Enamel and oil on canvas, 42⅝ × 56⅛ inches. The Museum of Modern Art, New York. Purchase

sault, the slashed black marking of the pubic triangle, the darting scarlet of an extended tongue. Color brings, finally, a rare intensity to the inset diamond shapes which stand in *Excavation* for the human eye; the eye of the onlooker fuses, in this painting, with the eye of the participant.

The format of *Excavation* was one often used by the Flemish 17th-century master Jacob Jordaens for the meaty confrontations that made his name; and something of the history of figure painting in the Low Countries could be said to survive in this de Kooning. But, unlike Jordaens, de Kooning looks at the scene from no one point of view. The subject matter of *Excavation* is not so much composed as mapped, with no one incident taking precedence over the others. (We should remember that one of de Kooning's black-and-white paintings reminded him of a 17th-century Dutch engraving of a naval battle.) Faces, limbs, whole bodies form up and dissolve before our eyes. The story which this picture tells us has no beginning and no end; we can come in and go out as we please. What we are looking at has the tautly structured allover scaffolding of Cubism—that moment in the development of European painting when, as de Kooning said in 1951, painters were given "a poetic frame where something could be possible, where the artist could practice his intuition." But whereas Cubist painting was about stillness and equilibrium, *Excavation* is about the ways in which energy can find outlet in action.

In *Woman I,* de Kooning gave painting its head with what looks to be a maximum of spontaneity. But in point of fact the picture cost him 18

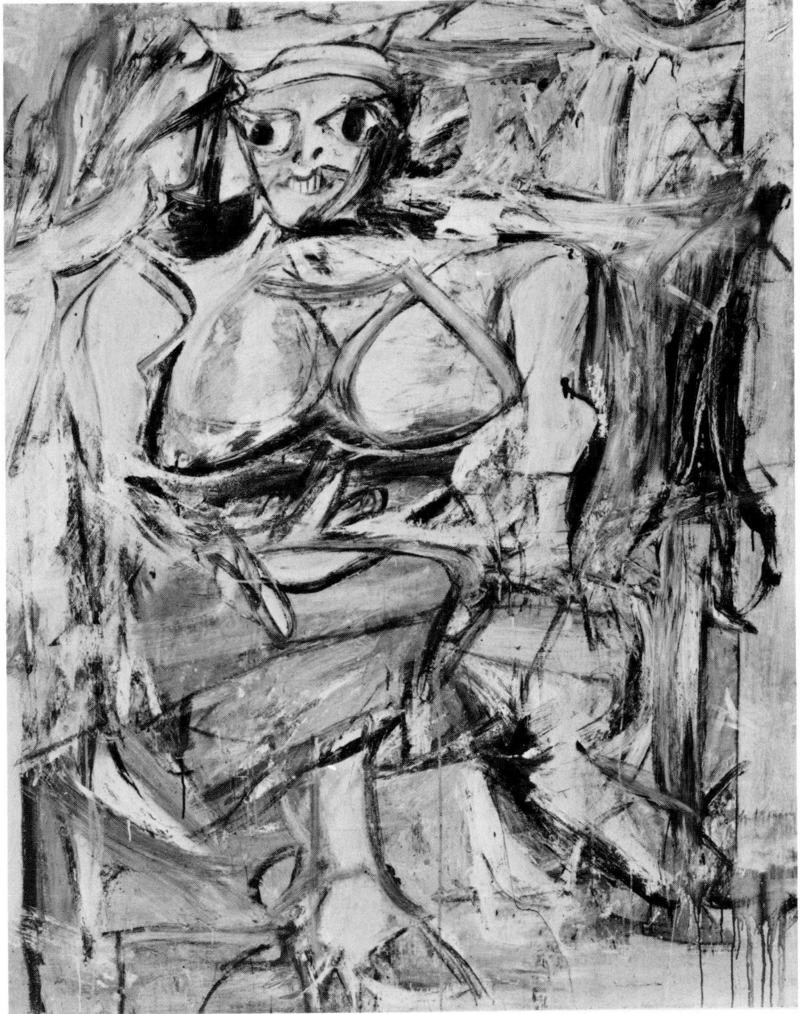

Willem de Kooning. *Woman I.* 1950–52. Oil on canvas, 6 feet 3⅞ inches × 58 inches. The Museum of Modern Art, New York. Purchase

months' hard work and was then put aside, only to be rescued at the suggestion of the art historian Meyer Schapiro and brought to a triumphal conclusion. The image was "painted out literally hundreds of times," Thomas B. Hess tells us; but it stood for a concept of imperious womanhood that would give the painter no rest until it had been set down on canvas.

In this painting, as in certain others of its date, what Ezra Pound had called a *style* came out of America. Action is what *Excavation* and *Woman I* are all about, and Action Painting (a phrase first used by Harold Rosenberg in 1952) is as good a generic name as any for the "shower of wonders" which was produced in New York in the late 1940s. It is not an all-inclusive name—how could it be?—but it fits much of the work for much of the time. Both words count. "Action" stands for the particular physical involvement which characterizes the work; and it also stands for a determination to get up and go, rather than to settle for nostalgic imitation. "Painting" stands for the belief that there was still a great future for the act of putting paint on canvas. The way to realize that future was, first, to assimilate the past; second, to open out the act of painting in such a way that it became, in itself and by itself, one of the most capacious forms of human expression.

The man who brought this mimetic element most vividly to the notice of the public was Jackson Pollock; and it is with the name of Pollock above

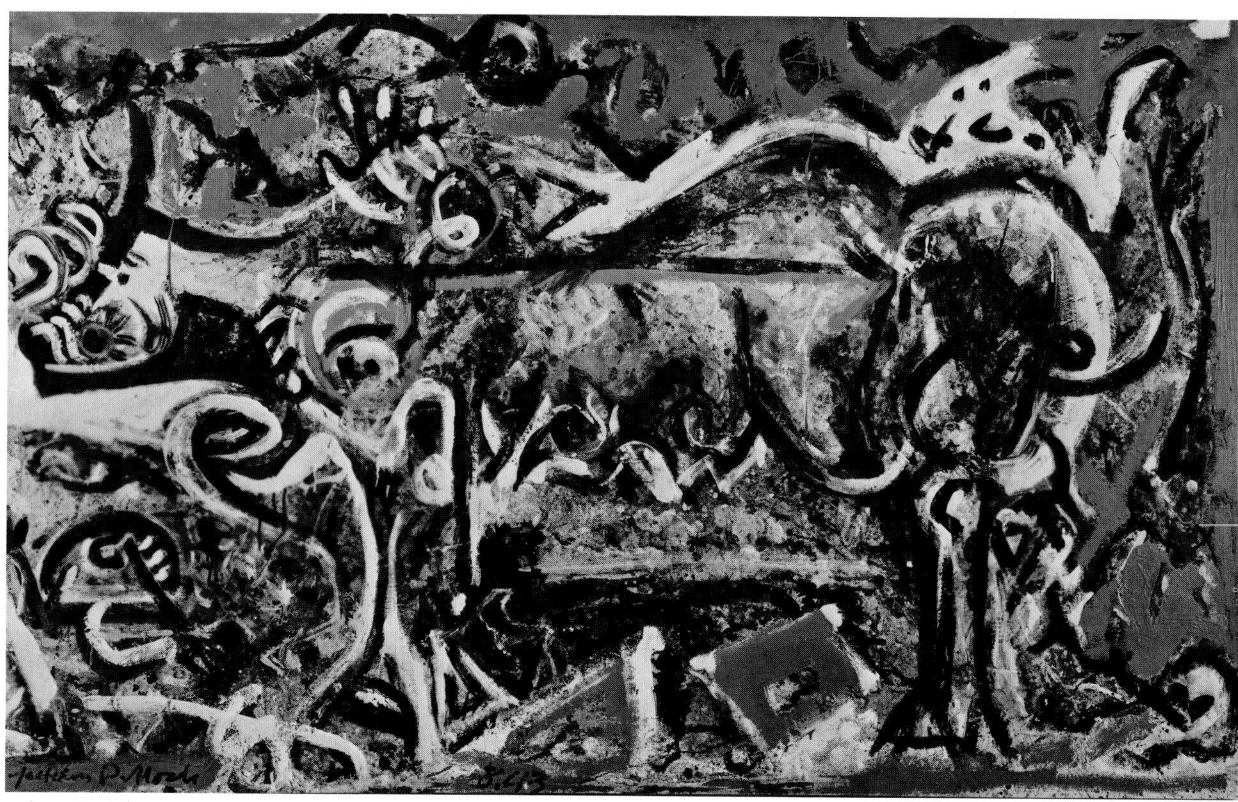

Jackson Pollock. *The She-Wolf.* 1943. Oil, gouache and plaster on canvas, 41⅞ × 67 inches. The Museum of Modern Art, New York. Purchase

all that the notion of the new American painting is still associated. That this should be so is natural on more than one score. Pollock's work has qualities of excitement and immediate seduction which make it stand out in any company; and Pollock was himself an archetypal American, a quasi-mythical figure who is as real to those who never knew him as Melville's Captain Ahab or Scott Fitzgerald's Dick Diver. When we look at a Pollock like *Autumn Rhythm*, 1950, we see the American dream made visible. A country boy with country ways has made it to what looks like immortality; and whereas we are embarrassed for Ernest Hemingway when he talks of "taking on Tolstoy," it is perfectly reasonable to believe that in 1949 and 1950 Pollock took on the great Europeans of this century and survived.

He had had to work for it. His was both a complex and wayward derivation, in which influences of a paradoxical and mutually contradictory sort had been not so much absorbed as fought through, year by year. Some of the experiences which formed him will already be familiar to the reader: the massive black-and-white structure of Picasso's *Guernica*, for instance, and the presence in New York in the early 1940s of artists like André Masson, who personified the concept of art as ritual. But whereas Masson was a sophisticated European who took a connoisseur's delight in the magical aspects of primitive art, Pollock thought of American Indians and painting as a part of his own inmost inheritance—to the extent, in fact, of keeping the Smithsonian Institution's publication on the subject under his bed. There was nothing slapdash or opportunistic about his development; he always knew that he had a great deal to work through as a human being and a great deal to work through as an artist; and already in the 1930s there was a physical truculence about his work which revealed just how much it had cost him. It is easy to say, with hindsight, that his development as a painter could have been enormously accelerated if he had learned earlier (and he first registered at the Art Students League in New York in September, 1926) about "automatic writing" as it had been practiced since the early 1920s by the European Surrealists. But automatic writing is mere affectation if the writer has nothing to write about; and Pollock in the 1930s was not yet ready to tackle the chaos of the unconscious.

Every major artist has, as we have seen, an inbuilt psychic mechanism which tells him when to stop and when to go, when to hold back and when to let the work impose itself. Pollock had this capacity in a rare degree; in the 1930s he had contacts with the Mexican mural painter David Alfaro Siqueiros, who at that time had a great reputation. He learned from Siqueiros that it was permissible for art to be "ugly," at first sight; that the wall, not the canvas on the traditional easel, was the natural dimension for a painter; and that the painter was entitled to shop around among the new materials and the new forms of industrial equipment which were then coming on the market. In this way Pollock in 1936 learned to use the airbrush and the spraygun. He also learned from Siqueiros to adopt a free, open, public approach to painting. Paintings were meant to be seen by everyone, Siqueiros said, and all means of attracting attention were valid. The painter was no longer a hermit, walled up in the studio with nothing between him and the taut little canvas but what Siqueiros called "a stick with hairs on the end of it." Painting had become a hand-to-hand encounter between the painter and the wall (or the floor); and the painter was free to spray, pour, drip, throw or scatter the paint as he pleased.

Heady stuff, one might think. But Pollock did not, in point of fact, make full use of it for another ten years. Nor was he drawn to the simplistic topical subject matter which made Siqueiros famous: he concerned himself with wild private notions that could be tamed in terms of mythology (private or public, ancient or modern). The images which resulted were thickly worked: clotted, as much as drawn, and packed with references to ritual (often of a cruel and destructive sort). Pollock was aiming at that time for a ruthless, hieratic art from which the idea of human sacrifice was never far away.

In the 1940s two radical changes came over the work. Pollock learned to trust the automatic

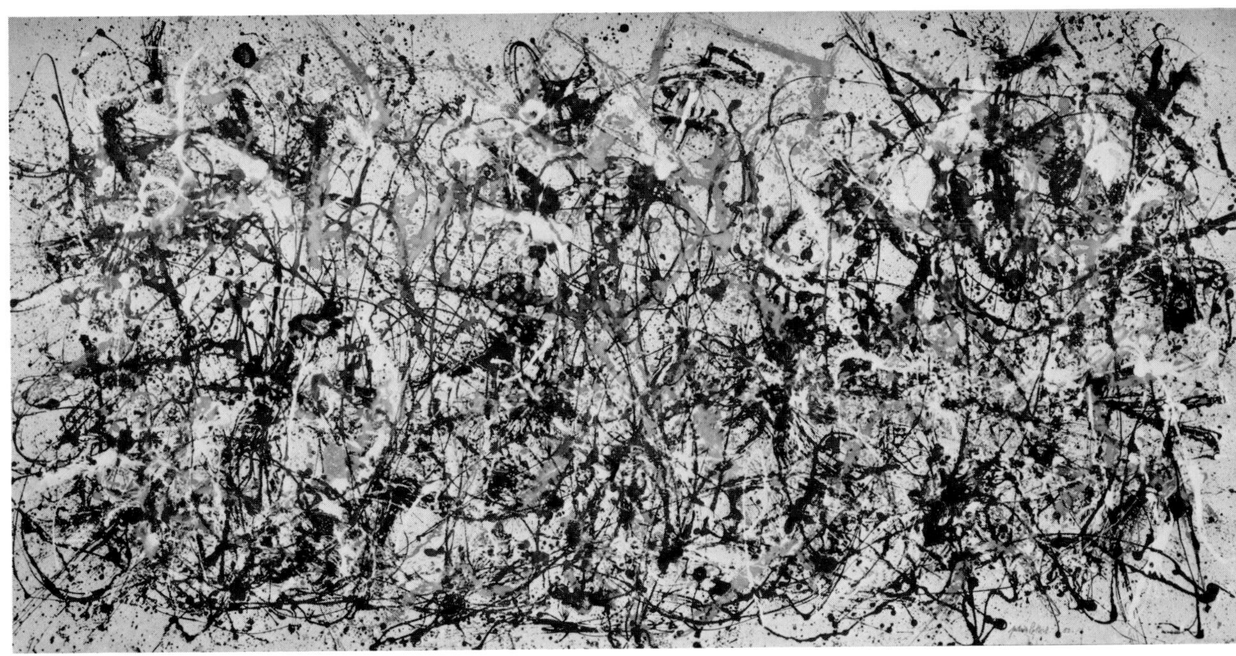

Jackson Pollock. *Autumn Rhythm.* 1950. Oil on canvas, 8 feet 9 inches × 17 feet 3 inches. The Metropolitan Museum of Art, New York. George A. Hearn Fund

procedures through which impulses long buried within him found outlet; and he learned that the myth with which he could best occupy himself had nothing to do with the ancient world. It was, on the contrary, the myth of the artist as a continuing creator. Here his friend Robert Motherwell sized up the situation exactly when he wrote of Pollock in 1944 that "his principal problem is to discover what his true subject is. And since painting is his thought's medium, the resolution must grow out of the process of his painting itself."

And so it did: in Pollock's completely realized wall-size paintings of 1947–50, painting itself is the subject matter. Time has robbed these pictures of the aggressiveness which once seemed their most obvious characteristic, and it has also allowed us to look for ancestors where no ancestry had seemed plausible. Already in 1961 Robert Rosenblum related Pollock's *Number 1,* 1948, to the visionary nature-painting of J. M. W. Turner. The visitor to The Museum of Modern Art can move from *Number 1* to Monet's *Water Lilies* and find in them a comparable continuum: a lateral expansion in which the tight focus of conventional landscape painting plays no part. Unknown to Pollock, there were the mountainscapes of the American Augustus Vincent Tack to foreshadow, however faintly, the concept of the picture as something to get lost in. In his ambitions, and in his achievement, Augustus Vincent Tack (1870–1949) was midway between the 19th-century Americans who attempted the sublime in landscape and the painters of the First New York School. The scale was there, and the sense of aspiration, and the defocused allover composition; but exalted effort still called at that time for specific subject matter—in Tack's case, mountain scenery.

But when all that has been said, a Pollock of 1947–50 is still quite unlike any painting that had been before. As to why this was and where the difference lay, some explanation is needed. Certain misapprehensions should also be got out of the way. For instance it is often believed that Action Painting was rhetorical, if not melodramatic, in character and that it corresponded in some way to the existentialism which was then in high fashion. The existential attitude can be summarized, however incompletely, as one of lucid despair at our inability to divert, and still less to arrest, the course of history. In conversational terms the general idea was, "You can't win, but at least you can lose with your eyes open." What was then called "the literature of extreme situation" was existential in tone; and it emerged in many cases from the experience of life in those parts of Europe which were overrun by the German Army in World War II.

There was nothing of this in Action Painting. But the lives of the Action Painters could be interpreted, then and later, in terms of misfortune. Jackson Pollock and David Smith were killed in motor accidents; Franz Kline died of a heart attack at 52; Arshile Gorky and Mark Rothko committed suicide. So it is worth emphasizing that the paintings done by Pollock in the late 1940s and early '50s are celebratory in intent. Pollock had his full share of private distresses, and some of them had found their way into his work with a ferocity not often paralleled; "birth, copulation and death" were his subjects, directly or indirectly, over and over again. Recognizable images pullulated in his work until 1945; they came back again after 1950; but in 1947–50 Pollock perfected a kind of picture in which the terms of painting—its basic predispositions—are redefined.

These pictures were abstract in a completely new way. Kandinsky had made large-scale abstract paintings before 1914; but, as was said earlier, there is no such thing as a form that has no likeness. Kandinsky's huge-scale Compositions are treasure houses of complex reference. Pollock in the late 1940s took the long history of line a stage further by inventing a formal statement that was neither a description nor an equivalence but the record of a self-sufficient activity. This activity was set free from the limitations of earlier art; whereas the drawn line is limited by the dimensions of the human arm, and whereas the line left by one loaded brush is further limited by the finite capacity of the brush itself, the poured or dripped line has a new elasticity and a power of extension which had not existed in painting before. (The sheer bigness of American Action Painting has, by the way, been exaggerated. Though large by the scale of the polite easel paintings which then ranked highest with the conservative collector, they were never large by the standards which Tintoretto or Rubens took for granted when an important commission was in question. Nor were they large by the standards of the prize paintings of the 19th century. The bigness of the new American painting lay rather in the size of the basic unit of expression: in this case, the line extended in such a way that the eye cannot establish either its beginning or its end. Newman, for one, liked the spectator to stand up close, so that he felt as if he were being sucked into the picture.)

Americans had learned in the 1930s to think of abstract painting in terms of either the strict blocking-out of geometrical forms or a jumble of evocative shapes which brought with them an immigrant's bundle of associations from the Old World. In 1944 Mondrian died in New York and Kandinsky died in Paris; thereafter, nothing much was forthcoming in the directions which they had pioneered. With Europe drained of energy by six years of war, there was room for an American art to assert itself. In two full-hearted sentences, Harold Rosenberg in 1952 said how it looked at the time: "The American vanguard painter took to the white expanse of the canvas as Melville's Ishmael took to the sea. On the one hand, a desperate recognition of moral and intellectual exhaustion; on the other, the exhilaration of an adventure over depths in which he might find reflected the true image of his identity."

A Pollock of 1947–50 undeniably acts out a drama of this kind: one man against the world. He was arguably the last great romantic artist: the last man to believe that with paint on canvas a man could encompass the whole and make new sense of it. Spontaneity was fundamental to what he did: "When I am *in* my painting," he wrote in 1947, "I'm not aware of what I am doing." But he was also a man who had thought through the whole adventure of European modernism and decided by 1944 that "American painters have generally missed the point of modern painting from beginning to end." The tensions of a great Pollock come from the fact that he did not simply "let go" in a self-indulgent way; impulse was the servant, in his case, of a profound historical understanding of what it remained for painting to do. A great painting is a painting about which people can differ widely and yet be right, every one of them; and in relation to a Pollock of 1950 we can accept the apocalyptic vision of Harold Rosenberg and yet equally well see what younger critics mean when they say that Pollock's true point of departure was the taut, allover weave of Cubist painting as it was practiced by Picasso and Braque in 1910.

Pollock was not alone, among the members of the New York School, in having gone over the masterpieces of the recent past in Europe and ransacked them, one by one, for relevance. He was preceded in this by Arshile Gorky, who from 1925 onward was developing what Meyer Schapiro called a series of psychic son-father relationships with the European masters. He had, in this, the shrewdest of eyes for quality. (In the year 1926 there were not many curators or historians who would have said in print, as Gorky did, that Picasso and Matisse were greater than the Old Masters and that Cézanne "is the greatest artist, shall I say, that has ever lived.") Yet Gorky had no cultural affinities with French painting. He had come to the United States at the age of 15 as a quintessential outcast. Neither boy nor man, he had been uprooted before he had anything to leave behind him, and he was pitched into American life with no money, no defined gift, and nowhere in particular to go. He was a member of a disregarded minority. He could not speak English. He was as denuded, outwardly, as a human being can be.

This was to become a classic 20th-century predicament: above all, in the late 1930s and early

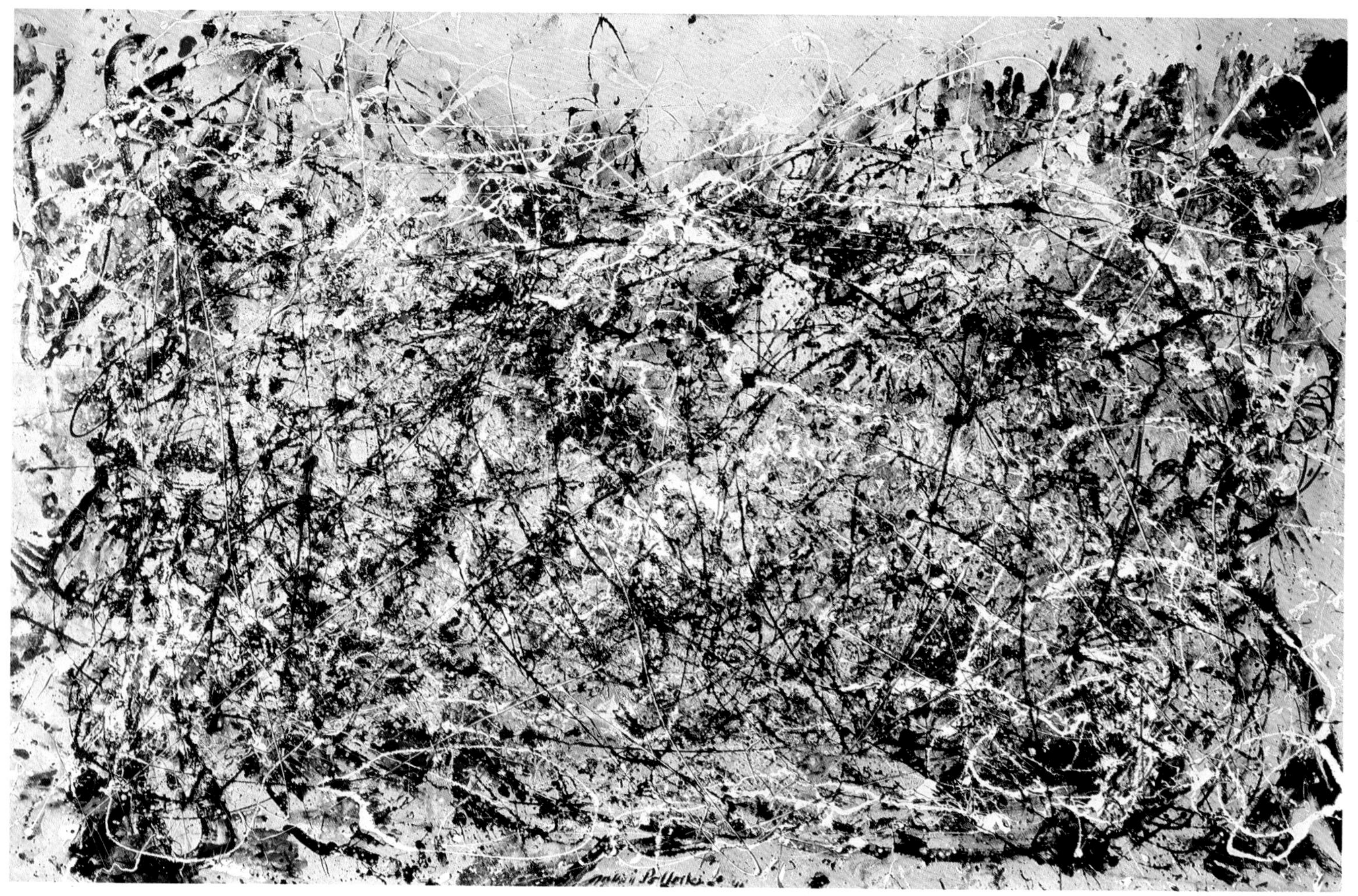

Jackson Pollock. *Number 1.* 1948. Oil on canvas, 5 feet 8 inches × 8 feet 8 inches. The Museum of Modern Art, New York. Purchase

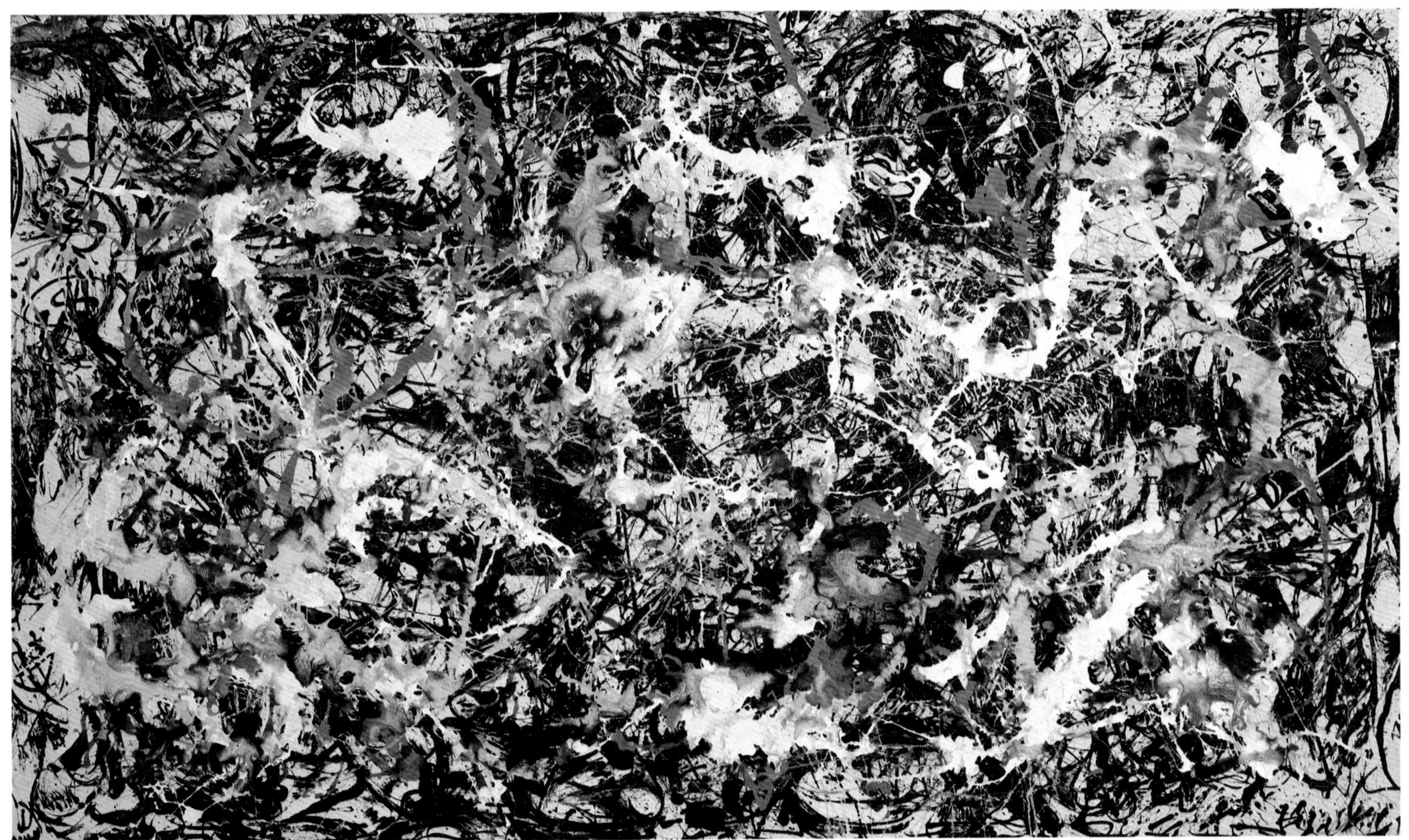

Jackson Pollock.
Convergence (Number 10, 1952).
1952.
Oil on canvas,
7 feet 9½ inches × 13 feet.
Albright-Knox Art Gallery, Buffalo. Gift of Seymour H. Knox

'40s. (The German poet Bertolt Brecht epitomized it when he enjoined posterity to "remember/The bleak Age/ Which you have escaped"—an age in which whole populations moved from place to place, involuntarily, "changing countries more often than shoes.") In the 1920s it happened above all to the young and obscure; such people had a sense of uncompleted identity when they came to America and could not even speak English. They had the privilege, unthinkable in most earlier times, of a social mobility to which no limits need be set; but for most of them that privilege was nominal, inert, nonfunctioning. Constitutionally speaking, their children could end up in the White House; but meanwhile the cultural break called for a tour de force of adjustment for which few human beings are equipped.

These were the circumstances in which Arshile Gorky decided in 1925 to become a painter. It was in modern painting, as Gorky saw it, that the dignity of modern man was most securely upheld; modern art spoke a universal language which was especially moving to one who came, as Gorky did, from a linguistic minority; and he set himself to master the idioms of Cézanne and Picasso and Miró in such a way that eventually they would speak through him, and he through them. Of course he was one of thousands of artists who had an ambition of this sort; but he was unique in the gravity, the fine judgment, the hard-won professional skill with which he went about it. Nothing was allowed to interfere: when other painters were deflected by the Depression, or by a will to politicization, or by the imminence of war, Gorky kept right on. His studio was an ark, and inviolable. When times got bad, he just quadrupled his order for paints and canvas. It could have been, and it may even sound like, the determination of a dogged but talentless crank; but Gorky made himself in the end into one of those rare artists in whom every generation discovers for itself new areas of meaning. Emulation became one of the fine arts when he practiced it: and when his work took on a character of its own, in the 1940s, it was soon recognized both as the fulfillment of tendencies which had been latent in European Surrealism and as a personal document, a *journal intime* in which a man of outstanding gifts came to terms with the century.

André Breton, for one, was in no doubt that among artists who might be claimed as Surrealists, Gorky was the most gifted to have appeared since the late 1920s. At a time when most of what passed for Surrealism was pedestrian and literal in its idiom, Gorky gave a completely new twist to the notion of ambiguous or hybrid forms. In particular his *The Liver Is the Cock's Comb*, 1944, seemed to Breton to open the door wide onto a world of analogy which till then had been sealed off from painting.

By 1944 Gorky had a voice of his own. In *The Liver Is the Cock's Comb*, he remembered the turbulence of Kandinsky's masterpieces of 30 years earlier. He also remembered the metamorphoses that Miró in the 1920s had inflicted upon the everyday life of the Catalan countryside. But what he made of the combination of these two was completely personal to himself. It had, in particular, a richness of color and a ferocity in the reinvention of form that corresponded to his own ardent, searching, all-or-nothing nature.

At a time when most Europeans either knew nothing of American art or frankly disdained it, Breton saw just what Gorky was about. "Those who like easy solutions will go unrewarded for their pains (such as they are)," Breton wrote. "Deter them as we may, they will insist on reading Gorky's pictures in terms of landscape, still life and the human figure. They will not dare to face up to those *hybrid* forms in which human feeling tends to present itself. A *hybrid* form results when we look at Nature and at the same time allow free passage to that flow of memories (from childhood and elsewhere) which an intense concentration before Nature will arouse in an observer who has the gift of emotion in its highest and rarest form. For I must emphasize that Gorky is, of all the Surrealists, the only one who maintains a direct contact with Nature and sits down in front of her to paint. Nature is not for him an *end*, however; he seeks in Nature such sensations as will serve him as a springboard toward the deeper exploration of certain states of being."

What this means, briefly, is that someone had come along who could renew and refresh the biomorphic imagery of the 1920s and '30s. Gorky was a master of ambiguity, and he gave it an accent that was all his own. His biomorphs were quite distinct from those of Miró, Arp, Henry Moore or (to name the newest arrival) Matta. Moreover, most European Surrealists had invoked the illusion of deep space in their paintings and many had held fast to old-style notions of composition; Gorky in the 1940s did neither of these things. The space in his paintings looked merely an inch or two deep, as it had been in the Cubist paintings of Picasso and Braque in 1910; and whereas Matta's paintings of the 1940s could usually be broken down in terms of self-contained illustrative incidents, Gorky's could not.

This was true even when Gorky appeared to have defined his subject matter exactly. In 1942, for instance, he produced the three versions of his *Garden in Sochi*. One of these was bought by The Museum of Modern Art, and Gorky prepared for the Museum's archives a long statement about the garden in question, which had belonged to his father and stood, by his own account, "about 194 feet from the house." Visitors to the Museum could scour the picture for the wild carrots, the porcupines, the barren apple trees and the "patches of moss, like fallen clouds" which Gorky spelled out for them. They could also bear in mind that this was a place known as the Garden of Wish Fulfillment, and that the village women used to come and rub their naked breasts on the rocks to

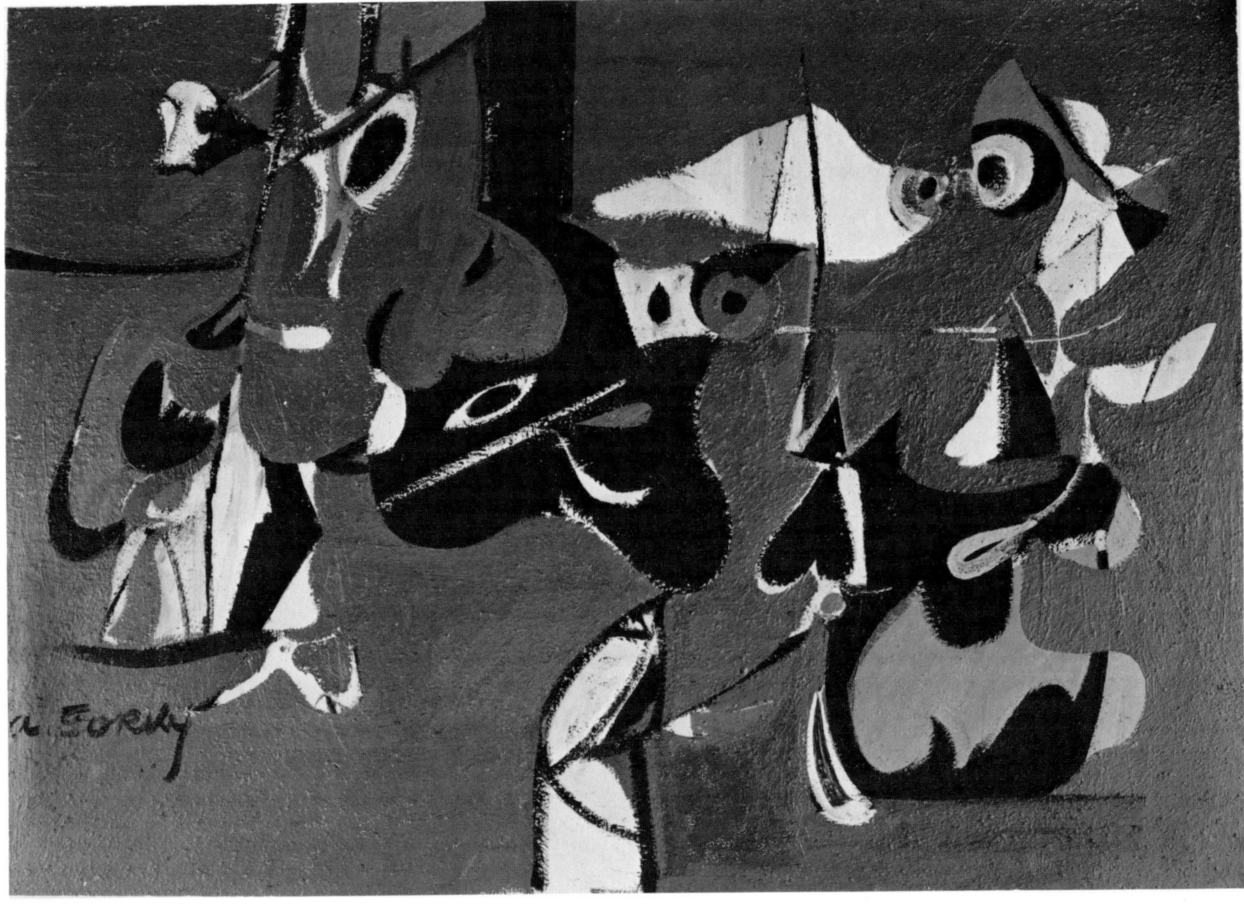

Arshile Gorky. *Garden in Sochi.* 1941. Oil on canvas, 44¼ × 62¼ inches. The Museum of Modern Art, New York. Gift of Mr. and Mrs. Wolfgang S. Schwabacher

make their wishes come true. They could look, finally, for the "Holy Tree," which was hung with strips of cloth that pilgrims had torn from their own clothes. This Holy Tree, itself leafless, had therefore a covering of pseudo-leaves which seemed to the young Gorky to rustle in the wind "like the silver leaves of poplars."

Chagall, for one, would have got a great deal of mileage out of detail of this sort; but the case of Gorky was more complicated. In the hybrid forms of these three paintings the things he spelled out for the catalogue reader were both *there* and *not there.* This is an extreme instance of the fact that no two people see the same picture. We can read into it what we will. Or, more exactly, it will summon, from our own unconscious, kindred but idiosyncratic memories with which we can complete the image. All pictures do this, in a varying degree; what is special about Gorky is that he unlocks the valve of private feeling with a particular sureness. It is a mistake, as Breton said, to read his pictures literally. They should be to us what Nature was to Gorky: a springboard.

It is legitimate, even so, to take up one or two of the clues which he offers us. Most commentators agree that the strong vertical form at the top of the *Garden in Sochi* is the Holy Tree; some see a porcupine, to the right below, and blue rock and black earth in the lower part of the picture to the left. The idea, part visual, part tactile, of a human female breast held in the hand and rubbed against a rock is pure Gorky in its alliance of the unexpected with the voluptuous; and I don't see why we should not find echoes of it in the *Garden in Sochi.* Gorky did not define his images, and he defies us to define them for him; but when we concentrate on his paintings as intensely as he concentrated upon Nature we shall find that memo-

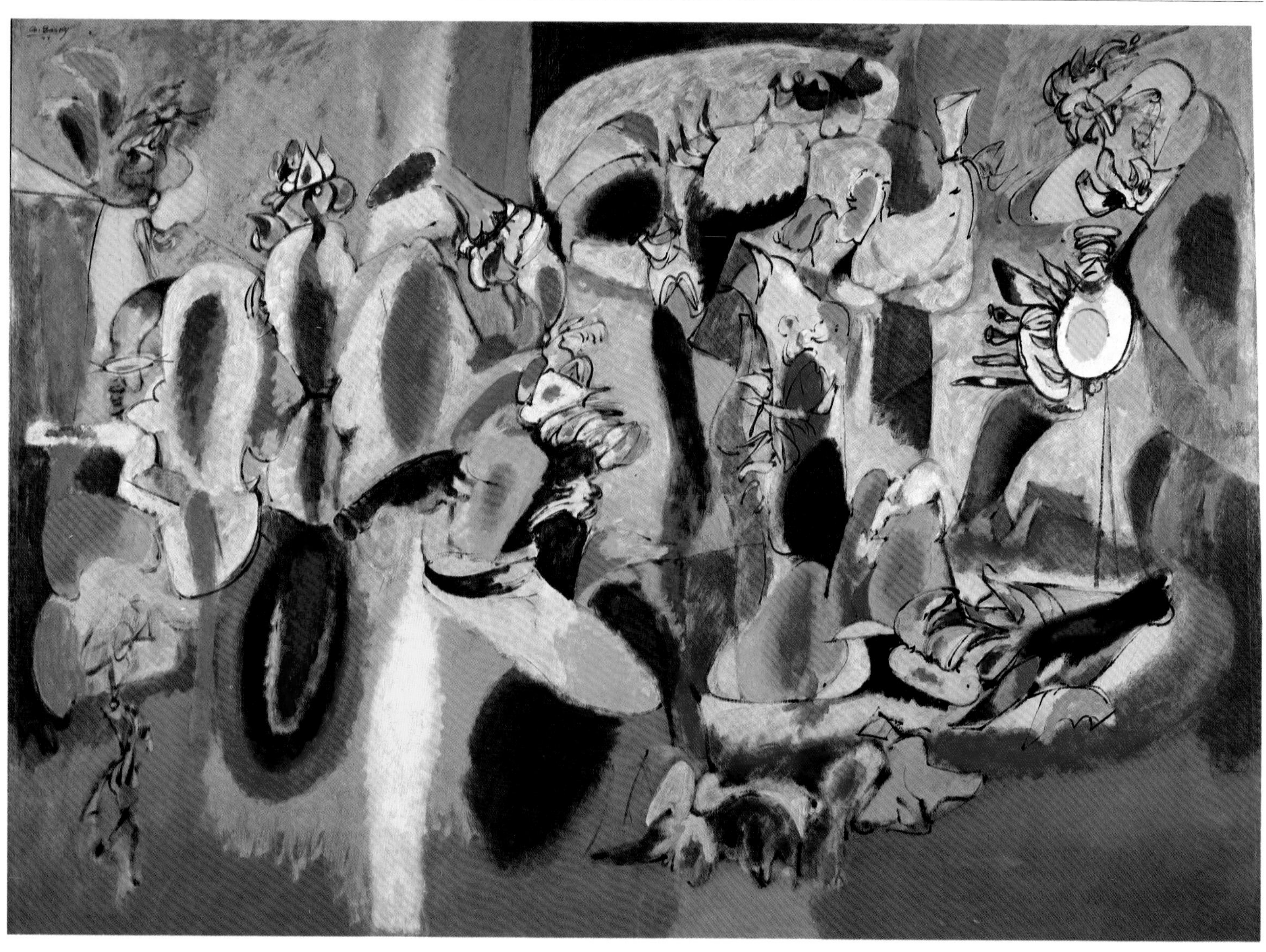

Arshile Gorky.
The Liver Is the Cock's Comb. 1944.
Oil on canvas,
6 feet × 8 feet 2 inches.
Albright-Knox Art Gallery, Buffalo. Gift of Seymour H. Knox

Barnett Newman.
Vir Heroicus Sublimis. 1950–51.
Oil on canvas, 7 feet 11⅜ inches × 17 feet 9¼ inches.
The Museum of Modern Art, New York. Gift of Mr. and Mrs. Ben Heller

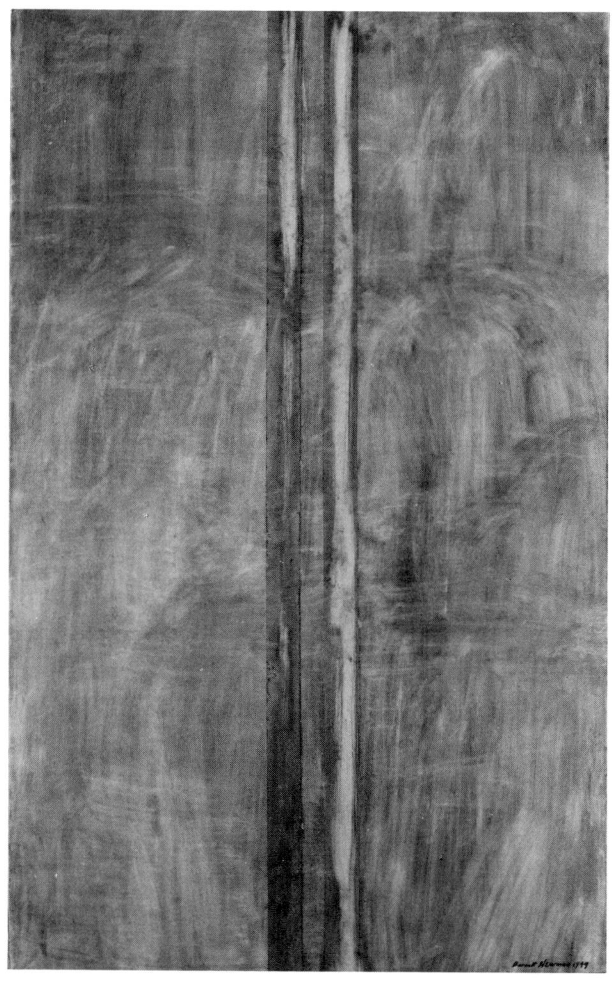

Barnett Newman.
Concord. 1949.
Oil on canvas,
7 feet 5¾ inches ×
53⅝ inches.
The Metropolitan
Museum of Art,
New York. George
A. Hearn Fund

ries long "forgotten" come back to us and that, as in a successful psychoanalysis, we make constructive connections between aspects of our experience which had previously seemed to us quite unrelated.

Gorky does this for us because he was prepared to risk himself. He opened himself out, where earlier artists had kept themselves shut. Like one of Arthur Miller's heroes, he allowed himself "to be completely known." His work had nothing of the grand public quality which was the mark of Hofmann and Pollock in their major statements. It was addressed to one pair of eyes at a time, and it set up an ideal of human intercourse in which everything can be said: without fear and without reserve. Gorky took from other artists and never tried to deny it; but where Picasso and Miró, Matta and André Masson in the last resort defended their own privacy—with wit, with panache, with masks borrowed from other places and other times—Arshile Gorky was the man who kept nothing back. Like John Berryman in poetry, he allowed art to eat him alive.

In his last paintings, of which *Agony* is an outstandingly fine example, Gorky was able to ally painterly eloquence to forms which epitomize the hurts which life had inflicted upon him. On the one hand, he opens the door upon the charnel house in which all human hopes and ambitions have their end; on the other, he achieved a fullness and subtlety of color that then were only just beginning to be within the reach of Abstract Expressionism.

Gorky's was an art of private reference: more so than Hofmann's, more so than de Kooning's, more so even than Pollock's. The other three had by implication a heroic stance which went beyond autobiography; and this was true, equally, of Barnett Newman.

Newman doubtless had, in private, his full share of those sensations of loss and unease which were mandatory among responsible human beings in the dark middle of this century. But in his art he was concerned with healing, and with restoration, and with the ways in which an individual human nature can be at one with itself and with the universe. *Onement* was the title he chose for the painting with which he broke through in 1948 to a way of painting that was entirely his own. *Concord* was the title of a major painting of the following year. Now, Newman was very sensitive to language, and he knew that *Onement* has overtones both of being "at one with the world" and of atonement in a specifically religious sense. *Concord* sets up likewise a complex vibration in our minds: concord as the aim of a fulfilled and humane society, Concord as a place-name that means much in American history, Concord the village as part of a pastoral New England still not too much contaminated. Newman thought everything through; and until he had thought everything through he refused to act.

It is relevant to all this that Newman was not a high-minded recluse but a home-bred New Yorker who delighted in the look and the life of the city. He was involved in New York City to the extent of running for mayor, in 1933, at the age of 28. Newman ran on a ticket of his own devising, and he didn't get in; but Mayor La Guardia took up at least two of his proposals (for free art schools and a municipal opera), and New York would be a better place today if some of the others had been adopted also: notably the Clean Air Department, the department which was to clean up the East River and the Hudson, and the establishment of extensive waterfront parks. He felt himself at home in every inch of New York, from the Metropolitan Museum to the improvised ballparks in out-of-the-way parking lots. He was at ease—more so than any of his colleagues—in the world of abstract thought; but he was also a man who could go to the corner for a newspaper and be found there, two hours later, still locking horns in argument with the news vendor. It was not his way to stand aside from life; and he gave his best, unstintingly, in all situations, never looking round the room to see if the company was worth his while. But when thinking and writing about art, above all when *making* art, he was an unsparing transcendentalist for whom art could be one thing only: a search for the hidden meaning of life.

In itself almost meaningless, that phrase was validated by Newman in the course of a five-years' period (1940–45) of preparation. Thinking, not doing, was fundamental to this: Newman made no pictures at that time, but he thought, and argued, and wrote—sometimes at great length—about what he saw as the central problem of mid-century art. "If we could describe the art of this, the first half of the 20th century, in a sentence," he wrote in 1944 or thereabouts, "it would read as the search for something to paint." One of the first facts about modernism was that the artist had at his disposal the art of all times and all places, much as Ezra Pound in the *Cantos* felt free to lift and transpose, and adjust as he thought fit, from the literature of other times, other peoples, other languages. "The new painter," Newman wrote, "has developed what is perhaps the most acute level of sensitivity to the grammar of art ever held by any painter in history." What to do with that grammar and that sensitivity was a problem not easily solved in 1944–45, when European art was out of sight and its derivatives were in decline. Art which relied on illustrative subject matter was clearly regressive, since (as Newman wrote in 1944) "the struggle against subject matter is the contribution the modern artist has made to world thought." "Yet," he went on, "the artist cannot paint without subject matter"; and when someone tried to do so the results were most often feeble. "Abstract art in America," he wrote on another occasion, "has to a large extent been the preoccupation of the dull, who by ignoring subject matter remove themselves from life to engage in a pastime of decorative art."

All this was the more dismaying in that the times called loud and clear for an art that would have something of their own dimensions. As a citizen, as a son and as a husband, Newman had worked to redefine America: a straighter, braver, more forthright man never lived. From 1945 onward he had his full share of what he called "the new sense of fate." By this he meant that, in the potential of America, tragedy had taken the place of terror; there was nothing to be frightened of but the fact that America might prove unworthy of her responsibilities. This is fundamental to the situation of whatever country dominates all the others; but it needs, each time round, a new resolution. The age cried out for wisdom, in 1945, and it was for the artist to respond as best he could.

It was in 1949 that Newman at last began to come up with his answer. As with much of the best art of this century, the results did not, to begin with, look like art at all. He was probably, in that sense, the most forbidding of the New York School. A big Pollock like *Number 1* gives off a

Barnett Newman.
Achilles. 1952.
Oil on canvas,
8 feet × 6 feet 7 inches.
Annalee Newman,
New York

sense of untrammeled energy which is highly contagious. There is about de Kooning's women a sexual provocation that is like a live wire left unsheathed. Hofmann had so meaty, so emphatic a way with paint that we just have to stop and look. But a Newman of 1949–51 is likely to consist of a large plain rectangle of uninflected color with one, two, three or at most four thin straight vertical stripes that run from top to bottom of the canvas. He did not make things easy.

Stripes of a comparable kind had been turning up in his paintings ever since he returned to the easel in 1945. They had, however, been combined either with textured backgrounds or with subject matter of a symbolic sort. Thomas B. Hess had described how Newman came to realize that a picture did not have to have embellishments of that sort: "He kept his motifs separate from the backgrounds by masking them with tape. On his birthday, January 29, 1948, he prepared a small canvas with a surface of cadmium red dark (a deep mineral color that looks like an earth pigment—like Indian red or a sienna) and fixed a piece of tape down the center. Then he quickly smeared a coat of cadmium red light over the tape, to test the color. He looked at the picture for a long time. Indeed he studied it for some nine months. He had finished questing."

It is possible to respond to Newman's paintings without knowing what he intended by them, just as it is possible to enjoy the Noh plays without understanding Japanese, or to enjoy the love-duet in act I of Wagner's *Die Walküre* without realizing that the two people concerned are brother and sister. It will somehow get through to any sympathetic observer that Newman was up to something very grand, and that the picture on the wall results from an exemplary commingling of science and hard labor and love. It could have been, as a matter of hypothesis, that there was nothing more to the pictures than what they yield at first sight; but this never quite accounted for the thralldom of paintings in which there was nothing whatever in the way of spectacular incident. Nor was it in line with Newman's ambitions for art, or with his low opinion of earlier American abstract painting, that they should yield no more than a retinal satisfaction.

At the very least—so it seemed at the time—there were complex and subterranean mathematical procedures behind the terminal simplicity of his paintings. Newman had been planning since 1944 to "achieve feeling," as he put it, "through intellectual content." He was interested in numbers, for their own sake, and he had that preoccupation with measurement which we earlier traced, as an American trait, way back into the

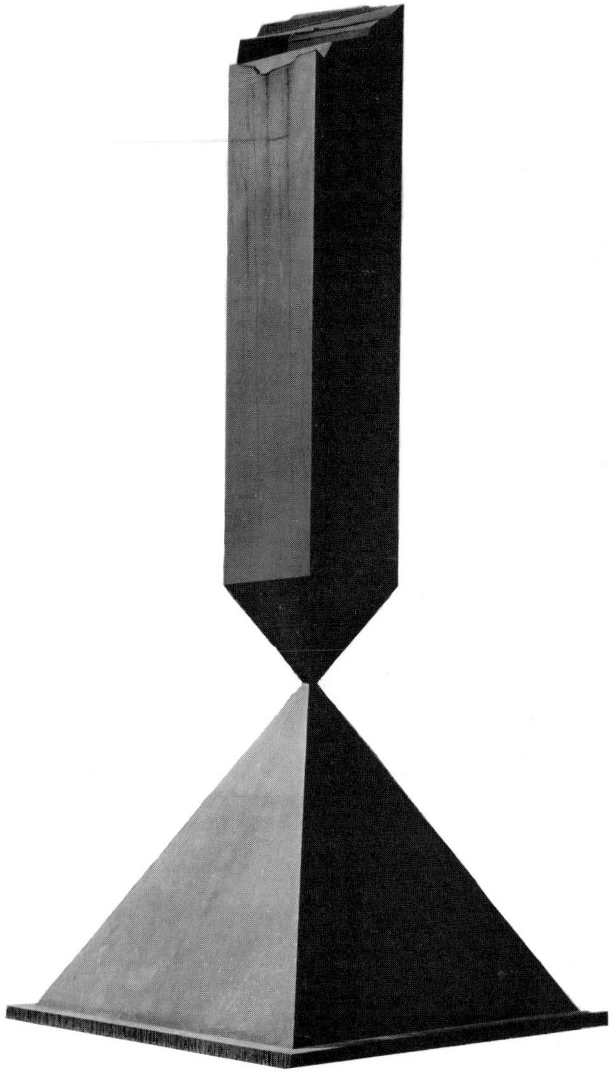

Barnett Newman. *Broken Obelisk.* 1963–67. Cor-ten steel, 25 feet 5 inches × 10 feet 6 inches × 10 feet 6 inches. Institute of Religion and Human Development, Rice University, Houston

19th century. He felt such things instinctively, but he did not exploit them as closed systems. He remembered, rather, that to measure the unmeasurable is a part of Jewish mystical experience.

In this, as in much else here, I follow the reading proposed by Hess, who was for many years a close friend of Newman's. Something in what he says could be inferred by any intelligent person: the difference, for example, between the clean, sharp, straight look of the vertical stripe ("zip" was Newman's name for it) as it appears in *Vir Heroicus Sublimis*, 1950–51, and the soft, smoky, irregular look of the same element as it appeared in the original *Onement* and in many later paintings. Even in reproduction that difference is quite clear: but when we are in front of the real thing the zips stand for a contrasted gamut of experience which runs all the way from a stark, wandlike look to something that has been breathed on, edged this way and that, smudged and softened, and yet retains the affirmative vertical principle.

Hess goes deeply into this, suggesting that the painterly zip, with its wayward but in the end resolutely upright thrust, may stand for the newly created Adam. Self-evidently the product of a human hand (of one of Adam's offspring, therefore, at however many removes), it also stands for "the physical sphere—that which is touched, felt, informed by the manipulation of the artist." "On the other hand," Hess goes on, "the taped, clean-edged smooth zip could refer to the more intellectual sphere, assuming the presence of an abstract force of division—as God separated the waters and the firmament in Genesis." (Mrs. Newman once proposed a simpler explanation: that the two forms of stripe stood for "the he and the she of it" —a form of polarization which Newman would neither confirm nor deny.)

Such notions can be ridiculed: but it is relevant that Newman believed that art should have subject matter and that he was not interested in making agreeable patterns on canvas. Few people would dispute the fact that his *Vir Heroicus Sublimis* is one of the monuments of the New York School in its opening phase (1945–51, let us say). It is possible to see it simply as a magisterial move in that long campaign for the liberation of color which began in France before 1900; the zips are there, on that reading, to intensify the effect of the great field of cadmium red that runs the whole length of the painting. Even the dimensions of the painting can be seen as an attempt to outdo the scale on which Jackson Pollock had lately been working. But the picture sustains a loftier interpretation—and one that is more in tune both with Newman's quality as a human being and with his exalted notion of the role of art in society. When the art historian Erwin Panofsky challenged the title of *Vir Heroicus Sublimis*—suggesting in effect that it was mere empty rhetoric—Newman was able to beat him down in open debate; and I think we can go along with Thomas B. Hess in believing that the secret symmetry which runs throughout *Vir Heroicus Sublimis* (and the use, for that matter, of the number 18, there and elsewhere in Newman's work) are not devices to pass an idle moment between one picture and another in a museum but references to Genesis, to the primal creative act and to the invisible God of the Kabbalists.

No one interpretation can exhaust this painting. But secreted in the middle of *Vir Heroicus Sublimis* is a red square, eight feet by eight exactly. The uniform cadmium red of the large plain panels of color is tested, disputed, modified and generally investigated by slender "zips" which vary both in their hue and in their intensity. As Hess said, "The effect of the painting is at the farthest remove from any idea of a diagram or a coldly articulated structure. The color envelops the spectator; the verticals stand as presences in it, like the angel sentinels who guard the Throne of the Lord." The title is to be taken literally and not as rhetoric: for what is being celebrated here is man's ability to master and order his experience as a fully responsible being.

Barnett Newman wrote in 1948 that "Greece named both form and content; the ideal form—

beauty, the ideal content—tragedy." It seemed to him that in that context the European artist was "nostalgic for the ancient forms, hoping to achieve tragedy by depicting his self-pity over the loss of the elegant column and the beautiful profile." The American artist had by contrast "an opportunity, free of the ancient paraphernalia, closer to the sources of the tragic emotion." Alike in *Achilles* and *Broken Obelisk*, Newman gave a new twist (literally, in the case of the obelisk) to formulae which long use had made flaccid. In *Achilles*, the hero's giant stature and broken sword are hinted at but not described. As for the obelisk, it is a potent symbol of man's flawed, divided nature.

I cannot claim in these few pages to have done more than touch on certain major figures of the New York School. Even in the period under review, which ends in 1951, other men, other works and other media should ideally be included. Other dialogues—with the American past, with the European masters, with the notion of an art that would lie beyond the range of the art market—could also be spelled out in detail. Something could also be said about the coincidence (if it is one) by which these artists came to fulfillment at the apogee of American power: political, military, economic. What I have tried to suggest is that art, like nature, abhors a vacuum; that there was a job to be done in the United States in the late 1940s, just as there had been a job to be done in Paris between 1885 and 1914; and that for the first time American artists proved equal to a span of involvement that ranged from the most intimate disorders of the psyche to what is called in Jewish mysticism "the everlasting unity and presence of Transcendence."

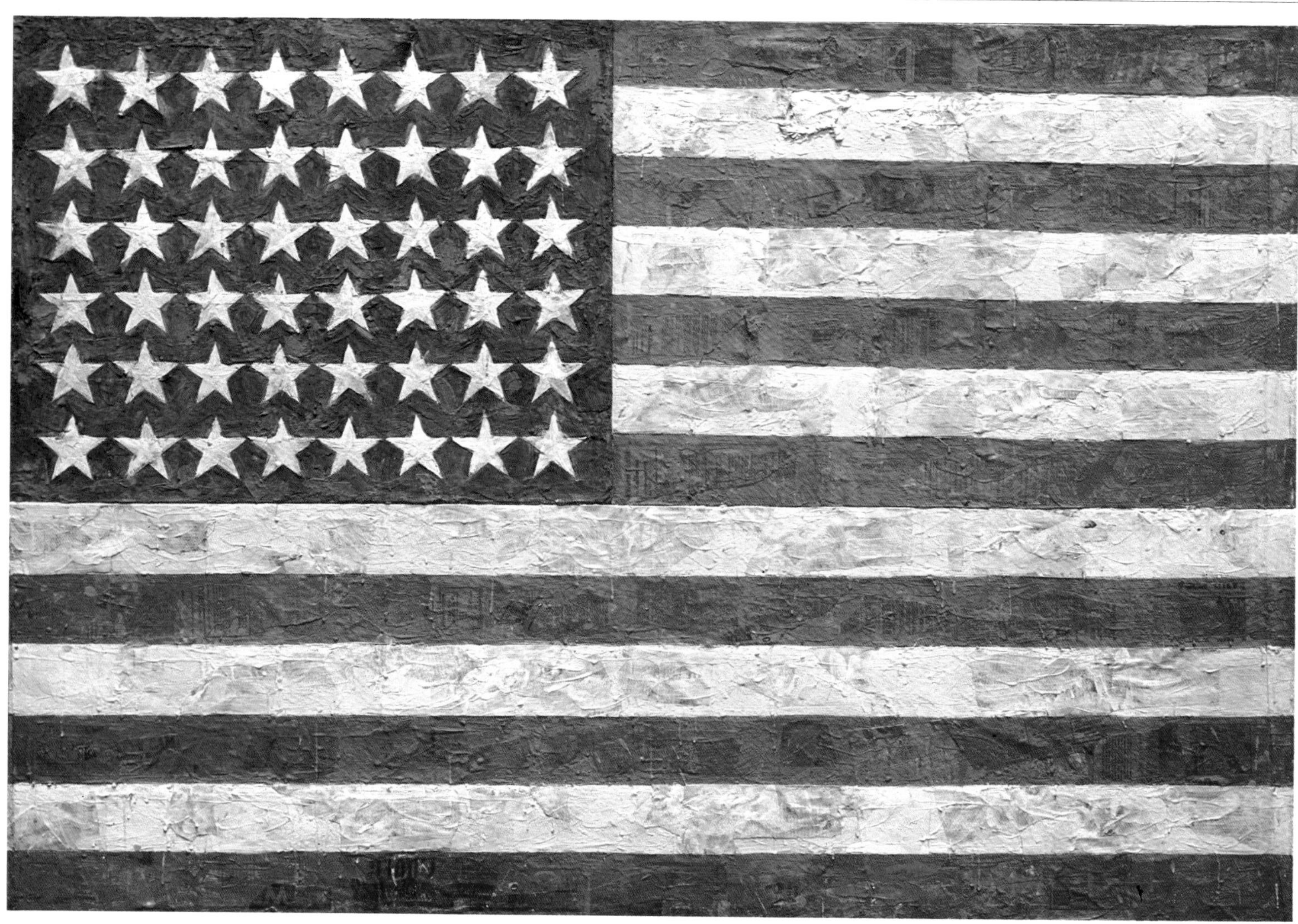

Jasper Johns.
Flag. 1954–55.
Encaustic on newsprint over canvas mounted on plywood, 42¼ × 60½ inches.
The Museum of Modern Art, New York.
Gift of Philip Johnson in honor of Alfred H. Barr, Jr.

THE GREAT DIVIDE 1950-70

The art of the second half of this century treads everywhere on tender ground. For what is true of people and of public events is also true of works of art: we have a special feeling toward the ones we grew up with.

This feeling is rooted in reason, for it is in first youth that we establish the modes of feeling, the canons of beauty, and the standards of truth and integrity by which we are to live for the rest of our lives. But it also goes beyond reason. We are committed, every one of us, in ways that are sometimes welcome, sometimes repugnant, to what is done in our own day. Its face is our face, its ways are our ways, its echo is the twin of our own. We may demur—"It has nothing to do with me," we may say, whether from modesty or from disgust—but posterity will not believe us. Posterity will say that to be alive at a given time and not to be marked by the events of the day is a disgrace and a diminution. We were there; this and that happened; how could we not bear the mark forever?

This is true above all of those moments in history at which a shift of sensibility occurs or the potential of human capacities is redrafted. People who come to maturity at such times are by that much the more alive. It would, for instance, be a very dull American who did not feel that the first years of the presidency of Harry S. Truman were a time unlike any other. In terms of political, economic and military power the United States dominated the rest of the world as never before or since. It had a primacy of the sort which can turn to tyranny; but the use made of it was more often than not both farsighted and responsible. It was also magnanimous: how often in history has a nation offered to renounce a decisive military superiority in the interests of the common good? Yet this is what happened in 1946. Had the Baruch plan been accepted by the United Nations, the United States would have destroyed her stock of atomic weapons and manufactured no more of them, in return for a general agreement that atomic power should be used for peaceful purposes only, with regular worldwide inspection to confirm that this was being done.

United States policy was magnanimous in other ways also. We should not forget that twelve million American men and women were given the chance of further education under the G.I. Bill of Rights; that relief to the devastated countries of Europe ran at around $700,000,000 a year; and that when George C. Marshall was Secretary of State, in 1947, he made it possible for those same countries to establish, by their own exertions but with American financial backing, "the political and social conditions in which free institutions can exist." That such institutions should exist was much to the advantage of the United States: to that extent the Marshall Plan can be interpreted in terms of American self-interest. But anyone who traveled in Europe in 1946 will know that the condition of victors and vanquished alike was appalling; and to both of them at that time the large-heartedness of the United States seemed as genuine as it was prompt.

It could be a coincidence, but I don't think it was, that American Action Painting came to the fore at precisely that time. Action Painting was not, as some people supposed, melodramatic or self-indulgent. It arose from an intelligent examination, on the part of people who had been serious artists for nearly half a lifetime, as to just why so much of European painting had run itself into the ground. And it stood for an idea current in public life also: that human nature had not said its last word.

Many of its manifestations had an evangelical character. In a major Jackson Pollock, as in a slashing, man-sized, black-on-white Franz Kline, painting comes into the open, baring its essential nature with a mimetic vivacity that can still carry us away. When Arshile Gorky unbandaged the wounds with which life had left him, he did it in such a way that we found new courage to face our own hurts. It was a time for the undefeated spirit. What was called an "American sublime" was brought into being: a mode of expression from which the contingent and the equivocal were banished. A painting like Barnett Newman's *Day One* is typical of that moment in history. Already its title suggests the beginning of a new era for all humanity; and it was typical of its time in being, as Thomas B. Hess pointed out, "not only unsaleable, but unexhibitable. There was no chance at all, with its 11-foot height, that it could be sold, or even seen by anybody but the artist and the friends he invited to his studio."

The all-or-nothing, backs-against-the-wall character of work such as this answered to experience of life not only during the Depression and during World War II, but even in the late 1940s, when the audience for radically new art in a country of 140,000,000 people was estimated at around 50: "a small circle," as Clement Greenberg described it in the fall of 1947, "of fanatics, art-fixated misfits who are as isolated in the U.S. as if they were living in Paleolithic Europe." Greenberg went on to describe their isolation as "inconceivable, crushing, unbroken, damning"; and it is natural that those who lived through that period either as participants or as sympathizers should consider that later generations of American artists have had a much easier ride. Certainly they have not had to draw for so long on the reserves of moral energy which were demanded of Pollock, de Kooning, Gorky and Newman. Nor were they called upon to make the kind of breakthrough to public acknowledgment which has to be made once and once only; by 1956, the year of Pollock's death, that job had been done. Thereafter it was taken for granted that painting and sculpture had a new rank among American modes of expression, and that they were redefining America as distinctly as it had been redefined by Emerson in the 1830s, by Herman Melville in the 1850s, and by Whitman in the laconic penetrations of his *Specimen Days in America* (first published in 1882–83).

It was a lot to ask of any artist that he do this; but in their different ways—and no group of men could have been more different, one from the other—the American Action Painters had trained hard and long for it. Nor were they in any doubt of the historic and definitive shift in sensibility which they were to bring about: "But surely our quarrel is with Michelangelo" was Newman's rejoinder when fellow artists, in a discussion, tried to scale down their ambitions to a more parochial level.

Theirs was, in fact, a prodigious commitment: but one that was in line with the changes that were coming about in many other departments of life in the late 1940s. "To every age, its own art" had been the motto of the Vienna Secession when it was founded in 1897; and the new American painting lived up to it. If life was different, art would be different too; and how different, how startlingly and unfathomably different was the life that came up over the horizon after World War II! It was not simply that the conditions of everyday existence were changed beyond recognition by antibiotics, by computerization, by the transistor, by the jet engine, by the prospect of atomic power. It was that the ingredients of metaphor had been turned upside down and would never be right way up again. It is by metaphor, and by analogy, that we feel our way through life; yet here were medicines that did away with many of the traditional terrors of illness, machines that performed feats of assimilation previously within the reach of one man in a million, and instruments of the size of a pocket-watch that could do the work of a freight locomotive. Ancient certainties toppled day after day. Standards accepted since long before the name of "American" was first spoken no longer made sense. The power of speedy and nimble adjustment to all this was as much a part of the postwar era as horns are part of a ram. And yet people could become too open to new ideas, too quick to assume that nothing could faze them; and they could end up feeling, with the bemused hero of Saul Bellow's novel *Herzog*, that "modern character is inconstant, divided, vacillating, lacking the stone-like certitude of ancient man, also deprived of the firm ideas of the 17th century, clear, hard theorems. . . ."

It was one of the strengths of American Action Painting in the late 1940s and early '50s that it offered, in contradistinction to all this, a new set of certainties: modes of feeling so wide in their range and so peremptory in their expression as to form the apparatus of survival in a world where preexisting landmarks were few. In pictures like Pollock's *Convergence (Number 10, 1952)* and Newman's *Vir Heroicus Sublimis* feeling was all of a piece, without reserve or equivocation. The new American painting covered the whole gamut of human experience, from the most exalted (Mark Rothko said that "subject matter is crucial, and only that subject matter is crucial which is tragic and timeless") to the undignified and the hilarious. (As much as anyone in modern times—poets, novelists, playwrights not excepted—Arshile Gorky makes clear the often grotesquely inconvenient nature of our deepest entanglements; and it is Willem de Kooning who has best carried forward into our own day the notion, so prevalent in the late 19th century, of the man-eating Venus.)

I have to say at this point that the history of the New York School is neither as simple nor as orderly nor as unified as I have made it appear. Making art is by its very nature an untidy, spasmodic, unequal business; and when there occurs a collective impulse to let more of life into art than had been admitted before, then human frailty is bound to come in along with other and more constructive qualities. The artists of the New York School had their flaws, like the rest of us. Operating on terrain that was largely untested, they found some of it spongy and had to withdraw. They had dry periods, as well as fertile ones. The moral energy which informed their finest works came and went. To speak of them as "a school" is a matter more of convenience than of historical truth. Yet one thing was common to all of them, and common to most thinking people in the late 1940s: a feeling of "either/or." In art, as in so many other departments of life, humanity was being given a fresh start. It was time to stand up and be counted; the question at issue was (or seemed to

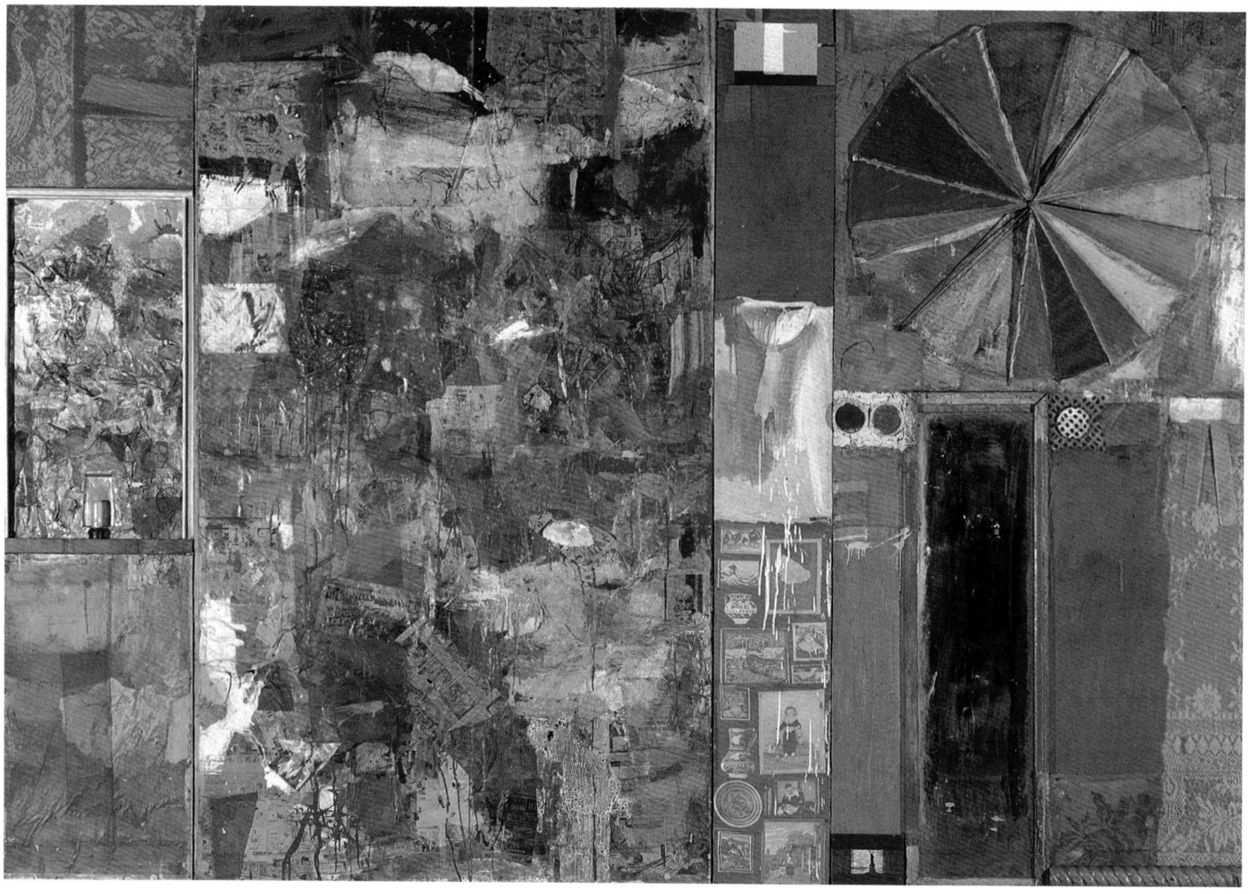

Robert Rauschenberg. *Charlene.* 1954. Combine painting in four sections, 7 feet 5 inches × 9 feet 4 inches. Stedelijk Museum, Amsterdam

be) *either* a decisive shift in sensibility *or* a genteel continuance.

That was how it looked around the time that Harry S. Truman put the pollsters to shame and got himself reelected by a large majority. By the time that Truman was out of the White House, in 1952, the world looked different. The unified salvationist outlook had given way to misgiving and disquiet at every level of society. The New World fancies of the late 1940s began to look too fanciful by half. Nothing was what it had seemed to be when Marshall was Secretary of State, when the United Nations was an immaculate phantom not yet localized by the East River, and when Southeast Asia was just a place where the French and the British were always getting into trouble. Of course there were still the spectacular novelties of technology: in fact there were more of them every day. But what if they got into the wrong hands for the wrong purposes? What was once called "a full life" was within the reach of more and more people. But what if that life turned out to be not so much full as empty? What if there were something sterile and self-defeating about the response to life which could be summed up as "I consume, therefore I am"?

In one way and another just about everybody felt let down in the early 1950s, and their feelings were acted out at the level of obsession in the long series of defections and betrayals, real or imagined, which were a feature of the period. Nobody who read, day by day, of the trial of Alger Hiss in the United States and of Otto John in Germany will forget how violent were the passions which these cases aroused. Nor could any scientist be quite unmoved by the fact that Fuchs and Pontecorvo, men of great consequence in their field, felt it better to leave the West and settle in the U.S.S.R. Something was dying at that time; and that something was the notion of humanity for

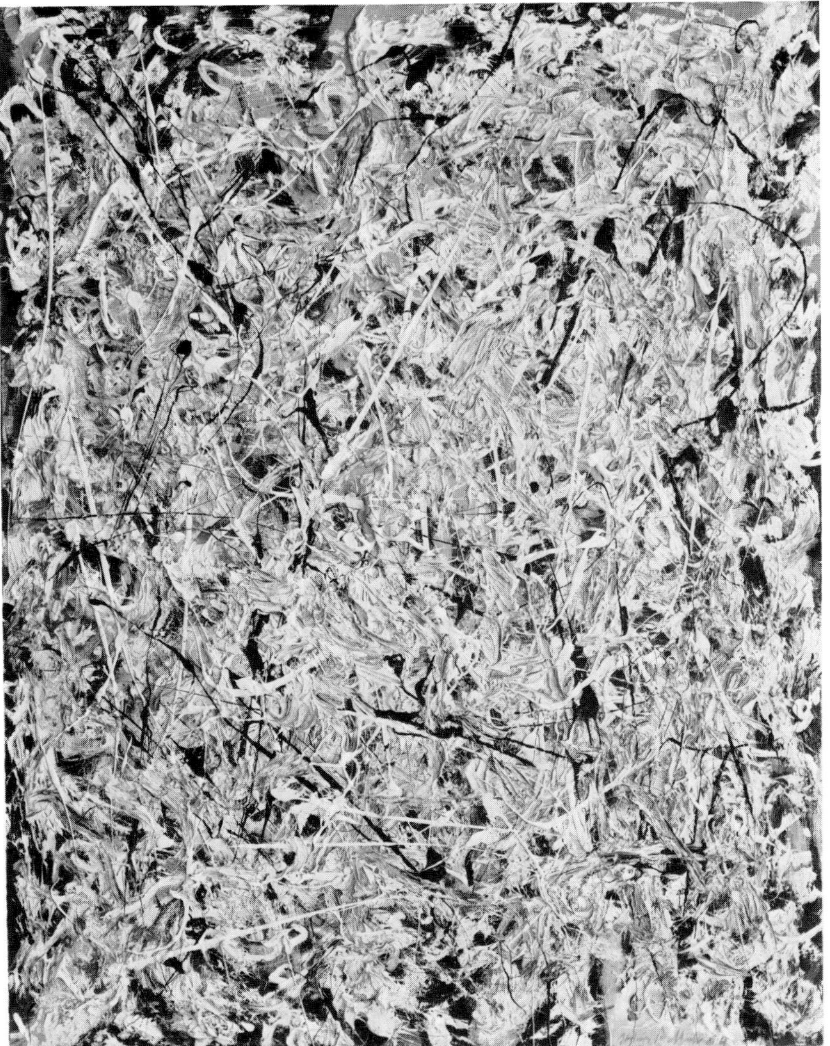

Jackson Pollock. *White Light.* 1954. Oil, enamel and aluminum paint on canvas, 48¼ × 38¼ inches. The Museum of Modern Art, New York. The Sidney and Harriet Janis Collection

which Barnett Newman had spoken up in his *Vir Heroicus Sublimis* as recently as 1950–51.

Just what came out of all this in art could be charted, day by day. But in our shorter space it may be more illuminating to follow the example set by Shakespeare's Hamlet when he wanted to explain the difference between his murdered father and his stepfather. Hamlet could talk his way through just about anything, but in that moment of crisis he fell back on the painted image. "Look here," he said, "upon this picture, and on this." It is difficult, admittedly, for us to particularize as exactly as Hamlet did. No one picture will serve for one extreme, no one picture for the other. But we can get some idea of the cross-generational confrontation if we put a late Pollock, *White Light*, 1954, side by side with *Charlene*, 1954, by Robert Rauschenberg. And it will become clearer still if we go on to put Jasper Johns's *Target with Four Faces* next to Clyfford Still's *1960-R*.

The impact of confrontations such as these has still not subsided. For the older generation, something holy had been defiled. The art historian Leo Steinberg remembers, for instance, "the reaction to Jasper Johns of two well-known New York abstract painters. One of them said, 'If this is painting, I might as well give up.' And the other said, resignedly, 'Well, I am still involved with the dream.' He too felt that an age-old dream of what painting had been, or could be, had been wan-

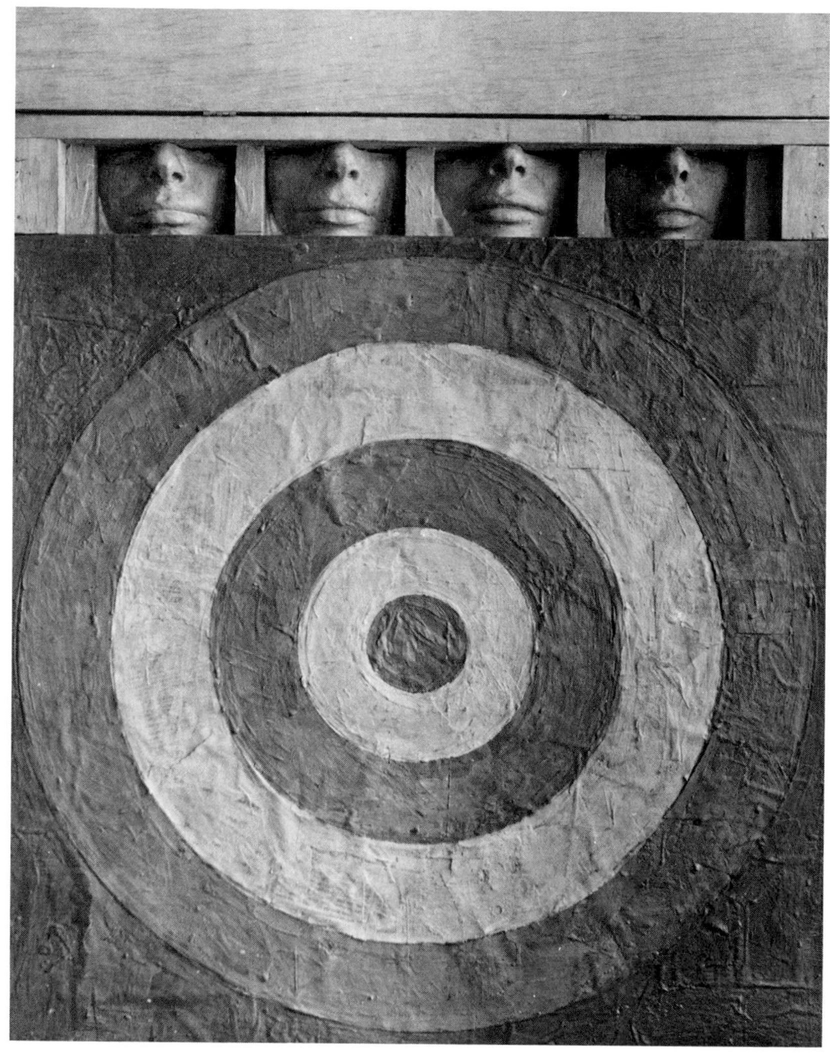

Jasper Johns.
Target with Four Faces. 1955.
Encaustic on newspaper on canvas surmounted by four tinted plaster faces in wooden box with hinged front, overall (with box open) 33⅝ × 26 × 3 inches.
The Museum of Modern Art, New York.
Gift of Mr. and Mrs. Robert C. Scull

tonly sacrificed—perhaps by a young man too brash or irreverent to have dreamed yet." As for Robert Rauschenberg, he is to this day a nonperson to champions of a certain direction in abstract painting: someone not to be named, let alone discussed. These are religious matters, in which loyalties are absolute. "He who is not with me is against me"; and the idea that it is possible to see very great merits on both sides once drew from Harold Rosenberg the rejoinder that "the eclectic critic is guaranteed extinction." On this matter, as on most others, Rosenberg was categorical: "1946 to 1952 or 1953 was a remarkable period in American art, and no period since has come close to equaling it."

This was in part, as I said earlier, a generational matter. An acute French observer of life, Jean de La Bruyère, wrote three hundred years ago, "We love only once. The other times are less involuntary"; and his remark has not gone out of date. Intelligent people know, of course, that art never stays the same; and they also knew by 1955 that it was time for the logic of history to intervene and bring forward something that had evolved naturally from Action Painting (or from Abstract Expressionism, as it was also called). It seemed most likely that that evolution would start from the basic premise of Action Painting: that the image was generated by the very act of applying the paint, without conscious reference to anything in the world outside the studio and with no conces-

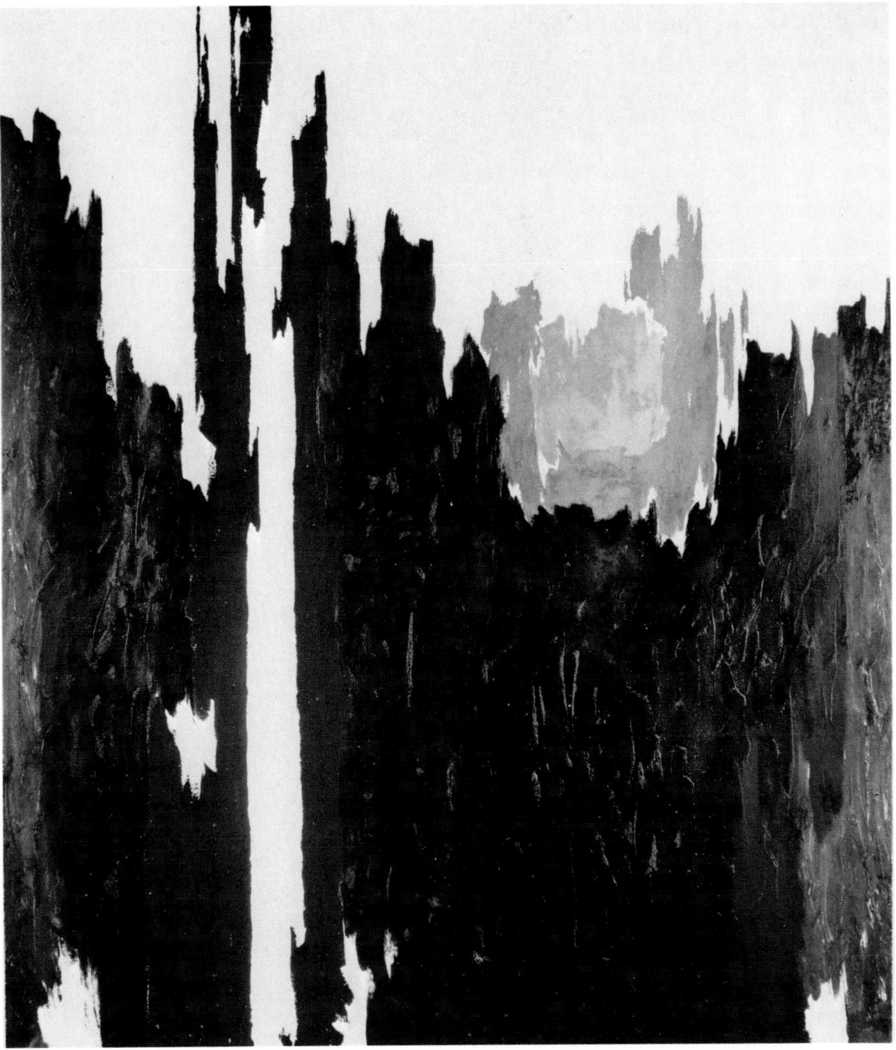

Clyfford Still. *1960–R.* Oil on canvas, 9 feet × 7 feet 3 inches. Hirshhorn Museum and Sculpture Garden, Smithsonian Institution, Washington

sions to the divide which once separated painting from drawing, foreground from background and light from shadow. A development of that sort had begun in 1953, in that the concept of staining the canvas, instead of applying the paint to its surface, had been investigated by a painter in her middle 20s, Helen Frankenthaler. Two gifted painters from Washington, D.C., by name Morris Louis and Kenneth Noland, had been to see her work in New York; and it was reasonable to look to all three of them for an uncompromising lyricism that would maintain the level of aspiration which had sustained Rothko and Newman and the others. All this was bound up not only with a specific notion of art but with a specific notion of human dignity; people felt deeply about it then, and they still feel deeply about it now.

But there were other young people—born around 1930, let us say—who had convictions which were no less strong, and no less firmly rooted in their historical situation. As they saw it, Action Painting had sprung from a climate of feeling that was distinctly that of an earlier generation. What had been right for 1947 was not right for 1955, any more than in Paris what had been right for 1905 (the Fauvist exploitation of heightened color) had been right for 1910, when the first masterpieces of Cubism were virtually colorless by the standards of five years earlier. Action Painting had had many facets, but it arose above all from a grand, high-souled opening out of the self which found expression in a large-scale unified eloquence. There were incidental exceptions: in one of his Women de Kooning had cut a pair of red lips out of an advertisement and collaged them to the canvas, and if we look closely at the vortex of Pollock's imagery we may find that fragmented objects from everyday life have been sucked into the whirlpool and left there. But fundamentally the materials of Action Painting were those of traditional painting, just as its aspirations were toward the amplest and most spectacular unveiling of an individual human nature.

Great works of art came out of this conviction. But by the mid-1950s it had lost its solitudinous and evangelical status and become an orthodoxy. Just about everyone was trying to act upon it. The "either/or" syndrome had impressed itself on hundreds of more or less gifted, more or less genuine artists, much as Cubism had ceased by 1914 to be an activity for just two or three supremely gifted people. But what if the "either/or" syndrome was not the only answer? When John Cage published *Jasper Johns: Stories and Ideas* in 1964 he put the dissenting point of view in two short sentences: "The situation must be Yes-and-No not either-or. *Avoid a polar situation.*" (The words italicized are Johns's own.)

In general conversation these would not be fighting words, but in the context of the art of the mid-1950s they caused a cultural divide to crack wide open, sundering father from son, husband from wife, and friend from friend. Too many people had too much at stake for the concept of "yes-and-no" to be accepted lightly. It was on the basis of "either/or" that a whole generation had seen its contemporaries win through to worldwide acceptance. "Either/or" was associated with a virile, fearless, all-enduring turn of mind; what could the "yes-and-no" approach of John Cage and Jasper Johns stand for if not a flabby, easygoing acceptance? A relaxation of all standards? A readiness to see the barriers go down between art and entertainment, art and interior decoration, art and merchandising? Such things should be resisted; meanwhile there was only one place for art to go to, and only one way for art to get to it.

It was in those terms, more or less, that the alarm was sounded. And there was undeniably a look of provocation about the paintings of Jasper Johns and Robert Rauschenberg when they first went on view. After the American sublime, a facsimile of the Stars and Stripes! After the exalted investigations of Rothko and Still, a bed smeared with paint and hung on the wall! After Gorky had probed the most tender places of the psyche, a target with plaster casts of parts of the body stuck on top of it! Anyone who learned of such things by hearsay might well think of them as acts of sabotage against the high art which had lately won through to recognition.

They were nothing of the kind. There was nothing destructive or nihilist about Johns and Rauschenberg, and the idea that they could be likened to the Dadaists was wide of the mark. The logic of history was on their side, as much as it had been on the side of Pollock and de Kooning; but it was a logic born of a different view of history. Their work was predicated on the belief that a mixed mode of utterance was true to life as it was being lived, and that it was not the role of the artist to censor and unify a flow of experience which in reality was made up of compound apprehensions which needed to be read in more than one way at once.

This point of view had been touched upon by two pioneers of modern sensibility. It was fundamental to the work of Marcel Duchamp that the observer should be challenged to take in several meanings at once, and that these meanings can operate on quite different levels of understanding. (How this worked has been discussed here in relation to *Fresh Widow* and *Apolinère Enameled*.) John Cage in the late 1930s had suggested more than once that there should no longer be a point at which life stopped and art began. In 1937, for instance, he foresaw the use of electronic instruments which would "make available for musical purposes any and all sounds that can be heard." Musical expression would be set free from the tyranny of existing musical instruments; "we can compose and perform," Cage went on, "a quartet for explosive motor, wind, heartbeat, and landslide."

As between Johns and Rauschenberg, there is no doubt that it was Rauschenberg who took over the Cage position in a wholehearted and single-minded way. In an often-quoted statement he said that he wanted to work "in the gap between art and life"; and in 1961 he told an interviewer that "there is no reason not to consider the world as one gigantic painting." So far from treating the picture as something set apart from the world, he welcomed the world into it. He saw it as the function of the artist to work with what is given; and in paintings like *Charlene* he sieved the dredged filth of New York City as a prospector sieves the sand of the riverbed: for gold. *Charlene* is as American, and as much a part of the American life of its epoch, as is the page in *Specimen Days* where Whitman describes Manhattan as he knew it in 1879. It is, in fact, a contribution to the roomy, meandering, accumulative tradition of American autobiography.

"Combine-paintings" was Rauschenberg's name for pictures of this sort; and they do, in effect, combine unaltered materials of the most heterogeneous kind with passages of straightforward paintwork. So far from making fun of Action Painting, they are the work of someone for whom the Abstract Expressionist brush stroke and the look of paint dripped straight from the can are an important part of art: but a part to be taken into the work as a phenomenon among others. It is not for them to bear sole responsibility for the picture; and they are, if anything, all the more eloquent for being made to coexist with newsprint, reproductions of Old Master painting, half-obliterated comic strips and (in *Charlene*) the outstretched spokes of an umbrella which have been fleshed out and painted over and can be spun around like the

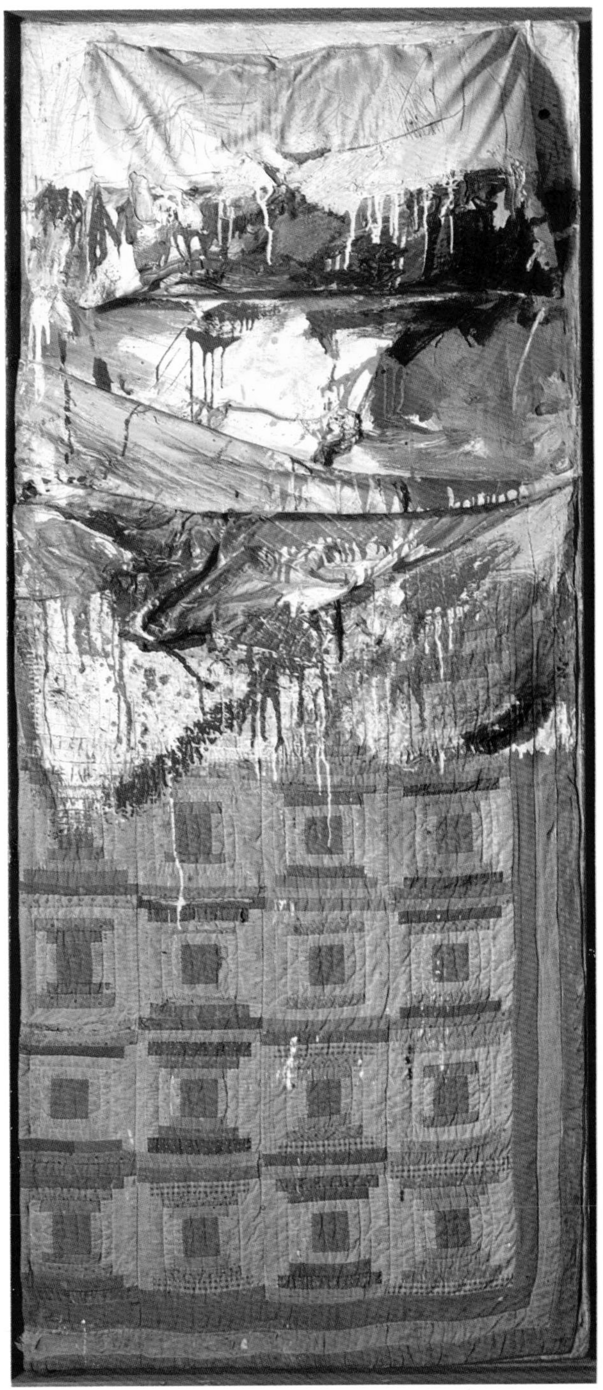

Robert Rauschenberg.
Bed. 1955. Combine painting,
6 feet 2 inches × 31½ inches × 6½ inches.
Mr. and Mrs. Leo Castelli, New York

arms of a windmill.

So dense is the deposit of allusion and association in *Charlene* that we can stay with it for weeks on end and still find new points of entrance, new appeals to memory, new combinations of sight and touch and feel and remembered smell. It is a part of the continuum of big-city experience; and as I said before it treats earlier, preexisting art as a part of that experience. Art is accorded equality with the rest: no less, and no more. A lost tradition of narrative painting reasserts its rights as we track back and forth in the accumulation of one man's experience. There are elements of abstract painting also in the tall thin vertical panels which structure the painting as a whole; and in the flattened umbrella in the top right-hand corner there is an after-echo of the severe geometrical painting of Europe in the 1930s—a time when *Circle* seemed a predestined name for a good art magazine. *Charlene* is a picture to live in, not to look at; and among the qualities for which it speaks is an open trust in the way things are.

The case of Rauschenberg's *Bed* is comparatively simple, though few works of art have caused so much exasperation. *Bed* is about paint's power to survive, as the instrument of human expression, in surroundings no matter how far removed from those of high art. Action Painting had claimed for the artist, and for what he produces, a place set apart. It relied on materials, and on a specific type of physical construction, that asserted the continuity of high art. Pollock may have spread his canvas on the floor and worked on it in ways that were quite new, but when the picture got up on the wall it was stretched taut and trim on a rectangular wooden support, just like an easel painting by Rubens or Velázquez. *Bed* gets away from all that and asserts, by contrast, that the eloquence of paint can be bestowed on the apparatus of everyday life. The bed in *Bed* is still a bed, but it is also a painting; Rauschenberg here works literally in "the gap between art and life," and he contrives to close it, so that art and life merge into one single experience and can no longer be separated one from the other.

These were difficult ideas, when they were first mooted. Too much was risked, too much was questioned, too much familiar ground was ruled "off limits." It was not immediately clear to what an extent the epic scale and the exuberant physicality of *Charlene* and the other combine-paintings of Rauschenberg were specifically American qualities that had found a completely new outlet. The facts of American abundance had always tempted American writers, poets, composers and painters, and many of them had tried one variant or another of the cumulative approach: Charles Ives piling one orchestra on top of another, Whitman listing his allegiances for page after page, John Dos Passos aping the crosscutting of the cinema in *U.S.A.*, Joseph Stella in 1913 working his heart out to get all Coney Island down on canvas. Rauschenberg was in the listing business, too; but he realized, as no one had realized before him, that raw material can be served up raw and that art and life could be made to interlock in the mid-1950s as they had never quite interlocked before. In *Rebus*, for instance, he took the detritus of the New York street—a political poster, two news photographs of track events, a comic strip and some objects of more mysterious provenance—and allied them to a small reproduction of Botticelli's *The Birth of Venus* and a page from an art magazine. The great art of the past took its chance, in other words, with metropolitan graffiti and with the kind of images to which no one gives more than a moment's attention. For all its chaotic appearance the picture is tautly organized and bound together with passages of pure painting.

Rauschenberg at this stage in his career was still very much the boy from out of town who had made it into the big city. He had just discovered the poetics of glut, and he couldn't wait to tell us about them. The paintings were a way of dealing with the unprecedented input that came the way of everyone in the postwar metropolis: and not merely "a way," but the only way of coming to terms with it without censorship or dilution. Raus-

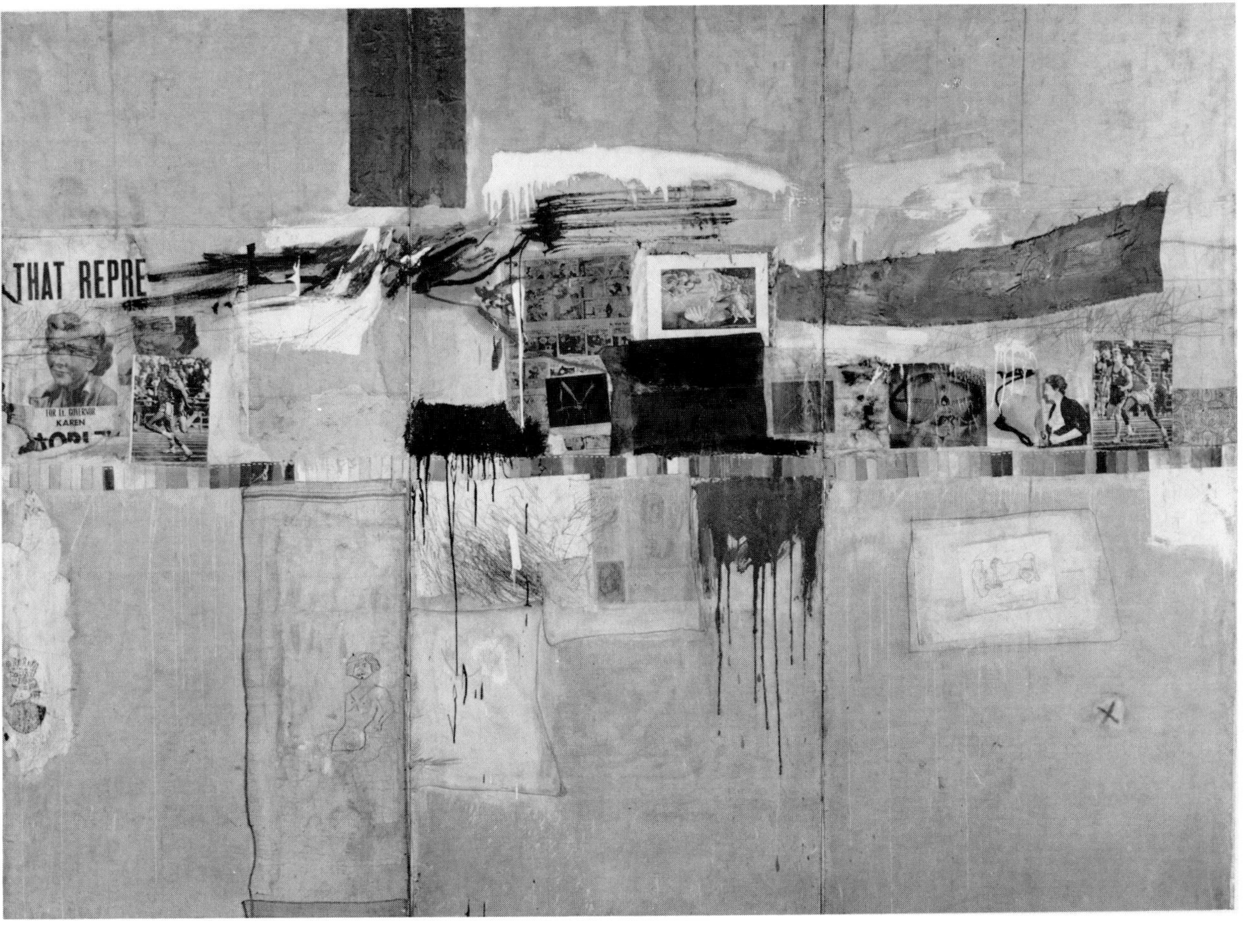

Robert Rauschenberg. *Rebus.* 1955. Combine painting, 8 feet × 12 feet. Mr. and Mrs. Victor W. Ganz, New York

chenberg gave himself, too: openhandedly. It is the paradox of his combine-paintings that although there is nothing so bizarre or so recalcitrant that it could not find a place in them (a stuffed hen, a deflated inner tube, a radio in full operation) Rauschenberg marks them all with his own identity. He is them, and they are him: the ancient sorceries of art are still in operation.

Rauschenberg's activity is basically outgoing in character. He has a gift for communication and an inbred sense of performance. Extravagances no matter how hazardous turned out to end well when he was in charge of them; and when he encroached upon the performing arts—whether as dancer, as artistic adviser to the Merce Cunningham Dance Company, as a founder-member of EAT (Experiments in Art and Technology), and as the inventor of art works that depended in part on activation by their audiences—it was with a consistent optimism. Rauschenberg worked for years with Merce Cunningham and his dance company. Cunningham is the agile figure in the top right-hand area in *Trophy I.* And Rauschenberg makes the most of Cunningham's seemingly effortless balance by introducing into the lower left-hand area of the painting an image which is the epitome of ungainliness—a fallen horse and its unseated rider. The point is rammed further home by the sign that reads "Caution: Watch Your Step." In *Empire II* Rauschenberg perpetuates the kind of image which he would improvise from whatever materials came to hand as Merce Cunningham and his company moved from city to city. An object familiar from the New York skyline in its less pretentious days is given a new and altogether grander identity by being mounted on

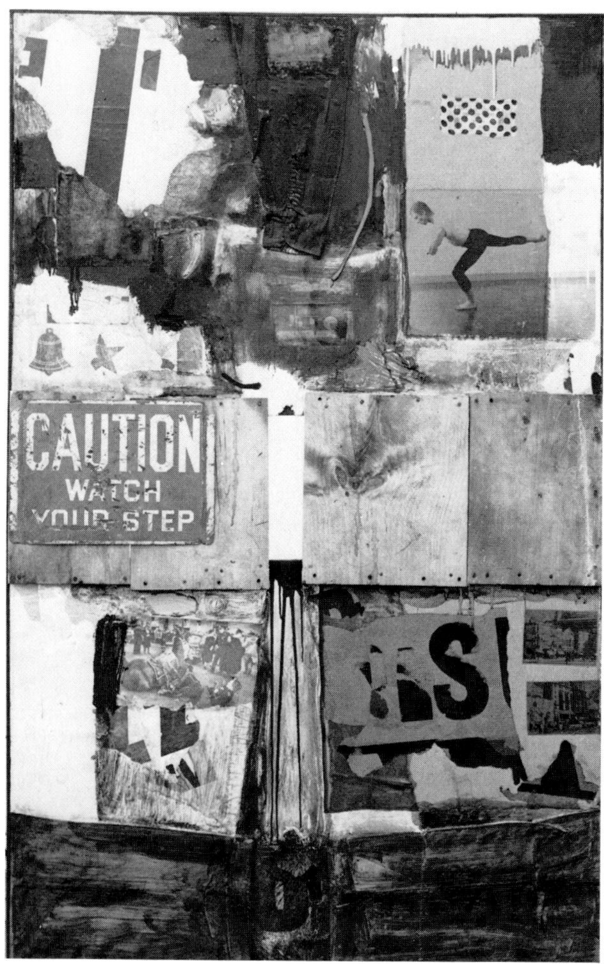

Robert Rauschenberg. *Trophy I (for Merce Cunningham).* 1959. Combine painting, 66 × 41 inches. Galerie Beyeler, Basel

what looks, in this context, to be a rough-and-ready chariot.

The case of Jasper Johns is entirely different. He stands for the lapidary, as against the garrulous; for ideas laid one on top of another, as against ideas spread out laterally; and for the thing thought over week after week, as against an overflowing generosity that can survive occasional lapses. Rauschenberg in the mid-1950s was like a faucet of ideas that just couldn't be turned off; Johns was, and is, more deliberate, more self-critical, more apt to say, "Is this really worth doing?"

His work presented from the first the kind of many-layered difficulty which is the surest indication that important art is on the way. The flag, for instance: was it a hoax? An affront to Old Glory? An inscrutable private joke? Discussion waxed hot. In point of fact it was none of those things. It was an intelligent man's response to the fact that the admired painting of the day had to do with images of an entirely idiosyncratic sort: signs never made before. Painting of this kind was running itself breathless by the time of Johns's first New York show in 1958, and in many cases it looked like self-indulgence. It seemed to Johns to be a good idea to see what could be made with an image which was, on the contrary, readymade and immutable. Such an image would ideally have length and breadth but no depth, since the flatness of the canvas was fundamental to painting at that time. If the basic image was so familiar as to bring about a virtual anaesthesia of the aesthetic faculty, people might be confronted as never before with the pure essence of painting: the primal shock, for which others had aimed in ways that had begun to look merely rhetorical. The American flag was just right, in this context. It was an image which in itself left no one indifferent; yet its associations were so far outside the domains of art as to suspend altogether the traditional art-gallery habits of mind. There occurred to every single person, when he first saw one of Johns's flags, a moment of disbelief; and in that moment he was accessible as never before to the primal shock of painting.

As it happened, no two of his flags were the same. People who said "Seen one, seen them all" were put in their places when it turned out that the unchanging face of Old Glory masked a series of raids upon the traditional uses of oil paint, together with a revival of the use of encaustic and a number of forays into territory not yet mapped. There was a ghost-flag—a huge, phantomatic expanse of whites on whites and grays on grays—and there were flags in which faces half-surfaced through the familiar red-and-white horizontals. There were flags on flags, most monumentally superimposed. There were flags which had a private reference, and as late as 1973 there was a double flag which came across with a brilliant, extroverted, public effect. There were flags which re-

Robert Rauschenberg. *Empire II.* 1961. Construction, 61 × 29 × 58 inches. Philip Johnson, New Canaan, Conn.

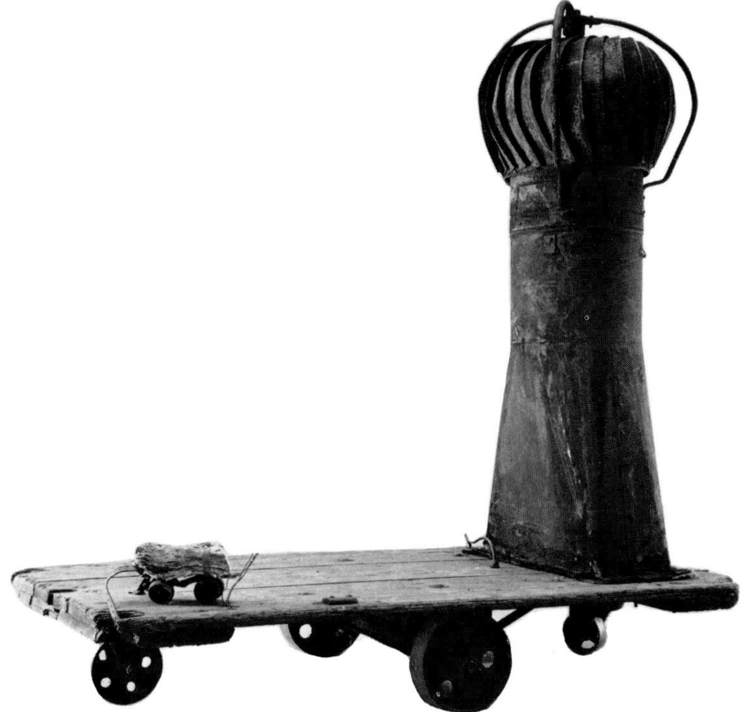

flected the large areas of melancholy in Johns's own nature; and there were flags which stood for the elemental cachinnations with which in private life he seems to reinvent the notion of laughter.

The flags did, however, have one thing in common: they were all painted on a flat, unbroken surface, and they were to that extent traditional pictures with no adjuncts or annexes. This was not the case with the *Target with Four Faces* of 1958, and it was not the case with many other, later works by Johns. The target, like the flag, was ideal subject matter, in that flatness was of its essence. It was readymade and immutable, like the flag; and in its everyday appearances it, too, probed the limits of impersonality. A target which showed individuality would be by that much the less of a target.

A target is made up, on the other hand, of concentric circles, and Johns was far too astute an observer of modern art not to know that concentric circles had been a favorite motif with abstract painters since the days of Robert Delaunay and the youthful Stanton Macdonald-Wright. Concentric circles did away with the necessity for composition, since the form of the image was dictated from the start. They made it possible for colors to "tell" with an intensity that would be modified and weakened if they had to overlap or interlock. In a fine-art context they also raised problems which in the past had been solved by giving the circles not the blank, frontal look of a target, but a fragmented or interrupted fine-art look. (This continued to be the case in the late 1950s and early 1960s when Kenneth Noland, for one, was working with concentric circles; he repudiated the unvarying readymade form of the target by varying the internal relationships of one circle to another.) Johns made no claims for this target as art. It was what the title said it was: two pairs of yellow and blue circles, centering onto a red bull's-eye. Their physical substance was mysterious, as was that of the wall-like surface of which they formed a part. There could hardly be a less personal image, and yet the impression which stayed with the observer could be owed to one man only.

Flag and target make demands upon us which have nothing to do with the demands of art, though with the one as with the other we associate an exceptional degree of involvement. When Johns paints them we shift to and fro, involuntarily, between the kind of recognition which is owed to a flag, or to a target, and the kind of recognition which is owed to art. Noticing this, we learn something new about living. In *Target with Four Faces*, Johns thickens this particular plot, and we come to know what John Cage meant when he wrote in his notes on Johns that "I thought he was doing three things (five things he was doing escaped my notice)." For the upper part of this picture is really very peculiar. Where the lower part has the total flatness of a paving-slab, the upper part has real three-dimensional recession: genuine depths in which plaster casts of a sightless head are secreted. This section is hinged, moreover, and has a lid which can be swung down at will. The four heads are identical, and they present themselves to us with an identical frontality. There is the sharpest possible contrast between the shadowed recesses, in which the heads sit in retreat from the world, and the light of open day which floods across the target. The one is a complex scale-model, in full working order, of an inscrutable situation; the other one of the simplest of man-made objects, and one of the most easily explicable. The complete image, as haunting as any in 20th-century art, has overtones of fairground and firing squad, jury box and old-style pharmacy.

It is basic to the work of Jasper Johns that he makes us question not only what we are looking at but what is entailed in the act of looking. All looking has to do with cognition; but do we look in order to know something completely? Or do we stop looking, in any real sense, as soon as we have made an initial act of recognition? Johns never lets us off that particular hook. Defying us to give in to laziness, he chips away at the sloven in all of us. Take the printed word "Blue," for instance. It is so keyed to our expectations of a certain color that if it happens to be colored red, as may well be the case in a painting by Johns, then we see it as if we had never seen it before.

In the 1960s Jasper Johns began to tackle these questions in bulk and simultaneously, in paintings on the scale of epic which have none of the small-scale concision of his earlier work. But in 1958–59, in his *Numbers in Color*, he was still working with a finite image drawn from the experience of everyday. The series of numerals that runs from 1 to 0 is a sign language so complete and so nearly universal that it would really be very difficult to get through life without it. Its rival, in this, is the alphabet (and Johns did once make a very beautiful painting called *Gray Alphabet*); but there are several kinds of alphabet, whereas the series 1–0 is as valid for a Russian as for an American, and as valid for a Pakistani as for a Moroccan. It is one of the great instruments of negotiation; without it, we should be stuck with the abacus.

What Johns did in his *Numbers in Color* was to set out the complete sequence from 1 through 0 eleven times over. The subject was *given*, and it recurred with an absolute regularity, just as in a passacaglia the bass line recurs unaltered over and over again. The paradox of *Numbers in Color* is that by accepting this fixed and immutable subject Johns gave himself a freedom of maneuver and an openness of expression which were total and unlimited. We can see just what this means if we compare *Numbers in Color* with Pollock's *White Light*. In the Pollock, freedom of expression is preordained. The painter has no obligations to anything except the dictates of his own psyche. The picture is the paint, and the paint is the picture: nothing else intrudes. And *White Light* is undeniably a beautiful picture, with all the luxuriance which we associate with a major artist who knows exactly what he is doing and is comfortably inside the limits of his potential. It might seem to be enough, and in terms of the embellishment of life it certainly is enough; but art has a higher and a more strenuous function, and a part of that function is to go on questioning the terms of art's validity. Art survives not because it gives pleasure, but because it goes on asking questions to which we need to know the answer. Pollock in *White Light* was giving pleasure of an exalted, hard-won kind. Johns in *Numbers in Color* gave that same pleasure—the delight of seeing paint handled superlatively well—plus something else. He used the alphabet of numerals to redraft the alphabet of feeling. *Numbers in Color* sets out the gamut of human emotion with reference (and herein lies the contribution of Johns) to an ordered schema from which feeling is traditionally excluded. Emotion plays no part in mathematics. Neither love nor hate will make 2 × 2 equal 5. Numerals are weightless, incorporeal, independent of time and place, above and beyond individual feeling. They form a closed system to which feeling has no access. The impersonal single subject, so valuable to Johns in 1954, was succeeded in 1958 by the impersonal system, with its even greater potential.

Questions of identity have always preoccupied Johns, and he is perfectly well aware that each of the ten numerals in question has a personality which is clearly defined. "Number One" stands for leadership, in common parlance, and Johns's number 1 has a broad, upstanding shaft, a sharp downward turn at the top (like the peaked cap of some archetypal field-marshal), and a square-built plinth-type base: all stand up for an impregnable solidity. Zero has also its associations; and Johns drafts a broad-bellied vacancy, an echoing oval that signals a moment of repose after the clattering activity of numbers 1–9. Himself conspicuous in life for sensitivity toward the identity of others, he gave each intervening numeral its own character: we remember, for instance, the enlarged teardrop which forms the stem of his number 7 and the swanlike curve of his number 2. But he tells us explicitly that the picture is about numbers in *color;* and as every word counts in a title by Johns we are warned that the picture is as much about color as it is about numbers.

What Johns does is to animate the entire surface of the canvas with an allover, in-and-out paint structure which has the vitality of Action Painting but is keyed to something outside itself. There are two separate and independent structures here: on the one hand 11 rows of numerals with their recurrent subliminal crescendo from 1 to 0, on the other the continually varied skeins and loops of paint which sometimes menace, and sometimes give way to, the mathematics of the basic design. Every great painting carries within itself the history of other great paintings; and in *Numbers in Color* we see something of the fugitive and vagabond humors of landscape painting, something of the verticals and horizontals of Mondrian, and something of the patient monitoring which we associate with still life. Everything is there, and every kind of statement. Looking at it, we realize all over again that it is not from the unsupported ego that great art is most likely to come.

There is, of course, an alternative hazard: the artist may fail to impose upon heterogeneous material that imaginative order which is the essence of what we call "art." If too much material is given the right of entry, and if the operating imagination is too weak to deal with it, chaos and triviality will result. The challenge of new and complex subject matter had to be met, even so; the highly energized character of new art in the 1950s made it mandatory. And it was not only Rauschenberg and Johns who gave the signal; on the contrary, the expansiveness, the limitless ambition and the bodily involvement for which Pollock set the definitive example were an inspiration to artists who wanted to get more and more of the world into their art. In 1958 this point was put by Allan Kaprow, artist and theoretician, when he wrote that "Pollock left us at the point where we must become preoccupied with and even dazzled by the space and objects of our everyday life. . . . Not satisfied with the *suggestion* through paint of other senses, we shall utilize the specific substances of sight, sound, people, movement, odors, touch. Objects of every sort are the material for the new art."

It was in this belief that from 1954 onward art made raid after raid into territory which it had traditionally disdained. The great divide grew ever wider between those who believed, with

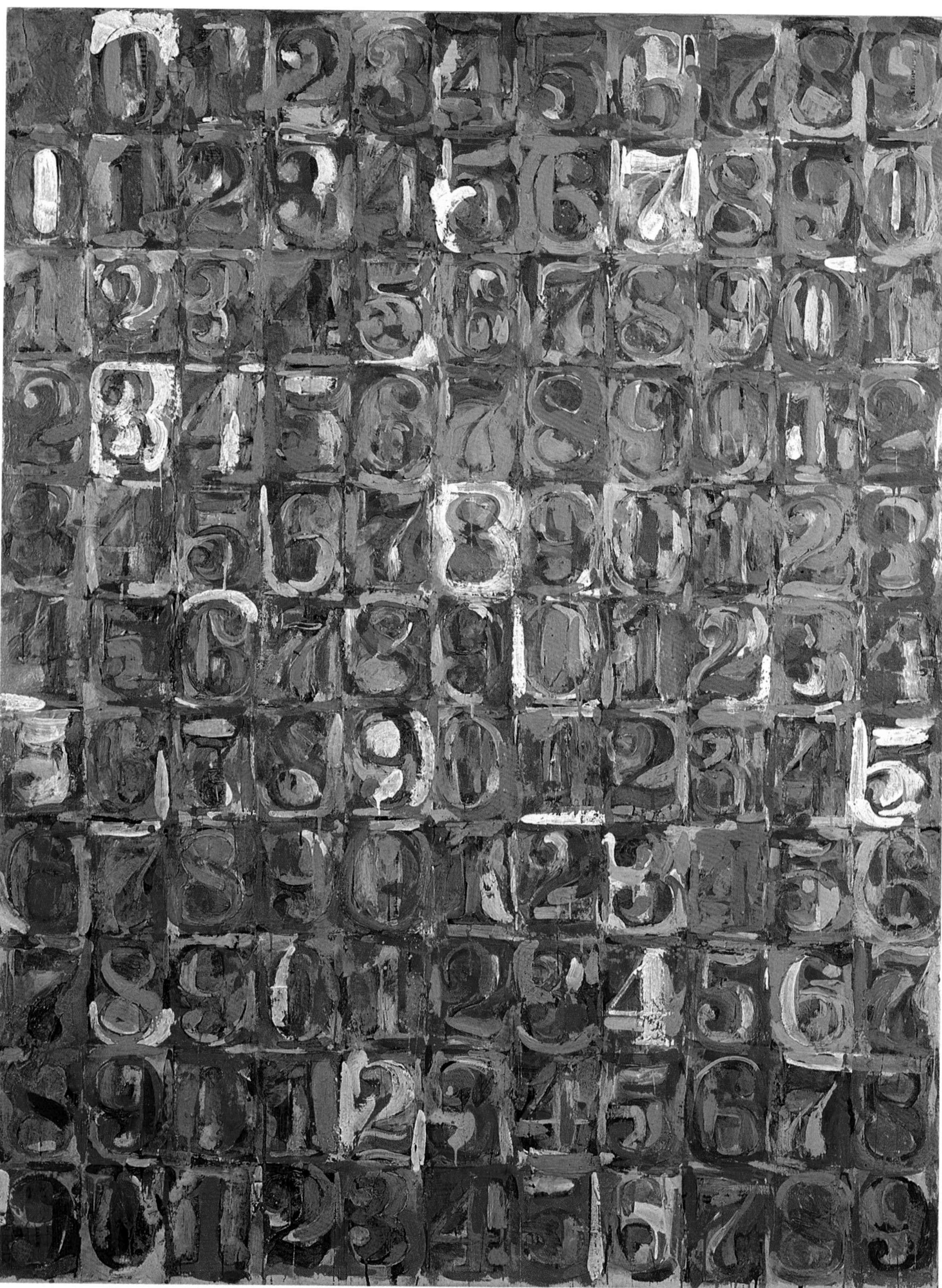

Jasper Johns.
Numbers in Color.
1959.
Encaustic and collage on canvas,
66½ × 49½ inches.
Albright-Knox Art Gallery, Buffalo.
Gift of Seymour H. Knox

Thomas B. Hess, that the only art worth talking about was "difficult, serious, remote, aristocratic" and those who believed that, no matter where the action was, art should get a piece of it. The two points of view looked to be irreconcilable, and many of the participants were determined that they should remain so. "Avoid a polar situation," Johns had said: but what common ground could there be between Ad Reinhardt, who said that "a museum is a treasure house and a tomb, not a countinghouse or an amusement center," and Claes Oldenburg, who said that he was for "an art which does something other than sit on its ass in a museum"?

The truth is that by the mid-1950s too much new energy had come into everyday life, and too many new forms of awareness were available to the artist, for any but the most steadfast of gifted natures to look neither to right nor to left. What Reinhardt called "Art-as-something-else" was irresistibly attractive when the world as it had previously existed was turning out to be obsolete and new ways of life were calling out for comment. Reinhardt stood, on the contrary, for what he called "Art-as-only-itself." In May, 1957, he wrote that "the first rule and absolute standard of fine art, and of painting, which is the highest and freest art, is the purity of it. The more uses, relations, and 'additions' a painting has, the less pure it is. The more stuff in it, the busier the work of art, the worse it is. More is Less."

Reinhardt himself acted on these principles, with an evergrowing stringency, till his death in 1967. "Looking is not as simple as it looks," he had said in 1946. And he went on to prove it with a long series of paintings which culminated in the black paintings of which *Number 119, 1958,* is one. It takes time and patience to decipher the cruciform image which lies within the matt, light-absorbing surface of the canvas; but Reinhardt's intention was to free the observer from the conventional time-span within which we look at art. A lifelong polemicist, cartoonist, demonstrator and writer of enraged letters on subjects that were dear to him, Reinhardt in his late paintings aimed at a terminal statement: a point beyond which easel painting could go no further.

One or two others, as we shall see, did the same and are still doing it with a singular scorn for compromise. Sometimes superb work resulted, with a critical follow-up remarkable for both cogency and conviction: the thing written and the thing done were one, almost. But the work that got itself talked about by laymen in the 1960s originated for the most part in what Rauschenberg had called the gap between art and life; and it overturned three of Thomas B. Hess's requirements by being not remote, not difficult, and not aristocratic. (Whether it was not serious would have to be debated case by case.) At the highest level there were points of contact—Johns and Noland both painted targets, as I said earlier, and the panoramic and environmental scale of Action Painting was common both among Pop painters (James Rosenquist, above all) and among sculptors of several persuasions (Louise Nevelson, George Segal)—but fundamentally the great divide was never deeper or wider than in the 1960s.

If the world can be thought of as one gigantic painting, as Rauschenberg had suggested in 1961, it follows that we can cut into it almost at random and come up with something that hangs together as art. "If I call it art, it's art," had been the implication of what Marcel Duchamp did when he signed a urinal in 1917 and sent it in for an exhibition. Pop art (as it came to be called) did not quite do that; its impact was owed to the combination of unprocessed material from everyday life with traditional fine-art procedures (paint on canvas, adjustments of scale, adroit reemphasis and the use of isolated details in the interest of irony or pathos). In fact it claimed for itself the privileges (and, eventually, the financial rewards) of high art, while sticking closely to subject matter with which high art had never associated before. "To think that I have been speaking prose all my life and never knew it!" says Monsieur Jourdain in

Ad Reinhardt.
Number 119, 1958 (Black). 1958.
Oil on canvas,
7 feet × 6 feet 3 inches.
Hirshhorn Museum and Sculpture Garden, Smithsonian Institution, Washington

Molière's *Le Bourgeois Gentilhomme;* in the same way, people learned from Andy Warhol and Roy Lichtenstein that they had lived amidst art all their lives and never known it.

Lichtenstein was always a great forager. The source material of *Girl with Ball* was an advertisement for vacations in the Poconos. Lichtenstein introduced into the painting allusions both to the technology of printing (the benday dots which serve as skin tone for the vacationing girl) and to the recent history of art (the curvilinear Art Nouveau forms which designated her hair, the cropping of the whole image at top and bottom to bring it closer to the spectator, and the firmly drawn line which unites the profile of the wave to the outline of the girl's body). What looks crude and simplistic to eyes nurtured on French Impressionism results in reality from a series of conscious and intelligent decisions. In the early 1960s Lichtenstein probed one after another the kinds of image we acknowledge, cherish, or in some cases have simply got used to and no longer notice. One such was the likeness of George Washington as it turns up over and over again in post-Colonial times. Another was the stylized notion of gods and goddesses.

Pop art was rooted, furthermore, in certain perennial aspects of American life: the element of insistent repetition, for instance. Repetition of this kind gives off a visual drumbeat that calls on us to stop and pay attention. It was always so: witness the photograph of a provincial druggist's shop which Charles Ellis Johnson took in the year 1888. That druggist knew his public; no matter what he had to sell—canker syrup, essence of ginger, "Essence of Life" or an all-purpose medicine called the "Valley Tan Remedy"—he knew that people wanted to get the message over and over again.

In Andy Warhol's *Green Coca-Cola Bottles*, 1962, ancestral memories of this kind were drawn upon. Whereas Jasper Johns in his *Numbers in Color* renewed the great tradition of oil painting with subject matter that seemed to be entirely impersonal, Warhol with his Coca-Cola bottles aimed at the effect of a print run that was not quite perfect. And it is with what would elsewhere be looked at askance, as errors of registration, that he sustains our interest from row to serried row. Further, Warhol was always interested in the demystification of art: in its reduction, in other words, to something that at first glance could be done by anyone. His *Numbers*, 1962, an adaptation of a do-it-yourself painting manual, is a particularly crisp and jaunty example; and it is one of the many paradoxes of Warhol's career that this image should be so inescapably his own.

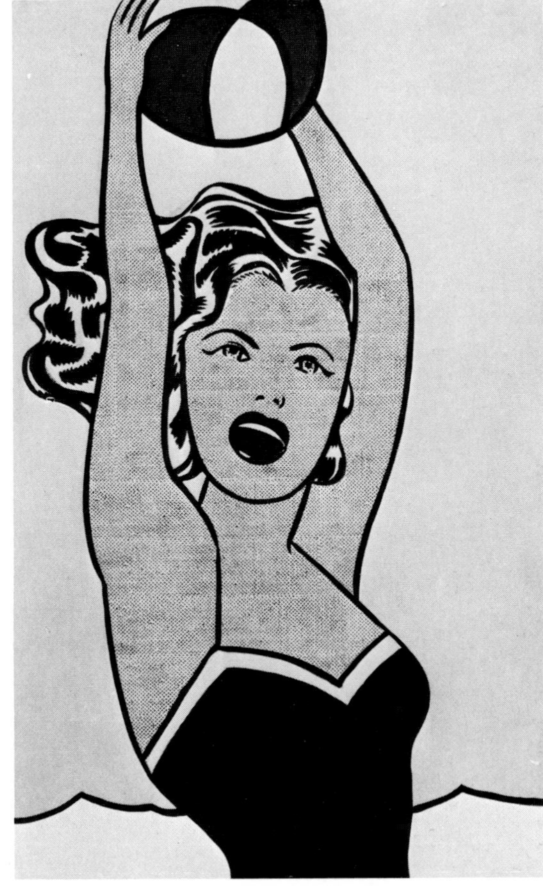

Roy Lichtenstein.
Girl with Ball.
1961.
Oil on canvas,
60½ × 36½ inches.
Philip Johnson, New Canaan, Conn.

Pop art could also operate with metamorphic effect upon objects of current use that would not at other times have been the material of art. New Yorkers look at the zip codes of Manhattan every day of their lives, for instance, and they also regard a juicer as indispensable to a well-furnished kitchen. It was left to Claes Oldenburg to wreak his peculiar white magic with these things. He took the zip-code map of Manhattan and built it, block by block, as a sculpture, with the tall thin shape of Central Park conspicuous in the center. We became conscious as never before of the interlocked segments which make up a mailman's Manhattan; and the piece also works as a work of art, to be hung from a nail on the wall and quizzed, day after day, for what it has to offer.

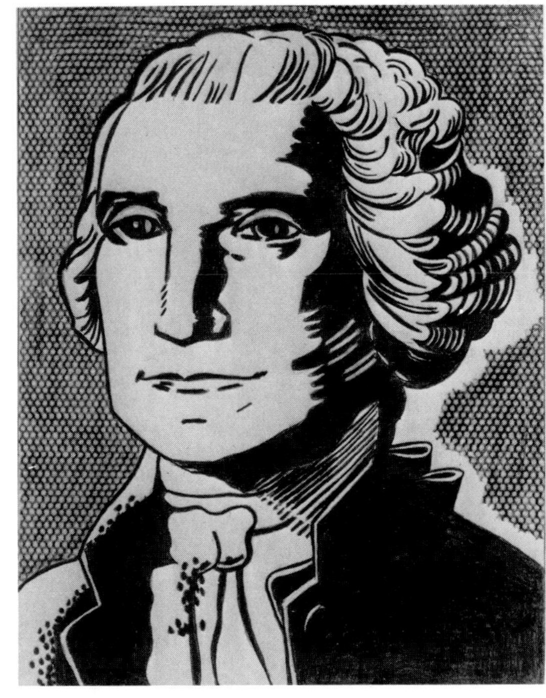

Roy Lichtenstein.
George Washington.
1962.
Pencil and frottage,
18¾ × 14½ inches.
Mr. and Mrs. Ned Owyang, New York

In the case of the juicer, Oldenburg took metamorphosis a step further. With vinyl, kapok and fake fur he produced a sculpture which is two things in one. It is the portrait of the way a juicer might look if it melted like wax while halfway through juicing an orange. And it is a self-portrait of the artist himself, complete with cap, a few strands of untidy fair hair, a half-hidden face, and what might be a parka several sizes too big for him.

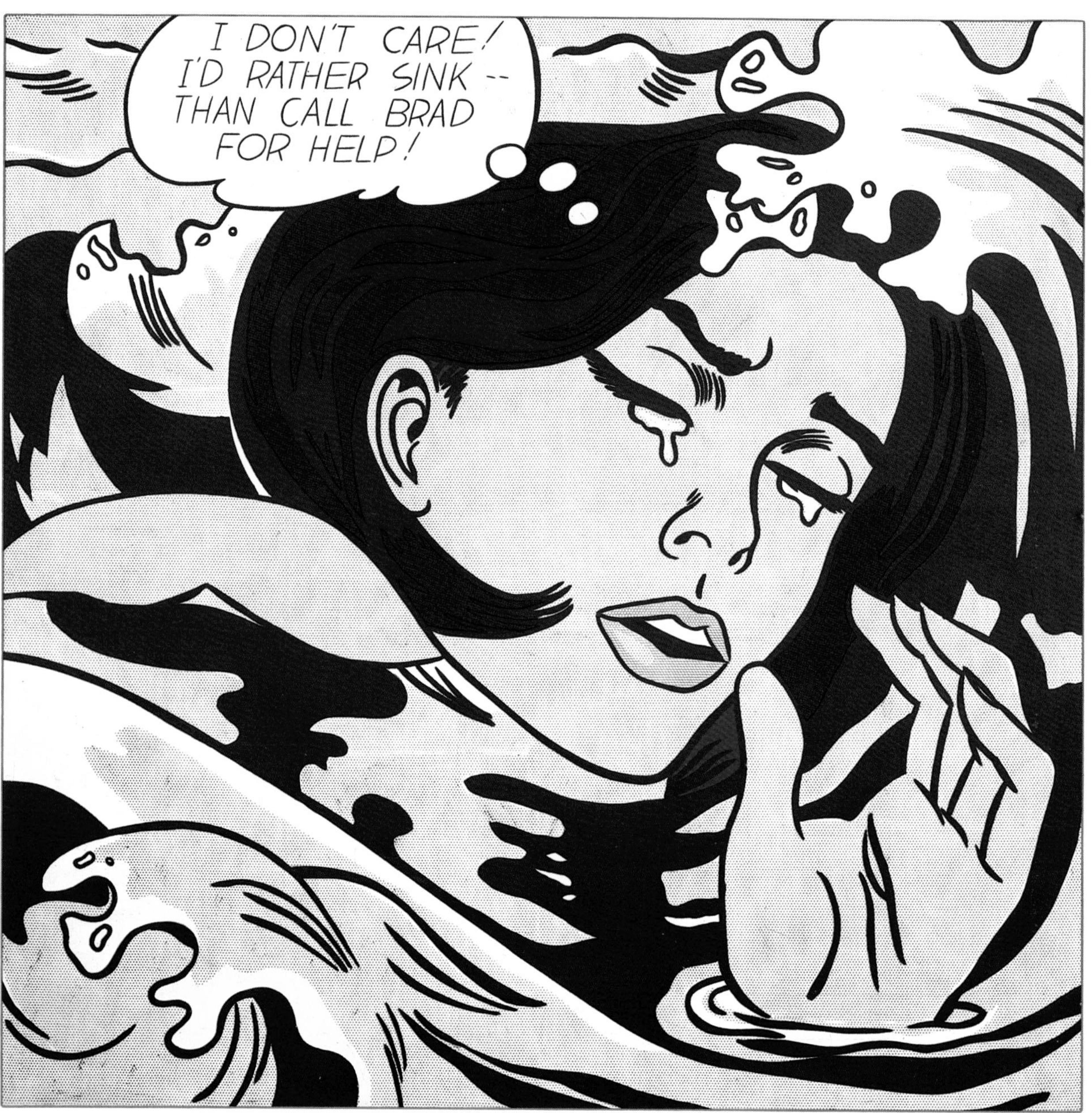

Roy Lichtenstein. *Drowning Girl.* 1963. Oil and synthetic polymer paint on canvas, 67⅝ × 66¾ inches. The Museum of Modern Art, New York. Philip Johnson Fund and gift of Mr. and Mrs. Bagley Wright

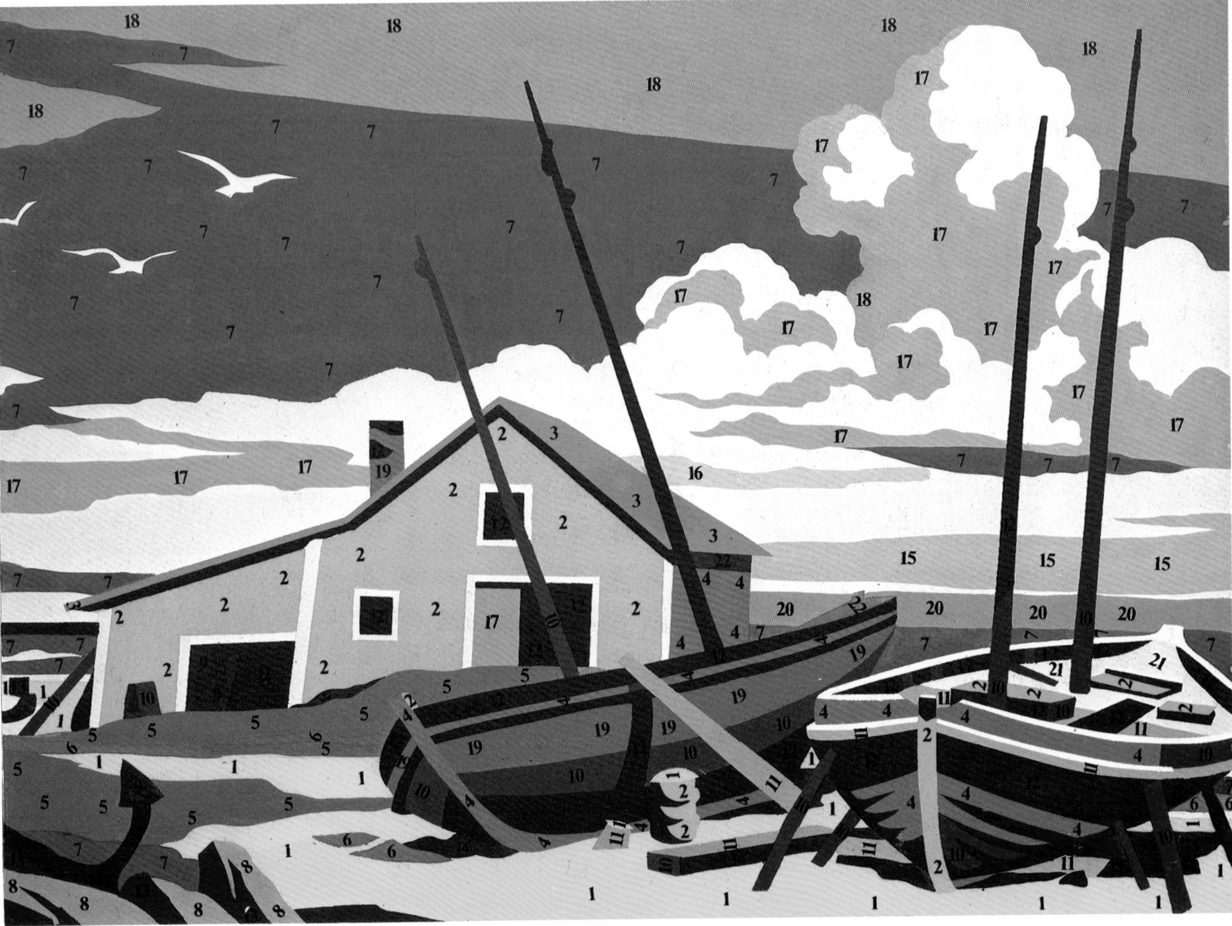

Andy Warhol. *Do It Yourself—Seascape.* 1962. Liquitex on canvas, 54 inches × 6 feet. Dr. Erich Marx, Berlin

Richard Lindner, though not a Pop artist, was related to Pop in his shrewd observation of American mores. For some years he lived on East 69th Street in New York City. His apartment was only a few doors away from the headquarters of the F.B.I.; and Lindner was much taken with the idea that on his very own street tabs were being kept on the mobsters and hoodlums in whom he had taken a lifelong and an immensely sardonic interest. *East 69th Street* has to do with the imagined arrest of a king of the underworld, a kid-gloved Lucifer for whom only the newest and most stylish men's wear will do. It has the relish with which George Grosz and Bertolt Brecht would seize on people of the same sort; but it also has a flat heraldic quality which is one of Lindner's contributions to the American painting of our day.

So Pop art had complex motives. One of them was to see just how far it could flout the expectations of the "cultivated" public (Roy Lichtenstein said that his ambition had been to produce a picture so hideous that no one would hang it). What was put to the test was the automatic reverence, the white flag of immunity from comment, which is accorded to the large framed painting *as such*, no matter how bitterly the status of individual paintings may be contested.

Next came an important social change, and one not yet definitively acknowledged. Generation after generation had taken for granted that the categories proposed by the novelist Sinclair Lewis in his *Babbitt* (1922) were eternal and unchangeable. They believed that there was such a thing as the cultivated life, on the one hand, and that on the other hand there was life as it was led by the vast majority of Americans. That majority was dis-

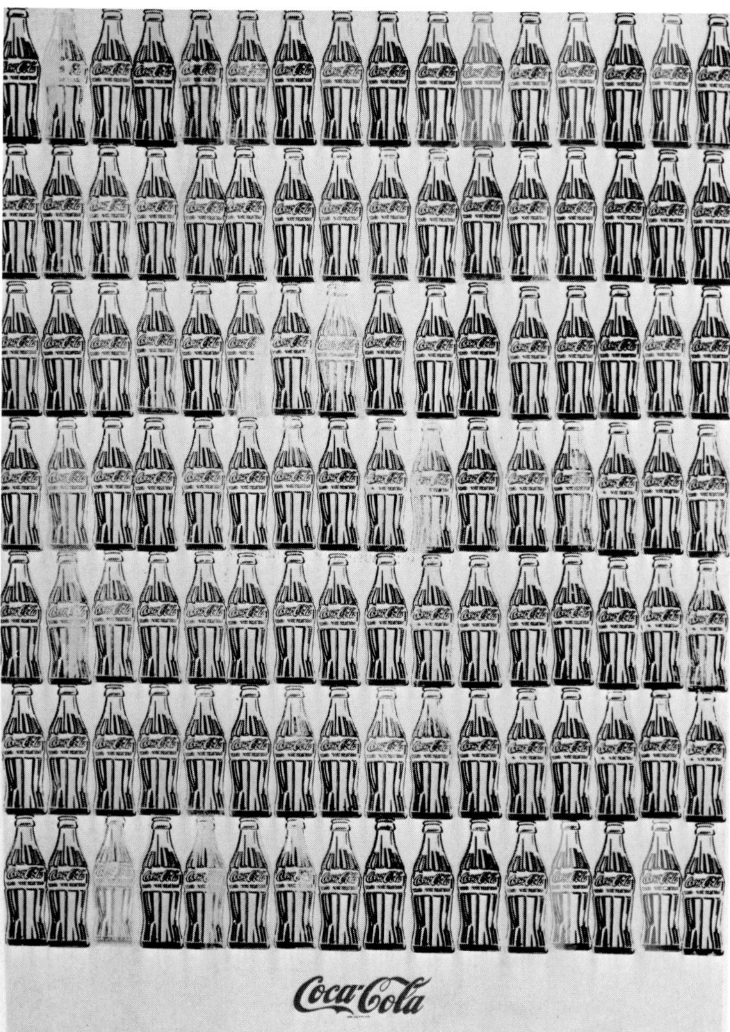

Andy Warhol.
Green Coca-Cola Bottles. 1962.
Oil on canvas,
6 feet 10¼ inches × 57 inches.
Whitney Museum of American Art, New York.
Gift of the Friends of the Whitney Museum of American Art

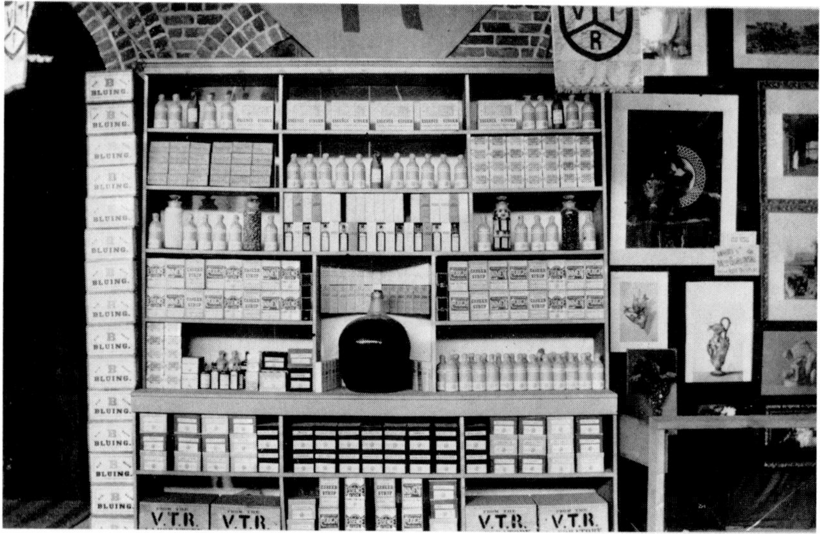

Charles Ellis Johnson.
Druggist's Display, Featuring Valley Tan Remedy. 1888.
Photograph.
Museum of Fine Arts, Boston. Photo courtesy of Dr. and Mrs. Avard T. Fairbanks

counted as mediocre, undiscriminating, herd-minded, all but illiterate. One of the best things that ever happened to America is that between 1950 and 1970 this idea got a thorough going-over and was to a large degree discredited. Of course there were still plenty of Babbitts around; but there was a new self-awareness on the part of other generations, and one of the rewards of this was the realization that there is such a thing as popular culture and that it is primarily in relation to the popular culture of the day that each generation defines itself. Anyone who happened to read J. D. Salinger's *The Catcher in the Rye* on the day of its publication in 1951 will have recognized not only the portrait of a new archetypal young American but the arrival of a new attitude to popular culture. Popular culture from that day onward was neither something to be overinflated, in fan-club style, nor something to be put down by set-faced heads of families: it was just *there,* once and for all, as a complete structure in relation to which young people could find out who they were.

Pop art had its place in all this. It was also one of its functions to demystify the procedures of fine art. One of the monuments of Pop is George Segal's *The Butcher Shop,* 1965—a reconstruction, as it happens, of the shop owned by Segal's father: the locus, therefore, of his deepest and earliest intimations of how life is carried on from one day to the next. *The Butcher Shop* has the stillness of the image of an ancient Greek stele, but it is also direct, immediate and actual in a way that is akin to the black-and-white movies of Segal's youth. It is of yesterday, but it is also of all time. It speaks for the ancient ritual by which we take life so that we ourselves may survive: but it has none of the stylization with which the sculptors of the 19th century hoped to make their work last forever. A complete society is somewhere there inside it, and yet it is made up of plaster casts and a summary architecture, with no pretensions to high art. (It is worth noting that *The Butcher Shop* has a hieratic, abstract quality—a feeling for ritual on an almost bare stage—which is in striking contrast to Bere-

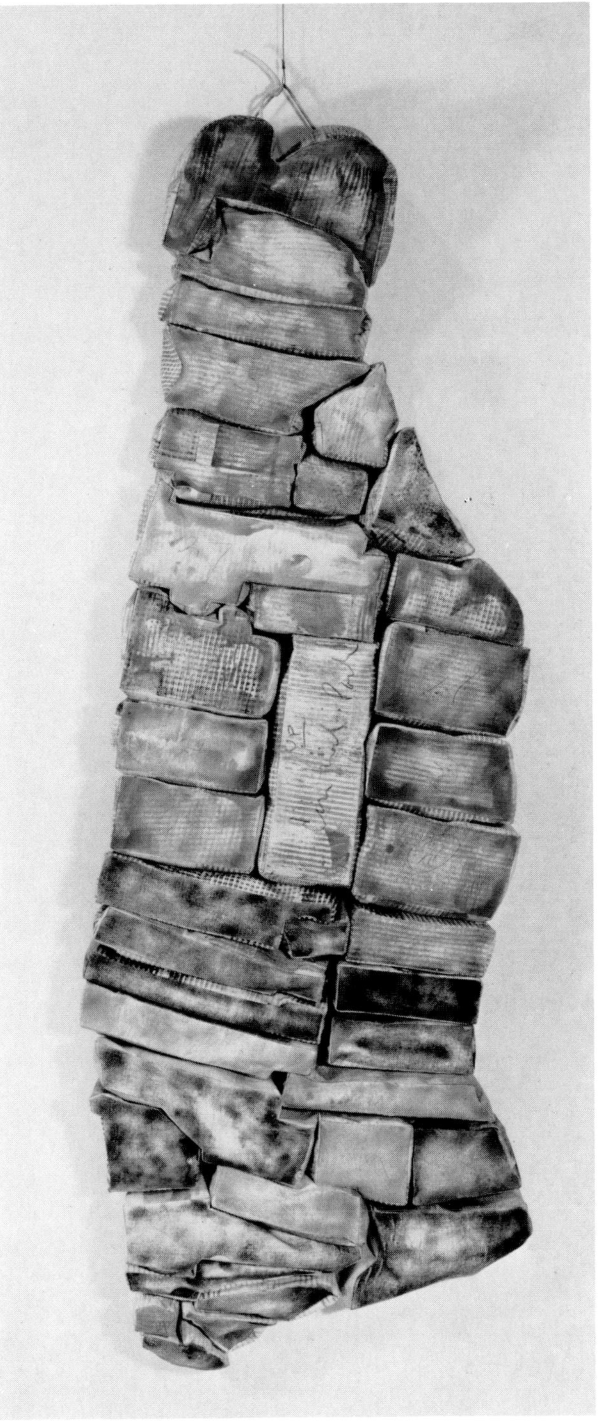

Claes Oldenburg. *Soft Manhattan #1 (Postal Zones).* 1966. Stenciled canvas and kapok, 6 feet 8 inches × 30 inches × 8 inches. Albright-Knox Art Gallery, Buffalo. Gift of Seymour H. Knox.

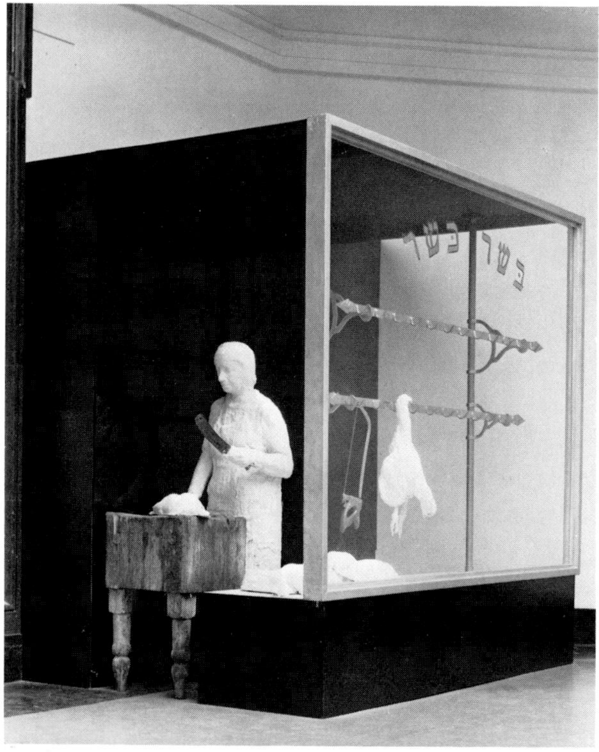

George Segal.
The Butcher Shop.
1965.
Plaster, wood, vinyl, metal and plexiglas, 7 feet 10 inches × 8 feet 3¼ inches × 48 inches.
Art Gallery of Ontario, Toronto. Gift from the Women's Committee Fund

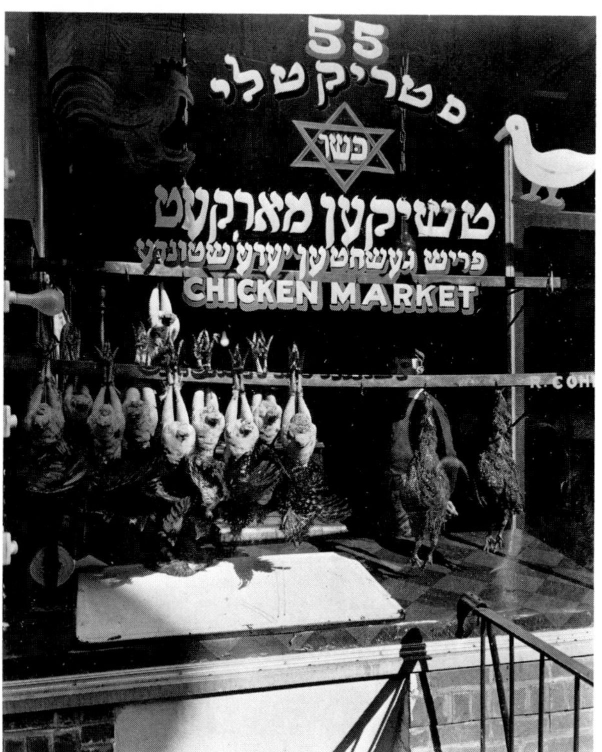

Berenice Abbott.
New York Shopfront.
c. 1936–37.
Photograph.
Museum of the City of New York

nice Abbott's photograph of the real thing as it was in the 1930s. The Segal has the look of classical drama; the Abbott—one of many in which she recorded a New York now largely vanished—has a Dickensian delight in detail.)

There was in Pop art an element of exorcism. It was made to banish evil memories, or to hoist them to a level on which they would lose their power to degrade. Segal's father, in effigy, has a dignity which society did not always accord him in life. Robert Indiana's numerals have none of the philosophical implications of Johns's; they are based on the memory of a time when the great numbered highways of the United States meant the possibility of escape from the grinding meanness of life in the Depression. James Rosenquist's *F-111* puts as cogently as anyone could wish the case against the uses to which the American Air Force was beginning to be put; "If I spell it out large enough," he seems to say, "someone's going to read it." With his panoramic *F-111* Rosenquist renewed the tradition of outrage which had produced Picasso's *Guernica* and Miró's *Head of a Woman.* The picture is polemical in intent; and it suggests, among much else, that something is wrong with a world in which the production of a new kind of aircraft allows one little girl to sit laughing under the hair-dryer while other little girls in a distant country will be burnt to death when that same aircraft gets into service. It is more difficult to ascribe any one motive to Andy Warhol, since Warhol operates behind a mask of inarticulacy, but his Electric Chair and his Car Crash series undoubtedly reminded people of what was being done in their name, in the one case, and of what they may well end up doing themselves, in the other. In the Happenings pioneered by Jim Dine, Claes Oldenburg and Allan Kaprow in 1959–60 there was, equally, a strong element of social protest.

Much in all this was subject before long to what the poet and novelist James Agee called "the emasculation of acceptance." It was difficult to sustain that point of maximum tension—fundamental

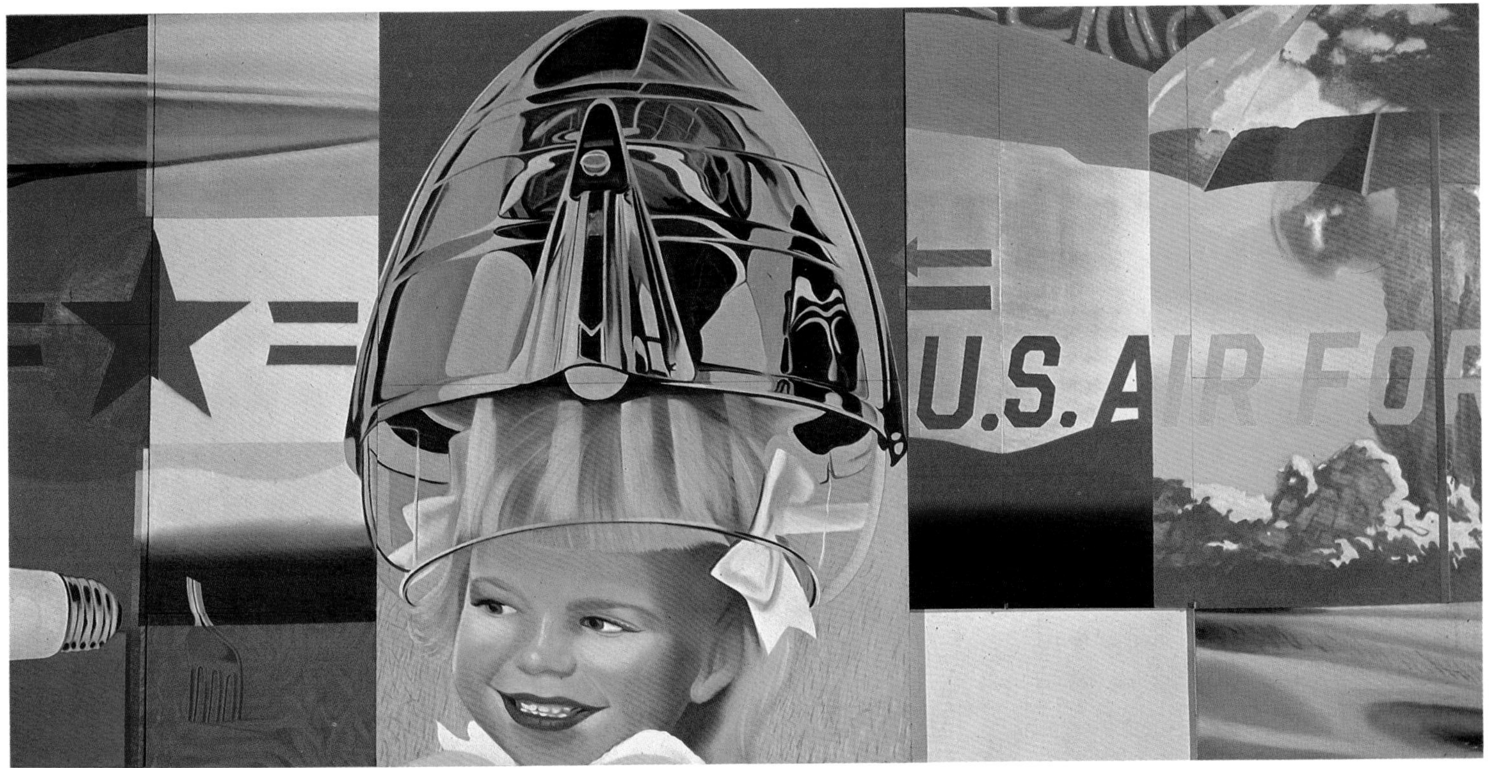

James Rosenquist.
F-111 (partial view).
1965.
Oil on canvas with aluminum, entire work 10 feet × 86 feet.
Robert C. Scull, New York

to the creation of a valid art—between what needs to be said and the means which are available for saying it. "Don't bother with that—just do it all over again" is the message of the market; and it was difficult in the mid-1960s to recapture the élan which powered Pop art when Claes Oldenburg rented a real store to sell his simulated pieces of pie. It was a time for evolution. Sometimes the evolution was merely toward the tactics of merchandising; in such cases the moral thrust of the work quite withered away.

Sometimes, on the other hand, it turned out that artists had been double agents for high art all the time. Jasper Johns, for one—though never a Pop artist in any strict sense—had been the source of much that was later taken over from him by other artists in simplified form, and when he produced his *Painted Bronze* in 1960 many people took it as an affront: the *Bed* all over again. How could two beer cans be art? Surely it was all part of a wager? (Someone had said of Johns's dealer, Leo Castelli, that "that so-and-so could sell beer cans as art if he put his mind to it.") People who went to see the work itself before making up their minds soon realized that the two cans had their place in high art, as securely as did Picasso's *Glass of Absinthe*, so clear at every point was the mark of Johns's governing hand. It turned out, equally, that Roy Lichtenstein was as capable of working from Monet's Cathedrals, or from his Haystack series, as from the comic strips which had made his name. As for the direct reproduction of objects of common use—well, it was plain to any unprejudiced person that Alex Hay's five-foot-high enlargement in paper, epoxy, fiberglass and paint of an E-ze brown paper bag, done in 1968, was one of the most elegant of art objects and not at all the put-on that it would have been assumed to be ten years earlier.

The great divide was in no way narrowed, however, by the fact that Reinhardt's "Art-as-only-itself" had infiltrated the enemy camp. These incidents were thought of, indeed, as gross improprieties. Historical allusions had at most a

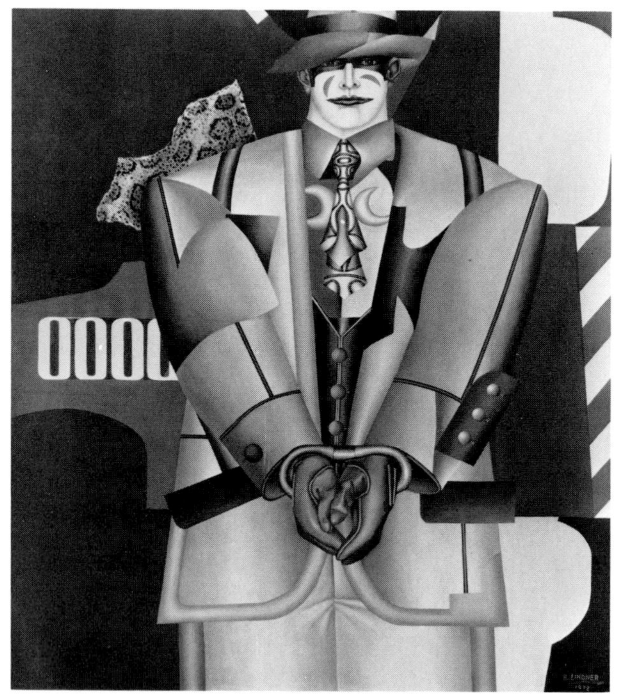

Richard Lindner. *The F.B.I. on East 69th Street.* 1972. Oil on canvas, 6 feet 8 inches × 70 inches. Museum Boymans-van Beuningen, Rotterdam

parasitic function: a play element quite out of place in serious art. As to that, a firm opinion was forthcoming from the Viennese-born philosopher Ludwig Wittgenstein, whose later books were required reading for all ambitious people in the 1960s (not least for those whose first and last experience of philosophy they were). Wittgenstein had said that "something new (spontaneous, 'specific') is always a language game"; and this was in line with the general trend of fashionable thought in the 1960s, when linguistics was all the rage in the paperback bookshops.

Play has, however, a quality of reaching outward. Play is a dramatization of our deepest concerns. In play, we mime the strategies for survival which are so fundamental to our equilibrium that we dare not reveal them in any other way. Chess, tennis, golf, baseball, football in its various guises —all serve to externalize our anxieties. ("No chess playing" was one of Ad Reinhardt's rules and regulations for a new art.) When Jasper Johns wanted to emphasize that the painter is the prisoner of a perfectly flat surface which can only be concealed by obsolete make-believe, he put a real drawer, complete with knobs, in the middle of the picture. But this was a device from outside of art, and as such unacceptable to those who believed that high art must ensure its continuance within the terms of its own physical existence and in no other way.

Clement Greenberg was an embattled supporter of this point of view, and what he had to say is worth quoting at length. He saw the predicament of art in the late 1950s and '60s as a part of a historical process that had begun with the German philosopher Immanuel Kant. It was by self-criticism that art survived; and around the beginning of our century, at a time when many of art's prerogatives were being taken away, a process of radical self-criticism began. The survival of art would depend on the thoroughness with which artists defined the areas in which art could still do incomparably well.

"What had to be made explicit," Greenberg wrote, "was that which was unique and irreducible not only in art in general but also in each particular art. Each art had to determine, through the operations peculiar to itself, the effects peculiar and exclusive to itself. By doing this, each art, would, to be sure, narrow its area of competence, but at the same time it would make its possession of this area all the more secure."

"It quickly emerged," Greenberg went on, "that the unique and proper area of competence of each art coincided with all that was unique to the nature of its medium. The task of self-criticism became to eliminate from the effects of each art any and every effect that might conceivably be borrowed from or by the medium of any other art. Thereby each art would be rendered 'pure,' and in its 'purity' find the guarantee of its standards of quality as well as of its independence. 'Purity' meant self-definition, and the enterprise of self-criticism in the arts became one of self-definition with a vengeance."

Whether or not Greenberg was aware of the overtones of the word "vengeance" in this context, the program that he set out had undeniably a punitive quality. Old scores were to be settled,

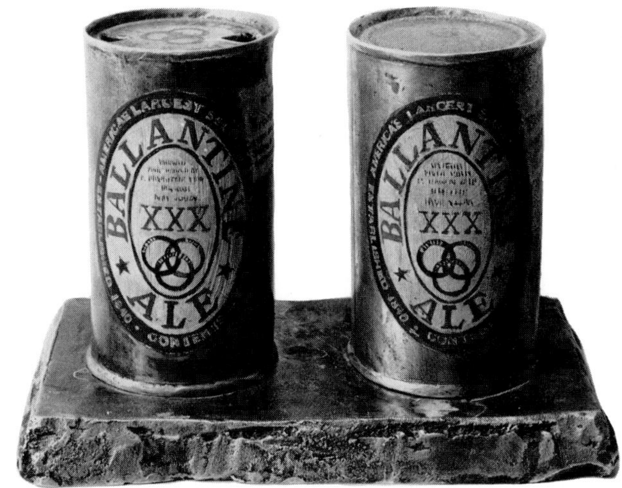

Jasper Johns.
Painted Bronze.
1960.
Painted bronze,
5½ × 8 × 4¾
inches.
Kunstmuseum,
Basel.
The Ludwig
Collection

old wrongs put right, sham heroes toppled from their pedestals, and the one true faith upheld. Good art—or "strong art," as it was called—was to be made within a set of conditions that grew ever more stringent until eventually everything that was not prohibited would be mandatory. One of the things to be said about all this is that it actually worked: good art and strong art were made, year by year, on the basis of a reductive program, a series of logical and ruthless decisions, that concentrated on the essential practicalities of art: the size and shape of the stretcher, the physical characteristics of the paint, the extent to which the final image was free from the taint of illusionism.

Fundamental to all of this was the role of color. Color had been set free, as we all know, by 1914. But was there such a thing as freer than free? The dying Matisse proved that there was, with the cut-paper paintings that he had produced in 1950–53. But those paintings were still not well known, and they were in any case a function of terminal illness, on the one hand, and of 60 years of research on the other. The problem was to make color freer than free as a logical next step forward from what had been done by Mark Rothko, for one, in America. It could be done, and it was done to stunning effect by Kenneth Noland in paintings like *Bend Sinister.* In the sideways thrust of that colossal image (it measures 7 feet 8 inches by 13 feet 5 inches) it seems as if color, incorporeal and unsupported, were pulling itself free from the absolute flatness: with just one unprecedented heave, the thing was done.

When seen by itself, *Bend Sinister* impresses by the authority with which a unified and seemingly quite simple image is made to carry the whole burden of art. It is even more arresting, however, if we know the paintings which immediately preceded it: chevron images which hang down with a perfect symmetry, blasting off from the two top corners of the canvas and hurtling straight on down toward the exact center of the canvas's lower edge. These centered chevrons have an added meaning, in their turn, if we know what came before *them:* and so on back to the beginning of Noland's career.

Even then, we need to know more: for Noland is one of the painters who bear out van Gogh's prediction that no one man could bring the art of the future into being. It would have to be done, van Gogh thought, by groups or teams, or at the very least by paired enthusiasts (like Gauguin and himself in their more harmonious days). Van Gogh was proved right by the history of subsequent art, in which not one consequential movement has been the work of a man on his own. Bonnard and Vuillard; Matisse, Derain, Vlaminck; Picasso and Braque; Kirchner and his friends in Dresden; Kandinsky and his friends in Munich; Lunacharsky's protégés in the U.S.S.R.; the Dadaists and the Surrealists in their heyday—in every case there was a collective impulse. How it was in New York in the 1940s we have seen; and although it is easy to exaggerate the degree of complicity which joins one coeval to another there is no doubt that in the 1950s the friendship of Kenneth Noland with Morris Louis, and to a lesser extent with the sculptor David Smith, was fundamental to the development of American art.

Louis and Noland met in 1952 in Washington, D.C., where they both lived. Morris Louis was by 12 years the older of the two, but it was Noland who had the kind of outgoing, combative temper-

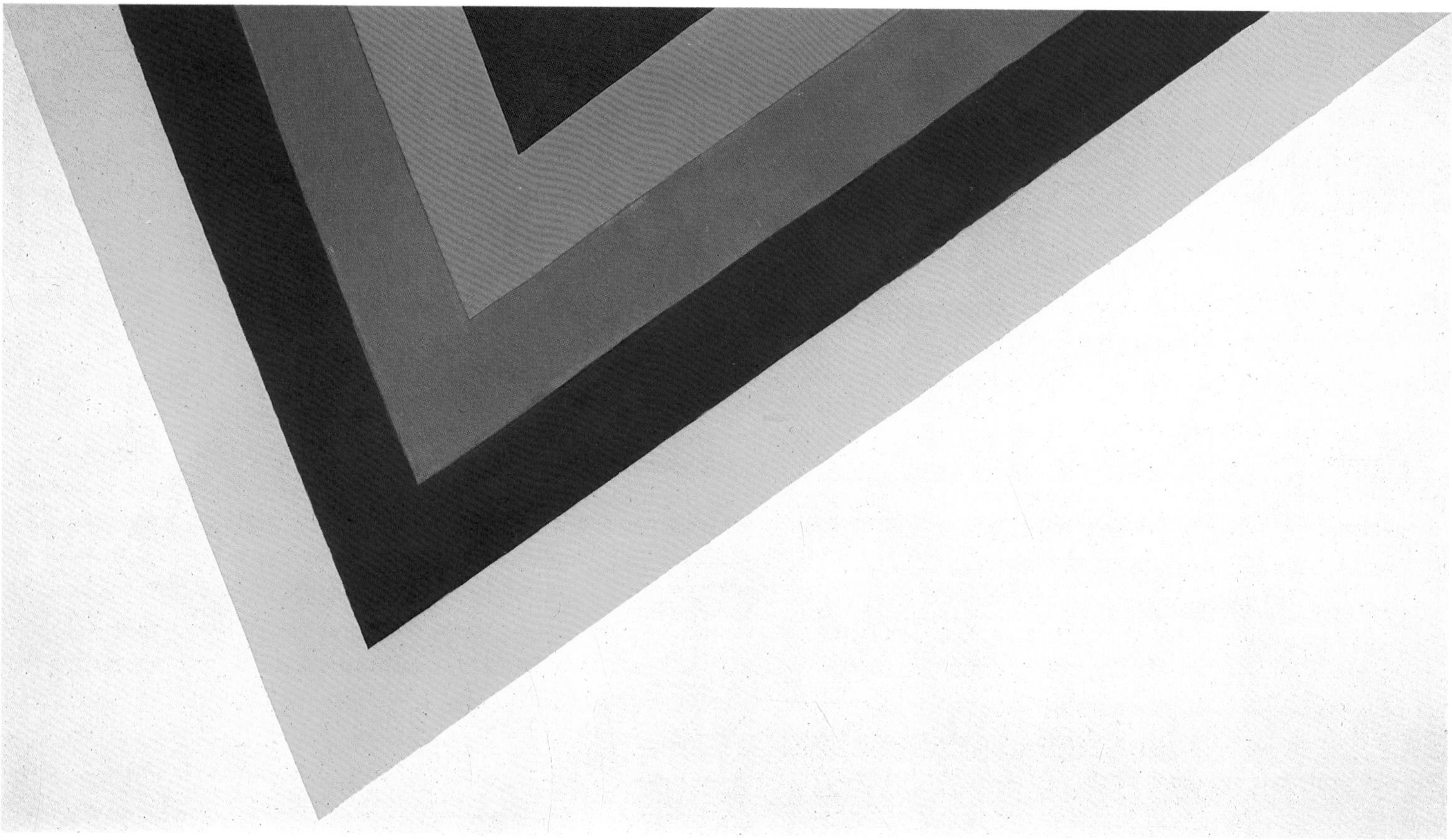

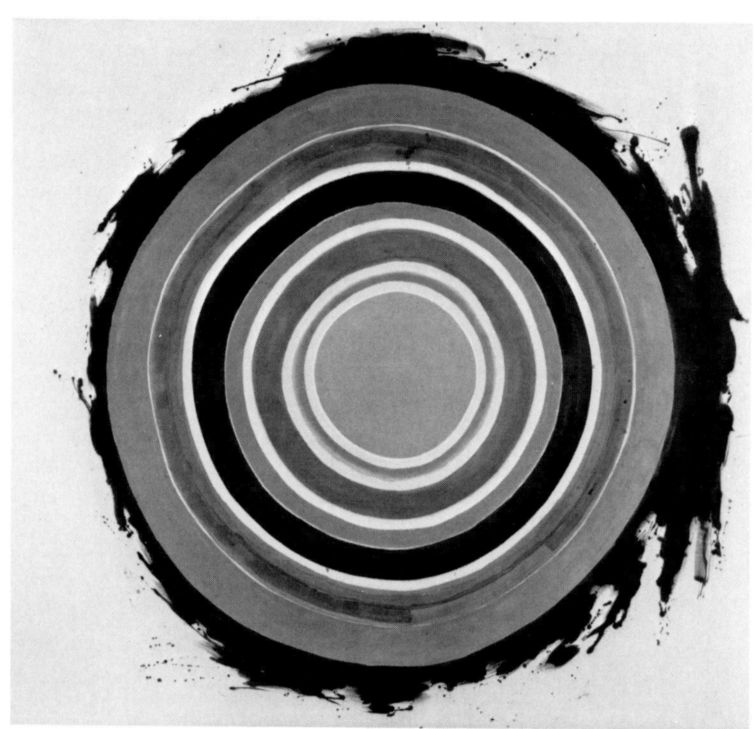

Kenneth Noland.
Bend Sinister. 1964.
Acrylic on canvas,
7 feet 8¾ inches ×
13 feet 5¾ inches.
Hirshhorn Museum
and Sculpture
Garden, Smithsonian
Institution,
Washington

Kenneth Noland.
Beginning. 1958.
Acrylic on canvas,
7 feet 6 inches × 8
feet.
Hirshhorn Museum
and Sculpture
Garden, Smithsonian
Institution,
Washington

ament which thrives on the definition of ideas: and for the three years—1952–55—of their close friendship they were able to effect a joint hammering-out of their intentions such as had rarely been paralleled since the first alliance of Picasso and Braque. (At one time they even painted on the same canvas.)

What were they doing? Well, they wanted to find out what was the predestined next thing in art: the step which history dictated, but which it was left to individual men and women to riddle out. As friends of Clement Greenberg, they proceeded by elimination: by defining their "area of competence," no matter how narrow it might turn out to be. Noland had spent some time at Black Mountain College as a student of the Russian-born painter Ilya Bolotowsky, who brought to his raw young audiences something of the European abstract tradition. He had worked in Paris, where the sculptor Ossip Zadkine (then one of the most famous artists in Europe) had singled him out in 1949 as someone of exceptional promise. Noland had steam up, by the end of the 1940s, but he had nowhere to go—until, that is, he and Morris Louis began to work on the impressions they had brought back from Helen Frankenthaler's studio in 1953. In her *Mountains and Sea* they found an answer to the question "What is it that art can still do, *and that nothing else can?*" In paintings like *Mountains and Sea* and *Other Generations* Frankenthaler in the 1950s was onto something all her own: the alliance of delicate freehand drawing with paint that was allowed to stain its way into the canvas rather than to sit, like a skin, on top of it. Hers was not the only answer: Matisse and Braque in France had lately come upon quite different ones, for instance. But it was an answer that they followed through to spectacular effect: Louis until he died in 1962, Noland to this day.

Certain things were eliminated from the start, as having lately exhausted their usefulness. One of them was the manual element in painting: the evident motion of the hand, whether with brush or tube or can, which left its mark on the canvas in the form of motor energy. Another was drawing, in any of its accepted forms, since anything

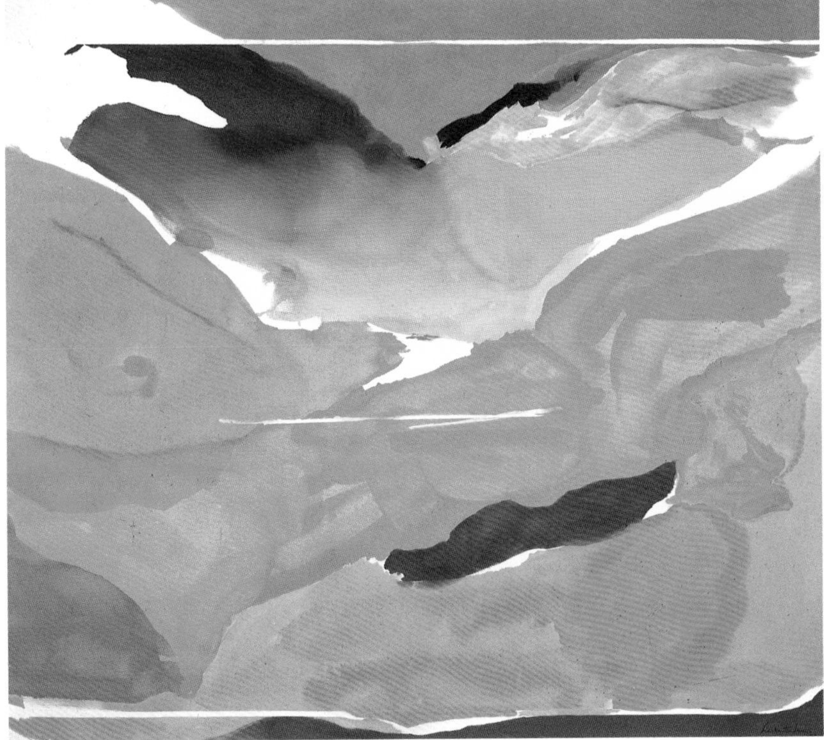

Helen Frankenthaler. *Nature Abhors a Vacuum.* 1973. Acrylic on canvas, 8 feet 7½ inches × 9 feet 4 inches. Private collection, New York

that could be read as drawing could also be read as illusion, or as metaphor: the pounding rhythms of a major abstract Pollock demand, for instance, to be described in terms of loops and skeins and lassos. A third thing to be eliminated was composition, as it was generally understood; for composition in Action Painting as often as not looked back to composition as it had evolved in Cubist painting, even down to the uneasiness which seized the Cubist painters as they got further and further from the closely argued central image and had to decide what to do at the edges of the canvas.

So a lot was going out. What was coming in? New ways of applying paint, to begin with: after that, new ways of structuring the image. Thinned pigment (the new synthetic paint called "acrylic") was to be soaked and stained into unsized canvas. Instead of building up on the surface of the canvas, in traditional style, the paint sank into the canvas and became one with it. Just how this was to be done—how the artist was to govern the nature of the image without being seen to direct it—was a matter for discussion. The paint could be poured onto a canvas laid flat on the floor; it could be allowed to run down a canvas that was held up as one holds up a sheet for folding; it could be rubbed in with a sponge; and it could be rolled on with a commercial paint roller. The important thing was that none of the traditional signs of "handling" should be present: no mark should be seen to result from a strong forward movement of the arm, a turn of the wrist, a well-judged dab with the brush held between two fingers and thumb. Color should seem to act spontaneously and of its own nature.

As to the structuring of the image, Louis and Noland proceeded according to their own very different natures. Louis was physically frail, and by temperament he was a quiet, inward sort of person. Noland liked to bring everything into the open, and to go to work from a position of armored certainty. Louis at more than one stage of his career echoed the aspirations of the American sublime; Noland did not want overtones of any kind, anywhere. In a top-class Morris Louis—in one of the "unfurled" paintings, for instance—color seems to go its own way, freer than ever before or since, down runnels which are never the same twice over. In a Noland, we know who's boss, down to the last millimeter of the surface. Louis

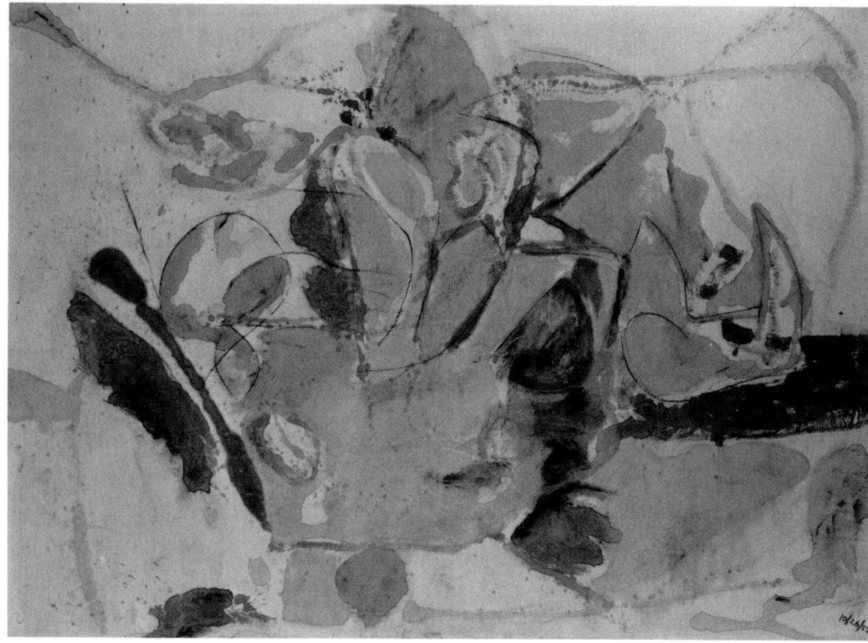

Helen Frankenthaler. *Mountains and Sea.* 1952. Oil on canvas, 7 feet 2⅜ inches × 9 feet 9¼ inches. Collection the artist, New York

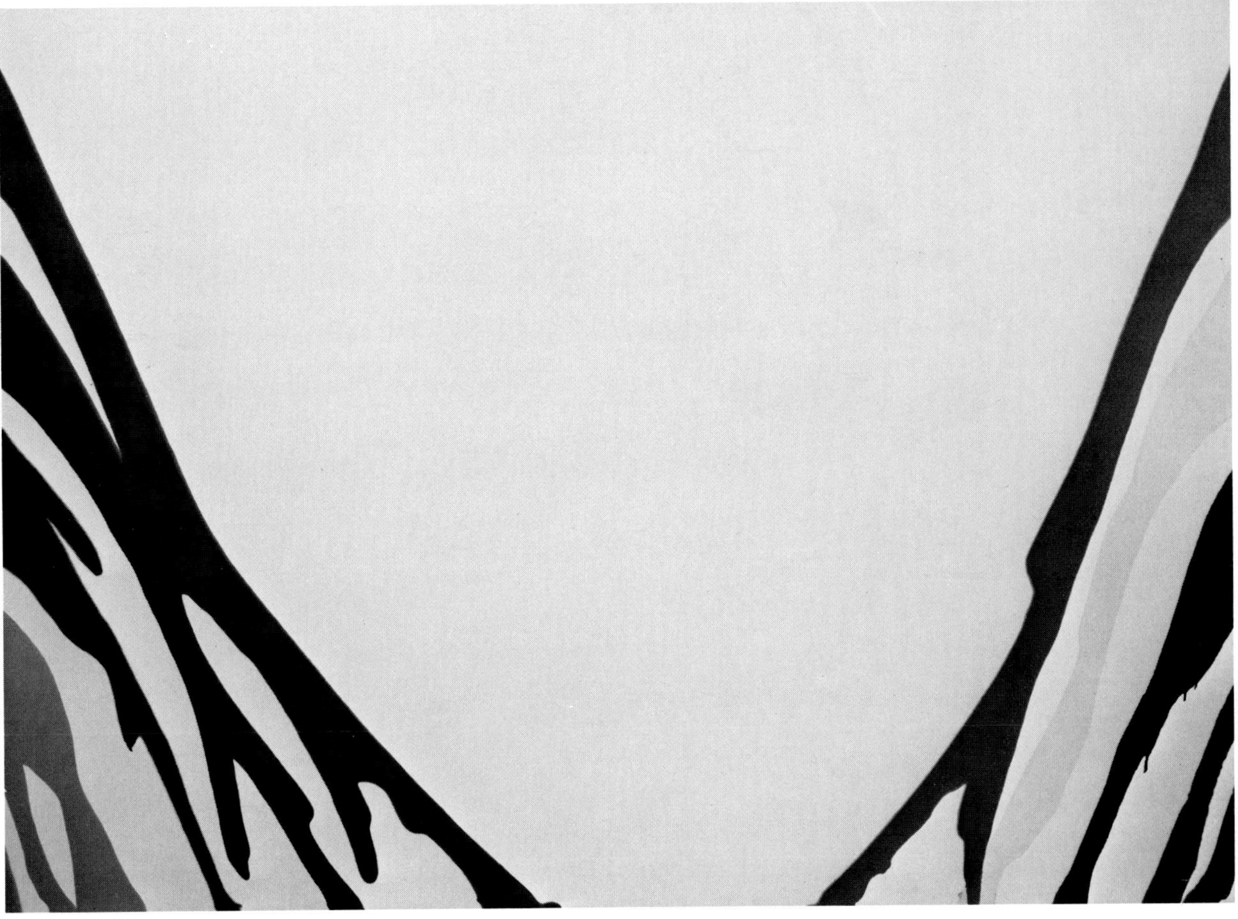

Morris Louis.
Alpha Gamma.
1960.
Acrylic on canvas,
8 feet 9 inches × 12 feet 1 inch.
The Detroit Institute of Arts

did not exclude a monumental ambiguity—above all, in the Veils series in 1954, and again in 1958—but a mature Noland is a statement-system in which clear thoughts find clear expression and there is never a conflict of intention, never a second thought, never an evocative fuzz. As much as Picasso and Braque, the two artists complement one another.

The American critic Michael Fried put the case for this when he said that "only an art of constant formal self-criticism can bear or embody or communicate more than trivial meaning." The self-criticism which he had in mind was limited to a very few areas of investigation. These were (i) the echoes or implications of the picture's physical format, (ii) the avoidance of anything that could be likened to freehand drawing, (iii) the nature of a specifically post-Cubist composition, (iv) the extent to which color could be given, not "freedom," but a total independence. These were severe prescriptions; and if we consider the area of competence which until quite recently was taken for granted in art there is no doubt that in the 1960s the field of permissible effort was dramatically narrowed. "On this ground," these painters and their friends seem to say, "painting will make its last stand."

There is here something of American folklore. The ghost of General Custer, face to face with Crazy Horse, comes over the horizon; and, with him, something of the first settlers' determination to build a new world, a Jerusalem untainted by the falling-short of their forebears in Europe. Plain talking and plain doing were the remedy: and we seem to hear an echo of those days when Frank Stella suggests in his black paintings of 1960 that

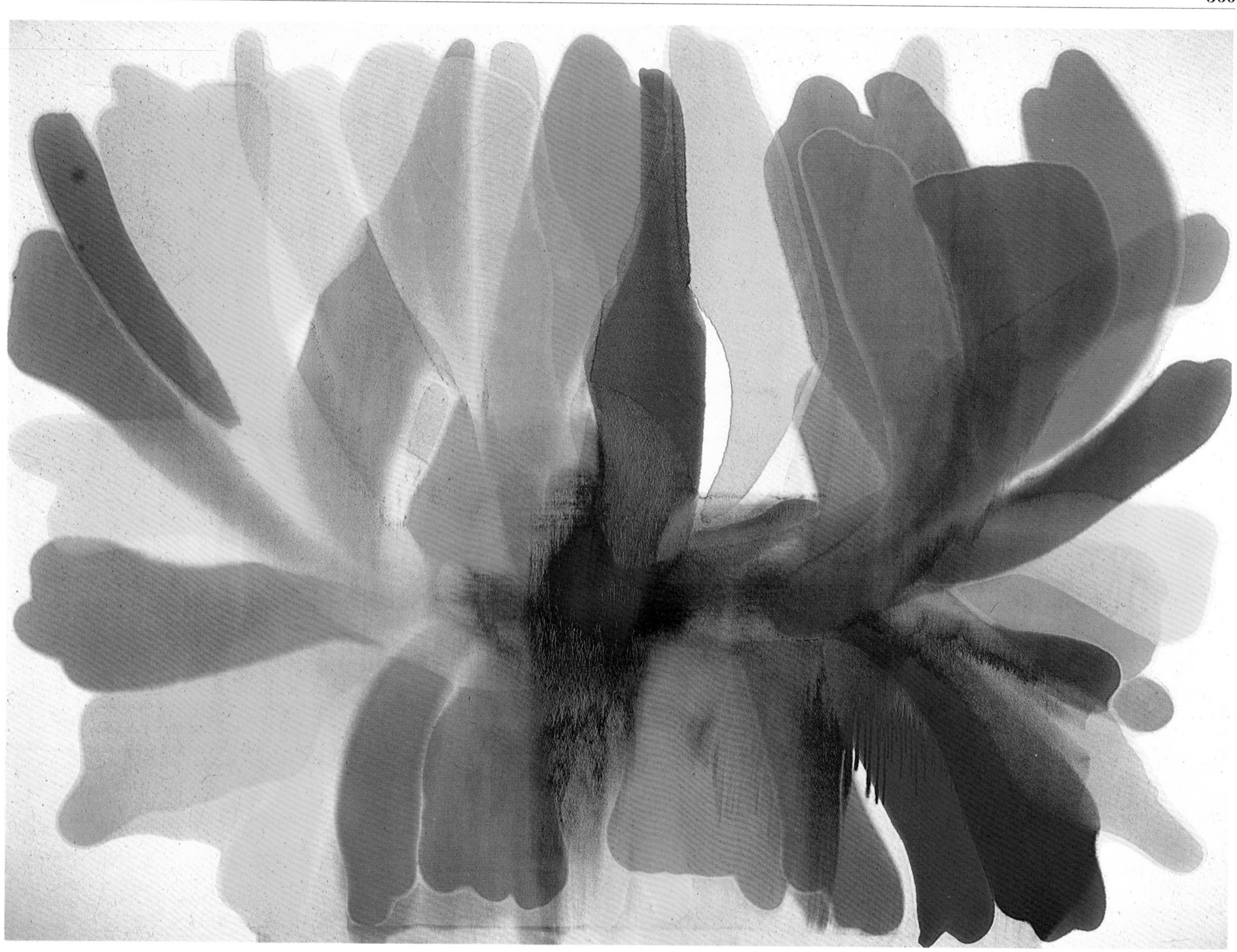

Morris Louis.
Point of Tranquillity. 1958.
Acrylic on canvas, 8 feet 5 inches × 11 feet 3 inches.
Hirshhorn Museum and Sculpture Garden, Smithsonian Institution, Washington

thereafter the only defensible basis for composition is the shape and size of the wooden strips on which the canvas has been stretched. After a decade and more when the subjectivity of Abstract Expressionism had dominated the New York art scene, it was Frank Stella, above all, who put the case for quite another kind of painting: one in which the image would be "given," centered, symmetrical and invariable. There is, too, that same delight in exact measurement which, as we have seen, was identified by Emerson in the 1830s as a specifically American trait. Literal truth is fundamental to this kind of painting; and the implication is that as long as painting sticks with literal truth it can never be dislodged from its functions. When trueing and fairing are mentioned in connection with these pictures, we remember that "true" and "fair" bear a moral connotation.

The work which results from all this could be dull and schematic, well-argued but unfeeling. So much is outlawed that was once among the painter's most valued prerogatives: allusion, ambiguity, freedom of reference, the right to establish ideal standards of beauty both in human beings and in Nature, and the power to make changes of pace and tone and intent within one and the same picture. It is a tribute to the artists whose work is reproduced here that they have been able, nonetheless, to make feeling flow where none flowed before. With a chevron, a set of immensely elongated stripes or five or six batons of pure color laid side by side, Louis and Noland gave back to painting a purity and an intensity of feeling such as we needed but did not dare to hope could still exist. What more natural than that those who have experienced this need most acutely should feel that there and there only lies the salvation of art? Between them and those who claim for art an altogether wider set of options, no compromise is possible. The great divide has never been wider; nor could the art of this generation have trodden more consistently on tender ground.

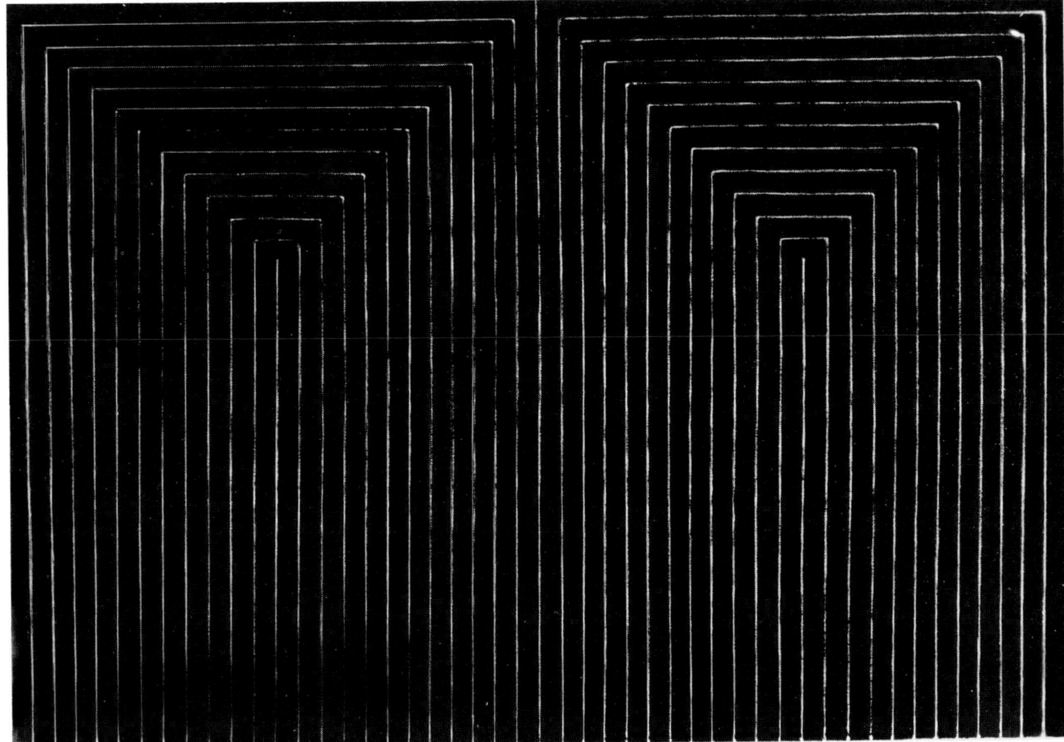

Frank Stella. *The Marriage of Reason and Squalor.* 1959. Oil on canvas, 7 feet 6¾ inches × 11 feet ¾ inch. The Museum of Modern Art, New York. Larry Aldrich Foundation Fund

HOW GOOD IS MODERN ART?

Face to face with new art, we begin a series of investigations. We test, and we taste. We refer back to what we know already. We think of what we always wanted to know but could never find anyone to tell us. We wait to see how the new art makes us feel: older or younger, richer or poorer, cleverer or more stupid, more at home in the world or less. These are true tests: and just very occasionally, when they all come out right, we burst out with the modern equivalent of a famous 19th-century cry, "Hats off, gentlemen, a masterpiece!"

It sounds pure gain. What is done in our time is done in our name, as I said earlier. We demand of new art that it leave our generation with its claim upon posterity substantiated. Yet great news can be a great inconvenience, and new art may force us to reconsider our ideas not only about earlier art but about ourselves. After Cézanne, after a Picasso of 1910, after a Kandinsky Improvisation, earlier art looked different. T. S. Eliot put this point very well when he said that "when a new work of art is created, something happens simultaneously to all the works of art that preceded it. The existing monuments form an ideal order among themselves, which is modified by the introduction of the new (the really new) work of art among them."

We ourselves are modified, also, by the arrival of "the new (the really new) work of art." We ourselves may look different too: whence the tension, the disquiet, the outright mutiny with which it is so often received. "Is it good enough for me?" is the unspoken question which lies behind all our judgments of new art. But when the new art is also great art we have to ask another, and a less comfortable question: "Am I good enough for it?" The German poet Rainer Maria Rilke understood this when he wrote in 1908 of a certain sculpture that "after this, we must live differently."

So it is a happy day when good new art is also good news, everywhere and without qualification. This was the case with Matisse's cut-paper paintings of 1951–53, which were received with universal delight and astonishment and have stood ever since as a true image of human nature at one with itself. The world had needed just those paintings at just that time. It was a hinge-point in human affairs, and nowhere better defined than in the long poem called *Winds*, which was written in the United States by the exiled French poet St. John Perse, who was later to be awarded the Nobel Prize. The poem was Whitmanesque in its scale and sweep, and it described how "very great winds" had passed over mankind, leaving us with "men of straw in the year of straw." "For man is in question," St. John Perse said elsewhere in the poem: "Will no one, anywhere, raise his voice? It is for the poet to speak and to guide our judgment."

Those who felt, with Perse, that mankind "had a rendezvous with the end of an age" did better with painters, as it turned out, than with poets. Still, the images had to be found. And where to look for them? It had seemed an insoluble question. So much of European painting was like Europe itself: worn out. The best American painting was for the most part tragic in intention, as we have seen: what it had to offer was a portrait, complete and unflinching, of a flawed humanity. It also restated in terms of art what Henry James had had to say about Nathaniel Hawthorne—that "an American could be an artist, one of the finest, without 'going outside' about it and just by being American *enough.*" These were great achievements, and they came to be recognized as such, but the strain showed; indeed, it was fundamental to the achievement. The early 1950s were a time of worldwide exhaustion and self-doubt; and to be what I have called "good news everywhere" the new art had to combat these states of mind. It had, in other words, to be as near as possible weightless, incorporeal, and exempt from all outward effort. It had to picture a world released from gravity and freed from guilt: a world in which Nature was wholly benign, the sick were made well, and the unloved were loved.

It fell to Henri Matisse to picture this world, in circumstances which were really very curious. As early as 1943 he had said to a friend that "all signs indicate that I am about to start working on large-scale compositions, as if I had the whole of life, or another life, before me." As Matisse was then 73 years old and was often as not too ill even to stand before an easel, let alone to ply a brush, this might have been a protective illusion of the kind which often settles over the victims of terminal illness. But in his case it was the literal truth: at no time in his life did he produce more work on the scale of epic than between 1951 and his death in November, 1954.

Matisse at that time was preoccupied, as he had been all his life, with color. He could no longer brush huge areas of canvas, but such was the effect of infirmity upon his imagination that he decided to see how color could be magicked into being in ways that had not been exploited before. When he was invited to design a chapel for the Dominican Order in the little town of Vence, where he lived from 1943 to 1949, he could have used the firm strong color which he had commanded with total virtuosity in his paintings of the 1930s. But he opted in the end for the simplest of general schemes, dominated by black line drawings on a bone-white background. If color dances every day through the Vence chapel, it is not because of what is on the wall, but because the stained glass windows flood the white interior space with the ghost of pure color: where all else is black and white, phantoms of palest blue, green, yellow cross and recross the floor, visible but impalpable.

Both in his designs for the Vence chapel and on individual sheets of paper, Matisse in the late 1940s was drawing with an exceptional power and freedom. The deep black of the ink, the summary unerring line, the breadth and force of the stroke: all added up to what can be called a "late" style, in which the game was for high stakes and no bets were hedged. It was an old man's summation of an activity that he had pursued day after day, without stint or remission, for 60 years. Color was laid

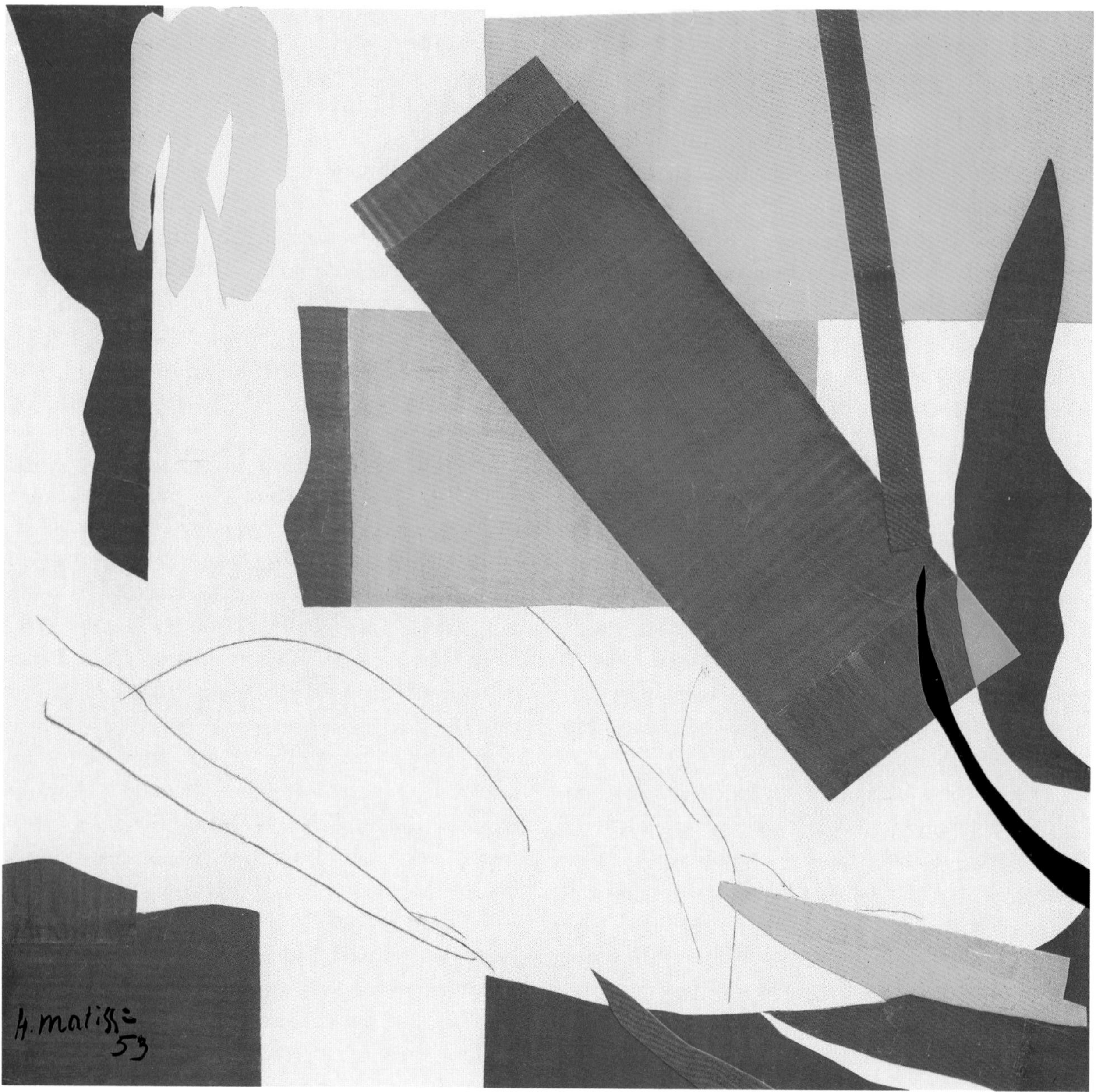

Henri Matisse.
Memory of Oceania.
1953.
Gouache and crayon on cut-and-pasted paper over canvas, 9 feet 4 inches × 9 feet 4⅞ inches.
The Museum of Modern Art, New York. Mrs. Simon Guggenheim Fund

aside—except, of course, insofar as black and white are colors. Yet, in respect of color also, a 60 years' experience demanded a last word; and it began to get it in 1947 in a book by Matisse: *Jazz.*

Jazz was something quite new for Matisse. Already the title was a whole world away from the stately evocations of the French past with which he had busied himself in wartime. Jazz music at that time and for a man of Matisse's generation was still something dashing, exotic, specifically American. It stood for snappy cross-rhythms and euphoric riffs of a kind unprecedented in high art. It also stood for something not written down, but conjured from nowhere by people for whom improvisation was the touchstone of talent.

None of this would apply to Matisse's normal methods of drawing. He never made a mark on paper that did not speak for a long schooling and a sense of moral responsibility toward high art. But in *Jazz* he did not make marks on paper. He took sheets which had already been colored (so brightly in fact that his doctor advised him to wear dark glasses when looking at them) and he cut into them with scissors. There was no drawing, as such: he felt as if he were cutting into pure color as a sculptor cuts into marble. The scruples and inhibitions of high art fell away, and images of a kind he had never tackled before rose up freely from his unconscious.

Sometimes they were images of violent action; sometimes memories of Tahiti come back after 20 years; sometimes fantasy took over after a long lifetime dedicated primarily to fact. The man who had largely eschewed pure invention turned out to be haunted by scenes from a Texan rodeo that he had never been to, by sword swallowers from an imaginary circus, and by the fate of Icarus as he fell soundlessly through space. The stay-at-home reinvented the marvels of the Polynesian seabed. The most matter-of-fact of great masters pictured for himself the funeral of Pierrot, with white horses drawing a monumental hearse and just one small splash of red to stand for the wreaths on the coffin. A feature of *Jazz* was Matisse's handwritten comments, which set out the general principles by which he had lived. Opposite his schematic sword swallower, for instance, he wrote that the artist needs all his energy, all his integrity, and the greatest possible modesty if he is not to fall back upon forms of expression that have already been done to death. In *Jazz,* Matisse completed himself. What had been left unsaid was said, and with an effect of long-pent-up excitement. It was unthinkable that so vivid and so rewarding a medium would be used once and once only.

There were difficulties, of course. The scale of *Jazz* was such that he could work on it in bed without exhausting himself. For anything larger, other methods would have to be found. Eventually, however, and with the help of his assistant, Lydia Delektorskaya, Matisse decided that he could work on very large sheets of colored paper by using long-handled shears. The cut-out forms could be first pinned down and later definitively stuck in place; as for the area to be covered, there was no need to set a limit to it. Twelve feet by twenty-five (as in *The Siren and the Parakeet* of 1952) was none too large. There was never a complete break with his own past: the emblems of Nature were such as he had often outlined in pen and ink, the heavy-limbed girls took poses of a kind he had often studied for his sculptures, the glimpses of the human body at full stretch in deep water harked back to the grouped dancers whom he had pictured with such authority in 1909 and again in the 1930s. But something had vanished from the work all the same; and that something was the evidence of hard labor.

The cut-outs did not look "easy," any more than *Dance* of 1909 had looked "difficult." They just seemed to have been wished out of the air, instinctively and instantaneously. It wasn't true, of course, but it seemed to be true; and when the big cut-outs were first put on show they came upon the world like an act of amnesty. All sins were forgiven; something had come into being that was perfect, whole and complete. That so large a body of work should be produced by someone who was in medical terms a dying man was really very extraordinary; it was as if the processes of nature had been reversed and death had been kept waiting at the door. So infectious and so all-pervasive was the effect of the cut-paper works that they caused, quite unjustly, a temporary decline in the reputation of those paintings on canvas by Matisse in which the evidence of hard labor is there for all to see. It can be argued that the very perfection of the cut-papers puts them lower in the scale of moral effort than the oils on canvas in which Matisse took the classic problems of painting and tussled with them in the traditional way; but in the convalescent Europe of the 1950s people were grateful enough to have set before them the image of an unflawed and primal happiness. Faced with something the like of which had not been seen before, they could have said, with Ralph Waldo Emerson, "I have enjoyed a perfect exhilaration. I am glad to the brink of fear."

Only one man could do it, however. It is the paradox of Matisse's cut-paper paintings, which look so quintessentially youthful and unburdened, that in point of fact they signal the old age of the European masterpiece. There had been nothing like them before, and there would be nothing like them again. Not only was there no one around who could do it, but Matisse's broad exalted confidence in the role of the masterpiece was even then ebbing away from the European consciousness. It was part of a more general decline. The demoralization of an entire continent is not something that can go unreflected in the mirror of art. If that decline and that demoralization were not more immediately apparent in art, it is because the dominant figures in that art were still men who had come to manhood at the end of the 19th century and had that century's belief in the absolute power of art. Not only had these artists a glorious past, but in more than one case they had a glorious future. Even those who had died (Klee in 1940, Mondrian in 1944, Kandinsky in 1944, Bonnard in 1947) left late work that came upon the world as a delayed revelation. Where they lived on (Matisse until 1954, Braque until 1963, Duchamp until 1968, Picasso until 1973) it was not as ancient monuments or revered seniors who happened not to have died, but as people who still had plenty to say. Braque was never better than in his late Studio series; Picasso reached perhaps his highest point of virtuosity in the variations on *Las Meninas* by Velázquez and *The Women of Algiers* by Delacroix; Duchamp overturned every assessment of his career by working in secret for 20 years on an environmental work (*Etant donnés: 1° la chute d'eau, 2° le gaz d'éclairage/Given: 1. The Waterfall, 2. The Illuminating Gas*, 1946–66), which was made known only after his death. Talk of decline makes no sense, in this context. But art is a collective as well as a personal matter; and in that regard times were changing too fast for comfort.

What went wrong with the idea of the masterpiece? One way to open up this question is to look at one of the last occasions on which the traditional certainties were asserted with maximum force. In 1902 Max Klinger completed a seated figure of Beethoven. White, black and violet marbles, alabaster and ivory—all were brought into play. The great man was dressed in Roman style and seated on a throne big enough for any two ordinary men. An eagle sat at his feet. Angels urged him on at shoulder-height. Klinger is best known now for his print series *The Glove;* but in the Beethoven statue he made the kind of grandiose public statement which in 1902 was still perfectly acceptable. So acceptable was it, in fact, that Klinger was welcomed by a salute from the trombones of the Vienna Philharmonic Orchestra when the statue was shown in Beethoven's own city.

What has caused Klinger's *Beethoven* to sink without a trace is not so much the overblown rhetoric of the sculpture itself as the collapse of belief in the role of art as the custodian of current values. The mid-century view has been that since most accepted values are pernicious, art is not art if it supports them. The art which has lately commanded respect is the kind which goes its own way, attentive to art's own historical necessities but indifferent to officialdom. Individual artists may or may not take a political stand. On January 1, 1966, Alexander Calder took a page in *The New York Times,* at his sole expense, to put himself and Mrs. Calder on record as believing that: "Our only hope is in thoughtful men. Reason is not Treason." There have been works of art which likewise take a specific stand: James Rosenquist's *F-111* is the outstanding example, and the cycle of David Smith's Medals for Dishonor should also be remembered. But basically the big rounded statement, such as was welcomed in 1902, is no longer tolerable to most artists. This is not because they have opted out, or because they refuse the challenge, but because the conditions of life no longer allow of that kind of panoramic certainty. Certainty has now a narrower compass; and even within that compass there are elements that are conditional or contingent.

This is in part because our view of the world is now permeated with the need to question and revise and readjust which was initiated in physics before 1914 by Albert Einstein and Max Planck and Ernest Rutherford. This is not to say that these august names can be invoked by anyone who looks at the state of the world and says, "It just doesn't make any sense"; but it does mean, as the English historian James Joll has pointed out, that "Einstein's theory of relativity not only led to a scientific revolution; it seemed in the popular mind to confirm a widespread belief that nothing was certain any more." If matter is not matter, and if the stone that stubs our toe is not really solid, what are we to choose as tokens of reality? The masterpiece as monolith—"a single block of stone, especially one of notable size," says the dictionary—is necessarily devalued if the "single block of stone" is not what it seems.

There is also the fact that the classic notion of the masterpiece has within it an element of self-congratulation. What people said to one another was that "a society which can produce *this* cannot have too much wrong with it." But the truth is that it is difficult to point to a great power which has not, at some point in this century, been ruled by buffoons or criminals; that it would be difficult to point to a great city, a landscape or a stretch of offshore water which has not been contaminated, during that same period, by human action; and that it would be difficult to point to a social system or a set of beliefs which has remained stable, intact and unchallenged since the days of our grandfathers. This being so, it is not the function of art to patch over the shortcomings of society. The function of art, as the composer John Cage once said, is something quite different: to awaken us to "the very life we're living."

In this context we should see the late works of Matisse as above all a triumph of continuance. Matisse is one of the rare men who have held time at bay: in his art, and in his own body. It was not that the clock was stopped, but rather that the clock had been thrown away and was never referred to. Matisse was armored against the world. Other and younger artists were not, however; nor did other great seniors—Picasso and Braque, for instance—maintain in their work quite that immunity from current events which characterized Matisse. (The slow rundown of life in occupied France during World War II was evoked by both Picasso and Braque with a power which was all the greater for its relative discretion.) But it was left for another generation to suggest that the whole structure of accepted art in France had been as much a fraud and a sham as the structure of military defense.

What happened in France by 1944 was that the previously established order was in total disrepute, that accepted systems of judgment were entirely discredited and that hierarchies long taken for granted were thrown into the shredder. There was a situation vacant, at that time, for someone who could make first-rate art and yet nowhere bear the taint of a pre-1939 aesthetic. The situation brought forward the man, as it often does; and the man was Jean Dubuffet, a wine wholesaler turned painter, who had his first exhibition in Oc-

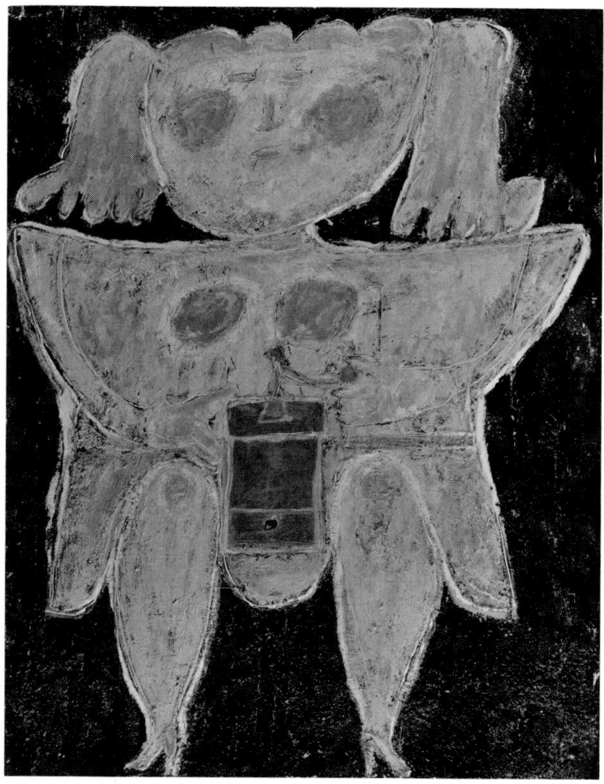

Jean Dubuffet. *The Coffee Grinder.* 1945. Oil and various materials on canvas, 45½ × 35 inches. Mr. and Mrs. Ralph F. Colin, New York

tober, 1944, just a few weeks after the Germans had been turned out of Paris.

Dubuffet belonged to that close-knit Parisian milieu in which art and literature overlap; and he was known there as an inimitable human being, an original among originals, with a strong line in the kind of elasticized dialectic which can be pulled this way and that, at will, and yet always snap back into place. He was a dazzling and prolific writer, whose published polemical writings for the years 1946–67 came to over a thousand pages. And in 1944–45, when most people longed only to see the return of French high culture as it had existed till 1939, Dubuffet outraged his countrymen by saying that museum art was grossly overrated and that there was quite as much to be learned from the art of madmen and guttersnipes. France had been producing great art in such quantity and for so many years that a lifetime was none too long for anyone who wanted to know it thoroughly. Rather than look around for the new and the difficult, people were delighted to settle, where the art of their own day was concerned, for the point of view epitomized once and for all by William Butler Yeats in his poem "The Nineteenth Century and After":

Though the great song return no more
There's keen delight in what we have:
The rattle of pebbles on the shore
Under the receding wave.

Dubuffet despised this point of view. Not only did he oppose it in print, but his paintings were the antithesis of the polite, well-made, undemanding work of those who followed the masters of the French School at a respectful distance. His pictures looked as if they had not been painted at all, but scored in mud with a pointed stick. Their subject matter was rudimentary, their awkwardness flagrant, their total effect nearer to metropolitan graffiti than to traditional painting. He spared nothing and nobody. Yet if the early Dubuffet now stands out, it is not as an iconoclast. He gave, on the contrary, a paradoxical, unforeseeable grandeur to what were derided at the time as impudent scrawls and scribbles. It is to him, against all the odds, that the European imagination attached itself; and it is through him that the dream of a freer, franker and yet not less humane mode of utterance was carried forward in art.

Dubuffet in all this looked both backward and forward. His ideas were in line, that is to say, with avant-garde attitudes as they had expressed themselves in Europe for many years past. As a young man he had been deeply impressed by Hans Prinzhorn's book, first published in 1922, on the paintings of the mentally ill; but Max Ernst had been preoccupied with such things since before 1914. Dubuffet welcomed chance into his art as a full partner—"It takes two," he wrote, "to dance this dance"—but then chance had been built into the notion of art since the early days of Surrealism. At a time when John Cage was quite unknown in Paris, Dubuffet had the same ideas as he about the expressive power of sounds from everyday life. "I know that musicians don't want to hear about them and consider them merely as 'noise,'" he

Jean Dubuffet. *The Cow with the Subtile Nose.* 1954. Oil and enamel on canvas, 35 × 45¾ inches. The Museum of Modern Art, New York. Benjamin Scharps and David Scharps Fund

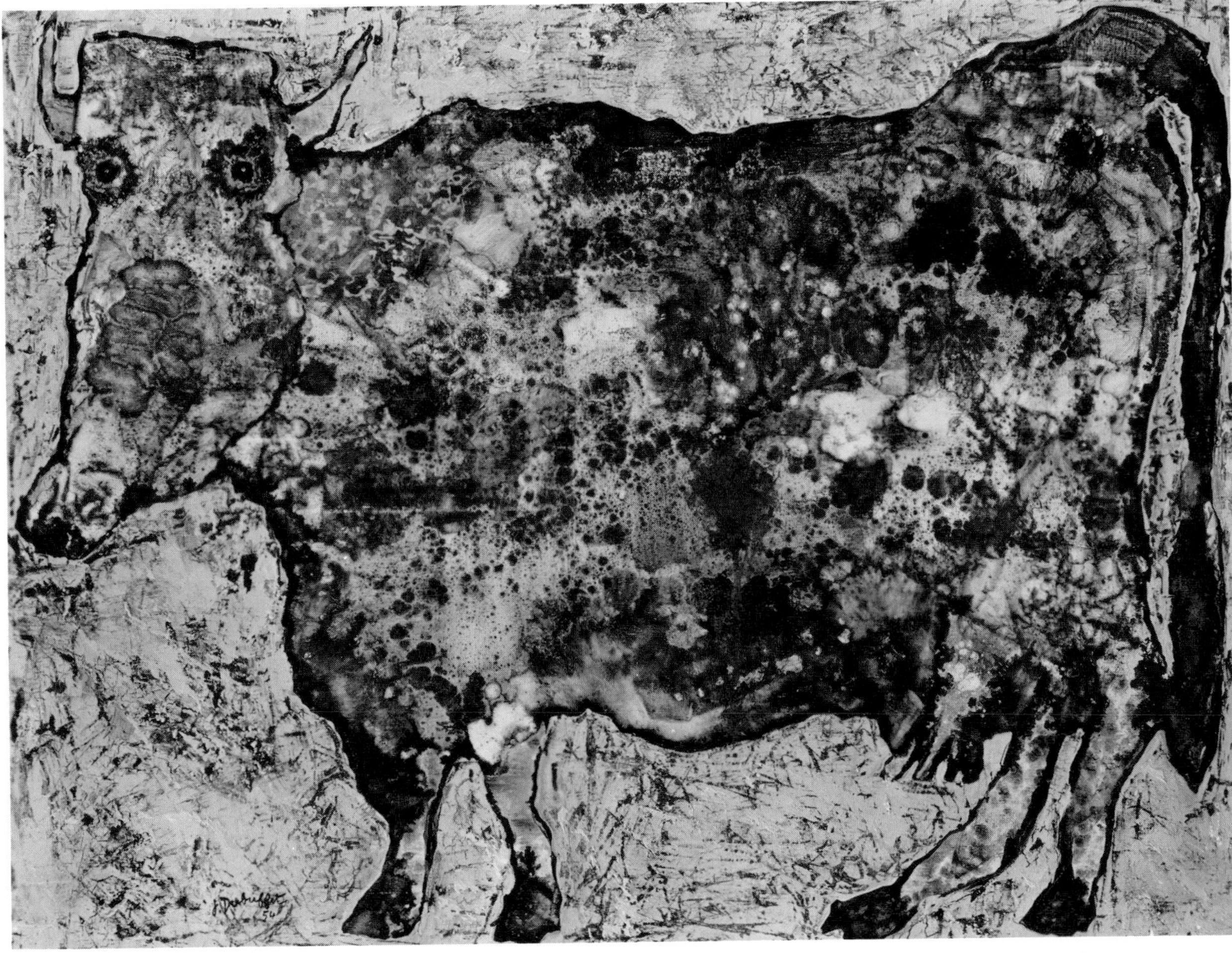

wrote in 1946; "but I don't see why the sound of a chair being dragged along the floor, of an elevator starting its ascent, or of the turning-on of a faucet of water should not have its place in music, every bit as much as the twelve starveling and arbitrary notes of the scale."

Dubuffet arrived by his own calculations at idea after idea which had been, or was to be, propagated elsewhere as basic to a modernist attitude to life. In 1944, for example, he wrote to a friend that he did not believe in the notion of artistic gifts and that there was no reason why one person should not paint as well as another. In this he paralleled one of the most radical ideas of R. Buckminster Fuller—that "every child is a genius until it is degeniused by education." Dubuffet was also, in those early days, for an anonymous art as distinct from the 50 years of adulation which causes a once-gifted artist to coast along on his signature alone; in this, he prefigured the revolt of the late 1960s against the kind of art which stands barely higher than autograph hunting in the hierarchy of human experience. His was an art that began from zero; but in this, once again, he had been preceded by Paul Klee, who once said that he wanted to work as if European art had never existed and everything had to begin again from the beginning. So he was both new and not new; but if some of his ideas had been in the air for a generation Dubuffet nonetheless brought to them an incisive, quizzical, unsparing turn of mind that was specifically his own. At what might otherwise have been a low point in the history of French creativity he was able to reassert that there is no imaginative need for which an image cannot be forthcoming.

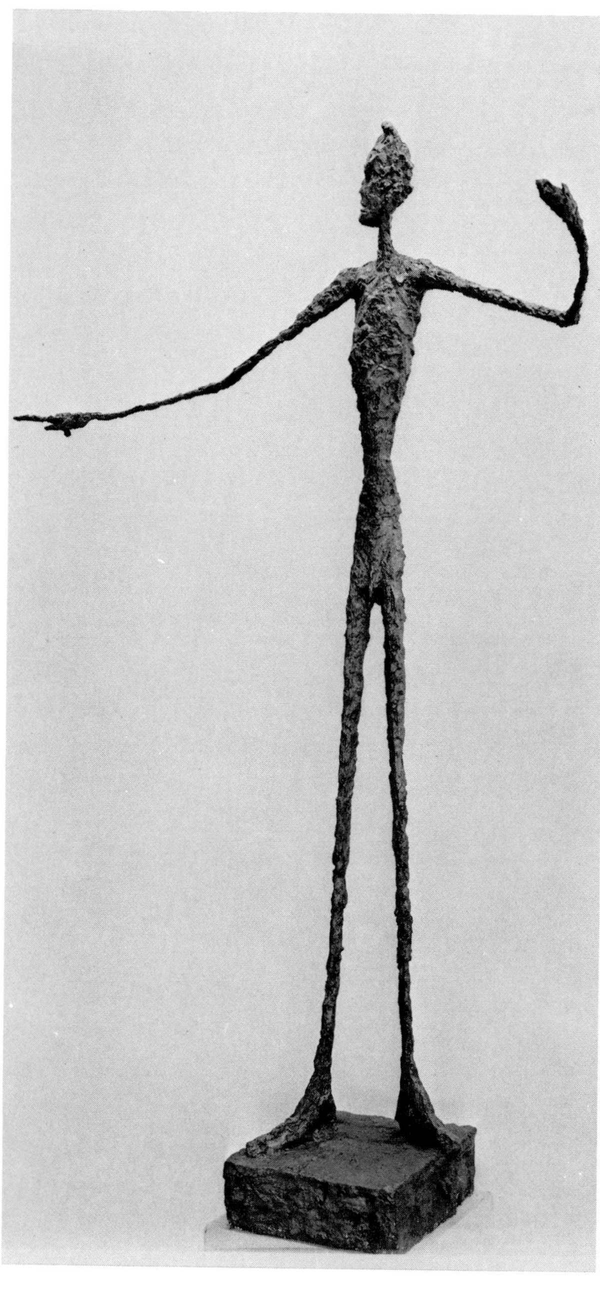

Alberto Giacometti. *Man Pointing.* 1947. Bronze, 70½ inches high. The Museum of Modern Art, New York. Gift of Mrs. John D. Rockefeller 3rd

Dubuffet was already over 40 when he turned to painting full time in 1942; but his was a new name in art and he brought to art itself a new attitude —one that was half-derisory, half-magical. He made magic from derision, in fact; but the magic was too strong for a genteel taste, and it was to be a number of years before the best of his early paintings were found to validate the very thing that he had made mock of: the continuity of high art in no matter how surprising a form. Beneath all his bravado Dubuffet turned out to have reinvigorated the ancient categories of art—the portrait that is searching but never merely malicious, the still life of familiar objects, the townscape that manifests a novelist's eye for detail.

That art should start again from zero was the concern of another artist in Paris in the late 1940s. Alberto Giacometti's was not a new name; as we have seen, his gift for the invention of cryptic and poetical objects had given him a place all his own in the history of Surrealism. But when Giacometti returned to Paris from his native Switzerland in 1945 he brought with him a new preoccupation, a new kind of physicality in sculpture, and an existential view of "the masterpiece." "Existential" was everyone's favorite adjective in Paris at that time; and it referred not only to the philosophy which was associated primarily with the name of Jean-Paul Sartre but, more colloquially, to the belief that in all human enterprises the odds are stacked against us and that all we can do is to play a losing game as lucidly as possible. This belief related exactly to the conditions of life in German-occupied France; and it found a most vivid outlet in such key works of the time as Sartre's play *No Exit* and Albert Camus's novel *The Stranger.* ("On Joue Perdant"—"You Can't Win"—is a classic title of the period.) But it had also a more general implication: that our century has eaten away at beliefs once taken for granted—the unity of human personality, the unity of matter, the unity of space and time—and that it is the role of art to come to terms with that erosion.

This is where Giacometti came in. Ever since he had read Nietzsche and Schopenhauer at the age of 12, he had been familiar with the tragic sense of human destiny which was fundamental to everyday life in France between 1940 and 1945. Nobody was more inventive than he when it came to finding a metaphor for imminent doom; we remember, here, the *Woman with Her Throat Cut* of 1932. But when that doom became a fact of political history with the coming to power of Hitler in Germany in 1933, Giacometti began to turn to quite another aspect of art.

"I knew that one day," he said later, "I'd have to sit down on a stool in front of a model and copy what I saw." His colleagues among the Surrealists were appalled—"As if everyone didn't know what a head is!" was André Breton's reaction—but to Giacometti it seemed that the most adventurous thing which remained for art to do was to reinvent the idea of likeness. On this one card, as Simone de Beauvoir said in her memoirs, he staked everything. He sat down and tried to say exactly what it was like to be in the presence of another human being. And he tried to do it as if no one had ever done it before: to start from zero. He did it, as he said himself, "with no hope of succeeding." What do we really see? What do we mean by likeness? What are we to do with the formless, blubberlike space which separates us from the person we are looking at? How can we possibly recapture the total experience? What if the sculpture, even if passable in itself, is falsified by its relation to the world around it? These were the problems which Giacometti tried to deal with. While dealing with them from 1935 to 1947 he never had an exhibition. Nothing satisfied him: his aim was, as Sartre wrote, to "cut the fat off space" until only the lean meat of experience was left; unlearning was as important as learning, in this context, and the work was bound to go through some peculiar phases. (Among other things, it got very small: the complete surviving work of the years 1942–45 could be transported in six matchboxes.)

It was as a result of these preoccupations that Giacometti eventually found three-dimensional equivalents for things that sculpture had not previously dealt with: the fugacity of sense-impressions, for instance, the unstable or at any rate unseizable nature of human personality, and the arbitrary deformations which are imposed on the human figure by memory, by its surroundings at any given time, or by the chance involvements of looking. We can see today that the break with the sculpture of the past was not as complete as it once seemed; the *Man Pointing* of 1947 had a look of Rodin, for instance. Nor did Giacometti

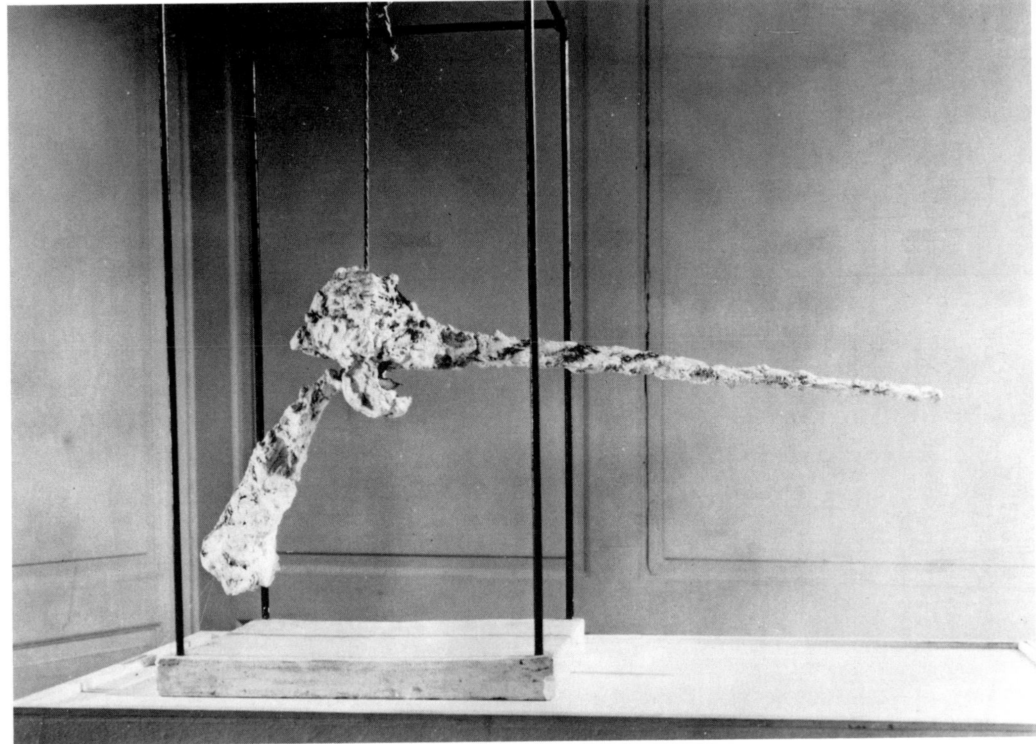

Alberto Giacometti. *The Nose.* 1947. Plaster, paint and iron, 32¾ × 16¾ × 16 inches. Alberto Giacometti Foundation. Deposed at the Kunstmuseum, Basel

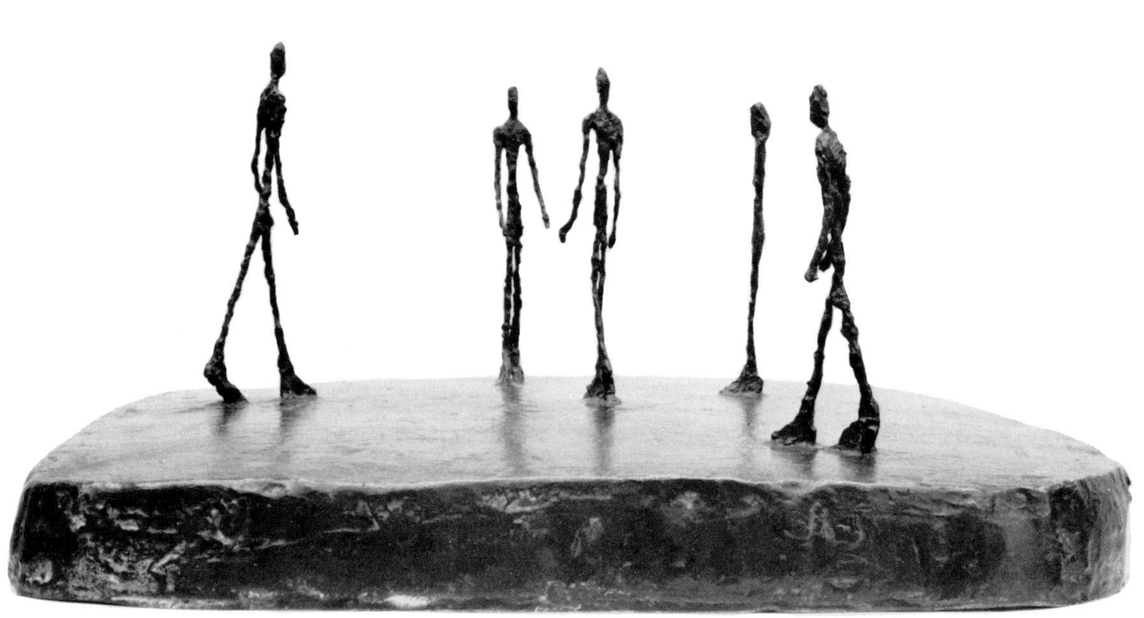

Alberto Giacometti. *City Square.* 1948. Bronze, 8 ½ × 25⅜ × 17¼ inches. The Museum of Modern Art, New York. Purchase

lose altogether the Gogol-like feeling for the grotesque which had marked some of his Surrealist pieces; the plaster version of *The Nose,* 1947, is a telling example of this. But in general what Giacometti had to say about the poignancy and the incompleteness of human relations was altogether new—as were, equally, his ways of saying it. Big-city life looks different when we have seen Giacometti's *City Square,* 1948; and as for the act of offering oneself, whether from love or for money, it was reimagined in the *Four Figures on a Pedestal* of 1950, just as it had been reimagined in Manet's *Olympia.* "Here we are. What are you going to do about it?" is what the four girls have to say: as with Dubuffet, the central themes of European art are recalled and furthered, even if the immediate obsessions are of an unprecedented sort.

Giacometti was the last person to make claims for his own work—he would invariably say, in fact, that it was a disaster from start to finish—but in his actions he was true to the European notion that a career in art should be cumulative and that ideally the work should grow in weight, and in density, and in its power of commitment, year by year. The remains of a great name were not enough; recruitment was for life, or not at all. This was what Matisse had believed, and Braque, and Klee. It was what Picasso lived up to, with a determination to put all of himself on record, no matter what the consequences. It was what Piet Mondrian thought, too; and of the Europeans who came to live in the United States in the 1940s it was perhaps Mondrian who best exemplified the principle—one could almost say the duty—of continual growth.

Mondrian was quite specific on this point. Already in 1924 he had written, "We are at a turning point in the history of culture. We are at the end of everything *old,* in a total and all-comprehensive sense. The divorce between the old and the new is now absolute and definitive." In 1942, when he was living in New York, he wrote: "Art must not only move parallel to human purposes. It must advance ahead of them." He believed, with the Indian mystic Krishnamurti, that it was the duty of every man to be "a force for evolution," and to do what he could to bring about a better world. "It is in human nature," Mondrian said toward the end of his life, "to love a static balance; the great struggle, and the one which every artist must undertake, is to annihilate a static equilibrium."

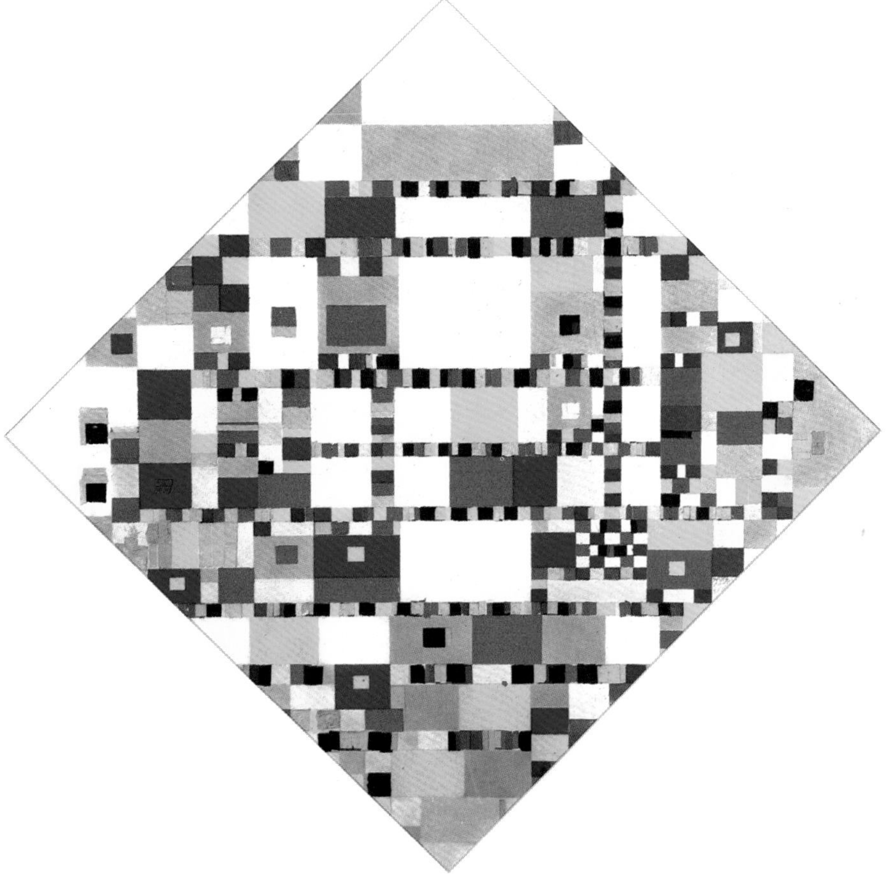

Piet Mondrian. *Victory Boogie-Woogie.* 1943–44. Oil on canvas, 70¼ × 70¼ inches (on the diagonal). Mr. and Mrs. Burton Tremaine, Meriden, Conn.

Mondrian had always abhorred "a static balance" in his own work. To avoid it, he went to enormous though largely invisible pains, working over and over until the finished painting was at every point the expression of a free man's hand—and, beyond that, of a free man's existence in the world. When he arrived in the United States he took the risk that every exile takes: that of total disorientation. There were Europeans in New York at that time who ate exiles' food, read exiles' newspapers, chased all over town for exiles' tobacco, and sought no company but that of other exiles. Mondrian was the opposite. "I feel here is the place to be," he said in 1943, "and I am becoming an American citizen. Where you live you belong to it, and when you feel a place is the nearest to you, you should become part of it."

Mondrian saw the new as a process of continual evolution. When he lived in New York, he felt that the best way for him to "advance ahead of human purposes" was to annihilate the "static equilibrium" which for many years had characterized the means which he allowed himself: the rectangular areas of red, blue and yellow, separated from one another by unbroken black lines of varying thicknesses. What if the black lines were to go, and unbroken lines of pure color—still red, blue and yellow—were to be allowed to overlap? What if he were to move on from there and work from a completely new constituent unit, the small square or rectangle, while retaining the linear crisscross as the basic compositional schema? Would not these changes correspond to evolutionary developments in other domains of life?

Behind these thoughts lay the conviction that life could still be mastered. This has now become something of a historical curiosity: a belief that it is very difficult to put forward with confidence. In the 17th century, and even in the 18th, people believed that everything worth knowing could be put within the covers of a single publication. Nor need that publication overtax a trained intelligence. It was in this belief that the Encyclopedia of Diderot and d'Alembert began publication in 1751. Everything was in that book, from the best way to make a pair of gloves to the latest thing in scientific research. Such a project today would make no sense. Not only is there more to know than any one person can encompass, but mankind has gone so far wrong in so many directions that it may already be too late to arrest the consequences of our errors. Life may be not only unmastered but unmasterable. The evolution which Mondrian believed in may lead only toward disaster. The role of the artist may become purely consolatory: that of a cool-fingered nurse at the bedside of someone who will never recover.

This was not how it looked at the time of Mondrian's death in February, 1944. But, given the premonitory nature of art, we should not see it as a mark of old age and declining health that Mondrian in more than one case was unable to complete his New York paintings. They were more complex than any he had attempted before—in fact they make many of his paintings of the 1920s and early '30s look almost epigrammatic—and they raised problems of resolution which it remained for a later generation to tackle completely. But their incompleteness was not of the kind that halted Michelangelo when he was carving his late *Pietà*, or of the kind that brought Haydn to a stop after the first two movements of his last string quartet. It was an echo of that incapacity to bring great undertakings to a formal conclusion which is one of the marks of this century. In this context we remember Arnold Schoenberg, who broke off his opera *Moses and Aaron* at the end of act II; Marcel Duchamp, who never quite finished the *Large Glass;* Ezra Pound, with his open-ended series of *Cantos;* Robert Musil, whose three-volume novel, *The Man without Qualities,* ends in midair. These were not men of puny energies; they had an intimation that a time was coming when the world could no longer be mastered, and that for that reason the 19th-century ideal of the well-rounded masterpiece was no longer true to the facts of life. Marcel Proust may have been the last man in history to undertake a complete survey of life as it presented itself to a supremely intelligent observer and bring it to a majestic and shapely conclusion; and he was only able to do it from a point of view that was by turns stoical and deeply pessimistic.

Mondrian had quite other ideas, and at the end of his life he wanted to devise a more complex metaphor for the encounters, the misadventures and the mutual accommodations of which life is made up. Once or twice, he succeeded. Art exists, as we know, to negotiate with life on our behalf, and if possible to come to terms with it in ways that will help us live. But if those negotiations cannot be brought to a successful conclusion, it is the duty of the artist to bring back a true bill: an unfinished work in which we glimpse both the nobility of the initial program and the point beyond which no one, no matter how gifted, could go further. That is the significance of Mondrian's unfinished paintings.

Art as an instrument of mediation between ourselves and the world was never in safer hands than during the first half of this century. Modern art as it then existed was the quintessence of modernity, if by modernity we mean an alert, resourceful and unprejudiced enquiry into those aspects of life which are specifically of our own day. But there is a fundamental difference between the art of the first half of this century and the art of earlier periods of high achievement. If we look at the art of the Italian Renaissance, or at Baroque art, or at Neo-Classical or Romantic art, we can go quite a long way down the ladder and still find work that commands our interest and our respect. The little masters of 17th-century Holland are not in the class of Rembrandt or Cuyp or Frans Hals, but they are good enough to look at, and to think about, and to talk about, year after year. Minor artists in these periods were lifted above and beyond themselves by collective and impersonal forces: a shared level of technical proficiency, a shared and luxuriant subject matter, a shared sense that art was speaking for the age in a way that nothing else did, a documentary interest now taken over by other forms of expression. We have none of these things. Such is our belief in individual and inimitable genius that, by definition, only a very few people at any one time can be accepted as artists of consequence. When André Gide was the most famous writer in Europe in the mid-1940s, he wrote that "the world will be saved by one or two people." Gide was born in 1869 and was the contemporary, therefore, of Matisse and Proust. He took it for granted, as they did, that the burdens of art and literature would be shouldered for eternity, as they had been shouldered in his own long lifetime, by "one or two people." He also believed that that elite could not, in the nature of things, be enlarged.

It was then taken for granted that the finite and stationary structure was the highest form of art. When Matisse and Picasso and Braque and Mondrian painted their last pictures, the norms to which they conformed were exactly what they had been in the days of Raphael and Titian. If it surprised Marshall McLuhan that the form of the printed page should not have changed in the five centuries that had passed since the printing of the Gutenberg Bible, it should have been equally surprising to those who cared about such things that the formats and the materials in use among the First New York School in 1947–52 were virtually identical with those of the panoramic landscapes of Rubens.

If this was taken as perfectly natural, it was in part because the work in question was so good as to delay any enquiry as to whether other formats and other materials would not be more apt for the time. It was also because the best new art still had, at most, the kind of almost clandestine success which had been the lot of serious new art since the time of the first Impressionist exhibition in 1874. There was continuity in that fact. Not only was art being made by "one or two people," but it was being admired and bought by one or two people, just as D.-H. Kahnweiler had only one or two clients when he began to show Cubist paintings in Paris in 1908.

And there was, finally, the question of quality. Quality is what matters most in new art, and it is the only sure guarantee for its continuance. Where quality is present in a very high degree, it usually results from a secret alliance with the past. That alliance may be concealed, as it was when Dubuffet literally dragged painting through the mud with his Corps de Dame series in 1950, or when the English painter Francis Bacon around the same time was producing what were then regarded as gratuitous scenes of horror, or when Roy Lichtenstein said that his ambition had been to paint pictures which were so despicable that nobody would put them on the wall. The secret was well kept in all three cases; but each had used a hot line to the past, even so.

Dubuffet had things to say about women's bodies that at first glance seemed merely coarse and derisive; but in point of fact he had truths to tell that had not been told in art before, and the final effect of these truths was to heal and not to wound. History caught up with Francis Bacon when every newspaper in the world carried photographs—presidential candidates in full spate, Adolf Eichmann on trial in his glass box in Jerusalem, unnamed prisoners in their cells—that looked like nothing so much as diluted Bacon. Before long it was clear, moreover, that Bacon's affinities were as much with Old Master painting as with the purely instinctive procedures which he freely acknowledged. Bacon in the 1970s was out to combine the grand formal statements of Old Master painting with a continual awareness of the imagery that is fed into us in our every waking moment: the police photographs, the standard portraits of political leaders (many times life-size), the discarded fragments of newsprint, the raised oval that sets the scene for high drama in theaters all over the

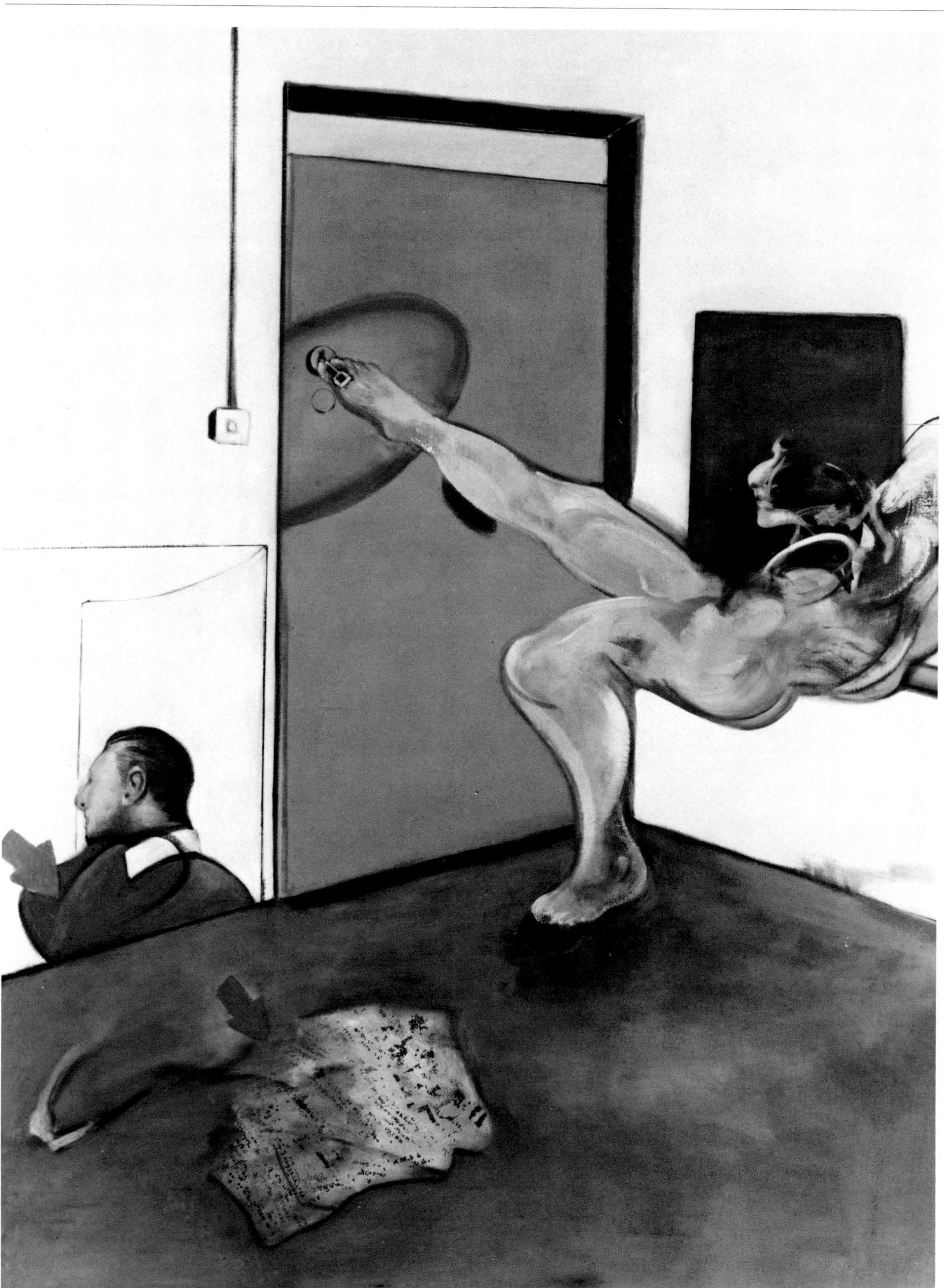

Francis Bacon.
Painting. 1978.
Oil on canvas,
6 feet 6 inches × 58 inches.
Private collection

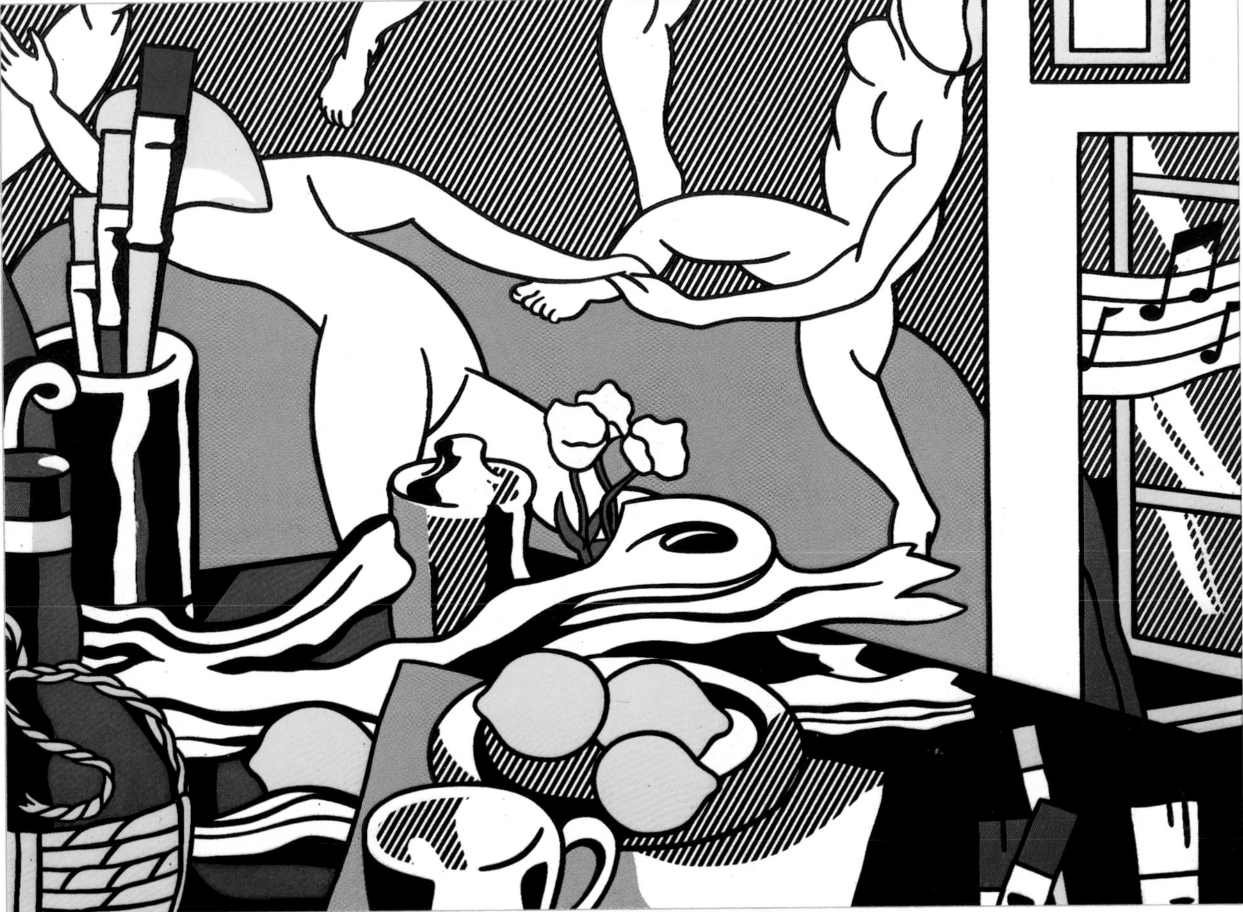

Roy Lichtenstein. *Artist Studio—The Dance.* 1974. Oil and magna on canvas, 8 feet × 10 feet 8 inches. Mr. and Mrs. S. I. Newhouse, Jr., New York

world. He also drew upon the memory of Michelangelo's incomparable evocations of male voluptuousness and upon that element of the irrational that has played so large a part in 20th-century art. From all these he fashioned compound images that move to and fro, like captive tigers, between the known and the unknown, the clear and the ambiguous, the dreamed and the real. After Roy Lichtenstein had been driving conservative connoisseurs to apoplexy for years it turned out that he had developed a subtle amalgam between an analytical awareness of past art and the modification of the image by industrial techniques. Remembering how in a famous painting which is now in the U.S.S.R. Henri Matisse took a part of his *Dance* and made it incidental to another composition, Lichtenstein took up this same idea more than 60 years later. After draining *Dance* of the color, which is its most spectacular attribute, he got the image to work with other elements from Matisse, and with memories of his own earlier preoccupations. In this way he was able to carry on a conversation with one of the supreme masters of modern art. His laconic manner of speech should not delude us as to the daring of the enterprise. The mid-1970s did not witness a more complex pictorial achievement.

In painting, at any rate, the finite and stationary structure—the picture that stayed flat on the wall, complete and in one of a few standard formats—had the advantage that no one had thought of anything better. Throughout the second quarter of this century, painting had all it could do to cope with what had been initiated by "one or two people" between 1900 and 1925. If we take what had been done by Matisse, Picasso, Braque and Mondrian by 1920, and if we add what came in with the Surrealists between 1920 and 1925—the element of automatism, that is to say, and the freedom to draw upon the unconscious—the basic energy sources of painting in the first half of this century are complete.

Such was the momentum of those energies that it was possible to feel even in the 1950s that they were operating in Europe at an undiminished pressure. If painting had to a large extent turned in upon itself for subject matter, it had plenty to turn in upon. If there was self-evidently a big gap between the best artists and the next best, the answer was that the same had been true of the Impressionists, the Post-Impressionists, the Fauves, the Cubists and the Surrealists. Inequality is intrinsic to life. Meanwhile living art as a whole seemed to have reserves of energy which were in no danger of becoming exhausted. As the 1940s turned into the 1950s, it seemed to Europeans and Americans alike that a great era for art might well be at hand. There was an element of self-satisfaction, as always, in prognoses of this kind. But it is not ignoble to wish for our grandchildren the specific excitement, the sense of invigoration and renewal, with which we first set eyes on the last works of Matisse and the first works of Jasper Johns.

Yet we should be rash to count on a continuity of this kind. We have to remember, disagreeable as it may be, that the great age of Athenian drama lasted only 70 years and that the great age of verse drama in England was even shorter. Between the middle age of Haydn and the death of Brahms, sonata form was one of the loftiest modes of human expression; how often since then has it been used to comparable effect? The great ages of Venetian painting, Dutch painting, Flemish painting went out as if at the turn of a switch. We have very good novelists today, but who could argue that the novel as a form has lately been renewed? In every age there are those who agree with Friedrich von Schiller, greatest of German dramatists, that "beauty too must die, though it holds gods and men in thrall." Change is the law of life. What we once needed, we need no more. What we once made, we make no more. Why should modern art be exempt from these cruel laws?

"Because we'd miss it," is one answer. "Because it still has a lot to give us," is another. Both could be upheld throughout the 1950s and '60s. The sheer intensity of intergenerational friction during those decades was significant: the future of art was very much a live issue. Painting might be referred to as "bow and arrow art" by those who thought of the future of art in terms of a typewritten message, a ditch in the desert, a suitcase filled with rotting cheese, or free access to an electronic toyshop; but the thralldom of color, in particular, was as strong as ever. There was color as extension, in the stripe paintings of Kenneth Noland; color liberated from drawing, as in the tinted vapors that were as if breathed onto the canvas by Jules Olitski; and color as conspiracy, in paintings by Ad Reinhardt in which time was recruited as an ally and only a long, slow look would reveal the true nature of the picture.

What people called "the mythic drive behind high art" was still in evidence, and it took many different forms. At a time for instance when abstract painting in the United States was much occupied with unequivocal statements conceived in terms of the straight line, a young British artist was concerned with just the opposite: the extent to which curved lines could act out a complete psychodrama which moved with an intransigent eloquence from initial statement to conflict, and from conflict to resolution. Bridget Riley's *Fall* has nothing to do with the trumpery distractions of "Op" art. It is about the ways in which inner stresses can be faced and worked out to our eventual advantage. It takes the formal language which Edvard Munch used in the background of his *The Shriek*, drains away the emotive color, strips the image of its anecdotal element, and ends up with a statement which is as terse as it is compelling.

The priority of painting was, however, much in dispute throughout the 1960s. There were many reasons for this. There was the argument that it was in sculpture that truly revolutionary work was

Bridget Riley.
Fall. 1963.
Acrylic on board,
55½ × 55¼ inches.
The Tate Gallery,
London

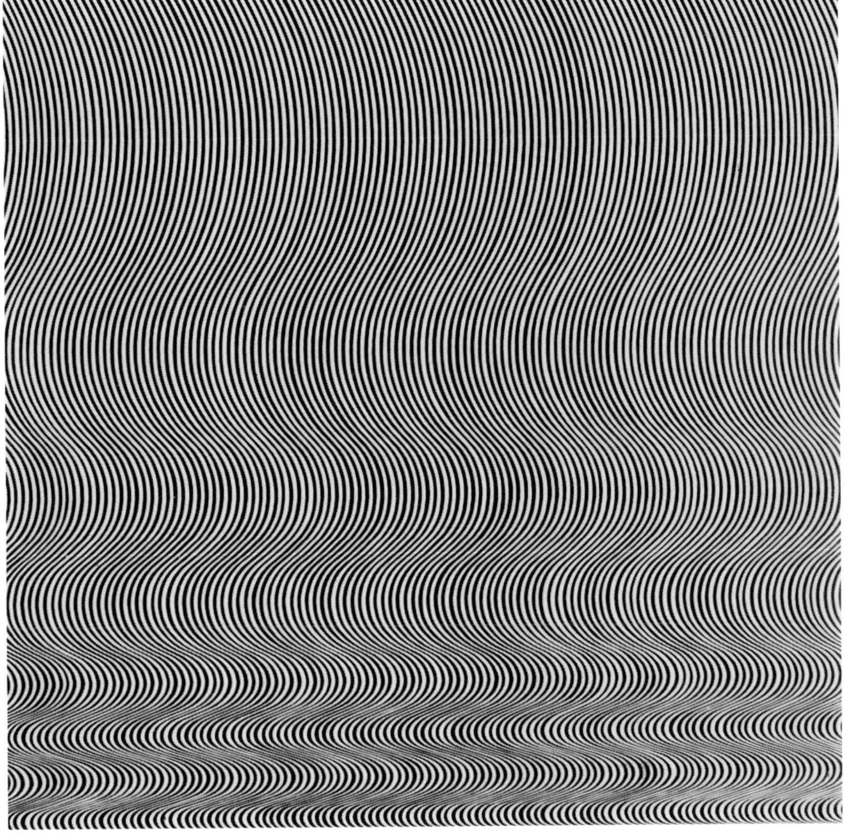

being done. There was the argument that a new world needed not "a new art" but new kinds of art. There was the argument that the fixed and finite physical nature of painting was bound to rule it out as the locus of some of the deepest of human concerns at a time when human expectations and motivations were in a state of radical change. There was the argument that both painting and painters were being exploited by economic forces of a detestable sort. There was the argument, finally, that the self-exploratory activities of painting were entering their terminal phase. Ad Reinhardt, for one, believed that he was painting the last pictures which would ever need to be painted. Frank Stella in the late 1970s renewed the potential of painting by annexing for it the energies inherent in the third dimension. What resulted was a form of painted sculpture which in its impact on the view was both galvanic and unsettling.

There was something in each and all of these arguments. Painters are people, before and after they are painters. They are as dismayed as the rest of us by what is being done to other people, and to the world, in our name. Painting is an edgy, lonely, uncertain business, and it is very disagreeable to feel that the end product of it is being used to make big money fast for a pack of speculators. It is legitimate in times of crisis for a painter to crave something more direct in the way of communication with other people. In bad times the to-and-fro of human contact is more than ever essential to us, and if that to-and-fro can have something of the urgencies of art, so much the better. Traditional art has a traditional audience, and that audience still excludes a large part of the human race. We should not ignore one of the central facts of our time: that new populations and new publics are coming of age all over the world. Such people have the same rights, in matters of art, as the handful of poets, connoisseurs and fellow artists who alone appreciated the best new art before 1914.

So it is natural to speculate as to whether the future of art may not lie in the new forms of communication in which our age has specialized. As recently as 1945 we were still deeply conservative in such matters. The formulas of the art world had set fast, like pack ice, and showed no signs of melting. The rituals of the opera house and the symphony orchestra had not changed for more than half a century. Going to the theater meant sitting in an auditorium in attitudes unchanged since the time of Sophocles and gazing across the footlights at a play that lasted exactly two and a half hours. A book bound in paper had something wrong with it. A phonograph record was both heavy and fragile and stopped after four minutes. Films were something you saw in a movie house; and movie houses, like the Moscow subway, were vast, ornate, and designed to blind the customer to the drabness of life outside.

All these things were accepted as immutable. Yet it took a bare 25 years for us to adapt to improvised theater, aleatory music, free-form architecture, magnetic tapes that run for three hours or more, and dance dramas that owed nothing to the formalized miming of *Swan Lake.* In all these and many other domains we saw what Mondrian had meant when he said almost 50 years earlier that "we are at the end of everything *old.*" Sitting through the 25-minute monologue which constitutes Samuel Beckett's play *Not I,* listening to Karlheinz Stockhausen's electronic *Hymnen,* watching Merce Cunningham and his dance company give a completely new idea of the ways in which life can be spelled out on the stage, we might find it really rather odd that much of painting and sculpture should still be stuck with the materials of Rembrandt and Rodin. Perhaps it is hardly less odd that so many of us should still think

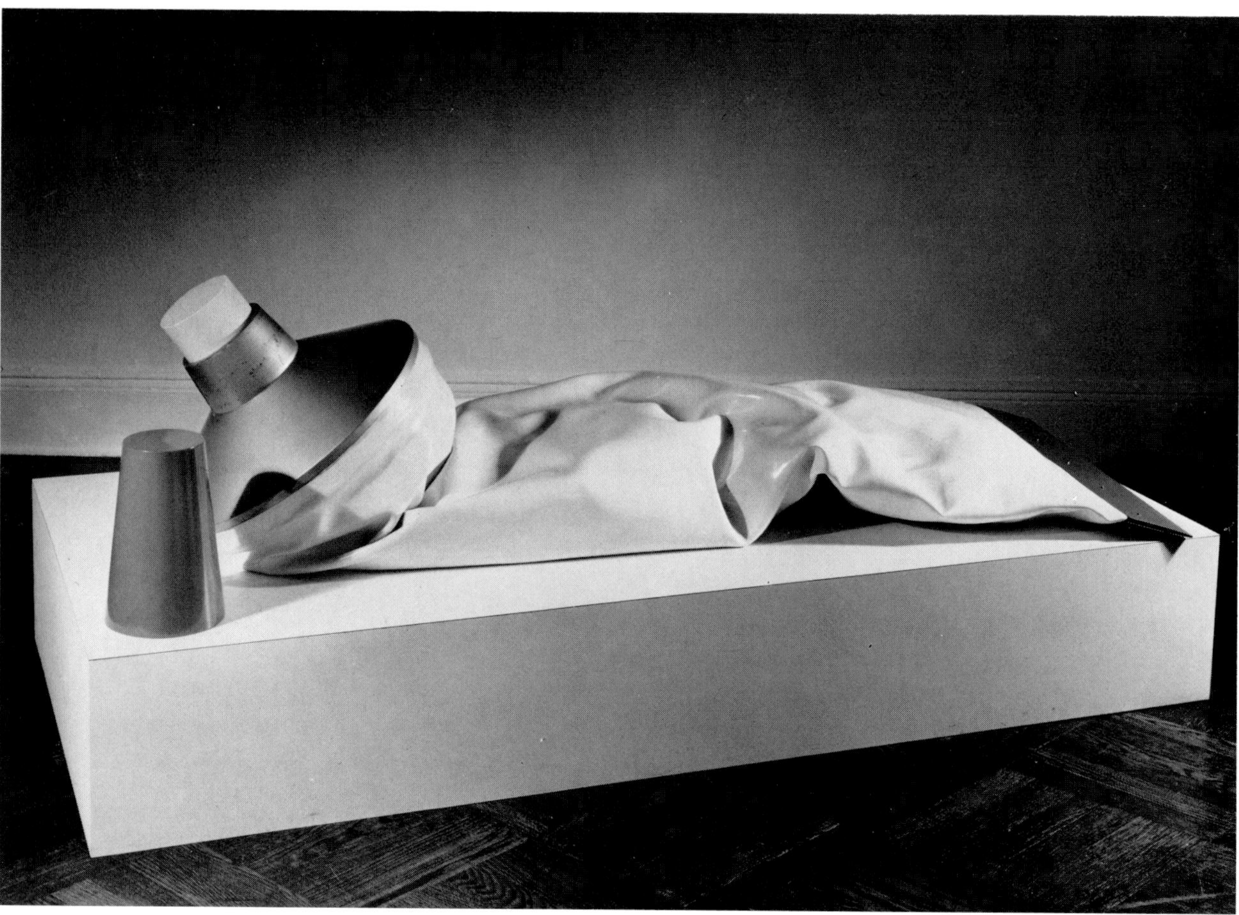

Claes Oldenburg. *Giant Toothpaste Tube.* 1964. Vinyl over canvas filled with kapok, 25½ × 66 × 17 inches. Private collection, Fort Worth, Texas

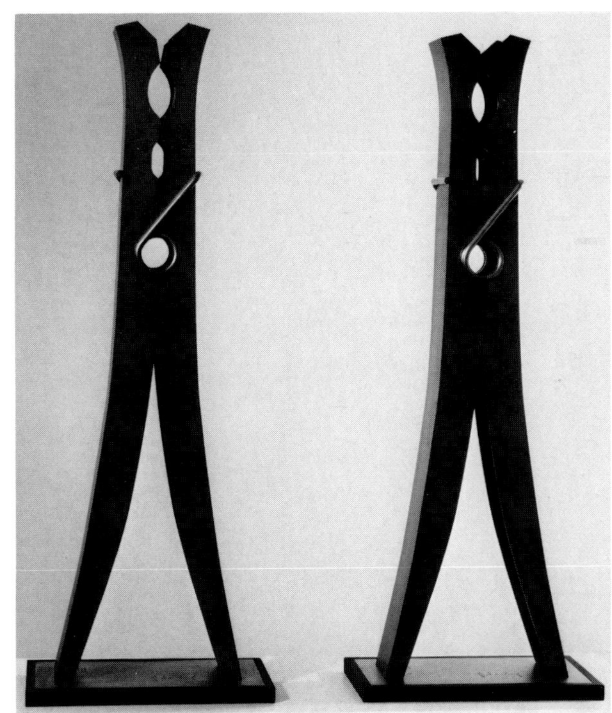

Claes Oldenburg. *Clothespin-4.* 1974. Bronze and steel (edition of 9), 48¾ inches high, including base. Courtesy Leo Castelli Gallery, New York

of painting and sculpture as separate entities, defined once and forever, when we acknowledge that the future of music may depend on new sources of sound and the future of the theater on modes of expression that owe nothing to theater as it was understood by the public of Alfred Lunt and Lynn Fontanne.

What we have witnessed, in this context, is the normalization of the avant-garde on the one hand and the abhorrence of existing conventions on the other. There is nothing new about new sources of sound: the symphony of factory chimneys as it was performed in Russia not long after the Revolution is evidence enough of that. There is nothing new about the boredom which many people feel when faced with the sterotyped subscription concert, the ritual "gallery opening" with its herd of free-loading nonentities, or the evening at the theater which costs a fortune and offers very lean pickings in terms of pleasure or enlightenment. Nor is there anything new about the freedom to restructure the arts, or to borrow freely and at will from one discipline in the service of another. To hear Kurt Schwitters recite his wordless poem was one of the great oratorical experiences of the 1920s and '30s. Poetry has arrogated to itself a total liberty on the page ever since Mallarmé published "Un Coup de Dés" in 1897. The Douanier Rousseau fancied himself as a playwright, and so did Picasso. Kandinsky wrote a drama to be performed by music, light and moving stage parts alone. But all these activities were incidental to a strenuous creativity in other domains; and they were done in a world which had not yet learned to exploit art for immediate advantage.

That is where the difference lies. There is something radically wrong with a world in which the effective life of most new books is between two and three weeks and in which works of art which are part of our universal inheritance can be hidden in vaults until the bankers' consortium which owns them can make a sufficient return on its investment. Things of this kind create a climate in which it is inordinately and unnecessarily difficult to produce good new work. They are the enemies of art; and in the 1960s artists began to fight back in the only way that was available to them—by making art that in one way or another was immune to the system.

The new art in question was of many kinds. Much of it was, and is, no good at all. How could it be otherwise? Art cannot function without an agreed social context. There must be some kind of contract, formulated or not, between the artist and the public which he wishes to reach. Contrary to popular belief, no art of consequence was ever produced in isolation. But there are times when both art and its audience are refugees from an environmental madness: this was the case with Dada in its Swiss and German phases, and it was the case with many manifestations of the new in the 1960s. When Claes Oldenburg set up his "Store" at 107 East Second Street, New York City, in the winter of 1961–62 and sold his simulated ray guns, wedding bouquets, wristwatches, pieces of pie, gym shoes, jelly doughnuts, airmail envelopes and inscribed birthday cakes, as a standard store would sell the real thing, he got under the guard of the system. Art was flourishing, but in what looked to be a nonart situation. Oldenburg had solved one of the central problems of the 1960s: how to make art without falling prey to the system, and he spelled it out in *Store Days* (1967), which deserves to be one of the classic texts of modern literature: "I know," he wrote, "that down to the last simple detail experience is totally mysterious." And he went on to assert an unexpected kinship: "The only person I know that tried to prove the simplest thing in the world, like a piece of candy, was utterly mysterious was Chirico (in his early days)."

Oldenburg in all this was not taking the dignity out of art. He was giving back to everyday objects the dignity which everyday life had taken away from them. "I am for an art," he said, ". . . that does something other than sit on its ass in a museum. I am for an art that grows up not knowing it is art at all, an art given the chance of having a starting point at zero. I am for an art that is smoked, like a cigarette, smells, like a pair of shoes. I am for an art that flaps like a flag, or helps blow noses, like a handkerchief. I am for an art that is put on and taken off, like pants, which develops holes, like socks, which is eaten, like a piece of pie, or abandoned with great contempt, like a piece of shit."

Nothing could be less like a recipe for an old-style masterpiece. But, as with Dubuffet, high art ended by getting its way; and those tiny and resolutely demotic pieces by Claes Oldenburg have an imaginative vitality which is very rare in mainstream scupture of their period.

Initially in 1964 the *Giant Toothpaste Tube* came across as an act of defiance. What could such an object have to do with high art? But in time the almost empty tube of toothpaste took shape in our minds as a traditional reclining figure. And if the detached top of the tube still contradicted this—well, there remained the parallel of the Crusaders' tombs of the 14th century in Europe, where the dead warrior was sometimes portrayed with his helmet at his side. Besides, Oldenburg knew that changes of scale always bring with them changes of implication. The humble clothespin when magnified and cast in bronze and steel assumes an imperious hominoid look, as if it were halfway through changing into the image of a born leader of men, with his two feet set firmly apart, his left hand tucked into his belt and his big ears cocked to catch the latest news. The toothpaste piece and the clothespin piece are ten years apart, but the aesthetic behind them is the same.

That we have to give the name of "sculpture" to the *Giant Toothpaste Tube* is in itself instructive, by the way. If we consider that that same word is applied to a Calder mobile, a fluorescent light piece by Dan Flavin, a totem in stainless steel by David Smith and a length of felt hung from a nail by Robert Morris, it will be clear that the word "sculpture" now has wider connotations than the word "painting." The emancipation of sculpture is one of the discreeter romances in the cultural life of our century.

Sometimes the new sculpture had a long ancestry. At a first glance Donald Judd's *Untitled*, 1970, might seem to be a work without precedent in art, so completely does it outlaw the traditional elements of sculpture: variety, surprise, "composition," personal handling and evidence of effort. But in point of fact Judd here draws upon the measured regularity and the austere plainness of statement which are fundamental to a certain specifically American aesthetic. That aesthetic turns up all over the place: in the high-backed chair made in the first half of the 19th century, in the Navajo blanket made some 50 years later, and in Charles Sheeler's painting of 1925, where the stately movement of the staircase is echoed in the ribbing of the ceiling on the right and turns up all over again in the roof. A recurrent America stands, therefore, behind Judd's sculpture, for all its deliberate modernity.

Meanwhile there was still a demand for public sculpture. Sculpture in a public context has both advantages and drawbacks. It was a drawback to its emancipation that for centuries it had a clearly defined public function. There are millions of people on this earth who have never seen an original painting of any quality; but it is difficult to live in a big city anywhere in the world and not have daily contact with sculptures to which at any rate a certain ambition must be conceded. (Even the badness of those sculptures can liberate the imagination; Giorgio de Chirico took a great deal, for instance, from the public monuments of Turin, in Italy, where the 19th century excelled itself in terms of absurdity.) Sculpture is built into big-city experience in a way that other kinds of art are not, and for that reason it has associations with officialdom which have lately fallen into disrepute.

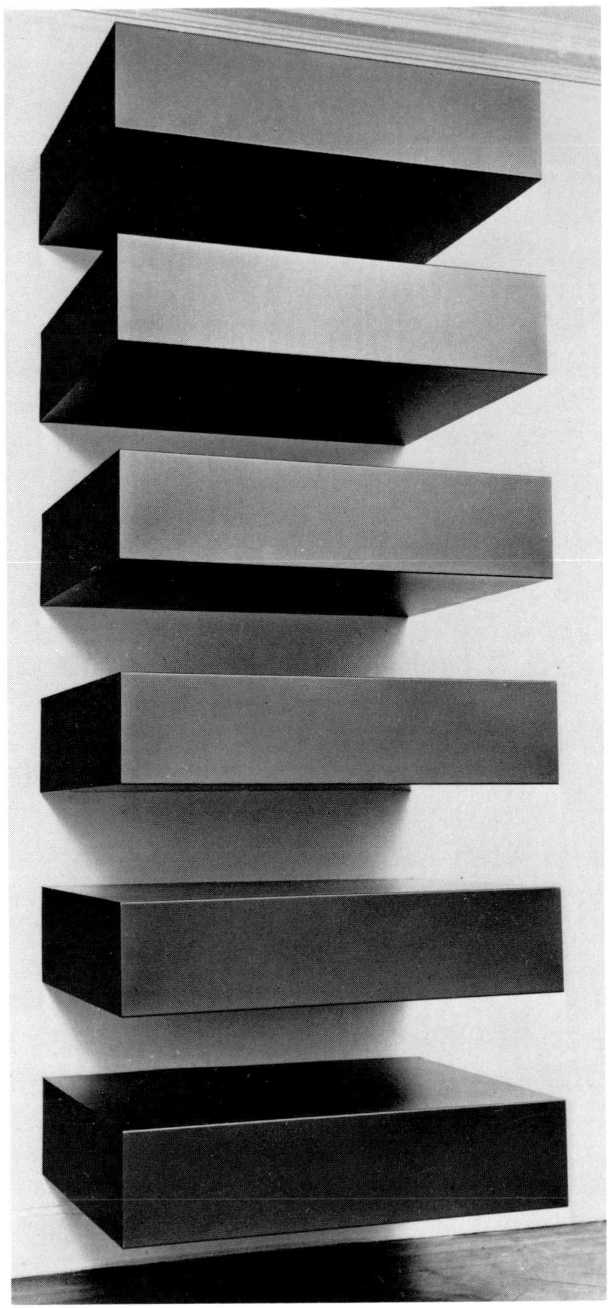

Donald Judd. *Untitled.* 1970. Anodized aluminum, 8 boxes (6 shown), each 9 × 40 × 31 inches. Courtesy Leo Castelli Gallery, New York

As against this, sculpture in a private context is very much a minority art. A picture on the wall is part of an almost universal currency of good living. By contrast, a sculpture in the living room very often causes dismay and embarrassment. Backs can be turned to a bad painting; a bad sculpture sits there and defies us to ignore it. Sculpture is apart from the mainstream of living in ways which ensure for it a certain privacy. Its mutations are not monitored as closely as are the mutations of painting. Until recently there was, moreover, a fundamental untractability about the materials of sculpture; this called for a degree of dedication and perseverance which does not arise in the case of the amateur painter. Making sculpture was real work, and the chances of a happy accident of the kind which enriches the life of the Sunday painter were very small. Sculpture has always had, finally, a magical quality—witness the myth of Pygmalion, the sculptor, whose statue of Galatea came to life—and the traditional sculptor stood next to God in his ability to create an unmistakable human being where none had existed before.

This apartness and this implicitly superior status have continued into our own time. Sculpture is a crusading art. The degradation of public sculpture in the second half of the 19th century drove the more thoughtful among younger sculptors to renew and purify the sculptural act. Raymond Duchamp-Villon, the brother of Marcel Duchamp, saw it as fundamental before 1914 that sculpture should be "a reaction against our business era, where money is the master." The great painter-sculptors—Degas, Matisse, Boccioni, Picasso, Giacometti—used sculpture with a freedom and an audacity and a determination to try something quite new. As for the sculptor-sculptors —Medardo Rosso, Naum Gabo, Julio Gonzalez,

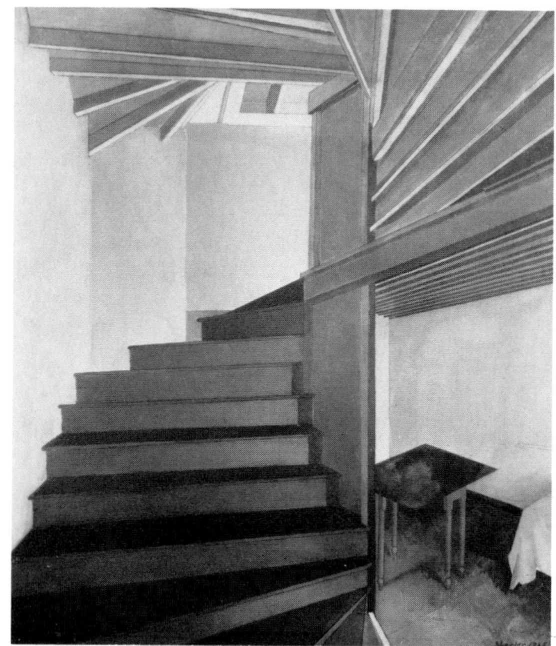

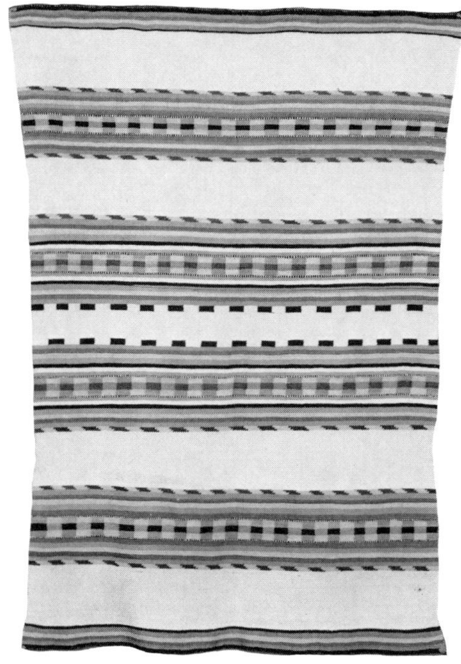

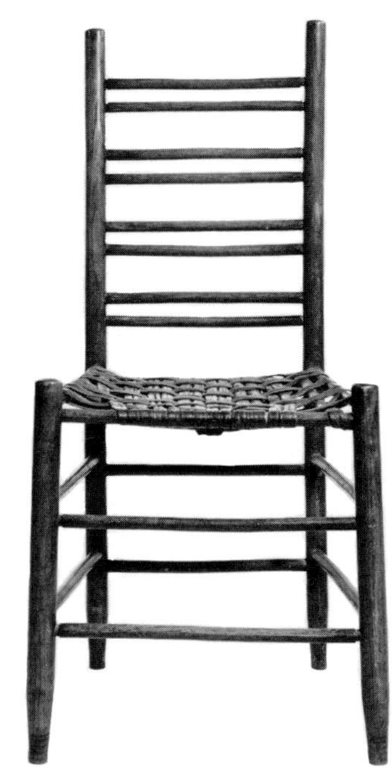

(left)
Charles Sheeler. *Staircase, Doylestown.* 1925. Oil on canvas, 24 × 20 inches. Hirshhorn Museum and Sculpture Garden, Smithsonian Institution, Washington

(center)
Man's Shoulder Blanket. Navajo Indian, 1875–90. Tapestry weaving, wool yarns, 6 feet 8 inches × 52 inches. Museum of Fine Arts, Boston. Gift of John Ware Willard

(right)
Side Chair, from Nacogdoches, Texas. c. 1830–45. Turned ash and elm, with hickory-bark seat. San Antonio Museum Association Collection, San Antonio, Texas

Henry Moore, David Smith, Anthony Caro—they inspired loyalty of a kind which few painters experience. People went to Brancusi's studio in Paris as they would have gone to visit a hermit in the desert. Something fundamental to human dignity was being carried on there: the search for an absolute perfection. In a general way Duchamp-Villon had been quite right when he said in 1913 that "In an era of floating ideas and aspirations, there can be no such thing as a definitive or durable monument"; but this is the sign of a decay in human affairs that must somehow be arrested. Whence the peculiar urgency of modern sculpture at its best; whence, equally, the fascination for sculptors of many kinds, before 1914, of what the art historian Albert E. Elsen has aptly called "the image of the powerful figure whose legs scissor space, whose past and future are measurable only by his tread and not by his name."

If sculpture produced, against all the odds, a definitive and durable monument in the 20th century it was not in the form of a striding figure. Nor did it have the public function which earlier ages had assigned to it. Much of the best sculpture went underground. The full extent of Picasso's activity as a sculptor was not revealed till the 1980s. Matisse's sculpture was always regarded as auxiliary to his painting, though he devoted an immense amount of time to it. Much significant work was lost or destroyed: above all, what was done by Tatlin and others in Russia after 1917. Brancusi's monumental works in Rumania must be the least readily accessible of all the major achievements of modern art. From Medardo Rosso to Joseph Cornell, the making of three-dimensional objects has kept an element of privacy.

Still, there are worse things than privacy when it comes to the making of great art. (When did Cézanne live in the limelight?) Original sculpture in the 20th century had the advantage that no publicity machine was behind it. Brancusi lived off the enthusiasm of "one or two people." Moore in his early 40s could rarely afford the materials for a major work. Henri Laurens lived and died on the edge of penury. David Smith in his studio at Bolton Landing, New York, was never favored (or oppressed, according to one's point of view) by the adulation which surrounded painters without a fraction of his gifts. It would almost be true to say that sculpture in our century has been the secret weapon of art.

This is not a mere form of words. At any time in

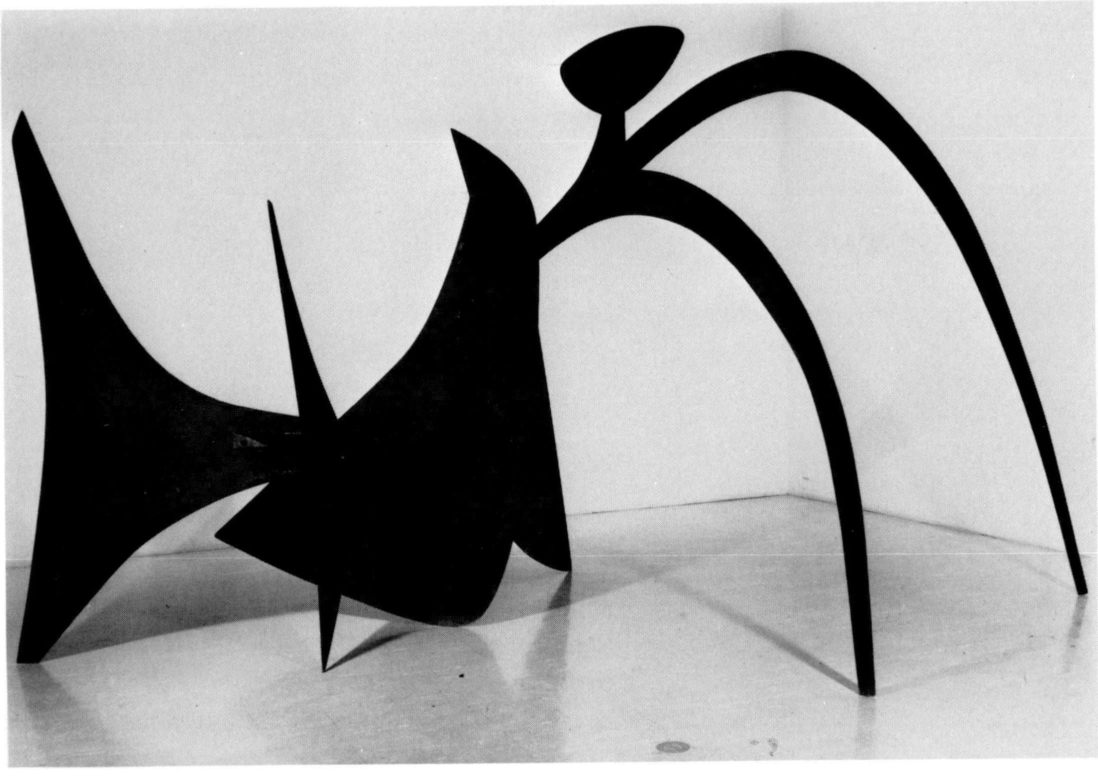

Alexander Calder. *Black Widow.* 1959. Painted sheet steel, 7 feet 8 inches × 14 feet 3 inches × 7 feet 5 inches. The Museum of Modern Art, New York. Mrs. Simon Guggenheim Fund

the recent history of art there is likely to have been one area which functioned as a touchstone of probity. "Drawing is the integrity of art," said Ingres when faced with the rivalry of Delacroix; he meant that drawing was the department of art in which no one can fake. In our own century, painting has carried the banner for modernism; and it is with painting above all that the public associates the idea of the new. But it can be argued that on many an important occasion sculpture darted ahead of painting. And sculpture endures to this day a degree of physical hostility which painting is spared; sculptures in public places attract a peculiarly mindless hostility. Sculpture is difficult to show and difficult to talk about. Sculptors incline to be pugnacious—often with good reason—and even if many bronzes are now cast in quite large editions there is still something about the firsthand experience of sculpture which cannot be counterfeited. Sculpture is immune, therefore, from the vulgarization which lies in wait for painting.

At the same time, a bad sculpture is one of the most blatant forms of environmental pollution. Thomas Mann in his essay on Wagner said that no one can make himself smaller than his true size—the point being that Wagner could not plan a light romantic comedy without turning out *Die Meistersinger,* which runs for five hours—and it is equally true that no one can make himself larger than his true size; a big sculpture which doesn't come off is intolerable. The case for the moral grandeur of sculpture in our century rests on the number and scope of the conventions which had to be overthrown before sculpture could regain its dignity. David Smith put the sculptor's point of view when talking to Thomas B. Hess in 1964. "Sculpture has been a whore for many ages," he said. "It had to be a commissioned thing. Sculpture was not sculpture till it was cast in bronze. Before it was cast, the man who paid for it had certain reservations and designations as to subject matter."

Initially, before 1914, the dignity of sculpture was reclaimed by an isolated piece here and there. Later, where a large body of work existed, it was

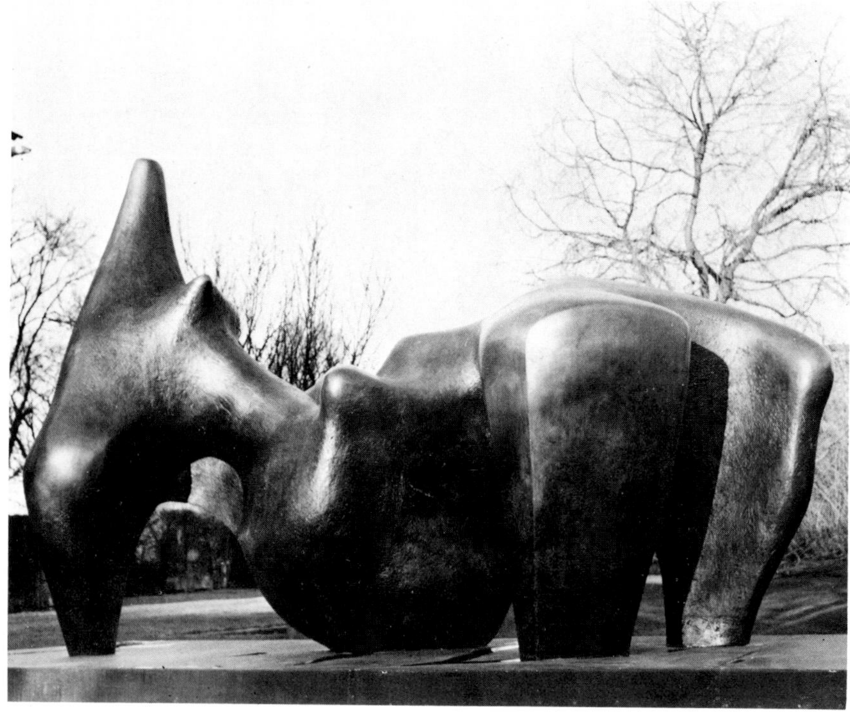

Henry Moore.
Reclining Figure.
1969–70.
Bronze, 13 feet long.
Schlesinger Organization, Johannesburg

overshadowed by the priority accorded to painting. If sculpture impinged on the general consciousness, it was likely to be in the form of artifacts remote from our own culture, such as those from pre-Columbian Mexico, from Benin or from Easter Island. One of the novelties of the last 50 years, in this context, is the emergence of modern sculptors with whom a whole generation could identify itself. Instances of this are Alexander Calder, Henry Moore and David Smith, all three of whom in their work got through to the public with a physical immediacy that is very rare.

Something in this is owed to personality. Calder, Moore and Smith come across in their work as men of open, straightforward, downright character, with a contempt for anything mean or evasive: whence comes our confidence in them as human beings. When Calder first made inert materials get up and dance, the world danced with them. Some of the ideas in his mobiles may have come from Joan Miró, whom Calder knew well for many years; but Calder was the master of a dynamic, free-running humor, and his feeling for life was distinctively that of the most glorious type of American. Quite apart from the contagious amusement of his work, he was in himself one of humanity's more presentable possessions.

At a time in history when it was possible to despair of human nature, Henry Moore likewise said in effect, "There is an alternative." Everything in his experience of childhood, everything in his education, everything in his watchful and undeceived understanding of adult life has suggested to him that if human nature is given the right opportunities it may even now redeem itself. This has lately been a very difficult case to argue. A discouraged "No" has been much easier to justify than a constructive "Yes"; and in Moore's affirmative position there was something of that earlier epoch in which D. H. Lawrence in one way and H. G. Wells in another looked forward to a radical change in the prospects for humanity. Lawrence in particular wanted people to know their rights, as human beings, and to act upon them. He wasn't too far, in this, from Henry Moore.

Moore throughout his long career has functioned as a concerned citizen. In the 1930s he was a master of the cryptic three-dimensional image that spoke for what was difficult and irreducible in the act of making our way through life. He gave full and free expression to the healing quiet of the hearth, in later times, but he also went on tussling away at the metaphorical implications of the human body in their relation to present-day concerns. Just as Rodin in the late 19th century was able on occasion to sound the note of national pride with a fiery awareness, Moore in more complicated and ambiguous situations was able to draw new echoes from our human apparatus. He fought, for instance, to make a human figure that was larger than life in more than a literal sense. He aimed to give it overtones of epic endurance, overtones of the bare, rounded headlands of his native Yorkshire, and overtones of a fierce and impulsive sexuality. He had learned from Rodin that when the human body is fragmented it can tug at our emotions in a way that is quite special.

In his two- and three-piece sculptures in the 1960s and '70s he often caught the body at a moment of vigorous and decisive action: a moment at which even the light had found it hard to catch up with it. Nor did he shrink from what sometimes seemed to younger people an element of illustration. When he was asked in the mid-1960s to commemorate the completion of the first nuclear chain reaction he came up with an image that was characteristically ambiguous and many-layered in its impact. It had elements of the human skull (shaven, as if for an operation on the brain); of the mushroom cloud which follows an atomic explosion; of the armored head, so often treated by Moore before; and of a form that is both fortress and prison. These were archaic concerns according to more than one reading of the state of sculpture, but Henry Moore addressed himself to them as a whole man who felt it his duty to say what could be said in no other way about a matter of supreme and lasting importance.

No one who has seen David Smith's Medals for Dishonor can doubt that he too had very strong feelings about his duties as a citizen. But he was also a man of panoramic curiosity—"I want to know everything," he once said, "that has ever been known by any man"—and he named among his own sources "the illustrations in the Bible of cuneiform, the Sumero-Akkadian style of writing, and other Mesopotamia Valley cultures." "I have always," he went on, "been more Assyrian than Cubist."

David Smith in this was at one with the major artists of this century, who almost without exception have had allegiances which went far beyond what was customary among the major artists of the past. Where formerly the standard progres-

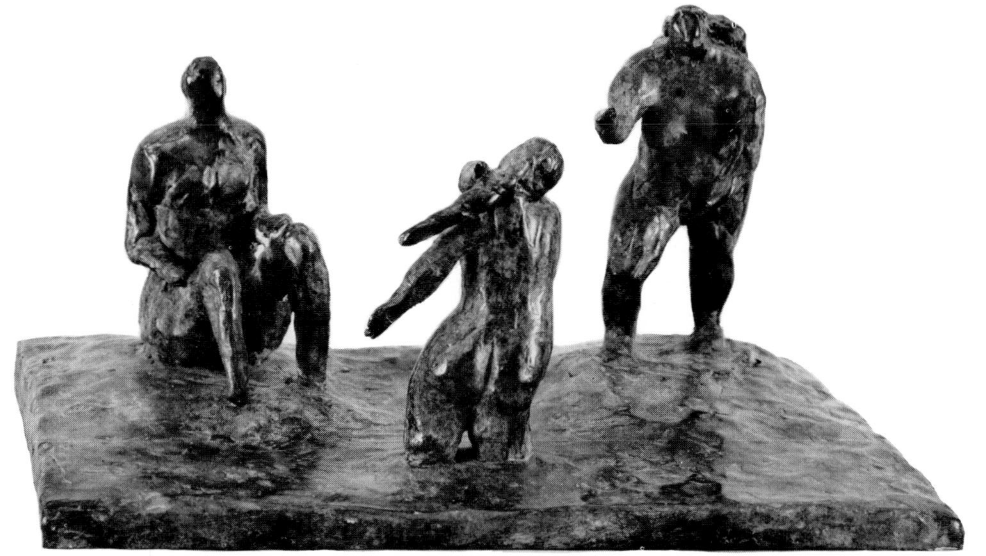

Henry Moore. *Three Bathers after Cézanne.* 1978. Bronze, 6¼ × 11¾ × 8⅝ inches. Private collection, England

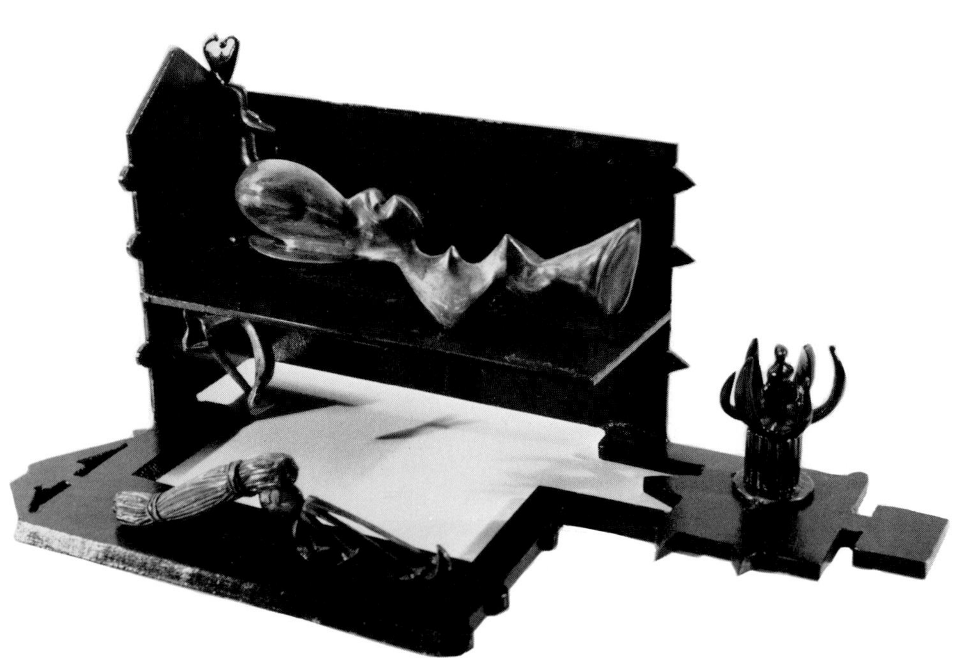

David Smith.
Reliquary House.
1945.
Bronze and steel,
12¼ × 23½ ×
11¾ inches.
Mr. and Mrs. David
Mirvish, Toronto

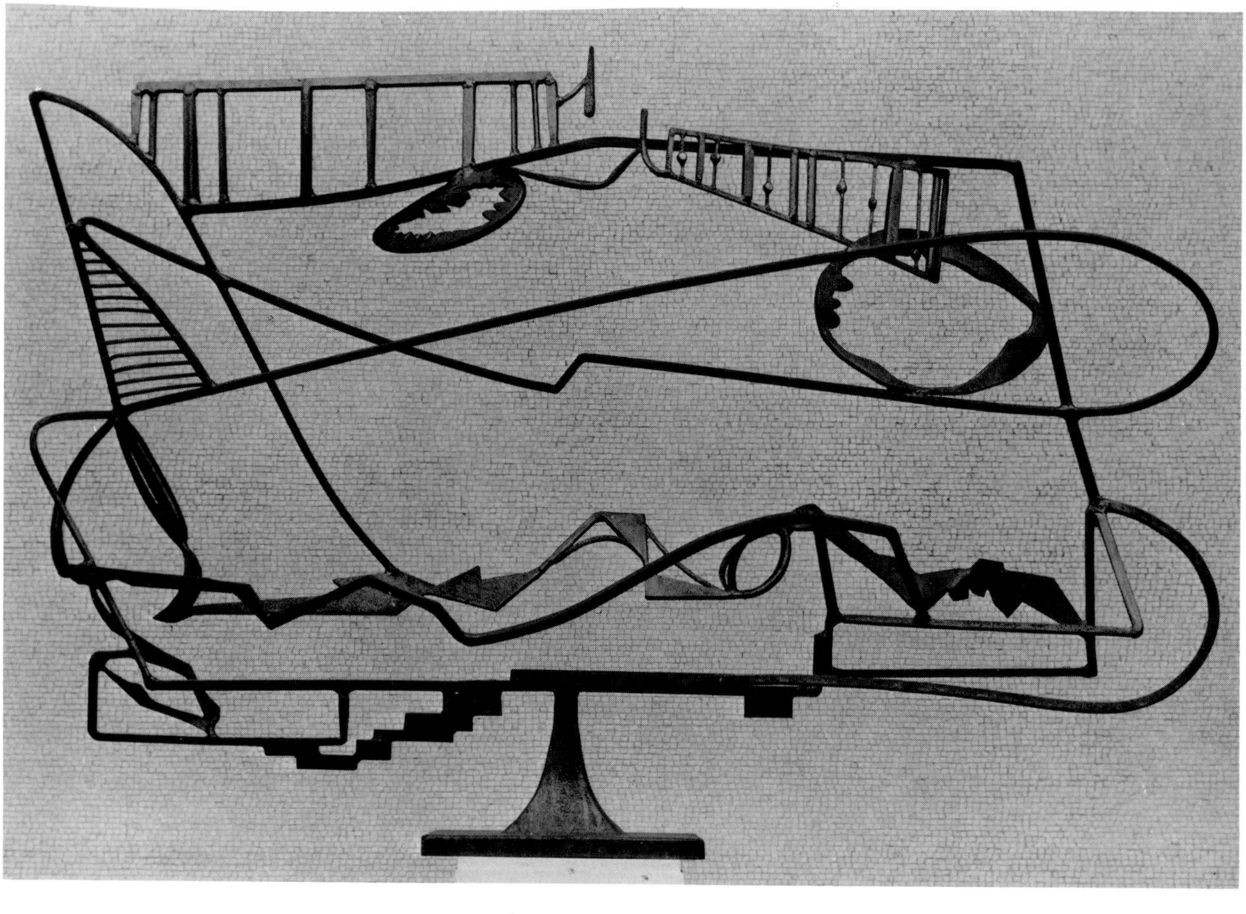

David Smith.
*Hudson River
Landscape.* 1951.
Steel, 6 feet 3
inches long.
Whitney Museum of
American Art, New
York

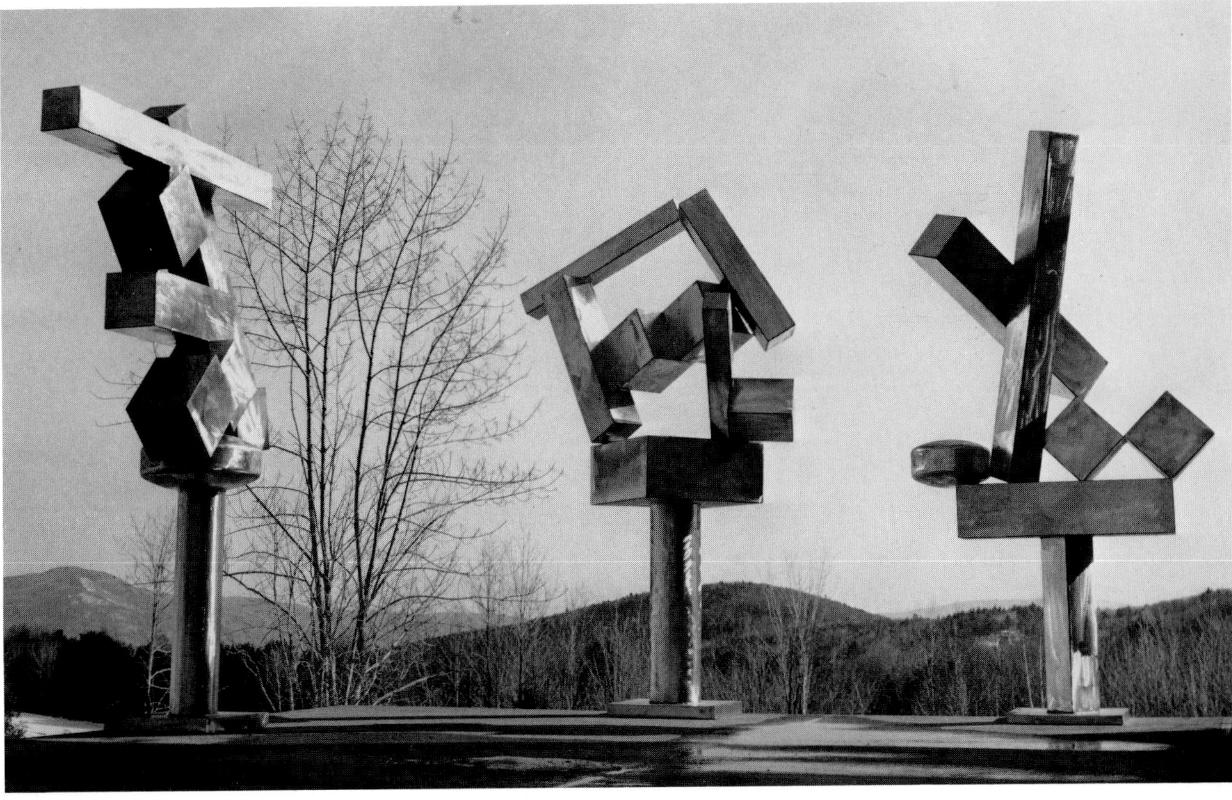

David Smith.
(left)
Cubi XVIII. 1964. Stainless steel, 9 feet 7¾ inches × 21¾ inches × 20¾ inches. Museum of Fine Arts, Boston. Anonymous Centennial gift

(center)
Cubi XVII. 1963. Stainless steel, 8 feet 11¾ inches × 64⅞ inches × 38⅛ inches. Dallas Museum of Fine Arts. Eugene and Margaret McDermott Fund

(right)
Cubi XIX. 1964. Stainless steel, 9 feet 5⅛ inches × 21¾ inches × 20¾ inches. The Tate Gallery, London. Photographed by David Smith at Bolton Landing, N.Y.

sion from classical antiquity to the Middle Ages and on through the Renaissance was thought to fulfill all needs, in our own century the mix is altogether more resourceful. There was something fundamental, inescapable, about the importance of Islamic art for Matisse, ancient Iberian art for Picasso, Russian folk art for Kandinsky, late 19th-century illustrated magazines for Max Ernst, American Indian sand-painting for Jackson Pollock. But David Smith had the specifically American characteristic that he wanted to bring the business of making art into line with the business of everyday life. Art was not something which called for a specialized posture. Smith wanted, on the contrary, to "draw in proportion to my own size, to draw as freely and as easily, and with the same movements, that I dressed myself with, or that I ate with, or worked with in the factory." What counted was not only the quality of the thing done: it was the quality of the stance before life—or, as Smith put it in 1960—"the freedom of gesture and the courage to act."

Sometimes, as in the *Reliquary House* of 1945, Smith set up a complete world of his own imagining. A reliquary in medieval times was a miniature storehouse in which small objects of particular significance were preserved. Smith had pasted a working drawing for a reliquary of this sort into one of his sketchbooks, and it served as the point of departure for one of the most enigmatic of 20th-century works of art. As elucidated by the art historian Edward Fry in his book on Smith, it was conceived as an opened-out model of a house, in the tradition of Giacometti's *The Palace at 4 A.M.* In his notes Smith urged himself to "put the hopes upstairs, put the wars below, and hang the past from the ceiling." The "hopes" in question related to the extravagantly voluptuous bronze figure of a naked woman who reclines in the upper part of the house; the "wars" to the conflict between man and woman which is symbolized by the struggle between the bundle of sticks (male) and the schematic image of the moon and its rays (female). (Smith derived the forms of this struggle from a

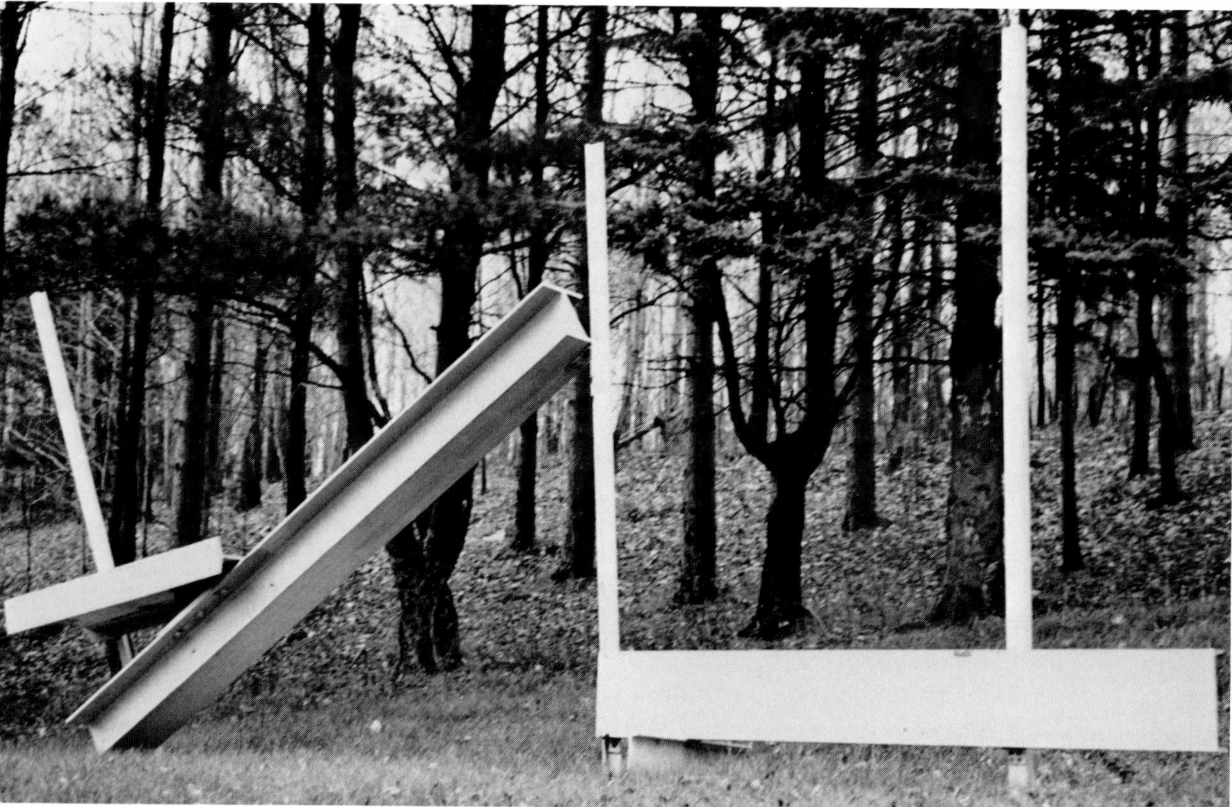

Anthony Caro.
Atlantic. 1962.
Steel, painted green,
10 feet 7½ inches
× 25 feet × 18
inches.
Kenneth Noland,
South Salem, N.Y.

French 17th-century engraving.) The "past" hangs from the ceiling in the form of a private symbol for a locked (and therefore inaccessible) woman. Smith once drew the opened-out sides of the reliquary (which now lie flat on the floor) as respectively male (to the left) and female (to the right). In completing the sculpture he added, on the female side, a small but perfectly proportioned human form which stands for what can emerge eventually, like a flower from unfolded petals, when the locked woman is unlocked and the male-female conflict is resolved.

Sometimes he drew on everyday experience, with nothing added or fantasticated. While traveling by railroad between Albany and Poughkeepsie, for instance, he habitually made drawings of the view from the window. He liked especially the spectacular view of the Hudson River; and he took note of the rocky banks, the staircaselike steps of land that led down to the water, the meandering movement of the river when its level was low toward the end of winter, and the slow circling of the huge clouds above. In *Hudson River Landscape*, 1951, he synthesized all these things in two-dimensional form with the effect of a man drawing in the air, bending the steel to his will as freely as a landscape draftsman bends the penciled line, and calling upon the memory of natural phenomena to help him to articulate space.

As he grew older, Smith in his art developed an ever-greater power of affirmation. In the last four years of his life (1961–65) he made a long series of monumental sculptures in stainless steel. He used a restricted number of basic forms: the cube, the rectangular flat slab, the cylinder, the circle, the square turned on its side. Most of the Cubi were conceived in frontal terms, and as a rule they greet us in the attitude of a man attempting to stop a runaway train. They celebrate what the poet W. H. Auden called "the vertical man." Though not organized expressly in human terms, they stand for a certain idea of American manhood: one that is free, open, outgoing, erect and not overly complicated. The glint and sparkle of the stainless steel

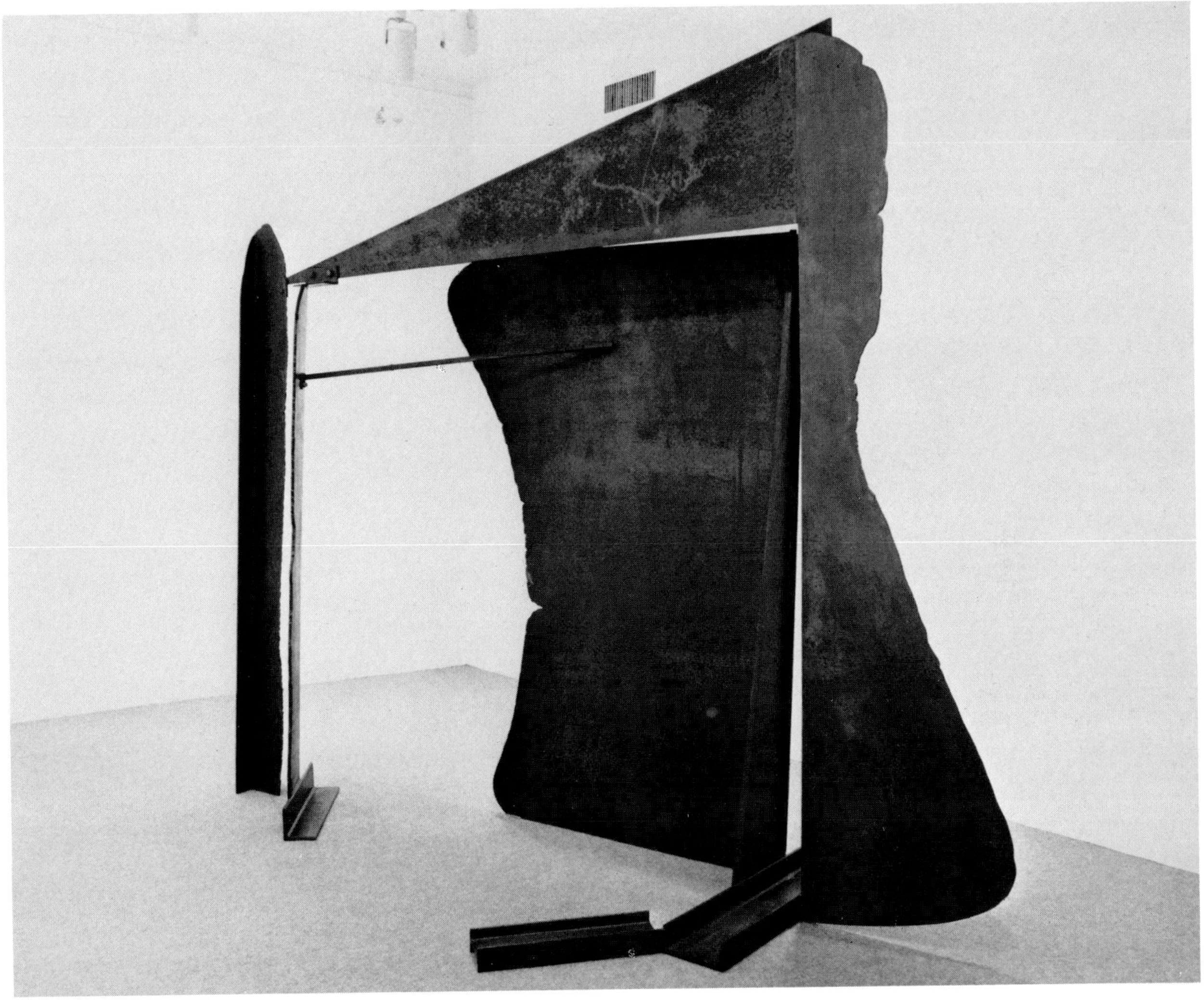

Anthony Caro.
Veduggio Sun. 1973.
Painted steel, 9 feet 3½ inches × 8 feet 2½ inches × 70½ inches.
Dallas Museum of Fine Arts. Gift of the Mr. and Mrs. Edward S. Marcus Fund

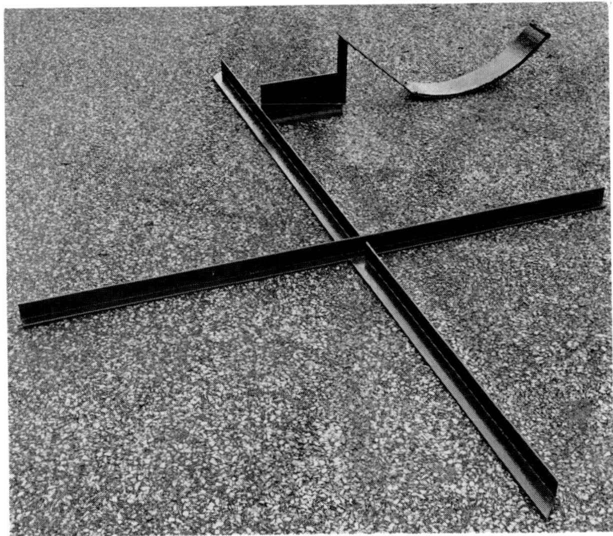

Anthony Caro.
Crosspatch. 1965.
Steel, painted red, 67½ inches × 56½ inches × 7¾ inches.
Stephen Mazoh & Co., Inc., New York

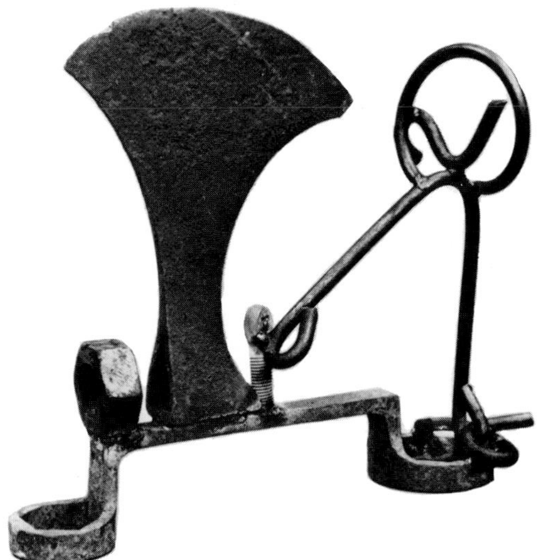

Anthony Caro.
Writing Piece 'Only.' 1979.
Steel, painted and blacked, 16½ × 19 × 5½ inches.
Private collection, New York

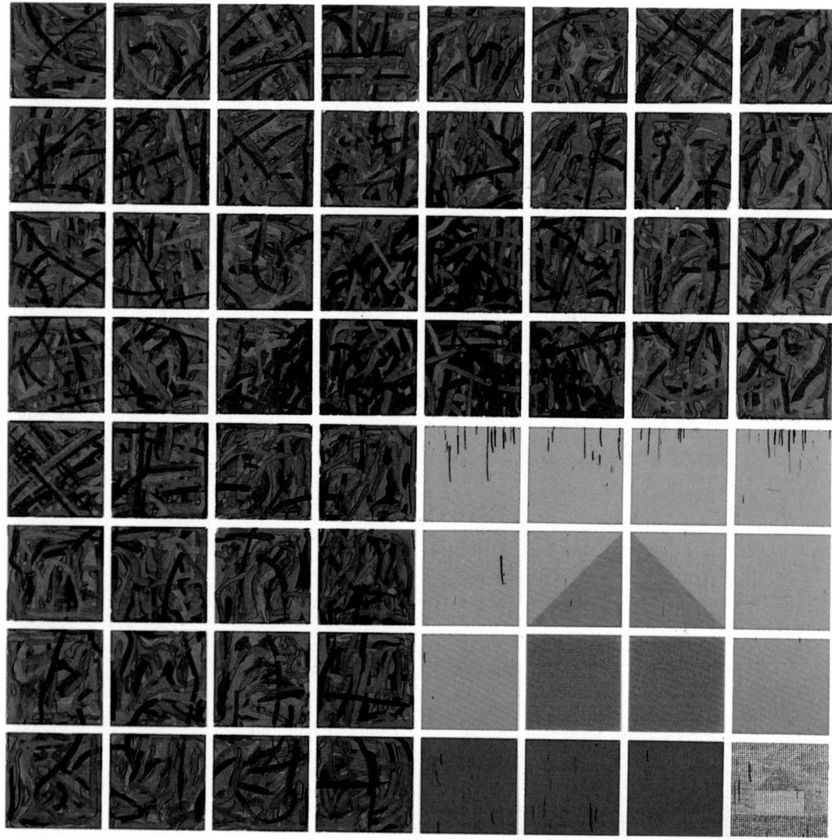

Jennifer Bartlett.
2 Priory Walk.
1977.
Baked enamel, silkscreen grid, and enamel on steel, 8 feet 7 inches × 8 feet 7 inches.
Philadelphia Museum of Art.
Adele Haas Turner and Beatrice Pastorius Turner Fund

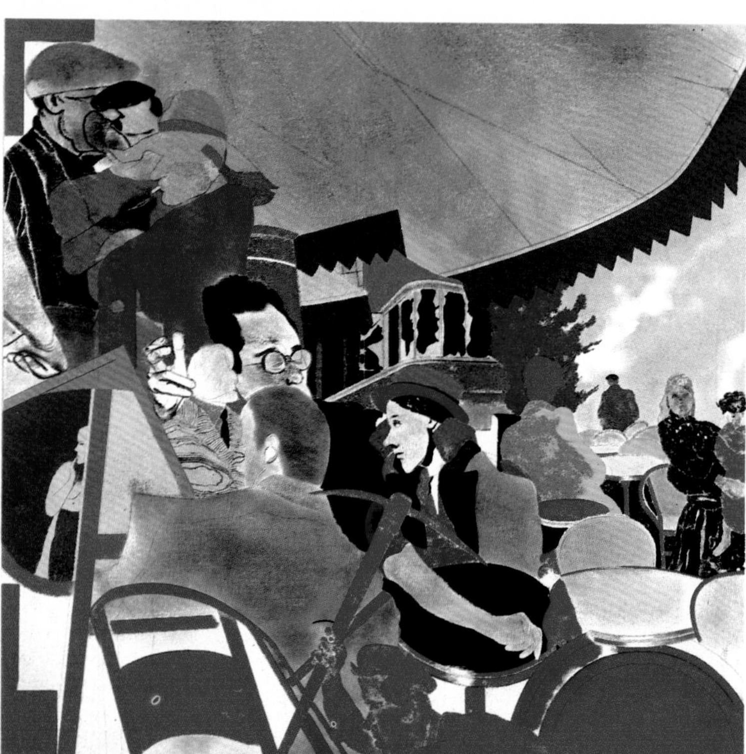

R. B. Kitaj.
The Autumn of Central Paris (After Walter Benjamin).
1973.
Oil on canvas, 60 × 60 inches.
Private collection, Paris.
Courtesy Marlborough Gallery, New York

Ellsworth Kelly.
Red Blue Green.
1963.
Oil on canvas,
7 feet × 11 feet 4 inches.
La Jolla Musem of Contemporary Art.
Gift of Dr. and Mrs. Jack Farris

is fundamental to them. So is their scale, which dominates but does not dwarf us. Smith's was, at the last, an optimistic art: one that suggests to us that there is nothing human beings cannot do if they put their minds to it.

David Smith may have been the last major artist to have an absolutely explicit, constructive and sanguine conception of the future of art. In this, as in everything else, he came on as one of Nature's frontiersmen. Art "has existed from the minds of free men for less than a century," he once said. Thus "the freedom of man's mind to celebrate his own feeling by a work of art parallels his social revolt from bondage. I believe that art is yet to be born and that freedom and equality are yet to be born."

Modern art could have no nobler charter than that. Written in 1950, it stands for a large-heartedness, a freedom from corruption and a breadth of ambition which have largely ceased to characterize the world of art. Smith at that time was as unsuccessful, in worldly terms, as an artist can be. (His income from the sale of his work in 1951 was $333. In 1952 it was nothing at all.) The boom years for art were yet to come, and conditions—for sculpture, at any rate—were roughly as they had been in 1937, when Smith was prompted by the example of the Spanish sculptor Julio Gonzalez to begin making welded sculptures: the work was done to define the sculptor's identity as a free human being, and with no rational prospect of financial success.

Smith was killed in 1965 when his truck overturned on the road. He had no successors, but he did have a friend and colleague whose work is in some respects a continuation of his. Anthony Caro began as an Expressionist figure sculptor: a manipulator of weighty full-bodied human forms that spread and sprawled in space. But by 1962 he had turned to loose-jointed lateral conjunctions of man-made forms which made no reference to nature. Not only gravity but function was denied—as in *Atlantic*, where the monumental I-beam stands at an angle which it would not conceivably adopt in "real life." The emphasis is on open and transparent sequences of form that get clear away from the monumental, earthbound associations of earlier sculpture. Not forms, but the relations between them, had become the true subject of art. Caro's contacts with David Smith in 1963–64 were fruitful for both of them. Working in the United States at that period, Caro at times used the square or near-square forms which Smith built up to such effect in his Cubi series. But where Smith used them to develop ever more imposing emblems of masculinity, Caro took the weight out of them and made them relate to one another, as in *Rainfall*, with a rare elegance. Where Smith worked by concentration, Caro worked by dispersion, setting his forms free from any overtone of menace and devising for them a whole new set of delicate relationships. Often he gave his collocations of form the sculptural equivalent of slender wrists and ankles. Fine-drawn in themselves, they are so lightly connected with one another as to make us wonder if they have not just floated together by mutual attraction. In a piece like *Crosspatch*, Caro explores the poetics of adjacency in ways that make us newly aware of the balance that should be inherent in our own bodies. In 1972–73 Caro paid three visits to Veduggio, Brianza, Italy, where he worked with a material quite new to him: soft-edged steel. Using scraps from plates and joists, he held fast to their ruddy, worked-over quality, so that the sculpture which resulted has none of the immaculateness of *Crosspatch*. The forms have on the contrary a flamboyant, eaten-into and yet spreading outward look, which is perhaps nearer to the paintings of Helen Frankenthaler (who had worked in Caro's studio in 1972) than to anything that Caro had done before. Yet the elements which lie flat on the ground are unmistakably Caro's, as is the flexible syntax of the piece as a whole. In this, as in the whole corpus of his work to date, Caro is the most creative sculptor to have emerged in any country since World War II.

By 1970 a vast machinery of promotion and speculation had fastened onto the making of art, which for most of David Smith's lifetime had been almost as private a matter as theology or pure mathematics. How this came about is a complex question. In part it was an authentic and justified tribute to the new role of art in the imaginative life of the United States. People acknowledged that something extraordinary had happened in art. They might not like it, any more than they liked the music of Elliott Carter or the prose of Gertrude Stein, but they knew that these things resounded to the credit of the United States. To wish to get a piece of the action is intrinsic to human nature. It is fundamental to the seduction of art that we hope to become what we look at; and if we can look at it every day in our own house the process may perhaps be accelerated. That was the most reputable of the motives which led people to pay high prices for modern art.

Other factors should be spelled out. New money breeds new collectors, and new collectors do not always have the patience, the knowledge and the discrimination which are basic to the enjoyment of Old Master painting. Much of the best modern art calls for these attributes, but in the art of the 1960s there was much that was altogether readier of access. Ambiguity and complexity played no part in it. There was no question of lingering before it as we linger before Giorgione or Vermeer. Frank Stella was categorical about that in 1964: "One could stand in front of any Abstract Expressionist work for a long time, and walk back and forth, and inspect the depths of the pigment and the inflection and all the painterly brushwork for hours. But I wouldn't ask anyone to do that in front of my paintings. To go further, I would like to prohibit them from doing that in front of my paintings. That's why I make the paintings the way they are." About much of the art of the 1960s there was a bluntness and a blankness which in time gave it the status of an ostentatious form of traveler's check.

Something in this bluntness and blankness came from a revulsion against the art of the 1940s and early '50s. Among the ideas most in disfavor were that of the heroic but foredoomed failure, the approximation that could never become complete, and the acting out, either on the canvas or in three dimensions, of any kind of private drama. There was believed to be something almost obscene about personalized brushstrokes, about sculpture that bore the mark of the shaping hand and about the traditional European idea of the balanced composition. ("With so-called advanced painting you should drop composition," said Stella.) Much of this was a natural reaction against the extreme subjectivity and the secular mysticism of much that had been made famous since 1950. But it was exploited by a public that did not want to look hard for more than a few moments and by promoters who preferred work that avoided the classic stance—the "now and never again," the "here and nowhere else"—of European art. From this emerged the impersonal series-painting of the 1960s, and the graphics industry which was often no more than an expensive form of souvenir hunting, and the multiples which cashed in on the prestige of art but ran none of art's risks. The remarkable thing was not that this situation should have come about, but rather that good work was done from time to time in spite of it.

And good work was done, right through the 1960s and the 1970s. The wish to make a monumental statement did not die out, either. Whether in the Ocean Park series of Richard Diebenkorn, or in the outsize provocations of Frank Stella, or in the three-dimensional autobiography of Joseph Beuys, or in the enormous paintings in which Jennifer Bartlett took image after image to the very point of disintegration, only to bring them safely back again, there were statements of a grand, searching, unsubdued sweep that spoke up for mankind as clearly as they spoke up for art. There were also compound statements, in which art raided archaeology, raided natural history, raided cartography, raided the skies and raided the seabed. Someone who did all this and much else besides, in painting and sculpture alike, was Nancy Graves. In her *Trace* an informed viewer will find

Richard Diebenkorn.
Ocean Park 115.
1979.
Oil on canvas,
8 feet 4 inches × 6 feet 9 inches.
The Museum of Modern Art, New York. Mrs. Charles C. Stachelberg Fund

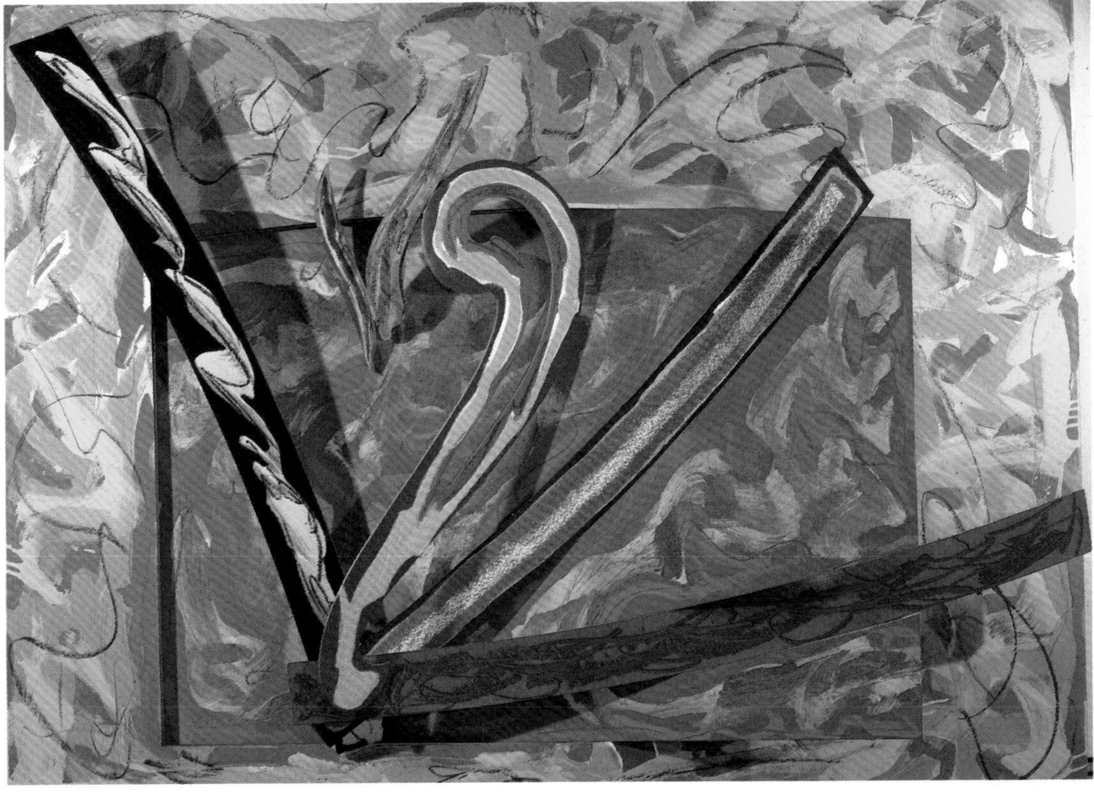

Frank Stella.
New Caledonian Lorikeet II. 1977.
Lacquer, oil, glitter, paintstick on metal relief, 10 feet × 13 feet × 30 inches.
Courtesy Leo Castelli Gallery, New York

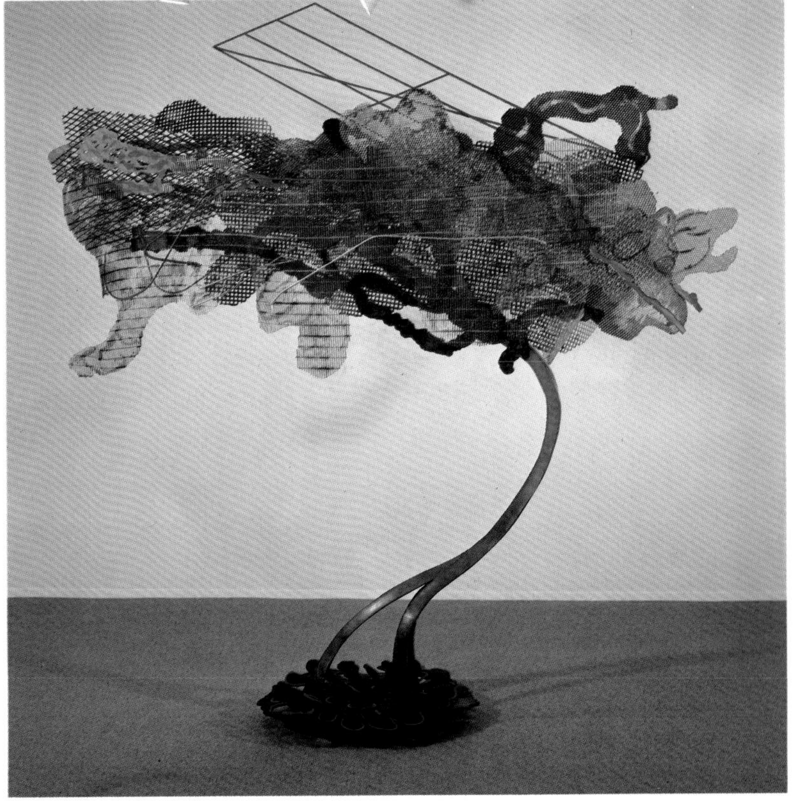

Nancy Graves.
Trace. 1979–80.
Bronze, steel, patina and paint, 9 feet 7 inches × 8 feet 11 inches × 50 inches.
Graham Gund, Cambridge, Mass.

the new openness of form that we expect from sculpture since David Smith and Anthony Caro. He will find an incorporeal lightness and radiance of color to which neither Smith nor Caro aspired. And he will also find a marriage, well and truly consummated, between art and natural history.

So there were people who stayed with gallery art, museum art, continuity art. But art did go underground, all the same. It had gone underground before, when nobody wanted it: when the audience for the best art numbered six or seven people and the artist—Picasso, at his very best, and Matisse, at his very best—did not even think of putting it on show. Now it went underground for the opposite reason: because everybody wanted it. As insistently as before 1914, the times called for an alternative art. It took many forms; but what these forms had in common was that they questioned the nature of art—and, more especially, of art that was susceptible to instant marketing. Art was to go about its own concerns, in private, and if necessary take forms that denied what was fundamental to marketed art: the possibility of possession.

No one can buy a work of art that consists in the temporary and all but invisible readjustment of the city that we live in. If a work of art exists in idea form only, the idea in time will belong to everyone, and the typewritten statement that can be bought and sold is no more than an outdated token. The alternative art of the late 1960s and early '70s took forms that were ephemeral, impalpable, sometimes purely notional. Sometimes it depended on the participation of the viewer: and although this in itself was not new—every work of art has always been completed by the person who looks at it—there was often a willed ephemerality about the new art which had not been met with before.

The instruments of art had never before been so varied. At one extreme there was brought into play every newest refinement of technology: the video-tape, the hologram that hung in the air, the android or humanized robot that clanked and stumbled along the streets of New York, the computer-generated environment, the labyrinth of light and sound that is activated by the public that penetrates it, the crystals in a glass sphere that turn from solid to gas in response to atmospheric conditions. At the other extreme, there were artists who made art with pebbles picked from the foreshore and a worn-down piece of chalk, or with a folded sheet of carbon paper and a few lines ruled in pencil. There were people who went further still and said, with Joseph Kosuth, "I want to remove the experience from the work of art." ("Actual works of art," he also said, "are little more than historical curiosities.") On this last reading, art as it had existed previously was a tautology: an acting-out, in other words, of something that existed already, in definition form, and did not need to be made visible.

These were heady matters, as tempting to the near-genius as to the charlatan, and as accessible to the near-saint as to the ravening opportunist. Among the technophiles there were some who simply ran wild, like small boys let loose in a candystore. Among the pseudo-philosophers there were some who could not tell "its" from "it's," let alone master Plato or Kant. Sometimes the wish that art once again become private was simply overridden by society. Claes Oldenburg once described how this came about; and his remarks ring true in other and later contexts. "I really don't think you can win. . . . The bourgeois scheme is that they wish to be disturbed from time to time, they like that, but then they envelop you and that little bit is over, and they are ready for the next. . . ." Sometimes, also, elements from marketed art, and from the market situation, made their way in, unbidden. The promotion of personality is as repulsive in this context as the promotion of art. The aesthetics of undifferentiated experience had been put forward to great effect by John Cage, in many of his later compositions, and by Andy Warhol (above all, in his films). It was dismal when the same point of view motivated people who had neither talent nor spontaneous impulse. Where

Dada had evolved in an economy of imminent starvation, the art of the early 1970s evolved in an economy dominated by technical superabundance; and something of the billion-dollar silliness of that economy rubbed off on the art.

It was not a healthy situation. On the one hand were artists who financially, and in terms of glamour, had replaced the movie stars of the 1930s as objects of popular attention. On the other were artists who went from town to town like wandering friars. Lodged and fed by small groups of sympathizers, they made and unmade their art wherever there was an audience, no matter how small. Both were in what is called "art"; yet on the one side a major work cost over a hundred thousand dollars, while on the other there might well be nothing to sell. Each group was pressured, however strangely, by the existence of the other. The established artist was rare in the early 1970s who did not feel that in some way he was the last of his line; many bought time, and bought silence, by stratagems of their own devising.

Absence was one of these stratagems. James Joyce's famous formula for survival ("Silence, exile, cunning") was taken up in one form or another in the 1960s and '70s by artists who wished to carve out their own space in the world. One of these was R. B. Kitaj, an American painter long resident in London who works with the recent past of Europe in much the same way as the Old Masters worked with the mythology of Greece and Rome. A voracious and adventurous reader, he constructs from his reading a vision of our times which he then sets down on canvas, mixing old-style "good drawing" with pictorial devices of altogether more recent date. *The Autumn of Central Paris* has for its main subject a Parisian café of the kind that Pierre Bonnard painted many times over. At that café is seated among others the German-born critic and essayist Walter Benjamin, who killed himself when the German army entered Paris in 1940. The nonchalance of the party at the table is well offset by the man with the pick, who is taking apart not only the sidewalk on which they are sitting but the society which Benjamin had evoked with such eloquence in his unfinished study of Paris.

Paris after World War II did not do as much, directly, for the American expatriate artist as it had done before and after World War I. But it did do something indirectly, most notably in the case of Ellsworth Kelly. Kelly lived in Paris from 1948 to 1954, at a crucial period in his life, and for this and other reasons his work has a particularly rich, complex and liberal derivation. There is a grand assurance about his use of color which has not quite been equaled by any other American painter. The shapes in his paintings could not be more abstract, but they are never either arbitrary or doctrinaire. A Kelly which many people supposed from its title to be an evocation of the Brooklyn Bridge was in point of fact derived from a drawing of a sneaker. His many triangular paintings originated from the look of a scarf which he happened to see on the nape of the neck of a young girl in Central Park. The rectangle and the ovoid form in *Red Blue Green* are further examples of Kelly's working method, in that they derived initially from (i) the shape of the window in his studio, (ii) the way in which that shape was distorted when it reappeared as a reflection on the other side of the street. These accidental, "given" motifs were refined and rethought until they were in perfect equilibrium, with the red shape and the blue shape ideally coordinated with the green one.

Sometimes in the period we are discussing an artist could "keep his distance" simply by staying home. This was the stratagem of Joseph Cornell, who occupied himself in his tiny house in Flushing, New York, with a form of poetic object—the collaged box—which served him for a lifetime. Himself an all-time champion stay-at-home, he nourished his imagination with notional journeys —in time, in space, and in matters of the heart. In time, he preferred the Romantic period in Europe. In space, he preferred the run-down European hotels in which his favorite 19th-cen-

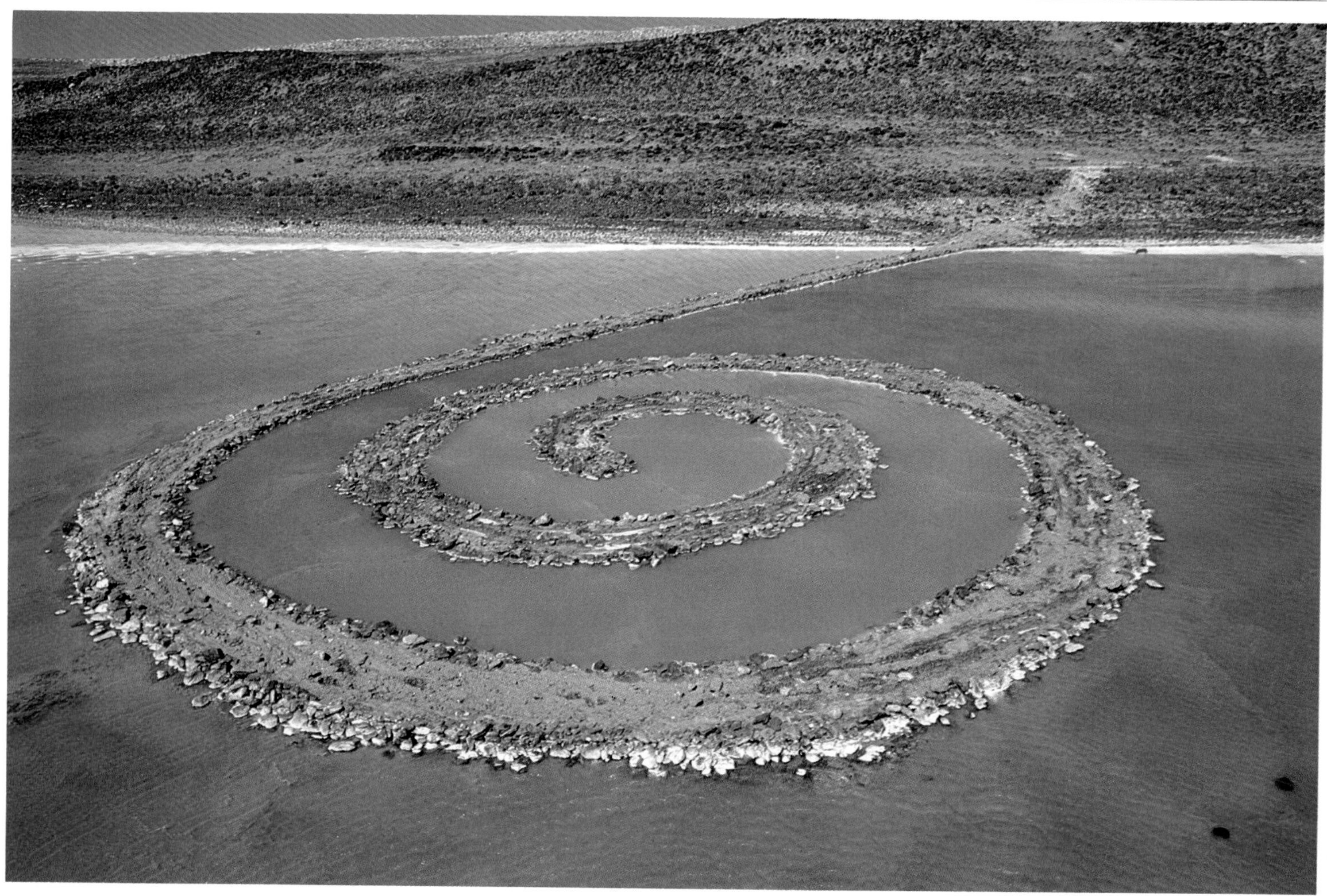

Robert Smithson. *Spiral Jetty,* Great Salt Lake, Utah. 1970. Photograph: Gianfranco Gorgoni/Contact

tury French poets eked out much of their lives. In matters of the heart his imaginary entanglements were with the great ballerinas—Cerrito, Taglioni, Grisi and Fanny Elsller—of the 1840s. He was also fascinated by archaic modes of transport. A long-extinct hotel in Belgium, a four-horse coach to a famous battlefield, a bird and a bell—these and other things add up to an image as magical as anything of its kind since Miró's *Object* of 1936.

Works such as those by Kitaj, Kelly and Cornell that I have just discussed have nothing in common except that all of them were studio products. One man in one room made them. But the studio product was not the whole of art in the 1960s and '70s, and indeed to many people it seemed to be an activity too much tied to an earlier era. Why should not the whole world be our raw material, the overarching sky our studio ceiling, and the puissance of our technology our paints and brushes and hammer and chisel?

Robert Smithson was one of the great proponents of this point of view. He was a mixture of poet, filmmaker, landscape gardener, draftsman, geologist and philosopher. He liked to work on a vast scale and in landscapes for which Nature appeared to have no further use. Both in the *Spiral Jetty* and in the *Amarillo Ramp* his working methods paralleled the use of pouring and dripping in Abstract Expressionism. But where the Action Painters had poured and dripped on a finite canvas, Smithson claimed for himself prerogatives hardly less absolute than those of Jehovah in the Old Testament. He remade the world in an image of his own devising. But he did not forget that all

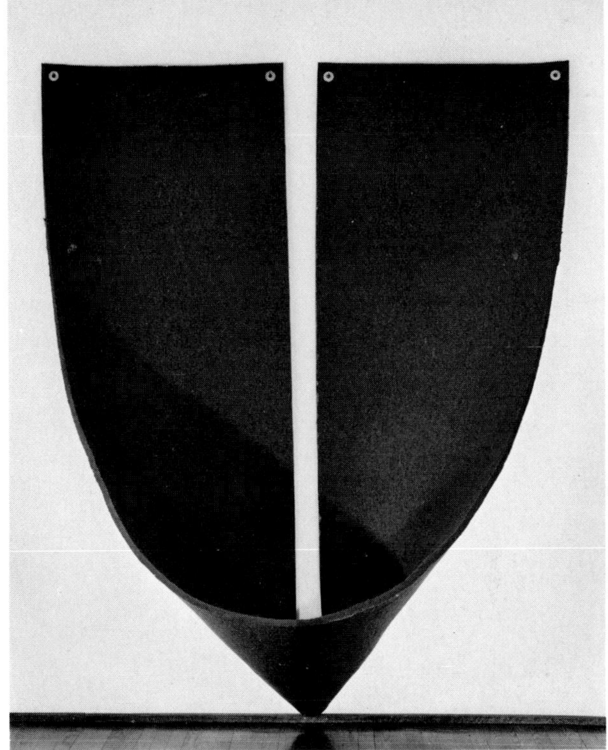

Robert Morris. *Untitled.* 1974. Felt and metal, 99 × 76¾ × 36¼ inches. Courtesy Leo Castelli Gallery, New York

such images have their echoes in the past. The spiral in the *Jetty* is a form that had dominated the imagination of artists and architects from Borromini in the 17th century to Tatlin in the 20th. Smithson also knew that the sun has been figured as a spiral nebula of smaller suns beyond number. And as the critic Joseph Masheck has pointed out, Smithson was aware of "the Jungian concept of the *circumambulatio*—a compulsive spiraling-in to one's undiscovered self." What we see in these gigantic works is not a privileged playground, but an attempt to come to terms with American landscape on a scale of which Walt Whitman would have approved.

A paradoxical situation then arose, by which major adventures in art were subject to a form of almost clandestine emigration. The best sculptures of Anthony Caro were shipped out of London, for instance, to American private collections; two German collectors made away with as much of the best American art as they could get their hands on; it was in Holland that Robert Morris and other American artists were encouraged to carry out environmental works for which no bidders were found in the United States. In this way there was reestablished on a worldwide scale something comparable to the pacific International which had existed in Europe before 1914. The energies inherent in the best modern art were in demand everywhere: in Japan, in Australia, in Israel, and not least in France, where most resolute efforts were made to recapture the ancient prestige of Paris as the city most receptive to the new.

All this gave a look of health and vigor to a situation which in point of fact was short of both these qualities. In America museums were built at enormous expense, only for the trustees to find that they could barely afford to keep them open, let alone find good things to put in them. To many younger artists the museum system as a whole seemed grossly paternalistic. Museums mirrored, in their view, a power structure and a chain of command which had proved so disastrous in other departments of life that it could not go unchallenged in art. They also stood for a star system in which people who themselves were in no way creative were paid to set one artist above another. Yet such was the elasticity of the museum system, and such the self-preservative instinct of society, that even those artists who had taken what amounted to a vow of apostolic poverty were likely to find in time that the museums were ready to take them on their own terms. No form of art was so resolutely antispectacular that some ambitious curator would not put it on view. The fear of being left out is as contagious in art as it is in every other area of life; Wilfred Trotter's *Instincts of the Herd in Peace and War* (1923) has yet to go out of date.

From this there results a profound uneasiness: and, with that, a tendency to reverse roles in ways that would have been unthinkable 50 years ago. Collectors once held on to their collections; today they are tempted to trade them in as they trade in their automobiles. Museum directors once planned for eternity when they made a new acquisition; today nothing in their world is stable—least

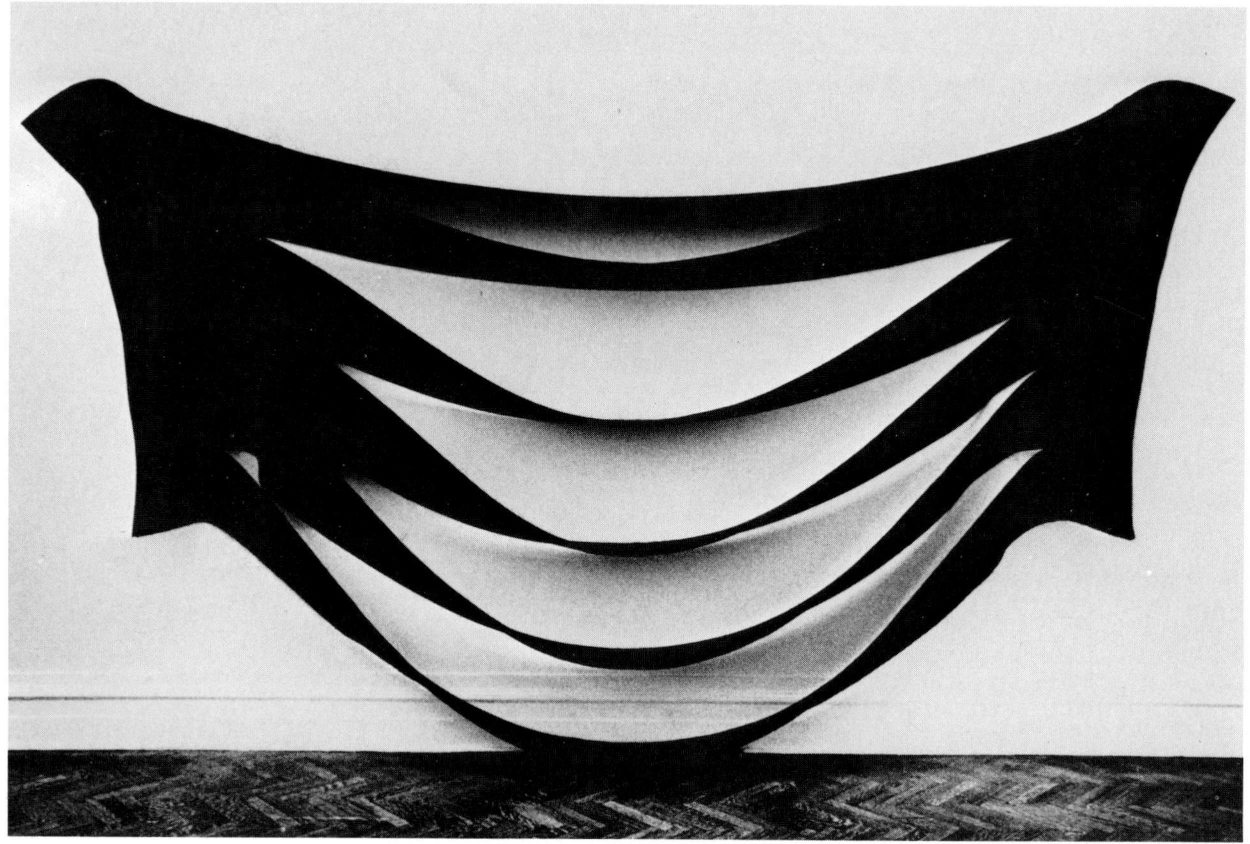

Robert Morris.
Untitled. 1969.
Felt, ¾ inch thick, installed 6 feet × 15 feet.
Bernar Venet, Paris

of all their own tenure of office. Artists once kept the past continually in mind, haunting it as Cézanne haunted the Louvre; today they may think, with the sculptor Donald Judd, that "if the earlier work is first-rate it is complete," and that that very completeness makes it no longer relevant. At the age of 40 Mark Rothko, Barnett Newman, David Smith and Willem de Kooning had still a protective obscurity in which to work; an artist of that age today may well seem to his juniors to be far gone in fogeydom—and the uncomplaining instrument, what is more, of a corrupt and loathsome system.

If we are to feel our way as to what will rank as art in the last decade of our century we have to bear in mind two fundamental aspects of the general situation. One is a degree of technological omnipotence which in the nature of things will grow ever greater. It is within our power to control and shape the environment in ways never before precedented, and perhaps to guarantee for our physical selves a longevity which formerly belonged to fable alone. Art would not be art if it did not negotiate with these new possibilities.

Art would also not be art if it did not sometimes take the simplest of everyday materials and give them an unprecedented eloquence. Over a period of around ten years, for instance, Robert Morris worked on the potentialities of felt as a sculptural medium. Felt in his hands could be made to stand up like steel or aluminum. It could roll on the ground like a gundog exhausted from the chase. It could fulfill any number of rhetorical purposes. It could also cross-refer to current developments elsewhere in art. Of the two untitled pieces reproduced here, for instance, the first can be taken to refer to the severe plain drawing, sculpture and architecture, whereas the other looks across to the downward-swooping runnels of pure paint that Morris Louis used to such magical effect.

The other factor which we should watch for is

something humbler and more conventionally human. It is what is called in German *Torschlusspanik:* the terror of the closing door. The end of art, as art has hitherto been conceived, is more than "the end of an era." It is the end of a god: the death of something which brought reassurance, and brought consolation, and brought an unshakable equanimity. It is very disagreeable, as I said at the outset of this survey, to think that art will one day come to an end. And it is particularly disagreeable when the art of the recent past has been of very high quality.

It is for this reason that the status of art has been claimed for activities which in themselves might seem to be no more than novelty hunting of a particularly fatuous kind. It is for this same reason, and to relieve the strain upon those rare individuals who still produce finite works of art at the highest level, that such efforts have been made to bring the notion of art into a public (if not actually into an anonymous) domain. If everything is art, and if the life of everyday can be monitored in terms of art, then we shall no longer have to apply to individual exertions the dreaded words "not good enough." We should aim, therefore, to arouse in every human being the kind of superior awareness which is in itself a form of creativity. If this were to become universal—so the argument runs—the gap between art and life would be closed once and for all.

That everyone should be an artist is, on one level, the noblest of dreams: the enfranchisement of one man in a million would give way to the enfranchisement of everyone, without exception. On a less conscious level it stands, however, for something quite different: the wish to spread among all mankind, and therefore to spread very thin, the responsibility for what is considered in the Bible, and in mythology, as a blasphemous act. It is not for mankind—so the primeval belief ran —to rival the gods. When Marsyas with his reed pipes challenged Apollo to a trial of skill, Apollo had him flayed alive. When Orpheus made music so beautiful that it overthrew the existing order of things, the gods saw to it that he lost his beloved Eurydice and was torn apart by Maenads. When the Hebrews got above themselves and tried to build a tower that would reach to Heaven, Jehovah put an end to it by destroying the unity of language that alone made possible the control of the vast and heterogeneous work force.

Somber warnings, these. Yet in bad times we need to believe that the problems before mankind are not insoluble. We know that the breakdown of art, like the breakdown of literacy, may portend a more general breakdown, and one that is irreversible. If it is forbidden to rival the gods, it is also despicable not to attempt it. That particular rivalry, with all that it involves in the way of risk and terror and possible retribution, may well be the supreme human act: the one that best justifies our existence and may prevent it from coming to an end.

This is not a belief that we need to abandon. Rarely in human history can a decade have begun less well than the 1980s. On every hand, and in every country in the world, the present is matter for misgiving and the future a matter for dread. It is natural that at such a time people should think of art as a thing of the past. But what is natural is not always laudable, and it is a pointless diminution of our status on earth to assume that "art as we knew it" can no longer be counted upon. "Art as *who* knew it?" is the answer to that. Now more than ever we need to remember that art is the constructive act, and that the artist is the person who puts the world together after everyone else has let it go to pieces.

For what is the alternative? The silence of the German poet Friedrich Hölderlin. The silence of the French poet Arthur Rimbaud. The silence in old age of the American poet Ezra Pound. The silence of Moses, in Arnold Schoenberg's unfinished opera, when he realized that people were turning away from the truths for which he, Moses, could not find the right words. We may never know why Hölderlin went mad, why Rimbaud left Europe to eke out a living in Africa or why Pound

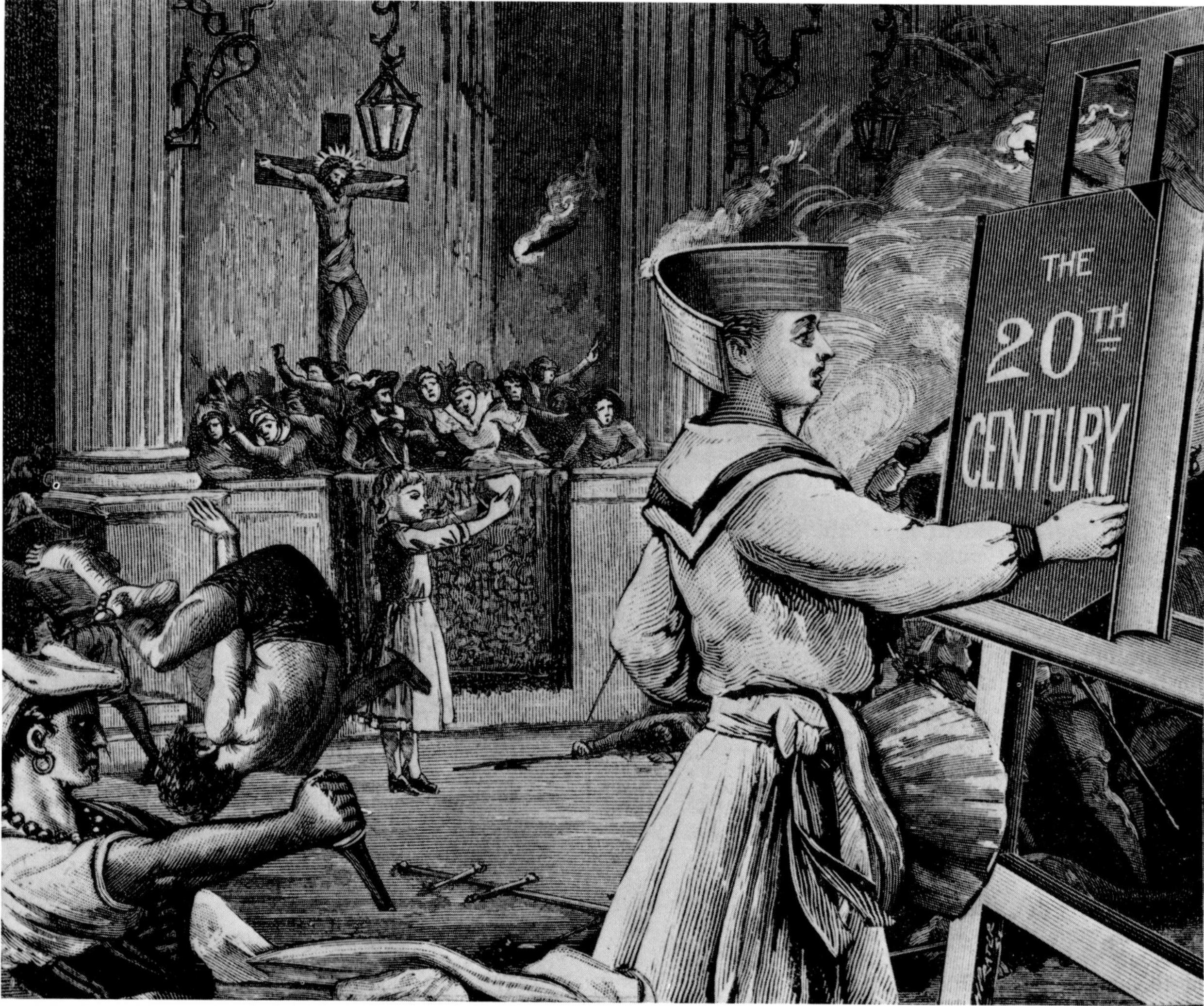

Max Ernst.
The Voice of the Holy Father. 1930.
Paper on paper, collage, 5¾ × 6¾ inches.
Private collection, New York

abjured the gift of tongues that he had used so unwisely. But we know that one of the last poets in classical Latin literature was right when he said that civilization lives by speech and dies by silence. For "speech," in our present context, we should substitute the image in all its forms, finite or variable.

It is difficult to think of today's world in terms other than those of crisis and emergency. What is at stake is the survival of the earth as a place fit to live on, and of the human race as something that will bear scrutiny. It was not in conditions such as these that the masters of early modern art grew to manhood; and a certain sympathetic indulgence should, I think, be accorded to those who aspire to be their successors. "What can we know for certain?" is a question which has haunted modern art ever since it was first posed by Cézanne. If it has lately been answered primarily in terms of art's own nature—if art, in other words, has aspired primarily to define itself—the lesson in self-knowledge which we can draw from it is nonetheless valid for being metaphorical. Art has provided us with models of our environment ever since cave paintings conjured up the bulls and the bisons that shook the earth as they passed overhead. It is still fulfilling this same function, whether in the panoramic and posthumous masterpiece of Marcel Duchamp which is now in the Philadelphia Museum, or in such more restricted studies as the miniature forest, to be viewed from what felt like a refrigerated trench, which Robert Morris contributed to an exhibition at The Museum of Modern Art in New York. Art is there to make sense of the world, and it should surprise nobody if over the last 50 years this has become progressively more difficult. In 1930, when Max Ernst made his *Voice of the Holy Father,* many of the secrets of our century were still intact. To open the book of the future was a perilous act: one to be watched, as it is watched in that little picture, with every symptom of dismay. But art could do it, and art until now has dared to do it.

It is possible, too, to be unduly discouraged. The French poet Paul Valéry was very bright indeed as a young man at the turn of this century, and he mixed with people in Paris whose business it was to know what was going on. But, like other very bright people who have been close to the work of their immediate seniors, he took a gloomy view of what was to come. To feel that nothing can be the same again is the most natural of human instincts, and Valéry may well have drawn only assent when he wrote to a friend in 1908 and said, "Will anything great ever again come out of Europe?" I shall have failed in my purpose if I have not convinced the reader that this question called for a full-throated "Yes!" The best art of our century may well remind us of what was written not long ago by the British scientist and Nobel prizewinner P. B. Medawar: "To deride the hope of progress is the ultimate fatuity, the last word in poverty of spirit and meanness of mind."

For no one can foresee in what forms of art the next generation will see itself fulfilled and justified. The poet William Carlos Williams spoke ideally well of the effect of great painting when he said that "It is ourselves we seek to see on the canvas, as no one ever saw us, before we lost our courage and our love." This sense of ourselves redeemed and made whole is the greatest gift which one human being can make to another. Art has always been there to give us that sense of ourselves, and never more so than since the springs of feeling were made over to us, unmuddied, by the Impressionists. Over and over again it has reminded us that all art consoles, and that great art consoles absolutely. What form art will take in the future no one can say; but no sane society will wish to be without it.

SUGGESTED READINGS

GENERAL

Arnason, H. H. *History of Modern Art.* New York, Abrams, 1968.

Ashton, Dore. *A Fable of Modern Art.* New York, Thames & Hudson, 1980.

Baigell, Matthew. *History of American Painting.* New York, Praeger, 1971.

Banham, Reyner. *Theory and Design in the First Machine Age.* New York, Praeger, 1960.

Barr, Alfred H., Jr., ed. *Masters of Modern Art.* 2nd. ed. New York, The Museum of Modern Art, 1955.

Bowness, Alan. *Modern European Art.* New York, Harcourt, Brace, Jovanovich, 1972.

Breunig, LeRoy C., ed. *Apollinaire on Art: Essays and Reviews, 1902–1918.* New York, Viking, 1972.

Brown, Milton W., and others. *American Art: Painting, Sculpture, Architecture, Decorative Arts, Photography.* New York, Abrams, 1979.

Brown, Milton W. *American Painting from the Armory Show to the Depression.* Princeton, N.J., Princeton University Press, 1955.

Buckle, Richard. *Diaghilev.* New York, Atheneum, 1979.

Burnham, Jack. *Beyond Modern Sculpture: The Effects of Science and Technology on the Sculpture of This Century.* New York, Braziller, 1968.

Chipp, Herschel B. *Theories of Modern Art: A Source Book by Artists and Critics.* Berkeley and Los Angeles, University of California Press, 1968.

Clay, Jean. *Modern Art, 1890–1918.* New York, Vendome Press (distributed by Viking), 1978.

Elsen, Albert E. *Modern European Sculpture 1918–1945, Unknown Beings and Other Realities.* New York, Braziller, 1979.

Elsen, Albert E. *Origins of Modern Sculpture: Pioneers and Premises.* New York, Braziller, 1974.

Gablik, Suzi. *Progress in Art.* New York, Rizzoli, 1977.

Geldzahler, Henry. *American Painting in the Twentieth Century.* New York, The Metropolitan Museum of Art, 1965.

Giedion, Sigfried. *Space, Time and Architecture.* Rev. and enl. 5th edition. Cambridge, Mass., Harvard University Press, 1973.

Gombrich, E. H. *The Story of Art.* London, Phaidon, 1972.

Greenberg, Clement. *Art and Culture: Critical Essays.* Boston, Beacon Press, 1961.

Haftman, Werner. *Painting in the Twentieth Century.* New ed. New York, Praeger, 1965.

Hamilton, George Heard. *19th and 20th Century Art.* New York, Abrams, 1970.

Hamilton, George Heard. *Painting and Sculpture in Europe 1880–1940.* Rev. ed. Baltimore, Penguin Books, 1972.

Hammacher, A. M. *The Evolution of Modern Sculpture: Tradition and Innovation.* New York, Abrams, 1969.

Herbert, Robert L., ed. *Modern Artists on Art.* Englewood Cliffs, N.J., Prentice-Hall, 1964.

Holt, Elizabeth Gilmore, ed. *From the Classicists to the Impressionists: A Documentary History of Art and*

Architecture in the Nineteenth Century. Garden City, N.Y., Doubleday, 1966.

Hunter, Sam, and Jacobus, John. *American Art of the 20th Century: Painting, Sculpture, Architecture.* New York, Abrams, 1974.

Kramer, Hilton. *The Age of the Avant-Garde: An Art Chronicle of 1956–1972.* New York, Farrar, Straus & Giroux, 1973.

Kuh, Katharine, ed. *The Artist's Voice.* New York, Harper & Row, 1962.

Lynton, Norbert. *The Story of Modern Art.* Ithaca, Cornell University Press, 1980.

Malraux, André. *The Psychology of Art.* New York, Pantheon, 1949.

Malraux, André. *Museum without Walls.* (Vol. 1 of *The Psychology of Art.*) Garden City, N.Y., Doubleday, 1963.

Porter, Fairfield. *Art in Its Own Terms: Selected Criticism, 1935–1975.* Rackstraw Downes, ed. New York, Taplinger, 1979.

Read, Herbert. *A Concise History of Modern Painting.* Rev. and enl. ed. New York, Praeger, 1968.

Read, Herbert. *A Concise History of Modern Sculpture.* New York, Praeger, 1971.

Rose, Barbara. *American Art since 1900: A Critical History.* Revised edition. New York, Praeger, 1975.

Schapiro, Meyer. *Modern Art, 19th and 20th Centuries: Selected Papers.* New York, Braziller, 1978.

Shattuck, Roger. *The Banquet Years: The Origins of the Avant-Garde in France, 1885 to World War I.* Rev. ed. New York, Vintage Books, 1968.

Steinberg, Leo. *Other Criteria: Confrontations with Twentieth-Century Art.* New York, Oxford University Press, 1972.

Walker, John A. *Glossary of Art, Architecture and Design since 1945.* 2nd. rev. ed. Hamden, Conn., Linnet Books, 1977.

MOVEMENTS

Impressionism, Post-Impressionism

Herbert, Robert L. *Neo-Impressionism.* New York, Solomon R. Guggenheim Foundation, 1968.

Lövgren, Sven. *The Genesis of Modernism: Seurat, Gauguin, van Gogh and French Symbolism in the 1880s.* 2nd. rev. ed. Bloomington, Indiana University Press, 1971.

Pool, Phoebe. *Impressionism.* New York, Praeger, 1967.

Rewald, John. *The History of Impressionism.* 4th rev. ed. New York, The Museum of Modern Art, 1973.

Rewald, John. *Post-Impressionism: From van Gogh to Gauguin.* 3rd ed. rev. New York, The Museum of Modern Art, 1978.

Roskill, Mark. *Van Gogh, Gauguin and the Impressionist Circle.* Greenwich, Conn., New York Graphic Society, 1970.

Symbolism

Delevoy, Robert L. *Symbolists and Symbolism.* New York, Rizzoli, 1978.

Jullian, Philippe. *Dreamers of Decadence: Symbolist Painters of the 1890s.* New York, Praeger, 1971.

Lucie-Smith, Edward. *Symbolist Art.* London, Thames & Hudson, 1972.

Milner, John. *Symbolists and Decadents.* London and New York, Studio Vista/Dutton Paperbacks, 1971.

Symons, Arthur. *The Symbolist Movement in Literature.* (First publ. 1899.) New York, Dutton, 1958.

Fauvism

Crespelle, Jean-Paul. *The Fauves.* Greenwich, Conn., New York Graphic Society; London, Oldbourne, 1962.

Duthuit, Georges. *The Fauvist Painters.* New York, Wittenborn, 1950.

Elderfield, John. *The "Wild Beasts": Fauvism and Its Affinities.* New York, The Museum of Modern Art, 1976.

Expressionism, Die Brücke, Der Blaue Reiter

Grohmann, Will. *Expressionists.* New York, Abrams, 1957.

Kandinsky, Wassily, and Marc, Franz, eds. *The Blaue Reiter Almanac.* New York, Viking, 1974.

Manvell, Roger, and Fraenkel, Heinrich. *The German Cinema.* New York, Praeger, 1971.

Miesel, Victor H., ed. *Voices of German Expressionism.* Englewood Cliffs, N.J., Prentice-Hall, 1970.

Myers, Bernard S. *The German Expressionists: A Generation in Revolt.* New York, McGraw-Hill, 1963.

Roethel, Hans K. *The Blue Rider.* New York, Praeger, 1972.

Roh, Franz. *German Art in the 20th Century.* Rev. ed. Greenwich, Conn., New York Graphic Society, 1968.

Selz, Peter. *German Expressionist Painting.* Berkeley and Los Angeles, University of California Press, 1957.

Cubism

Apollinaire, Guillaume. *The Cubist Painters.* New York, Wittenborn, 1962.

Barr, Alfred H., Jr. *Cubism and Abstract Art.* Reprint. First publ. 1936. New York, Arno for The Museum of Modern Art, 1967.

Cooper, Douglas. *The Cubist Epoch.* London, Phaidon Press (distributed by Praeger), 1971.

Fry, Edward F. *Cubism.* London, Thames & Hudson; New York, McGraw-Hill, 1966.

Golding, John. *Cubism: A History and an Analysis, 1907–1914.* Rev. ed. New York, Harper & Row, 1972.

Rosenblum, Robert. *Cubism and Twentieth-Century Art.* New York, Abrams, 1968.

Futurism

Apollonio, Umbro, ed. *The Futurist Manifestos.* New York, Viking, 1973.

Kirby, Michael. *Futurist Performance.* New York, Dutton, 1971.

Marinetti, Filippo Tommaso. *Selected Writings.* R. W. Flint, ed. New York, Farrar, Straus & Giroux, 1971.

Martin, Marianne W. *Futurist Art and Theory, 1909–1915.* New York, Oxford University Press, 1968.

Taylor, Joshua C. *Futurism.* New York, The Museum of Modern Art, 1961.
Tisdall, Caroline, and Bozzolla, Angelo. *Futurism.* New York, Oxford University Press, 1978.

ORPHISM
Spate, Virginia. *Orphism: The Evolution of Non-Figurative Painting in Paris, 1910–1914.* New York, Oxford University Press, 1979.

VORTICISM
Cork, Richard. *Vorticism and Abstract Art in the First Machine Age.* Berkeley, University of California Press, 1976.

DADA
Barr, Alfred H., Jr. *Fantastic Art, Dada, and Surrealism.* Reprint. First publ. 1937. New York, Arno for The Museum of Modern Art, 1970.
Bigsby, C. W. *Dada and Surrealism.* London, Methuen, 1972.
Foster, Stephen C., and Kuenzli, Rudolf E., eds. *Dada Spectrum: The Dialectics of Revolt.* Madison, Wisc., Coda Press, and Iowa City, Ia., University of Iowa, 1979.
Hülsenbeck, Richard, ed. *Dada Almanach.* Millerton, N.Y., Something Else Press, 1966.
Lippard, Lucy R., ed. *Dadas on Art.* Englewood Cliffs, N.J., Prentice-Hall, 1971.
Motherwell, Robert, ed. *Dada Painters and Poets.* New York, Wittenborn, 1951.
Richter, Hans. *Dada: Art and Anti-Art.* New York, McGraw-Hill, 1965.
Rubin, William S. *Dada, Surrealism, and Their Heritage.* New York, The Museum of Modern Art, 1968.
Rubin, William S. *Dada and Surrealist Art.* New York, Abrams, 1969.
Tashjian, Dickran. *Skyscraper Primitives: Dada and the American Avant-Garde 1910–1925.* Middletown, Conn., Wesleyan University Press, 1975.
Verkauf, Willy, ed. *Dada: Monograph of a Movement.* New York, Wittenborn, 1957.

SUPREMATISM, CONSTRUCTIVISM
Bann, Stephen, ed. *The Tradition of Constructivism.* New York, Viking, 1974.
Barron, Stephanie, and Tuchman, Maurice, eds. *The Avant-Garde in Russia, 1910–1930: New Perspectives.* Exhibition catalogue, Los Angeles County Museum of Art. Cambridge, Mass., MIT Press, 1980.
Bowlt, John E. *Russian Art 1875–1975: A Collection of Essays.* New York, MSS Information Corporation, 1976.
Bowlt, John E., ed. *Russian Art of the Avant-Garde: Theory and Criticism, 1902–1934.* New York, Viking, 1976.
Gray, Camilla. *The Russian Experiment in Art: 1863–1922.* London, Thames & Hudson, 1971.
Shvidkovsky, O. A., ed. *Building in the USSR, 1917–1932.* New York, Praeger, 1971.

DE STIJL
Jaffé, Hans L. C. *De Stijl.* New York, Abrams, 1971.
Jaffé, H. L. C. *De Stijl, 1917–1931: The Dutch Contribution to Modern Art.* Amsterdam, Meulenhoff, 1956.
Overy, Paul. *De Stijl.* New York, Dutton, 1969.

BAUHAUS
Bayer, Herbert; Gropius, Ise; and Gropius, Walter. *Bauhaus, 1919–1928.* Introduction by Alfred H. Barr, Jr. New York, The Museum of Modern Art, 1938.
Gropius, Walter. *The New Architecture and the Bauhaus.* Shand, P. Morton, tr. First publ. 1936. Boston, Charles T. Branford, 1955.
Itten, Johannes. *Design and Form: The Basic Course at the Bauhaus.* New York, Reinhold, 1964.
Naylor, Gillian. *The Bauhaus.* London, Studio Vista; New York, Dutton; 1968.
Neumann, Eckhard, ed. *Bauhaus and Bauhaus People.* New York, Nostrand Reinhold, 1970.
Roters, Eberhard. *Painters of the Bauhaus.* New York, Praeger, 1969.
Wingler, Hans M. *The Bauhaus: Weimar, Dessau, Berlin, Chicago.* Cambridge, Mass., MIT Press, 1969.

SURREALISM
Breton, André. *Manifestoes of Surrealism.* Seaver, Richard, and Lane, Helen, tr. Ann Arbor, University of Michigan Press, 1972.
Breton, André. *Surrealism and Painting.* Watson Taylor, Simon, tr. New York, Harper & Row, 1972.
Gershman, Herbert S. *The Surrealist Revolution in France.* Ann Arbor, Mich., University of Michigan Press, 1969.
Jean, Marcel, ed. *The Autobiography of Surrealism.* New York, Viking, 1980.
Jean, Marcel. *The History of Surrealist Painting.* New York, Grove, 1960.
Levy, Julien. *Surrealism.* Reprint. First publ. 1936. (Co-publ. by Worldwide Reprints.) New York, Arno, 1968.
Lippard, Lucy, ed. *Surrealists on Art.* Englewood Cliffs, N.J., Prentice-Hall, 1970.
Read, Herbert. *Surrealism.* New York, Praeger, 1972.
Waldberg, Patrick. *Surrealism.* New York, McGraw-Hill, 1966.

NEW YORK SCHOOL
Ashton, Dore. *The New York School: A Cultural Reckoning.* New York, Viking, 1973.
Geldzahler, Henry. *New York Painting and Sculpture: 1940–1970.* New York, The Metropolitan Museum of Art, 1969.
Hess, Thomas B. *Abstract Painting: Background and American Phase.* New York, Viking, 1951.
Janis, Sidney. *Abstract and Surrealist Art in America.* Reprint. First publ. 1944. New York, Arno, 1970.
Motherwell, Robert, and Reinhardt, Ad, eds. *Modern Artists in America: First Series.* New York, Wittenborn, Schultz, 1951.
O'Doherty, Brian. *American Masters: The Voice and the Myth.* New York, Random House, 1974.

Rosenberg, Harold. *The Tradition of the New.* New York, Horizon, 1959.

Sandler, Irving. *The Triumph of American Painting: A History of Abstract Expressionism.* New York, Praeger, 1970.

Sandler, Irving. *The New York School: The Painters and Sculptors of the Fifties.* New York, Icon/Harper & Row, 1978.

Tuchman, Maurice, ed. *The New York School: Abstract Expressionism in the 40s and 50s.* London, Thames & Hudson, 1970.

POP AND AFTER

Amaya, Mario. *Pop Art . . . and After.* New York, Viking, 1965.

Battcock, Gregory, ed. *Minimal Art: A Critical Anthology.* New York, Dutton, 1968.

Battcock, Gregory, ed. *The New Art.* New York, Dutton, 1966.

Battcock, Gregory, ed. *Super Realism: A Critical Anthology.* New York, Dutton, 1975.

Benthall, Jonathan. *Science and Technology in Art Today.* New York, Praeger, 1972.

Burnham, Jack. *Great Western Saltworks: Essays on the Meaning of Post-Formalist Art.* New York, Braziller, 1974.

Cage, John. *Silence: Lectures and Writings.* Middletown, Conn., Wesleyan University Press, 1961.

Cage, John. *A Year from Monday: New Lectures and Writings.* Middletown, Conn., Wesleyan University Press, 1967.

Celant, Germano. *Arte Povera.* New York, Praeger, 1969.

Davis, Douglas. *Art and the Future.* New York, Praeger, 1973.

Klüver, Billy; Martin, Julie; and Rose, Barbara, eds. *Pavilion: Experiments in Art and Technology.* New York, Dutton, 1972.

Lippard, Lucy. *Pop Art.* New York, Praeger, 1966.

Lippard, Lucy, ed. *Six Years: The Dematerialization of the Art Object.* New York, Praeger, 1973.

McShine, Kynaston L., ed. *Information.* New York, The Museum of Modern Art, 1970.

Meyer, Ursula. *Conceptual Art.* New York, Dutton, 1972.

O'Hara, Frank. *Art Chronicles, 1954–1966.* New York, Braziller, 1975.

Pincus-Witten, Robert. *Postminimalism.* New York, Out of London Press, 1978.

Popper, Frank. *Origins and Development of Kinetic Art.* Greenwich, Conn., New York Graphic Society, 1968.

Russell, John, and Gablik, Suzi. *Pop Art Redefined.* New York, Praeger, 1969.

Seitz, William C. *The Art of Assemblage.* New York, The Museum of Modern Art, 1961.

Walker, John A. *Art since Pop.* New York, Barron's, 1978.

ARTISTS

JOSEF ALBERS

Spies, Werner. *Josef Albers.* New York, Abrams, 1970.

JEAN (HANS) ARP

Arp, Jean. *On My Way: Poetry and Essays 1912–1947.* New York, Wittenborn, Schultz, 1948.

Jean, Marcel, ed. *Arp on Arp.* New York, Viking, 1972.

Read, Herbert. *The Art of Jean Arp.* New York, Abrams, 1968.

Soby, James Thrall. *Arp.* New York, The Museum of Modern Art, 1958.

Trier, Eduard. *Jean Arp: Sculpture. His Last Ten Years.* New York, Abrams, 1968.

FRANCIS BACON

Russell, John. *Francis Bacon.* Greenwich, Conn., New York Graphic Society, 1971.

Sylvester, David. *Francis Bacon, Interviewed by David Sylvester.* New York, Pantheon, 1975.

GIACOMO BALLA

Dorazio, Virginia D. *Giacomo Balla: An Album of His Life and Work.* New York, Wittenborn, 1969.

MAX BECKMANN

Kessler, Charles S. *Max Beckmann's Triptychs.* Cambridge, Mass., Belknap Press of Harvard University Press, 1970.

Selz, Peter. *Max Beckmann.* New York, The Museum of Modern Art, 1964.

JOSEPH BEUYS

Adriani, Götz, and others. *Joseph Beuys: Life and Works.* Woodbury, N.Y., Barron's, 1979.

Tisdall, Caroline. *Joseph Beuys.* New York, Solomon R. Guggenheim Foundation, 1979.

UMBERTO BOCCIONI

Taylor, Joshua C. *The Graphic Work of Umberto Boccioni.* New York, The Museum of Modern Art, 1961.

PIERRE BONNARD

Fermigier, André. *Bonnard.* New York, Abrams, 1969.

Soby, James Thrall, and others. *Bonnard and His Environment.* New York, The Museum of Modern Art, 1964.

Terrasse, Antoine. *Bonnard.* Geneva, Skira, 1964.

Vaillant, Annette. *Bonnard.* Greenwich, Conn., New York Graphic Society, 1966.

CONSTANTIN BRANCUSI

Geist, Sidney. *Brancusi: A Study of the Sculpture.* New York, Grossman, 1968.

Giedion-Welcker, Carola. *Constantin Brancusi.* Basel, Benno Schwabe; New York, distributed by Wittenborn, 1959.

Jianou, Ionel. *Brancusi.* New York, Tudor, 1963.

Spear, Athena T. *Brancusi's Birds.* Catalogue raisonné. New York, New York University Press, for the College Art Association of America, 1969.

GEORGES BRAQUE
Cooper, Douglas. *Braque: The Great Years.* Chicago, The Art Institute of Chicago, 1972.
Mullins, Edwin. *The Art of Georges Braque.* New York, Abrams, 1968.
Ponge, Francis; Descargues, Pierre; and Malraux, André. *Georges Braque.* New York, Abrams, 1971.
Richardson, John. *Georges Braque.* Greenwich, Conn., New York Graphic Society, 1961.
Russell, John. *Georges Braque.* London, Phaidon, 1959.

MARCEL BREUER
Jones, Cranston. *Marcel Breuer: Buildings and Projects,* 1921–1961. New York, Praeger, 1962.

ALEXANDER CALDER
Arnason, H. Harvard, intro. *Calder.* New York, Viking, 1971.
Calder, Alexander. *Calder: An Autobiography with Pictures.* New York, Pantheon, 1966.
Lipman, Jean. *Calder's Universe.* New York, Viking, 1976.

ANTHONY CARO
Rubin, William. *Anthony Caro.* New York, The Museum of Modern Art, 1975.
Whelan, Richard. *Anthony Caro.* Additional texts by Michael Fried, Clement Greenberg, John Russell and Phyllis Tuchman. Harmondsworth, Middx., Penguin, 1974.

PAUL CÉZANNE
Andersen, Wayne. *Cézanne's Portrait Drawings.* Cambridge, Mass., MIT Press, 1970.
Fry, Roger. *Cézanne: A Study of His Development.* 6th rev. ed. First publ. in 1927. New York, Noonday Press, 1970.
Lindsay, Jack. *Cézanne: His Life and Art.* Greenwich, Conn., New York Graphic Society, 1969.
Rewald, John, ed. *Paul Cézanne: Letters.* 4th ed. rev. and enl. New York, Hacker, 1976.
Rubin, William, ed. *Cézanne: The Late Work.* New York, The Museum of Modern Art, 1977.
Schapiro, Meyer. *Paul Cézanne.* New York, Abrams, 1969.

MARC CHAGALL
Chagall, Marc. *My Life.* New York, Orion Press, 1960.
Crespelle, Jean-Paul. *Chagall.* New York, Coward-McCann, 1970.
Meyer, Franz. *Marc Chagall.* New York, Abrams, 1963.

GIORGIO DE CHIRICO
Carrà, Massimo. *Metaphysical Art.* Rathke, Ewald; Waldberg, Patrick; and Tisdall, Caroline, eds. New York, Praeger, 1972.
Chirico, Giorgio de. *The Memoirs of Giorgio de Chirico.* Crosland, Margaret, tr. Coral Gables, Fla., University of Miami Press, 1971.
Far, Isabella. *Giorgio de Chirico.* New York, Abrams, 1969.
Soby, James Thrall. *Giorgio de Chirico.* Reprint. First publ. 1955. New York, Arno for The Museum of Modern Art, 1966.

JOSEPH CORNELL
Ashton, Dore. *A Joseph Cornell Album.* New York, Viking, 1974.
McShine, Kynaston, ed. *Joseph Cornell.* Essays by Dawn Ades, Lynda Hartigan, Carter Ratcliff and P. Adams Sitney. New York, The Museum of Modern Art, 1980.
Waldman, Diane. *Joseph Cornell.* New York, Braziller, 1977.

SALVADOR DALI
Bosquet, Alain. *Conversations with Dali.* New York, Dutton, 1969.
Dali, Salvador. *Dali by Dali.* New York, Abrams, 1972.
Soby, James Thrall. *Salvador Dali.* Reprint. First publ. 1946. New York, Arno for The Museum of Modern Art, 1970.

STUART DAVIS
Blesh, Rudi. *Stuart Davis.* New York, Grove, 1960.
Kelder, Diane, ed. *Stuart Davis.* New York, Praeger, 1971.

ROBERT AND SONIA DELAUNAY
Buckberrough, Sherry A. *Sonia Delaunay: A Retrospective.* Exhibition catalogue. Buffalo, Albright-Knox Art Gallery, 1980.
Cohen, Arthur, ed. *The New Art of Color: The Writings of Robert and Sonia Delaunay.* New York, Viking, 1978.
Damase, Jacques; Delaunay, Sonia; and others. *Sonia Delaunay: Rhythms and Colors.* Greenwich, Conn., New York Graphic Society, 1972.
Vriesen, Gustav, and Imdahl, Max. *Robert Delaunay: Light and Color.* New York, Abrams, 1969.

ANDRÉ DERAIN
Diehl, Gaston. *Derain.* New York, Crown, 1964.
Sutton, Denys. *André Derain.* London, Phaidon (distributed by Doubleday), 1959.

THEO VAN DOESBURG
Baljeu, Joost. *Theo van Doesburg.* New York, Macmillan, 1974.

JEAN DUBUFFET
Messer, Thomas M., intro. *Jean Dubuffet: A Retrospective.* New York, Solomon R. Guggenheim Foundation, 1973.
Selz, Peter. *The Work of Jean Dubuffet.* New York, The Museum of Modern Art, 1962.

MARCEL DUCHAMP
Cabanne, Pierre. *Dialogues with Marcel Duchamp.* New York, Viking, 1971.
d'Harnoncourt, Anne, and McShine, Kynaston, eds. *Marcel Duchamp.* New York, The Museum of Modern Art, 1973.

Duchamp, Marcel. *Notes and Projects for the Large Glass.* New York, Abrams, 1969.
Lebel, Robert. *Marcel Duchamp.* New York, Grossman, 1967.
Paz, Octavio. *Marcel Duchamp or The Castle of Purity.* London, Cape Goliard Press in association with New York, Grossman, 1970.
Schwarz, Arturo. *The Complete Works of Marcel Duchamp.* New York, Abrams, 1969.
Tomkins, Calvin. *The World of Marcel Duchamp.* New York, Time-Life, 1966.
Tomkins, Calvin. *Bride and the Bachelors: The Heretical Courtship in Modern Art.* Rev. ed. New York, Viking, 1968.

RAYMOND DUCHAMP-VILLON
Hamilton, George H. *Raymond Duchamp-Villon, 1876–1918.* New York, Walker, 1967.

RAOUL DUFY
Werner, Alfred. *Dufy.* New York, Abrams, 1970.

THOMAS EAKINS
Hendricks, Gordon. *The Photographs of Thomas Eakins.* New York, Grossman, 1972.
Hendricks, Gordon. *The Life and Work of Thomas Eakins.* New York, Grossman, 1974.
Porter, Fairfield. *Thomas Eakins.* New York, Braziller, 1959.

MAX ERNST
Di San Lazzaro, G., ed. *Homage to Max Ernst.* New York, Tudor, 1972.
Ernst, Max. *Beyond Painting and Other Writings by the Artist and His Friends.* New York, Wittenborn, 1948.
Lieberman, William S. *Max Ernst.* Reprint. First publ. 1961. New York, Arno for The Museum of Modern Art, 1972.
Quinn, Edward. *Max Ernst.* Boston, New York Graphic Society, 1977.
Russell, John. *Max Ernst: Life and Work.* New York, Abrams, 1967.
Schneede, Uwe M. *The Essential Max Ernst.* London, Thames & Hudson, 1972.
Spies, Werner, ed. *Max Ernst, Oeuvre-Katalog.* Houston, Menil Foundation, 1975—in progress.
Spies, Werner. *The Return of La Belle Jardinière: Max Ernst, 1950–1970.* New York, Abrams, 1971.

HELEN FRANKENTHALER
Rose, Barbara. *Frankenthaler.* New York, Abrams, 1972.

NAUM GABO
Read, Herbert, and Martin, Leslie, intro. *Gabo: Constructions, Sculpture, Paintings, Drawings, Engravings.* Cambridge, Mass., Harvard University Press, 1957.

PAUL GAUGUIN
Andersen, Wayne. *Gauguin's Paradise Lost.* New York, Viking, 1971.
Goldwater, Robert. *Paul Gauguin.* New York, Abrams, 1957.
Jaworska, Wladyslawa. *Gauguin and the Pont-Aven School.* Greenwich, Conn., New York Graphic Society, 1972.
Rewald, John. *Paul Gauguin.* New York, Abrams, 1969.

ALBERTO GIACOMETTI
Lust, Herbert. *Giacometti: The Complete Graphics.* New York, Tudor, 1970.
Hohl, Reinhold. *Alberto Giacometti.* New York, Abrams, 1972.

VINCENT VAN GOGH
Barr, Alfred H., Jr., and Brooks, Charles M., Jr. *Vincent van Gogh: A Monograph.* Reprint 1942 ed. New York, Arno for The Museum of Modern Art, 1967.
Gogh, Vincent van. *The Complete Letters of Vincent van Gogh.* Reprint 1958 ed. Boston, New York Graphic Society, 1978.
La Faille, J. B. de. *The Works of Vincent van Gogh: His Paintings and Drawings.* Rev. and enl. ed. New York, Reynal, 1970.

ARSHILE GORKY
Levy, Julien. *Arshile Gorky.* New York, Abrams, 1968.
Rosenberg, Harold. *Arshile Gorky: The Man, The Time, The Idea.* New York, Horizon Press, 1962.

JUAN GRIS
Cooper, Douglas. *Juan Gris: catalogue raisonné de l'oeuvre peint établi avec la collaboration de Margaret Potter.* 2 vols. Paris, Berggruen, 1977.
Kahnweiler, Daniel-Henry. *Gris: His Life and Work.* New York, Abrams, 1969.
Soby, James Thrall. *Juan Gris.* New York, The Museum of Modern Art, New York, 1958.

WALTER GROPIUS
Giedion, Sigfried. *Walter Gropius: Work and Teamwork.* New York, Reinhold, 1954.
Gropius, Walter. *Apollo in the Democracy: The Cultural Obligation of the Architect.* New York, McGraw-Hill, 1968.

GEORGE GROSZ
Hess, Hans. *George Grosz.* New York, Macmillan, 1974.
Schneede, Uwe M. *George Grosz: His Life and Work.* New York, Universe, 1979.

PHILIP GUSTON
Ashton, Dore. *Yes, But . . . : A Critical Study of Philip Guston.* New York, Viking, 1976.
Feld, Ross. *Philip Guston.* New York, Braziller, and The San Francisco Museum of Modern Art, 1980.

EVA HESSE
Lippard, Lucy. *Eva Hesse.* New York, New York University Press, 1976.

HANS HOFMANN
Hofmann, Hans. *Search for the Real and Other Essays.* Cambridge, Mass., MIT Press, 1967.

Hunter, Sam. *Hans Hofmann.* New York, Abrams, 1963.

Seitz, William C. *Hans Hofmann.* Reprint. First publ. 1963. New York, Arno for The Museum of Modern Art, 1972.

WINSLOW HOMER

Flexner, James Thomas. *The World of Winslow Homer, 1836–1910.* New York, Time-Life, 1966.

Goodrich, Lloyd. *Winslow Homer.* Greenwich, Conn., New York Graphic Society, 1973.

Hendricks, Gordon. *The Life and Work of Winslow Homer.* New York, Abrams, 1979.

EDWARD HOPPER

Goodrich, Lloyd. *Edward Hopper.* New York, Abrams, 1971.

JASPER JOHNS

Crichton, Michael. *Jasper Johns.* New York, Abrams, 1977.

Kozloff, Max. *Jasper Johns.* New York, Abrams, 1969.

Steinberg, Leo. *Jasper Johns.* New York, Wittenborn, 1963.

DONALD JUDD

Judd, Donald. *Donald Judd: Complete Writings 1959–1975.* New York, New York University Press, 1975.

Smith, Brydon. *Donald Judd, Catalogue Raisonné of Paintings, Objects, and Wood-Blocks, 1960–1974.* Ottawa, The National Gallery of Canada, 1975.

WASSILY KANDINSKY

Grohmann, Will. *Wassily Kandinsky: Life and Work.* New York, Abrams, 1958.

Kandinsky, Wassily. *Concerning the Spiritual in Art and Painting in Particular, 1912.* New York, Wittenborn, 1970.

Kandinsky, Wassily, and Marc, Franz, eds. *The Blaue Reiter Almanac.* New York, Viking, 1974.

Overy, Paul. *Kandinsky: The Language of the Eye.* New York, Praeger, 1969.

Roethel, Hans K., and Benjamin, Jean K. *Kandinsky.* New York, Hudson Hills Press, 1979.

ELLSWORTH KELLY

Coplans, John. *Ellsworth Kelly.* New York, Abrams, 1972.

Goossen, E. C. *Ellsworth Kelly.* New York, The Museum of Modern Art, 1973.

ERNST LUDWIG KIRCHNER

Gordon, Donald E. *Ernst Ludwig Kirchner.* Cambridge, Mass., Harvard University Press, 1968.

Grohmann, Will. *E. L. Kirchner.* New York, Arts Inc., 1961.

PAUL KLEE

Grohmann, Will. *Paul Klee.* First publ. 1954. New York, Abrams, 1966.

Haftmann, Werner. *The Inward Vision: Watercolors, Drawings, Writings.* New York, Abrams, 1958.

Klee, Felix, ed. *The Diaries of Paul Klee 1898–1918.* Berkeley and Los Angeles, University of California Press, 1964.

Klee, Felix. *Paul Klee: His Life and Work in Documents. Selected Posthumous Writings and Unpublished Letters.* New York, Braziller, 1962.

Klee, Paul. *The Nature of Nature: The Notebooks of Paul Klee.* New York, Wittenborn, 1973.

Klee, Paul. *The Thinking Eye: The Notebooks of Paul Klee.* New York, Wittenborn, 1961.

GUSTAV KLIMT

Hofmann, Werner. *Gustav Klimt.* Greenwich, Conn., New York Graphic Society, 1972.

Novotny, Fritz, and Dobai, Johannes. *Gustav Klimt, with a Catalogue Raisonné of His Paintings.* New York, Praeger, 1968.

FRANZ KLINE

Dawson, Fielding. *An Emotional Memoir of Franz Kline.* New York, Pantheon, 1967.

OSKAR KOKOSCHKA

Bultmann, Bernhard. *Oskar Kokoschka.* New York, Abrams, 1961.

Wingler, Hans M. *Oskar Kokoschka: The Work of the Painter.* Salzburg, Galerie Welz, 1958.

WILLEM DE KOONING

Hess, Thomas B. *Willem de Kooning.* New York, The Museum of Modern Art, 1969.

Hess, Thomas B. *Willem de Kooning Drawings.* Greenwich, Conn., New York Graphic Society, 1972.

Rosenberg, Harold. *De Kooning.* New York, Abrams, 1974.

LE CORBUSIER

Besset, Maurice. *Who Was Le Corbusier?* Geneva, Skira (distributed by World Publishing Co.), 1968.

Boesiger, Willy, and Girsberger, Hans, eds. *Le Corbusier, 1910–1965.* New York, Praeger, 1967.

Choay, Françoise. *Le Corbusier.* New York, Braziller, 1960.

FERNAND LÉGER

Delevoy, Robert L. *Léger: Biographical and Critical Study.* Geneva, Skira, 1962.

Francia, Peter de. *Léger's "The Great Parade."* London, Cassell, 1969.

Fry, Edward F., ed. *Fernand Léger: The Functions of Painting.* New York, Viking, 1973.

Green, Christopher. *Léger and the Avant-Garde.* New Haven, Yale University Press, 1976.

SOL LEWITT

Legg, Alicia, ed. *Sol LeWitt.* New York, The Museum of Modern Art, 1978.

ROY LICHTENSTEIN

Coplans, John, ed. *Roy Lichtenstein.* New York, Praeger, 1972.

Waldman, Diane. *Roy Lichtenstein.* New York, Abrams, 1971.

Waldman, Diane. *Roy Lichtenstein: Drawings and Prints.* New York, Chelsea House, 1969.

RICHARD LINDNER

Ashton, Dore. *Richard Lindner.* New York, Abrams, 1969.

Kramer, Hilton. *Richard Lindner.* Boston, New York Graphic Society, 1975.

JACQUES LIPCHITZ

Lipchitz, Jacques, and Arnason, H. H. *My Life in Sculpture.* New York, Viking, 1972.

EL LISSITZKY

Lissitzky, El, and Arp, Jean. *The Isms of Art.* New York, Arno, 1968.

Lissitzky-Küppers, Sophie, ed. *El Lissitzky: Life, Letters, Texts.* Introduction by Herbert Read. Greenwich, Conn., New York Graphic Society, 1968.

MORRIS LOUIS

Fried, Michael. *Morris Louis.* New York, Abrams, 1969.

RENÉ MAGRITTE

Gablik, Suzi. *Magritte.* Greenwich, Conn., New York Graphic Society, 1970.

Passeron, René. *René Magritte.* Chicago and Los Angeles, O'Hara, 1972.

Soby, James Thrall. *René Magritte.* New York, The Museum of Modern Art, 1966.

Sylvester, David. *René Magritte.* New York, Praeger, 1969.

Torczyner, Harry. *Magritte: Ideas and Images.* New York, Abrams, 1977.

Waldberg, Patrick. *René Magritte.* New York, Wittenborn, 1965.

KASIMIR MALEVICH

Andersen, Troels. *Malevich.* (Catalogue raisonné.) Amsterdam, Stedelijk Museum, 1970.

Malevich, Kasimir. *Essays on Art: 1915–1933.* Andersen, Troels, ed. New York, Wittenborn, 1971.

MAN RAY

Penrose, Roland. *Man Ray.* Boston, New York Graphic Society, 1975.

FRANZ MARC

Lankheit, Klaus. *Franz Marc: Watercolors, Drawings, Writings.* New York, Abrams, 1960.

ANDRÉ MASSON

Rubin, William, and Lanchner, Carolyn. *André Masson.* New York, The Museum of Modern Art, 1976.

HENRI MATISSE

Barr, Alfred H., Jr. *Matisse: His Art and His Public.* Reprint. First publ. 1951. New York, The Museum of Modern Art, 1974.

Elderfield, John. *The Cut-Outs of Henri Matisse.* New York, Braziller, 1978.

Elderfield, John. *Matisse in the Collection of The Museum of Modern Art.* New York, The Museum of Modern Art, 1978.

Elsen, Albert. *The Sculpture of Henri Matisse.* New York, Abrams, 1972.

Flam, Jack D., ed. *Matisse on Art.* New York, Phaidon, 1973.

Gowing, Lawrence. *Matisse.* New York, Oxford University Press, 1979.

Lieberman, William S. *Matisse: Fifty Years of His Graphic Art.* New York, Braziller, 1956.

Marchiori, Giuseppe. *Matisse: The Artist and His Time.* New York, Reynal, 1967.

Russell, John. *The World of Matisse 1869–1954.* New York, Time-Life, 1969.

LUDWIG MIES VAN DER ROHE

Blaser, Werner. *Mies van der Rohe: The Art of Structure.* New York, Praeger, 1965.

Drexler, Arthur. *Ludwig Mies van der Rohe.* New York, Braziller, 1960.

JOAN MIRÓ

Dupin, Jacques. *Miró: Sculpture.* New York, Macmillan, 1972.

Greenberg, Clement. *Joan Miró.* Reprint. First publ. 1948. New York, Arno, 1970.

Penrose, Roland. *Miró.* New York, Abrams, 1969.

Rubin, William. *Miró in the Collection of The Museum of Modern Art.* New York, The Museum of Modern Art, 1973.

Soby, James Thrall. *Joan Miró.* New York, The Museum of Modern Art, 1959.

Sweeney, James J. *Joan Miró.* Reprint. First publ. 1941. New York, Arno for The Museum of Modern Art, 1970.

Tapié, Michel. *Joan Miró.* New York, Abrams, 1970.

LÁSZLÓ MOHOLY-NAGY

Kostelanetz, Richard, ed. *Moholy-Nagy.* New York, Praeger, 1970.

Moholy-Nagy, László. *Vision in Motion.* Chicago, Theobald, 1947.

Moholy-Nagy, László. *Painting, Photography, Film.* Cambridge, Mass., MIT Press, 1969.

PIET MONDRIAN

Jaffé, Hans L. C. *Piet Mondrian.* New York, Abrams, 1970.

Seuphor, Michel. *Piet Mondrian: Life and Work.* New York, Abrams, 1956.

Welsh, Robert P., and Joosten, J. M., eds. *Two Mondrian Sketchbooks, 1912–1914.* Amsterdam, Meulenhoff, 1969.

CLAUDE MONET

Isaacson, Joel. *Claude Monet: Observation and Reflection.* New York, Dutton, 1978.

Seitz, William C. *Claude Monet.* New York, Abrams, 1960.

Seitz, William C. *Claude Monet: Seasons and Moments.* New York, The Museum of Modern Art, 1960.

HENRY MOORE
James, Philip, ed. *Henry Moore on Sculpture.* New York, Viking, 1966.
Melville, Robert. *Henry Moore: Sculpture and Drawings, 1921–1969.* New York, Abrams, 1970.
Read, Herbert. *Henry Moore: A Study of His Life and Work.* New York, Praeger, 1965.
Russell, John. *Henry Moore.* New York, Putnam, 1968.
Sylvester, David. *Henry Moore.* New York, Praeger, 1968.

GUSTAVE MOREAU
Paladilhe, Jean, and Pierre, José. *Gustave Moreau.* New York, Praeger, 1972.

ROBERT MOTHERWELL
Arnason, H. H. *Robert Motherwell.* New York, Abrams, 1977.

EDVARD MUNCH
Benesch, Otto. *Edvard Munch.* London, Phaidon, 1960.
Heller, Reinhold. *Edvard Munch: The Scream.* New York, Viking, 1973.
Hodin, J. P. *Edvard Munch.* New York, Praeger, 1972.
Langaard, Johan H., and Revold, Reidar. *Edvard Munch: Masterpieces from the Artist's Collection in the Munch Museum in Oslo.* New York, Universe, 1972.
Messer, Thomas M. *Edvard Munch.* New York, Abrams, 1972.
Rosenblum, Robert, intro. *Edvard Munch: Symbols and Images.* Washington, National Gallery of Art, 1978.
Stang, Ragna. *Edvard Munch: The Man and His Art.* New York, Abbeville Press, 1979.
Timm, Werner. *The Graphic Art of Edvard Munch.* Greenwich, Conn., New York Graphic Society, 1969.

LOUISE NEVELSON
Glimcher, Arnold B. *Louise Nevelson.* New York, Praeger, 1972.

BARNETT NEWMAN
Hess, Thomas B. *Barnett Newman.* New York, Walker, 1969.
Hess, Thomas B. *Barnett Newman.* New York, The Museum of Modern Art, 1971.
Rosenberg, Harold. *Barnett Newman.* New York, Abrams, 1978.

BEN NICHOLSON
Russell, John, intro. *Ben Nicholson: Drawings, Paintings and Reliefs, 1911–1968.* London, Thames & Hudson, 1969.

KENNETH NOLAND
Moffett, Kenworth. *Kenneth Noland.* New York, Abrams, 1977.

GEORGIA O'KEEFFE
O'Keeffe, Georgia. *Georgia O'Keeffe.* New York, Viking, 1976.

CLAES OLDENBURG
Baro, Gene. *Claes Oldenburg: Drawings and Prints.* New York, Chelsea House, 1969.
Oldenburg, Claes. *Store Days.* New York, Something Else Press, 1967.
Oldenburg, Claes. *Injun and Other Histories.* New York, Something Else Press, 1967.
Rose, Barbara. *Claes Oldenburg.* New York, The Museum of Modern Art, 1969.

FRANCIS PICABIA
Camfield, William A. *Francis Picabia: His Art, Life, and Times.* Princeton, N.J., Princeton University Press, 1979.

PABLO PICASSO
Ashton, Dore, ed. *Picasso on Art: A Selection of Views.* New York, Viking, 1972.
Barr, Alfred H., Jr. *Picasso: Fifty Years of His Art.* Reprint. First publ. 1946. New York, The Museum of Modern Art, 1974.
Blunt, Anthony. *Picasso's "Guernica."* New York, Oxford University Press, 1969.
Brassaï, Jules Halasz. *Picasso and Company.* Garden City, N.Y., Doubleday, 1966.
Cirlot, Juan-Eduardo. *Picasso: Birth of a Genius.* New York, Praeger, 1972.
Daix, Pierre, and Boudaille, Georges. *Picasso: The Blue and Rose Periods: A Catalogue Raisonné of the Paintings, 1900–1906.* 2nd ed. Greenwich, Conn., New York Graphic Society, 1967.
Daix, Pierre, and Rosselet, Joan. *Picasso: The Cubist Years, 1907–1916: A Catalogue Raisonné of the Paintings and Related Works.* Boston, New York Graphic Society, 1979.
Gilot, Françoise. *Life with Picasso.* New York, McGraw-Hill, 1964.
Jaffé, Hans L. C. *Pablo Picasso.* New York, Abrams, 1964.
Leymarie, Jean. *Picasso: The Artist of the Century.* New York, Viking, 1972.
Penrose, Roland. *Picasso: His Life and Work.* London, Victor Gollancz, 1958.
Penrose, Roland. *Portrait of Picasso.* 2nd rev. and enl. ed. First publ. 1957. New York, The Museum of Modern Art, 1971.
Penrose, Roland, and Golding, John, eds. *Picasso in Retrospect.* New York, Praeger, 1973.
Rubin, William, ed. *Pablo Picasso: A Retrospective.* New York, The Museum of Modern Art, 1980.
Rubin, William. *Picasso in the Collection of The Museum of Modern Art.* New York, The Museum of Modern Art, 1972.
Stein, Gertrude. *Gertrude Stein on Picasso.* New York, Liveright in cooperation with The Museum of Modern Art, 1970.

JACKSON POLLOCK
Friedman, B. H. *Jackson Pollock: Energy Made Visible.* New York, McGraw-Hill, 1972.

O'Connor, Francis V., and Thaw, Eugene V., eds. *Jackson Pollock: A Catalogue Raisonné of Paintings, Drawings and Other Works.* New Haven, Yale University Press, 1978.

O'Hara, Frank. *Jackson Pollock.* New York, Braziller, 1959.

Robertson, Bryan. *Jackson Pollock.* New York, Abrams, 1960.

Rose, Bernice. *Jackson Pollock: Drawing into Painting.* New York, The Museum of Modern Art, 1980.

ROBERT RAUSCHENBERG

Forge, Andrew. *Robert Rauschenberg.* New York, Abrams, 1972.

ODILON REDON

Selz, Jean. *Odilon Redon.* New York, Crown, 1978.

Werner, Alfred. *The Graphic Works of Odilon Redon.* New York, Dover, 1969.

BRIDGET RILEY

Sausmarez, Maurice de. *Bridget Riley.* London, Studio Vista, 1970.

LARRY RIVERS

Hunter, Sam. *Larry Rivers.* New York, Abrams, 1969.

Rivers, Larry, and Brightman, Carol. *Drawings and Digressions.* New York, Clarkson N. Potter (distributed by Crown), 1979.

ALEXANDER RODCHENKO

Elliott, David, ed. *Rodchenko and the Arts of Revolutionary Russia.* New York, Pantheon, 1979.

Karginov, German. *Rodchenko.* London, Thames & Hudson, 1979.

AUGUSTE RODIN

Descharnes, Robert, and Chabrun, Jean-François. *Auguste Rodin.* New York, Viking, 1967.

Elsen, Albert Edward. *Rodin's Gates of Hell.* Minneapolis, University of Minnesota Press, 1960.

Elsen, Albert Edward. *Auguste Rodin: Readings on His Life and Work.* Englewood Cliffs, N.J., Prentice-Hall, 1965.

Sutton, Denys. *Triumphant Satyr: The World of Auguste Rodin.* New York, Hawthorne, 1966.

MEDARDO ROSSO

Barr, Margaret Scolari. *Medardo Rosso.* New York, The Museum of Modern Art, 1963.

MARK ROTHKO

Waldman, Diane. *Mark Rothko, 1903–1970, a Retrospective.* New York, Abrams, 1978.

GEORGES ROUAULT

Courthion, Pierre. *Georges Rouault.* New York, Abrams, 1961.

HENRI ROUSSEAU

Rich, Daniel Catton. *Henri Rousseau.* Reprint. First publ. 1942. New York, Arno for The Museum of Modern Art, 1970.

Vallier, Dora. *Henri Rousseau.* New York, Abrams, 1964.

KURT SCHWITTERS

Schmalenbach, Werner. *Kurt Schwitters.* New York, Abrams, 1967.

Steinitz, Kate Trauman. *Kurt Schwitters: A Portrait from Life.* Berkeley, University of California Press, 1968.

Themerson, Stefan. *Kurt Schwitters in England.* London, Gaberbocchus Press, 1958.

GEORGE SEGAL

Seitz, William C. *Segal.* New York, Abrams, 1972.

GEORGES SEURAT

Courthion, Pierre. *Georges Seurat.* New York, Abrams, 1968.

Herbert, Robert L. *Seurat's Drawings.* New York, Shorewood, 1962.

Homer, William I. *Seurat and the Science of Painting.* Cambridge, Mass., MIT Press, 1964.

Rewald, John. *Georges Seurat.* New York, Wittenborn, 1943.

Russell, John. *Seurat.* London, Thames & Hudson; New York, Praeger, 1965.

JOHN SLOAN

St. John, Bruce. *John Sloan.* New York, Praeger, 1971.

St. John, Bruce, ed. *John Sloan's New York Scene, from the Diaries, Notes, and Correspondence 1906–1913.* New York, Harper & Row, 1965.

DAVID SMITH

Fry, Edward, F. *David Smith.* New York, Solomon R. Guggenheim Foundation, 1969.

Gray, Cleve, ed. *David Smith by David Smith.* New York, Holt, Rinehart & Winston, 1968.

Krauss, Rosalind E. *Terminal Iron Works: The Sculpture of David Smith.* Cambridge, Mass., MIT Press, 1971.

McCoy, Garnett, ed. *David Smith.* New York, Praeger, 1973.

ROBERT SMITHSON

Holt, Nancy, ed. *The Writings of Robert Smithson.* New York, New York University Press, 1979.

CHAIM SOUTINE

Castaing, Marcellin, and Leymarie, Jean. *Soutine.* New York, Abrams, 1964.

Wheeler, Monroe. *Soutine.* New York, The Museum of Modern Art, 1950.

FRANK STELLA

Rosenblum, Robert. *Frank Stella.* London and New York, Penguin Books, 1970.

Rubin, William S. *Frank Stella.* New York, The Museum of Modern Art, 1970.

JOSEPH STELLA

Baur, John I. H. *Joseph Stella.* New York, Praeger, 1971.

CLYFFORD STILL
O'Neill, John P., ed. *Clyfford Still.* New York, The Metropolitan Museum of Art, 1979.

MARK TOBEY
Russell, John; Cage, John; Feininger, Lyonel and Julia. *Mark Tobey.* Basel, Beyeler, 1971.
Seitz, William C. *Mark Tobey.* New York, The Museum of Modern Art, 1962.

JOAQUÍN TORRES-GARCÍA
Jardí, Enric. *Torres-García.* Boston, New York Graphic Society, 1973.

EDOUARD VUILLARD
Preston, Stuart. *Edouard Vuillard.* New York, Abrams, 1972.
Ritchie, Andrew C. *Edouard Vuillard.* Reprint. First publ. 1954. New York, Arno for The Museum of Modern Art, 1969.
Russell, John. *Edouard Vuillard 1868–1940.* London, Thames & Hudson (distributed by New York Graphic Society), 1971.

ANDY WARHOL
Coplans, John. *Andy Warhol.* Greenwich, Conn., New York Graphic Society, 1970.
Crone, Rainer. *Andy Warhol.* New York, Praeger, 1970.
Warhol, Andy. *Andy Warhol's Index Book.* New York, Random House, 1967.

FRANK LLOYD WRIGHT
James, Cary. *The Imperial Hotel: Frank Lloyd Wright and the Architecture of Unity.* Rutland, Vermont, Charles E. Tuttle, 1968.
Drexler, Arthur. *The Drawings of Frank Lloyd Wright.* New York, Horizon, 1962.
Farr, Finis. *Frank Lloyd Wright: A Biography.* New York, Scribner's, 1961.
Scully, Vincent, Jr. *Frank Lloyd Wright.* New York, Braziller, 1960.
Wright, Frank Lloyd. *Frank Lloyd Wright: Writings and Buildings.* Kaufman, Edgar, Jr., and Raeburn, Ben, eds. New York, Horizon, 1960.
Wright, Frank Lloyd. *Buildings, Plans and Designs.* New York, Horizon, 1963.

INDEX

A page number preceded by an asterisk indicates an illustration; if the number is boldfaced, the illustration is in color.

Abbott, Berenice, *New York Shopfront,* 352, *352
Abstract Expressionism, 322, 334, 361, 395, 400; *see also* Action Painting
Abstract painting, 136, 137, 139, 140
Abstraction on Spectrum (Organization 5) (Macdonald-Wright), ***161**
Achilles (Newman), *324, 327
Acrobat with a Ball (Picasso), 59
Acrylics, 358
Action Painting, 311–15, 330–31, 334–36, 337, 338, 343, 345, 358
A.D. MCMXIV (Man Ray), 162, *163
African sculpture, 100
Age d'or, L' (film), 215
Agee, James, 352
Agony (Gorky), ***301,** 322
Akhmatova, Anna, 244
Albers, Josef, 246
Alchemy, 175
Allegory, 72
Almanac (Blue Rider publication), 135, 136, 143
Alpha Gamma (Louis), *359
Altdorfer, Albrecht, 41
Amarillo Ramp (Smithson), 400
Ambroise Vollard (Picasso), 110
American Abstract Artists, 298, 300
American Indian art, 382, *384, 389
"American sublime," 330
Anatomy Lesson (Rembrandt), 291
André Derain (Balthus), 54, *54
Angel of Hearth and Home, The (Ernst), 209
Angelico, Fra, 34
Anshutz, Thomas Pollock, 294, 296; *Steelworkers—Noontime,* 295, *295
Anti-Semitism, 222, 223
Anxiety (Munch), *79
Apocalyptic Landscape series (Meidner), 91
Apolinère Enameled (Girl with Bedstead) (Duchamp), 170, ***172,** 179, 336
Apollinaire, Guillaume, 102, 104, 106, 127–30, 132, 143, 146, 147, 150–52, 157, 168, 170, 175, 182, 186, 196, 206, 255, 259, 260; *Alcools,* 127; *Calligrammes,* 127, 130, 146; portrait of (Picasso), *127
Aragon, Louis, 200
Architectonic Painting (Popova), *233, 234
Architecture, 83, 225, 226, 231, 232, 235, 245, 247, 255–57
Arensberg, Walter, 159, 167, 178
Armored Train, The (Severini), *151
Armory Show (New York, 1913), 43, 86, 154, 155, 159, 166, 167, 297, 303
Arp, Jean (Hans), 179–81, 184, 265, 309, 318; *Madame Torso with a Wavy Hat,* *180; *Squares Arranged According to the Laws of Chance,* *181
Art Deco, 267, 272
Art Institute of Chicago, 159
Art Nouveau, 30, 89, 134, 227
Art of This Century (gallery), 302
Art Students League, N.Y., 313
Artist and His Model (Matisse), 278, *279, 284
Artist and His Mother, The (Gorky), *300
Artist Studio—The Dance (Lichtenstein), 377, ***377**
Artist's Father, The (Duchamp), *152
Atlantic (Caro), *390, 394
Atomic power, 329–31
Attributes of the Arts (Chardin), 112, 270
Auden, W. H., 14, 390
Autumn of Central Paris (After Walter Benjamin) (Kitaj), ***393,** 399
Autumn Rhythm (Pollock), 312, *313

Baader, Johannes, 183
Baargeld, Johannes, 183, 184
Bacchanalian Scene (Poussin), 66
Bacon, Francis, 375–77; *Painting,* *376
Baignade à Asnières, Une (Seurat), 27
Baldung, Hans, *Temptation of Eve,* 83, *83
Ball, Hugo, 182
Balla, Giacomo, 149, 151; *Car in a Race,* *154; *Dog on a Leash,* 154, *155; *Girl Running along a Balcony,* 154
Ballet mécanique (Léger), 255
Ballet Russes, 119, 201, 260
Balthus, *André Derain,* 54, *54
Barnes, Albert C., 159, 279, 280
Barnes Foundation, Merion, Pa., 159, 279, 280
Barr, Alfred H., 61, 101, 114, 297
Bartlett, Jennifer, 395; *2 Priory Walk,* ***392**

Baruch Plan, 329
Bathers (Cézanne), 51
Bathers by a River (Matisse), ***156**, 157, 264, 300
Baudelaire, Charles, 15, 16, 28, 71, 76, 194
Bauhaus, 226, 245–48, 251, 253
Bauhaus Stairway (Schlemmer), *246, 247
Bayer, Herbert, 246
Bazille and Camille (Monet), *18
Beardsley, Aubrey, 89, 90
Beatles (group), 127
Beaumont, Sir George, 46
Beauvoir, Simone de, 371
Beckett, Samuel, 380
Beckmann, Max, 91, 157; *Declaration of War,* 92, 93; *Family Picture,* ***93**, 95; *Night,* 93–95, *94; *Young Men by the Sea,* 92
Bed (Rauschenberg), 336, ***337**, 338
Bedroom at Arles (van Gogh), ***44**
Beethoven, Ludwig van, 15, 366
Beethoven (Klinger), 366
Beflagged Street, Le Havre (Dufy), *55
Beginning (Noland), *356
Behrens, Peter, 226
Bellmer, Hans, *Machine Gun,* 209
Bellow, Saul, 331
Bend Sinister (Noland), 355, ***356**
Benda, Julien, 259
Benin, 386
Benjamin, Walter, 399
Berg, Alban, 182
Bergson, Henri, 31, 32, 149
Berlage, H. P., 225
Berlin, Dada in, 183, 187; Expressionism in, 86
Bernard, Emile, 56
Bernheim-Jeune gallery, 56, 146–47, 274
Berryman, John, 322
Beuys, Joseph, 395
"Beyond Painting" (Ernst), 203
Bicycle Wheel (Duchamp), *169, 170
Bierstadt, Albert, 294
Big Dryad (Picasso), 104–05
Bingham, George Caleb, 293
Bird in Space (Brancusi), 265, *267
Birth of Venus, The (Botticelli), 338
Bishop, John Peale, 300
Bismarck, Otto von, 15, 24
Black Mountain College, 246, 357
Black Rose, The (Braque), *282, 283
Black Widow (Calder), *385
Blaue Reiter, 86, 132, 135, 136, 140–42, 143, 160, 235
Blaue Reiter Almanac, 135, 136, 143
Blavatsky, Madame, 138
Bleyl, Fritz, 81
Bliss, Lillie P., 159
Blue Horse, The (Marc), 142
Blue House, The (Vlaminck), ***45**
Blue Nude (Matisse), 40
Blue Rider, *see* Blaue Reiter
Blue Room, The (Picasso), *59, 60
Blunt, Anthony, 288
Boccioni, Umberto, 126–27, 146–47, 149, 150, 151, 152, 266, 383; death of, 152; *City Rises,* *146; *Dynamism of a Soccer Player,* *147; *Unique Forms of Continuity in Space,* *151, 152
Böcklin, Arnold, 134
Bolotowsky, Ilya, 357
Bonnard, Marthe, 273, 274, 275
Bonnard, Pierre, 35, 38, 47–50, 76, 195, 202, 253, 259, 263, 268, 273–79, 306; death of, 366; *Man and Woman,* *49, 50, 273; *Nude in Bath,* 274, *274; *Nude in Bathroom,* ***273**, 275
Borges, Jorge Luis, 192
Borromini, Francesco, 401
Botticelli, Sandro, 34, 338
Boy Leading a Horse (Picasso), 59
Brancusi, Constantin, 259, 264–67, 306, 384; *Bird in Space,* 265, *267; *Caryatid,* 259; *Figure (Little French Girl),* 266, *266; *Fish,* 266, *266; *Kiss,* 159, 265, *265; *Magic Bird,* *264; *Mlle Pogany,* 265, *265; *Torso,* 266, *267
Braque, Georges, 135, 157, 158, 166, 201, 263, 276, 281–87, 297, 300, 322, 375; *Black Rose,* *282, 283; *Café-Bar,* 123, ***125**, 282; and Cubism, 101–25, 128, 197, 230, 306, 318; death of, 366; *Guéridon (Round Table),* ***281**, 282; *Harbor in Normandy,* *104, 105, 106; *Landscape at L'Estaque,* *55; *Man with a Guitar,* ***109**; *Portuguese,* *111, 112; *Road near L'Estaque,* *103; *Roche-Guyon: The Château,* 122–23, *123; *Still Life with Fruit,* 105, *105, 106; *Still Life with Violin and Jug,* *110, 111; *Studio (with Wooden Stool),* *283, 285; *Studio Interior with Black Vase,* 283, *** 285**
Breakfast (Gris), 117, ***117**
Brecht, Bertolt, 317, 349, 351
Breton, André, 171, 177, 195–212 *passim,* 302, 318, 319, 371
Breton Eve (Gauguin), 34
Breton Women at a Well (Corot), 33
Breuer, Marcel, 246, 300; Whitney Museum of American Art, 246
Bride, The (Duchamp), 167, 175, *177
Bride Stripped Bare by Her Bachelors, Even (Large Glass) (Duchamp), 169, 171, ***173**, 174, 175, 177, 190, 374
Broadway (Tobey), 296
Broken Obelisk (Newman), *325, 327
Brooklyn Museum, 297
Browne, Sir Thomas, 14
Bruce, Patrick Henry, 130, 159–60; *Composition II,* *160
Brücke, Die, 35, 81–87
Building the L-Platz (Klee), ***249**, 251
Buñuel, Luis, 212, 215
Burial at Ornans (Courbet), 58
Burne-Jones, Edward, 89
Burning House (Chagall), *142, 144
Butcher Shop, The (Segal), 351–52, *352

Cabaret Voltaire (periodical), 182
Cabinet of Dr. Caligari, The (film), 132
Café-Bar (Braque), 123, ***125**, 282
Café Singer Wearing a Glove (Degas), 20, ***21**, 22
Cage, John, 151, 336, 337, 342, 367, 368, 398
Cahill, Holger, 299
Calder, Alexander, 367, 382, 386; *Black Widow,* *385
Calvary (Chagall), ***145**, 146
Camus, Albert, 370
Cantos (Pound), 100, 268, 323, 374
Canudo, Ricciotto, 146
Car Crash series (Warhol), 352
Car in a Race (Balla), *154
Card Players, The (Cézanne), *33
Card Players (Léger), 157–58, *158
Carnival of Harlequin (Miró), 203
Caro, Anthony, 384, 394, 398; *Atlantic,* *390, 394; *Crosspatch,* *391, 394; *Rainfall,* 394; *Veduggio Sun,* *391, 394; *Writing Piece 'Only,'* *391
Carrà, Carlo, 149, 184, 198; *Funeral of the Anarchist Galli,* *150; *Metaphysical Muse,* 198, *198
Carroll, Lewis, 194
Caryatid (Brancusi), 259
Cassirer, Paul, 92
Castelli, Leo, 353

Catalan Landscape, see Hunter, The
Catcher in the Rye, The (Salinger), 351
Cendrars, Blaise, 130, 146
Cesnola, Louis Palma di, 295
Cézanne, Paul, 17, 22, 23, 25, 26, 30–35, 43, 45, 51, 54, 55, 56, 61, 103, 105, 132, 159, 242, 279, 297, 306, 315, 404; *Bathers,* 51; *Card Players,* *33; death of, 56, 124; *Five Bathers,* 99; *Grandes Baigneuses,* 33, *34, 58, 61, 99, 105, 170, 275; memorial exhibition of 1907, 120; *Still Life with Peppermint Bottle,* 31–32, ***32;** *Table and Fruit,* 120; *Three Bathers,* *50
Chagall, Marc, 39, 128, 130, 143–46, 222, 223, 234–38, 247, 319; *Burning House,* *142, 144; *Calvary,* ***145,** 146; *Forward!,* 222, ***224,** 237; *Homage to Apollinaire,* *144, 146; *Over Vitebsk,* *143, 144
Chahut, Le (Seurat), 27, 30
Chaliapin, Fyodor, 143
Charcot, Jean-Martin, 23
Chardin, Jean-Baptiste, 14; *Attributes of the Arts,* 112, 270
Charlene (Rauschenberg), ***332,** 333, 337–38
Charnel House, The (Picasso), 15, 271
Chekhov, Anton Paviovitch, 239
Chéret, Jules, 30
Chesterton, Gilbert Keith, 236
Chiaroscuro, 293
Children's art, 135
Child's Brain, The (de Chirico), 207
Chinese Restaurant (Weber), 160, *162
Chirico, Giorgio de, 128, 184, 195–99, 207, 209, 221, 382, 383; *Child's Brain,* 207; *Mystery and Melancholy of a Street,* 198; *Philosopher's Conquest,* *197, 198; *Song of Love,* ***193,** 196
Chocolate Grinder, No. 1 (Duchamp), 168, *168
Chocolate Grinder, No. 2 (Duchamp), 168, *168
Church, Frederic Edwin, 294
Churchill, Winston, 158
City, The (Léger), 254, *254, 255
City Rises, The (Boccioni), *146
City Square (Giacometti), 372, *372
Claudel, Paul, 207
Climbing Path, The (Pissarro), 22, *22
Clothespin-4 (Oldenburg), *381, 382
Coffee Grinder, The (Dubuffet), *368
Collage, 113–19, 187–91, 210
Collaged box, 399
Collectors, 401
Cologne Dada, 183, 184, 187
Color, 28, 30, 35, 37, 38, 39, 42–67, 103, 112, 113, 119, 132, 134, 135, 137, 140, 142, 355, 358, 363, 365, 378
Colossus, The (Goya), 70–71
Column (Gabo), *234, 235
Combine-paintings, 337–39
Commedia dell'arte, 260–61
Composition, 358, 361, 395
Composition (Mondrian), ***229,** 231
Composition C (Mondrian), ***229,** 230
Composition II (Bruce), *160
Composition 8 (Kandinsky), *245
Composition with Color Planes V (Mondrian) 230, *231
Concord (Newman), 322, *322
Conquest of the Air, The (Fresnaye), 132, ***132,** 153
Conrad, Joseph, 167, 259
Constable, John, 46
Constructivism, 247, 248
Contrast of Forms (Léger), 120–22, ***124**
Convergence (Number 10, 1952) (Pollock), ***317,** 331
Coq d'or, Le (Rimsky-Korsakov), 144
Corbière, Tristan, 72, 73
Corinth, Lovis, 134
Cornell, Joseph, 384, 399, 400
Corot, 61, 112; *Breton Women at a Well,* 33
Corps de Dame series (Dubuffet), 375
Courbet, Gustave, 16, 26, 102, 208, 291, 292; *Burial at Ornans,* 58
Couture, Thomas, 291
Cow with the Subtile Nose, The (Dubuffet), *369
Crafts, 135
Cranach, Lucas, 83
Crommelynck, Fernand, 239
Crosspatch (Caro), *391, 394
Cubi XVII (Smith), *389
Cubi XVIII (Smith), *389
Cubi XIX (Smith), *389
Cubi series (Smith), 390, 394
Cubism, 101–25, 128, 132, 150, 160, 166, 181, 230, 232, 262, 268, 271, 274, 282, 284, 306, 309, 310, 358; Analytical, 119, 154; Synthetic, 111, 119, 123, 191, 197, 275, 283
Cunningham, Merce, 339, 380
Cuyp, Albert, 374

Dada, 118, 178–87, 191, 195, 199, 200, 207, 264, 336, 381, 399; *Die Schammade,* 184; manifesto, 182
Dad's Coming (Homer), 293
Dali, Salvador, 195, 199, 207, 209, 212, 213, 214; *Persistence of Memory,* *208, 209; *Soft Construction with Boiled Beans: Premonition of Civil War,* 213, ***216,** 268
Dance (Matisse), 43–44, ***65,** 66, 67
Dance II (Matisse), 280, *280, 281
Dance of Life, The (Munch), ***68,** 78–79
Daumier, Honoré, 223, 262
David, Jacques-Louis, *Marat Assassinated,* 14; *Oath of the Horatii,* 46
Davis, Stuart, 298, 303; *House and Street,* *298; *Lucky Strike,* 303
Day One (Newman), 330
Death Chamber, The (Munch), 77
Death of Sardanapalus (Delacroix), 58
Declaration of War (Beckmann), 92, 93
"A Definition of Neo-Traditionalism" (Denis), 43, 103
Degas, Edgar, 20, 22, 26, 37, 39, 60, 65, 74, 98, 159, 162, 383; *Café Singer Wearing a Glove,* 20, ***21,** 22
Déjeuner sur l'herbe, Le (Manet), 16
Déjeuner sur l'herbe, Le (Monet), 58
Delacroix, Eugène, 45, 159, 385; *Death of Sardanapalus,* 58; *Liberty Leading the People,* 288; *Women of Algiers,* 366
Delaunay, Robert, 30, 128–32, 143, 151, 160, 180, 191, 279, 300, 306, 341; *Eiffel Tower,* *130; Eiffel Tower series, 132; *Homage to Blériot,* ***133,** 153
Delaunay, Sonia, 180
Delektorskaya, Lydia, 365
Demoiselles d'Avignon, Les (Picasso), 53, 59, 64, ***96,** 97, 104, 106, 108, 170, 259
Denis, Maurice, 35, 43, 47, 49, 103
Departure of Kaiser Wilhelm from Berlin on July 31, 1870, to Join the Troops at the Front (Menzel), 80
Depression, Great, 298, 317, 330, 352

De Quincey, Thomas, 194, 197
Derain, André, 35, 39, 43, 46, 53–55, 59, 61, 63, 128, 135, 157; portrait of (Balthus), *54; *Portrait of Matisse,* ***52;*** *Three Trees, L'Estaque,* ***53**
Dessert, The (Matisse), 51
De Stijl (magazine), 223, 225, 227, 255
De Stijl group, 225, 231–32, 255
Diaghilev, Sergei Pavlovich, 119, 143, 144, 201, 260, 261
Diebenkorn, Richard, 395; *Ocean Park 115,* ***396**
Dine, Jim, 352
Disposable art, 152
Distortion, 40
Do It Yourself—Seascape (Warhol), ***349**
Doesburg, Theo van, 225, 227, 231, 232, 247, 255, 297
Dog on a Leash (Balla), 154, *155
Doges' Palace, Venice, 71–72
Dongen, Kees van, 54, 135
Dos Passos, John, 338
Dostoevsky, Fyodor, 76, 84
Dove, Arthur G., 159, 162; *Nature Symbolized, No. 2,* *163
Drawing-Collage (Miró), 210, *211
Dream, The (Rousseau), ***129,** 130
Dreams, 192, 194, 195, 206, 207, 216, 221
Dreier, Katherine, 159, 297
Dresden, 80–81, 82, 86
Drowning Girl (Lichtenstein), ***348**
Druggist's Display, Featuring Valley Tan Remedy (Johnson), 346, *350
Dubuffet, Jean, 367–70, 372, 375, 382; *Coffee Grinder,* *368; Corps de Dame series, 375; *Cow with the Subtile Nose,* *369; writings of, 368
Duchamp, Marcel, 30, 128, 153–55, 166–81, 186, 190, 259, 297, 336, 345, 404; *Apolinère Enameled (Girl with Bedstead),* 170, ***172,** 179, 336; *Artist's Father,* *152; *Bicycle Wheel,* *169, 170; *Bride,* 167, 175, *177; *Bride Stripped Bare by Her Bachelors, Even (Large Glass),* 169, 171, ***173,** 174, 175, 177, 190, 374; *Chocolate Grinder, No. 1,* 168, *168; *Chocolate Grinder, No. 2,* 168, *168; corrected readymades, 170; death of, 366; *Etant donnés: 1° la chute d'eau, 2° le gaz d'éclairage,* 366; *Fresh Widow,* 179, *179, 336; *Nude Descending a Staircase, No. 2,* 153, *153, 154, 155, 167, 168, 169, 171; *Passage from the Virgin to the Bride,* 175, ***176;** *Portrait of Chess Players,* 153; readymades, 170; *Three Standard Stoppages,* 179; *Why Not Sneeze, Rose Sélavy?,* 178, *178; *With Hidden Noise,* 178, *178
Duchamp-Villon, Raymond, 153, 266, 383, 384; *Horse,* *152, 153
Dufy, Raoul, 54, 55, 128; *Beflagged Street, Le Havre,* *55
Durand, Asher Brown, 294
Duranty, Edmond, 18
Dürer, Albrecht, 15, 45, 83
Dynamic Hieroglyph of the Bal Tabarin (Severini), ***148**
Dynamism of a Soccer Player (Boccioni), *147

Eakins, Thomas, 291–92, 293, 295; *Gross Clinic,* *290, 291; *Max Schmitt in a Single Scull,* ***292**
Easter Island, 386
EAT (Experiments in Art and Technology), 339
Echaurren, Sebastian Matta, *see* Matta
Eddy, Arthur Jerome, 159
Edison, Thomas, 245
Egyptian art, 100
Eiffel Tower, The (Delaunay), *130
Einstein, Albert, 127, 247, 258, 300, 367
Electric Chair series (Warhol), 352
Elektra (Strauss), 80, 90
Eliot, T. S., 100, 127, 167, 270, 297, 362
Elmer, Edwin Romanzo, *Mourning Picture,* 195
Elsen, Albert, 76, 278, 384
Eluard, Paul, 212
Emerson, Ralph Waldo, 292, 293, 330, 366
Empire II (Rauschenberg), 339–40, *341
Encaustic, 340
End of the Last Act of a Drama, The (Klee), *250, 251
Endell, August, 134
Engineer Heartfield, The (Grosz), *182
Environmental works, 400, 401
Ernst, Max, 128, 155, 157, 183, 187, 196, 199–15, 221, 253, 297, 302, 368, 389, 405; *Angel of the Hearth and Home,* 209; "Dadamax," 184, 199; *Europe after the Rain,* 213–14; *Here Everything Is Still Floating,* 186, *186; *Horde,* 213, 268; *Horse, He's Sick,* *183; *Little Tear Gland That Says Tic Tac,* 200, *200; *Loplop Introduces Members of the Surrealist Group,* 212, *214; *Pietà,* 207; *Postman Cheval,* 210, *210; *Revolution by Night,* 207; *Stratified Rocks, Nature's Gift of Gneiss Lava Iceland Moss 2 Kinds of Lungwort 2 Kinds of Ruptures of the Perineum Growths of the Heart (b) The Same Thing in a Well-Polished Box Somewhat More Expensive,* *184; *Two Children Are Threatened by a Nightingale,* ***204,** 206; *Voice of the Holy Father,* *404, 405
Erwartung (Schoenberg), 15, 228
Etant donnés: 1° la chute d'eau, 2° le gaz d'éclairage/ Given: 1. The Waterfall, 2. The Illuminating Gas (Duchamp), 366
Europe after the Rain (Ernst), 213–14
Evans, Walker, 296
Evening Star III (O'Keeffe), *166
Excavation (de Kooning), 308–10, ***309**
Execution of the Emperor Maximilian, The (Manet), 288
Existentialism, 314, 370
Experiments in Art and Technology, *see* EAT
Expressionism, 14, 84, 86, 90–91, 100, 118, 182, 270, 297

F-111 (Rosenquist), 352, ***353,** 367
Fall (Riley), 378, *379
Family of Saltimbanques (Picasso), 59, *63, 64–65, 66
Family Picture (Beckmann), ***93,** 95
Faulkner, William, 297
Fauvism, 53–58, 137, 202, 274
F.B.I. on East 69th Street, The (Lindner), 349, *354
Fear (Angst) (Klee), *286
Feininger, Lyonel, 248
Female Nude (Picasso), *108, 110, 112
Fénéon, Félix, 273
Feydeau, Georges, 171, 174
Figaro, Le, 147
Figure (Little French Girl) (Brancusi), 266, *266
Film, 86, 71, 255, 398
Fire in the Evening (Klee), 251, ***252**
Firebird, The (Stravinsky), 260, 265

First New York School, *see* New York School
First Surrealist Manifesto (Breton), 195, 199
Fish (Brancusi), 266, *266
Fitzgerald, F. Scott, 253, 312
Five Bathers (Cézanne), 99
Flag (Johns), ***328,** 336, 340
Flaubert, Gustave, 18, 155, 210
Flavin, Dan, 382
Flöge, Emilie, ***89,** 90
Fogg Art Museum, Harvard University, 19
Folkestone Boat, Boulogne, The (Manet), ***12,** 18
Form, 44, 62
Fortune Teller, The (La Tour), 194
Forward! (Chagall), 222, ***224,** 237
Four Figures on a Pedestal (Giacometti), 372
Four Seasons (Poussin), 15
Fourier, Charles, 207
Franco-Prussian War, 24
Frankenthaler, Helen, 335, 394; *Mountains and Sea,* 357, *358; *Nature Abhors a Vacuum,* ***357;** *Other Generations,* 357
Franz Josef, Emperor, 26
Frazer, J. G., 23
French Impetuosity (Picabia), 166
Fresh Widow (Duchamp), 179, *179, 336
Freud, Sigmund, 23, 25, 61, 69, 74, 88, 126, 179, 192, 206, 259
Fried, Michael, 359
Friedrich, Caspar David, 70, 72, 74, 91; *Frozen Sea,* 70, 71, *71, 76; *Grave of One Who Fell for Freedom,* 70
From Material to Architecture (Moholy-Nagy), 248
Frozen Sea, The (Friedrich), 70, 71, *71, 76
Fruit Dish (Picasso), 114
Fry, Edward, 124, 389
Fuller, R. Buckminster, *152, 369
Funeral of the Anarchist Galli (Carrà), *150
Futurism, 126, 128, 146–55; manifestos, 147, 151

Gabo, Naum, 235, 236, 238, 248, 257, 383; *Column,* *234, 235; *Head of a Woman,* *234; *Kinetic Construction,* 235
Galerie Dada, 182
Gallatin, Albert Eugene, 297
Gance, Abel, 255
Garden in Sochi (Gorky), 318, 319, *319
Gare Saint-Lazare, The (Monet), 18, ***20**
Gare Saint-Lazare series (Monet), 19–20
Gates of Hell (Rodin), 75, *75
Gauguin, Paul, 24, 26, 30, 34–38, 43, 45, 47, 48, 51, 55, 74, 75, 80, 103, 130, 273, 355; *Breton Eve,* 34; *Loss of Virginity,* 130, *131; *Marie Lagadu,* 35, ***36;** *Moon and the Earth (Hina Tefatu),* 37, *37; *Whence do we come? What are we? Where are we going?,* *25, 26–27; *Yellow Christ,* 34, 35
Geist, Sidney, 266
Genet, Jean, 268
George Washington (Lichtenstein), 346, *347
Géricault, Théodore, 14; *Raft of the "Meduse,"* 58
German Dada, 181, 182, 184
German Expressionism, 84, 86, 91, 182, 297
German Impressionism, 83, 84
Giacometti, Alberto, 195, 199, 210, 212, 216, 219, 221, 370–72, 383; *City Square,* 372, *372; *Four Figures on a Pedestal,* 372; *Man Pointing,* *370, 371; *No More Play,* *217, 219; *Nose,* *371, 372; *Palace at 4 A.M.,* 216, *217, 389; *Reclining Woman Who Dreams,* 216; *Spoon Woman,* 219; *Woman with Her Throat Cut,* 212, *215, 370
Giant Toothpaste Tube (Oldenburg), *380, 382
Gibson, Charles Dana, 296
Gide, André, 375
Giorgione, 395; *Pastoral,* 63; *Tempest,* 194
Girl before a Mirror (Picasso), 300
Girl Running along a Balcony (Balla), 154
Girl with a Mandolin (Picasso), 110
Girl with a Ball (Lichtenstein), 346, *347
Glackens, William, 295, 296
Glass, Art Nouveau, 227
Glass of Absinthe (Picasso), 353
Gleizes, Albert, 128, 150; *Harvest Threshing,* 129
Glove, The (Klinger), 366
Goethe, Johann Wolfgang von, 46
Gogh, Theo van, 27, 40
Gogh, Vincent van, 26, 27, 30, 38–41, 42, 43, 45, 47, 49, 53, 55, 69, 74, 75, 80, 104, 202, 227, 355; *Bedroom at Arles,* ***44;** *Night Café,* 39, ***40;** *Potato Eaters,* 38, *38; *Self-Portrait,* *26; *Starry Night,* 41, *41; *Street in Les Saintes-Maries,* *39
Gogol, Nikolai, 222
Golden Age, 61, 62
Golden Age, The (Ingres), 61, 63
Golding, John, 106, 171, 174
Gombrich, E. H., 14
Gontcharova, Natalie, 128, 143–44
Gonzalez, Julio, 383, 394
Gordon, Donald E., 86
Gorky, Arshile, 298, 303, 306, 308, 315–22, 330, 331, 336; *Agony,* ***301,** 322; *Artist and His Mother,* *300; death of, 314; *Garden in Sochi,* 318–19, *319; *Liver Is the Cock's Comb,* 318, ***320**
Gothic art, 83, 92, 182, 271
Gottlieb, Adolph, 303, 307, 308
Gowing, Lawrence, 270
Goya, Francisco, 23, 87; *Colossus,* 70–71; *Third of May, 1808,* 287
Graham, John, 298
Grande Chaumière, Paris, 300
Grand Déjeuner, Le, see Three Women
Grande Revue, La, 56
Grandes Baigneuses (Cézanne), 33, *34, 58, 61, 99, 105, 170, 275
Grave of One Who Fell for Freedom, The (Friedrich), 70
Graves, Nancy, *Trace,* 395–98, * **397**
Gray Alphabet (Johns), 342
Greco, El, 100; *View of Toledo,* 111
Green Coca-Cola Bottles (Warhol), 347, *350
Greenberg, Clement, 268, 292–93, 300, 330, 354, 357
Grien, *see* Baldung, Hans
Gris, Juan, 101, 104, 114–20, 128, 130, 306; *Breakfast,* 117, ***117;** *Man in the Café,* *114, 115, 117; *Playing Cards and Glass of Beer,* *115, 117; *Portrait of Picasso,* 115; *Violin and Engraving,* *115, 117
Grohmann, Will, 286
Gropius, Walter, 226, 245, 246, 247, 253; Pan Am Building, 246
Gross Clinic, The (Eakins), *290, 291
Grosz, George, 182, 183, 198, 223, 349; *Engineer, Heartfield,* *182; *Metropolis,* 91, *92
Grünewald, Matthias, 92
Guéridon, Le (Round Table) (Braque), ***281,** 282
Guernica (Picasso), 271, 287, 288, *288, 289, 302, 312, 352
Guggenheim, Peggy, 302
Guggenheim Museum, *see* Solo-

mon R. Guggenheim Museum
Guimard, Hector, 223
Guitar (1913, Picasso), ***116,** 117, 118
Guitar (1919, Picasso), 123
Guitar and Wineglass (Picasso), 113–14, *113, 118
Guston, Philip, 303

Haan, Meyer de, 48
Hals, Frans, 374
Hamilton, Richard, 171
Happenings, 352
Harbor in Normandy (Braque), *104, 105, 106
Harlequin (Picasso), 119–20, ***121**
Harper's Weekly, 223
Hartley, Marsden, 155, 160, 242; *Portrait of a German Officer,* 160–62, *162
Harvest Threshing (Gleizes), 129
Hausmann, Raoul, 182, 183
Hawthorne, Nathaniel, 292, 363
Hay, Alex, 353
Haydn, Franz Josef, 374
Haystack series (Monet), 353
Head of a Peasant Girl (Malevich), 242
Head of a Woman (Gabo), *234
Head of a Woman (Miró), 213, ***213,** 352
Heartfield, John, 183
Heckel, Erich, 80, 81, 84; *Two Men by a Table,* 84, *84
Hemingway, Ernest, 267, 297, 312
Henri, Robert, 295, 296
Henry, Charles, 28
Here Everything Is Still Floating (Ernst), 186, *186
Herkomer, Hubert von, *On Strike,* 75
Hess, Thomas B., 306, 307, 309, 311, 325, 326, 330, 345, 385
Hesse, Hermann, 137
Hindemith, Paul, 267
Hirschfeld-Mack, Ludwig, 247
Hiss, Alger, 332
Hitler, Adolf, 46, 370–71
Höch, Hannah, 183
Hoffmann, Ernst Theodor Wilhelm, 194
Hoffmann, Josef, 226, 247
Hofmann, Hans, 300, 302, 303, 306, 308, 322, 325; *Magenta and Blue,* 302, *302
Holbein, Hans, *Dead Christ,* 84
Hölderlin, Friedrich, 403
Holland, 233
Homage to Apollinaire (Chagall), *144, 146
Homage to Blériot (Delaunay), ***133,** 153
Homer, Winslow, 223, 294; *Dad's Coming,* 293; *Nooning,* 293; *Snap the Whip,* 294
Hopeless Ones, The (Klee), *250, 251
Hopper, Edward, 299; *House by the Railroad,* *299
Horde, The (Ernst), 213, 268
Horse, The (Duchamp-Villon), *152, 153
Horse, He's Sick, The (Ernst), 183
House and Street (Davis), *298
House Beautiful, 226
House by the Railroad (Hopper), *299
Houses on the Hill, Horta (Picasso), *108
Hudson River Landscape (Smith), *388, 390
Hugo, Victor, 194, 225
Hülsenbeck, Richard, 182, 187, 191
Hulten, Pontus, 175
Hunt, William Morris, 295
Hunter, The (Catalan Landscape) (Miró), 202, *203, 206
Huszár, Vilmos, 225
Huysmans, Joris Karl, 74

I See Again in Memory My Dear Udnie (Picabia), ***165,** 167
I Want a Child (set by Lissitzky), *238, 239
Iberian art, 100, 389
Ibsen, Henrik, 23, 75, 80
Illuminations (Rimbaud), 23, 29
Immigration to U.S., 315, 317
Impressionism, 15–25, 51, 74, 79, 83, 84, 274, 275
Imprisoned Animal (Klee), *287
Improvisation No. 27 (Kandinsky), 159
Improvisation No. 30 (Kandinsky), *138
Indiana, Robert, 352
Ingres, Jean-Auguste-Dominique, 46, 61, 63, 159, 208, 385; *Golden Age,* 61, 63; *Odalisque with a Slave,* 61
Insel, 81
Institute of Design, Chicago, 246
Intérieur à l'Etang-la-ville (Vuillard), *48
Interpretation of Dreams (Freud), 126, 130, 192
Intimists, 49
Invitation to the Sideshow (Seurat), 28, *28, 29
Isenheim Altarpiece, Colmar, 92
Islamic art, 126, 389
Italy, 147
Itten, Johannes, 247
Ives, Charles, 241, 338

Jallais Hill, Pontoise (Pissarro), *24, 25
James, Henry, 33, 43, 293, 294, 363
Japanese art, 49, 201–02
Jarry, Alfred, 186
Jasper Johns: Stories and Ideas (Cage), 336
Jazz (Matisse), 365
Jealousy (Munch), 77, *78
Jeanneret, Charles-Edouard, *see* Le Corbusier
Jewish Bride, The (Rembrandt), 14
John, Otto, 332
Johns, Jasper, 198, 333, 336, 337, 340–45, 353, 354; *Flag,* ***328,** 336, 340; flag series, 340–42; *Gray Alphabet,* 342; *Numbers in Color,* 342, 343, ***344,** 347; *Painted Bronze,* 353, *355; *Target with Four Faces,* 333, *334, 341, 342
Johnson, Charles Ellis, *Druggist's Display Featuring Valley Tan Remedy,* 346, *350
Johnson, Eastman, 294
Johnson, Philip, Seagram Building, 246
Joll, James, 367
Jordaens, Jacob, 310
Joy of Life (Matisse), 62, *62, 63, 64, 66, 99, 170, 202
Joyce, James, 69, 72, 167, 177, 268, 399
Judd, Donald, *Untitled,* 382, *383, 402
Judgment of Paris, The (Rubens), 97, *99
Judith I (Klimt), ***88,** 90
Jugend, 81, 134
Jung, Carl Gustav, 70, 192, 194
Jurisprudence (Klimt), 87, 88, 89

Kafka, Franz, 70, 81, 95, 177
Kahnweiler, Daniel-Henri, 106, 375
Kandinsky, Wassily, 30, 35, 39, 86, 128, 134–43, 160, 180, 234, 236, 238, 243, 244, 246, 248, 268, 297, 300, 306, 314, 362, 381, 389; *Composition 8,* *245; death of, 315, 366; *Improvisation No. 27,* 159; *Improvisation No. 30,* *138; *Landscape near Murnau,* 137, ***137;** *Mountain,* 139; *Russian*

Beauty in a Landscape, *134; *Study for "Composition II,"* ***136;** *Study for "Landscape with a Tower,"* *135
Kant, Immanuel, 44, 45, 46, 354
Kapital, Das (Marx), 15
Kaprow, Allan, 352
Kazin, Alfred, 297
Kelly, Ellsworth, 399, 400; *Red Blue Green,* ***392,** 399
Kessler, Count Harry, 92
Kiesler, Frederick, 298
Kinetic Construction (Gabo), 235
King Kong (film), 71
Kirchner, Ernst Ludwig, 35, 38, 79–87, 91, 92, 157, 158, 241; death of, 87; *Portrait of Erich Heckel,* 79, *82; *Standing Nude with a Hat,* *87; *Street, Berlin,* ***85,** 86; *Street, Dresden,* 79, ***81,** 86
Kiss, The (Brancusi), 159, 265, *265
Kitaj, R. B., 399, 400; *Autumn of Central Paris (After Walter Benjamin),* ***393,** 399
Klee, Felix, 286
Klee, Paul, 30, 39, 140, 248–53, 268, 286–87, 297, 369, 372; *Building the L-Platz,* ***249,** 251; death of, 366; *End of the Last Act of a Drama,* *250, 251; *Fear (Angst),* *286; *Fire in the Evening,* 251, ***252;** *Hopeless Ones,* *250, 251; *Imprisoned Animal,* *287; *Letter Ghost,* 286–87, *287; *Monument, on the Edge of Fertile Country,* 251; *Pastorale,* 251; *Struck off the List,* 286; *Upper Egypt,* 251
Klimt, Gustav, 87–91; *Judith I,* ***88,** 90; *Jurisprudence,* 87, 88, 89; *Medicine,* 87, 88, 89; *Park,* *91; *Philosophy,* 87, 88, 89; *Portrait of Emilie Flöge,* ***89**
Kline, Franz, 303, 306, 307, 308, 330, 336; death of, 314; *Two Horizontals,* 308, *308
Klinger, Max, 194, 366; *Beethoven,* 366; *Glove,* 366
Koklova, Olga, 260
Kokoschka, Oskar, 77, 91, 182, 247
Kollwitz, Käthe, 75
Kooning, Willem de, 298, 303, 306–10, 322, 325, 330, 331, 336, 402; *Excavation,* 308–10, ***309;** *Painting,* 309, *310, ; *Woman I,* 310–11, *311
Kosuth, Joseph, 398
Krafft-Ebing, Richard von, 23
Kropotkin, Pyotr, 24
La Bruyère, Jean de, 334
Laforgue, Jules, 72, 155, 169, 182, 186
La Fresnaye, Roger de, 132; *Conquest of the Air,* 132, ***132,** 153
Landscape at L'Estaque (Braque), *55
Landscape near Murnau (Kandinsky), 137, ***137**
Landscape with Mantis (Masson), 209
Lane, Fitz Hugh, 294
Large Glass, The, see Bride Stripped Bare by Her Bachelors, Even
Larionov, Mikhail, 128, 143–44, 157; *Soldier on a Horse,* ***141**
La Tour, Georges de, *Fortune Teller,* 194
Laurens, Henri, 384
Lautréamont, Le Comte de, 186, 196, 197, 200
Laval, Charles, 48
Lawrence, D. H., 32, 259, 386
Lebel, Robert, 171
Leck, Bart van der, 225
Le Corbusier, 223, 226, 255–57; Villa Savoye, 226
Le Fauconnier, Henri, 128
Léger, Fernand, 120–23, 126, 128, 132, 157–58, 186, 241, 253–57, 259, 279, 282, 299, 300, 302, 303; *Card Players,* 157–58, *158; *City,* 254, *254, 255; *Contrast of Forms,* 120–22, ***124;** *Mechanic,* 253–54, *253, 255; *Nudes in a Landscape,* 120; *Three Women (Le Grande Déjeuner),* ***256,** 257; *Village in the Forest,* 122, *122
Le Nain, Louis, 33, 257; *Peasants in a Landscape,* 33
Le Nain, Mathieu, 257
Lenin, Vladimir Ilich, 223, 233, 234, 240
Leonardo da Vinci, 41
Letter Ghost (Klee), 286–87, *287
Lewis, Sinclair, 349
Liberty Leading the People (Delacroix), 288
Lichtenstein, Roy, 346, 349, 353, 375, 377; *Artist Studio—The Dance,* 377, ***377;** *Drowning Girl,* ***348;** *George Washington,* 346, *347; *Girl with Ball,* 346, *347
Liebermann, Max, 134
Light-Space Modulator (Moholy-Nagy), *247, 248
Linde, Ulf, 175
Lindner, Richard, 349; *F.B.I. on East 69th Street,* 349, *354
Lissitzky, El, 235, 236, 237, 239, 240, 248, 297; set for *I Want a Child,* *238, 239; "The New One," *237
Little French Girl, see Figure
Little Girls in Aasgaardstrand (Munch), *80
Little Review, 259
Little Street, The (Vermeer), 275
Little Tear Gland That Says Tic Tac, The (Ernst), 200, *200
Liver Is the Cock's Comb, The (Gorky), 318, ***320**
Loos, Adolf, 26
Loplop Introduces Members of the Surrealist Group (Ernst), 212, *214
Lorrain, Claude, 294
Loss of Virginity, The (Gauguin), 130, *131
Louis, Morris, 335, 355–61, 402; *Alpha Gamma,* *359; death of, 357; *Point of Tranquility,* ***360;** Veils series, 359
Louvre, Paris, 127, 147
Lucky Strike (Davis), 303
Luks, George, 295, 296
Luminists, 294
Lunacharsky, Anatoli, 234–38, 240, 244
Luncheon of the Boating Party (Renoir), ***17**
Luxe, calme et volupté (Matisse), 51
Lyly, John, 262

Macdonald, Margaret, 89
Macdonald-Wright, Stanton, 160, 341; *Abstraction on Spectrum (Organization 5),* ***161**
Machine Gun (Bellmer), 209
Machines, 168, 169
Macke, August, 140, 157, 158, 183; *Making Fun of the Blue Rider,* *139, 140
Macke, Marie, 140
Mackintosh, Charles Rennie, 89
McLuhan, Marshall, 375
Macnish, Robert, 69
Madame Torso with a Wavy Hat (Arp), *180
Madrid, 23
Maeterlinck, Maurice, 273
Magenta and Blue (Hofmann), 302, *302
Magic Bird (Brancusi), *264
Magnanimous Cuckold, The (set by Popova), 239, *239
Magritte, René, 195, 196, 199, 216, 221; *Menaced Assassin,* ***220,** 221; *On the Threshold of Lib-*

erty, *219, 221; *Reckless Sleeper,* *218, 221
Mahler, Gustav, 88–89
Making Fun of the Blue Rider (Macke), *139, 140
Malevich, Kasimir, 235, 237, 238, 240, 241–44; *Head of a Peasant Girl,* 242; *Morning in the Village after Snowfall,* ***240,** 241; *Suprematist Composition,* ***241,** 243; *Suprematist Composition: White on White,* 242, 243, *243: *Suprematist Painting,* 243, *244; *Woman with Water Pails,* *242
Mallarmé, Stéphane, 36, 72, 73, 169, 381
Malraux, André, 270
Mama, Papa Is Wounded! (Tanguy), ***205,** 207
Man and Woman (Bonnard), *49, 50, 273
Man in the Café, The (Gris), *114, 115, 117
Man Pointing (Giacometti), *370, 371
Man Ray, 159, 162, 195, 212; *A.D. MCMXIV,* 162, *163; *Rope Dancer Accompanies Herself with Her Shadows,* 162, ***164**
Man with a Guitar (Braque), ***109**
Man with a Hat (Picasso), 111, *112
Mandelstam, Nadezhda, 244
Manet, Edouard, 16, 19, 22, 26, 65, 73–74, 282; *Déjeuner sur l'herbe,* 16; *Execution of the Emperor Maximilian,* 288; *Folkestone Boat, Boulogne,* ***12,** 18; *Olympia,* 16, *16, 34, 275, 372; *Portrait of Stéphane Mallarmé,* 73, *73
Manguin, Henri-Charles, 43
Mann, Thomas, 134, 258, 259, 268, 300, 385
Mantegna, Andrea, 45
Marat Assassinated (David), 14
Marc, Franz, 86, 136, 140–42, 158, 160; *Blue Horse,* 142; death of, 157; *Unfortunate Land of Tyrol,* *140, 142
Marcotte, Léon, 294
Marie Lagadu (Gauguin), 35, ***36**
Marin, John, 159, 296
Marinetti, Filippo Tommaso, 146, 147, 149, 152
Marquet, Albert, 43, 54; *Two Friends,* 276
Marriage of Reason and Squalor, The (Stella), *361
Marshall, George C., 330
Marshall Plan, 330
Marx, Karl, 15
Masheck, Joseph, 401
Massacre of the Innocents (Poussin), 15
Massine, Léonide, 261
Masson, André, 195, 199, 202, 206, 209, 302, 312, 322; *Landscape with Mantis,* 209
Matisse, Henri, 30, 35, 37, 43–46, 51–66, 84, 102, 126, 157, 160, 208, 266, 272, 273, 275, 276–81, 282, 284, 299, 300, 306, 315, 375, 389, 398; *Artist and His Model,* 278, *279, 284; *Bathers by a River,* ***156,** 157, 264, 300; *Blue Nude,* 40; cut-paper works, 355, 362–67; *Dance,* 43–44, ***65,** 66, 67; *Dance II,* 280, *280, 281; death of, 363, 366; *Dessert,* 51; *Jazz,* 365; *Joy of Life,* 62, *62, 63, 64, 66, 99; *Luxe, calme et volupté,* 51; *Memory of Oceania,* ***364;** *Moorish Screen,* 276, ***277;** *Moroccans,* *263, 264; *Music,* 66, *67, 279; *Painter and His Model,* *278; *Portrait of Madame Matisse with a Green Stripe,* ***57;** *Red Studio,* ***64,** 66, 67; sculpture of, 383, 384; *Self-Portrait,* *51; *Siren and the Parakeet,* 365; *Studio, Quai St-Michel,* *276; Vence chapel, 363; *Window,* 276, 285
Matta, 302, 318, 322
Maturin, Charles, 196
Max Schmitt in a Single Scull (Eakins), ***292**
Mechanic, The (Léger), 253–54, *253, 255
Medals for Dishonor cycle (Smith), 367, 387
Medawar, Peter Brian, 405
Medicine (Klimt), 87, 88, 89
Meidner, Ludwig, 86, Apocalyptic Landscape series, 91
Melville, Herman, 292, 293, 312, 315, 330
Memory of Oceania (Matisse), ***364**
Menaced Assassin, The (Magritte), ***220,** 221
Meninas, Las (Velázquez), 366
Menzel, Adolf, *The Departure of Kaiser Wilhelm from Berlin on July 31, 1890 to Join the Troops at the Front,* 80
Merce Cunningham Dance Company, 339, 380
Mercure de France, 56
Merz 19 (Schwitters), ***188**
Merz 83: Drawing F (Schwitters), *187
Merz 380: Schlotheim (Schwitters), ***189**
Metaphysical art, 197, 198
Metaphysical Muse (Carrà), 198, *198
Metropolis (Grosz), 91, *92
Metzinger, Jean, 128, 150
Metropolitan Museum of Art, New York, 159, 225, 295
Meyerhold, Vsevolod, 239
Michelangelo, 40, 331, 377; *Night,* 278; *Pietà,* 374
Michelson-Morley experiment, 23
Mies van der Rohe, Ludwig, 248, 258, 300; Seagram Building, 246
Miller, Arthur, 322
Milton, May, 60
Miró, Joan, 199–206, 210, 213, 214, 297, 309, 318, 386; *Carnival of Harlequin,* 203; *Drawing-Collage,* 210, *211; *Head of a Woman,* 213, ***213,** 352; *Hunter (Catalan Landscape),* 202 *203, 206; *Object,* 210–11, ***212;** *Portrait of a Woman,* 202; *Portrait of E. C. Ricart,* 201; *Rope and People I,* 213, *215; *Spanish Dancer,* 203; *Table with Glove,* 202, *202; *View of Montroig,* *201, 202; *Writer,* 206
Mlle Pogany (Brancusi), 265, *265
Moby Dick (Melville), 292, 293
Modernism, 296, 297, 298, 323
Moholy-Nagy, László, 246, 247–48, 253, 302; *Light-Space Modulator,* *247, 248
Molière, 346
Mondrian, Piet, 128, 195, 208, 225–33, 255, 258, 297, 302, 306, 372–74, 375, 377; *Composition,* ***229,** 231; *Composition C,* ***229,** 230; *Composition with Color Planes V,* 230, *231; death of, 315, 366; Pier and Ocean series, 230; *Painting I,* *232; *Red Amaryllis with Blue Background,* 227, *227; *Self-Portrait,* 227, *227; *Still Life with Ginger Pot,* 228, *230; *Victory Boogie-Woogie,* ***373;** *Woods near Oele,* 227–28, ***228**
Monet, Claude, 17, 19, 22, 26, 42, 47, 58, 72, 80, 140, 253, 274, 306; *Bazille and Camille,* *18; Cathedral series, 31, 353; *Déjeuner sur l'herbe,* 58; *Gare Saint-Lazare, Paris,* 18, ***20;** Gare Saint-Lazare series, 19–20; Haystack series, 353; *Water Lilies,* 314
Monet Painting in His Garden at Argenteuil (Renoir), *19
Monfried, Daniel de, 49, 51

Montjoie, 146
Monument on the Edge of Fertile Country (Klee), 251
Moon and the Earth (Hina Tefatu), The (Gauguin), 37, *37
Moore, Henry, 318, 384, 386–87; *Reclining Figure,* *386; *Three Bathers after Cézanne,* *387
Moore, Marianne, 297
Moorish Screen, The (Matisse), 276, ***277**
Moréas, Jean, 72, 73
Moreau, Gustave, 72, 73, 74, 76, 87; *Oedipus,* 74; *Salome Dancing before Herod,* 74
Morning in the Village after Snowfall (Malevich), ***240,** 241
Moroccans, The (Matisse), *263, 264
Morosov, Ivan, 143, 241
Morris, Robert, 382, 405; *Untitled* (1969), 402, *402; *Untitled* (1974), *401, 402
Moses and Aaron (Schoenberg), 374, 403
Motherwell, Robert, 307, 314
Motley, John Lothrop, 292
Mount, William Sidney, 295
Mountain (Kandinsky), 139
Mountains and Sea (Frankenthaler), 357, *358
Mourning Picture (Elmer), 195
Munch, Edvard, 15, 35, 39, 74–87, 92, 101, 227; *Anxiety,* *79; *Dance of Life,* ***68,** 78–79; *Death Chamber,* 77; *Jealousy,* 77, *78; *Little Girls in Aasgaardstrand,* *80; *Shriek,* 378; *Virginia Creeper,* 78; *Voice,* ***77**
Munich, 132, 134
Munich Secession, 134
Münter, Gabriele, 140
Murphy, Dudley, 255
Murphy, Gerald and Sara, 253
Museum of Modern Art, New York, 66, 159, 297, 300, 405
Museum of Non-Objective Painting, New York, 297
Museum without Walls (Malraux), 270
Museums, 401
Music (Matisse), 66, *67, 279
Musil, Robert, 268, 374
Mussolini, Benito, 149
Mystery and Melancholy of a Street, The (de Chirico), 198

Nabokov, Vladimir, 300
Napoleon III, 26
National Gallery, London, 29, 66
Nature Abhors a Vacuum (Frankenthaler), ***357**
Nature Symbolized, No. 2 (Dove), *163
Navajo Indians, Man's Shoulder Blanket, 382, *384
Nerval, Gérard de, 199
Neue Kunstlervereinigung, 135
Neumann, J. B., 297
Nevelson, Louise, 345
New Bauhaus: American School of Design, Chicago, 246
New Caledonian Lorikeet II (Stella), ***397**
New Deal, 298
"The New One" (Lissitzky), *237
New Vision, The (Moholy-Nagy), 248
New York, 162, 166, 167, 170, 294, 295, 300–11, 347
New York School, 302–27, 331, 375
New York Shopfront (Abbott), 352, *352
New York Times, The, 367
Newman, Barnett, 303, 306, 307, 308, 315, 322–27, 330, 331, 335, 402; *Achilles,* *324, 327; *Broken Obelisk,* *325, 327; *Concord,* 322, *322; *Day One,* 330; *Onement,* 322, 326; *Vir Heroicus Sublimis,* ***321,** 326, 331, 333
Nietzsche, Friedrich Wilhelm, 23, 26, 35, 37, 46, 299, 370
Night, The (Beckmann), 93–95, *94
Night (Michelangelo), 278
Night Café, The (van Gogh), 39, ***40**
1960-R (Still), 333, *335
No More Play (Giacometti), *217, 219
Nobel, Alfred, 15
Noland, Kenneth, 198, 335, 341, 345, 355–61, 378; *Beginning,* *356; *Bend Sinister,* 355, ***356**
Nooning, The (Homer), 293
Nose, The (Giacometti), *371, 372
Novak, Barbara, 293
Nude Descending a Staircase, No. 2 (Duchamp), 30, 153, *153, 154, 155, 167, 168, 169, 171
Nude in Bath (Bonnard), 274, *274
Nude in Bathroom (Bonnard), ***273,** 275
Nudes in a Landscape (Léger), 120
Number 1 (Pollock), 314, ***316,** 323
Number 10 (Rothko), ***305**
Number 10, 1952, see Convergence
Number 119, 1958 (Black) (Reinhardt), 345, *346
Numbers (Warhol), 347
Numbers in Color (Johns), 342, 343, ***344,** 347

Oath of the Horatii, The (David), 46
Object (Miró), 210–11, ***212**
Ocean Park 115 (Diebenkorn), ***396**
Ocean Park series (Diebenkorn), 395
Oceanic art, 272
Odalisque with a Slave (Ingres), 61
Oedipus (Moreau), 74
O'Keeffe, Georgia, 159, 162, 296; *Evening Star III,* *166
Old Man and Death, The (Wright), 14
Old Masters, 14, 15, 44, 119, 206, 375, 395, 399
Oldenburg, Claes, 345, 347, 353, 381–82, 398; *Clothespin-4,* *381, 382; *Giant Toothpaste Tube,* *380, 382; *Soft Manhattan #1 (Postal Zones),* 347, *351; *Store Days,* 382
Olitski, Jules, 378
Olympia (Manet), 16–17, *16, 34, 275, 372
On Strike (Herkomer), 75
On the Spiritual in Art (Kandinsky), 140, 243
On the Threshold of Liberty (Magritte), *219, 221
O'Neill, Eugene, 299
Onement (Newman), 322, 326
Op art, 378
Orphism, 30, 128
Other Generations (Frankenthaler), 357
Oud, J. J. P., 225
Over Vitebsk (Chagall), *143, 144
Ozenfant, Amédée, 255, 257

Pach, Walter, 167
Pacific International, 127, 134, 143, 155, 180, 235, 244–45, 247, 260, 401
Painted Bronze (Johns), 353, *355
Painter and His Model, The (Matisse), *278
Painter and His Model (Picasso), 272, *284, 285
"A Painter's Notes" (Matisse), 56
Painting (Bacon), *376
Painting (de Kooning), 309, *310
Painting (Still), ***304**
Painting I (Mondrian), *232
Painting vs sculpture, 385
Palace at 4 A.M., The (Giacometti),

216, *217, 389
Pan, 81, 134
Pan Am Building, 246
Panofsky, Erwin, 326
Parade (ballet), 260
Parade, La (Seurat), 28, *28, 29
Parade du boulevard, La (Saint-Aubin), 29
Paris International Exhibition, 287
Paris Salons, 16, 18, 43, 47, 53, 56, 61, 120, 128, 154
Park, The (Klimt), *91
Passage (painting technique), 103
Passage from the Virgin to the Bride, The (Duchamp), 175, ***176**
Pasted-paper technique, 115–19, 355, 362–67
Pastoral (Titian/Giorgione), 63
Pastorale (Klee), 251
Paz, Octavio, 169, 171, 174, 177
Peasants in a Landscape (Le Nain), 33
Perret, Auguste, 226
Persistence of Memory, The (Dali), *208, 209
Perspective, 31
Petrouchka (Stravinsky), 241, 260
Phalanx (art school), 135
Philadelphia, art-teaching tradition, 294, 295
Philadelphia Museum of Art, Arensberg Collection, 159
Philadelphia Press, 296
Philip IV, 14
Philosopher's Conquest, The (de Chirico), *197, 198
Philosophy (Klimt), 87, 88, 89
Photography, 25, 296
Photomontage, 183
Piaget, Jean, 102
Picabia, Francis, 128, 153, 155, 159, 166–69, 174, 175, 179, 200, 201; *French Impetuosity,* 166; *I See Again in Memory My Dear Udnie,* ***165,** 167; *Plumes,* ***185**
Picasso, Pablo, 38, 53, 58–61, 64–66, 129, 135, 235, 260–64, 270, 271, 276, 284, 288, 289, 300, 306, 315, 322, 362, 367, 375, 381, 389, 398; *Acrobat with a Ball,* 59; *Ambroise Vollard,* 110; *Big Dryad,* 104–05; Blue Period, 35, 60, 99, 100; *Blue Room (La Toilette),* *59, 60; *Boy Leading a Horse,* 59; *Charnel House,* 15, 271; constructions, 118, 190; and Cubism, 101–25, 128, 197, 230, 262, 318; death of, 366; *Demoiselles d'Avignon,* 53, 59, 64, ***96,** 97, 104, 106, 108, 170, 259; *Family of Saltimbanques,* 59, *63, 64–65, 66; *Female Nude,* *108, 110, 112; *Fruit Dish,* 114; *Girl before a Mirror,* 300; *Girl with a Mandolin,* 110; *Glass of Absinthe,* 353; *Guernica,* 271, 287, 288, *288, 289, 302, 312, 352; *Guitar* (1913), ***116,** 117, 118; *Guitar* (1919), 123; *Guitar and Wineglass,* 113–14, *113, 118; *Harlequin* (1915), 119–20, ***121;** *Houses on the Hill, Horta,* *108; *Man with a Hat,* 111, *112; *Painter and Model,* 272, *284, 285; *Pipe and Musical Score,* ***120;** portrait of, 115; *Portrait of Apollinaire,* *127; Rose Period, 64, 65, 66, 99, 100, 110; sculptures by, 383, 384; *Seated Bather,* 209, *209; *Self-Portrait,* *58; sketches for *Pulcinella,* 261, 262; *Still Life,* 118; *Still Life with Bread and a Fruit Dish on Table,* 106, *107, 202; *Still Life with Liqueur Bottle,* 106, *106; *Still Life with Red Bull's Head,* 289, *289; *Studio with Plaster Head,* 270, 271, ***272,** 288; *Study for Les Demoiselles d'Avignon,* *98; *Three Dancers,* ***269,** 270, 271, 287, 288; *Three Musicians* (MoMA), 119, 261–64, ***261,** 268; *Three Musicians* (PMA), 119, *260, 261–64, 268; *Two Nudes,* 99, 100, *101; variations on *Las Meninas,* 366; *Vie,* 59, 61; *Violin (Violin and Compote of Fruit),* 114, *114; *Woman Ironing,* 60, *60; *Woman's Head,* 107; *Woman with Pears,* 107
Picasso: Fifty Years of His Art (Barr), 101
Piero della Francesca, 30
Pietà (Ernst), 207
Pietà (Michelangelo), 374
Pipe and Musical Score (Picasso), ***120**
Pissarro, Camille, 17, 26, 38, 42, 47; *Climbing Path,* 22, *22; *Jallais Hill, Pontoise,* *24, 25
Planck, Max, 367
Playing Cards and Glass of Beer (Gris), *115, 117
Plumes (Picabia), ***185**
Poe, Edgar Allan, 155, 194, 196, 221
Point of Tranquility (Louis), ***360**
Pointillism, 28, 51, 132
Polish Rider (Rembrandt), 194
Pollock, Jackson, 302, 303, 306, 307, 308, 311–14, 315, 322, 330, 331, 336, 338, 358, 389; *Autumn Rhythm,* 312, *313; *Convergence (Number 10, 1952),* ***317,** 331; death of, 314; *Number 1,* 314, ***316,** 323; *She-Wolf,* *312; *White Light,* 333, *333, 342, 343
Pop art, 345, 346, 347, 349, 351, 352, 353
Popova, Liubov, *Architectonic Painting,* *233, 234; set for *The Magnanimous Cuckold,* 239, *239
Porter, Cole, 127
Portrait of (a), Apollinaire (Picasso), *127; *Chess Players* (Duchamp), 153; *E. C. Ricart* (Miró), 201; *Emilie Flöge* (Klimt), ***89;** *Erich Heckel* (Kirchner), 79, *82; *German Officer* (Hartley), 160–62, *162; *Madame Matisse with a Green Stripe* (Matisse), ***57;** *Matisse* (Derain), ***52;** *Picasso* (Gris), 115; *Stéphane Mallarmé* (Manet), 73, *73; *Woman* (Miró), 202
Portuguese, The (Braque), *111, 112
Postal Zones, see Soft Manhattan #1
Postcards, 210
Postman Cheval, The (Ernst), 210, *210
Potato Eaters, The (van Gogh), 38, *38
Pound, Ezra, 100, 159, 167, 259, 267, 268, 276, 297, 303, 311, 323, 374, 403–04
Poussin, Nicolas, 30, 31, 288; *Bacchanalian Scene,* 66; *Four Seasons,* 15; *Massacre of the Innocents,* 15
Pravda building, 237
Pre-Columbian art, 386
"Primeval Sonata" (Schwitters), 187
Primitive art, 126, 134, 266, 312
Prinzhorn, Hans, 368
Project for the Leningrad "Pravda" Building (Vesnin brothers), *236, 237
Project for the Monument to the Third International (Tatlin), *235, 236–37
Proudhon, Pierre Joseph, 26
Proust, Marcel, 14, 259, 268, 374, 375
Psychology of Art, The (Malraux), 270
Pulcinella (ballet), 261, 262
Pushkin, Alexander, 299
Puvis de Chavannes, Pierre, 37, 62

Quinn, John, 159, 167, 259

Raabe, Wilhelm Carl, 83
Racine, Jean-Baptiste, 30
Raft of the Méduse, The (Géricault), 58
Rainfall (Caro), 394
Raphael, 45, 375
Rauschenberg, Robert, 334, 336, 337–40, 345; *Bed,* 336, ***337,** 338; *Charlene,* ***332,** 333, 337–38; *Empire II,* 339–40, *341; *Rebus,* 338, *339; *Trophy I (for Merce Cunningham),* 339, *340
Readymades (Duchamp), 170
Rebus (Rauschenberg), 338, *339
Reckless Sleeper (Magritte), *218, 221
Reclining Figure (Moore), *386
Reclining Woman Who Dreams (Giacometti), 216
Red Amaryllis with Blue Background (Mondrian), 227, *227
Red Blue Green (Kelly), ***392,** 399
Red Studio, The (Matisse), ***64,** 66, 67
Redon, Odilon, 72, 74, 155, 194
Reinhardt, Ad, 345, 353, 354, 378, 379; *Number 119, 1958 (Black),* 345, *346
Reliquary House (Smith), *388, 389–90
Rembrandt, 14, 25, 374, 380; *Anatomy Lesson,* 291; *Jewish Bride,* 14; *Polish Rider,* 194
Renaissance, 31
Reni, Guido, 288
Renoir, Pierre-Auguste, 17, 72, 73, 159, 274, 279; *Luncheon of the Boating Party,* ***17;** *Monet Painting in His Garden at Argenteuil,* *19
Reverdy, Pierre, 201
Revolution by Night (Ernst), 207
Revolving (Schwitters), *190, 191
Richardson, Henry Hobson, 223
Richardson, John, 282
Richter, Hans, 179
Rietveld, Gerrit, 225, 233
Riis, Jacob A., 296
Riley, Bridget, *Fall,* 378, *379
Rilke, Rainier Maria, 64
Rimbaud, Arthur, 23, 29, 200, 403
Rimsky-Korsakov, Nikolai, 144
Rite of Spring, The (Stravinsky), 127, 259, 260
Road near L'Estaque (Braque), *103
Robie House (Wright), 226
Roche-Guyon: The Château, La (Braque), 122–23, *123
Rodchenko, Alexander, 240
Rodin, Auguste, 73, 75, 76, 78, 159, 266, 371, 380, 386; *Gates of Hell,* 75, *75
Rome Prize, 47
Roosevelt, Franklin Delano, 299
Rope and People I (Miró), 213, *215
Rope Dancer Accompanies Herself with Her Shadows (Man Ray), 162, ***164**
Rosenberg, Harold, 296, 302, 306, 311, 315, 334, 336
Rosenberg, Paul, 264
Rosenblum, Robert, 307, 314
Rosenquist, James, 345; *F-111,* 352, ***353,** 367
Rosso, Medardo, 149, 150, 383, 384
Rothko, Mark, 303, 306, 307, 308, 331, 335, 355, 402; death of, 314; *Number 10,* ***305**
Rouault, Georges, 47, 135, 262
Roue, La (film), 255
Rousseau, Henri ("Le Douanier"), 128, 129, 194, 279, 381; *Dream,* ***129,** 130; *Sleeping Gypsy,* 130, *131
Roussel, Raymond, 168, 169
Rowell, Margit, 206
Rubens, Peter Paul, 72, 279, 315, 375; *Judgement of Paris,* 97, *99
Rubin, William, 112, 118, 119, 123, 206, 263, 271
Rubinstein, Arthur, 181
Ruskin, John, 46, 47
Russell, Bertrand, 104
Russia, 222, 223, 233–45, 381; folk art, 389; Revolution, 222, 233, 237
Russian Beauty in a Landscape (Kandinsky), *134
Russolo, Luigi, 149, 151
Rutherford, Earnest, 127, 367

Saint-Aubin, Gabriel de, 29
Salinger, J. D., 351
Salome Dancing before Herod (Moreau), 74
Salons, 16, 18, 120; d'Automne, 43, 47, 53, 56, 61; des Indépendants, 128, 154
Sargent, John Singer, 296
Sartre, Jean-Paul, 370, 371
Schammade, Die (magazine), 184
Schapiro, Meyer, 311, 315
Schauspielhaus, Munich, 134
Schiller, Friedrich von, 378
Schlemmer, Oskar, 198, 247; *Bauhaus Stairway,* *246, 247
Schmidt-Rottluff, Karl, 80, 81
Schoenberg, Arnold, 15, 88, 182, 228, 247, 258, 268, 282, 300, 374, 403
Schoenmaekers, M. H. J., 227, 231
Schopenhauer, Arthur, 197, 370
Schwarz, Arturo, 170
Schwitters, Kurt, 181, 187–90, 247, 381; *Merz 19,* ***188;** *Merz 83: Drawing F,* *187; *Merz 380: Schlotheim,* ***189;** "Primeval Sonata," 187; *Revolving,* *190, 191
Sculpture, 118, 151–52, 235; public, 382–94; *vs.* painting, 385
Scriabin, Aleksandr, 143
Seagram Building (Mies van der Rohe), 246
Seated Bather (Picasso), 209, *209
Segal, George, 345, 351; *Butcher Shop,* 351–52, *352
Self-Portrait, Matisse, *51; Mondrian, 227, *227; Picasso, *58; van Gogh, *26
Seurat, Georges, 26, 27–30, 51, 59, 65, 80, 162, 279, 295; *Baignade à Asnières,* 27; *Chahut,* 27; *Invitation to the Sideshow (La Parade),* 28, *28, 29; *Sunday Afternoon on the Island of La Grande Jatte,* 27, ***29**
Severini, Gino, 149; *Armored Train,* *151; *Dynamic Hieroglyph of the Bal Tabarin,* ***148;** "Futurist Manifesto," 151
Shakespeare, 299, 333
Shawm Player, *84
Shchukin, Sergei, 66, 143, 241
She-Wolf, The (Pollock), *312
Sheeler, Charles, *Staircase, Doylestown,* 382, *384
Shinn, Everett, 296
Shriek, The (Munch), 378
Side Chair from Nacogdoches, Texas, 382, *384
Signac, Paul, 59
Simplicissimus, 134
Siqueiros, David Alfaro, 313
Siren and the Parakeet, The (Matisse), 365
Sleeping Gypsy, The (Rousseau), 130, *131
Slevogt, Max, 134
Sloan, John, 295, 296
Smith, David, 298, 303, 308, 355, 382, 384, 385, 387–94, 395, 398, 402; *Cubi XVII,* *389; *Cubi XVIII,* *389; *Cubi XIX,* *389; Cubi series, 390, 394; death of, 314, 394; *Hudson River Landscape,* *388, 390; Medals for Dishonor cycle, 367, 387; *Reliquary House,* *388, 389–90
Smithson, Robert, 400; *Amarillo Ramp,* 400; *Spiral Jetty,* 400–01, ***400**

Snap the Whip (Homer), 294
Société Anonyme, 297
Soft Construction with Boiled Beans: Premonition of Civil War (Dali), 213, ***216,** 268
Soft Manhattan #1 (Postal Zones) (Oldenburg), 347, *351
Soirées de Paris, Les, 128, 144
Soldier on a Horse (Larionov), ***141**
Solomon R. Guggenheim Museum, New York, 246, 298
Solzhenitsyn, Aleksandr, 15
Song of Love (de Chirico), ***193,** 196
Soupault, Philippe, 200
Soutine, Chaim, Céret landscapes, 302
Spanish Dancer (Miró), 203
Spear, Athena T., 264
Specimen Days in America (Whitman), 330, 337
Spinoza, Benedict, 233
Spiral Jetty (Smithson), 400–01, ***400**
Spoon Woman (Giacometti), 219
Squares Arranged According to the Laws of Chance (Arp), *181
Staircase, Doylestown (Sheeler), 382, *384
Standing Nude with a Hat (Kirchner), *87
Starry Night, The (van Gogh), 41, *41
Steelworkers—Noontime (Anshutz), 295, *295
Steichen, Edward, 259
Stein, Gertrude, 63–64, 107, 118; portrait of, 100
Steinberg, Leo, 100, 333
Steiner, Rudolf, 138, 139, 140
Stella, Frank, 359, 379, 395; *Marriage of Reason and Squalor,* *361; *New Caledonian Lorikeet II,* ***397**
Stella, Joseph, 296
Stern, J. P., 82
Stieglitz, Alfred, 159, 160, 166
Still, Clyfford, *1960-R,* 333, *335; *Painting,* ***304**
Still Life (with), (Picasso), 118; *Bread and Fruit Dish on a Table* (Picasso), 106, *107, 202; *Fruit* (Braque), 105, *105, 106; *Ginger Pot* (Mondrian), 228, *230; *Liqueur Bottle* (Picasso), 106, *106; *Peppermint Bottle* (Cézanne), 31–32, ***32,** *Red Bull's Head* (Picasso), 289, *289; *Violin and Jug* (Braque), *110, 111
Stock Exchange building, Amsterdam, 225
Stock market crash of 1929, 298
Stockhausen, Karlheinz, 380
Store Days (Oldenburg), 382
Story of Art, The (Gombrich), 14
Strand, Paul, 296
Stratified Rocks, Nature's Gift of Gneiss Lava Iceland Moss 2 Kinds of Lungwort 2 Kinds of Ruptures of the Perineum Growths of the Heart (b) The Same Thing in a Well-Polished Box Somewhat More Expensive (Ernst), *184
Strauss, Richard, 74, 80, 90
Stravinsky, Igor, 127, 171, 241, 258, 259, 260, 261, 262, 265, 270, 300
Street, The (film), 86
Street, Berlin (Kirchner), ***85,** 86
Street, Dresden (Kirchner), 79, ***81**
Street in Les Saintes-Maries (van Gogh), *39
Strindberg, August, 23, 76, 77
Struck off the List (Klee), 286
Stuck, Franz von, 134
Studio, The (periodical), 81
Studio (with Wooden Stool) (Braque), *283, 285
Studio, Quai St-Michel (Matisse), *276
Studio Interior with Black Vase (Braque), 283, ***285**
Studio with Plaster Head (Picasso), 270, 271, ***272,** 288
Study for "Composition II" (Kandinsky), ***136**
Study for "Landscape with a Tower" (Kandinsky), *135
Study for "Les Demoiselles d'Avignon" (Picasso), *98
Sturm, Der, 140, 180
Suitor, The (Vuillard), ***48**
Sunday Afternoon on the Island of La Grande Jatte (Seurat), 27, ***29**
Suprematist Composition (Malevich), ***241,** 243
Suprematist Composition: White on White (Malevich), 242, 243, *243
Suprematist Painting (Malevich), 243, *244
Surrealism, 118, 129, 178, 195–221, 264, 274, 302, 306, 307, 318, 370, 372; manifestos, 195, 199; word origin, 128
Sutter, David, 28
Symbolism, 72–76, 83, 84, 95, 100, 169, 227
"Symbolist Manifesto" (Moréas), 73

Table and Fruit (Cézanne), 120
Table with Glove (Miró), 202, *202
Tack, Augustus Vincent, 314
Talks on Art (Hunt), 295
Tanguy, "Père," 42
Tanguy, Yves, 196, 199, 212, 214, 302; *Mama, Papa Is Wounded!,* ***205,** 207
Target with Four Faces (Johns), 333, *334, 341, 342
Tatlin, Vladimir, 235–38, 248, 384, 401; *Project for the Monument to the Third International,* *235, 236, 237
"Technical Manifesto of Futurist Painting," 149
Technology, 398
Tempest, The (Giorgione), 194
Temptation of Eve, The (Baldung), 83, *83
Texture, 117
Théâtre de l'Oeuvre, 273
There and Back Again (Hindemith), 267
Third of May, 1808, The (Goya), 287
Thomson, J. J., 23
Thoreau, Henry David, 292, 293
Three Bathers (Cézanne), *50
Three Bathers after Cézanne (Moore), *387
Three Dancers, The (Picasso), ***269,** 270, 271, 287, 288
Three Musicians (MoMA) (Picasso), 119, 261–64, ***261,** 268
Three Musicians (PMA) (Picasso), 119, *260, 261–64, 268
Three Standard Stoppages (Duchamp), 179
Three Trees, L'Estaque (Derain), ***53**
Three Women (Le Grand Déjeuner) (Léger), ***256,** 257
Tiepolo, Giovanni Battista, 23, 72
Tiffany, Louis Comfort, 227
Tintoretto, Jacopo, 72, 279, 315
Titian, 15, 25, 44, 375; *Pastoral,* 63; *Venus of Urbino,* 16
Tobey, Mark, 296; *Broadway,* 296
Toilette, La (Picasso), *59
Tolstoy, Leo, 15, 26, 27, 31, 312
Torso (Brancusi), 266, *267
Toulouse-Lautrec, Henri de, 60, 98, 159, 162, 182
Trace (Graves), 395–98, ***397**
Trophy I (for Merce Cunningham) (Rauschenberg), 339, *340
Trotter, Wilfred, 401
Truman, Harry S., 329, 332
Turner, J. M. W., 14, 46, 294, 314
Two Children Are Threatened by a Nightingale (Ernst), ***204,** 206
Two Friends (Marquet), 276

Two Horizontals (Kline), 308, *308
Two Men by a Table (Heckel), 84, *84
291 Fifth Avenue (gallery), 159
Two Nudes (Picasso), 99, 100, *101
2 Priory Walk (Bartlett), ***392**
Tzara, Tristan, 179, 182, 200, 220

Ulysses (Joyce), 69, 167, 268
Unconscious in art, 126, 130, 179, 192
Unfortunate Land of Tyrol, The (Marc), *140, 142
Unique Forms of Continuity in Space (Boccioni), *151, 152
Untitled, (Judd), 382, *383; (Morris, 1969), 402, *402; (Morris, 1974), *401, 402
Upper Egypt (Klee), 251

Valentine Gallery, New York, 300
Valéry, Paul, 200, 405
Vantongerloo, Georges, 225
Vauxcelles, Louis, 105
Veduggio Sun (Caro), *391, 394
Veils series (Louis), 359
Velázquez, 14; *Meninas,* 366
Velde, Henry van de, 92, 225, 235, 245
Vence chapel (Matisse), 363
Venetian art, 23, 71–72
Venus of Urbino (Titian), 16
Verdi, Giuseppe, 299
Vermeer, Jan, 44, 275, 395; *Little Street,* 275
Verne, Jules, 194, 195
Veronese, Paolo, 44, 71
Vesnin, Alexander, 236, 237
Vesnin, Alexander and Victor, 235; *Project for the Leningrad "Pravda" Building,* *236, 237
Victory Boogie-Woogie (Mondrian), ***373**
Vie, La (Picasso), 59, 61
Vienna, 87–90
Vienna Secession, 89, 331
View of Montroig (Miró), *201, 202
View of Toledo (El Greco), 111
Villa Savoye (Le Corbusier), 226
Village in the Forest (Léger), 122, *122
Villiers de l'Isle-Adam, Philippe, 169
Villon, Jacques, 153
Violin, The (Violin and Compote of Fruit) (Picasso), 114, *114
Violin and Engaving (Gris), *115, 117
Vir Heroicus Sublimis (Newman), ***321**, 326, 331, 333
Virginia Creeper (Munch), 78
Vision in Motion (Moholy-Nagy), 248
Vlaminck, Maurice, 39, 43, 53, 54, 55, 135; *Blue House,* ***45**
Voice, The (Munch), ***77**
Voice of the Holy Father, The (Ernst), *404, 405
Vollard, Ambroise, 42, 201, 273; portrait of, 110
Vuillard, Edouard, 35, 38, 46–49, 51, 73, 76, 274; *Suitor (Workshop) (Intérieur à l'Etang-la-ville),* ***48**

Wagner, Richard, 76, 134, 194, 325, 385
Walden, Herwarth, 140, 146, 180
Walpole, Horace, 195, 196
Warhol, Andy, 346, 352, 398; Car Crash series, 352; *Do It Yourself —Seascape,* ***349**; Electric Chair series, 352; *Green Coca-Cola Bottles,* 347, *350; *Numbers,* 347
Waste Land, The (Eliot), 100, 127, 167, 270, 297
Water Lilies (Monet), 314
Watteau, Antoine, 14, 37, 62, 63, 65
Weber, Max, 159, 160; *Chinese Restaurant,* 160, *162
Wedekind, Frank, 84
Weimar, 245, 247; Republic, 268
Wells, H. G., 194, 386
Wharton, Edith, 267
Whence do we come? What are we? Where are we going? (Gauguin), *25, 26–27
White Light (Pollock), 333, *333, 342, 343
White on White, see Suprematist Composition: White on White
Whitehead, A. N., 104
Whitman, Walt, 82, 292, 293, 330, 337, 338, 401
Whitney Museum of American Art (Breuer), 246
Why Not Sneeze, Rose Sélavy? (Duchamp), 178, *178
Wilhelm II, Kaiser, 26, 80, 82, 87
Williams, William Carlos, 405
Wils, Jan, 225
Wilson, Edmund, 244
Window, The (Matisse), 276, 285
Window on Russia, A (Wilson), 244
Winged Victory of Samothrace, 147, 152
With Hidden Noise (Duchamp), 178, *178
Wittgenstein, Ludwig, 354
Woman I (de Kooning), 310–11, *311
Woman Combing Her Hair (Picasso), 99
Woman Ironing (Picasso), 60, *60
Woman with Her Throat Cut (Giacometti), 212, *215, 370
Woman with Pears (Picasso), 107
Woman with Water Pails (Malevich), *242
Woman's Head (Picasso), 107
Women, depiction of, 76, 207, 208, 209, 212
Women of Algiers, The (Delacroix), 366
Woods near Oele (Mondrian), 227–28, ***228**
Workshop, The, see Suitor, The
World Crisis (Churchill), 158
World War I, 92, 93, 95, 101, 119, 123, 142, 157, 158, 159, 183, 184, 195, 230, 233, 234, 255, 259, 286, 300, 302
World War II, 258, 280, 300, 302, 330, 331, 367, 399
World's Fair of 1867 (Paris), 17
WPA (Works Progress Administration), 299
Wright, Frank Lloyd, 225, 243; Robie House, 226
Wright, Joseph, 14
Writer, The (Miró), 206
Writing Piece 'Only' (Caro), *391

Yale University, 246; Art Gallery, 159
Yeats, William Butler, 368
Yellow Christ (Gauguin), 34, 35
Young, G. M., 207
Young, J. Z., 221
Young Men by the Sea (Beckmann), 92
Young Rhineland group, 184

Zadkine, Ossip, 357
Zola, Emile, 17, 25
Zurich, Dada in, 179–84

PHOTOGRAPHY CREDITS

Photographs reproduced in this volume have been provided, in the majority of cases, by the owners or custodians of the illustrated works of art (see captions). The following list, keyed to page numbers, applies to photographs for which a separate acknowledgment is due: E. Irving Bloomstrann, New Britain, Conn.: 19; Brigdens, Toronto: 154; Bulloz, Paris: 50, 55 bottom; Rudolph Burckhardt, New York: 181, 341, 347 top, 355, 383; Richard Cheek, Cambridge, Mass.: 384 right; Geoffrey Clements, Staten Island, N.Y.: 162 top, 298, 300, 302, 350, 356 top and bottom, 359, 388 bottom; Prudence Cuming Associates, London: 376; Eeva-Inkeri, New York: 392 bottom; André Emmerich, New York: 390; Jonathan L. Fairbanks, Boston: 350; Frequin-Photos, Voorburg, Holland: 219, 354; Claude Gaspari, St-Paul, France: 283; Giraudon, Paris: 16, 73; Gianfranco Gorgoni/Contact, New York: 400; Greenberg-May Prod. Inc., Buffalo: 155, 351; Hickey & Robertson, Houston: 325; Colorphoto Hinz, Basel: 125, 133; Bruce C. Jones, Huntington, N.Y.: 339, 349, 401; Jones-Gessling Studio, Huntington, N.Y.: 380; Peter A. Juley & Son, New York: 37, 299; Kate Keller, New York: 204, 229 top and bottom, 237; Robert E. Mates, New York: 136, 137, 266; James Mathews, New York: 38, 54, 147, 169, 190, 215, 227 bottom, 231, 284, 333, 372; O. E. Nelson, New York: 335; Mali Olatunji, New York: 116; Fotostudio Otto, Vienna: 88; Mario Perotti, Milan: 198; Hans Petersen, Copenhagen: 57; Rolf Petersen, New York: 131 bottom, 150, 178 bottom; Eric Pollitzer, New York: 377, 381, 385, 397 top; Sandak, Inc., New York: 64, 65, 81, 85, 91, 93, 96, 109, 117, 124, 129, 132, 145, 148, 165, 193, 205, 212, 220, 241, 252, 301, 305, 321; Soichi Sunami, New York: 39, 41, 78, 79, 92, 103, 106, 112, 115 top, 146, 151 bottom, 166, 179, 182, 183, 184, 186, 187, 200, 202, 203, 208, 209, 211, 214, 215, 217, 232, 233, 234 top, 242, 243, 246, 250 bottom, 263, 264, 265 bottom, 266, 267 top, 279, 287 left, 288, 310, 311, 312, 319, 368, 369, 370; Joseph Szaszfai, New Haven, Conn.: 188, 189; Taylor & Dull, Inc., New York: 295; Rodney Todd-White & Son, London: 235; Charles Uht, New York: 55 top, 108 top, 289; O. Vaering, Oslo: 68; Malcolm Varon, New York: 121, 164, 261, 304, 316, 328, 348, 364; John Webb, London: 141, 236, 238, 239; A. J. Wyatt, Philadelphia: 58, 114 top and bottom, 163 top, 168 right, 254, 260.